Russian Women and the End of Soviet Socialism

Judith McKinney

# Russian Women and the End of Soviet Socialism

## Everyday Experiences of Economic Change

palgrave
macmillan

Judith McKinney
Hobart and William Smith Colleges
Geneva, NY, USA

ISBN 978-3-030-16225-2 ISBN 978-3-030-16226-9 (eBook)
https://doi.org/10.1007/978-3-030-16226-9



This Palgrave Macmillan imprint is published by the registered company Springer Nature Switzerland AG
The registered company address is: Gewerbestrasse 11, 6330 Cham, Switzerland

# Preface

It has been over twenty-five years since Mikhail Gorbachev presided over the dissolution of the Soviet Union, and over thirty since his accession to the position of General Secretary of the Communist Party. Gorbachev's rule marked the beginning of the country's transition from central planning of economic activity and state ownership of the means of production to an economy where markets and private ownership play important roles. Those who expected the smooth and rapid emergence of a textbook version of a private-enterprise, free-market economy functioning in an American-style democracy have been proved wrong; those who look at political and economic life in Russia after Vladimir Putin's return to the presidency in 2012 as proof that nothing in Russia ever really changes are also mistaken. While there is no doubt that Putin has reintroduced central control over much of the political sphere and key elements of the economy, the everyday lives of ordinary Russian citizens are dramatically different from what they were in the late 1980s, in ways both great and small, and for reasons having as much to do with systemic changes and policy shifts as with technological advances.

I made my first trip to Russia in the summer of 1968, just before the Soviet invasion of Czechoslovakia, and spent a semester at Leningrad

State University in spring of 1971 with one of the first groups of American undergraduates to have this opportunity. Over the course of that semester we witnessed—and sometimes personally experienced—many of the consequences of the Soviet system. Letters from home were occasionally opened before we received them. Russian friends requested that we not acknowledge them when we were on buses or subway cars together or when we encountered them on the street unless they—and we—were alone. And late one night, as I took a walk to get some fresh air after a long bus ride, I realized that I was keeping some poor KGB informant out in the cold and snow as he watched to make sure I wasn't meeting someone the authorities would want to know about. There were few cars on the streets in that era and little variety in the shops. Buying anything was a long and complicated process, and could be impossible if the clerk took a dislike to you. While tickets for concerts and the ballet were astonishingly inexpensive, oranges were so rare that if one of us managed to find any we would hold a party to celebrate. Twice a week we joined the lines of students in our dorm waiting for the showers, hoping to reach one of the stalls before the hot water was cut off.

Twenty-four years later—in December of 1995—I returned to the city, now rechristened St. Petersburg, and was greeted by Russian friends waiting openly for me in the lobby of a hotel. They joined excursions with the small group of Americans I was escorting and invited me to one of their apartments for dinner and wide-ranging conversation. They talked openly with me about the sharp increase in economic inequality and the new prevalence of crime and antisocial behavior, as well as about the toll that our friendship had taken on their early career opportunities. Litter, which simply had not existed during my earlier visit, was now conspicuous and, when I bent to pick up a piece of paper I had inadvertently dropped, a friend told me not to bother since everyone now tossed everything everywhere. The *babushki*—literally, grandmothers, but routinely used to refer to any older women—who had earlier considered it their duty to scold anyone guilty of misbehaving (by littering, by not having a loop with which to hang one's coat over a hook, by wearing slacks while female, or by breaking any one of hundreds of other implicit rules of appropriate behavior)—were now too busy trying to sell items at sidewalk kiosks or in the subways to worry about such violations of the social norm. At the same time, the stores were full (of both products and shoppers) and during this ten-day visit I had more opportunity to eat apples, oranges and tomatoes than I had during the entire four months I spent in the country in 1971. Ads were often in English, a McDonald's had opened in Moscow, and the dollar was accepted for payment in most situations.

Despite having studied—and indeed taught—about the changes taking place under Gorbachev and Boris Yeltsin, I spent that short visit in 1995 in a state of culture shock, stunned not by the differences between life in the United States and life in Russia, but by the differences between the Soviet Union I remembered and this new unfamiliar Russia. Subsequent visits—four since 2005—have deepened my awe at the adjustments, both psychological and practical, that were required by those who lived there. These visits have also provided me with a richer understanding of how the government policies of liberalization, privatization and stabilization—the cornerstones of the neoliberal prescription for the economic transition—were experienced on the ground and how the policies introduced by Putin in the 2000s have further reshaped life in Russia.

This book, based on interviews I conducted in the city of Yaroslavl as a Fulbright Scholar in the fall of 2012, offers a look at the adjustments and experiences of a particular subset of Russian citizens—female, mostly middle-aged, middle-class professionals—during the economic, political and social transformations of the post-Soviet period. These conversations provided examples of how everyday life changed for the women and suggested how these changes challenged their views of the government and of the appropriate relationship between the government and the population. How the women shaped their narratives also offers insight into what they thought their responses to the changes revealed about themselves. Some of the challenges and hardships they faced were openly acknowledged and blamed squarely on government policy; other situations were sanitized, as if acknowledging the difficulties would have reflected badly on their own capabilities.

In all, during the fall of 2012 I interviewed over 30 women, ranging in age from 31 to 74. I also draw on a small number of interviews that

I conducted in the ethnically diverse southern city of Astrakhan in the summer of 2010 while participating in an intensive language course run by SUNY Stony Brook. All interviews were conducted in Russian and were semi-structured. I had a set of standard questions that I used to begin the conversation or restart it if it flagged, but for the most part, the women simply told me stories of their lives, in their own way at their own pace with their own emphases. Because my intention was to focus on economic experiences, I did not always pursue other topics the women raised as fully as, in hindsight, I wish I had. As I transcribed the interviews and organized the material, I became aware of lost opportunities for richer discussions and illuminating details, and some of the stories presented here will raise questions that could not be answered with the material I have.

Most of the interviews lasted for roughly an hour, although the shortest were only a little over half an hour and two continued for well over three hours. I used a digital pen in most cases, although in one interview the woman requested that I simply take notes without turning on the recording device and there were a couple of instances when a casual encounter developed into a quasi-interview and I believed it would be awkward to interrupt the conversation to bring out the pen. There were also, inevitably, a few cases where I turned on the pen too late or turned it off too early and had to try to reconstruct the content from memory a few hours later. I transcribed the recordings and then sent them to a young Russian woman who filled in many holes and corrected many errors; when translating, I received invaluable assistance from a Moscow-born colleague with years of experience teaching Russian to college students in the United States.

To Stanislava Voronina and Marina Aptekman, who helped with the transcription and translation, to my colleague Renée Monson, Professor of Sociology, who allowed this economist to sit in on her course in Qualitative Research Methods and encouraged me to believe that the project was feasible, to the Russian friend who helped in innumerable ways and offered invaluable introductions to potential respondents, to anonymous reviewers who offered suggestions that significantly improved the project, to the friends and family members who offered support along the way, and, of course, most of all to the many women in Russia who were willing to share their stories with me, my deepest thanks. Thanks also to Hobart and William Smith Colleges and the Fulbright Scholar Program for the funding that made this all possible.

Geneva, USA Judith McKinney

# Contents


1 Introduction 1

2 Before the Fall: The Soviet System 13

3 Challenges and Opportunities of the Early Post-Soviet Years 35

4 Rising Prices and Irregular Wages 63

5 Coping Strategies 89

6 Jobs: Formal, Informal, Multiple 113

7 Working for Oneself: Small Business Ventures 139

8 Voucher Privatization 163

9 Economic Inequality: Income and What It Says about You 187

10 Dissolution of a Multinational Empire: Migration Flows and Ethnic Relations 215

11 New Freedoms 243

12 Conclusion 273

Index 281

# 1
# Introduction

As identified by Western analysts, the key concepts marking Mikhail Gorbachev's efforts to reform the Soviet system were *glasnost* (usually translated as "openness" and associated with a greater willingness to allow public discussion of a broad range of issues from a variety of perspectives), democratization (the introduction of contested elections and greater voice for workers in enterprise management), and economic restructuring. The key policies during Boris Yeltsin's rule were liberalization (of prices in particular but also of economic activity more broadly), macroeconomic stabilization (reining in inflation and avoiding excessive unemployment) and the privatization of state-owned property. Reading about these policies in the late 1980s and early 1990s had given me a sense of sharp discontinuity from the Soviet past.

As I spoke with women in Yaroslavl in the fall of 2012, however, I realized that for those who lived through these changes the boundaries between the eras and the differences among the policies were blurred. It proved difficult—sometimes impossible—to map their personal experiences onto either the historical periodization or the economic


J. McKinney, *Russian Women and the End of Soviet Socialism*,
https://doi.org/10.1007/978-3-030-16226-9_1

concepts.[1] To take just one example, there was rationing of some food products under Brezhnev, there was rationing of some food products under Gorbachev, and it wasn't always possible to assign a clear date to the women's stories of shopping for food under these circumstances. Some of this was no doubt due simply to the passage of time, but it is also true that the everyday is experienced in ways that don't fit neatly into textbook definitions; what happened at the macro level in the country certainly had a powerful impact on the lives of the women, but not always at the moment and in the ways one might have predicted.

Similarly, the terminology the women used differed considerably from that of the (Western) academic discourse.[2] When the women did use the terms *perestroika* [restructuring] and *perekhod* [transition] they did so loosely and often interchangeably. This is consistent with the practice noted by Shevchenko in Moscow roughly a decade earlier: "official designations for the period—'time of transition' (*perekhodnyi period*) and 'changes' (*peremeny*)—did not take root in popular discourse" (Shevchenko 2009: 19). Instead, people used terms with much more negative connotations, terms like disintegration, collapse, crisis, or catastrophe.

There are a number of studies by economists analyzing the negative consequences of Russia's transition policies—how price liberalization led to hyperinflation, how voucher privatization led to the concentration of wealth and the rise of the oligarchs, how stabilization led to a web of payment arrears.[3] Here I look at how the policies were viewed and interpreted by a group of Russian women and how, looking back, they assess the impact these policies have had on their lives. Some changes which received a great deal of attention from Western scholars and the media—for example, voucher privatization—had barely registered with

---

[1]Ilic (2013: 11) notes a similar pattern in her interviews with women of the interwar generation: "the dates of these events appeared to be less seared in the memories of my interview subjects than they are in my own mind as a historian of the Soviet Union."

[2]The one striking exception, "the liberalization of prices," was, perhaps not coincidentally, also the policy of which their recollections seemed clearest and most accurate.

[3]See for example Hedlund (1999), Gustafson (1999), Gaddy and Ickes (2002), and Klein and Pomer (2001).

the women I spoke to, or, at least, had been largely forgotten, although the concentration of wealth resulting from that program remained a source of sharp resentment. Thus, although almost all of the women brought up the nouveaux riches "New Russians" without prompting, almost none mentioned vouchers unless I asked specifically about them, and their recollections of how the system worked were hazy and frequently incorrect. Similarly, almost none of the women who spoke with me thought of themselves as having experienced wage arrears. Since the data about the prevalence and severity of wage arrears are quite clear, the denial by the women raises a critical point. What I present here is based on the memories and interpretations of those I interviewed. Much has been forgotten, much has been transformed to fit the women's sense of identity and the storyline of their lives, much of the technical no doubt has been only partially understood. Like all oral history, this thus offers the particular truth of this group of individuals rather than historical fact.

There are, of course, many commonalities in the demands the systemic changes placed on women in Russia no matter where they lived, and studies of the 1990s and early 2000s in Moscow and St. Petersburg (for example, Shevchenko 2009; Patico 2008 respectively) or in very small-town Russia (White 2004) offer vivid descriptions of experiences my interviewees would find familiar. On the other hand, the opportunities and challenges in provincial capitals like Yaroslavl differ in important ways from those in places either much larger or much smaller. Thus, the women living in Yaroslavl were generally more optimistic and enjoyed considerably less constrained lives than the small-town women interviewed by White, although this also reflects the later date of my interviews. At the same time, the opportunities for those in Yaroslavl to be employed at "Western" salaries—far higher than the Russian norm—are quite limited, since, unlike Moscow, Yaroslavl does not serve as the Russian base for international organizations[4] nor has it attracted anywhere near as much foreign

[4]Dmitri Medvedev, during his term as President, did initiate a Global Policy Forum to be held in Yaroslavl annually, but it seems to have met for only three years and has not survived the return of Putin to the presidency.

investment as the capital, which in the latter half of the 1990s received almost half of all direct foreign investment in the country. A number of the women I spoke with had studied in Moscow and some had children living and working there at the time of our conversations; many stressed the differences in the way of life in the two cities, occasionally with regret but frequently with pride. Seeing how life evolved in Yaroslavl from the 1980s through the first decade of the twenty-first century thus adds to our understanding of this historical moment and reminds us of the importance of the lenses through which we view it.

## The City

As a medium-sized provincial capital (population a bit over 600,000), Yaroslavl is the sort of place in which a significant portion of the Russian population lives. According to the 2010 census, just under three-quarters of the Russian population is defined as "urban", but the term is used quite loosely, including as it does both Moscow, with over 10 million residents, and settlements of under 5000 (White 2004: 13). Of this "urban" population, roughly as many people live in the 23 cities which, like Yaroslavl, have populations of between half a million and a million as live in Moscow and St. Petersburg combined; slightly fewer live in the 10 cities with populations of one to one and a half million. Thus, about 38% of the "urban" population lives in cities of 500,000 or more, with another 17% living in cities between 200,000 and 500,000.[5]

Yaroslavl itself has a varied economy and a long history, having celebrated the 1000th anniversary of its founding. Located on the Volga River and part of the famous Golden Ring of cities to the northeast of Moscow, it is a popular tourist destination for both Russians and foreigners and serves as the site of study-abroad programs for a number of colleges and universities. Outside the lovely historic district, with its many onion-domed churches, its popular promenades along the embankment of the Volga and the adjoining Kotorosl River, and several museums and centers of education, sprawls a not especially attractive

[5]www.worldpopulationreview.com/countries/Russia-population/cities.

industrial city, home to several large Soviet-era factories and some newer post-Soviet enterprises. Among its major Soviet factories—not all of which have survived the end of central planning and state ownership—there have been an oil refinery and plants producing diesel engines, tires, paint for automobiles, sewing machines and dairy products. In the post-Soviet period, thanks to investment from companies in Japan and Sweden, a pharmaceutical plant and factories producing steel structures and road-building equipment have been added, along with a smattering of foreign businesses in the service sector such as McDonald's and the German supermarket giant Globus. Thomas Remington, in his book *The Politics of Inequality in Russia,* classifies the Yaroslavl region (of which the city of Yaroslavl is the administrative center) as one with a "market-adaptive regime" and describes the regional government as having used political pluralism and careful coordination of the transition to "[foster] economic growth through gradual but consistent adaptation of local firms to market conditions" (Remington 2011: 97, 101–103).

In addition to the tourists and international students who pass through the city, Yaroslavl has seen a number of foreign scholars and has been the focus of several studies on the political dimensions of post-Soviet change (for example Ruble 1995; Stoner-Weiss 1997; Hahn 2001). Foreign visitors are thus not a novelty: I was one in a long line of foreigners to whom my landlady offered room and board, and several of the women I interviewed teach Russian to students from a variety of countries. On the other hand, there is not a significant expatriate community in Yaroslavl, so the city seems free of the tensions that such a community can generate. As far as I could tell, I was neither a curiosity nor an object of resentment, the latter certainly helped by the fact that my visit preceded the crisis in Ukraine and America's response to Russian actions there.

## The Women

Many of the women I spoke with had worked as teachers at some point, although several of these had either changed careers or taken additional jobs to supplement the low salaries they received in their primary employment. Most of those who were never teachers were nonetheless highly educated professionals, members of the former Soviet *intelligentsia*. Three women were running their own businesses, and a few others had owned small businesses in the past. Two women worked with foreign direct sales companies, two others worked in municipal offices. Roughly half of the women were receiving pensions from the government, but, like a great many Russian pensioners, they continued to work. A few had parents who were still alive; all had at least one adult child and a few had grandchildren. Some were widowed, some divorced, some in long-term marriages. They certainly do not constitute a random sample of women in Russia, or even in Yaroslavl. I located these women with the generous assistance of a Russian friend, so most are people with whom she has worked or studied or socialized. There was also, of course, self-selection. Several women declined to meet with me, offering a variety of reasons—from a lack of time or interest, to a reluctance to revisit times of hardship or fear of speaking freely with someone they didn't know (especially an American). Also missing from the sample are those for whom the hardships of this period were truly devastating or even fatal—victims of trafficking or of extreme domestic abuse[6]—as well as those who chose to leave the country and build a new life elsewhere.

In order to help readers interested in seeing how recollections about different aspects of their lives fit together, I offer here brief descriptions of the women whose comments I draw on most frequently. I have, in all cases, used pseudonyms.

- Ekaterina—born in 1956 in Moscow, married, with a grown daughter. She moved to Yaroslavl with her family as a teen and later graduated from a pedagogical institute there, eventually receiving a doctorate from a university in Moscow. A foreign language teacher (and academic administrator), she has embraced the freedom to travel and openly express political opinions. She is one of the few who mentioned being politically active in the late 1980s.

[6]For discussions of these darker experiences, see for example Johnson (2009) and Stoecker and Shelley (2005).

- Feodosia—the oldest and poorest of my respondents, born in 1938 in a small village, where she lived until she married a man from Yaroslavl. It was an unhappy marriage because he drank heavily, but it lasted until his death when she was 70. She graduated from a vocational school and worked as a sanitary engineer, although she said she was already receiving a pension and no longer working in 1988.[7] Although she has two children and a suitor has suggested she move in with him, she lives alone. She volunteers at her Russian Orthodox Church, occasionally receiving very modest financial assistance from the church, cast-off clothing from others in the congregation and gifts from the suitor.
- Klara—born in 1942, widowed at 57, although her husband had been on disability from a stroke for many years before he died. Before his stroke he had been in an upper management position at a power plant; she taught French. She no longer works, but receives income by renting out rooms in her apartment to foreign students. Her son lives in Yaroslavl, her daughter in Canada.
- Liza—born in 1957, educated in Moscow, where her grown son now lives. She is a university teacher, married to a doctor. She stressed that she joined the Communist Party because of her genuine commitment to its values and remained a member until the Party was outlawed after the 1991 coup.
- Regina—born in 1951 in Yaroslavl, she grew up in a number of places in the former Soviet Union because her father was in the military. She returned to Yaroslavl to study engineering. In the early 1990s the enterprise she worked for was unable to pay her and she lost her job. At the same time, funding dried up at the research institute where her husband worked, so he left and started his own company, which is still in operation. She spent some time at home, some time in a job she did not enjoy, but now again works in her field and is pleased with that. She is very reserved, very conscious of being a member of the *intelligentsia*, disappointed that her daughter chose not to complete university.

[7]The usual retirement age for women was 55, but she may have been entitled to an early pension introduced in 1991 for women 53 or 54 who lost their jobs and had no chance of being employed elsewhere (see Posadskaya 1994: 170).

- Renata—born in 1967, divorced, with a daughter born in 1991. She has spent almost all of the post-Soviet period developing and running small enterprises dealing with energy in the field of construction (*konstruktsionnye-energeticheskie kompanii*). She has had only one business at a time, but has had to start over several times because of legal or financial difficulties. After the second failed endeavor, she worked for a while as a manager at a company selling uniforms to various businesses but left that to start another company of her own.
- Sofia—born in 1951, educated in a boarding school for gifted orphans, she was an idealistic and active Komsomol member, but became disenchanted and left the party in the late 1980s, at which time she was quietly baptized in a neighboring village. Her religion is a source of comfort and support for her and she speaks of it often. The only woman to mention the KGB, she is certain that a former student (and friend) had informed on her over the course of a number of years. She and her husband both hold doctorates. She teaches Russian to foreigners and he owns a small company. They have a grown son.
- Yulia—born in 1960, married and divorced twice, with a long and varied employment history that includes stints in a factory, as a secretary, as a teacher, as an entrepreneur and as a civil servant. While most of the job changes were the result of her dissatisfaction with the working conditions or pay, she has amassed a large collection of awards and certificates testifying to her many accomplishments. Her only daughter lives in the United States. We met when I was interviewing someone else where she worked, and she requested that I interview her as well.
- Zoya—born in 1960, but already a pensioner, because she was eligible after 20 years working for the Migration Service. Both her father and husband were in the military. She spent some of her adolescence in Germany, where her father was posted, and some years in Kazakhstan, where her husband was serving. She graduated from a pedagogical institute and taught history while living in Kazakhstan, but could not find a teaching position when they moved to Yaroslavl. She and her husband have two sons.

What follows is my attempt to capture the spirit and resiliency of these women—and the others I spoke with—as they survived wage arrears, hyperinflation, physical dislocation, shortages of goods and rampant uncertainty, managing to care for their families and, in most cases, going on to create fulfilling and successful lives. Earlier studies, carried out when most Russians were still struggling to find their footing,[3] are invaluable for the richness of details they provide, details which may have blurred for my respondents, but the emphasis of these is understandably on the enormous hardship people faced. For example, Judyth Twigg, writing in 2002, says, "The Russian people have been subjected to seemingly unbearable humiliation and hardship over the last decade. It is hard not to ask why they have tolerated it" and then lists various explanations offered by observers—from a love of martyrdom, a retreat into alcohol or drugs, and "centuries-old Russian stoicism" to a fear of letting chaos loose (2002: 161). My interviews with women in Yaroslavl more than two decades after Gorbachev first began to introduce policies that fundamentally transformed their lives allow us to see not just the hardship but also the way the women found opportunities within the challenges.

If earlier studies left one wondering how long the Russian people could cope and whether they could possibly rebuild their lives, my respondents provide striking evidence that they could and indeed they have. Some marriages failed, at least a couple of children, especially those in late adolescence in the late 1980s, seem to have lost their way, but few of the women had their lives fundamentally damaged. The others adapted, adjusted, and in several cases flourished. One hopes that the challenges posed by conflict in Ukraine, sanctions imposed by the West, and sharply reduced petroleum revenues since 2012 have not seriously derailed these successes.

I began this project expecting to find a direct relationship between age and the degree of hardship experienced—that those who were young adults at the time of the upheavals would find it easier to adapt than

[3]See, for example, Bridger et al. (1996), Klugman and Motivans (2001) and Kuehnast and Nechemias (2004).

those who were already well-established—but the reality was more complex. Two of the most enterprising and successful of my respondents were born in the late 1950s; two of those who seemed least happy were born in the 1960s. For obvious reasons, my sample includes no one who was already elderly in the early 1990s—those for whom the transition was almost certainly both logistically and emotionally most difficult. The story of Feodosia, born in 1938, was definitely the saddest I heard, but it is unclear how much of this was due to her age and how much to a combination of lack of education and an unfortunate marriage.

If age did not predict how positively the women viewed the changes in their country, it did appear to influence what they considered to be the dominant issues of the periods of perestroika and transition, as well as the coping strategies they adopted. Women born in the early 1950s were more likely to speak about new opportunities to travel abroad and collaborate with foreign institutions; they were also more likely to emphasize the deterioration of relations among the former republics and the erosion of government assistance with education and employment. Women who were just entering the work force in the late 1980s or early 1990s, on the other hand, spoke most about the challenges of earning enough money and the difficulties of providing for young children. These younger women were more likely to have started a business—the oldest to do so was born in 1956—and more likely to mention receiving help from parents. Although my sample is small and generalization risky, these conversations do remind us that how the policies and changes of the 1980s and 1990s are viewed varies not only with the passage of time but also with individual situation.

## Plan of the Book

To understand how the changes of the late 1980s and early 1990s affected the lives of my respondents and how they responded to these changes, it is important to have a sense of what they were raised to expect. I therefore begin with a review of key features of the Soviet economic and political system. After that, I present an overview of the challenges and opportunities the women identified most frequently in our conversations, and the wide range of responses they had to these changes. The following six chapters offer more detailed exploration of particular aspects of the women's economic lives. In Chapter 4, I look at the challenges of providing for one's family in the face of rapidly rising prices and low and irregular wages and in Chapter 5, I discuss the typical ways in which the women sought to cope with these challenges. Chapter 6 looks at employment, contrasting the Soviet experience with the immediate post-Soviet situation, as well as with that faced by the women's children as they enter the labor market. In Chapter 7, I look at the experiences of those women who have chosen not to work for others and have instead created their own businesses. Chapter 8 explores the women's experiences with and assessment of the voucher privatization program and Chapter 9 looks at their reactions to the greater economic inequality that characterizes post-Soviet society. The next two chapters move from the economic to the political and social, exploring first ethnicity—primarily in the context of the migration flows that followed the dissolution of the Soviet Union into fifteen independent countries—and then the increased freedoms to travel, practice religion, and express political opinions. The conclusion offers a brief description of what has happened in the Russian economy and, where possible, in the lives of my respondents since the time of my interviews.

## References

Bridger, Sue, Rebecca Kay, and Kathryn Pinnick. 1996. *No More Heroines? Russia, Women and the Market.* London: Routledge.

Gaddy, Clifford G., and Barry W. Ickes. 2002. *Russia's Virtual Economy.* Washington, DC: Brookings Institution Press.

Gustafson, Thane. 1999. *Capitalism Russian-Style.* Cambridge: Cambridge University Press.

Hahn, Jeffrey W. (ed.). 2001. *Regional Russia in Transition: Studies from Yaroslavl.* Washington, DC: Woodrow Wilson Center.

Hedlund, Stefan. 1999. *Russia's 'Market' Economy: A Bad Case of Predatory Capitalism.* UCL Group: Taylor and Francis.

Ilic, Melanie. 2013. *Life Stories of Soviet Women: The Interwar Generation.* Abingdon/New York: Routledge.

Johnson, Janet Elise. 2009. *Gender Violence in Russia: The Politics of Feminist Intervention*. Bloomington: Indiana University.

Klein, Lawrence R., and Marshall Pomer (eds.). 2001. *The New Russia: Transition Gone Awry*. Stanford, CA: Stanford University Press.

Klugman, Jeni, and Albert Motivans (eds.). 2001. *Single Parents and Child Welfare in the New Russia*. Basingstoke: Palgrave.

Kuehnast, Kathleen, and Carol Nechemias (eds.). 2004. *Post-Soviet Women Encountering Transition*. Washington, DC: Woodrow Wilson Center Press.

Marsh, Rosalind (ed.). 1996. *Women in Russia and Ukraine*. Cambridge: Cambridge University Press.

Patico, Jennifer. 2008. *Consumption and Social Change in a Post-Soviet Middle Class*. Stanford, CA: Stanford University Press.

Posadskaya, Anastasia (ed.). 1994. *Women in Russia: A New Era in Russian Feminism*, trans. Kate Clark. London/New York: Verso.

Remington, Thomas F. 2011. *The Politics of Inequality in Russia*. New York, NY: Cambridge University Press.

Ruble, Blair A. 1995. *Money Sings: The Changing Politics of Urban Space in Post-Soviet Yaroslavl*. Cambridge: Cambridge University Press.

Shevchenko, Olga. 2009. *Crisis and the Everyday in Postsocialist Moscow*. Bloomington/Indianapolis: Indiana University.

Stoecker, Sally, and Louise Shelley (eds.). 2005. *Human Traffic and Transnational Crime: Eurasian and American Perspectives*. Lanham, MD: Rowman & Littlefield.

Stoner-Weiss, Kathryn. 1997. *Local Heroes: The Political Economy of Russian Regional Governance*. Princeton: Princeton University Press.

Twigg, Judyth L. 2002. What Has Happened to Russian Society? In *Russia after the Fall*, ed. Andrew C. Kuchins. Washington, DC: Carnegie Endowment for International Peace.

White, Anne. 2004. *Small-Town Russia: Postcommunist Livelihoods and Identities: A Portrait of the Intelligentsia in Achit, Bednodemyanovsk and Zubtsov, 1999–2000*. London and NY: Routledge-Curzon.

World Population Review. 2018. *Population of Cities in Russia*. Accessed online at http://worldpopulationreview.com/countries/russia-population/cities/. December 2018.

# 2

# Before the Fall: The Soviet System

The world today is a fundamentally different place from that which existed at the end of World War II. Empires have disbanded, alliances have shifted, truths assumed to be eternal have proved ephemeral. In this book I examine how a number of women have adapted to a particular combination of these changes, brought about by the transfer of power in the Soviet Union to a new generation of leaders in the mid-1980s. For these women, almost everything they had been taught (and some, but not all of them, had believed) was repudiated by the new leaders; much of what they had prepared for as students and young adults had become obsolete; much of what they encountered was entirely unexpected. The "social contract" between rulers and the population—popular acceptance of the right of the Party leadership to remain in power in return for basic economic security and stability—was being rewritten (Cook 1993). So too was the "working mother gender contract," which captured the expected roles and responsibilities of men, women and the state in family life.[1] The women were bombarded

[1]For discussion of the development and impact of the working mother gender contract see, among others, Temkina and Rotkirkh (2002), Rotkirkh (2003), Temkina and Zdravomyslova (2003), Zdravomyslova (2003) and Zdravomysolova (2010).


J. McKinney, *Russian Women and the End of Soviet Socialism*,
https://doi.org/10.1007/978-3-030-16226-9_2

by new information, new possibilities, and new challenges. Twenty-five years later most of them had adapted with considerable grace and considerable success.

Although one of the women I interviewed had been a child during World War II, most grew up during the years of Nikita Khrushchev and Leonid Brezhnev. The terror of Stalinism and the extreme deprivation of the war years were in the past, but the basic economic and political arrangements remained those of Soviet-style communism. In this chapter, I provide an overview of that system.

## Economic System[2]

Originally intended to eliminate the inequality and exploitation that Marxists believed was made possible by private ownership of the means of production and the "anarchy" of the marketplace, the Soviet economic system was based on two fundamental principles. The first was that there should be social rather than private ownership of the means of production. In theory, this meant that Soviet workers collectively owned the country's capital stock–its factories and machinery, its oil rigs and coal mines, its shops and restaurants; in practice, however, social ownership meant ownership by the Soviet state.[3] The second key principle of the Soviet economic system was that the country's resources should be allocated among competing uses by means of central planning. The leaders of the Communist Party had the responsibility, enshrined in Article 6 of the Constitution, to guide the country and this authority included determining the direction of economic development. The dozen or so members of the Politburo set overall

[2]For a much more detailed description of the Soviet economic system, see such classic studies as Campbell (1974), Bergson (1964) and Nove (1977). For a brilliant fictional portrayal of the system in the early 1960s, see Spufford (2012). For a discussion of the strengths and weaknesses of the system at the time Gorbachev began his reforms, see Hewett (1988).

[3]The one significant exception to state ownership was found in agriculture, where in addition to state farms there were the collective farms, officially owned by the members who lived and worked there but responsible for obligatory delivery of crops to the state.

priorities and often set specific output targets for key products. The State Planning Committee (*Gosplan*), in collaboration with dozens of industrial ministries, was then responsible for determining output levels for individual producers in such a way that the goals of the Party leaders would be met.

In the early days of the Soviet Union, priorities were stark—to maintain power, to rebuild productive capacity destroyed during the years of war (first World War I and then the Civil War that followed the Bolshevik Revolution of 1917), and to create a heavy industrial base sufficient to defend the country in a future war. Such a war was considered inevitable by early Soviet leaders, who were certain that the capitalist West would not willingly accept the challenge posed by a country based on such fundamentally different principles. The relatively low level of industrial development in Russia at the time also meant that the number of products and producers to be taken into account was limited. It was therefore possible in those early years to approximate central planning, or at least to create the illusion of doing so.

Official ideology emphasized that central planning would ensure the best possible use of the country's scarce resources. Any effort to achieve a truly efficient use of the resources, however, was overwhelmed by the drive to produce impossibly high levels of output. Because there was no slack in the plans, minor problems could snowball, disrupting operations in many different industries and locations and wasting resources. Still, the relatively narrow focus of the leaders made it possible to concentrate resources where they were (believed to be) most needed and to achieve impressive rates of growth in heavy industry.[4]

Over time, as the economy modernized and living standards rose, albeit modestly, actual practice increasingly diverged from the formal process. Because it was impossible to create a plan from scratch each

[4]Official statistics on the growth rate were certainly exaggerated. Contemporaneous studies by Western analysts, as well as archival material which became accessible in the post-Soviet period, suggest considerably less dramatic achievements (see Jasny 1957; Bergson 1961; Ofer 1987; and Khanin and Seliunin 1987, for example). Nonetheless, there is no question that the country underwent an impressive degree of industrialization in this period.

year, most factories and ministries received annual plans that were simply more demanding versions of the previous year's plan. While this approach greatly simplified the planning process, it had at least two clearly undesirable consequences—the dampening of any significant innovation and the reluctance by enterprise managers to push their enterprises to achieve maximum possible performance, since to do so meant receiving an even higher target the following year. Because the planning task was so large and so time-consuming, the "final" plans—often still being modified well into the period of operation—were inevitably riddled with inconsistencies.

A vast bureaucracy attempted to direct economic activity and an equally vast bureaucracy attempted to monitor the results, rewarding those who performed well and punishing those who did not. Those in the bureaucracy were rewarded on the basis of how well those under their jurisdiction performed, clearly creating a perverse incentive to collude in over-reporting achievements and masking problems. Without Stalin's brutality, there was little to check this behavior in the 1960s and 1970s, and attitudes toward the plan and toward economic performance more generally became increasingly cynical, as captured in the oft-quoted Brezhnev-era line, "They pretend to pay us and we pretend to work."

The first part of this sentiment points not so much to a failure to give workers money to spend as to the failure (or refusal) to make this money meaningful. Soviet workers did receive wages and salaries on a regular basis (something that was definitely not true during the early post-Soviet years). This income, however, mattered far less than it would have in a market economy, since money was neither necessary nor sufficient to provide a claim on goods and services, and was often little more than a unit of account.

Because the leaders' priorities rather than consumer demands were supposed to determine the composition of output, prices did not play the important roles they do in a market system. In competitive markets, relative prices, determined by the interaction of supply and demand, indicate relative scarcity. In the Soviet system, however, prices were set by bureaucrats within the State Price Committee. (As with planning, the task was far too great for the designated committee to handle, so much of the price-setting was in practice delegated to the industrial ministries.) Given the magnitude of the task, prices were changed infrequently. As a result, supply and demand for specific goods were often extremely unbalanced, so queuing and connections were at least as important as money for the acquisition of goods. At times—in particular during both the early and final years of the Soviet system and during World War II—basic goods were rationed, so that one needed a coupon (and often money as well) to acquire them. Even when formal rationing was not in place, acquiring the goods one needed was never just about earning the money to pay for them.

Between World War II and the early 1980s, most Soviet citizens could count on having their basic needs met. Rents were low and stable, as were prices of basic foodstuffs and children's necessities. Medical care and education—from pre-school through graduate school—were provided free of charge. Even those with low income could therefore generally obtain these goods and services. At the same time, a high income did not guarantee access to something more or better. That required connections, luck, a willingness to engage in the second economy, or some combination thereof. There were two significant avenues for acquiring especially desirable goods or services—Party channels and networks of friends and family.

Those in the upper levels of the Communist Party hierarchy had access to special stores, special health clinics, and special cafeterias, as well as the occasional opportunity to travel abroad and shop in countries offering a wider array of consumer goods. For ordinary citizens, acquiring goods involved being in the right place at the right time—being first in line when a new shipment arrived or being in a position to trade favors. In some periods, work as a truck driver or sales clerk was considered especially desirable, since it provided some control over access to goods (Grossman 1977: 29). In all periods, having a family member (usually an older woman) who could devote hours to standing in line made a great difference to the quality of one's life.

As the *New York Times* correspondent in Moscow wrote in the mid-1970s:

> I noted in the Soviet press that Russians spend 30 billion man-hours in line annually just to make purchases. That does not count several billion more man-hours expended waiting in tailor shops, barbershops, post offices, savings banks, dry cleaners and various receiving points. (Smith 1976: 83)

The role of queues in Soviet life and the complicated cultural rules that arose to shape the operation of these queues are brilliantly captured in Vladimir Sorokin's aptly named novella *The Queue*, written in the early 1980s and first published in the West (Sorokin 2008). Although the number of situations requiring queuing today has fallen sharply, the unwritten rules for navigating queues do not seem to have changed much and can be a source of considerable frustration for a foreigner attempting to purchase a postage stamp or a train ticket.

Soviet wages and salaries, like prices, were centrally set and the leaders struggled to find the right degree of differentiation within the wage structure. This was a delicate balancing act. It was important to have a small enough difference between the top and bottom tiers to justify claims that the Soviet system was more egalitarian than the capitalist system. At the same time, there needed to be a large enough gap to provide incentives to acquire the skills needed by the country and to encourage effort in the workplace, especially as the role of terror waned. In the later years, as growth rates slowed and consumer expectations rose, this balancing act became increasingly difficult. As wages and salaries rose faster than prices, the total amount of money in the hands of the public grew and eventually exceeded the total value of the consumer goods and services available for them to buy (Katsenelinboigen 1977). This macroeconomic imbalance further exacerbated the problems caused by the widespread mismatch between the particular goods and services people wanted and those the system was producing.

In addition to providing the population with income, wages and salaries played a role in the allocation of workers across industries and occupations. Within constraints posed by the total number of slots in the various education and training programs and by targets for employment and wage bills in the annual plans of enterprises, Soviet citizens were largely free to respond to wage and salary incentives when deciding what careers to pursue and which jobs to hold. Like most of the rest of the planned system, however, this arrangement was shot full of exceptions and loopholes and could be used to punish or to privilege.

Admission to universities and other education al establishments was determined by application and testing rather than by official assignment. In the early years, admission was heavily influenced by the Party's desire to protect the state from "class enemies" (those who had been privileged prior to the Revolution and could therefore be expected to look unfavorably upon the new system) and to advance the careers of those from the proletariat. Later, access to education, like most other coveted goods and services, became subject to corruption and bribery. Upon graduation, a young person received a three-year assignment to a particular job as a way to compensate the state for his or her education.

Since wage rates were set by the state, it should have been impossible for enterprises to compete for workers, but in the face of strong excess demand for workers Soviet managers devised a variety of ways to get around this—reclassifying positions, for example, or offering a higher position in the waiting list for enterprise-controlled housing—and labor turnover in the post-Stalin period was not significantly lower than in other industrial countries (Wiles 1984). This labor turnover was almost entirely initiated by the workers themselves. It was extremely rare for someone to be fired from a job under the Soviet system. Not only did the Soviet Constitution, in both its 1936 and 1977 versions, guarantee employment, but the pressures of fulfilling the annual plan and the lack of attention to costs ensured that enterprises had an incentive to keep as many workers on hand as possible. Even in the 1960s, as the country experimented with efforts to increase productivity and efficiency, enterprises were encouraged to find new roles for workers whose positions were eliminated rather than laying them off. Only those perceived by the state as politically unreliable–the dissidents and "refuseniks" of the 1960s and 1970s—were likely to have any trouble finding or keeping jobs.

From the perspective of the ordinary Soviet citizen, then, the economic system, especially under Brezhnev, provided the security of employment and stable prices, with considerable freedom to choose one's place of work. It also ensured that for most of the citizens most of the time basic economic needs were met. It did not, however, meet the rising expectations of an increasingly urban, increasingly educated population.

## Standard of Living[5]

Contrary to Karl Marx's expectations, the first proletarian revolution did not take place in Germany or England, countries which had experienced the Industrial Revolution relatively early and had large populations of urban industrial workers. Instead, it occurred in predominantly rural Russia. The industrial backwardness of the country, coupled with its isolation from the rest of the world, meant that the first priority of the new Soviet leadership was to develop the industrial base. The development of heavy industry was to be carried out at a relentlessly rapid pace. In the meantime, it was believed, the basic needs of the population could be met by reducing inequality: if no one consumed too much, there would be enough for everyone to consume what was essential.

In the early years, rationing seemed the surest way to achieve this, and access to food (and at times other critical goods) was granted via ration coupons, with different quantities allocated to those with different "scientifically determined" physiological requirements—for example, those involved in heavy manual labor versus members of the intelligentsia. Although explicit rationing was abandoned by the mid-1930s, it was reintroduced during World War II and again, much later, for particular food products. With or without official rationing, the availability of consumer goods was always a low priority. For decades Soviet citizens were told that they were preparing for a glorious future and that sacrifice today was necessary to achieve the promised abundance later. A combination of ideological fervor and harsh repression kept near-term expectations under control and the population had little choice but to accept the crowded housing, limited diet, drab clothing and dearth of consumer durables and services. While post-Stalin leaders did allocate more resources to household consumption, the sector

[5]Much of this and the following section draws on my article (2004).

remained vulnerable to cuts during both the revision and the implementation of plans.

Prior to Khrushchev, there was very little investment in housing. For the entire period from 1918 through the first quarter of 1941, only about 409 million square meters of new useful living space were created. Khrushchev and Brezhnev made housing construction a higher priority. More useful living space was introduced during the Sixth Five-Year Plan (1956–1960) than for the entire period between the revolution and the German invasion during World War II, and the volume of new housing continued to increase through 1985, except for a slight dip in the Tenth Five-Year Plan (1976–1980). Nonetheless, at the end of 1986, when the Soviet population was almost 280 million, there were only about 4 billion square meters of useful living space in the country (Gosudarstvennyi komitet SSSR 1987: 373, 509, 514, 517). At less than 14.5 square meters per person, this is not much more than the typical American college student enjoys in half of a dormitory double.[6]

This lack of housing space created significant stress in the lives of Soviet families, especially those living in cities, where communal apartments were the norm. In these, several unrelated families shared a single kitchen and bathroom, with each separate family crowded into its own small room. Younger workers, even married couples, were often housed in dormitories. Young couples who managed to avoid worker dormitories often lived with the parents of one of them. This had its benefits: despite the lack of privacy, it expanded the circle of adults who could cooperate in acquiring goods, providing child and elder care, and taking care of household responsibilities.

Consumer durables and consumer services were also in short supply. Despite efforts by Khrushchev and Brezhnev, the stock of household appliances remained low throughout the Soviet period, especially in rural areas.[7] The picture for consumer services was even bleaker

---

[6]According to http://dormstormer.com/average-dorm-room-size/, accessed 3 October 2018, a college dorm room is "typically smaller than 130 square feet" or 180 square feet for a double (Dormstormer 2018).

[7]The one exception seems to have been sewing machines, which in the 1980s were more common in rural households, presumably because the need was greater in areas with little access to retail outlets for clothing.

than that for goods. Such services grew extremely slowly until late in the Khrushchev years, and the level remained inadequate up to the end. The number of retail trade outlets per 10,000 people had barely increased from 1940 to 1986, rising from 21 to 25 over that period (Gosudarstvennyi komitet SSSR 1987: 496). By comparison, in 1997 there were approximately 22,649 trade retail establishments per 10,000 people in the United States, roughly 1000 times the 1986 density for the Soviet Union (US Census Bureau 1997: 11).

In addition to the inadequate supply of goods and services, Soviet consumers endured low quality and little variety. Soviet refrigerators, for example, were very small and, as late as 1973, two-thirds of the washing machines available required that one wring out the clothes by hand (Schroeder and Severin 1976: 634). Central planning functioned at all only by keeping output targets highly aggregated, and the incentive system ensured that those aspects of production not specified in the plan would get short shrift. Enterprises had nothing to gain and much to lose from shortening production runs in order to diversify output, while the push to meet the month's output target meant that even flawed units would be counted toward that target.

Despite the rhetoric of a classless society and the elimination of one key cause of inequality in capitalist economies—the income received because of assets owned rather than work performed—the Soviet system did not eradicate economic inequality. While in most periods there were meaningful differences in pay based on skills and experience, the real roots of inequality lay elsewhere. What mattered most was not wages received but access to goods, and that depended primarily on the distribution system. The leaders and planners determined where goods would be sent; if there were no attractive goods in the stores to which one had access, earning more money wasn't much help.

There was both a political/social hierarchy and a geographic hierarchy in the distribution of goods. As mentioned above, Party members, especially those in leadership positions, had access to special stores, cafeterias, hospitals, and apartments. Similar privileges were accorded to select members of the cultural and sports elite. In addition to the privileges that came with occupation and Party membership, there were privileges that came from having a permit (*propiska*) to live in Moscow or

Leningrad, since access to goods varied sharply depending on where one lived.[8] Moscow was in a class by itself, other large cities followed, then provincial capitals, other cities, and finally the small villages scattered throughout the countryside. To some extent this allocation mirrored the allocation of money income and so made sense, but the inadequate attention paid to all but the primary cities went far beyond what would have occurred under a market system. As a result, train stations in Moscow and Leningrad were crowded with women surrounded by piles of bags and boxes, waiting to return home with the goods they could buy only by traveling to these centers.

## Situation of Women, or the Working Mother's Gender Contract

The low priority accorded consumption by Soviet planners took its greatest toll on women, who bore almost complete responsibility for maintaining the household despite holding full-time jobs in the formal sector. Early Bolshevik visions of freeing women from virtually all household and childcare responsibilities through the development of public institutions for those purposes were soon abandoned, but the state's need to have women performing both waged labor and reproductive labor continued. To make it possible for women to fulfill both roles, the government provided support to working mothers in the form of both financial assistance and daycare facilities. Thus, women's dual burden was not only recognized but actively encouraged by the state, which was an important third party to the gender contract that developed under Stalinism. Following Temkina and Rotkirkh (2002: 4), I include in gender contract "institutional support, practices and the symbolic representation of gender relations, roles and identities (translation mine)" but I do not here address sexual norms and practices.

[8]Often described as a means of controlling migration flows within the country, the residence permit also served as a means of rationing scarce goods and services, since only those with the necessary documentation were eligible to receive housing, education, health care, or particular "deficit goods." See Buckley (1995).

The emphasis on working mothers was especially critical in the 1930s and 1940s since the high male death rates for most of the first half of the twentieth century—the result of two world wars, a civil war, famine, forced collectivization and purges—meant both fewer male workers and large numbers of women who would never marry. If the country wanted women to fill jobs in industry (or elsewhere in the economy) to make up for the missing men, it needed to provide care for their children during the hours they were away from home; if the country wanted women to have children, it needed to make it possible for them to raise those children outside of marriage.

As a result, the Family Code adopted in 1944 included provisions for the state to support children of unmarried women up to the age of 12 (McKinney 2004: 42–43; Harwin 1996: 19–20). In the post-World War II period, although demographic and economic conditions improved considerably, the basic elements of the working mother gender contract continued and, in the early 1980s, in response to concern over a falling birth rate, maternity benefits were increased. In 1983, in the final decade of the Soviet system, the total paid by the state in the form of child-related allowances—consisting of payments to pregnant women, to children up until their first birthday, to lone mothers and mothers of large families, and to children in poor families—was 4.4 billion rubles, out of total social spending of 125.6 billion. The state also spent four times that amount providing child-care services such as infant care, pre-school and after-school care, boarding schools and summer camp (Tsentral'noe statististicheskoe upravlenie SSSR 1985: 84–85; *Narodnoe khoziaistvo SSSR v 1985 g*: 559). The share of school-age children in after-school facilities rose in the 1970s from about 10% to over 26% (Harwin 1996: 38–40); the number of children served by pre-school facilities reached 15.5 million in 1983 (Tsentral'noe statististicheskoe upravlenie SSSR 1985: 8); in 1990, 66.4% of all children of pre-school age were enrolled in such facilities (Gosudarstvennyi komitet rossiskoi federatsii po statistike 1992: 231).

Soviet women participated in the paid labor force at a very high rate by international standards, reflecting both the Marxist belief that such employment was essential for their liberation and the stark reality that few Soviet families could subsist on the wages of a single earner. This was especially true because wages were only one—and not always the most important—way in which employment contributed to economic well-being. Workplaces often controlled access to housing, childcare, medical care, vacation spots, garden plots, and a variety of scarce goods (Rotkirkh 2000: 17).

Despite state assistance to working mothers, Soviet women continued to struggle to meet the demands of their jobs and the needs of their children. Although they spent only slightly fewer hours a week than men in paid employment and meeting their physiological needs, according to time-budget studies carried out in the 1960s they spent more than twice as much time as men performing housework (Lapidus 1978: 270–271). A government survey conducted in March of 1980 found that, on average, Soviet women who worked for state enterprises (virtually all employed women except those on collective farms) spent over 6 hours a week acquiring goods and services and an additional 29.5 hours a week on housework (Tsentral'noe statististicheskoe upravlenie SSSR 1985: 89). The lack of labor-saving appliances increased the workload, as did the lack of retail outlets. Ironically, Khrushchev's efforts to provide more housing contributed to the demands on women's time, since the new apartment buildings were built on the edges of cities, and the construction of shops in the area usually lagged far behind.[9]

The dual burden, combined with the low priority given to consumer goods and services by the state, meant that providing for their children often required the support of both extended family and a sizeable social network. Colleagues shopped for one another, shared information about where to acquire scarce (*defitsitnyi*) goods, covered for one another on the job, and otherwise exchanged the favors without which life would have been much harder.

[9]The challenges and stresses of daily life for women are captured beautifully in Natalia Baranskaya's novella *A Week Like Any Other*, published in 1969 but still germane twenty years later (Baranskaya 1993).

## Political System

After it became clear that the Bolshevik Revolution would not serve as a catalyst for proletarian revolutions across the industrialized world and that the Soviet leaders would need to "build socialism in one country"—at least for the foreseeable future—ideological purity gave way to practical necessity (and to Stalin's paranoia). Marx's prediction that the state would "wither away" was not borne out. Instead, the role of the state expanded as the government and Party apparatus attempted to control economic, political and cultural activity in the country, channeling all toward the intermingled goals of maintaining power within the country and defending the country against external enemies. While these goals were never abandoned, after victory in World War II, the establishment of Soviet-style systems in the countries of Eastern Europe, and recognition of the USSR's status as a global superpower, the nature of the compact between the leadership and the population shifted and Stalinist terror was largely replaced by political stability and economic security. Always, however, the power of the state was there, often in the background, but available to be exercised whenever any threat was suspected.

Probably the most important—and most confusing—aspect of the Soviet political system was the existence of dual bureaucracies, the parallel yet overlapping structures of the Soviet government on the one hand and the Communist Party on the other. As stipulated in Article 6 of the Soviet Constitution, "The leading and guiding force of Soviet society and the nucleus of its political system, of all state organizations and public organizations, [was] the Communist Party of the Soviet Union."[10] Real authority thus rested with the Party—all candidates for government positions were named by the Party organization, all elections were uncontested, and all laws and policies were initiated by the Party—but the Party did not, itself, constitute the formal government.

[10]An online copy of the 1977 Soviet constitution is available in English at the website http://www.departments.bucknell.edu/russian/const/77cons01.html, accessed 27 June 2017 (Constitution (Fundamental Law) of the Union of Soviet Socialist Republics 1977).

The distinction between Party and Government was often murky. Both Stalin and Khrushchev served simultaneously as head of the Communist Party (Stalin as General Secretary, Khrushchev in the briefly renamed position of First Secretary) and as head of the government (as Chairman of the Council of Ministers or Prime Minister). Neither man, however, ever served as the country's president, the largely ceremonial position of Chairman of the Presidium of the Supreme Soviet.

Following Khrushchev's ouster in the mid-1960s, the distinction between Party and State was sharper, as the offices of President of the Soviet state, Prime Minister of the government and General Secretary of the Party were briefly held by three different individuals, respectively Nikolai Podgorny, Alexei Kosygin and Leonid Brezhnev. This division of labor, intended to avoid the dangers of one-man rule, was short-lived. By 1977, Brezhnev had assumed the presidency—though he never became Prime Minister—and Kosygin's more liberal views had been discredited, although he remained as Prime Minister until late 1980, when he resigned in poor health shortly before his death. The three leaders who followed Brezhnev—Yuri Andropov, Konstantin Chernenko, both very briefly, and Mikhail Gorbachev—continued the practice of serving both as General Secretary and as Chairman of the Presidium of the Supreme Soviet.

The shifting titles of those at the top of the hierarchy reflected and reinforced the confusing relationship between the two bureaucracies. To some extent they were parallel structures, with many similar offices. Since the Party apparatus was charged with ensuring that the policies adopted by the Party leadership were implemented and since these policies addressed virtually all aspects of life, the structure of that bureaucracy necessarily reflected the increasing complexity of the society and the economy. Thus, there needed to be a Party office with responsibility for foreign affairs, another with responsibility for agriculture, another with responsibility for culture, and so forth. Furthermore, because the government was organized as a federation of fifteen republics, the national structure was largely replicated at the union-republic level for fourteen of the republics. In recognition of its special "first among equals" status, the lone exception was Russia (the Russian Soviet

Federated Socialist Republic), the capital of which, Moscow, served as the seat of each of the union-wide entities.

Further complicating the picture were the primary party organizations connected to every place of employment. These organizations formed the lowest tier of the Party hierarchy and sent delegates to Party conferences that elected the members of the Party committees. Thus, the Party was intertwined with both the government structure and the economic structure. At the same time, the government and economy were also intertwined, since there was a government bureaucracy responsible for drawing up and overseeing the implementation of the plans that directed economic activity. Despite this Byzantine bureaucratic structure, the details of which changed fairly frequently in an attempt to improve the flow of information and increase effective control, the essence of the system was simple and constant. That remained the dominant role of the Party and the small group of men who ran it, even as that group became less and less capable of overseeing a large and complex economy and a population that had changed dramatically since the time of the Revolution.

By the time Mikhail Gorbachev became General Secretary of the Communist Party and thus head of the country, the population had become accustomed to elderly and somewhat embarrassing leaders. Leonid Brezhnev had held the top post from the fall of 1964, when Nikita Khrushchev was ousted, until his death in November of 1982, by which time he was both physically and mentally frail. Brezhnev was followed by two more leaders born before the Bolshevik Revolution, both of whom died in office and neither of whom served for much more than a single year. The selection of Gorbachev initially injected new energy into the system and his reforms eventually led to wide-ranging and remarkably open discussion, but his popularity within the country soon waned, as life for most Soviet citizens became more rather than less difficult.

Although the roughly 10% of the adult population who belonged to the Communist Party were expected to shoulder certain political responsibilities in their workplaces and neighborhoods, by the 1960s and 1970s true ideological fervor was no longer demanded. It was widely understood that Party membership was an important qualification for a successful career and the mandatory participation in Party meetings and Party work was often *pro forma*.[11] It was, however, sufficiently time-consuming that it represented a real burden for working mothers, and women frequently sacrificed both Party and professional advancement in order to devote necessary time to caring for the home and family.

While even in the mid-eighties 53% of the Soviet population was female—the long-lasting result of the high number of male deaths during the early decades of the century—just 28% of Party members were women (*Zhenshchiny i deti v SSSR* 1985: 28). Representation in the Central Committee of the Party was lower still, never reaching even 5% after 1917, and only two women ever served on the Politburo prior to Gorbachev's time as General Secretary (Lapidus 1978: 219).[12]

Women did, however, serve in the representative bodies of the state, since quotas guaranteed them seats. In 1984, 33% of seats in the Supreme Soviet of the USSR and on average 50% of the seats in soviets at the *oblast*, *krai* and local level were held by women (*Zhenshchiny i deti* 1985: 25). Until the late 1980s these representative bodies voted unanimously and rousingly for all proposals and candidates put forward by the Party leaders so this guaranteed right to participate provided no real power or voice.[13] Nonetheless, when compared to data for the USA (where a total of 10 women served in the House of Representatives at some point in the 1960s and only one woman served in the Senate), the presence of women in the Soviet government and Communist Party was noteworthy.

For those Soviet citizens who did not join the Communist Party, political activity was largely confined to casting ballots for those serving

[11]See Yurchak (2006) for an intriguing analysis of the way young members of the Party used *pro forma* observation of many responsibilities in order to have the opportunity to carry out a kind of Party work they considered more meaningful.

[12]The two women on the Politburo were Elena Stasova in the very early years and Yekatarina Furtseva under Khrushchev. Furtseva also served as Minister of Culture.

[13]According to Carol Nechemias (1996: 21), from 1966 to 1973 women made up 10.5% of those who spoke on the floor of the USSR Supreme Soviet (roughly equivalent to the share for the US Congress) while filling approximately 30% of the seats. Nechemias cites Hough (1977: 142).

in the various levels of government. Voting was required by law, but since races were always uncontested this was not a challenging task. In fact, in some cases one's vote was cast without one's personal presence or involvement. Party members were judged on turnout in their districts, so even if someone were ill or otherwise unwilling or unable to go to the polls he or she might be counted as having voted. This, of course, contributed to widespread cynicism. This cynicism, however, was tempered by a lack of understanding of how things worked outside the borders of their country, since even the educated, professional urban population had limited exposure to the rest of the world and to alternative news media.

Control over contact with and access to information about the rest of the world remained an essential component of Soviet rule. This control was achieved in a variety of ways, including censorship of the media, tight restrictions on travel abroad, confiscation at the border of material deemed inappropriate, and warnings against interaction with foreigners spending time in the country. In fact, even communication among Soviet citizens was made difficult since there were few private telephones and no publicly available telephone directories. City street maps were also limited and there were virtually no non-Party civic organizations in which like-minded people could come together.

## Late Soviet Period

Despite frequent changes in the details, the basic features of the Soviet economic and political system—the leading role of the Party, the allocation of resources according to centrally determined economic plans, the limits to freedom of expression and opportunities to travel—remained constant for decades. Nonetheless, by the late 1970s Soviet society had changed dramatically and the ways in which the population and the system interacted had changed in response.

The economic successes—industrialization, urbanization, rising standard of living—brought new challenges. The possibilities for extensive growth (increasing output by increasing the quantity of inputs used) had largely been exhausted and intensive growth (increasing output by increasing the productivity of inputs) was possible only with continuous innovation and increased attention to quality, goals the system had struggled to achieve. The rate at which the economy was growing continued to slow, while the telecommunications revolution in the West upset the balance in the Cold War arms race.

The rising standard of living led to rising expectations, and the Brezhnev-era social contract, which promised economic security and stability in return for support of the Party's leadership, began to fray. Increased education levels made the population less susceptible to the Party's rhetoric, and increased interaction with the rest of the world made censorship less effective. As Alexei Yurchak argues, "the performative dimension of authoritative discourse started to play a much greater role than its constative dimension" (2006: 37). As a result, ideological pronouncements became more difficult to interpret (50–54), making it possible for "late socialism [to become] marked by an explosion of various styles of living that were simultaneously inside and outside the system" (128).

For decades the leadership struggled unsuccessfully to adapt to the demands placed on it by the new conditions. Early attempts at reform were too limited and tentative and when Gorbachev presided over more far-reaching and fundamental reforms the system imploded, leaving the population to try to create and adapt to a whole new economic, political and social reality. The following chapters explore what this meant in the lives of a number of Russian women in Yaroslavl, both in the early years of rapid and unpredictable changes and in the period of greater stability during which I spoke to them.

## References

Baranskaya, Natalia. 1993. *A Week Like Any Other*, trans. Emeryville, CA: Seal Press.

Bergson, Abram. 1961. *The Real National Income of Soviet Russia since 1928*. Cambridge, MA: Harvard University Press.

Bergson, Abram. 1964. *The Economics of Soviet Planning*. New Haven: Yale University Press.

Buckley, Cynthia. 1995. The Myth of Managed Migration: Migration Control and Market in the Soviet Period. *Slavic Review* 54 (4): 896–916.

Campbell, Robert W. 1974. *The Soviet-Type Economies: Performance and Evolution*. Boston: Houghton Mifflin.

Constitution (Fundamental Law) of the Union of Soviet Socialist Republics. 1977. Accessed online at http://www.departments.bucknell.edu/russian/const/77cons01.html. June 2017.

Cook, Linda. 1993. *The Soviet Social Contract and Why It Failed*. Cambridge, MA: Harvard.

Dormstormer. 2018. Average Dorm Room Size. Accessed online at http://dormstormer.com/average-dorm-room-size/. October 3.

Gosudarstvennyi komitet rossiskoi federatsii po statistike. 1992. *Narodnoe khoziaistvo rossiiskoi federatsii*. Moscow: Respublikanskii informatsionno-izdatel'skii tsentr.

Gosudarstvennyi komitet SSSR po statistike. 1987. *Narodnoe khoziaistvo SSSR za 70 let*. Moscow: Finansy i statistika.

Grossman, Gregory. 1977. The 'Second Economy' of the USSR. *Problems of Communism* 26 (5): 25–40.

Harwin, Judith. 1996. *Children of the Russian State: 1917–1995*. Aldershot/Brookfield: Avebury.

Hewett, A. (eds.). 1988. *Reforming the Soviet Economy: Equality vs. Efficiency*. Washington, DC: Brookings Press.

Hough, Jerry F. 1977. *The Soviet Union and Social Science Theory*. Cambridge, MA: Harvard.

Jasny, Naum. 1957. *The Soviet 1956 Statistical Handbook: A Commentary*. East Lansing: Michigan State University Press.

Katsenelinboigen, Aron. 1977. Disguised Inflation in the Soviet Union: The Relationship Between Soviet Income Growth and Price Increases in the Postwar Period. In *The Socialist Price Mechanism*, ed. Alan Abouchar, 170–183. Durham, NC: Duke University.

Khanin, Grigorii, and Vasilii Seliunin. 1987. Lukavaia tsifra. *Novyi Mir* (2), 181−201.

Lapidus, Gail Warshofsky. 1978. *Women in Soviet Society: Equality, Development, and Social Change*. Berkeley: University of California Press.

McKinney, Judith Record. 2004. Lone Mothers in Russia: Soviet and Post-Soviet Policy. *Feminist Economics* 10 (2): 37–60.

Nechemias, Carol. 1996. Women's Participation: From Lenin to Gorbachev. In *Russian Women in Politics and Society*, eds. Wilma Rule and Norma C. Noonan, 15–30. London: Greenwood Press.
Nove, Alec. 1977. *The Soviet Economic System*. London: George Allen & Unwin.
Ofer, Gur. 1987. Soviet Economic Growth: 1928–1985. *Journal of Economic Literature* 25 (4): 1767–1833.
Rotkirkh, Anna. 2000. *The Man Question: Loves and Lies in Late Twentieth Century Russia*. Accessed online at https://www.academia.edu/2643465/. May 2019.
Rotkirkh, Anna. 2003. 'Coming to Stand on Firm Ground': The Making of a Soviet Working Mother. In *On Living Through Soviet Russia*, eds. Daniel Bertaux, Anna Rotkirch, and Paul Thompson, 144–173. London: Routledge Studies in Memory and Narrative.
Schroeder, Gertrude E., and Barbara S. Severin. 1976. Soviet Consumption and Income Policies in Perspective. In *Soviet Economy in a New Perspective*, 620–660. Washington, DC: US Government Printing Office.
Smith, Hedrick. 1976. *The Russians*. New York: Quadrangle Press.
Sorokin, Vladimir. 2008. *The Queue*, trans. from the Russian by Sally Laird. New York: New York Review of Books.
Spufford, Francis. 2012. *Red Plenty*. Minneapolis: Graywolf Press.
Temkina, Anna, and Elena Zdravomyslova. 2003. Gender Studies in Post-Soviet Society: Western Frames and Cultural Differences. *Studies in East European Thought* 55 (1): 51–61.
Temkina, A.A., and A. Rotkirkh. 2002. Sovetskie gendernye kontrakty i ikh transformatsia v sovremennoï Rossii [The Contracts Between the Sexes in the USSR and Their Transformation in Contemporary Russia]. *Sotsiologitcheskie Issledovania* 11: 4–14.
Tsentral'noe statististicheskoe upravlenie SSSR. 1985. *Narodnoe khoziaistvo SSSR v 1985 g*. Moscow: Finansy i statistika.
US Census Bureau. 1997. *Economic Census: Retail Trade, 1997*. Accessed online at http://www.census.gov/prod/ec97/97r44-sm.pdf. November 2002.
Wiles, Peter. 1984. Wage and Income Policies. In Leonard Schapiro and Joseph Godson, eds. *The Soviet Worker from Lenin to Andropov*, 15–38. New York: St. Martin's Press.
Yurchak, Alexei. 2006. *Everything Was Forever, Until It Was No More: The Last Soviet Generation*. Princeton: Princeton University Press.

Zdravomyslova, Elena. 2010. Working Mothers and Nannies: Commercialization of Childcare and Modifications in the Gender Contract (A Sociological Essay). *Anthropology of East Europe Review* 28 (2): 200–225.
Zdravomyslova, O.M. 2003. *Sem'ia i obchtchestvo: gendernoe izmerenie rossiiskoï transformatsii* [The Family and Society: Gender-Based Measures in Russian Transformation]. Moscow.
*Zhenshchiny i deti v SSSR.* 1985. Moscow: Finansy i statistika.

# 3

# Challenges and Opportunities of the Early Post-Soviet Years

## Introduction

The dissolution of the Soviet system posed an enormous array of challenges for the population, both logistical and psychological. Once again, as in the years of Stalin's big industrialization push, people were told that the hardships were temporary, that struggle today was needed to achieve a brighter future—this time one marked by the innovation, consumer abundance and freedoms of democratic market capitalism. The hardships to be endured along the way included severe shortages, steep price increases, long delays in the payment of wages, extreme uncertainty—and a significant change in the relationship between the state and the population. At precisely the moment when life was becoming more difficult, the government was retreating from its practice of heavily subsidizing housing, childcare and essential consumer goods, its active involvement in the allocation of jobs and housing, and its commitment to provide for all, leaving people to fend for themselves under circumstances for which they were largely unprepared.

At the same time, the end of the Soviet system offered both economic and political opportunities for those eager to take advantage of the



J. McKinney, *Russian Women and the End of Soviet Socialism*,
https://doi.org/10.1007/978-3-030-16226-9_3

situation. People who had chafed under the restrictions on free speech and travel, those who suspected the KGB of hindering their professional advancement, and those who saw the chance to give free rein to their entrepreneurial spirit (or to exploit being in a position to appropriate state resources for personal benefit) believed, at least at first, that the future was indeed promising.

The stories my respondents shared illustrated both the challenges and the opportunities of the early post-Soviet years and talking about the period evoked a wide range of emotions. There was sadness and anger, of course, but also pride and some amusement. Some of the women focused on the hardships of those early years, others on the excitement and optimism they had felt. For some, the memories were clearly painful and talking about the difficulties brought them to the edge of tears. For others, looking back provided the opportunity to highlight how well they had managed to cope and how much they had achieved, accomplishments that would not have been possible under the Soviet system. Still others—women who had been politically active when elections first became contested and saw Putin's reelection in the spring of 2012 as evidence that the early promise of democracy had been betrayed—viewed the early years with nostalgia.

These differences in the tenor of their recollections naturally lay in part in how successful they had managed to be, but since all but one of the women I spoke with fell into the mid-range of Russian material well-being, income was not a significant distinguishing characteristic. I spoke to only one who lived in poverty and none who lived in luxury (although the former husband of one now owns "a large company in Moscow" and a couple have sons who seem to be highly successful). The differences in tone seemed primarily to reflect differences in personality and in the relative weight they gave to material comfort, political empowerment and intellectual freedom.

While no one—except for a woman who was working for an oil company—suggested that the period of the late 1980s and early 1990s had been anything but difficult, there was considerable variation in the nature of the challenges the women emphasized. For some what was most vivid were the practical difficulties of feeding and caring for their children, for others it was the struggle to find and hold jobs that provided an adequate income. Several of the women dismissed the economic difficulties in a few brief sentences, focusing instead on the emotional pain of watching their children adrift in a society so unfamiliar that none of the old norms of behavior seemed to hold or of being forced themselves to behave in ways that made them feel ashamed. Even those women who rejoiced in some of the ways the state became less involved in and controlling of day-to-day life found its withdrawal from other aspects troubling, in particular the abdication of its commitment to economic security and stability. Below I offer glimpses of this range of responses before exploring them in more depth in later chapters.

## "So Offended by the Government": Failure to Care for the Disabled, the Elderly and the Young

The most negative assessments of the period were offered by women who felt that the government had broken faith with them or with members of their families. Despite the dissolution of the USSR and the fall from power—and temporary abolition—of the Communist Party, the women who were angry at the government's failure generally did not distinguish between the Soviet-era government and that which followed. It was clear that they did not believe that the change in leadership and political system in any way exonerated those newly in power from responsibility for anything that had been carried out or promised by their predecessors. The "government" (whoever happened to be in power) had stopped fulfilling its side of the social contract and this was seen as a betrayal.

One particularly striking example of the refusal to distinguish between Soviet and post-Soviet governments is found in this complaint from the oldest, poorest and least-educated woman I interviewed.

> Our stupid Soviet laws—they're the reason I'm against [Russia], the reason I don't love our country and our authorities. My daughter had a husband. [He] died. They had a one-room apartment. And her son chased his mother out of that apartment. We (his grandfather and I) had given the son an education; he finished the military-medical academy. And it turns out that we raised an idiot. The same one we held in our arms [crooning], "Dear little Sasha." And that Sasha drove his own mother out of the

> apartment and sold it. And the laws allowed him to do all that, to drive his own mother out of her apartment.... All of this was allowed by our laws, even though it seems to me that she should have been protected by the law and the government. She is an invalid of the Second Group.[1] And how is it possible to kick an invalid out of her apartment? It's good that I had a two-room apartment. If I hadn't..., the two of us would have been BOMZHi [acronym for the Russian expression "without definite place of residence," that is, homeless]. I just don't know where we would have spent the night, where we would have slept. That's the kind of strange laws we have in Russia, there's no other way I can put it. [Feodosia, 74]

Note that Feodosia blames "Soviet" laws for the loss of her daughter's apartment, even though what happened would have been impossible in the Soviet period. Only in the 1990s was the sale of apartments allowed. As with several other changes introduced in the 1990s, the attempt to create a housing market was carried out on the advice of Western experts, with insufficient attention to the characteristics of Soviet-era housing arrangements and inadequate preparation of the population to protect them from those eager to capitalize on the new economic opportunities and lagging legal code.[2] Failure to prepare the population adequately played a major role in widespread dissatisfaction with any number of post-Soviet policies and arrangements. As shown in Chapter 8, for example, a prominent theme when the women talked about voucher privatization was how little they understood about the program or its possibilities, and how easily they were duped.

Much of the dissatisfaction, however, had less to do with lack of understanding than with the sense of betrayal mentioned above. Both my oldest and youngest respondents spoke at length about the state's failure to care for the elderly, blaming the post-Soviet leaders for reneging on obligations incurred by the Soviet state.

---

[1]Beginning in 1932, the Soviet government classified the disabled based on the degree to which they could be expected to carry out productive labor. Group II "includes those not perceived to require constant nursing care who have lost some capability to work but may work in special conditions" (Phillips 2011: 51). I inferred that the daughter suffered a stroke that destroyed her short-term memory.

[2]For an examination of the attempts to develop a housing market and the dissatisfactions this has created, especially among the young, see Zavisca (2012).

Feodosia, born in 1938, said:

> This is why I am so offended by the government. I am very offended. People like me, children of the war, we grew up, we lived after the war and during the war with nothing. [Weeping] My feet were all blackened and now they pain me. And we, the children of the war, we see nothing, we receive nothing.

Oksana, only ten years old at the time of the dissolution of the Soviet Union, lamented the treatment of her grandparents:

> What was most offensive [was what happened to] people the age of my grandfather—he was born in 1926. These men… had worked all their lives in the Soviet Union and had retired. They had worked in difficult conditions, surviving the war, surviving the post-war period, surviving the repression…. That generation received nothing at all…. I'm talking about my grandmother, too, who worked her whole life as an engineer. And my grandfather in the 1960s [was recognized] for saving the Soviet government 2.5 million rubles, an enormous amount of money, as the head of a design bureau[3]…. He died of cancer in a tiny old house without even [an indoor] bathroom because we couldn't find or pay for anything more. And he wasn't the only one. There he lay in the hospital, interacting with others of his age, who [all] had given everything and received nothing in return.

Several of the other women who blamed the government for failing to take care of the population focused on the inadequate support they received as mothers of young children, although it is important to note that even some of those who gave birth well before the end of the Soviet system criticized the state for inadequate financial support. In fact, one of the most dismissive comments about government assistance came from a woman whose daughter was born in 1982.

> As it turned out, I raised her alone. For Russian women, this is a problem. We don't have the security of "child support," [using air quotes

[3]A design bureau was part of the research, development and innovation system, not part of the fashion industry.

> around the English phrase] and therefore all child care falls on the shoulders of moms who have no husband. It is really very difficult. It is difficult financially, because... Well, in 1983 I received 30 rubles [per month].... This was the support from the government for Russian moms until their child reached the age of one year.... At that time according to the official exchange rate—where one dollar was worth 60 kopeks—this would have been 50 dollars but in reality it was [worth]15 dollars. Fifteen dollars a month, that was the support. [Yulia, 52]

Another woman, who gave birth in 1990, near the very end of the Soviet period, received even less. She contrasts the lack of state support at that time not with what had been received by earlier generations, however, but with what is currently available under Vladimir Putin's pro-natalist policies.

> Today a woman who gives birth to a child—her first, her second—she receives help from the government. There's this maternal capital and even something more, but of course at that time it wasn't like that at all. Because it was right at the time of perestroika... and I received basically nothing at all from the government for my child, not a single kopek. Nothing at all. [Veronika, 51]

The maternal capital to which she refers is a sizeable lump sum—roughly $12,000—payable to women giving birth to or adopting a second or third child in Russia. A woman can receive this amount only once, so payment for a third child goes only to those whose second child was born before the program was introduced in 2007. These funds, which can be accessed only after the child reaches the age of three, must be used for specifically designated purposes: to improve a family's housing, to provide education for the child or, if the child has disabilities, to facilitate his or her "social adaptation and integration," or to fund a pension for the mother.[4,5]

---

[4]From the website of the Pension Fund of the Russian Federation, http://www.pfrf.ru/en/matcap/, accessed 28 June 2017. The program, originally intended to last ten years, has been extended to 2021 for families below the poverty level (Manuilova 2018). In his 2019 address to the Federal Assembly Putin called for an increase in the income level below which people qualify for child allowances, so that about 70% of families with one or two children will be eligible for government assistance, as well as for the lump-sum payment for those having a third or subsequent child (Presidential Address to the Federal Assembly 2019). Accessed March 2019 at http://en.kremlin.ru/events/president/news/59863.

[5]For an analysis of the use of these funds in the early years of the program, see Borozdina et al. (2011).

Putin's program, although far more generous than anything seen earlier, continues a long-standing practice of trying to boost birth rates in the country as a way to address population losses. In the Soviet period, the losses were due primarily to wars and repression; efforts to boost birth rates included making abortion illegal (from 1936 to 1955), celebrating Heroine Mothers (those giving birth to at least ten children), providing paid maternity leave, making one-time payments at birth, and providing monthly allowances for the first few years of a child's life. In the early post-Soviet period, the population losses were due primarily to sharp increases in mortality rates and sharp drops in life expectancy, especially for males, associated with alcoholism, suicides, accidents and an increase in cardiovascular disease (Kontorovich 2001: 234; Vishnevsky and Shkolnikov 1999: 59). According to official statistics, deaths per 1000 were 10.4 in 1986 and 15.7 in 1994; male life expectancy, which was 63.9 years in 1990, had fallen to 57.7 in 1994 (Goskom 1987: 407, 409; Goskom 1991: 94; Gorzev 1996: 35). Some critics have argued that Putin's emphasis on birth rates is therefore misplaced, and that efforts to reform the health care system and address health problems would be more effective. Although the birth rate has risen since the introduction of the maternity capital, demographers attribute this not to an increase in the total fertility rate but rather to an increase in the number of women of prime child-bearing age, and to the typical response to pro-natalist policies, which is to have one's children sooner than one might otherwise, without increasing the total number of children one has (Blank et al. 2017: 637–638).

Few of my respondents were still of child-bearing age when Putin introduced his policy, and none had been persuaded by earlier pro-natalist efforts to have lots of children. Many of the women had only one child, several had two, and only one had three. It is perhaps significant that the woman with three children spent her early married years in the Soviet republic of Kazakhstan, where the birth rate was far higher than in Russia, although not as high as in the other, more predominantly Muslim, Central Asian republics. In 1987, for example, while in the Russian Republic there were 17.1 births per thousand, in Kazakhstan there were 25.5 and in the other Central Asian republics there were between 32.6 and 41.8 (Goskom 1988: 354).

While my respondents may have viewed Soviet-era programs as inadequate, they had nonetheless clearly received the message that the working mothers' gender contract meant the government had a responsibility to help women raise their children. They considered the abdication of this responsibility one of the most serious failures of the post-Soviet leaders. The formal commitment to help provide for children and single-parent families was not actually eliminated after the dissolution of the Soviet Union, but declining output and an inability to collect taxes meant that the federal government lacked the funds to finance that commitment and it soon shifted responsibility to lower levels of government. Those too were short of funds, however, and found it necessary to rely more and more on in-kind transfers (McKinney 2004: 46; Manning et al. 2000: 59, 212; Foley and Klugman 1997: 194).

The economic difficulties of raising children during the period of perestroika and transition were compounded by psychological strains, strains that have lingered even after the economic challenges have eased. One of my respondents, after discussing how hard life had been for her in the late 1980s and early 1990s, spoke sorrowfully about how difficult this period was for her children, expressing both anger at those who flourished during the period and regret that she had somehow failed her children.

> My older son was born in 1980, and the younger in 1986, that is just before perestroika.... When I remember those years, I don't know how I survived. You know, I even suffered from depression. I was in such a state that I didn't even want to wake up in the morning or open my eyes, it was so hard.... It's terrible, what the country has lived through, and how many families fell apart at the time.... I wouldn't want to return to that time, to the 1990s, I wouldn't wish that for anyone....
>
> [My sons] didn't say anything to me, they didn't complain, but they also suffered, I saw it, and when I talk about it now I get goosebumps. Now that I've begun to remember, I see the whole picture. The things we didn't give our children in those years, when we should have given them. You understand, 15-16-year-old youths, when their childhood still hasn't ended.... And you want to prolong it for them. [Zoya, 52]

Other respondents offered an even more sobering view of what it was like to be young in the late 1980s and early 1990s. These were women grieving over their adult children, whom they saw as having been derailed or damaged by coming of age during a time of such confusion. The saddest of these cases was one I heard about in an unrecorded conversation. This woman's only son is an alcoholic in his thirties, unable or unwilling to keep a job, sometimes living with his parents, sometimes with a girlfriend, and so destructive when drunk that he has effectively made it impossible for his parents to enjoy a social life or keep their apartment in good repair. Despite the high incidence of alcoholism in Russia, there are few sources of real support, either for those struggling with their own addiction or for those who love them. It was clear that the situation caused my respondent not only enormous pain but also great shame and guilt.

While this was the saddest example I encountered, several women spoke with regret about the gap between their own values and those of their children, a gap they attributed to the situation in Russia at the time their children were adolescents. One woman, whose daughter chose not to attend university and has tried to make a living first in tourism and then as a photographer—that is, in what her mother sees as commerce—described it this way:

> This bad time left a stamp [*opechatok*, literally a misprint] on the young people. Even though ours was always a family of the *intelligentsia* and all of our circle belonged to the *intelligentsia*—we did not associate with other social layers at all—but all the same, this wave, it somehow engulfed all the young people, in my opinion.… It spoiled this generation; this generation was lost. Not all, of course, but we were not lucky in this regard. [Regina]

As this woman notes, "not all" Russians of the transition generation were lost. And, of course, whether one considers a child "lost" depends not only on the path the child follows but also on how that path conforms to the expectations of the parents. As we will see in later chapters, although several women regretted their children's decision not to pursue university education, others were able to take pride in the ways in which their offspring managed to navigate the new system, even if the careers were not those the parents would have chosen for them.

Failure to provide adequate support to the most vulnerable—the elderly and the very young—were not the only ways in which the post-Soviet government was seen as retreating from its Soviet-era commitment to the population. Several other forms of "betrayal"—such as allowing prices of necessities to rise, failing to pay wages on time, no longer guaranteeing education or employment, allowing the former non-Russian republics to become independent and allowing their titular nationalities to make their resentment of the Russians clear—are explored in later chapters.

## "Women Were Stronger Than Men"

In addition to changing the relationship between the state and the population, the events of this period forced adjustments in gender relationships as well. The conventional wisdom within Russia is that women coped better with the difficulties of transition than men did (Kay 2006: 27) and many of my respondents shared this belief. In some cases, this arose from painful personal experience; in others it seemed simply to reflect acceptance of the gender norms deeply embedded in the culture.

Sarah Ashwin has argued that these norms involved significant internal contradictions and rested on an unhappy union of traditional gender roles (man as provider, woman as caregiver) and Soviet institutional needs (women as well as men should participate in the labor force and the relationship of individuals with the state should matter more than relationships within the household). The result of these contradictions, Ashwin claims, was "strong, independent women who nevertheless ended up doing all the housework, and weak, 'feminine' men who none the less had the autonomy to relax, drink and escape the domestic arena (2000: 18). Anna Rotkirkh challenges the idea that the Soviet state should be seen as having supplanted the husband as family provider, noting that rural Russian women traditionally worked outside the walls of the home—usually "under the dictate of somebody else," that Russian households have traditionally consisted of extended rather than nuclear families, and that Russian women have long relied heavily on informal social networks as well as husband and/or state to meet the needs of the family (2003: 157–158). Despite these important qualifications, it seems clear that as the state withdrew from its commitment to provide for women and children, many Russian men were unprepared to take over that responsibility and the "strong, independent women" were forced to assume the additional task of figuring out how to navigate the new economic conditions (Kay 2006: 27).

This was in stark contrast to the vision, held by Gorbachev and other leaders, that the reforms would "make it possible for women to be returned to their purely womanly mission (Gorbachev 1987: 116)." It was hoped that as they shed the double burden of being employees as well as mothers, women would both refrain from taking jobs from the men who were believed to need them more and be in a position to address any number of social ills by staying home and tending to both their children and their husbands. This, it was believed, would prevent the children from becoming drug abusers, prostitutes or juvenile delinquents and the men from becoming alcoholics or emasculated drones (McKinney 2004: 45).

Instead, women found their contributions to providing for the family more critical than ever. The inability or unwillingness of some Russian men to rise to the challenges of the transition added to the difficulties the women faced, especially when the stresses led to the failure of their marriages or, in a couple of cases, to the death of a spouse. It also casts into sharp relief the initiative and coping skills displayed by the women, and my respondents often shaped their narratives to highlight this contrast. At the same time, it was clear from several of the stories I heard that many of the husbands had worked hard to support their families, had found ways to navigate the new system successfully, and had done what they could to help their wives navigate it as well. Here, I offer comments that express the standard view. In later chapters, especially in the discussion of employment and entrepreneurship, I present a number of recollections that call this view into question.

One woman, in her mid-twenties at the time the Soviet Union dissolved, described the experience of her circle of friends.

> I think that at that time women were stronger than men, during the period of perestroika. We all had a university education, a good education, and yet when there was no salary, there was no work, some [of us] washed floors, [some] went to market. I know a lot of girls who just became shuttle traders. They went to Poland or Turkey, they brought goods from there, and then they resold them, because they had to earn money.
>
> For many men, this seemed very strange, that with such an education one would deal with such matters. [Instead] they lay on the couch, then they began to drink, then there were divorces… I think the divorces were initiated by the women. It was because of alcohol, it was because of the men's unwillingness to work.… [We women think] 'I know that I need to make money, I will do any work.' [A man will say] 'Yes, I have a certain status, I have an education, I will not do it.' Women do not think that way. Russian women will go to wash floors, go to wash dishes, go to carry newspapers to the post office if they need money. [Marta]

Despite the difference in ages and, I believe, social position, a woman born in 1945 offered a remarkably similar view of Russian men and the reasons for divorce. Our conversation took place at a municipal social service center that provided a gathering space and activities for the retired.

> Yes, I lived with my husband [in the early 1990s], but we have such husbands! They sit on the couch and say, "We don't need anything more, we don't want anything more." We have such men, you know? They depend on women.… All the responsibility for the family fell on me; I saw that there was no one else but me, no one.… They just thrust their chest forward and it's all about themselves. We have such infantile men … [Malvina]

She emphasized the sharp contrast between her husband's response to the employment challenges of the period and her own. When perestroika began, they were both employed at a design bureau. When "everything there broke" and they weren't receiving their pay, they both left. She first went to work in a transportation enterprise and, when that failed to provide a living, she embarked on shuttle trading. Her husband, however, "was so dejected that he just went on disability." If he had been "a real man," she insisted, he would have taken a job in construction, which paid more, but "he just sat there.... Do you understand? This is what our men are like. Who is to blame for this? I don't know." When a woman sitting nearby suggested that not all men are the same, she replied, "No, it seems to me... Well, maybe in America they are not the same, after all, I don't know." (The other woman ended up winning the argument, however, because she then asked about Malvina's son, a successful businessman in Moscow of whom Malvina is extremely proud.)

Other women, while expressing sympathy for the struggles of the men, nonetheless also stressed the difference in ability to cope.

> I became a widow at 39.... When restructuring happens in countries, women ... are more resilient to change, we have more reserves of strength. And men, they have a very hard time going through that crisis. After all, they are responsible for the family. My husband was a manager. We lived very well, and then the plant began to fall apart and started not to pay the workers, and then laid off workers. In 1991, 1992, people were not paid a salary. He had to cut workers, then the shop itself. It was clear that the whole factory would be closed. Of course, he was in a terrible panic, because he did not understand how he could support his family at all, and he became ill.... Just because of the nervous system and the stress on the body, he had cancer of the blood and in 1995 he died, he was gone. He was only 42, still a young man. [Vera, 56]

While most comments about the differences in behavior and attitude between men and women focused on the period of the 1980s and 1990s, one observation took a longer perspective. Mentioning that most of the students who were coming to her for tutoring in 2012 were female—and adding parenthetically that she has never considered herself to be a feminist—Marta, aged 45, remarked: "And all the men have disappeared somewhere, they're involved in these political games and do nothing for the country."

Although several of my respondents remained in long-term, apparently successful marriages, only one explicitly mentioned the importance of that relationship in helping her survive the difficulties of the late 1980s and early 1990s. This woman's comments were also unusual because of her suggestion that women's unreasonable demands, not just men's weaknesses, contributed significantly to the marital difficulties of the time. Also obvious is her contempt for those who benefited during this period in ways she considered inappropriate.

> Many families did fall apart then, because the wife would say to her husband, 'You're incompetent, you can't provide for us, look at how our neighbors are living. He drives a foreign car, he has lots of money and it doesn't matter how he got the money, that's not important.' And very many families broke apart at that time and the children were left unhappy, they didn't matter to anyone. And so I think that a huge asset of my family is that we were able to preserve the family, not to quarrel, not to fall apart, but rather to come closer together. [Zoya, 52]

Zoya and her husband both worked for the Federal Migration Service at the time.

## "I Lived Through Perestroika with Great Difficulty": Poverty, Dissolution of the Soviet State, and Moral Bankruptcy

The three women for whom recollections of the late 1980s and early 1990s seemed most painful were my oldest respondent, born in 1938, my youngest, born in 1981, and a woman born in the 1960s. Not only did their ages vary, so did the nature of their grievances. For the oldest it was poverty, for the youngest it was the toll emigration from one of the non-Russian republics had taken on her mother, for the third, it was the loss of the moral values she identified with the Soviet system.

The elderly woman had little positive to say about any period of her life and was angry at the government for all she has endured. Sometimes it was the state itself which harmed her; at other times the state simply failed to protect her from harm inflicted by others, including a husband and a grandson.

> When perestroika began, in general it was worse in Russia than after the war. Just like after the war, there was nothing and I just barely survived,

> I just barely raised my children, I just barely gave them an education. I lived through perestroika with great difficulty. There was nowhere to work; nowhere took on pensioners; there was nowhere for the young to work and nowhere for pensioners. We lived badly, we were hungry, we saw nothing worthwhile in life, absolutely nothing. [Feodosia]

That this woman considered her situation during perestroika and the transition worse than during World War II is a particularly powerful indictment, given that she had just finished describing to me the poverty she had experienced in the earlier period, a subject to which she returned a bit later in the conversation.

> When the war began, we lived in such poverty. Only in 1957, when the first Sputnik flew, did my mother and I taste white bread [considered a luxury in contrast to the staple dark rye bread]. My father died in the war. We were very poor, very poor.

Feeling betrayed by her country, she insists she feels no loyalty to it. After praising her children for their patriotism, she says:

> But me? If they invited me, I'd trade Russia for dollars.... If they told me, "look here ... you'll have bread and meat to eat." I don't even know what the word meat means any more, I've forgotten what meat is.... I'm speaking honestly about this. So that I could have a worthwhile old age, I would leave Russia. I'd sell Russia along with Putin. It's a bad trait, but I don't hide it.

My youngest respondent, quoted earlier expressing bitterness about how hard the upheaval was for her grandparents, was equally bitter about the toll it took on her mother. For this family the challenges of adjusting to new economic, political and social realities were compounded by migration from Baku, the capital of Azerbaijan, to the smaller, more provincial Russian city of Yaroslavl. Oksana summed up the experience with the comment, "For my family, as a result of perestroika we lost basically everything."

What they lost included a home, both literal and emotional, many of their belongings, much of their money, their social network, their status and their way of life—even, eventually, the family, since Oksana's Russian mother's marriage to an Azeri didn't survive the move. As a Russian she no longer felt welcome in Azerbaijan and her husband found life in Yaroslavl unpleasant. Their first move to Yaroslavl was temporary and they moved back to Baku briefly to try again. Eventually, however, Oksana, her mother and her mother's parents returned to Yaroslavl, leaving the husband behind.

Life in Yaroslavl was a great shock. Social norms were very different.

> There was a completely different mentality, completely different social order and views on life.... Here the norms were harsher, with obscenities [*mat*] and drunkenness. In Baku, especially in our circle, it wasn't like this at all... [There] people were always very respectful, always so calm, so when we came... we had a hard time. It took Mama a long time to get used to it, probably 5-6 years. When she got off the trolley if someone were rude to her she would fall into a stupor and just stare at the person; she couldn't believe it.

The differences in norms were exacerbated by a dramatic loss of status. Oksana's mother had taught rhythmic and artistic gymnastics at a conservatory.

> [My mother] graduated with a red medal, a red diploma and a gold medal [which means that she received very high grades.] She was always active and proper. She went to work at a conservatory right after she graduated. She worked in a very refined place.

Unable to find similar work when she arrived in Yaroslavl, she spent a few years struggling to get by, accepting any job she could find. Eventually she landed a permanent teaching job, but it did not offer the same pleasure and status as had her job in Baku. In her daughter's dismissive comment,

> And then after that, at the age of 33, to end up teaching at a public school in Yaroslavl!

All of this took its toll.

> Mama aged so much when we moved. Even the climate was worse. There in the south, on the sea, there was a marvelous climate, plenty of iodine. But if you live here in the Yaroslavl Region your thyroid gland works badly. So … there was a poorer climate and she lived through so much psychologically and it was physically hard and [she had to deal with] the move and a new job and everything. She aged so much.

Oksana herself seems to have weathered the difficulties of the disruption and dislocation well. Now in her thirties, she is married, has a job at an educational institution and is raising a child. She seems content with her own situation but continues to feel nostalgic about Baku and angry about how her mother and grandparents fared.

Unlike Feodosia and Oksana, the woman born in 1966, who requested that I not record our conversation, focused more on the fate of the country than on personal experiences. For her, the biggest regret was what she sees as the degradation of people's character. While noting that of course materially the population is better off than in the Soviet period, she insisted that this had come at the cost of their "spiritual" well-being; she noted that there are more opportunities today, but only for those willing to elbow their way forward. She mourned the fact that no one does anything for anyone else any more, neither the government nor individuals, and claimed that the situation was much worse than before for non-Russian members of the population. In the past, the government guaranteed them a decent education; now, having lost access to that education, they are limited to jobs involving hard, unskilled, manual labor.

## "1990 and 1991 Were the Happiest Years of Our Lives": Political Engagement, International Travel and Youth

In stark contrast to the laments presented above were descriptions of the excitement generated by the new openness and the belief that the sway of the KGB and the Party apparatus might be overturned. One woman expressed this view particularly strongly.

> These were the happiest years. First, we felt then that the unimaginable had occurred, something about which we had never even dared dream. I had thought that the Soviet Union and the web of the KGB were so strong that nothing short of the atomic bomb could ever destroy them. I knew that my entire life would be here in this Soviet space. [*v etom sovke*]

She then tried to explain this slang term.

> It has many meanings and expresses all the negative things tied to Soviet power. One can say of a person that he is a *sovok,* that he retains these traits. One can say it of something that takes place in our lives today, that it is *sovok.* For example, if you go into a store and the clerk is rude to you, that is *sovok*.... It is a very good word.[6]

Returning to her theme, she described the excitement of being able to be politically active and to believe that one could actually bring about important changes.

> And suddenly this world unexpectedly opened up to us and all these ties broke apart and the Soviet Union exploded. I don't know. Probably there are few people who agree with me, but I was among those who were in support of the Soviet collapse. And I still think this way. I considered this to be very positive, because in Russia it was very hard to hold firm to oneself....
>
> And then we, who had only talked about this at home, in the kitchen, those of us who were caught up in all these KGB-related problems... we suddenly felt what freedom is, such freedom without the KGB. And we told ourselves that we were afraid of nothing. My husband ran for a position as deputy of the city council, as part of a wave during this wonderful period. He had several rivals, but he was elected and became a deputy. And he could do what we had dreamed about, he could speak from the podium and fight for it and he did a lot for Yaroslavl. He was a deputy of this first free city council, serving for four years, I think. [Sofia, 61]

---

[6]For a fuller discussion of the term, see Sharafutdinova (2019: 182–183).

НИКОЛАЙ
АЛЕКСЕЕВИЧ
НЕКРАСОВ
1821 1877

A colleague of this woman was also delighted with the political changes and for a while was an active participant in trying to bring them about.

> At that time I was already feeling very revolutionary. That is, it's not that I wasn't a Communist, I was simply very anti-Soviet. I can tell you that I simply hated that system and this realization developed very, very quickly.... At that time, in the 90s, we had all these attempts, where my husband and I and my colleague and her husband were part of some sort of democratic movement... the Union of Right Forces.[7] We met at the general meeting. There were sometimes meetings at the Nekrasov Monument and we'd go there. And we could meet at some other places, too. And I really wanted to join this [democratic] party, but somehow I never did. And, of course, everything changed.... You see, the democratic movements in Russia have had their own crisis. I think you will agree with me that there is no consistency, no real structure to it. That said, I think that some moments bring forth democratically minded people. [Ekaterina, 56]

In addition to appreciating the increased political freedom, these women spoke with pleasure about the increased freedom to travel abroad. As a teacher of German, Ekaterina relished the opportunity to visit first the German Democratic Republic (part of the Soviet bloc, generally referred to in the USA simply as East Germany) and eventually the Western part of united Germany. By the time we talked she estimated that she had made almost 60 such trips, as well as a number of trips to other parts of the world. She contrasted this to the limited travel opportunities during the Soviet period.

> In general, the very word "perestroika" gave great joy to those of us connected with a foreign language, I have to say, because as you understand we had been a closed country...a very closed country. And if sometimes perhaps our foreign partners believe that it was easy to travel to the German Democratic Republic that isn't correct. Even to get to the GDR wasn't

[7] The current association with this name was not established until 1999, when a number of small somewhat liberal parties merged. Presumably, she had in mind an earlier liberal group.

simple. In the whole time I was studying I could go to the GDR only once. That was in 1977 and it was a happy event. When they sent anyone to study in the GDR or Hungary or Czechoslovakia, this was a happy event.

Freedom to travel offered more than intellectual and psychic benefits, of course. When shops in Russia were nearly empty, travel abroad gave people the opportunity to buy all manner of goods not available at home. In addition, ties with foreign organizations or individuals increased the likelihood of receiving packages from abroad. Although this certainly didn't make daily life easy for these women it may have lessened the strain slightly, making it easier for them to focus on the joys of greater freedom—a freedom which the two women quoted in this section both saw as eroding under Putin. Since our conversations took place before Russia's annexation of Crimea and support for the separatists in eastern Ukraine renewed tensions between Russia and much of the West, the concern they expressed in the fall of 2012 has almost certainly heightened by now.

For those who were in their early twenties during the country's upheaval, life was in many ways especially difficult, since the state mechanisms by which they had expected to find housing, employment and child care were falling apart and nothing had yet developed to replace the former arrangements. Nonetheless, several women of this age looked back at the period with considerable nostalgia, a sentiment that was no doubt heightened by the fact that when we spoke some were divorced, with grown children, and seemed very conscious of having an empty nest.

One woman who was studying in Moscow in the late 1980s and early 1990s put it this way.

It was hard, but, you know, somehow life goes on and you forget the bad stuff. And, of course, although it was a very complicated time in the life of the country, in my personal life it was a very happy time. There were my studies and the birth of my child and I was young. It was the happiest period.... We had an interesting profession and we very much loved what we were studying. It was all very interesting, life was hectic, not at all boring. We sketched portraits on the Arbat [a street in the historic center

> of the city]. Artists sold their drawings, their portraits and that's how we earned money. They [the state agencies who in the Soviet past would have been paying stipends to all university students] weren't paying students anything. [Veronika]

Another put it more succinctly. "Well, it was hard, but I can't say that I was dying. Not at all. I was young, I was attractive, I fell in love…and I was successful."

A third woman, who during the early years of the transition lived with her husband in a teachers' dormitory in the small city of Uglich, not far from Yaroslavl, recalled the conditions of daily life and expressed amusement at their youthful optimism.

> There was only one bathroom. It was terrible, old, broken, cold….Today it seems very strange that I couldn't take a shower every day. We went to the *banya* [public bathhouse], the city *banya*. We had only cold water for personal care. We boiled water to make it hot [so we could] wash. It's only now that I'm analyzing it this way; at the time, we didn't think about it…. We were teachers, intellectual people, what we call "the grain of the city." We came there and we had such a life. We had a good education and the town is small and ancient. We organized different holidays, parties for our students. We lived very actively. We didn't think about the fact that there were no products in the shops. My parents usually brought us food. I was pregnant, so I was supposed to eat fruits, fish, meat. We didn't have anything in the shops and I didn't give it a thought… We thought everything would be fine. I was young, happy, my husband loved me. What's most interesting is that now that I'm remembering it I can't say that this was happiness, but all the same it was youth, it was love… We smiled, we went out, we danced, and relaxed and were delighted that we had a daughter. [Marta, 45]

As is suggested by the preceding comment, this woman is aware that the conditions of the period took a toll, among other things, on the health of the children born at that time.

> I think that such children, my friend's children, who were born in that period have health problems. Most of them do…. When my daughter

> was little, she was sick a lot. She caught all the viruses. Her immune system was very weak. She was often ill until she was seven or eight years old. Every month she had a temperature, flu, any virus.... We would go out and somebody would sneeze and right away she would get sick, she'd have a temperature in the evening.... But gradually things got better.

She also clearly considers life today to be far better materially than during these turbulent years of her early adulthood. Nonetheless, she just as clearly feels real nostalgia for that period, as do the women for whom the political changes mattered more than the economic hardships.

The affectionate amusement with which this woman viewed her younger, more naïve self and her disbelief at how little she knew then is echoed by the way many of the women talk about the post-Soviet generations of Russians and how incapable these young people are of understanding what life used to be like.

> Now, it's all been forgotten—what ration cards are, what lines are, what it is to be a member of the Komsomol [the Young Communist League], a Pioneer. The children don't know that there was nowhere to buy jeans, just from speculators [black marketeers]. Nobody knows this. Or to travel, to buy tickets, how you couldn't simply buy them—they don't understand this. [Liza, 55]

> The situation was such that it is now impossible to describe to the younger generation, but it was our truth. [Ekaterina, 56]

## The Challenges of Choice

As the experiences of the women I interviewed clearly demonstrate, the collapse of the Soviet system and the struggle to create a viable replacement brought a complicated mix of good and bad. Even after the initial upheaval ended and life in a material sense improved, the women continued to face sometimes unexpected challenges. One source of considerable psychological difficulty—at least initially—was the increased availability and variety of consumer goods. From the perspective of those from the developed West, especially Americans, variety is a good thing, making it possible for each consumer to find exactly the desired combination of features in a product. For the Russian women I spoke with, however, the far greater variety brought by the transition was seen as a very mixed blessing. While everyone welcomed having goods more readily available, some of the most powerful recollections I heard dealt with the stresses arising from the sudden exposure to an abundance of choices.

A woman of around 60 in Astrakhan described the discomfort she felt during early attempts to buy clothes under the new circumstances.

> Here is an interesting personal observation: I want to buy a coat and I go to the store. And they offer me 50 different coats. I want to buy a pair of shoes. I go to the store and they offer me 100 different styles of shoes, right? At first, because most of my life was spent in the Soviet period, I would leave the store without anything at all because I wasn't used to having a choice.... [During the Soviet period] let's say I need a coat. Whether I like this color or not, whether it's my size or perhaps a little bit too big, I have to buy it anyway because otherwise there's nothing for me to buy. And now I come and they say, 'Here is this kind of coat, do you want this kind? Do you want this style? Do you want this color?' And I understand that I want this one and also this one and also this other one, but I can't [have them all] and I leave without making a choice. Now it's changed, but at first when choices appeared... Having lived a long time without any choice I had a lot of trouble making a choice when it became possible.

A slightly younger woman living in Yaroslavl described a similar experience, although hers actually took place on a trip to Germany. An excellent story-teller, she set the stage by describing her quest for a simple pair of black shoes—first in Yaroslavl, and then during a trip to Moscow:

> I dreamed of buying myself a pair of black shoes.... It didn't matter at all whether they had heels or not, whether they were patent leather or not–it just didn't make any difference to me. The most important thing was that they be black, because black is a neutral color, so one could wear them at

> any time, but in Russia, this is what one would call a 'Mission Impossible' [said in English]. This was a mission that was simply impossible to carry out, simply absolutely decidedly impossible to fulfill in Russia, in Yaroslavl [at that time]—and by the way this doesn't mean that it was better in the preceding period—one couldn't see black shoes anywhere.
>
> I often had to go to Moscow to process the documents [associated with getting her graduate degree]… In Moscow if you stood in these huge lines, you too could become a happy owner of shoes. And [a special kind of] sausage too would be provided to you when you stood in some enormous line… And I waited through this enormous line… at some big shoe store until I became the proud possessor of [dramatic pause] a pair of orange shoes! … Made in Yugoslavia! … Picture this—there's this huge line, of 100 people or so, and every single one acquired only orange shoes, there simply weren't any others. And then you have to think, how do I live with this orange color, how do I work with it, what will go with it? And then you begin to hunt, to think maybe you can find an orange brooch…
>
> And then in a different store I waited through another line and bought a different pair of shoes, a turquoise pair…. I acquired shoes of this color, another bizarre color, but I couldn't acquire black ones anywhere. And so I set out on my journey [abroad] with these new shoes.

She then recounted her experiences in 1991, on her first trip to Western Europe. She and the rest of the group she was traveling with were amazed by the array of foods at the breakfast table and the comforts of what she now describes as a modest little hotel, but the real shock came when she took advantage of some free time to hunt for that elusive pair of black shoes in a Western department store. Taking the escalator to the shoe department, she was already overcome by a sense of having been utterly deceived by her government, with its claims that Soviet accomplishments far surpassed those of the rest of the world. And then she arrived amid all the shoes.

> And what happened next was completely awful. … I was completely disoriented, I absolutely couldn't concentrate, I didn't understand that I didn't need to try on all the shoes on the shelf, that these are shoes sized

> 30-33, for example, which I don't wear, and these are size 41, which I also don't wear, so they have nothing to do with me. But I absolutely could not differentiate. Do you understand? For me it was this flood of shoes. When I realized that I had to make a choice of some kind I couldn't do it. I couldn't do it. And in the end I simply cleared out of the store, not wanting to be there any longer. At the end of my stay I came to my senses a little and in the end I returned home with both black shoes and red shoes. …That is, later I could orient myself. [Ekaterina, 56]

## Conclusion

While most of my respondents clearly had, like Ekaterina, managed to "orient themselves" over the years following the end of the Soviet system, it is just as clear that most of them view the old system with at least some degree of nostalgia. Their mixed feelings are captured well in the words of one of my respondents, a woman born in 1951: "We were waiting for something, a paradise of some kind, which of course does not exist. We just… we were expecting a different system, and we got it, but it was not at all what we were waiting for." In the following chapters I explore how most of them managed nonetheless to find their footing in this new, unexpected system and to carve out lives that were a source of both pleasure and pride—emotions that, though very real, for many did not entirely erase a sense of loss.

## References

Ashwin, Sarah (ed.). 2000. *Gender, State and Society in Soviet and Post-Soviet Russia*. London/New York: Routledge.

Blank, Stephen J., Steven Rosefielde, Stefan Hedlund, Harley Balzer, and Janusz Bugajski. 2017. Politics and Economics in Putin's Russia. *Current Politics and Economics of Russia, Eastern and Central Europe* 32 (4): 567–692.

Borozdina, E., E. Zdravomyslova, and A. Temkina. 2011. Maternal Capital: Social Policy and Family Strategies. Published on genderpage.ru., December 2011. Accessed in *Demoskop Weekly* (495–496) at http://www.demoscope.ru/weekly/2012/0495/analit03.php. May 2019.

Foley, Mark C., and Jeni Klugman. 1997. The Impact of Social Support: Errors of Leakage and Exclusion. In *Poverty in Russia: Public Policy and Private Responses*, ed. Jeni Klugman, 189–210. Washington, DC: The World Bank.

Gorbachev, Mikhail. 1987. *Perestroika: New Thinking for Our Country and the World*. New York: Harper and Row.

Gorzev, Boris. 1996. The Demographic Burden of Empire. *Moskovskie novosti*, trans. *Current Digest of the Post-Soviet Press* 48 (13): 35, March 17–24.

Gosudarstvennyi komitet SSSR po statistike. 1987. *Narodnoe khoziaistvo SSSR za 70 let*. Moscow: Finansy i statistika.

Gosudarstvennyi komitet SSSR po statistike. 1988. *Narodnoe khoziaistvo SSSR v 1987 g*. Moscow: Finansy i statistika.

Gosudarstvennyi komitet SSSR po statistike. 1991. *Narodnoe khoziaistvo SSSR v 1990 g*. Moscow: Finansy i statistika.

Kay, Rebecca. 2006. *Men in Contemporary Russia: The Fallen Heroes of Post-Soviet Change*. Aldershot: Ashgate.

Kontorovich, Vladimir. 2001. The Russian Health Crisis and the Economy. *Communist and Post-Communist Studies* 34: 221–240.

Manning, Nick, Ovsey Shkaratan, and Natalya Tikhonova. 2000. *Work and Welfare in the New Russia*. Aldershot: Ashgate.

Manuilova, Anastasya. 2018. *Russia Launches Cash Incentives to Boost Birth Rate*. Accessed online at https://www.globalgovernmentforum.com/russia-launches-cash-incentives-boost-birth-rate/. June 2018.

McKinney, Judith Record. 2004. Lone Mothers in Russia: Soviet and Post-Soviet Policy. *Feminist Economics* 10 (2): 37–60.

Pension Fund of the Russian Federation. Maternity (Family) Capital. Accessed online at http://www.pfrf.ru/en/matcap/. June 2017.

Phillips, Sarah D. 2011. *Disability and Mobile Citizenship in Postsocialist Ukraine*. Bloomington, IN: Indiana University Press.

Presidential Address to the Federal Assembly. 2019. Accessed online at http://en.kremlin.ru/events/president/news/59863. March 2019.

Rotkirkh, Anna. 2003. 'Coming to Stand on Firm Ground': The Making of a Soviet Working Mother. In *On Living Through Soviet Russia*, ed. Daniel Bertaux, Anna Rotkirch, and Paul Thompson, 144–173. Routledge Studies in Memory and Narrative.

Sharafutdinova, Gulnaz. 2019. Was There a 'Simple Soviet' Person? Debating the Politics and Sociology of 'Homo Sovieticus'. *Slavic Review* 78 (1): 173–195.

Vishnevsky, Anatoly, and Vladimir Shkolnikov. 1999. Russian Mortality: Past Negative Trends and Recent Improvements. In *Population Under Duress: The Geodemography of Post-Soviet Russia*, ed. George J. Demko, Grigory Ioffe, and Zhanna Zayonchkovskaya, 59–71. Boulder, CO: Westview.

Zavisca, Jane R. 2012. *Housing in the New Russia*. Ithaca/London: Cornell University.

# 4

# Rising Prices and Irregular Wages

## Introduction

Leonid Brezhnev, who became General Secretary of the Communist Party in 1964 and remained in that post until his death in 1982, oversaw significant improvement in the economic well-being of Soviet citizens. It was during his years that Soviet households, at least those in the cities, finally acquired refrigerators, televisions, vacuum cleaners and washing machines, that per capita consumption of services grew rapidly and that the shared bathroom and kitchen of the communal apartment became for most of the population a (not very distant) memory. And yet by the end of his time in office, as the growth rate of the economy slowed significantly and wage growth outpaced productivity growth, the standard of living still lagged far behind that in the major Western industrialized countries.[1] Soviet women were still spending long hours in lines waiting for the opportunity to acquire food products and other

[1]Brainerd (2010: 87) notes that although estimates vary—not surprising given the low quality and reliability of Soviet statistics—per capita consumption in the Soviet Union was probably only about one-third that in the USA by the mid-1970s, after which the gap probably widened.





J. McKinney, *Russian Women and the End of Soviet Socialism*,
https://doi.org/10.1007/978-3-030-16226-9_4

consumer goods, and in some cases needed to present ration coupons as well as money to make the purchase (Burns 1982). In general, the markets for consumer goods were characterized by shortages, wildly uneven geographic distribution, poor quality and little variety.

Under Mikhail Gorbachev, who became General Secretary in 1985, shopping became even more difficult as distribution channels broke down, output fell, and uncertainty added a new source of stress. Gorbachev had attempted to revitalize the Soviet economy with a number of reforms he called *perestroika*, the "restructuring" of the economy. Intended to address the problems of low quality and slowing growth, his approach was initially little more than a minor variation on a familiar theme as he tried to channel investment to sectors—especially machine-building and metal-working—which would support the modernization of industry. Soon, however, he tried bolder initiatives, giving state enterprises far more responsibility for determining their output mix and choosing their suppliers and customers, yet retaining a role for "state orders" for some of the output. This mix of central plan and enterprise freedom in an environment with state-controlled prices led not to revitalization but to serious disruption and in 1991 Soviet GDP fell 17% (Cooper 1996: 306).

With the dissolution of the USSR in December of 1991 and Boris Yeltsin's introduction of "shock therapy"—which was supposed to involve the simultaneous introduction of price liberalization, privatization of enterprises, and a sharp reduction in government spending—still another source of stress was added—the dramatic increase in prices. For many of the women I spoke with, the challenges of feeding and clothing their families were among the strongest memories they held of the 1980s and 1990s. For the most part, they did not distinguish clearly between the two decades or between Gorbachev's *perestroika* and Yeltsin's shock therapy. For them, the change in economic system was a gradual process rather than one sharply delineated by the end of the USSR. Although they spoke of "then" and "now," when the topic was the acquisition of goods and services, they used "then" to refer to the entire difficult period, lasting about two decades, from the "era of stagnation" under Brezhnev through the financial crisis of August 1998 up to the early 2000s, when crisis finally appears to have stopped being "perceived as a routine and unchanging condition" (Shevchenko 2009: 2). The one striking exception to the women's blurred timeline was the moment when price controls were lifted, an event they all remembered vividly and almost all located precisely in time, on January 2, 1992. Because this liberalization of prices followed so closely upon the official dissolution of the USSR on December 26, 1991, I use "Late Soviet Period" and "Post-Soviet Period" below, distinguishing between the periods in a way the women themselves did not.

## Late Soviet Period: Low Prices, Empty Shelves

As a provincial capital, Yaroslavl was neither especially privileged nor especially disadvantaged by Soviet distribution practices. The city was far less well-provided with foodstuffs and other consumer products than Moscow and Leningrad, but far better off in this regard than smaller cities, more remote cities, and rural villages. What proved especially valuable in improving the lot of many of my respondents was the city's relatively close proximity to Moscow. This meant that they could often ride the "sausage train," the ironic name given to the train running between Moscow and Yaroslavl because it was often filled at the end of the day with women laden with bags and bundles of food products acquired during a day or two spent shopping in the better-provisioned capital.

> [At that time] in order to have meat in the home—after all there were children in the home—once every month or so Mama and I and whoever else could go with us would ride the train to Moscow and stand in line where they sold [literally, "gave out"] meat. They'd give, let's say, one kilo, two kilos per person. I'd stand in line, my mother would stand in line, and my husband would stand in line, for example. That way [we'd get] 6 kilos of meat. Everywhere in the warm train [on the way home] it was all wrapped up in newspaper, so that it wouldn't spoil. It was a dreadful thing, as you can imagine. The meat was in a warm railroad car for four hours without ice. We brought meat from Moscow, we brought eggs from Moscow, we brought sausages from Moscow, cheese. We didn't

> have cheese. Here near Yaroslavl there is a milk-processing factory, which makes wonderful cheese, but there wasn't any in our stores. This was in the 1980s, what was called the period of stagnation, when everything good that was produced one had to buy in Moscow, not here in Yaroslavl [*ne u nas*]. [Vera, 56]

Even those who did not make special trips to Moscow to buy food would take advantage of any visit to the city to stock up on whatever they could find there.

> I always used my trips to Moscow [taken in connection with work on an advanced degree] to acquire something for my daughter, for my husband.... Well, really, I didn't think quite so much about him, to be honest. I mostly thought about my daughter...to bring back some sausage, to bring back some candy, to bring back some mayonnaise. You know, these 'strange' things that simply didn't exist [here in Yaroslavl]. There wasn't any of this anywhere. I'd bring back cheese, I'd bring back butter. There was nothing [here]. [Ekaterina, 56]

That Moscow held a very special place in the distribution system was understood by all, including young children, as illustrated by the following anecdote, told by a woman who worked in the Soviet equivalent of Yaroslavl's city hall at that time.

> [At my work place] the food was of course not the same as it was everywhere else. My daughter would always say, 'My mom works in Moscow, because she brings cottage-cheese pancakes with raisins home from work.' These were sold only in Moscow; we didn't have them here. [But at work] we had our own buffet and provisions were different.... I remember that there was nothing in the stores. [Inessa, 53]

As these recollections suggest, both during the Soviet period and during its aftermath it was not enough to have money in order to acquire goods and services. In addition to cash, one needed time, a social network, ingenuity, and more than a little luck. For some goods one also needed *talony*, a sort of ration coupon which entitled the holder to purchase a certain amount of that good each month.

The use of ration coupons was introduced periodically throughout Soviet history. In the 1920s the practice was both a practical necessity and an ideological statement, since the Bolsheviks envisioned a moneyless society, where goods would be available in such abundance that everyone would simply be able to consume whatever he or she wished. Until such abundance could be achieved, however, rationing was a way to ensure that everyone's basic needs were met. Both in that early period and again during the Siege of Leningrad in World War II, the amount of a food product one could receive depended on age and occupation, with those performing hard manual labor entitled to a larger caloric intake. My respondents did not mention this sort of distinction in the 1980s and 1990s, although one woman did say that children were entitled to a larger ration of milk than adults.

In fact, as argued by Caroline Humphrey in an article first published in 1991, the situation in the late 1980s and 1990s was far more complex than the term "rationing" suggests, and was distinctly non-egalitarian (2002: 7–9). Access to goods might require *talony* or food coupons or having one's name on a list; this access might be granted by regional organizations or local governments or places of employment and might require possession of a local residence permit. In contrast, under rationing one would expect that everyone would receive coupons and present them in order to acquire the rationed products. For this to work, however, the government needs a clear sense of how much of each rationed good will actually become available. By the final years of the Soviet period, the government did not have the necessary information; not only was it hard to predict output, but the center had lost control of the distribution system and could not enforce the shipment of output from one region to another.

The wide variety in how coupons were distributed and how they could be used is clearly reflected in the variety of recollections offered by the women I spoke with. While all of them remembered that there had been *talony*/coupons, they offered different versions of exactly how the system operated and exactly when it was in effect. Among the details they disagreed about were which goods required the coupons and whether for these goods one needed to pay cash as well. According to one woman, the system was quite comprehensive:

> We got all sorts of products with the ration cards. For example, tinned meat. What else did we get? Well, everything was through the ration cards, just like during the war. Only bread was not rationed. Bread was simply sold. [Anna, 56]

Although the coupons were clearly used for a variety of goods, the good that mattered most for many of the women was milk. While the first three comments below refer to the early 1980s, before Gorbachev's *perestroika*, the last two recollections date from a decade later; it is thus clear that the struggle to provide milk for young children existed for many years, both before and after shock therapy.

> At that time, in 1982, to get milk one had to get up at 6:00 and go…. It was in kegs, they brought the milk in kegs. And you'd go and stand in line. The line was very long. My husband's grandmother would go and stand in line for milk for us. [Liza, 55]

> My father would get up every morning at 5:00 in order to go and stand in line to buy some milk [for my daughter, born in 1982]. [Yulia, 52]

> My son was born in 1981. I remember that time well. In the winter at six in the morning, it was freezing. At the milk store we'd stand in line in order for them to put a liter of milk in our hands—they wouldn't give more than a liter—so that I could cook kasha for the children. So [my husband] would go and stand in line beginning at 6:00 in the morning, and by the time the store opened at 7:00 I'd go with my child and they'd pour out the milk. It's awful to imagine that it was like that. [Vera, 56]

> Before prices were freed there was a milk store right near us, and it was necessary to get in line early in the morning. I'd always go there with my older daughter because if there were two people then they'd give out products for two. I remember the two of us would buy this three-liter jar of sour cream, but there wouldn't be three liters in it, only two liters, because it was [limited to] one liter per person…. [Anna, 56]

A woman who asked not to be recorded—explaining that she would find it hard to talk naturally under those circumstances but entirely willing to share her story—described pulling her two-year-old son (born in 1988) on a sled in the winter. They would stand in line outside for a long time, waiting for milk to be delivered to the store and distributed.

As these recollections make clear, the effort to acquire goods was a family undertaking. Some suggested that this was because they could only receive quantities for those physically present at the distribution point, but most described a system where goods were allocated on the basis of the number of coupons presented rather than on how many members of the family were in line. The more likely explanation for having the entire family involved is the enormous amount of time it took to acquire the goods and to accomplish the many other tasks that constituted daily life. Note, for instance, that family members sometimes took shifts standing in line.

One of the peculiarities of the coupon period was that the "essential goods" for which coupons were distributed apparently included vodka and cigarettes. Several of the women I spoke to indicated that although no one in their family consumed either of these items, the coupons nevertheless came in handy, since they—or the goods they entitled one to acquire—could be used as a form of payment in the informal sector of the economy.[2]

One young woman, for example, described how her family was able to construct a small *dacha* by paying their ration of vodka to workers in exchange for a delivery of scrap lumber. The term *dacha* is usually translated as a "country home or cottage." During the Soviet period these "homes" were subject to strict regulations regarding size and such amenities as heating; in fact, they were sometimes little more than a shed in which tools were stored until the summer, when the owners could work the land and grow some food (Caldwell 2004: 106). In more recent years, although the term has remained the concept has been broadened: some buildings referred to as dachas are now very substantial houses, suitable for year-round occupation. In this case, the original meaning

[2]Humphrey notes that in some regions there were workplace committees to decide who could receive coupons for vodka in an attempt to keep them out of the hands of those known to have problems with alcohol (2002: 9).

was closer to the truth, as was made clear in a later conversation. The woman I spoke with had mentioned my research to her mother, who encouraged her to explain that the dacha they built was very, very small. Her mother had clearly been worried that I would think they had been living well during this period and wanted that impression corrected.[3]

Less happy than the dacha anecdote—however small the dacha may have been—was the account by another woman, who described having her purse stolen several times on the subway in Moscow.

> Several times they robbed me. They simply cut my bag on the public transport. In Moscow at that time there was this buyer's booklet or buyer's card or something like that, so that one could buy [things]… That is, sometimes one had to present this in the store in order to buy certain products, *talony* for sausage, *talony* for vodka. I never drank vodka, but when one bought vodka it was like some kind of money, that is, one could pay vodka for something…. I don't remember what I could pay for with this vodka. I never did this, but they gave me the *talony* because I was supposed to receive them and there were several times in the metro that they cut my purse. And suddenly there you are, you're alone there, without any money. [Veronika, 51]

For some women, the problem was not that they received coupons for goods they had no interest in buying but rather that they found it difficult to use the coupons they received even for goods they did want to consume. A woman in Astrakhan described the impossibility of keeping up with the constantly changing rules governing the use of the *talony* and of finding the time actually to get to the appropriate distribution point.

> I don't remember the exact years… 1989-90, 1993, it's hard to remember… but [around then] was the period of the *talony*, when products—the most important, the most necessary—had to be purchased with *talony*.

---

[3]Unfortunately, this mother was one of the women who declined to meet with me herself, saying that it had been bad enough to live through the hard times and she had no desire to spend time recalling them.

> And there was a big problem with this because the conditions changed frequently. For example, one condition was that you could buy products with these *talony* only in a particular store which served that street—that is, it was tied to the region where you lived. Then the conditions changed and there was some sort of a base store, let's say. For the whole region [there would be] two such stores…, very big stores, and that's where one could buy things. Or other conditions, when you could use them in any store at all where the products were available. But if you're working you can't keep track of all these conditions and you know that, let's say, before the tenth of the month you can get the products if you go to a particular store, but then they say, "You've come to the wrong place, you need to go to a different place." [She mimics the saleswomen here, speaking in disdainful bureaucratic tones.]

A woman in Yaroslavl whom I interviewed in her office said she wished she had thought to bring along some unused, expired coupons from home to show me since she had not been able to use them in the period they covered.

> I still have them…just as a souvenir of those times… You know what's curious? There were these coupons and on them such correct things were written, that is, for example, that one is due 500 grams of meat in a month or 500 grams of sugar or something else, but really there already was nothing [in the stores] so you'd come with these coupons for the three members of your family—for your daughter, your husband and yourself—but there was nothing anywhere, there was nothing. And so I have at home this entire booklet, with only a few coupons torn out of it.
>
> What's important is that maybe you could acquire some sort of groats, maybe you could somewhere get some sort of sausage, *maybe*, but not necessarily and not always. Do you understand? That's how it was. So I've saved the coupons. It was a light blue booklet, at least in the Yaroslavl *oblast'*. It consisted of several pages; it was for the year and for each month it had written how much you could get. And here I have an entire booklet that remains practically untouched. That's the truth. The cards didn't save us, they absolutely didn't save us. There was nothing [to buy, even with the cards]. [Ekaterina, 56]

The scarcity of basic goods in shops in Yaroslavl during the late 1980s and early 1990s was a dominant theme in the recollections of the women I talked to. The woman who saved her coupon booklet as a souvenir, an accomplished raconteur, offered the following description about a shopping expedition she made with her daughter in late 1991.

> As you know, eleven-year-old children want to eat, they're growing and they want to eat, so [my daughter] and I set out with our ration coupons to hunt through the stores of Yaroslavl for something edible. I'm telling you the truth here, just for anything at all that was edible. And she and I arrived at the main grocery store in Yaroslavl—back then there weren't supermarkets and all these other stores that have sprung up along Kirov Street and near the intersection with First-of-May Street. And this store was the best known and largest food store in Yaroslavl, so we walked to this store together… We walked and walked and there wasn't anything [to buy] anywhere. And finally we reached this grocery store. And we had our coupons with us but in the entire store there were only—I remember this clearly—exactly six items for sale. There were matches, there were plastic bags, cellophane packets. In Russia at that time, there weren't many of these bags so if you managed to get one you would wash it out and hang it up to dry so you could reuse it….There were bay leaves to add to soup to flavor it…..I think maybe there was bread—I don't want to mislead you—but basically everything was inedible. That is, you're not going to eat bay leaves, you're not going to eat plastic bags, you're not going to eat matches. In short, it was terrible, you understand, terrible. This isn't simply a metaphor about the plastic bags. In those days except for potatoes the Russian people basically had nothing to eat. Sometimes you couldn't even find salt to put on the potatoes. These were very, very hard times, monstrous times.

Others recalled slightly different but no more attractive sets of products available. One said:

> We had empty shops, we had just seaweed, tins of preserves and some sort of sprats, these little anchovies you call them, tiny sprats in tomato sauce. [Yulia, 52]

And another remembered it this way.

> And I remember clearly that time before prices were freed and there was nothing in the stores, absolutely nothing. There were three-liter bottles of birch syrup and other than that there was nothing for sale in the stores. [Anna, 56]

She went on to describe an alternative approach to acquiring produce, which was to participate in the harvest at nearby collective farms, a common form of "volunteer" activity during the Soviet period, when enterprises and schools would be expected to send contingents out to the fields to provide help to the farmers.[4]

> As I recall all these moments, I don't know whether to laugh or cry (*i smekh, i grekh*). For example, I remember how we went to the collective farm for potatoes in the fall. That is, we would dig up these potatoes and put them into bags and send them to the warehouse, and we could take every fifth bag. Four you collected for the state, and the fifth bag for yourself. This was at the end of the 80s, probably. There was nothing, there were no vegetables, no cabbage, no potatoes [in the stores]. I remember the potatoes were small and very bad. Half of them were rotten. Those that weren't rotten we washed and spread on the floor to dry. Our whole apartment was full of drying potatoes.... We had these narrow pathways between them.

For one woman what was most difficult was not the specific shortages but rather the fear that these conditions might never end.

> In the stores there was nothing, especially not food. It was awful. There was nothing to take, there were shortages of everything [everything was "*defitsitny*"] ... Can you imagine? At home there's your family, and you have to feed them, there are your kids, and there's absolutely nothing anywhere. And the most important thing is that it's not going to be over tomorrow, it's not going to be over the day after tomorrow, you just don't have any idea when it will be over. [Zoya, 52]

[4]While participation in these harvests had long been more or less compulsory, Yurchak notes that in the late 1970s and early 1980s some people were given days off from work or bonus pay in return for this activity (2006: 155).

Surprisingly few of the younger women I talked to, those who gave birth in the very late 1980s or early 1990s, mentioned the struggle to find goods in the stores. The most likely explanation is that the brunt of the shopping effort was borne by the mothers of these women, especially because many of them were still living with their parents at the time. One woman, who had moved to a nearby town with her husband, explicitly described the help they received:

> My parents brought us food, since I was pregnant and needed to eat fruit, fish and meat. There was nothing in the stores, but I didn't give that a thought.... At the time we didn't think about what a child needed, what it didn't need, what we'd eat tomorrow... We didn't think that it was necessary to eat a certain cottage cheese, certain fruit. What cottage cheese, what fish? What we could buy, that's what we ate. [Marta, 45]

Although shortages of consumer goods had always been part of the Soviet economic landscape, they intensified in the late 1980s. In part, this was due to the slowdown in production that accompanied the breakdown in central control, but it was no doubt exacerbated by responses to the expectation that prices were going to increase. As early as fall of 1987, Gorbachev was publicly stating that food subsidies would be reduced (*New York Times* 1987) and Soviet consumers and sellers had strong incentives to hoard—with consumers trying to buy as much as possible before the price increases and sellers, when possible, holding on to goods until the higher prices were in effect.

## Post-Soviet Period: Rising Prices, Wage Delays

These higher prices came almost immediately after the dissolution of the USSR. One of the first policies introduced by Boris Yeltsin as President of the newly independent Russian Federation was the removal of many—though not all—price controls so prices could provide meaningful signals of relative scarcity (Berkowitz et al. 1998: 739).[5]

[5] Among the few consumer prices that continued to be controlled were those for bread and milk, electricity and other utilities, and residential rents (Rock and Solodkov 2001: 452).

It is therefore ironic that over the first several years of transition the Russian economy actually became increasingly de-monetized, with the ruble less and less useful as either a medium of exchange or a store of value. If in the Soviet period limiting the usefulness of money was at least in part ideologically driven (given the complicated relationship between money as a measure of value and Marx's labor theory of value), in the early 1990s, when normal market transactions were viewed as an important characteristic of the system being developed, de-monetization was an unintended and undesired consequence of government policies. Below I look first at the rise in prices and later at the way de-monetization played out for wage earners.

## Price Liberalization

Because they were set by government bureaucrats and changed only infrequently, Soviet-era prices were unable to serve one of the key functions of prices in a market economy—that of allocating scarce goods to those willing to pay the highest prices for them and thus, presumably, valuing the goods most highly. At the same time, the lack of flexible prices offered a significant benefit to Soviet consumers: people knew exactly what prices they would face. This price stability was an important aspect of the high degree of economic security enjoyed by the Soviet population, security that to some extent compensated for the relatively low level of economic well-being overall. The typical Soviet citizen might be frustrated by the lack of variety in clothing, the limited diet, the crowded living conditions and the enormous expenditure of time and effort required by even routine shopping, but she had no reason to fear that a sudden sharp increase in rent or food prices would force her out of her home or make it necessary to choose between food and medicine for her child.

The shock experienced by those facing market prices for the first time was thus considerable. The initial increase in prices for consumer goods, most of which had been heavily subsidized by the government, was often several hundred percent. On average, in January 1992, consumer prices rose by 296% (Ferguson and Granville 2000: 1079). Nor was this simply a one-time increase. Because of its inability to collect taxes, the government relied heavily on money creation to finance its spending and prices therefore continued to rise sharply over the next several years, with annual inflation rates in the triple digits—and, in the first year, one of over 1500% (Rock and Solodkov 2001: 452).

When my respondents spoke of this period of price liberalization, they tended to shake their heads in remembered amazement, laughing ruefully.

> If before, prices had been government prices, fixed prices, then by 1993 the producer could indicate whatever price he thought was realistic. And I remember very clearly the moment before the release of prices in the stores.... Sour cream cost one ruble, 70 kopeks—one ruble, 70 kopeks—and the very next day it cost 42 rubles per kilogram. You can imagine how many times more expensive it had become—about thirty-five times [actually, closer to 25, but her mistake reflects the sense that the new prices were inconceivably high]. Thirty-five! And we arrived and had such a shock. How are we going to live now? What are we going to eat now? Because [before] even if there had been nothing in the stores, it was somehow possible to get by. [Anna, 56]

> At that time when we went to bed at night we didn't know what the morning would be like, what prices would be, when there was such extreme chaos. And those prices! Tomorrow there would be absolutely different prices, they'd grow 10 times in a single night. [Zoya, 52]

This shift to market prices, especially as it played out under conditions of significant monopoly power and very high inflation, made an indelible impression on these women. The speaker in the first quotation above was not unusual in stating with absolute certainty exactly how much various items had cost; others stated exactly how prices compared to the wages and government benefits being received at the time. (The absolute certainty does not guarantee absolute accuracy, but does underscore that this part of the transition was one the women found particularly disconcerting and challenging.)

Difficult though this was, according to one woman it was considerably easier in Yaroslavl than in Moscow, since the local government in Yaroslavl, as in many other parts of the country, resisted this part of the economic reform for some time—an act of defiance that further complicated the central government's attempt to manage the transition.

> Everything was easier at home. In Yaroslavl they kept the old prices for food products for a long time, they didn't just suddenly raise them like in Moscow. [Veronika, 51, a student in Moscow at the time]

While a one-time realignment of prices could be viewed as a painful but ultimately beneficial necessity, there was nothing good about the hyperinflation of these years. Although much of the blame for the hyperinflation goes to the director of the Russian Central Bank, there were strong systemic forces at work as well. (With five heads of the RCB in the years between 1991 and 1998, no single individual can be held responsible for the problem.) One problem was the lack of effective tax collection; another was the initial attempt, on Western advice, to maintain the "ruble zone" throughout the territory of the former USSR, rather than having each former republic adopt its own currency. Recent experience in the "euro zone" has illustrated just how hard it can be to maintain a common currency even when there is a single central bank in charge.[6] In the late Soviet and early post-Soviet space, no such institution existed: the all-Soviet monetary and financial institutions had lost control and there was no infrastructure in place to coordinate monetary policy (Alexashenko 1993: 262). That this appears to have been ignored by those Western economists who initially argued for the maintenance of the zone serves as ammunition for those Russians who claim that

[6]The euro was not introduced until 2000, so there was no precedent for having independent countries sharing a currency. Granville, in fact, argues that the anticipated creation of the euro was an important factor in shaping Western advice, since "the last thing European officials wanted [as the ratification process for the Maastricht Treaty began] was the awkward spectacle of the failure of a similarly constituted monetary union on Europe's doorstep (2016: 22)."

Western "advice" was actually intended to weaken Russia rather than to help it.[7] (This belief is discussed at greater length in Chapter 11.)

Compounding the problem of hyperinflation were the serious microeconomic imbalances inherited from the Soviet period. Since relative prices of specific goods were, for the most part, unrelated to their relative scarcity, as controls were lifted the prices of especially popular and hard-to-find items could be expected to rise especially sharply. Economic theory tells us that this is a good thing: the higher prices would serve to discourage people from buying more of the scarce goods than necessary and at the same time would encourage firms to produce more of those goods, bringing the composition of output more in line with the structure of the population's demand. In practice, however, the supply-side response was slow in coming. The breakdown of the distribution system that accompanied the end of central planning and the rupture of relations among the former republics slowed the process considerably, so for some time the women faced both shortages of many goods and much higher prices for those goods that could be found.

## Wage Arrears

As the government finally attempted to rein in inflation in the mid-1990s and stopped making new money easily available, the problem of arrears—wage arrears, pension arrears, payment arrears between enterprises—became acute. This was the era of the "virtual economy," the term coined by Clifford Gaddy and Barry Ickes (2002) to describe the system of redistribution of assets via non-monetary exchanges and non-market prices associated with the rise of the Russian oligarchs. There was a huge disparity between the economy described by official statistics and the real economy of production and exchange. People were officially "employed" but did not receive regular wages. Often, indeed, they were not engaged in actual production, even though they remained

[7]For an interesting debate over the IMF's role in shaping ruble zone policy, see Odling-Smee and Pastor (2002a), the responses to that article by Pomfret (2002), Granville (2002) and Odling-Smee and Pastor's own response (2002b).

on the books of the employer. Those who were lucky enough to receive wages were often paid not in cash but in kind[8]: they might be given part of the output of the factory where they were employed or granted access to goods available at heavily subsidized prices in shops located at and run by the factory.

In marked contrast to the memories of price changes offered above, relatively few of my respondents recalled having experienced wage arrears themselves, and those who did remember generally dismissed the arrears as unimportant. Given how widespread and persistent wage arrears were in this period, this is surprising. One possible explanation is that none of the women I spoke to were employed in heavy industry, and many were teachers. Caroline Humphrey, writing about the situation in early 1993, contrasted the low but reliable pay of state employees such as teachers and doctors with the higher but very irregular pay of factory workers (2002: 23). On the other hand, Earle and Sabirianova, drawing on information through early 1998—by which time total wage arrears amounted to the equivalent of about eight billion USD—emphasize that the phenomenon was observed across a wide range of regions, industries and organizations, including the state sector (2002: 662).

One woman explicitly credited her position as a teacher with having protected her from arrears. In contrast, another claimed that she and her husband suffered simultaneous wage arrears specifically because they were both employed in the public sector.

> I can tell you that we never had any delays in our salary, no. The school is after all a government institution. We didn't have any wage arrears. [Anna, 56]

> [At this time, I was teaching and my husband had just started working for the police.] All the government structures of course—teachers and police—received very little money, and this was the period when they delayed payment of salaries, when they didn't pay it for several months. That is, this was a very bad period. [Marta, 45]

[8]As Caldwell (2004) notes, payment in kind made certain jobs, for example those in food service, especially attractive (54).

A third woman, 59, who has spent her entire life working in academia, first in a school, then in an institute of urban planning and then in a private business and technology institute, said, "We always received our pay regularly [at the same time]. The problem wasn't with [receiving] the pay. The only problem was that it was too little." She did not attribute this to the transition, however, adding, "But here teaching has never earned much money…. It is a creative profession, and therefore you work here just because you love it."

When pressed, most of the women acknowledged that perhaps there had been some "irregularities" in pay, but that these generally took the form of spreading the pay out over installments rather than failure to pay on time (a distinction I fail to appreciate). One woman said "Yes, we were paid on a regular basis. That is, payments were relatively regular. They were almost regular." Perhaps they wanted to distinguish their personal (minor) difficulties from the serious struggles of the less privileged. Certainly, as discussed more in Chapter 9, they wanted to distinguish themselves both from the very poor and from the undeserving rich.

Most of those who admitted to some experience with arrears stressed that it was not a serious problem for them. They assured me that they always managed to get by, and were never really without resources, expressed most bluntly as "There was always something to eat." This is an interesting contrast to their presentation of the challenge of acquiring goods, about which they were quite eager to provide anecdotes. They seemed to see the challenges of acquiring goods to reflect badly on the state rather than on themselves (which it certainly did)—and indeed to demonstrate their resourcefulness in addressing these challenges. In contrast, many of them seemed to equate failure to receive their salary with personal failing and failure to budget adequately.

Several of the respondents, for example, answered my question about arrears by telling me that they spent their money wisely, had savings to fall back on, and were never completely without funds—none of which actually addresses the question of whether their employer occasionally—or frequently—failed to pay them. For me, the question was one of employer (and government) behavior, but for them it was clearly a question of personal capabilities. In the second quotation below, for example, there is a seamless transition from the assertion that there had been no arrears to the point, offered as evidence for this claim, that there was always enough money for them somehow to get by.

The comments below are arranged, roughly, from the most positive to the least, from those who claimed to have no personal experience with arrears at all to those who acknowledged considerable difficulties. Although the first speaker supplemented the family income by moonlighting as a cleaner in the school her son attended, the main sources of income were her pension and her husband's disability payments.

> We received [our pension and disability payments]. I don't remember any problem at that time. That is personally we had no delays. In some places, in certain regions, in agricultural places, I know that at the factories they held back the pay. But for us this somehow didn't happen. We always lived, we always had some sort of savings. [Klara, 70]

The next two quotations are from women who worked as chemists in factories. The first spoke proudly of having been chosen to participate in the special program of quality control introduced by Gorbachev in the early years of his reforms. This gave her increased responsibility and increased pay. In addition, she was married to a man in a position of relatively high income and status. The second held a much less prestigious position as a lab assistant. Her experience was unusual, since the manager of the factory at which she worked chose to lay off workers, herself included, when unable to meet wage payments, rather than adopting the far more common practice of continuing to employ them while delaying their pay or placing them on involuntary "vacation".

> We lived normally, to put it bluntly. Yes, we lived normally. Our wages were occasionally delayed. But at our factory they sold things [to the employees], everyone knew this, that one could take [goods] as part of one's wages. There was this little store and there they sold goods. Frankly, I simply didn't use it, thanks to what my husband received. If they held back our wages, we somehow overlooked it. So we lived, I can't complain. We were lucky. My husband earned well, he was head of a department. [Lidia, 70]

> [When I worked at the factory—from 1990 to 1996] I received my salary regularly, there were no delays. The pay was good. [Liubov, 56]

Unlike the women quoted above, those offering the following recollections acknowledged the challenges caused by the arrears, but even here the first two speakers continue to emphasize the role their own frugality and common sense played in making the delays unimportant.

> Were there delays in our pay? There were, but they weren't very big. There were delays, there were, at one point. Today we've lived normally for so long that one quickly forgets. There were [delays], but somehow it was all normal. But then we always live within our means. We don't need to be given the moon out of the sky, we live within our means, and therefore I can't say that we didn't have money. Because we try to spend it wisely. Well, of course there was a difficult period in 1991, when I was defending my dissertation in Moscow. Then we did have to economize a lot from paycheck to paycheck. [Liza, 55]

> [Responding to a question about whether she had moonlighted in order to have additional sources of income]: No, we survived, we were able to survive. You understand, we didn't lose our jobs, neither my husband nor I. You understand, there were big arrears, but all the same they paid something, some kopecks, and that was enough for us. That is, it wasn't that we were completely without money, completely without anything. We received money nonetheless. We never lived luxuriously, so it wasn't hard for us to survive this situation. We got used to it. [Regina, 61]

> They stopped paying my husband [who was in the military] his salary for 3 months and I had to figure out how we could we live. That is, with three children one must somehow take care of feeding them, [take care] of the most essential. [Eva, 55]

> That's how we lived [on what I earned from petty trading] because there was no money. Generally [the military] didn't pay [my husband] and the school generally didn't pay me. Neither of us received wages, not him, and not me. [Vasilisa, 56]

That employers retained staff they couldn't pay and employees continued to go to work under these conditions can be explained by a number of features of the Soviet system. Because all Soviet enterprises were state-owned, the distinction between enterprise and government was blurred, and many of the services provided by the government (or by separate private-sector entities) in market economies were the responsibility of the enterprises in the Soviet Union. Depending on the size of the enterprise, this could include housing, daycare, health clinics, sports facilities, vacation resorts, dining facilities, vegetable gardens, and/or small shops. Access to these goods and services was thus tied to employment at the enterprise and in the turbulent and difficult early years of the transition many enterprise managers did their best to continue to provide such services even when they were unable to meet payroll. Quitting one's job meant forgoing whatever assistance the enterprise might be providing and there was little chance of finding another large enterprise that was in better shape and interested in taking on more workers. Rather than laying off the workers, the managers kept them on and paid them what they could when they could; rather than quitting, the employees tended to stay at their official jobs and supplement their pay with all manner of informal sources of income. Sometimes, this would involve working off the books for a new, private-sector enterprise.

Another explanation for the fact that the economic difficulties experienced by enterprises did not translate into widespread official unemployment is offered in the following quotation from a woman whose husband was an enterprise manager.

> In 1990 they stopped paying people money. People went to work but they didn't get paid, not for a month, not for two, not for three. I remember that foreigners would come and they would ask, 'why do they go to work?' and the women would correctly answer, 'If my husband didn't go and stand at his machine, he would simply get drunk. He needs somewhere to go.' Because for men it's very important that they have something to do in this life. [Their attitude was basically], 'So they don't pay me this month, but they've promised to pay next month.' [Vera, 56]

In some cases, rather than delaying the payment of wages, enterprises chose to make the payments in kind. Workers would receive part of the factory's output and have to sell it for cash or use it to barter for goods they wished to consume. Even institutions that provided services might offer payment in unusual form, as the last quotation in this section illustrates. The challenges and occasional absurdities of this arrangement are reflected in the recollections offered here.

A woman I interviewed in Astrakhan approached me a couple of days later to say that the interview had sparked an exchange of reminiscences in her family. One of the phenomena they recalled was seeing people attempting to sell the goods they had received in place of wages. On one occasion, arriving by boat in Uglich, about 1000 miles north of Astrakhan along the Volga River (and about 70 miles from Yaroslavl), they were greeted at the dock by a crowd she estimated at 50 people, all apparently employed at a local watch factory and all trying to sell the same nice watches to those on board. On another occasion, while driving between Moscow and St. Petersburg, roughly every kilometer they would encounter people trying to sell their "salaries" by the side of the road—pails in one location, glassware in another. Adding to the already considerable challenges of receiving one's pay in kind was the Soviet practice of concentrating the country's entire production of a particular good in a very small number of extremely large factories. As a result, there were many cities in which employment was heavily concentrated in a single plant, so that a large share of the city's population would be trying to hawk the same good at the same time.

For a college professor in Yaroslavl payment in kind had a more direct personal impact.

> I worked at a university....and suddenly it turned out that they weren't going to give us our salary. Not in cash, you understand.... And the university came up with the following solution. Now don't fall off the chair, as we say, don't fall off your chair.... Somewhere they had somehow acquired through barter some Finnish boots. These thick quilted boots... and they were violet. Imagine! The entire university staff received its salary...Well, it's true that there were some white boots but there weren't enough of those. They handed us as the equivalent of our salary two pairs

of violet boots. No doubt this was for one month's salary, though I'm no longer quite sure. But I do remember that they didn't pay us and then they wanted to be able to put something into our hands. And maybe we'd be able to sell these boots to someone. How the university acquired these boots I don't know.... In my department we didn't receive the white boots, so I gave one pair of violet boots to my mom and the others I just wore. That is, the idea was somehow to exchange them, but I couldn't exchange those boots for anything else, for example for food. No one would trade. Everyone else wanted to eat too. Boots were less important than food. And that's how they paid my salary. [Ekaterina, 56]

## Putin: Political Stability, Economic Growth and ... Sanctions

Eventually, things improved, helped by the collapse of the ruble in August of 1998,[9] which sharply raised the price of imported goods and reduced competition for Russian producers, and by high world prices for petroleum,[10] which sharply increased Russian export earnings and government revenue. By 2000, inflation rates had fallen to the low double digits, and since 2006 they have often been in the single digits. At the same time, growth of GDP was positive for all but one year between 1999 and 2014, the exception being 2009, when, like so many countries, Russia was hurt by the global financial crisis (World Development Indicators). When I spoke to the women in the fall of 2012, the staggering inflation rates and unreliable wages were described as distant experiences that they sometimes had trouble believing they had really lived through.

Less than a year and a half after our conversations, Russia annexed Crimea, reclaiming territory that Nikita Khrushchev had transferred to

[9]The ruble fell from a value of about 0.17 USD (6.7 rubles to the dollar) in August of 1998 to less than 0.07 USD in September and about 0.05 in December of that year (19.99 rubles to the dollar) (Federal Reserve Bank of Saint Louis Economic Research 2019).

[10]The price of crude oil was about 19 USD at the end of 1991 and only a little over 12 USD at the end of 1998. By 2000, it had risen to 26.72 USD and by 2007 to 95.95 USD. More recently, although it has fluctuated considerably, it has not dropped below 35 USD (Macrotrends 2019).

Ukraine in 1954. This, and the subsequent conflict in eastern Ukraine, prompted the USA and European Union to impose sanctions against a number of Russian officials and banks and to restrict the export of goods of potential military importance.[11] Although the sanctions were aimed at those in power and were not intended to have serious consequences for the general Russian population, President Putin responded in August of 2014 by introducing a ban on the import of foodstuffs from the USA, the European Union and other countries imposing sanctions. As a result, food prices have risen, certain kinds of foodstuffs have become scarce,[12] and real wages have fallen. The situation nonetheless remains far better than in the 1990s and does not demand the kind of ingenuity, explored in the next chapter, the women had to call on to care for themselves and their families in that challenging earlier period.

## References

Alexashenko, Sergey. 1993. Macroeconomic Stabilization in the Former Soviet Republics: Dream or Reality. In *Economic Consequences of Soviet Disintegration*, ed. John Williamson, 261–302. Washington, DC: Institute for International Economics.

Berkowitz, Daniel, et al. 1998. Quantifying Price Liberalization in Russia. *Journal of Comparative Economics* 26 (4): 735–760.

Brainerd, Elizabeth. 2010. Reassessing the Standard of Living in the Soviet Union: An Analysis Using Archival and Anthropometric Data. *The Journal of Economic History* 70 (1): 83–117.

Burns, John F. 1982. Soviet Food Shortages: Grumbling and Excuses. *New York Times*, Jan 15, A8.

[11]For a comprehensive list of the sanctions and of Russian responses, see Gutterman and Grojec (2018).

[12]Kalinina (2017) cites official figures saying average prices rose 32% between August 2014 and August 2017, while Novinite, a Bulgarian news agency, reports that in 2017 "about 40 percent of Russia's families do not have enough money for food and clothing." Ironically, some of those benefiting from the sanctions are members of the business and political elites, who are choosing to invest in Russian agriculture—especially in greenhouses (Kalinina).

Caldwell, Melissa L. 2004. *Not by Bread Alone: Social Support in the New Russia*. Berkeley/Los Angeles: University of California.

Cooper, William. 1996. The Economy. In *Russia: A Country Study*, Chapter 6, ed. Glenn E. Curtis. Washington: GPO for the Library of Congress.

Earle, John S., and Klara Z. Sabirianova. 2002. How Late to Pay? Understanding Wage Arrears in Russia. *Journal of Labor Economics* 20 (3): 661–707.

Federal Reserve Bank of Saint Louis Economic Research. 2019. National Currency to US Dollar Exchange Rate. Accessed online at https://fred.stlouisfed.org/graph/?id=CCUSMA02RUM618N. January 2019.

Ferguson, Niall, and Brigitte Granville. 2000. "Weimar on the Volga": Causes and Consequences of Inflation in 1990s Russia Compared with 1920s Germany. *The Journal of Economic History* 60 (4): 1061–1087.

Gaddy, Clifford G., and Barry W. Ickes. 2002. *Russia's Virtual Economy*. Washington, DC: Brookings Institution.

Granville, Brigitte. 2002. The IMF and the Ruble Zone: Response to Odling-Smee and Pastor. *Comparative Economic Studies* 44 (4): 59–80.

Granville, Brigitte. 2016. Lessons from the Collapse of the Ruble Zone and the Transferable Ruble System. CESifo Forum 4. Accessed online at https://www.cesifo-group.de/DocDL/forum-2016-4-granville-ruble-zone-collapse-december.pdf. January 2019.

Gutterman, Ivan, and Wojtek Grojec. 2018. A Timeline of All Russia-Related Sanctions. RFE/RL, September 19, 2018. Accessed online at https://www.rferl.org/a/russia-sanctions-timeline/29477179.html. January 2019.

Humphrey, Caroline. 2002. *The Unmaking of Soviet Life: Everyday Economies after Socialism*. Ithaca, NY: Cornell.

Kalinina, Kira. 2017. Three Years of Embargo in Russia: The Winners and Losers. *Russia Behind the Headlines*. August 2017. Accessed online at https://www.rbth.com/business/2017/08/06/3-years-of-embargo-in-russia-the-winners-and-losers_816898. January 2019.

Macrotrends. 2019. Crude Oil Prices—70 Year Historical Chart. Accessed online at https://www.macrotrends.net/1369/crude-oil-price-history-chart. January 2019.

*New York Times*. 1987. Soviet Says Food Prices Will Rise, October 3. Accessed online at https://www.nytimes.com/1987/10/03/world/soviet-says-food-prices-will-rise.html. May 2019.

Novinite. 2017. 40 Percent of Families in Russia with a Shortage of Money for Food and Clothing. Accessed online at https://www.novinite.com/articles/185589/40. January 2019.

Odling-Smee, John, and Gonzalo Pastor. 2002a. The IMF and the Ruble Area, 1991–93. *Comparative Economic Studies* 44 (4): 3–29.

Odling-Smee, John, and Gonzalo Pastor. 2002b. The IMF and the Ruble Area: Response to Comments, 1991–93. *Comparative Economic Studies* 44 (4): 81–84.

Pomfret, Richard. 2002. The IMF and the Ruble Zone. *Comparative Economic Studies* 44 (4): 37–47.

Rock, Charles P., and Vasiliy Solodkov. 2001. Monetary Policies, Banking, and Trust in Changing Institutions: Russia's Transition in the 1990. *Journal of Economic Issues* 35 (2): 451–458.

Shevchenko, Olga. 2009. *Crisis and the Everyday in Postsocialist Moscow*. Bloomington/Indianapolis: Indiana University.

Yurchak, Alexei. 2006. *Everything Was Forever, Until It Was No More: The Last Soviet Generation*. Princeton, NJ: Princeton University Press.

# 5

# Coping Strategies

High prices, inconsistent payment of wages, and continued scarcity of goods posed enormous challenges for Russians in the early 1990s and, as one woman said, in order to get by they "contrived, used cunning, and cooked porridge." This "contriving" included methods that had been honed during the Soviet period—such as receiving help from family and close friends and growing vegetables on a small personal plot of land—as well as those that were newly permissible—such as engaging in petty trading (selling either goods brought from elsewhere or one's own possessions) and small-scale entrepreneurial activity. Some women changed jobs or took on additional employment, often informally, and a few took advantage of the new freedom to engage with foundations, institutions or individuals from other countries. This last source of support has become more difficult to tap since a law was adopted in 2012 requiring all organizations in Russia that receive funding from abroad and are engaged in political activity (interpreted quite broadly) to register as foreign agents.[1]

[1]Daucé (2015) provides a nuanced study of the government's policy toward NGOs, especially those focused on human rights. For a compilation of Russian articles discussing the regulation of NGOs, see Reynolds (2007).


J. McKinney, *Russian Women and the End of Soviet Socialism*,
https://doi.org/10.1007/978-3-030-16226-9_5

## Help from Family and Friends

Help from the extended family and social networks came in a variety of forms—including time (performing chores, providing child and elder-care, standing in line to acquire rationed or otherwise hard-to-come-by goods), information (about job opportunities, availability of goods, successful coping strategies), housing, food and, occasionally, money. My respondents spoke often about assistance received from parents and occasionally about assistance provided by partners. They seldom mentioned help provided by friends, probably because I never steered the conversation in that direction rather than because such help was unimportant to them.

### Housing

Despite significant construction of apartment buildings in the 1960s and 1970s, urban housing in Russia remained inadequate at the time the Soviet Union dissolved. At the same time, rent everywhere was heavily subsidized. Rents had not been raised since 1928 and constituted a tiny fraction of household spending (Morton 1984: 70). The official Soviet claim in the 1970s was that the average family spent only 4–5% of its income on housing. In comparison, for a long time the standard recommendation for people in the USA has been that they should pay no more than around 30%.[2]

The combination of inadequate housing construction and very low rents meant that queues for acquiring one's own apartment were very long. Even as the communal apartment, with unrelated families forced to share kitchen and bathroom, became less common, it was still normal for multiple generations of a family to share a single small apartment. One woman put it simply, "I was lucky because at that time I was

[2]A recent study by the Joint Center for Housing Studies of Harvard University found, however, that in 2014 some 11 million American renters were paying over half of their income for rent (Vasel 2016).

living with my parents [with my newborn]. They somehow kept me fed [and, of course, housed]." Another, also a new mother at the time, said, "At that time we were living with my parents. My husband kept trying to find one job or another…but he couldn't find anything in his field."

An alternative arrangement involved having the older and younger generations swap apartments, so that the younger would have access to more rooms, making it easier to raise a child. Such practices had long characterized Soviet housing arrangements: housing space was continually reallocated within extended families in response to births, deaths, marriage and divorce.

In the Soviet period, many workers received apartments through their place of employment; others received them from the city in which they lived. Although these apartments were all technically owned by the state (either by the state-owned enterprise which had jurisdiction over them or by the municipal government), once a person received an apartment it became essentially that person's private property. The recipient could live in the apartment for life, trade it for a more suitable apartment as family circumstances changed, and even bequeath it to children or grandchildren. There were official housing exchange bureaus, as well as an informal market; apartment exchanges sometimes involved multiple families, a complex chain of transactions, and side payments (Morton 1984: 76–77).[3] During the transition, those living in an apartment could acquire it for free from the state, so that this previously implicit ownership became explicit.[4] As with so many changes in the early 1990s, this policy created opportunities for the unscrupulous to benefit from the inexperience and naïveté of others—sometimes, as illustrated in Chapter 3, even from that of family members.

Some sense of how family life cycles were reflected in the use of apartment space can be gained from the experience of my landlady.

---

[3]The absurdities, awkwardness and venality associated with informal housing reallocation in the Soviet Union have been captured in a number of fictional works, including Yuri Trifonov's novella *The Exchange* (1973) and Vladimir Voinovich's *Ivankiad* (1977).

[4]The differences between Russian and American understanding of "ownership" of living space is explored in depth in Zavisca (2012), which examines both Soviet housing practices and the attempt to develop a housing market in the post-Soviet period.

She owns a relatively large apartment in one of the nicest parts of Yaroslavl, along the Volga embankment in the historic district. The apartment, on the second floor of a four-story building, consists of a small entrance hall, the typical two-part Russian bathroom (one small room with bathtub and sink and, adjacent but separate, an even smaller room containing toilet and possibly some storage space), a kitchen, and three other rooms. The apartment had belonged to her husband's family, and in the early years of her marriage she lived there with her husband's mother and aunt.

After her son and daughter were born, the four immediate members of her family lived in one of the bedrooms, her mother-in-law in another, and her husband's aunt in the third. Once her husband was allocated an apartment through his workplace, the aunt moved to that new, smaller apartment and the children moved into what had been the aunt's room. Later still, the mother-in-law died, and my landlady's own mother, no longer capable of living alone, then moved in and shared what had been the mother-in-law's room with her adolescent granddaughter, leaving what had been the children's room for the teen-aged son. The mother died in 1995, the husband in 1999, and the children are grown and married. For many years, beginning when the children were still living with her, she has been renting out bedrooms to foreign students.

Such complicated arrangements were common. One couple, for example, first lived with the husband's grandmother after they married, and then traded places with his mother once they had a son. The young family moved into the apartment the husband had grown up in and his mother moved from that apartment to live with her own mother. The practice of sharing and trading apartments has continued to the present, despite the significant increase in construction and the introduction of some aspects of a housing market. At the same time, these changes in the housing market have created additional channels through which parents can provide assistance. For example, one woman, quoted in the next section, describes how she used land inherited from her grandmother as the site for a house she and her husband are paying to have built for their older son.

## Childcare

Because so many of the women I interviewed lived for at least a few years with parents or in-laws during the early years of the transition period, they generally received help with childcare as well as a place to live. Although only one respondent spoke explicitly of receiving her parents' help with childcare, this is more likely to reflect how common the practice was than to suggest that it was rare. Relying on family members for childcare was common during the Soviet period[5] and became increasingly important during the transition as the number of places in state-run facilities declined and private facilities had not yet developed.

Despite Soviet reliance on and ideological commitment to having women holding jobs outside the home, it had always been challenging to find a slot in daycare facilities and this became even harder in the early 1990s, as enterprises attempted to reduce costs and municipal governments struggled to find funding for even the most basic of operations. According to a study carried out by the OECD, enterprises were more inclined to cut childcare services than many of the other benefits they provided (Le Cacheus 1996: 20). By 1995, the number of preschool slots per thousand children under the age of seven had fallen to 658 (Gosudarstvennyi komitet statistiki 1996: 201). Four years later, fewer than 1.7 million children were enrolled (McKinney 2004: 47; Itar-TASS 1999). Exacerbating the difficulties was the elimination of most state and employer subsidies, so the care that was available was far more expensive than it had been and in 1998 cost on average 16% of the minimum subsistence income (Lokshin 2004: 1; Mezentseva, n.d.).

The options for most women with young children at this time were thus extremely limited: they could rely on a female family member (mother, mother-in-law, aunt) to provide childcare or they could adapt their employment to accommodate their parental responsibilities. The consequences for employment and career decisions are explored in greater length in Chapter 6. Here I focus on the role of the extended family.

[5]For a comparison of North American intensive mothering and Russian extensive mothering, see Rotkirkh (2000: 116–121).

While being able to leave one's child with a trusted older female family member was generally recognized as a blessing, this didn't necessarily mean that the new mother was entirely happy with the arrangement. The first woman I quote below expressed deep gratitude for her good luck, but the second clearly struggled emotionally. Her situation was complicated by the fact that her parents lived in Yaroslavl, her husband, a foreign student, had returned to his home country, and she was studying in Moscow.

> In 1992 my daughter was born. I stayed with her for one year. And then I had such a wonderful possibility. I had an aunt, a single woman. She helped me; she freed me to go to work. I couldn't put my daughter in the nursery, she was so little. I was lucky. My aunt stayed with the child and I went to work. I just needed to find somewhere a little closer to home. [Marta, 45]

> I gave birth to my child and [my parents] took us to Yaroslavl… I came to the institute [in Moscow] just to work for the diploma. I did the diploma work, but constantly, constantly I went to Yaroslavl. I took the train between Moscow and Yaroslavl because … well, my mother was living here and I felt uncomfortable. I was worried. [My son] was too small [to be away from me] and I was always commuting. [Veronika, 51]

One of the women whose mother and mother-in-law both worked and were thus not available to take care of her son and daughter chose to be with her children during the day, while teaching art in the evenings.

> My husband took good care of me; he loved me very much. And I took care of the children [a son and daughter]. The work in the studio made it possible for me to raise my children myself. I had classes from 6:00 in the evening. That meant that I could see the children off to school, prepare dinner [the main meal, consumed closer to mid-day than evening], and bring the children back home. I fed them dinner and stayed with them while they did their lessons.… And then I would head out. [If] my husband came home late, then we had an aunt who would come over. She would stay with the children and I'd work here in the studio until ten. I specifically chose such work so that I could raise my children myself. [Vera, 56]

Not everyone was able to arrange for regular childcare. As described in the following quote, sometimes great flexibility and multiple sources of support were necessary, especially if one's work schedule were unusual.

> In the early 1990s my daughter was born. I had to somehow combine work and raising her. And I was already working in the theatre. You understand, that was convenient on the one hand, but the basic work day was modified. That is, rehearsals began at 11:00 and ended around 2:00 or 3:00. Then there'd be a break, and then there was an evening rehearsal from 6:00 to 9:00, or an evening performance. That means I came to work twice, with a break in between. On the one hand, in the morning it was very convenient. I would take the child to kindergarten and manage to do some housework until 11:00. But kindergarten was only until 5:00 or 6:00…Then I'd collect the child and either I'd bring her to the theater, or her father would pick her up, or her grandmother. But really, well, [the children of those in the theatre] grow up here, in the theater, in the evenings. [Once] we were putting on a play. She was little, just 5 or 6 years old, and she attended all the rehearsals. She knew the whole script, everyone's part, she could recite the whole thing. [Aleksandra, 54]

## Money

Sometimes the assistance from family members took the form of cash, received either regularly or sporadically. One woman received gifts of money from her parents at intervals determined by when they received their pensions. Because the pensions were paid irregularly, so was the assistance from her parents.

> [My parents] were retired. In general pensions were paid irregularly, and how we managed to live then is truly hard to understand. It's hard to understand, because there were really strong delays in pensions, there were even delays for half a year. …At some unexpected time they would bring money. [But] we could survive it all, not because it was at all simple but…because at that time I was connected to my husband. [Veronika, 51]

Although it is possible that she was referring to the modest financial support her husband, also a student at the time, was providing, it is more likely that she was referring to the emotional support that came from a happy (and at the time quite new) marriage. Like several of the women I talked with, she was no longer married. She still mourned the end of the relationship, especially because she was the one who had decided to leave and was no longer confident that this had been the right choice.

Another woman was able to count on regular support from her parents.

> It was of course difficult during 1991, when I was defending my dissertation in Moscow. Then it was necessary to economize from paycheck to paycheck.... My husband and son were in Yaroslavl and I was in Moscow, but I returned every week. My parents told me that they would pay for all the tickets to and from Moscow, so I came every week while I was studying in Moscow. [Liza, 55]

Unlike the women quoted above, one respondent expressed deep embarrassment at having needed help from her mother during this period. Although roughly the same age as the other two, she was no longer acquiring education—which made such assistance normal—but was employed, as was her husband, in the government bureaucracy.

> It's amusing what it came down to, what I had to do. My mother, a pensioner, helped me, helped my family. With her pension, with her miserly little pension, she helped us with money. Can you imagine?! And we were two grown independent people! There were delays with the pensions, yes, there were delays, but somehow as with all the pensioners, she always had the ability somehow to set a little bit aside for a rainy day [literally, for a dark day], to create some sort of reserve. If we were the same, more enlightened about our reality and the uncertainty about the future, then we, too, would have set a little bit aside. [Zoya, 52]

Twenty years later, she and her husband were providing significant assistance to their grown son by helping him to build a house. This involved their taking out a loan, and she continued to be embarrassed by their failure to have "set a little bit aside" so that this loan was necessary.

> One son is married. There, on that land in the village that was left to us by my grandmother, we built the older son a house. We took out a mortgage, we borrowed credit [embarrassed laugh]. My husband and I now are paying on the mortgage, but we built him a house.

That "borrowing credit" made her uncomfortable reflects the experiences and values of her generation. A woman and her husband of about the same age made it clear that they personally have never borrowed, although their son has taken out a mortgage. The reference to America in this quote was one of several times in the course of the interview at which she delivered jabs about the USA and its culture—always with a smile, but clearly disparaging.

> Everyone lost their savings [to the pyramid schemes of the mid-1990s][6].... Therefore we [Russians] no longer save. We live like Americans, on credit. [Laughter] We live on credit. My son has a mortgage; he has a mortgage on a second apartment. [At this point her husband interjected, "You and I have never taken out a loan."]... No, we never have, not even once, but our children live [this way]. And we understand the children. We don't tell them they're wrong. [Liza, 55]

Not everyone of the generation shared this discomfort, however. One woman offered an interesting perspective, somehow seeing buying on credit as the post-Soviet equivalent of the Soviet practice of acquiring goods through connections. After explaining how price liberalization had led to increased availability of goods, she continued:

> Furniture appeared, and carpets. If earlier it was practically impossible to buy anything except through *blat,* through acquaintances, now people can buy things on credit. For example, we bought our furniture on credit.... It's good furniture and we somehow paid off a loan in one year and it wasn't a big deal. There were no difficulties. [Anna, 56]

[6] I discuss these more in Chapter 8.

One of my respondents, born in 1941, was the source rather than the recipient of assistance. As her comments make clear, she helped her daughters in a variety of ways, not just by giving them money. Note that although she was already receiving a pension at the time, she was still working as well—a very common technique for getting by. With women eligible to receive a pension at age 55,[7] many chose to continue working, at least part time. Note also the role played by the factory in making it possible to acquire goods. As discussed in Chapter 4, this was often at least as important a benefit of employment as wages were.

> It was hard for the young people. There wasn't work and there wasn't money, so it was necessary to help. There wasn't food in the stores. While I was working—I was still working for a while during perestroika—at the factory I could buy butter, sugar, meat. [These goods were available] only in the beginning, and only at the factories. The factory took care of its workers. But my daughters—they didn't work or where they worked they didn't receive anything and their wages [voice trails off]…. It was a very hard time. My older daughter finished a technical institute, the younger entered university but didn't finish, she got married. The older one changed [jobs] several times, but all the same she was working. My son-in-law, the husband of my younger daughter, wasn't working. We had to help them with our pensions [laughs]. We helped with food and with money. [Food] from our dacha, and whatever we bought at the factory, we bought for them.

## Growing One's Own Food

As suggested by the preceding quote, food grown or gathered by individual families played a critical role in Russia during the early 1990s. This might be food provided to urban residents by parents still living in the countryside, or food grown by city-dwellers in the small gardens

[7]In October 2018, Putin signed a law which will gradually raise the age of eligibility for pensions to 60, while raising that for men from 60 to 65. That women are able to retire at a younger age than men is ironic, given their significantly longer life expectancy. The initial plan called for the new age for women to be set at 63, but this proved so unpopular that it was changed to 60.

attached to their *dacha*. Most dachas had been allocated by Soviet-era enterprises as part of a policy to increase food production, and they continued to be a source of fruits, vegetables, and especially potatoes after the dissolution.[8] In the words of my landlady:

> At that time, we had a sort of garage here in the yard for the car, and there was a pit in it where you could store the potatoes we grew in the country. And we could harvest all kinds of fruits and berries and store them all winter…The main thing is that I don't like the kind of potatoes they sell in stores; I don't like those grown on the collective farms. They're somehow not very tasty, not quite right. These days it's hard to grow them [presumably because of her age], but I don't care. Even if it's just one sackful, I want my own potatoes because they taste better than all the others. I don't know all they do [on the farms], maybe they don't work the soil right or they add a lot of fertilizer, but I cannot eat those potatoes. And my family and I love potatoes. [Klara, 70]

Although almost all of the women I spoke with had access to a plot of land during the 1980s and 1990s and grew vegetables and fruits there, only two of them identified this land as genuinely important to their survival during these difficult years. The first described the sale of what she grew as her primary means of surviving during this period.

> I had a vegetable garden. Everything I harvested from the garden I sold, so that I could give the children bread and milk.[9] Everything I gathered I sold, beginning with dill in the early spring and ending with, well, literally, with whatever was in the garden—carrots, onions, whatever grows in this region, I sold it all. [Feodosia, 74, on pension and not working by 1988]

[8]For an exploration of the potato as "an important material artifact in a certain household ecology," "a symbolic resource that represents…some key aspect of political and social economy," and "a cognitive resource [and]…irreducible vehicle of thought about and action in the world," see Ries (2009).

[9]Her daughter was born in 1961 and her son in 1969, so it is not clear what period she is describing. It is also possible that the children she refers to are her grandchildren. It is also possible that she is using bread and milk symbolically.

The other woman, a decade younger, held a prestigious and well-paid job in the Gorbachev period. (Note that she uses "perestroika" for the post-Gorbachev period.) Although she did not sell the food her family grew, being able to consume it at home was a great help.

> These were hard times for me, this perestroika. I quit work and stayed home without pay… My husband taught at an art school; he was an artist. And we lived in tight financial circumstances. My son was ill, I wasn't working, only my husband worked. Yes, that was a hard time. We bought a house in the country—not really a dacha, but almost one. We lived thanks to that, because my husband had the summer off, and we would go out to the country. And there we would hunt for mushrooms and berries, and we grew our own. We didn't sell any of it; it was just to provide for ourselves. [Maria]

A third, much younger, woman spoke about the important role played by gardens for the population in general:

> Of course, people were saved by their vegetable gardens… Every family has a garden where they grow vegetables, fruit trees. It was a great help to many, because without this, it would probably not have been easy to survive.

This was echoed by a middle-aged woman, participating in a conversation among three friends. I had asked about wage arrears and after a brief discussion they had agreed that it hadn't been that bad, since people weren't starving to death. (Again, we see the tendency to dismiss the idea that wage arrears were a problem as long as people could get by.) This led naturally to a discussion of the role of the *dacha*.

> At that time, horticulture was widely developed, dachas. At that time they gave everyone land, divided it into plots. And a great many people grew things there, at least vegetables in the summer. In the winter we survived due to this. [Emilia, 57]

More typical, however, were the comments, often delivered with resigned laughter, that given the climate the gardens weren't actually all that much help. This was stated most succinctly by a woman who dismissed the whole idea of being able to use gardens with the comment, "Everything grew poorly" and is seen again in the following quotations.

> Yes, we had a place not far from Yaroslavl, a village home. This was the home of my grandmother. She had already died and the house in the village remained. There of course was a vegetable garden there and we planted and grew whatever it is possible to grow in our northern zones. [Zoya, 52]

> Our husbands served [in the military] and all the women dug gardens, we all planted vegetable gardens. We planted potatoes, we planted cabbage, we planted tomatoes. But there in the Urals everything grows badly, because it's an area not favorable for agriculture. [Vasilisa, 56, at the time living at a military post in the Urals]

One woman shared the following story, which highlights the mistakes she and her husband made, perhaps deliberately reinforcing the point that they were members of the *intelligentsia* rather than practical peasants for whom agriculture was a natural activity.

> At that time [the city administration] was giving plots of land to teachers so they could build dachas there, gardens, vegetable gardens, and in that way [feed] themselves.... These were just empty plots in the dacha section [outside of town]. And even though we [already] had a wonderful dacha on the Volga, my husband became excited by the idea that we would build our own home, lay out our own garden, and things would be much better than at my parents'.... This was sometime around 1990, '91, '92. We built the house, we planted potatoes, carrots, beets, and next to us was a local man from the village on the outskirts of which we had our land and he said, "Nothing will grow for you." I said, "Why will nothing grow for us?" He said, "What kind of land is that, then? It's poor land." And, indeed, nothing grew for us. Just these little bits and pieces [literally, tag ends] and potatoes smaller than an egg. In general, by the second year we already understood that we had wasted our money to build this house... Fortunately, we were able to sell it. Such a crazy life! [Anna, 56]

The contrast between the widespread view that growing one's own food had been essential during this period and the recollections of the women for whom such activity had been unsuccessful or unimportant is striking. Although these stories might be interpreted as describing "failure," they may also be seen as demonstrating a more important form of "success"—that of being true to one's identity even during hard times. As we see below, the importance of the women's sense of self also influenced their attitudes toward engaging in petty trade.

## Petty Trading

Despite severe restrictions on private economic activity during the Soviet period, legal, illegal and quasi-legal private activity was quite common, especially in the 1970s and 1980s, when the fear of draconian punishment had largely evaporated. The most extensive and conspicuous venue for legal private transactions was the *rynok*, the farmers' market where those living and working on collective or state farms could sell output from small household plots to supplement the meager wages they earned in the collective operation of the farms. It was also generally legal to supplement employment in the formal sector by selling services or personal property, provided one did not employ others in the activity. (Millar 1981: 88–96). The line between legal and illegal sale of services was blurred, however, since it was quite common for doctors, plumbers, carpenters, drivers and others to use state enterprise materials and often state employment hours to sell their services to those who wanted work done more promptly or with greater effort than was likely to be found in the state sector. Finally, there was the entirely illegal activity carried out by black marketeers, those who managed to gain access to scarce—often Western—goods (the iconic example was blue jeans) and to sell them for a hefty profit.

Thus, there was considerable experience with small-scale private economic activity before Gorbachev experimented with cooperatives and "individual labor activity" reforms in the late 1980s.[10] Nonetheless, prior to these reforms the authoritarian discourse portrayed such activity in decidedly negative terms. Good Soviet citizens worked for the collective, for the Soviet people, not for personal gain. If the private sale of services was considered bad, "speculation"—the purchase of goods in one location for the purpose of selling them elsewhere at a profit—was considered even worse. Speculators were described as parasites, simply sponging off the work of others. Under Stalin, their activity was punishable by death, and condemnation of the behavior continued long after the severity of the punishment had relaxed.

In the late 1980s and early 1990s, as the economy collapsed and people struggled to find ways to supplement their meager state incomes or support themselves while waiting for their wages to be paid, many were forced to engage in petty trade despite their deeply engrained distaste for it. This activity came in a variety of forms—the most desperate were forced to sell their personal belongings at flea markets or outside subway stations, others engaged in "suitcase trade," traveling to neighboring cities (and, after international travel was permitted, to neighboring countries) to buy goods and bring them back to sell, and some produced goods at home for sale. The last activity often developed into real entrepreneurial efforts and is discussed at greater length in Chapter 7.

There was considerable variation in the way my respondents discussed petty trading, and in their personal decisions about whether to engage in it. Although there was some difference across generations, with younger women more matter-of-fact about having spent time in petty trade, the sharpest differences seemed based on class identity, with those who were part of the *intelligentsia* most likely to express personal distaste, saying that to engage in trade would have been "against my character." While this could mean simply that it requires a resilience and entrepreneurial spirit that they lacked, in most cases I received the strong impression that they considered this kind of work to be beneath them. This distaste was expressed both by those who managed to avoid

[10]For a description of the goals and provisions of these 1986–1987 reforms, see Hewett (1988: 327, 340–342).

engaging in trade and by those who were forced to violate their principles—the former explaining that they simply weren't the type of people who would engage in trade and the latter clearly feeling a need to justify their involvement in these activities.

The women who managed to avoid engaging in petty trade expressed either relief or self-congratulation that they had escaped this fate. For example, an engineer in her early 60s said:

> In the beginning it was somehow very unattractive. Everyone went… to Poland, to Turkey, then to China. Everyone had these huge suitcases which they dragged along. In the end, many teachers lost their jobs, engineers.…What were they to do? So they engaged in this trading. We thank God, in our family this didn't happen, but I know that for many people it was simply impossible to live [otherwise]. [Regina]

A university teacher in Astrakhan of roughly the same age was also clear about how demeaning ("discrediting") such work would have been—worse than sweeping the street—although she softens the condemnation by suggesting that perhaps she lacks the necessary traits:

> Unfortunately, I am incapable of doing anything else [other than teaching]. If I lost my job, I just don't know what I'd do. Of course, I could wash floors, but I couldn't be involved in trade. If a person… if one is discredited one loses everything. I have a different kind of head. Well, I could do some sort of housework—let's say, sew, cook, clean—but other serious work I couldn't do. It would be a tragedy for me if I lost my job because for my whole life I've been involved in only this one thing.… No doubt if life required that I went to some other work, I don't know, maybe I could sweep the streets or maybe [sell] flowers on the street, but I don't know what else I could do. …If I lost this work I honestly don't know.

A woman in her mid-50s in an important position in the cultural sphere made the point even more bluntly, without any qualification.

> We [my husband and I] are the kind of people who simply could never [engage in trade]. Look, some people can, you understand, and some cannot. And we cannot.

This sense that only a particular kind of person could or would engage in trade is captured in the following exchange between two friends, both in their seventies and both relatively shielded during the most difficult years by good positions, which they retained, and by the positions of their husbands. They are speaking about Maria's sister-in-law.

> She worked at the Rubber Design Institute. She was laid off—the whole department was dismissed—and she started trading. She traveled to Poland to get products and then she sold them here. She and my brother had two children, too. It was hard. But at least she didn't just sit back and fold her hands. [Maria]

Lidia comments, "Of course, one had to know how to do this," and Maria responds, "Well, she did this, I think, for about four years. And, actually, she works this way even now, she got used to it, and she works now as a salesclerk. Only now she doesn't travel to Poland, she just works in a store." Lidia then repeats, "Well, you have to have the habit, too; there are those who can sell, and others cannot."

Not everyone who would have preferred not to engage in trade could avoid it, however, and so they offered explanations and justifications for their behavior, emphasizing that they did this kind of work only because they had no choice.

A young woman who was a student in the late 1980s explained her involvement in trade as necessary but short-lived. That she repeated this idea of necessity so many times in this short section of the interview underscores how much she considers it to have been beneath her. She is now employed in a way that uses abilities of which she is proud, working as regional director for an organization that runs a number of centers for teaching computer skills. It is also possible that her response was shaped by the fact that the conversation took place in the presence of her boss, an older woman, who was a professor of law and the only person I spoke to who never once brought the conversation around to the practical and personal, preferring instead to speak in terms of grand theories and social systems.

> I was a student and it was really necessary [to trade] just to survive, because there was no work anywhere. There simply was nowhere to get money and everyone here—teachers, lawyers, economists—everyone was forced to go sell at the market, you understand? I also did not refuse to do this. At that time it was necessary somehow to survive, to endure and still remain there in that niche.... Yes (I traded), it was probably about two years. I simply had to do this, because otherwise it would not have been easy to survive.

The loss of status was greater, and felt more keenly, by a woman forced to sell off family possessions in order to survive. This woman had been employed at a conservatory in Baku and her daughter (my respondent) explained that the family had lived well before they felt forced to move from Azerbaijan to Yaroslavl when the Soviet Union dissolved. Although the mother did eventually end up with a teaching job in Yaroslavl, her daughter stressed that even this involved a serious loss of status, since it was at a school far inferior to where she had previously taught.

> My mother was divorced, and my grandmother and grandfather were also in the position that their pensions weren't being paid. They weren't being paid anything, and Mama for the first time in her life sold a lot of things, whatever it was possible to sell, in order that we could live. Jewelry, gold, the television set—because it was necessary to feed me, an adolescent, it was necessary to [pay fees to] fill out documents, my grandparents had nowhere to live...Of course, it was hard. [Oksana, 31]

Other women I spoke to were not as psychologically invested in seeing themselves as *intelligentsy*, even though in a couple of cases they could indeed have identified as such. For one woman, now retired, shuttle trade was simply one of many ways she had found to support herself during her long life, one of the many experiences that, she claimed, made her life worthy of a book all by itself. She clearly relished talking about these experiences and the pleasure she got from this outweighed any embarrassment she may once have felt about engaging in trade.

She begins her account by providing her credentials as an educated, competent woman, who held a good job until it all "fell apart."

> I worked at a design institute. I worked with documents, that is to say, in the technical department. I graduated from an institute. At the time of perestroika, I had already left. I worked there twenty-two years, from 1979 to 1992. [As was often the case, her use of 'perestroika' extends past the Gorbachev period into the period of Yeltsin's market-based reforms.] I left because everything had fallen apart [literally, was broken], they weren't paying wages, there wasn't any money.

She briefly found work in another company, but when she lost that job, too, she began to sell goods on the street.

> I went to a motor company, and worked there in the personnel office until I was laid off. In 1994, everything fell apart and after that I was an entrepreneur. And then I gave it all up and went on pension. I worked for 40 years, from childhood. I was in trade. I traveled to Poland, to China and to many countries besides these. I've been in 17 countries. These 17 countries, that was simply as a tourist, but those two I went to for clothing…. I've lived through a lot, I could write a novel. Yes, I could write a novel. All that there's been in my life, if I told you, you wouldn't believe it. [Malvina, 67]

Other women, who may have initially viewed petty trading as a temporary expedient, actually ended up turning it into a way of life, either by opening their own businesses or by becoming associates for foreign direct sales operations. For them, embarrassment at having been involved in trade had given way to pride in their ability to run a successful business (or, in one case, pride in the perseverance and grit that enabled her to keep starting new businesses after several earlier attempts had failed). The challenges of entrepreneurship are considered in Chapter 7. In the following quotes, the emphasis is on the petty trading which was their early introduction to self-employment.

A college teacher in her late 50s who embarked on trade after participating in an American-sponsored training program described the role this played in changing her attitude. This woman today runs a relatively successful transportation company with her husband, who is retired from the military. Despite her success, there is a certain level of defensiveness noticeable in her comments, perhaps because in the early years she was engaged in "speculation".

> In 1995, I was at a workshop here, and you know I realized then that I had to get involved in something. I tried. You know why I showed you those socks? I went to the Tambov region and bought socks, since I was taught [by the Americans] that it's not shameful when you have no money to sell something. It isn't shameful. It's your business, it's your job, it's your work. What was hammered into our heads for decades was that reselling is bad, it's trade. But it seems to me that what is bad is when you have no money, then that's really bad.
>
> So I went and bought these socks in the Tambov region, and sold the first batch. Then I bought military shirts at a Voentorg [shop selling military uniforms] because in [the town where I was born] there are a lot of Vietnamese living, actually there are a lot of them working. They work at the knitting factory, and they love the "military" style, the military shirt. I figured, well, they love them, so I'll buy these shirts in Voentorg—they're cheaper there—and sell them the shirts and buy up socks [to sell]. And that's just what I did…And that's the way we lived, because there was no money. [Vasilisa, 56]

Another military wife, who began her career as a research chemist and then taught high school chemistry, also ventured into trade as a necessary evil when her husband had not received his pay for several months. Although trading clearly initially involved a loss of status, by the time we talked to one another she was entirely comfortable with her choices, happily describing the luxury items this work enabled her to buy for herself. Indeed, this woman eventually found herself so comfortable with the idea of trading that she now works as an active and enthusiastic sales representative for a major international cosmetic company.

> I knitted [things to sell] and I sold newspapers.... And at home I had housework to do.... For half a day I'd be a 'business-lady' [using the English term] and more or less for half a day I'd be a homemaker. But it turned out that I tended to devote more time to business. And, by the way, it turned out to be a good business with the newspapers. I even bought myself a fur coat. They imported Greek coats of fox fur, and I bought one for myself. [Eva, 55]

Being able to use one's ability to sew or knit to earn money, often to supplement income in a job in the formal sector, was generally a source of pride rather than embarrassment, a sign of resourcefulness rather than desperation. One owner of a fabric store initially engaged in petty trade but soon turned to selling goods she sewed. As is clear from her comments, she is happy to have left trade behind and to have focused on "creativity"; even though she continued to be engaged in business, it was no longer "just business," and that removed any stigma in her eyes.

> Yes, when it was difficult, yes, I traded.... But we only went to Poland and bought a little bit there, and I wasn't successful. They stole from me a little. But then I realized that for me creativity is closer [to my heart], to make something from something, not just to buy and sell. I'm more creative. There is such a thing as just business—you buy and sell, buy and sell—and that's a different mentality. And before, here, it was considered speculation. So then I opened a shop in my apartment. At first, two girls and I worked in my apartment. I have two rooms and I equipped one room as a workshop and rented sewing machines.... And we sewed curtains and skirts. [Tamara, 61]

Another woman, whom I interviewed while in Astrakhan, spoke with great pride about her sewing ability and the wonderful clothes she had created and sold in order to earn money. She made fashionable clothes, including wedding dresses, to order for friends and others. She never had to sell at the market (*rynok*), which, she implied, would have been a step down. (It was, however, a matter of pride that she could *buy* food at the market—the extra income her sewing provided made it possible for her to acquire the food sold there at higher prices and thus avoid the constraints imposed by the ration coupons.) This is a woman who takes great pride both in her own accomplishments and in the opportunities she has been able to provide for her daughter. When I spoke with her in 2010, she was still earning income from many different sources, supplementing her job as head of a department in a university with teaching at other academic institutions, offering private tutoring for high school students and selling theses to those preferring to buy their degrees rather than to work for them. She justified the last by arguing that her primary asset is her mind and she should be allowed to be compensated for making it available to those less well endowed.[11,12]

## International Ties

One of the major changes associated with *perestroika* and later with the dissolution of the Soviet Union was the relaxation of controls on interaction with foreigners. At the same time, many in the West were eager to participate in the transition. For neoliberal economists, the country seemed to offer a perfect laboratory: they hoped to help Russia create a textbook version of the market system, free of the kinds of "distortions" and "adaptations" that had evolved over centuries of Western capitalism. For members of Christian denominations with a strong proselytizing commitment, this was an opportunity to bring religion to people long forced to espouse atheism. For others, Russia, with its large population, rich endowment of petroleum and other natural resources, and woefully underdeveloped consumer sector, offered an exciting new market.

For a few of the women I interviewed, this opening up to the rest of the world offered new economic opportunities. Yaroslavl, of course, was not like Moscow, or even St. Petersburg, and none of these women was employed in major Western corporations (although some of their children have had that opportunity). Nonetheless, Western organizations

[11]Sadly, I wasn't very familiar with my equipment at that point and I failed to record my conversation with this exceptionally interesting woman. What I include here is from my written notes.

[12]This attitude toward educational assignments is similar to that described by Caldwell (2004: 72–74). Knowledge or information should not be viewed as a private resource, but as something to be shared for the benefit of one's group.

did offer an additional source of income. Two of my respondents have developed careers as sales representatives for foreign businesses—one in the cosmetics field and the other for a company that sells a wide range of products advertised as promoting wellness. Western organizations also played a role in providing key training to a couple of women, enabling them to pursue independent activities–in one case in the commercial sphere, in the other in the non-profit sector. These experiences will be examined in greater length in Chapters 7 and 11. As we will see in the latter chapter, the interaction between Russians and the West was complicated and could present unexpected pitfalls for those on both sides.

## Conclusion

As the women in my group of respondents dealt with the challenges and uncertainties arising from the state's economic policies—and its inability to implement those policies as intended—they both relied on familiar coping strategies and devised new ways of providing for their families. They continued to turn to extended family and social networks for assistance and were resourceful in identifying and developing skills that proved useful in the new environment. While some of the tactics they adopted challenged their sense of identity as highly-educated professionals, they were generally able to take pride in their capabilities and ingenuity. This chapter has focused on strategies falling outside of the formal labor market. Next I explore the way the women used employment—both formal and informal—as a coping strategy—not merely as a source of income, but also as a source of housing, childcare, access to scarce goods, and sense of identity.

## References

Caldwell, Melissa L. 2004. *Not by Bread Alone: Social Support in the New Russia*. Berkeley/Los Angeles: University of California.

Daucé, Francoise. 2015. The Duality of Coercion in Russia: Cracking Down on "Foreign Agents". *Demokratizatsiya* 23 (1): 57–75.

Gosudarstvennyi komitet statistiki. 1996. *Semiia v rossii, Statisticheskii sbornik*. Moscow: Finansy i statistika.

Hewett, EdA. 1988. *Reforming the Soviet Economy: Equality vs. Efficiency*. Washington, DC: Brookings Press.

Itar-TASS. December 3, 1999. Available in Johnson Russia List 3660. Accessed online at http://www.cdi.org/russia/johnson/archives.cfm. November 2002.

Le Cacheus, Jacques. 1996. The Current Situation and Key Issues for the Long Term. In *The Changing Social Benefits in Russian Enterprises*, 17–29. Paris: Organisation for Economic Co-operation and Development.

Lokshin, Michael M. 2004. Household Child Care Choices and Women's Work Behavior in Russia. *The Journal of Human Resources* 39 (4): 1094–1115.

McKinney, Judith Record. 2004. Lone Mothers in Russia: Soviet and Post-Soviet Policy. *Feminist Economics* 10 (2): 37–60.

Mezentseva, Elena. n.d. Gender Inequality in Today['s] Russia: Who Bear[s] the Social Cost of Reform. Accessed online at http://www.indiana.edu/~ree-iweb/newsEvents/pre2006/mezentseva%20paper.pdf. May 2019.

Millar, James R. 1981. *The ABCs of Soviet Socialism*. Urbana/Chicago/London: University of Illinois Press.

Morton, Henry W. 1984. Housing in the Soviet Union. The Soviet Union in the 1980s. *Proceedings of the Academy of Political Science* 35 (3): 69–80.

Reynolds, Sarah J. (ed.). 2007. Spies, Politics, and Charities: Regulation of Nongovernmental Organizations in Russia (I). *Statutes & Decisions: The Laws of the USSR and Its Successor States. A Journal of Translations* 42 (1): 4–8.

Ries, Nancy. 2009. Potato Ontology: Surviving Postsocialism in Russia. *Cultural Anthropology* 24 (2): 181–212.

Rotkirkh, Anna. 2000. *The Man Question: Loves and Lies in Late Twentieth Century Russia*. Available online at https://www.academia.edu/2643465/. Accessed May 2019.

Trifonov, Yuri. 1973. The Exchange. In *The Long Goodbye: Three Novellas*, 17–97. New York: Harper and Row.

Vasel, Kathryn. 2016. *11 Million Americans Spend Half Their Income on Rent*. CNNMoney. Accessed online at http://money.cnn.com/2016/06/22/real_estate/rent-affordability-housing-harvard/. January 2019.

Voinovich, Vladimir. 1977. *The Ivankiad*, trans. David Lapeza. New York: Farrar, Straus and Giroux.

Zavisca, Jane R. 2012. *Housing in the New Russia*. Ithaca, NY: Cornell University Press.

# 6

# Jobs: Formal, Informal, Multiple

## Introduction

Soviet propaganda touted the absence of unemployment as one of the key advantages of the Soviet system. Soviet citizens had, it was claimed, both the right and the responsibility to perform socially useful labor. The official line was that victory over unemployment had been achieved by the late 1920s. After that, unemployment "ceased to exist" in the Soviet Union and unemployment data were never again collected or published.

To some degree, the Soviet claim was legitimate. There was in fact no cyclical unemployment—the unemployment that arises during an economic downturn as aggregate demand falls and businesses cut back on production. This, however, was due less to the nature of the system itself—that is, to state ownership of the means of production and the use of central planning to direct economic activity—than to impossibly high output targets, reflecting unreasonably high levels of demand on the part of the government, and the system's reliance on extensive rather than intensive growth (see Chapter 2). Enterprise managers needed every pair of hands they could find in order to come close to meeting


J. McKinney, *Russian Women and the End of Soviet Socialism*,
https://doi.org/10.1007/978-3-030-16226-9_6

these goals. Because the overwhelming bulk of demand for output came from the state, there were no recessions caused by lack of consumer or business confidence, no worry that aggregate demand would fall and leave idle plant capacity, and thus no worry about being saddled with redundant workers.

There are other kinds of unemployment, however, and the Soviet Union was not immune to those. There was structural unemployment, the result of a mismatch between the jobs available and the skills of available workers. Stalin's obsession with size—his country should boast the largest dam, steel mill, power plant in the world—played a role in creating structural unemployment, as did the desire to streamline control over the economy. For many products there was a single gigantic firm somewhere in the country; as a corollary, many cities were basically one-industry towns. Because the composition of the labor force at these enterprises was often heavily gendered, the partners of those working in the town's major employer might have difficulty finding appropriate industrial jobs close to home.[1]

There was also some frictional unemployment, which arises when people leave one job, whether voluntarily or involuntarily, before having secured another. For much of the Soviet period, workers were generally free to change jobs at will and the very high level of demand for labor made leaving one's place of employment low-risk. Most studies found that the rate of labor turnover in the Soviet Union was comparable to that in industrialized capitalist countries, despite the fact that geographic mobility was seriously constrained by the system of internal passports and residence permits. Indeed, the Soviet press often featured articles lamenting "excessive labor turnover" (Kirsch 1972: 154) and an official estimate for the 1970s suggested a loss from turnover equivalent to the output that could have been produced by an additional 1.5

[1]Coal and steel towns, for example, had unusually low female labor force participation rates, due in part to the lack of good jobs for women and in part to the above-average wages paid to the male workers (Granick 1987: 83). Towns with predominantly "female" jobs, on the other hand, were more likely to be characterized by relatively small male populations than by significant male unemployment. Thus, Ivanova, a textile town, became known as "The City of Brides" because of its demographic imbalance.

million workers (Powell 1981: 117). The average length of unemployment when changing jobs in the USSR was estimated to be 28 days (Godson 1984: 120).

Still, the systemic ability to avoid cyclical unemployment meant that open unemployment in the Soviet Union was comparatively low. While acknowledging this, Western analysts of the Soviet system tended to focus on the country's problems with hidden unemployment and underemployment (see, for example, Millar 1981: 112–114). In theory, planning should match jobs and workers flawlessly, with every worker engaged in productive work at all times and every task accomplished with just the right input of labor. Soviet reality differed from theory, however, and Western analysts regularly decried such Soviet practices as paying people to perform unnecessary tasks, establishing almost insurmountable barriers for enterprises wishing to lay off unproductive workers, and tolerating the practice—widespread in the Brezhnev period—of running errands during work hours.

While these practices did reduce efficiency, their impact on daily life was not entirely negative. One benefit of Soviet labor policies was the high degree of economic security they provided. Soviet workers never had to worry about losing their jobs (unless they chose to engage in questionable political activities or otherwise aroused the distrust of those in authority). Another benefit of these "inefficiencies" was that they provided the elderly, the uneducated, and others who might have had difficulty competing in a labor market the opportunity to earn an income and provide for themselves, thereby relieving the state of the need to support them through welfare payments (Lane 1985: 61).

One of the major fears of Russian reformers in the late 1980s and 1990s, as they devised a strategy for replacing the Soviet economic system with one that was market-based, was that the transition would lead to a sharp and painful rise in unemployment. Enterprises would simultaneously be freed from the obligation of meeting state plan targets and deprived of state subsidies. They would therefore shift from focusing on plan fulfillment to focusing on profits, and this would require them to reduce costs by making significant cuts in their labor force, especially in cases where some workers were clearly redundant. Furthermore, as consumer demand replaced government demand as the major determinant of the composition of output, many large enterprises would shut down altogether, since they were designed to produce industrial and defense goods rather than household products.

To the surprise of many, mass unemployment did not in fact occur. While the real unemployment rate was well above the official rate—many of those laid off did not bother to register with the authorities—it remained lower than had been feared, especially outside of heavy industry and the defense sector. This resulted both from the managerial practice of keeping workers on the books even when they couldn't be paid in cash or on time and from workers' fear of losing access to whatever enterprise-based benefits they received. Thus, much of the hidden unemployment and underemployment that had characterized the Soviet period continued after it had ended, although the reasons for these phenomena were different, as were the forms they took.

While a few of the women I spoke to did experience unemployment in the 1990s, more often the changes in the labor market affected the kind of work they did, where they did it, and how many jobs they held. Strategic decisions about employment served as another major coping mechanism in the 1990s and, as with the methods described in Chapter 5, were influenced by both familiar and new forces.

As was true in the Soviet era, a woman might take a job to be near her home, making it easier to care for her children; she might take a job because it granted access to a slot in a nursery or kindergarten; she might take a job because it gave her access to housing. In the late 1980s and early 1990s she was more likely than before to take on supplemental work and there was now, for a few, the option of not holding a paid job at all. The change about which the women expressed deepest regret was the disappearance of the Soviet job placement system for those leaving school. Given their stage in life, their regret was less for themselves, than for their children, whose career paths, they believed, had been made more difficult and whose career opportunities had been reduced.

## Choosing a Job

Not only did Soviet workers enjoy great job security, they did not have to try very hard to find a job in the first place. The consistently high level of aggregate demand and relative unimportance of costs in the calculations of enterprises ensured that there were always plenty of job openings. In addition, as mentioned in Chapter 2, the government played a role in matching workers to jobs at the beginning of their careers. Because all education, from kindergarten through the most advanced post-graduate studies, was paid for by the government, those who received this education were expected to repay the investment by accepting an initial job assignment wherever the authorities decided. For many young professionals, this meant three years in an unattractive and/or remote posting; for those with better academic performance or better connections, the initial placement could be entirely satisfactory.

> I graduated from university at that time. My degree was as a software engineer, a mathematician-programmer. I was "distributed" to Kostroma [one of the Golden Ring cities, located about 50 miles northeast of Yaroslav] … to an electromechanical plant, to the automation department of the enterprise management system. I worked there until I took maternity leave. [Yulia, 52]

> I graduated from the Teacher Training University of Yaroslavl in 1990, from the Department of Pedagogy and Methods of Primary Education…. After university all young specialists were supposed to go to the place which the university chose for them and work for three years there… Where were most students sent? To the countryside, where they didn't have specialists…. [But] I was a good student and I was sent to Uglich [a town of about 40,000 people located 70 miles west of Yaroslavl]. There was a Pedagogical College there, where teachers were trained. It was not a university but a college; that is, it was at a lower level [than a university]. And I taught Pedagogy in this college. I taught for only one year, because I was married and became pregnant. I didn't complete the three years. I became pregnant and my husband and I returned to Yaroslavl. [Marta, 45]

As the above excerpt indicates, the placement process did not always work exactly as the authorities intended. In addition to cases where the period of service was abbreviated for some reason, there were cases where graduates simply failed to report to the assigned locations (Dyker 1984: 40–41). Nor were the employees the only ones who resisted official assignments; sometimes, the blame lay with the enterprises. Although the general weakening of central planning in the late 1980s certainly contributed to worker and enterprise willingness to ignore the labor distribution system, the problem was not new. According to figures cited by Steven Solnick, in 1965 4.2% of graduates in the Russian Republic were denied jobs by the enterprises to which they were assigned, and by 1970 this had risen to 7.2%. By the 1980s, it was clear that the assignment system was not working as intended. Although a survey published in early 1988 found that within six months of graduation about 85% of new graduates in the Soviet Union were at the job to which they had been assigned, only 59% of specialists who had graduated between 1985 and 1987 were even working in their field of study (1998: 132–134).

The reasons for this job mobility were varied, and, as is clear from the examples below, few were unique to the Soviet system. Women continued, as they had for decades, to choose jobs in order to facilitate caring for their children. While the daughter of the first speaker quoted below was born in the 1970s, the daughter of the second was born in the early 1980s and that of the third in 1992.

> I was an upbringer [*vospitatel'*].[2] My husband—my first husband—studied in Moscow at an institute, and I lived with my parents. I had a daughter and somehow so that I could earn something I went to work as an upbringer in the children's home.... I worked there for 5 years. When I moved here to Yaroslavl I went to work again as an upbringer so that I could get my daughter into the kindergarten. [Liubov]

[2]Although this is often translated as "educator," it was clear that these women did not view themselves as teachers. They did not consider this to be professional work or to require qualifications.

> I sat at home for a year after my child was born. When the state allowances ended, I set out to arrange childcare. This was a problem because there weren't enough places in the nurseries, and our city, you understand, is stretched out. It's pretty big, so naturally everyone tried to find a place close to home with a nursery, otherwise you'd have to travel on public transportation with a little one. Cars at that time were prohibitively expensive; a car would cost 5000 rubles and the salary of an engineer was 100 rubles… Buying a car was impossible. So it was only natural that I looked for a place close to home with a nursery. I was hired as an upbringer, even though I didn't have special pedagogical education or other education dealing with children. They hired me to work in the nursery. They even gave me 10 rubles extra salary because I had a higher education. Those with just secondary education, those from a vocational school, received a little bit less. I worked in the nursery for two and a half years, just so that my child could attend the kindergarten. If I hadn't gone to work there, there wouldn't have been a place for her in the kindergarten. Those were what the times were like. [Yulia]

> I couldn't put my daughter in a nursery, because she was very young…I just had to find somewhere to work close to home, so I worked in a school. [Marta]

Another reason to choose a job was to get a place to live, since enterprises and government agencies often controlled apartment buildings. This motivation had its flip side, since the employer's responsibility to provide housing was one of the factors contributing to problems with the distribution system for new graduates. Young people might refuse to stay in their assignment if an enterprise failed to make the promised accommodations available, or an enterprise might turn someone away because it had no housing to offer.

> In 1989… I worked at the City Executive Committee. This is the mayor's office today…. I worked as a secretary, nothing remarkable. I went to work there to get a place to live. At that time, in such organizations, housing was allocated. Then perestroika began, and they stopped giving out housing. I managed to receive housing, though I did not get the apartment I'd been promised when I was hired. I just got a room. I quit

> work there after a week, just as soon as I received a room. It was very unpleasant to work there. They did not like one another. [Inessa, 53]

Sometimes, job choice was simply a matter of geography, something familiar to two-career professional families throughout the developed world.

> At first [after graduating] I worked at a research institute. Before I married, I worked at a research institute in biology…. My specialty was biochemistry. I could have taught biology and chemistry, or I could have worked in a research institute and I worked in an institute. But when I got married and moved to a new place, it was hard to arrange things… You take what you can find. I worked in a hospital and I taught chemistry to students in eighth and tenth grades. [Eva, 55]

> How long did I work in a school as a history teacher? I worked in my specialty for four years. And then in 1989 we moved back here and it turned out that I couldn't find work. [We moved back] because I missed Yaroslavl, I missed my parents, who were living here…. I graduated from the Yaroslavl Pedagogical University with a specialty as a history teacher. How it turned out that I ended up going to work for the police, in the passport-visa service, I don't even understand myself. It's just that my husband was working for the police at that time and he suggested that I go work there. We had just moved to a new address and … in the part of the city where we lived there weren't any openings in a school for me to be a history teacher and I thought, "Where am I going to work?" They offered me a job in the Passport-Visa Service in 1991, and it turned out that I worked there from 1991 to 2011. [Zoya, 52]

Although this new job was not one for which she had been educated, it may well have offered comparable status and better pay than teaching and definitely offered the possibility of early retirement. It is thus unclear that accepting the position meant settling for something she would have preferred to avoid. For another woman, taking a position outside of her specialty seems to have offered greater satisfaction.

> In 1989 I worked in a school. I taught home economics and sewing… even though I graduated from a completely different department. My degree is in chemistry. At that time, our career guidance was poor and somehow I didn't end up in that line. I enjoy creative work; I've always liked to sew. I've always liked to work with cloth, that's what I love. [Tamara, 61]

Another respondent, who chose not to be recorded but was willing to share her story, also offered an example of a failure in the job placement system. Her experience casts light on issues tied to the migration flows prompted by increased nationalism in the non-Russian republics and the eventual dissolution of the USSR. This woman, trained as an engineer at a technical institute in Moscow, was assigned with her husband, a fellow graduate, to work at an electronics scientific-research institute in Yaroslavl. When they arrived in the city in 1990, however, it was to learn that both the jobs and the institute-controlled apartment they had been promised had been given instead to refugees (almost certainly of Russian ethnicity) from Azerbaijan. They soon found jobs at a different research institute in the city, positions that were available, ironically, because they had been held by Jewish scientists who chose to take advantage of the new freedom of movement to emigrate to the United States.

Despite such wrinkles, the system of initial post-graduation job placement had generally worked sufficiently well for its disappearance to be regretted by a large number of my respondents. A few had suffered directly from the challenges of finding the right job in the new labor market.

Speaking of her somewhat complicated job history—losing a job, staying at home, taking a new job in an unrelated field and disliking it, and finally, after many years, again finding a position that used her training, one woman said, "It is always difficult to find work, that is, to get exactly the right job. In my opinion, this is very difficult everywhere [Regina, 61]."

Another woman, who had married a foreigner and lived abroad during much of the 1990s, saw the changes with particular clarity.

> When I returned, I still wanted to work either in the field of design or in architecture. I didn't want to just work casually, accidentally, in some position I stumbled into. I didn't want to change my profession. But, you understand, it was hard to find something right away. I returned to a completely different government from the one I left. During that time when I wasn't here, from 1990 to 1997, everything changed. Everything was different.... All this change took place without me, and then, when I moved back here, I had to work, I had to find my niche and figure out what I wanted to do, where I could work [in my field]. And it turned out it wasn't that easy. [Veronika, 51]

As they adjusted to the new labor market, these women used a variety of strategies to find employment. The couple mentioned above who learned after moving to Yaroslavl that the positions they had been promised were no longer available found new jobs by looking at want ads in the newspapers. Some, discussed in the next chapter, began their own businesses. Only one respondent—a woman who had been laid off from a factory job—mentioned using the government employment service created in the mid-1990s to help cope with the mass unemployment that was anticipated.

Indeed, only a small number of Russians overall who lost their jobs in the 1990s bothered to register with these labor bureaus. The choice not to register seems to have been the result of several factors, including inconvenient locations and hours, very low levels of unemployment benefits, and the shame people felt at being unemployed in a country where this had for decades been both rare and condemned as parasitism (Bridger et al. 1996: 52–53). This particular woman, however, was entirely matter-of-fact about her use of the service as a way to acquire training.

> I worked as a lab assistant at a fuel equipment factory. I worked there until 1996. Then they laid people off. After the downsizing, I went to the labor bureau for the unemployed. I completed a training course for secretaries and went to work at the Yaroslavl Pedagogical University. I worked as the secretary of the director. [Liubov]

The other women who mentioned having lost their jobs during the 1990s made no mention of using a labor bureau and instead found jobs on their own or, like the woman who worked for the passport service and the second woman quoted below, with the assistance of their husbands.

> I worked at a design bureau… in the technical department. I worked there 22 years, from 1979 to 1992. I left because everything fell apart, they didn't pay wages, there was no money…. I went to a transportation company and worked there in human resources until I was laid off there too. [Malvina, 67]

> My husband helped to some extent. He arranged something for me, I checked it out and didn't like it. But they liked me and advised me to try this job [the one she ended up with]. [Regina, 61]

Husbands also, counter to the stereotype, often worked hard to support their families during this period through their own employment.

## Husbands' Work

As discussed in Chapter 3, the women often explicitly contrasted their ingenuity and willingness to do whatever was necessary to support their families with the behavior of Russian men. Educated men, I was repeatedly told, refused to stoop to jobs they considered beneath them. This claim that men were less able than women to adapt to the new economic and social circumstances and less willing to take jobs that were below their qualifications, though a cultural trope, was not universally valid. Some of my respondents spoke with admiration of their husbands' struggles to find work of any kind, even when these efforts were unsuccessful; others expressed gratitude for the way their husbands' efforts had made their lives easier. While some men may have been eager to take advantage of new entrepreneurial opportunities, others sacrificed their professions and associated status to try to provide for their families any way they could.

Some men, like those discussed in the following two quotes, made the shift to the new economy relatively early, and did so by starting their own businesses.

> My husband worked in science and these institutions lost funding. A great many projects were shut down, many areas did not receive funding, and simply ceased to exist. But he was smart, and decided that he should open his own business, in product certification. Earlier, we did not have such services ... but a huge need arose, because out there in the [non-Soviet] world products without certification are believed to be of poor quality. They are not valued; they're not in demand in the market. Therefore, if our enterprises produced something they wanted to sell abroad, they needed to get a certificate stating it was of a certain quality standard... High-quality products need documentation, and that's what he did ... Now he runs the business. It is a private business. He created it. He worked with a German organization, which certified him for this kind of activity.... I do not remember exactly [when he opened the business] but around the time when the fall began in research and development, so around 1990. [Regina, 61]

> My husband is an entrepreneur. He works in the field of furniture, doors. He started his business in 1993. The [economic] difficulties drove him to do this. He was working at a machine-building enterprise and privatization affected him negatively. There were delays in payment of wages, so he began to look for some means to live and began to work as a businessman. At first there were partners; he left the enterprise with a group of men and they began to produce doors. Later they split up into several small companies. Now he works alone. There were some problems... Sometimes one or two men work with him. When there are orders he invites them; when there aren't [enough] orders, it's just him. [Ksenia, 48]

In another case, the shift occurred several years later and involved taking a job with a private bank rather than starting up a business. This man's decision to change jobs was motivated by the fact that husband and wife worked for the same agency, which meant that any problem with wage arrears hit them at the same time. Because the agency was connected with the military, the man was eligible to receive a pension after twenty years of work rather than waiting until the normal legal retirement age of 60. By retiring from that position and taking a job in the private sector, he was able both to add to the family's income and to give them greater economic security by diversifying the sources of that income—even though he started this path in 1997, just before the financial crisis led to the closing of many banks. (He has since left that line of work and now is director of a sports school.)

> [Life] became easier…sometime around 1998-99, when…a sort of stability had appeared…. My husband left the *militsia* in 1997; he retired. He left for some commercial structure—a bank—so it became a little easier for us. He was there, let's say, in security, to protect the money of the bank. There was the [government] default at that time, but for my family it was easier, because there was a steady paycheck. And besides in the bank they could manipulate salaries, whether there's a default or not, and find some additional money. Therefore, by 1998 it had become a little easier for my family. [Zoya, 52]

A couple of women suggested that they were able to stay home with their children during this period thanks to the success of their husbands, but in one case this interpretation was immediately challenged by another woman taking part in the conversation.

> *Emilia (57)*: I worked as an engineer at a design bureau. In 1992 I stopped working there and didn't work anywhere after that. I stayed at home with my children. My husband allowed me [*pozvolil*] not to work. [The Russian word means both "to permit" and "to make possible"; my sense was that here she meant that her husband made the choice possible by earning enough on his own.] …My husband was also an engineer and worked at a factory. When I stopped working, he became involved in commerce.
>
> *Inessa (53)*: You had the opportunity not to work, yes, and also at that time the labor market here was unusual. Probably the design bureau was shut down then.
>
> *Emilia*: Yes, they were shutting design bureaus down or laying people off.

Given the economic upheaval and decline of the period, not all of the men were successful, of course. One woman, married to a non-Russian who eventually returned to Central Asia because he could neither find satisfactory employment nor adapt to life in Yaroslavl, put it this way.

> My husband tried to find some job or another. He graduated from a technical institute. He is an energy specialist by training, but he couldn't find anything in his specialization. As a man he really tried to feed the family [any way he could]. [Renata, 45]

Another respondent's husband faced challenges of a different kind. He worked in the Communist Party bureaucracy and had just received his doctorate from the Academy of the CPSU when the Party was outlawed.[3]

> The Party was no more. No one needed his education, no one needed his doctoral dissertation. For a while he suffered. Yes, for him the 1990s were really the hardest time.... To understand that the Soviet Union was destroyed, that on the next day there would be a new government. It was impossible. It took time to understand.... It was very hard to change his way of thinking. He changed jobs frequently. He didn't really commit himself and the career that he could have had in other circumstances didn't happen.... Now he works in a bank, he's head of an administrative department ... He [always] earned something, he just changed jobs often—after a year, or two, or three or four. [Alexandra, 54]

Although both of these men struggled, they clearly did not simply give up, lie on the couch, and take to drink, as the standard argument I was offered about Russian gender differences would lead one to expect. Whatever the men in their lives did—giving up, walking out, struggling

[3]The Communist Party of the Soviet Union (CPSU) was dissolved in late August 1991, after the attempted coup by hardliners opposed to Gorbachev's reform efforts. It was then officially abolished in the Russian Federation by President Boris Yeltsin on November 6 of that year, just prior to the anniversary of the Bolshevik Revolution. In February of 1993, the Communist Party of the Russian Federation was established and continues to function today, a distant second to Putin's United Russia in the number of delegates to the Russian legislature, the State Duma.

valiantly, or simply carrying on—many of the women found it necessary to supplement the family's earnings by taking on additional work.

## Moonlighting

Many of the women I interviewed were teachers and able to earn extra income in ways which were, at least tangentially, related to education. One possibility was private tutoring.

> At the time my daughter was little. I offered some private lessons for children who were not doing well in Russian or in mathematics. There were only a few of them. It wasn't the way it is now. Now, of course, a lot of teachers give private lessons, and this is considered normal. But back then, in the early post-Soviet period… [people believed that] the teacher should teach everything at school, and it was unclear why a teacher would take money [after hours]…. My mother was also a teacher, and she always said: 'What private lessons?! What is this?' That's why I had only a few students, but it was a way to get money. [Marta, 45]

The next speaker first took on extra work at one school and later supplemented her regular teaching job by offering classes at other institutions.

> My working day at that time started at 8:00 in the morning and I worked until 9:00 in the evening, or 10:00. I was practically constantly at the school. I'd take the very last trolley home. I'd leave at 11:00 at night. And I had a daughter [who was around three at this time]…. [At work] I had a lot of responsibilities. They paid me for this and for that… We have in Russia—it was the same in the Soviet Union—this understanding of shifts, of a rate [*stavka*]. This is the norm of work time for a given category of worker. And at that time I had three and a half *stavki*. You can imagine, right? That was quite a workload!
>
> [Later] while I was working at a [new private] institute, I was also conducting classes with students from several of our colleges in mathematics. It wasn't completely private, that is, the university would invite me as a teacher. I'd give a course in informatics or technology or economics,

> something like that. There were groups of students who were already working. Even the directors of some factories studied there—not of big factories, of course. This was in 1996 through 1998. [Yulia, 52]

Other women found additional work that departed significantly from what they viewed as their career and source of identity.[4] One, who was already receiving a pension at the time, did janitorial work at her son's school (not that in which she had been employed as a language teacher).

> I'd get up early in the morning and run to the school and wash the gym. Until eight o'clock in the morning or 8:30, I cleaned. I'd get up at 6:00 and do this as exercise and even so I earned more than the salary I would have received [teaching] at school. [Klara, 70]

Although at the time of my interviews the Russian economy was doing quite well, the practice of moonlighting had continued as a way to earn money to supplement irregular income or for special purchases, most often for the women's children, even though most of these were now grown. The same woman offered both of the anecdotes below, first describing her own experience and then that of a friend.

> There was a time quite recently when I worked in a kindergarten for a month or two. My daughter was finishing school, my husband had left us, and she had her final exams. For her graduation party she needed to buy a dress and go out to a restaurant. And I didn't have any students at the university. My pay is hourly. If I work during a month, I get paid, but if there aren't students then I receive nothing from the university. So I simply went and worked in a kindergarten. What did this mean? These are little kids; I was a nursemaid. I just washed them and walked with them and tended them. Let me repeat: Here I am, a university professor, and for two months I went to work in a kindergarten in order to buy my daughter a dress for her graduation evening....

---

[4]As Bridger and Kay note, this loss of status and identity held as well for many women who needed to find new primary employment after being laid off, since most available jobs involved manual or low-skilled work (1996: 22).

> My friend, who has a higher education, works as a nanny. She has two children and she works to send them abroad for vacation. She is a librarian, that's her main job, but she holds a second job at night in order to send her children to Europe in the summer. [Marta, 45]

At the time of our conversation, this speaker was engaged in a temporary part-time job tied to the upcoming elections, supplementing the income from what she views as her "real" job—her professional job—with other earnings. In fact, she was holding two different regular jobs in addition to whatever temporary work she picked up.

> The election commission work is very temporary; this is just when there are elections. I am a teacher of Russian as a foreign language. I work at [a private technical institute]… Since our salary is very small everywhere, I work two regular jobs: I work at the institute and I work for the military. We have a military school and I work there in the library. There are foreign students there, too—from Angola, Mongolia. I work at the circulation desk, to help them choose the literature for an essay or some assignment.

## The Next Generation

While most of the women I spoke to were far enough along in their work life in 1991 not to be affected personally by the end of the Soviet approach to education and job placement, they clearly worried about how its disappearance might hurt their children. As members of the *intelligentsia*, these women placed especially high value on education and expressed more concern about the kind of career their children attained than the money they might earn. A few mothers took clear pride in their children's ability to navigate the new economic environment successfully, but even in those cases there was sometimes an undercurrent of disappointment in the paths their children had chosen.

Two women lamented that a good education and acquisition of specialized training no longer guarantee a job. Although they viewed this as a new problem, as noted above even in the mid-1980s 41% of recent graduates were not working in their specialties. Indeed, neither of the women had herself followed a "normal" Soviet career trajectory. The first speaker had chosen to move to Uzbekistan in her early twenties for an adventure, while the second had spent most of her own working life in a job completely unrelated to her field of study.

> Now there's something to worry about. My daughter finished an art institute, specializing in artistic jewelry. She has a natural ability, she draws very well…but very sadly she finished four years ago and having received that education she has not been able to find work in her field. [In the meantime, she has taken up competitive windsurfing and is now teaching that sport; when I spoke with her mother she had recently also taken up snowboarding.] She plans next year to enroll in a university to study sports medicine and become a sports doctor. [Renata, 45]

> My older son is a lawyer… The younger son also finished law school this year … but so far he hasn't found work. I don't know how he will arrange work; so far, he's not even talking about it. He can give it some thought while he's working in a bank, the same bank where his dad worked…. You understand, when we lived in Soviet times, it was all defended in the plan. If I enrolled in an institute, I studied for free, the government educated me. If I didn't make it through the entrance exams—there were limited spaces—if I blew it, then…Well, then you go to a technical school. You go to some institute, lower in rank, right? But as long as you enroll, they educate you for 5 years. Then they assign you a job, they send you to work in your profession… where you gain experience. Today there isn't this at all. Today education has to be paid for; …there are very few places paid for by the government, very few government spots. Afterwards, you must find work yourself, you try to find work, but everywhere requires experience. Where is the poor young specialist, who just yesterday graduated from the university, going to get experience? To gain experience, you have to be able to work somewhere. And if it turns out that you have a mama or a papa with connections, then you're all set. But if your mom and dad don't have connections, that means you have to work outside of your specialty. And for that you spent five years studying! [Zoya, 52]

This speaker's regret for the good old days when connections were not so important in shaping opportunities is challenged in the next quote, which captures Malvina's belief that the old Soviet-era system of social networks and *blat* has been replaced by a new emphasis on merit. She attributes her son's success in the post-Soviet economy to his skills and education rather than to any sort of pull he might have exercised.

> [My son went to Moscow] and he arranged things there and found good work. I thought it was all still the way it used to be, where it was, let's say, "by acquaintance." But no, now you write a résumé and then they give you tests, and then they take you for a trial period. And it turned out that he found good work. He is head of an audit department. [Malvina, 67]

These different perspectives allow each woman to believe in the personal merits of her son: the one who has not been able to find the "right" job has been hindered by a lack of connections, while the one who has succeeded has done so without needing such assistance.

Some of the children who have succeeded have done so while remaining in Yaroslavl; some, like the young man in the previous quote, went to Moscow; still others left Russia altogether—for Israel, for Western Europe, for North America. Some have found jobs that aligned well with their education, while others ended up pursuing other career paths or taking jobs that they (or their mothers) hoped were temporary detours from their intended career.

None of this is peculiar to Russia, of course. In the USA, job-hopping and multiple career changes, relatively rare for earlier generations, are considered the norm for millennials and Generation Z, who must adapt to the vagaries of labor market demand in a period of rapid technological and structural changes. In the Russian case, however, the discomfort arising from uncertainty due to changing technology has been greatly intensified by the disappearance of the state's guarantee of employment for all. How my respondents felt about the careers of their grown children was also influenced by the reordering of social rankings (and relative pay) of occupations brought about by the economic changes.

Two women with successful sons expressed both considerable pride in their accomplishments and some regret about the fields they had chosen.

> My son finished university here in Yaroslavl this year.... Right now he's in the process of getting a job, let's put it that way. He has a spot where he is going to work; he's just waiting for the invitation because the place is undergoing repair. It seems as if everything is taking shape nicely. He graduated from the radio-physics department... Despite this, he will be working for a bank, but somehow with software security ... I don't know; I can't say anything more precisely. What he does is just a dark forest for me, in such a different field. I wanted him to paint, he was an artist, but he has chosen a different life path and is a physicist. [Veronika, 51]

> We think that our greatest success is our son. He has two degrees. He's a medical doctor and...he has an MBA. He works in Moscow. He's successful and has already bought an apartment in Moscow. He has a family. He doesn't work as a doctor, he works in a pharmaceutical company.... So we consider this our main treasure in life. We think that all that we have invested has paid off well. But our son does not work in medicine. This is for us–well, how can I put it gently? We wanted him to work in medicine because we have a dynasty. My husband's mother worked in this field, my husband works in this field, both as dermato-venereologists. We would have liked him to do the same, but, unfortunately, he changed his work profile. But we are glad that he can stand on his own, that he can achieve his goals. He's very ambitious.... So we are very satisfied. [Liza, 55]

Not all parents were satisfied with where their children have ended up, of course. Among those in the next generation who have had the most difficult time forging a successful path are several who were adolescents in the early 1990s, as social, economic and political changes occurred at dizzying speed. This was the cohort that analysts and reformers had initially expected to flourish in the new market conditions, since they would be starting their careers under the new circumstances and would find it easier to adapt, having less to unlearn, than their parents. In at least a couple of cases I heard of, however, the changes came at precisely the time when these young people were most vulnerable.

Unable to look to their parents for much guidance in navigating the new world, they tended to reject their parents' values even more forcefully than is typical of the age. Inundated by images of life in the West and the promise of access to a wide array of new and enticing Western goods, these adolescents often set themselves the goal of making a lot of money as quickly as possible and dismissed education, seeing it as unnecessary in that pursuit and unlikely to guarantee them a decent job in any case (Bridger and Kay 1996: 28). One frequently-cited survey of young women conducted in this period found that a high percentage aspired to work as prostitutes in high-end hotels patronized by Western businessmen (Bridger and Kay 1996: 32). Another avenue the adolescents believed would lead to wealth and success was trade.

> This was not a good time. It left its mark on the young. [My daughter] quit [threw away] the institute for no clear reason…There was a good education at the college, but, unfortunately, we couldn't persuade her [to return]. Then a while later she studied the tourist business and now she's involved with photography. Unfortunately, this generation was lost [literally, spoiled]. [Regina, 61]

This woman, who stressed that she and her husband socialized only with other members of the intelligentsia—"we did not associate with other social layers at all"—clearly mourned her daughter's decision to follow a different path. The situation of another women I spoke to was even sadder: her son, now in his thirties, has continued to drift aimlessly, holding short-term jobs but mostly remaining unemployed. Whether as cause or consequence of his lack of meaningful employment, he has become an angry and destructive alcoholic.

Another man, in his early 40s at the time of my interview with his mother, navigated the challenges of the new system with much greater success, forging a path that involved two very different opportunities that opened up in the 1990s. Initially, he went into banking, focusing on foreign exchange transactions, which prior to 1992 were strictly controlled and carried out at highly artificial exchange rates. Later he set up his own businesses, first in Moscow and later back in Yaroslavl. His mother's account, which I have edited to make the chronology clearer, suggests that he approached these opportunities with enormous confidence—possibly even bravado—although his ultimate success, I think, was real. There are also hints in her account of why this early period came to be known as "wild capitalism" or "violent entrepreneurship" (Volkov 2002) and clear indications of the generational gap.

> In 1992 my son was moonlighting in a bank as a student, working as a translator..... At that time it was necessary just to [do anything to] survive, and so he went to the bank. At the bank, he worked as head of the currency department, in spite of not having any specialized education. [Amused laughter][5] He finished some courses there... so he could work and then he did not like it. He changed banks more than once. There are people for whom settling down to work in a bank is hard.
>
> He told the director [of this first bank], 'You aren't thinking about the long term; you're living one day at a time, without a business plan.... I'm no longer interested in working in your bank. I'm quitting." Just like that. [The bank director] was close to retirement age; she should have left. When he told her he didn't want to stay at her bank, that he was leaving, she stared at him with such an expression. 'What are you saying? Do you think you're anointed? People are striving to land at a bank and you say this?' But he just handed in his notification and left. It had really become uninteresting to him.
>
> And I said, 'How could you?! At least you should have found a new job first!' He answered, 'Mama, I already have five offers. You think I'm such a fool? Look, I have five offers and I'm going to work something out. So he went to another bank and worked there for a while, some Moscow bank. They promised him a good salary, but he worked there only about half a year. Everything was wonderful and then suddenly they cut his pay, or something like that.

[5]That her son was given this responsibility is less strange than it might seem. Because the ruble had long been inconvertible (not freely exchanged for other currencies) there would have been almost no one in Russia with any "specialized education" or experience in the field.

> He said, 'Fellows, that's not what we agreed,' and he gave up on them and went to still another bank. And in that other one, too, it seemed to him that he was doing most of the work. The bank dealt with foreign currency. He said, 'My department provides 90 percent of the bank's income and the salary doesn't correspond.' He demanded a good salary.... He laid out his conditions to the directors, but the conditions weren't accepted and so he left there, too.
>
> He decided to leave banking altogether. He said—he probably worked in banking ten years—but then he said, 'Mama, this isn't right for me. I'm tired of stuffy offices, I don't want that. I want to be the boss. I don't want to be under someone else. I'm not stupid.' ...
>
> So he was, let's say, swimming free, and he went to Moscow. He wanted to set up a business in Moscow. At first, he had a business there. He led excursions somewhere, I think, and it was profitable, so he decided to set up another business. He was there with a friend, but they had a disagreement. My son had one opinion; the friend had a different opinion. The other one said, "We should buy new equipment at once." And my son said—well, I don't know which one of them said what, but there were two opinions... I think it was my son who said, 'Let's buy second-hand equipment and see how the business goes for us, and then we can develop.' Either way, they did not agree and then [my son] realized that the people who lent money for the business were not good. Naturally, they demanded some kind of percentage, but he told me, 'I realized that this was dirty money that they gave us and I decided not to be connected with such people.' So he left Moscow and decided to return to Yaroslavl.
>
> Now he has his own business.... It involves stoves, furnaces—both for homes and for bathhouses. He took some courses, learned to do everything and organized everything. I feel that it is not easy for him. It's grown a lot. [He now has three stores that sell this equipment.] The volume is big, and he's taken a lot on himself. I feel that he is tired.... On the one hand, he's still young; on the other, I worry about his health and his two children and his wife, who utterly lacks initiative. [Klara, 70]

Several others in the younger generation achieved professional success by taking advantage of the greater freedom to study, travel and work abroad after the Soviet Union dissolved. Given the sharp contrast between the values and personal characteristics likely to be most rewarded in international corporations in the current decade and those most assiduously cultivated, at least in theory, within the Soviet system, one might anticipate a certain disappointment, or at least ambivalence, on the part of the mothers of these young people. Perhaps they felt it, but none of the mothers of those living abroad revealed such ambivalence in their conversations with me; instead, they stressed the educational achievements that had made such success possible.

> My daughter lives in Paris. Two years ago, she began university as an English-French translator…She's married. Now she has finished a degree from a second institute there. [My children] take after me. I have two [higher] education degrees and they have two apiece. Now she works in the fashion industry. She finished an economic … program [and works] as a specialist for turning out the collection [of new clothes each season]. [Vera, 56, whose son also lives abroad, in Israel]

> [My daughter] received a cultural education here, she knows French perfectly. She lived in Paris for 4 years and received a third higher education there. And then for some reason the French authorities decided that they didn't need that kind of specialist. She had problems with her visa and she gave it all up and left. Now she works in Moscow, for a well-known French publicist, for an advertising company. She works there. [Alexandra, 54]

One woman even expressed a strong desire that her daughter leave Russia when she graduates.

> I am no doubt saying unpatriotic words, but I would like it very much if my daughter left Russia for somewhere where she could use her mind, because it's unreal when talented people—I see their salaries and it makes me so sad. And when the children of my relatives go somewhere to study foreign languages, travel to Europe, I'm happy that they are fulfilling themselves, I am happy that the young people, who are finding themselves and who can make a contribution to people, can realize their potential, even if it's not in my country. [Marta, 45]

## Conclusion

As the state retreated from its commitment to provide a job to every citizen and enterprises found it difficult to pay their workers, most Russians needed considerable flexibility and ingenuity to earn enough to support themselves and their families. Sometimes this involved changing jobs, sometimes it involved moonlighting, sometimes it involved embarking on the path of creating a business for oneself—and sometimes it required all three. Not only did this introduce the stress of uncertainty, it demanded adjustment to new social norms and values.

For the women who managed to avoid having to take on additional hours or kinds of work, either through their husband's successful navigation of the new system or through their own ability to live frugally, it was possible to cling to old norms. At least for some, moonlighting, like petty trading, was considered demeaning; it was thus the lot of those less fortunate or skillful. When I asked one woman if she had taken on additional work, she responded:

> In our family there was nothing terrible, no horrible shocks, no complete lack of money, no real decline. There was nothing like that in our family. We lived through it calmly. If a person has a good head, he can survive. [Regina, 61]

In contrast, most of those who *did* take on additional work expressed pride in the path they followed, viewing their own choices as testament to their ingenuity and capacity to survive, characteristics they associated with "the [true] Russian woman." Adopting new values was even more necessary for those who chose to create their own businesses. How they made this adjustment is the topic of the next chapter.

## References

Bridger, Sue, and Rebecca Kay. 1996. Gender and Generation in the New Russian Labour Market. In *Gender, Generation, and Identity in Contemporary Russia*, ed. Hilary Pilkington, 21–38. London: Routledge.

Bridger, Sue, Rebecca Kay, and Kathryn Pinnick. 1996. *No More Heroines? Russia, Women and the Market*. London/New York: Routledge.

Dyker, David. 1984. Planning and the Worker. In *The Soviet Worker from Lenin to Andropov*, ed. Leonard Schapiro and Joseph Godson, 39–76. New York: St. Martin's Press.

Godson, Joseph. 1984. The Role of the Trade Unions. In *The Soviet Worker from Lenin to Andropov*, ed. Leonard Schapiro and Joseph Godson, 108–134. New York: St. Martin's Press.

Granick, David. 1987. *Job Rights in the Soviet Union: Their Consequences*. New York: Cambridge University Press.

Kirsch, Leonard. 1972. *Soviet Wages: Changes in Structure and Administration Since 1956*. Cambridge, MA: Massachusetts Institute of Technology.

Lane, David. 1985. *Soviet Economy & Society*. Washington Square, NY: New York University Press.

Millar, James R. 1981. *The ABCs of Soviet Socialism*. Urbana/Chicago/London: University of Illinois Press.

Powell, David E. 1981. Labor Turnover in the Soviet Union. In *The Soviet Economy: Continuity and Change*, ed. Morris Bornstein, 101–117. Boulder, CO: Westview Press.

Solnick, Steven L. 1998. *Stealing the State: Control and Collapse in Soviet Institutions*. Cambridge, MA: Harvard University Press.

Volkov, Vadim. 2002. *Violent Entrepreneurs: The Use of Force in the Making of Russian Capitalism*. Ithaca, NY: Cornell University Press.

# 7

# Working for Oneself: Small Business Ventures

## Introduction

Although one of the central tenets of Soviet socialism was that all means of production were to be owned by the state, there remained some scope for private enterprise. As discussed in Chapter 5, it was legal for Soviet citizens to sell homemade or homegrown products at the collective farm market and to provide for pay such personal services as tutoring, tailoring and housework. By the late Soviet period it was also common (though not legal) for individuals to moonlight, for example as cab drivers or plumbers, using equipment or supplies from their official state employment, or to profit from speculation by selling scarce—often Western—goods that they managed to acquire.

Key ingredients of entrepreneurship—private economic activity and initiative, the ability to identify and meet consumer needs—had thus not been eradicated during the Soviet period, even if private ownership of capital had been. Nonetheless, the official view that such activity (particularly trading) was bad—immoral, antisocial, parasitic, unclean—had been internalized to some degree by much of the population. Mikhail Gorbachev's attempts during perestroika to bring existing



J. McKinney, *Russian Women and the End of Soviet Socialism*,
https://doi.org/10.1007/978-3-030-16226-9_7

private activity out of the shadows and onto the tax rolls and to harness the potential for more such activity, carefully circumscribed, ran into considerable skepticism and opposition, not just from the Party leadership but also from the population at large.

The deeply-entrenched negative attitudes toward private economic activity were reinforced by the behavior of the "New Russians" who emerged in the early 1990s. Not only was their conspicuous consumption an affront to the many who were struggling, they were widely (and for the most part accurately) believed to have acquired their riches through privileged access, lack of regulation and unscrupulous means, often by appropriating state property—"everyone's" property—for their private businesses. As a result, the women I spoke with had initially felt considerable ambivalence about setting up a business of their own, just as they did about engaging in petty trade. Most, however, had at some point at least considered taking such a step, and several had actually done so, with varying degrees of success.

All of the enterprises owned by my respondents were modest in size. The largest had ten employees; many had none. At the time privatization of state enterprises was introduced, none of the women was in a position to acquire one or even to spin off a small unit from a parent enterprise.[1] They thus had nothing in common with those Thane Gustafson describes as forming the core of the early "surge of Russian entrepreneurship"—first those who had been part of the underground economy in the Soviet period and then those who seized state assets during the "spontaneous privatization" that took place as the Soviet system collapsed (1999: 109–110). Rather, these women built their modest businesses from scratch, through hard work, individual initiative and the social and cultural capital they had developed. In some ways, they are thus much more representative of the private-enterprise, free-market economic system—the textbook version—that was *supposed* to be the result of transition from Soviet-style socialism.

Starting even a small business in any country at any time is not easy. Doing so in Russia in the early post-Soviet period was especially

[1]The privatization process is discussed in Chapter 8.

difficult. Bridger, Kay and Pinnick describe a process of registering a business so Byzantine as to be almost impossible to navigate, confiscatory taxes, and criminal predation as among the obstacles to be overcome (1996: 135–141). The women I spoke to seldom highlighted such problems, even when I asked about them explicitly.

Everyone responded to my question about registering the business with the assertion that it posed no difficulty whatsoever, including a woman who registered her first business, providing engineering and construction services to power companies, in 1994. That the second woman did not find it difficult is less surprising, since by the time she registered her business, a 2002 law introducing "one-stop" registration and setting a limit on how much it could cost was in effect (Buyske 2007: 89).

> I incorporated my own company. It wasn't hard at all. It's not difficult today, and it wasn't difficult then [in 1994]. It presented absolutely no difficulties. The problems were of another nature. [Renata, 45]

> At first, I thought, "How can I do this?" but it turned out to be very simple. I just went—here we have a chamber that records things—and took the necessary documents. The documents were such straightforward things as my passport, my diploma, nothing special. I don't remember exactly, because it was all a long time ago, but it didn't take a lot of time, for the registration and the tax inspectorate and everything. [Veronika, 51]

The "problems of another nature" mentioned by the first woman included the difficult macroeconomic conditions and the Russian mafia.

> [The problems] were due to instability, to the economic instability which existed at that time, and which actually still exists….I organized and registered my business in 1994. If you know our sad history, you are aware that in 1998 there was a default and the ruble fell, it was very serious.[2]

[2]For the first several months of 1998, the Russian government maintained the value of the ruble at around 6 to the US dollar, although it was allowed to creep up gradually, from 5.96 on January 1 to 6.29 on August 17. On August 18, the government took a series of actions to address its unsustainable financial position. It defaulted on its domestic debt and imposed a moratorium on

> And that period was connected with the loss of my business. Truly, the state ruined me. I lost all my money, I lost not only all my money but also my apartment. I had to pay my creditors. After all the debts I had taken on, I had to sell my apartment. The apartment had been a present from my parents.... After that it was very complicated, very hard, but I recovered. It took enormous effort, but I was able to recover—not to the same level I had achieved, but all the same I restored my business and began again in the same field. It took me four years to restore it all.
>
> Then there is the criminal component.[3] It was necessary to maneuver around that. Therefore, I had no ambition to create a large corporation.

A couple of the women also spoke about the challenges of figuring out how to pay taxes, especially before Putin's tax reform dramatically simplified what had been an impossibly complex and inconsistent maze of tax laws, as alluded to in the second quote.

> At first, I paid taxes but I didn't have a bookkeeper, but then I understood that I couldn't do it right without a bookkeeper so I hired one. She began to help me and pay the taxes and all the bills. [Tamara, 61]
>
> In the beginning, it was very difficult to handle the taxes, because I am not at all an accountant, I have no talent for this sort of thing. It was very difficult for me to understand, but then I just consulted with friends, I tried somehow to do it on my own, I found some sort of form. Now there's what's called a simplified system. And that's how I work. [Veronika, 51]

One woman did explicitly blame bureaucratic obstructionism and red tape for some of her business difficulties—both in the 1990s and in 2012. In the earlier period, the government prevented her from

---

payments owed on foreign debt. It also devalued the ruble and allowed it to float. By August 20, a dollar could buy 7.00 rubles and by December 31, it could buy 20.65 rubles. Thus, over the course of 1998 the ruble fell in value from almost 17 cents to less than 5 cents. For an analysis of the problems leading to the government's decision, see Desai (2000).

[3]For more on the role of "the criminal component" in the Russian economy, see Volkov (2002).

establishing an enterprise; in the latter, government regulations made it more difficult than necessary for her company to operate. In the 1990s, the problems may have arisen from very particular circumstances—she was a military wife, living in a military town, and had an American mentor. A woman from a Western agency proposed that they set up a bread factory, but it was not permitted.

> They had done this project in a [different] military town. But here, what happened? I was prohibited from having these contacts. [Vasilisa, 56]

Later she and her husband moved to Yaroslavl, where she contemplated setting up a private school, until deciding that the market was already saturated. When I spoke with her in 2012, she had been running a small urban transportation business (a *marshrutka*) with her husband for several years. They started with one passenger van, then expanded to four before downsizing to their current level of three. She attributed the difficulties the company faced to government interference.

> This business is not profitable. Cars are destroyed on our roads. You can see here all these documents that I haven't had time to put away. These are the documents for our cars. We fill them in every day…. When we are asked about small and medium business in Russia, I answer: 'No way; they don't let you work.' Our government doesn't need small and medium businesses, it needs only oligarchic big business. That's what it feels like today. Maybe I am mistaken. I don't know, but we don't feel any support.

> Absolutely nobody is interested in our issues, they only interfere with them. They told us that we can't set the fares because the state does that. We can't determine the route because the state does that. We can't take even a single step without the state. …We had these little "gazelles," Russian cars – there was support for their production and we all bought Fiats. We were all "asked" to buy Fiats; that's a euphemism for being pressured to buy them. We took out more loans. These cars are not well suited for Russian roads; they're intended for civilized roads, not for the kind of roads we have in Russia. They are intended for civilized

roads, without bumps, without holes, where half the asphalt hasn't been stolen. You understand, they are used to normal Italian, American, Polish, German roads but not to Russian roads. And that is why we run through spare parts every day. We don't have Saturdays or Sundays off because we have to go to Moscow to order these parts. We don't have them here.

The primary reasons offered by most of the women for struggling or failing, however, were not the fault of the government, but simply a lack of experience and poor choice of business partners. Although these are problems for entrepreneurs worldwide, they would have been exacerbated considerably by the lack of potential mentors, reliable sources of information and advice, and well-established contract law in early 1990s Russia.

When I left [my job at] the Pedagogical Institute, I was immediately asked by a colleague to establish together a Center of Russian Language. This was in 1989. At first he wanted to do this in connection with an [established] enterprise, but he had a conflict with the woman who was in charge of that center and so he said, let's do it on our own. We did that. Because he wasn't a Russian-language specialist…I was supposed to handle all the academic work and he would handle all the organizational work. So he and I were partners. Then I received an invitation to go to England, and we agreed that when I returned we'd resume working together. I came back in 1991 and discovered that he had organized everything without me and that he really wanted to take me on to work there [just] as a senior methodologist or something. I was simply stunned, because this had been our joint cause…. We had wanted to do it together. Nowadays I would probably be more mature…but at that time I was just bewildered and I agreed [to become] this methodologist, with a very small salary, and I worked there until 1993. In 1993 I left, having got the center up and running…. Now I see my mistakes, which perhaps should not be called mistakes, but…. As I see it now, I didn't need to do it that way, I was wrong to do it that way, I should have handled it differently. It's interesting to analyze now. [Sofia, 61]

> The first time I didn't do it alone, I did it as a sort of conglomerate, with people that, at the time, it seemed were close to me, people I could trust…. Well, people are not straightforward. People can live together for a long time and still not really know each other….I did not understand the people. I made a mistake twice. Twice I made a very serious mistake in my partners. [Renata, 45]

The first mistake involved a long, unsuccessful effort to help the woman with whom she was working deal with alcoholism. The second involved the courts.

> I ended up in the hospital. While I was in the hospital, my partners… [borrowed heavily]. I was the director, but somehow this all took place legally without me, and in the end, they threw me out of the business. Not only did they throw me out, they threw me out with four years' worth of debts. I went to court to try to retain [the business] but the decision was not in my favor.

For another woman, an interior designer, even having employees (not partners) posed challenges she preferred not to deal with.

> I work alone. When I had a lot of work, when there were a lot of orders, I tried to get a student, for example, to draw for me. I do the work from the very beginning to the very end. That is, I come to an empty room where there's complete disorder, one that's just been built or alternatively has just been torn apart, and I work there until it's ready for people to enter [to use it]. I put flowers in vases and put up curtains. That is, I do it all myself. It's such varied work. At every stage it's completely different. On the one hand, one has to deal with the electrician and, on the other, one has to select plants for decorating and fabrics and other things. Completely varied, but I'm now used to conducting the entire process myself. Because when you give some part of the work to another person, it does not remove one's own responsibility… that all this work is done correctly and well. I must double check the calculations, I must check the products, the tiles and the fabric and other things, and it turns out that I'm doing double duty and I'm still paying the [assistant]. I tried once.

> I tried a second time. Maybe I just did not have the talent for organization but maybe I just can't trust anyone. There was just some unpleasantness.... And in addition to that, there are deadlines. If you guess wrong about how long it will take, the workers will just stand around. That is, you are responsible for making sure that people are constantly working on the projects and that there is no delay, there are no changes, it's not necessary to reorder some materials. So it's somehow more peaceful for me when I do everything myself. Let me have only three orders, rather than six, but I'll do them myself and for each little part I am personally responsible. That way is easy for me. [Veronika, 51]

In addition to being small, most of the businesses were in spheres the women explicitly identified as "feminine"—interior design, craft supplies, fabrics, cosmetics, health and well-being. The subtext was that although being in business is not a feminine activity, being in business in certain fields is acceptable. One woman said:

> I sewed professionally, making things to order. For example, at New Year's, everyone else celebrated New Year's but I had orders, I had to sew all night. I enjoyed this a lot. It's woman's work. And so are cosmetics [her current line]. [Eva, 55]

Another, who is involved with a direct sales company which rewards her for recruiting additional sales representatives, put it this way:

> Now I'll tell you about my main profession....This is my love, my business [Later in the conversation she called it 'my mission on earth'] ... It interests me so much because here it's not only possible to achieve personal development but also to help a great many people. Because that's woman's nature, isn't it? To help people. And when people in the post-Soviet space come to me, to us, and join the project, within 3-4 years they begin to earn thousands of dollars a month, these would-be pensioners. [Vera, 56]

A third, who owns a fabric store, stressed that her strengths lay in being creative and artistic and she is pleased that her grown son can now handle the "business" aspects of the operation.

> My classmates once said that I'm not at all a "business-lady" [using the English word] type. I'm a rather gentle person. But there are, of course, moments that are demanding, for marketing, for management…My son works with me. He is educated in this, he's completed a program at a business school. … He now handles the office, studies the market, figures out what is needed, what isn't needed. He is already involved in this work. He understands it better than I do. [Tamara, 61]

This gendered view of business was shared and fostered by the state. According to Bridger and Kay,

> From the very beginnings of the market reforms, women have been urged to take responsibility for their own survival by using domestic skills to make money. Women made redundant from the defence industries research institutes and former USSR Ministries have been encouraged to think in terms of setting up small businesses providing tailoring, knitwear, embroidery, catering or a whole range of other domestic crafts. (1996: 24)

For most of the small business owners I spoke with, however, these "domestic crafts" were actually where their interests lay. One had long worked as an artist, another had studied interior design in the 1980s—that is, when there was still guaranteed state employment—and a third, although holding a degree in chemistry, had never used that education and maintained that what she "really loved" was working with fabric. The women I interviewed who had been working in scientific fields in the Soviet period did not choose to go into business for themselves, in the "domestic" sphere or otherwise.

I did speak to two women who were running businesses in the traditionally "masculine" sectors of transportation and energy. The owner of the transportation company was in business with her husband, who, having retired from the military, was also the director of a driving school. The other explained her decision to establish her business by saying she thrives on challenges:

> I have a lot of different blood, that is, genetically. My great-grandmother was from Sicily. I have Sicilian, Jewish, Polish, Belarusian blood, and this explosive mixture gives me inner strength and temperament. It won't let me sit still. I always need some kind of excitement, to have things happening around me.... [Renata, 45]

As is clear from the descriptions that follow, setting up a small business in post-Soviet Russia did not necessarily imply a thirst for excitement. For some entrepreneurs, the impetus came rather from a lack of alternatives in the formal economy and the need to find some source of income. In a different time and place, under different circumstances, these women would not have chosen this path. Their life's trajectory was thus fundamentally altered by the transition, even after the dust had settled and everyday crisis was a thing of the past. While the initial decision to become an entrepreneur may have seemed forced upon them, they did not express regret at how their careers had evolved, but instead spoke proudly of their accomplishments. In contrast, some of the women who never had set up a business of their own indicated that they wished they had.

## The Go-Getter

Of the handful of women who seemed, like Renata, incapable of "sitting still," not all were running a business at the time we spoke, although all had done so at some point. These women were distinctive in the way they were constantly seeking new opportunities, new ways to achieve. For them, there always seemed to be a better (or additional) way to use their talents to provide for themselves. Initially, perhaps, simply a means of survival, by the time I spoke with them it had transformed into a satisfying approach to life and a fundamental part of their sense of identity. They were not content to hold uninteresting jobs for the sake of stability and security; even when given the opportunity to advance quickly, they became bored. Because the variety of their work experience was an essential part of the way they adapted to the post-Soviet environment, I present their stories at some length.

The most openly ambitious woman I spoke with recounted an employment history that was almost dizzying in its variety.[4] This woman was exceptional not only in the number of different jobs she had held, but also in the way she framed her story. Although the reasons she gave for leaving one job for the next included the need for housing or access to a kindergarten slot for her daughter, exhaustion, low pay, frustration with the sense of entitlement of the "New Russians," and the financial crisis, she nonetheless described a career full of triumph after triumph, accomplishment after accomplishment. I spoke with her at her workplace, where she pulled out a box full of certificates and awards to show me, telling me of the grant she received from an international organization, the articles she had published, the accolades she had earned. This was not an elderly woman reminiscing about past glory, but a woman in her early fifties, employed in still another new job and full of ideas about how to make positive changes in the organization. Below are some brief quotes, starting with her initial assignment after completing higher education in the early 1980s. (Before graduation she had held a job on a factory floor.)

> I was assigned to Kostroma…to an electromechanical plant, to the department of automated control systems for enterprises. I worked there until I went on maternity leave…. [After maternity leave] I returned and was immediately let go because they were required to provide me with housing, childcare. They gave me a single place in the hostel. I would have been living with someone else in the room. And I'm an engineer with a higher education, right?…Therefore, I was entirely fine with being let go. [Yulia, 52]

She stayed at home with her child for a year. When she stopped receiving maternity benefits, she worked for a couple of years in a

[4]Her lengthy work history reflects both a number of themes discussed in earlier chapters—such as the role of housing and childcare in job choice—and some themes that will be discussed in later chapters—such as the role of foreign organizations in providing training and the emotions raised by the increasingly noticeable inequality.

kindergarten affiliated with the Komsomol,[5] so that she could enroll her daughter there. This led to her next job, with the Komsomol Committee at a plant that produced engines, and the opportunity to pursue a career with the Komsomol.

> They offered me the chance to develop a career there, but it was always uninteresting to me. I did not understand, honestly, the significance of this work and I declined.

She then took a job in the university department from which she had graduated, but the salary was too low and she moved on after a year.

> Since I'm an engineer-programmer, I offered my services as a teacher, in the new discipline of computer science. It was just starting to be introduced into the schools, and the director of one of the vocational schools lured me. He said he would give me an apartment.... I couldn't turn that down.... I worked there for ten years....
>
> And then I decided to end my career in education, because my health gave out.... In order to achieve this kind of result it was necessary to sacrifice a lot of personal time...I was disenchanted by the private school.... We had to admit rich idiots... because ordinary kids couldn't pay that kind of money.... At that time, then, I suffered from what they call cognitive dissonance....I would have had to adapt to this reality, to lose my individuality, to lose my status...I couldn't adapt to it. And so, in 1998, I stopped working altogether in the field of education.

Although unwilling to work as a teacher without the respect traditionally associated with that position in the USSR, she was willing to take a job which she described as having very little status at all and became a secretary.

> Then I started over from scratch. I went to work—you won't believe it—I went to work as an ordinary secretary in a commercial firm. As a nobody.

---

[5]Komsomol refers to the *Vsesoyuznyi leninskii kommunisticheskii soyuz molodyezhi* or All-Union Leninist Young Communist League, the stepping stone to membership in the Communist Party.

> A secretary in Russia is someone who washes cups, empties ashtrays, dusts the director's desk. And, of course, answers e-mail and the phone…. My husband said, 'I can't believe you. You're out of your mind.'…
>
> I worked [there] for two and a half years and I brought [it], as they say, up to international standards throughout—the way it was organized, … the equipment. The office was completely redone, everything was done differently. Bit by bit [the director] began to give me [all kinds of administrative responsibilities], the kind of work that a secretary never has.

Despite the increase in responsibilities, the pay was too low and she found it necessary to move on again, in order to help her daughter, who was about to start university.

> I was invited to work at a [private] educational center in administration….and my pay was four times more than I'd been earning…. I worked there two and a half years and rose as high as I could. The only higher position would be to own the business…. Then a different educational organization asked me to be assistant director…and very quickly, within three months, I became director….

Finally, she decided to start her own business, a consulting firm.

> I decided to start my own organization…. I developed it for 5 years. It worked successfully, here in Yaroslavl, in Vologda, in Kostroma, in Ivanovo, that is, in the central region. I came up with a new business line, completely new. Now because of the crisis, it's not very dynamic, because people are holding onto their money and are not investing in training and consulting. But I know for sure that it will move forward. I have left this company now, I passed it to another manager but I myself remain the founder there.

When I spoke with her, she was at the end of her first month in a managerial position at the Yaroslavl City Hall.

Although there were some holes and inconsistencies in her account and I had trouble establishing an accurate chronology, it was absolutely clear that this woman simultaneously views herself as having been exploited by both the Soviet system and the "New Russians" and as having triumphed repeatedly through personal initiative, talent, organizational and managerial skills, and sheer hard work.

If Yulia was remarkable for the variety of jobs she had held over the course of many years, another woman was juggling a remarkable number of activities simultaneously. When I spoke with her, she was working as an artist in various capacities (painter, illustrator, interior designer, and floral designer), as a teacher, as a salesperson, as an entrepreneur and as a volunteer in community organizations. A representative for a foreign direct sales company, she had risen through the ranks and was overseeing many other representatives in a number of locations in Russia, giving her responsibility for 1600 clients in all.

> I get up with the sun.... My alarm clock doesn't work. I [just] open my eyes when the sun begins to rise.... Then I have various meetings. I've already had three meetings today about different things. [She and I met at 2:00 pm.] One meeting was with a dear friend who brought a whole library of books for my colleagues. The second meeting was with a client, because I am helping her design a country house and she had some questions. The third meeting was at the company's office; it was time to prepay for a client's order. Now I'm meeting with you, and then from 5:00 to 8:00 I have a series of meetings and will arrange things with the director of the office. At eight o'clock, I'll drive home...and from 8:00 to 9:00 I'll have a light dinner. Then at 9:00, I'll get on Skype. I have consultations via Skype with Kiev and with Pereslavl. I have four private offices.... I have an office in Pereslavl, an office in Kostroma, an office in Tutaev, ... and an office in Rybinsk [all towns near Yaroslavl]. I just oversee things. I ask how was your day, what happened, but it's like a consultation. And then, since there's a 3-hour time difference with Paris, I call my daughter when it's midnight here. At midnight, I talk with my daughter. From midnight to 1:00, I try to read something or listen to something and then at 1:00 or 1:30 I go to bed. [Vera, 56]

The company for which she works, which has offices in many countries, is based in Asia and, she claims, protects people from susceptibility to disease by reducing stress. It takes a holistic approach, addressing nutrition, water quality, air quality, magnetic forces, and the like. She credits the company's products with enabling her to lead the very full and active life she does.

> And [their] sleep system makes it possible for me to get enough sleep from 1:30 to 8:00, that is in 6.5 hours. The system saves me two hours! A person sleeps in general for 8 hours, right? And I simply open my eyes after 6 hours.

Another reason she is able to devote so much time and energy to so many activities is that she no longer has any close family living in Russia. Her husband died when she was 39 and she has never remarried. Her daughter lives in Paris, her son and her parents live in Israel. While her husband was alive, she chose not to emigrate to Israel herself because he was deeply reluctant to leave Russia. (She is Jewish; her husband was not.) Now, she says, she has chosen not to emigrate because she relishes her freedom and wants to avoid the fate of many older Russian women, who end up with responsibility for their grandchildren.

Ironically, it was in Israel that she embarked on her most fully entrepreneurial—and least successful—venture. One of very few of my respondents to feel that she benefited from the voucher privatization scheme, discussed in detail in the next chapter, this woman decided to invest her earnings from that program into a café in Israel.

> And when three years ago I decided to open a café in Israel with an acquaintance, I sold half of my vouchers [actually, half of the shares that she purchased with her vouchers—this sort of confusion between the government-issued vouchers and the shares of stocks one could purchase with them was very common among the women I spoke with]. And I opened a café in Israel… It lasted half a year. One needs to be right there on the spot. When you're involved in this sort of traditional business, you have to control everything. The man who was my partner turned out to be unprofessional. He had the same good desire as I had, but he did not deliver. [And] taxes there strangle you…

Another woman who spoke openly about the failure of her business was one of my younger respondents. Born in Belarus, she moved with her family to Yaroslavl when she was a teenager and at 22 moved on her own to Tashkent, the capital of the Soviet republic of Uzbekistan, for an adventure and a taste of the "exotic". Her eagerness to tackle new experiences, plus the need to provide for an infant daughter when her marriage fell apart, led her to start her own business.

> If I were to try to start from scratch now it would be very complicated, but back then with the strength of youth, the arrogance, [I thought] I could do anything, I could do it all. I had absolute confidence in myself. It wasn't awful, I wasn't afraid, I wasn't scared of anything.

> At that time, I started engaging in business. With no education, I did everything myself. I sat down at the books and I studied the literature; I studied the legal literature, I studied the economic literature… I simply had no time for [formal] study because I had to take care of my child… So I had to learn, I had to combine theory and practice, and I had to do it quickly, under pressing circumstances. As a result, I haven't finished and only this year am I arranging to study formally. It was never an option, it was postponed indefinitely, there was always something else….

> I drew up a point-by-point plan for the goals and objectives I needed to achieve. For me it was important to provide for myself and my child… because I knew that after the divorce my husband would not help economically. [Renata, 45]

Despite relatively modest ambitions—she wanted to stay under the radar of the "mafia"—and a strategic approach, she encountered crisis after crisis and her business failed twice. She attributes the first failure to the financial collapse of 1998, during which credit dried up completely, leaving her with no way to borrow the money she needed. As described above, she attributes the second to the behavior of her partners and the courts.

> So once again I was left with nothing. Again, I had to start from scratch. Again, I had to organize everything. I took a "time out" [she used the English expression] because I realized that I had to collect my thoughts and focus. I took a "time out" and I got a job, went into management. … It turned out that there was very fast career growth—in half a year I went

> from being a mere manager to being head of the department.... This was with an organization that sells uniforms, that is, special clothing for different kinds of jobs.
>
> But then I started to get bored. It was very routine work and even though I understood from the beginning that I could grow to become the commercial director, that it was a career with great prospects, I began to feel suffocated within such narrow limits. Therefore, after I worked there about a year, I quit and again undertook my own business [again in energy] ...

In this third iteration of her business, Renata believes she has figured out how to make things work.

> Right now, my partner is again a young woman. We have everything very concisely arranged–all the priorities, all the responsibilities, that is, the economic components, the partnership—so that actually at the same time we depend on one another but are independent of one another. We have an agreement, and everything is structured in such a way that she is on her own and I am on my own; we are protected in case one partner leaves. I have simply learned from bitter experience. The knowledge has not been in vain. I tried to insure myself so that I can exit without unnecessary troubles.

Renata seems to relish the challenges of being a business owner, attributing this at one point in our conversation, as noted above, to her multi-ethnic genetic makeup and at another to Russian history and culture.

> For Europe, a crisis means, 'It's chaos, all is in ruins.' It's a state of fear, of [worrying about] what to do, what is going to happen next. But here in Russia, for us a crisis...is about the adrenalin, it means you need to gather yourself. You need this constant level of adrenalin, it's like a disease, we're constantly in this state.

Not all of the women relished the adrenaline rush of a crisis, nor did they choose to establish their own businesses out of a sense of boredom. Rather, they stumbled into entrepreneurship out of a lack of alternatives or as a gradual expansion of activity that began on a very small scale in an attempt to find a way to support themselves.

## The Accidental Entrepreneur

In this category, I place two of the three women I spoke with who are engaged in some aspect of interior design, one an interior designer and the other the owner of a couple of fabric stores. The first woman spent the early years after getting her training living with her husband outside of Russia and when she returned began working for a former classmate. This eventually proved insufficiently satisfying artistically and she sought orders through acquaintances and finally embarked on her own.

> For a whole year while I was working, I tried to find some orders or some sort of design work somewhere…simply to work in my specialty. And so finally I found something…I completed a few orders with builders. At first the builder would just give me an order and I would do it, but when my circle of clients grew, acquaintances among the builders, among furniture shops… I decided that I was ready and I could work on my own. I registered as an individual business and I've worked that way ever since [for about a dozen years]. [Veronika, 51]

Although she seems successful—she has enough work, her son is grown and educated and has been offered a job in his field—she clearly feels that she has not achieved all she could have. She continues to regret the failure of her marriage, which ended because she decided to return to Russia for her son's education and her husband was unwilling to make that move himself. At the same time, she regrets having been away during what would have been the important early years of her career. Returning when she did was particularly hard. The macroeconomic situation was extremely poor, and she was years behind her peers in understanding the new economic order. Thus, she views having been away during the extremely challenging initial post-Soviet years as a disadvantage rather than a lucky escape.

> When I returned it was very hard, because it was 1998 and there was the default. I wasn't really standing firmly on two feet, that is, I wasn't as financially well-off as others among my friends, who had found work right after graduation and by 1998 had achieved something. Many of

> them had their own businesses, many had joined the Union of Artists, the Union of Designers, they had bought an apartment. But I had nothing.

In contrast, the woman who owns the fabric stores seems to have succeeded far beyond her expectations. She describes herself as a most unlikely businessperson, even though she now owns a couple of stores with a total of ten employees and serves as the only agent in the area for a major foreign fabric firm.

> I am very retiring, I was not a star in the classroom, I was far from being a star. I studied conscientiously but… [she left the sentence incomplete]. And then life put me in a situation without money [when she was teaching home economics in a school]…. Of course, I could have sat quietly, worked peacefully with my hands, worked in the school, and received this very low salary, but I felt a potential of some sort, some sort of strength…. [Tamara, 61]

While she agreed with her friends' assessment that she does not have the personality expected of someone in business, by 2012 her business was flourishing.

> We have two workshops and a warehouse…. We have four workers who sew… A couple of years ago we switched from one bank to another bank and we had monthly turnover of somewhere around 50-60,000 rubles. And today our monthly turnover is between 500-600,000 rubles a month[6]…There was nothing, nothing at all, and now with ten people we have a turnover of half a million a month, and sometimes more.

Despite her disclaimers, she clearly has at least one essential business trait—the ability to see an opportunity and persuade others to let her take advantage of it. She also had learned important skills from her mother and grandmother, skills that they had used at home, but she was able to turn to advantage in the marketplace.

---

[6]Roughly 16,000–19,500 USD at the time we spoke.

> I happened to travel to St. Petersburg to visit an acquaintance and saw decorated shop windows, beautifully decorated shop windows…I went into Gostinnyi Dvor[7] and I was impressed.… It just struck me as so beautiful, and we did not have anything like it in Yaroslavl, so I returned to Yaroslavl and shyly approached the director of our department store and suggested, 'Let's hang beautiful curtains and drapes like that.' 'Well,' I was told, 'No one needs that. But here, we have some fabric that has been lying around for five years, no one wants it. Go ahead and try. See if it works out. Let's give it a try.' And I did it myself. I knew how to do it. My mother and grandmother, they all knew how to sew. It's in my blood. I sewed it and hung it, and on the second day it sold, so then they gave me a second fabric that hadn't been claimed, that no one wanted, and I did it again, I hung it again and again it sold. And that's how it all began.

Actually, it began before that, since in the early 1990s she had already turned her sewing abilities to use, producing clothes for sale. Her initial foray into the market economy was quite modest.

> Yes, when it was hard, I engaged in petty trade… but one time misfortune befell me. I was robbed, and I understood that I was more about creativity, about creating something out of something, not just buying and selling. I was closer to creativity.… And of course there was still the [Soviet] mentality, we believed that buying and selling was speculation. Then I opened a workshop in my apartment. Well, two girls came to work in the apartment. I had two rooms and I fitted one out as a workshop and rented out sewing machines. And then one of my relatives came to me and said, 'They can arrest you, the police, because you're not handling this the way you're supposed to.' I was buying labels.… We were sewing skirts. 'Made in Italy.' [She laughs.] Then they came to me and said, 'You watch out, be careful, this is very dangerous.'[8] Nothing happened, but then I registered legally as a private businessperson, and I began to pay taxes.

---

[7]Gostinnyi Dvor, originally constructed in the eighteenth century, is a huge, upscale shopping center on one of the main streets in St. Petersburg.

[8]For a fascinating discussion of the role of the '*leibl*'—Western label or logo—in the late Soviet period, see Yurchak (2006: 196–198).

Although neither of these women viewed themselves as having entrepreneurial characters—and both were far less outgoing and spirited while talking to me than those I have labeled "go-getters"—they have nonetheless carved out successful places in the new economic environment as small business owners.

## The Entrepreneur Manqué

Two women who did not become entrepreneurs (or, at least, did not identify themselves that way) expressed regrets that they had not displayed more initiative. Both are academics—the first in her early 60s and the other in her late 50s.

> And all this time my husband said to me, I will create a Russian language center for you, you'll run it. I'll do this for you.... But of course life was such that no one ever had any time. He didn't have any time and since I always had some sort of work—first this, then that, then a third thing, and a fourth—we never opened the center.... He promised me support, but I didn't receive it from him. I don't tell him this, since it feels like 100 years ago, but that's how this period went.... And now I think that I was simply waiting for something. I was counting on [my husband] to do something. I should have dared to do this business myself, calmly. I had a Soviet fear, this Soviet feeling. I was afraid. I didn't know how, I didn't have any experience organizing something like this, although maybe it would have worked and been successful. But I was a coward, a coward. [Sofia]

This woman actually did attempt to start a business in the early days of perestroika under Gorbachev but, as described above, her business partner did not behave as they had agreed and she found herself working as a poorly-paid employee rather than as a co-owner. When I met her, three decades later, she was offering Russian language classes to foreigners. She rented space from an institute and when there was sufficient demand employed a couple of other women to help teach. While I was there, however, there was not much demand for her services, she was working alone and worried that she could not bring in enough income to cover the rent. She then came up with the idea of creating a program teaching Russian to immigrant Muslim men at a local mosque. She was thoroughly enjoying the challenge of figuring out ways to bridge the large gap between cultures and finding new teaching strategies so the men would be comfortable with a female instructor.[9] Despite the initiative she displayed in identifying a need and the success she has had meeting it, she does not think of herself as a successful entrepreneur. As the quotation above illustrates, she attributes this both to her own character ("I was a coward") and to her upbringing as a Soviet citizen.

The woman quoted next also blames her failure to become a successful entrepreneur on the values and ambitions instilled in her by her Soviet-era education.

> [In 2005], the second time I went to the US, I met a man who owned 27 businesses, and I realized that *I* could have had that many businesses. But during the 1980s and early 1990s I was a graduate student in Moscow. I thought completely differently. All these years I haven't regretted it, because I love my profession. I am a teacher. I love my profession, but now looking back, I think that I could have achieved a lot more in life. [Liza, 55]

Despite her claim that she hasn't regretted her choices, this woman clearly wonders what she might have accomplished as an entrepreneur. There was no indication, however, that she had any interest at this point in tackling such a role. The slightly younger woman quoted below, on the other hand, is contemplating—though rather casually—taking this step now that she is retired. Because she worked for one of the branches of the police, she was able to retire early, so was only 52 when we talked. Her children are grown and living on their own and her husband, also receiving his pension, was still working (at a new job) so there was no strong financial need for her to act and she was clearly in no rush.

[9]Six years later it is clear from social media that she continues this endeavor with great success.

> We are trying, my partner and I—she also just retired, we served together—we have for a long time wanted to have a business, but, so far, we're just thinking about it, planning what we'll do. It will be tied to helping foreign citizens, in general tied to the Migration Service [where they had worked], help filling out documents, representing their interests to government agencies….
>
> [On the other hand] in my whole life this is the first year when I can rest a little bit freely, when I have a little free time, you understand. Simply even to rest, to sleep an extra hour, not to hurry, to get up slowly, collect myself, not to run with my tongue hanging out. [Zoya, 52]

Both her matter-of-fact willingness to consider starting a business and the clear lack of urgency she feels demonstrate how much Russia has changed since the early 1990s, when starting a business required overcoming deeply-engrained negative feelings toward such an action and yet was often seen as the only possible means of supporting oneself.

## Conclusion

While none of the women I interviewed described any experience with private enterprise, legal or otherwise, during the Soviet period and none gave any indication of having aspired to owning a business, several of them had achieved considerable entrepreneurial success by 2012. Their successes are especially impressive given the economic and political context in which they have operated. Even in the USA, where there is a strong culture of starting one's own business, 80% of new businesses fail in the first eighteen months (Wagner 2013). In Russia in the early 1990s, where none of the institutional infrastructure needed to help small businesses survive were in place, the prospects of success were even dimmer. There was effectively no commercial lending; there was no Small Business Administration offering advice on everything from finding a location and securing licenses and permits to developing a sales strategy; there were no convenient guides to relevant laws and regulations—in fact, there were no clear laws and regulations on the books.

Even for the women whose difficulties seemed rooted largely in the behavior of the people with whom they tried to work, the incomprehensible and unstable legal code of the transition period militated against finding an equitable and appropriate resolution of those difficulties.

Becoming an entrepreneur and starting one's own business is not the only way in which a person can become a "capitalist," that is, can earn income not merely from his or her own labor but rather—or in addition—from the ownership of productive assets. An alternative approach is to acquire shares in an already existing company. It was in an attempt to create a sizeable class of owners of capital—people who would then have a strong interest in maintaining the new economic system—that Western advisors encouraged the Russian government to undertake a program to transfer ownership of the country's capital stock from the state to private individuals. I discuss this program and its role in the lives of my respondents in the next chapter.

## References

Bridger, Sue, and Rebecca Kay. 1996. Gender and Generation in the New Russian Labour Market. In *Gender, Generation, and Identity in Contemporary Russia*, ed. Hilary Pilkington, 21–38. London: Routledge.

Bridger, Sue, Rebecca Kay, and Kathryn Pinnick. 1996. *No More Heroines? Russia, Women and the Market*. London: Routledge.

Buyske, Gail. 2007. *Banking on Small Business: Microfinance in Contemporary Russia*. Ithaca, NY: Cornell University Press.

Desai, Padma. 2000. Why Did the Ruble Collapse in August 1998? *The American Economic Review* 90 (2): 48–52.

Gustafson, Thane. 1999. *Capitalism Russian-Style*. Cambridge, UK: Cambridge University Press.

Volkov, Vadim. 2002. *Violent Entrepreneurs: The Use of Force in the Making of Russian Capitalism*. Ithaca, NY: Cornell University Press.

Wagner, Eric T. 2013. Five Reasons 8 Out of 10 Businesses Fail. *Forbes*. Accessed online at http://www.forbes.com/sites/ericwagner/2013/09/12/five-reasons-8-out-of-10-businesses-fail/. February 2019.

Yurchak, Alexei. 2006. *Everything Was Forever, Until It Was No More: The Last Soviet Generation*. Princeton, NJ: Princeton University Press.

# 8

# Voucher Privatization

## Introduction

One of the distinguishing characteristics of the Soviet economic system was that the capital stock—the means of production—was owned by the state. As a result, enterprises were not required to make a profit—and, indeed, if they did happen to earn a profit most of it went into the state budget to support other less profitable enterprises. This practice was less unfair than it might at first seem, since prices of both inputs and output were set by the state rather than the market and remained unchanged for long periods of time. Profit and loss were therefore more a reflection of arbitrary prices than an indication of the quality of management or the usefulness of the output. Financial reward and career prospects were tied to plan fulfillment rather than to profits, and Soviet managers therefore had little incentive either to focus on efficiency or to care about satisfying their customers.

To transform this system into one based on market forces and at least some degree of consumer sovereignty it was necessary to introduce a number of important changes. As discussed in Chapter 4, one was to liberalize prices so that they could begin to reflect both the true costs


J. McKinney, *Russian Women and the End of Soviet Socialism*,
https://doi.org/10.1007/978-3-030-16226-9_8

of production and the relative desirability of the goods. Another was to transfer ownership of the capital stock into private hands, so that the owners would have a genuine stake in using the resources wisely.

Privatization was thus a key element of the transition blueprint. In several of the East European economies, this process required making difficult decisions about whether to return property to those who had owned it before the adoption of Soviet-style socialism at the end of World War II, but in Russia, where state ownership had been in effect for considerably longer—and most of the enterprises had not even existed prior to the Bolshevik Revolution—this was not an issue. Instead, the problem was to figure out a way to distribute ownership of a vast array of very different kinds of enterprises in dramatically different physical condition to roughly 150 million people.

There was, of course, no stock market in Russia as the privatization process began in the early 1990s. Even had there been one, investors could not reasonably predict the value of enterprises which were soon to be operating in totally new circumstances, with new (as yet unknown) prices and a new (as yet unknown) structure of demand. Past performance could not be seen as a reliable indicator of future prospects. Even for Westerners familiar with market economies and experienced in investing, this would have been a challenge; for people who had lived their entire lives under central planning and state ownership it was nearly impossible.

Mark Mobius's description of the early days of the Russian stock market helps make the challenges clear:

> In the early 1990s, Russia's stock market was primitive. Trading began around three o'clock in the afternoon, give or take, when a vehicle would pull up to the stock exchange building carrying loads of cash. Brokers would sit at long tables waiting for workers and ordinary citizens who had been given share vouchers—which could be exchanged for shares in newly privatized Russian companies—to sell them on the exchange. Around six o'clock in the evening, the vehicle would return to collect the vouchers the brokers had bought on the cheap. (2012)[1]

[1]Further illustrative anecdotes can be found in Klebnikov (1994). Paul Klebnikov was editor of the Russian edition of *Forbes* when he was shot and killed in Moscow in 2004.

In addition to the absence of experienced and knowledgeable investors and the primitive way the market operated, there was the question of who could actually afford to invest. Most Russians had very low savings at that point, in part the result of the monetary "reform" of January 1991. At that time, hoping to prevent extreme inflation when prices were freed by first absorbing excess liquidity, Soviet leaders introduced new 50- and 100-ruble notes and gave citizens a mere three days in which to exchange old notes for new, while severely limiting the total number of rubles that could be exchanged and the amount that could be withdrawn from personal savings accounts (Sputnik 2011). This was justified by the claim that those wishing to exchange large sums must have accumulated them through illegal operations, but in fact many ordinary Russians lost much of their life's savings, acquired perfectly honestly, while many of those with money from questionable activities found ways to circumvent the rules.

One woman described the reform this way:

> And when the reform of the ruble took place—when they carried out that reform literally in a single day—that was a terrible affair. It's terrible, what the country has lived through. [Zoya, 70]

Another woman, who was a student at the time and the mother of a newborn, had no savings to lose herself, but she still remembered the shock people experienced:

> And this was such a hard period. They changed the money, they carried out a monetary reform and it was unexpected. It turned out that you had money [one day] and then suddenly you didn't, it was gone. All of this wasn't easy to deal with. [Veronika, 51]

Exceptions to the rules governing the exchange of old rubles for new were possible with the approval of special commissions. By the time the "reform" was completed, it was widely believed—and for the most part accurately—that anyone who still had money must have come by it dishonestly, or at best through connections and positions of privilege within the Party or state bureaucracy, an obvious inversion of the official line.

## Privatization Program

Given these challenges, those who designed the Russian privatization program had a number of not entirely compatible goals. They wanted the process to be quick, they wanted it to be perceived as fair, and they wanted it to generate revenue for the state. The arrangements ultimately put into effect failed on most (some would say on all) counts. It was not particularly quick, because the government was (and remains to this day) reluctant to give up control over strategic enterprises and sectors of the economy; it was seen, at least by most of the women I spoke with, as just another way in which those in power or with connections grabbed the wealth of the country for themselves[2]; and it generated far less revenue for the government than initially envisaged, in part because of the decision to try to give every citizen the opportunity to acquire some shares and in part because corruption and manipulation of sales meant that selling prices were sometimes shockingly low.[3]

Anatoly Chubais, the bureaucrat most conspicuously associated with the privatization program, remains an object of particular scorn among the women I spoke with.[4] Few of them had anything particularly positive to say about *any* of the Soviet or post-Soviet leaders,[5]

---

[2]According to Blasi et al. (1997: 76–77), this negative view was more common before privatization occurred than while it was underway. Polls conducted in the third quarter of 1992 showed 43% of respondents believing the program was "a deception that would make some people richer and the rest poorer," while those conducted in September 1994, found that 15% felt they had personally lost, 50% indicated they were unaffected and 19% gave no answer. While not strictly comparable, the two polls do suggest that the initial suspicion had waned during the first few months of the program. It is therefore striking that two decades later, the belief in deception and corruption was strong among those I spoke with.

[3]One example given by Klebnikov (1994) was the purchase of a 25% share in the Cosmos Hotel in Moscow, which at the time was netting about USD 10 million a year, for only USD 2.5 million.

[4]Somewhat surprisingly, there were almost no references—unfavorable or otherwise—to Yegor Gaidar, the economist most responsible for the design and implementation of the policies comprising Russia's economic "shock therapy."

[5]One woman, after complaining about several former leaders, was asked jokingly by a friend if she approved of *anyone*. She responded that Andropov had been okay, but that turned out to be simply because he had spent some years as organizer of the Komsomol in Yaroslavl and was thus considered a "local" boy.

but Chubais stood out as the most despised, blamed both for the fact that the voucher program resulted in little or no benefit to their families and, more seriously, for the emergence of the super-rich class of oligarchs and New Russians. One older woman referred to him as a deceiver; another mentioned his "henchmen" and said of privatization "It was all thought up by that…Chubais, the redhead. People still call him that. He was very unpopular, 'Tolik the Redhead'." (Tolik is a nickname for Anatoly.) The only significant exception was a woman who indicated that she used her vouchers wisely because she followed Chubais's advice to buy shares in Gazprom. (Although a few other respondents also bought Gazprom shares, most attributed the decision to a clever male in their family. No one else suggested that Chubais had been behind their decision, nor that he had made specific recommendations about what sectors to invest in.)

Given the magnitude of the task, it was decided that privatization would proceed in stages. Small businesses were to be sold immediately. The market for these businesses was local; the expectation was that the buyers would be the managers and workers of the enterprises being sold. This stage proceeded quickly and was generally accepted as reasonable. It generated very little in the way of revenue, however, since the enterprises being sold were small and there was little competition among bidders.

Privatization of large-scale enterprises was to take place a bit later and to be spread out over a longer period of time, with certain industries and sectors temporarily remaining in the hands of the state because of their economic or strategic importance—an approach reminiscent of the New Economic Policy introduced by the Bolshevik s in the 1920s. In both periods, the goal was a temporarily mixed economy, with the state in control of the most important industries and the market handling the rest. The tasks involved, however, were fundamentally different in the two periods. Allowing small private businesses to remain in business or to arise spontaneously in the 1920s was a far simpler matter than selling off the mammoth state-owned enterprises that existed seven decades later.

The first stage of large-scale privatization in the 1990s was voucher privatization. Every Russian citizen, from new-born to elderly, was to receive a voucher with a face value of 10,000 rubles. Since these vouchers were virtually free (there was a nominal handling fee of a few rubles), this part of the privatization process clearly could not generate revenue for the government. The focus instead was to be on fairness: the enterprises had been built through the sacrifices of the Russian people and by rights belonged to all of them. The clarity of that vision was soon muddied, however, by the alternative position that those working at a particular enterprise should have special claim to it. It was *their* work that had sustained these enterprises and *their* work that should be rewarded by the opportunity to acquire ownership shares. This latter argument rested on an implicit assumption that the success of a Soviet enterprise was primarily due to the acumen of its manager and the effort of its workers and clearly ignored the distorting effects of planners' decisions and non-market prices on enterprise success.

In practice, voucher privatization was a messy combination of these two visions: all citizens received vouchers of equal face value and these vouchers could then be used to acquire shares in any of the businesses being sold off by the state, yet the timing and logistics of the sale of shares generally gave a huge advantage to those with ties to that enterprise. As described by Blasi, Kroumova and Kruse, enterprises being privatized could choose among three options, of which two were widely adopted. The choice of 73% of the enterprises was to give workers the right to buy 51% of the shares at 1.7 times the book value before the remaining shares were auctioned off to anyone wishing to buy them. Another quarter of the enterprises chose to give the workers 25% of the shares for free and allow them to buy up to 10% more at a considerable discount (1997: 41).

Not everyone used the vouchers to buy shares in enterprises directly. Many lacked the time, the information or the energy to take the opportunity seriously. Some sold their vouchers for a few rubles or bartered them for goods or services they needed; others stashed them away and forgot about them. Still others turned to one of the investment funds—some legitimate, many not—that quickly sprang up. These funds claimed to offer an easy alternative for those overwhelmed by the challenge of choosing a particular enterprise. The most notorious of such funds was MMM, a Ponzi-style pyramid scheme frequently mentioned by my respondents, which took in vast sums of money (the exact amount is uncertain) from millions of Russians who were promised staggeringly high rates of return and invested far more than their vouchers, many losing their life savings. Although the founder, Sergei Mavrodi, was eventually arrested and jailed, he was later freed and, until his death in 2018, was suspected of various nefarious activities in other countries, including manipulation of the value of the digital currency Bitcoin.

## Experiences with Vouchers

Although one of my respondents raised the topic of vouchers on her own—her apartment is overflowing with mementos and the vouchers were among the many items she brought out for me to look at over the course of a conversation spanning several hours and several small meals—most of the women had to be prompted. My questions elicited a wide range of responses, from bitterness to resignation and shrugged shoulders to pleasure and pride that they had been able to navigate this unfamiliar terrain successfully and benefit in some way, however modest. The differences in the experiences of this group of women echo those found for the population in general. Roughly 14% of the population used their vouchers to buy shares directly, 8% in the enterprises where they worked and 6% in other enterprises. Almost one-third (30%) entrusted the investment decision to the investment funds that sprang up. The rest either did not use them for investment at all—39% simply sold them for cash or gave them away—or provided no information (17%) (Blasi et al. 1997: 77).

As the following exchange between a couple of good friends in their seventies shows, those who were least satisfied with voucher privatization saw it as just another part of the theft of society's assets by the oligarchs.

> *Maria*: They had it all thought out. They artificially stopped the enterprises.
>
> *Klara*: And then they bankrupted the enterprises…

*Lidia*: And they bought up vouchers and then they bought up Norilsk Nickel[6] and all sorts of others for nothing. In order not to lose it completely, people sold [their vouchers] for even just a bottle of vodka. Some just drank it up.
*Klara*: They did not explain it to the people. We still were not ready for it.... It's disgusting, scary. People were unhappy and angry about this privatization.
*Lidia*: And now again comes a new wave of privatization.[7]

Clearly, the efforts by the reformers to communicate the details of the voucher program—and the concept of private ownership more generally—were largely unsuccessful. Even the women I spoke with—for the most part well-educated and politically aware—tended to be confused about what exactly had been involved and did not differentiate clearly or consistently between the vouchers they received from the state and the stocks to which these vouchers were intended to provide access. Some of the confusion was no doubt due to the passage of time, since the vouchers were distributed twenty years before my interviews, but many of the women had clearly found it difficult to figure out how to participate, and some had simply dismissed it as not worth their efforts.

> We are just simple people. We didn't understand what this thing, this voucher, was. And they played on that. [Klara, 70]

[6]Norilsk Nickel, a huge mining and metallurgical complex located north of the Arctic Circle, was originally built in the 1930s by forced labor under the jurisdiction of the NKVD. The enterprise was not actually offered for sale during the voucher privatization program. Instead, it was privatized in the mid-1990s as part of a "loans for shares" program in which shares in state enterprises served as collateral for the Russian government as it took out large loans from commercial banks. Because the government could not repay the loans, the bank owners ultimately acquired the shares in these enterprises at extremely low prices. The loans for shares program is widely seen, both inside Russia and abroad, as having been thoroughly corrupt.

[7]She is referring to the proposal, first put forth in 2009, to sell off some of the key state-owned enterprises in energy, transportation and other sectors in order to raise government revenues, which had been sharply reduced by the fall in world oil prices that year. The plan was not put into effect, having been strongly opposed both by the managers of the enterprises and by much of the government bureaucracy, but it had received considerable attention and this woman clearly anticipated that the idea would be raised again. A detailed chronology of this unsuccessful privatization push can be found at Gaaze (2016).

> It was very hard, very hard. [There were] constant meetings of some sort, constant demonstrations, constant slogans. It was on TV, it was in the streets, who it was needed for, what they wanted, what they wanted from the people. Then they began to pull [enterprises] apart, to make off with these plants—a tire plant, a motor plant, such huge plants.... That is, at a time when someone was starving, someone was surviving these difficult times with their children, someone at that time was profiting and carrying off bits of the state, using this hullabaloo. [Zoya, 52]

In dealing with the completely unfamiliar task of deciding how to use the vouchers, the women relied on a very familiar coping strategy and turned to their social network. Several described the decision-making process as involving the extended family: in some cases, all members of the family agreed to invest in the same way, while in others they deliberately diversified the family's stock purchases. Other women spoke of relying on husbands or brothers to make the decision, and in one case advice about how to invest the vouchers came from an adolescent son (advice which turned out to be excellent). Many listened to advice from co-workers or friends, and some were swayed by hearsay.

Although most of the women emphasized that they had not benefited from the program, there were a few exceptions. Both in fact and in popular perception, those most likely to have enjoyed some benefits were those who had the luck or foresight to invest in Gazprom, the natural gas company that evolved from the Soviet Ministry of Natural Gas and is still today owned in considerable part by the state. Buying shares in Gazprom was at least formally an option for all, but several of the women suggested that only the privileged were in a position to avail themselves of this opportunity.

## "We Received No Vouchers"

A few of the women I spoke with insisted that they had received no vouchers because they were ineligible for the program by virtue of their position/occupation. One of these women was working at the time for migration services, part of the same ministry as the police:

> Vouchers? We didn't receive vouchers. I don't remember, but I think the police didn't get vouchers. No, we didn't get anything like that. I think the ones who received vouchers were those who worked in factories and so forth, in [industrial] production. I don't remember that we received any. [Zoya, 52]

This woman's apparent confusion can probably be explained by the fact that although all citizens were supposed to receive vouchers the program did grant special rights to the employees of industrial enterprises. Because migration services did not undergo privatization, Zoya would not have had an opportunity to acquire shares anywhere on preferential terms. Since she and others in her family did not benefit significantly from the vouchers, she has simply forgotten receiving them.

Another woman believed that those in her family were not eligible to receive vouchers because at the time of the program they were living in Germany, where her husband was serving with the Russian military. It seems unlikely, however, that the state would have deliberately excluded those in the military from a universal benefit. As another participant in the conversation pointed out:

> And why would you be without vouchers? Even my little daughter got a voucher… [Turning to me] She just didn't succeed in using them.

She was probably right. Certainly the logistical difficulties, considerable even for those living in cities in Russia at the time, would have been far greater for those living abroad—just as for those living in rural areas of the country, where there were no large local enterprises undergoing privatization.

## "I Kept Them as a Memento"

Another military wife definitely received vouchers, but also "didn't succeed in using them." In fact, she still had them in her position, and brought them out to show me. Her explanation for the failure to make good use of her vouchers rested more on lack of knowledge than on logistical challenges.

> I want to show you something. You know that popular privatization started in the 1990s. [By "popular" she meant open to the general population, not that it was well-regarded.] This is a voucher [handing it to me]. I kept them because I didn't have an opportunity to put them somewhere [invest them]. I am not telling you the story of a typical Russian woman, I am telling you the story of a woman whose husband was in the military. It is a very specific [experience]. When there was privatization we [the speaker, her husband and their young daughter] received three vouchers. Like most of our friends we didn't know where to put them. We received them and that was that. I didn't sell them, I kept them for the sake of the memory. [Vasilisa, 56]

In a later conversation, not recorded, this woman talked about traveling to St. Petersburg and seeing men carrying suitcases full of vouchers.[8] This reinforced her sense that she and her friends were out of their league and that it made no sense to try to use their vouchers for investment. Her belief that being employed outside of the industrial sector put her family at a disadvantage was shared by several of those I spoke to, although working in industry was no guarantee that things would go more smoothly. Not all industrial enterprises were equally attractive and investing in one's place of employment, though relatively easy, was no guarantee of future earnings. Some people were deliberately duped by management, others simply worked for enterprises that weren't attractive investments.

> With the vouchers, we can generally say that we made a mistake, we couldn't do anything. The company where my husband worked took the vouchers and asked [us] to invest them in the People's Fund. This was a fiction. They took the vouchers from us and we received nothing and were left without any kind of support from that side. What they did further with them, nobody knows. At least, *we* didn't know. [Taisia, 59]

[8]This closely parallels the description, given above, of the early days of the Russian stock market and the arrival of vehicles full of cash. Given the low level of development of commercial banking and of telecommunications at the time, the transportation of large quantities of vouchers and of cash was necessary.

The next speaker, like many others, confuses the vouchers with the shares that they allowed her to buy.

> I bought vouchers. Right at our plant they sold some. I went out and bought these vouchers. I do not remember, about ten or so. I don't remember exactly, but I bought a small number. And then they lay there and lay there. Lord, I thought, what should I do with them? My son arrived from Moscow and said, "Mom, there in Moscow they are buying these vouchers, these pieces of paper that are worthless to you." I said, "So sell them." I didn't make any money. I sold them for what I paid for them. But thank God that I sold them, so they didn't just turn into [worthless] bits of paper. But many people bought shares of Gazprom. [Lidia, 70]

This comment prompted the following exchange with another woman in the room, highlighting not just the recurring theme of the benefits of investing in Gazprom but also the dislike of Chubais.

> *Klara*: [My son] invested his voucher in the VAZ [the Volga auto factory] and it too came to absolutely nothing. There were no dividends, nothing. And it was like this for the majority of the people.
> *Lidia*: And what would we have today? After all, they promised that we'd all get a car [out of this privatization]. But if right now I still had those ten shares, what then?
> *Klara*: But if you had invested in Gazprom…
> *Lidia*: And what if I had sat and waited for Chubais to give me a car?

Using the car to represent the benefits to be expected from voucher privatization was not accidental. Even as late as 1985, average car ownership in the Soviet Union was only 45 per thousand (Pyle 1993: 49). Nor was this a matter simply of expense. As Lewis Siegelbaum explains:

> Between the desire to purchase a car and actually doing so lay a minefield of obstacles - most erected by the state as a crude form of rationing. In addition to formal restrictions associated with signing up to receive a car (and the possibility of having one's name removed or getting bumped as a form of punishment for work-related infractions), they included hefty

> prices amounting to several years' wages, the requirement of a 25 percent down payment at the time of order and the balance paid in cash on delivery, and waits on average of four-to-six and occasionally as many as ten years to receive the precious item. (2009: 6)

## "We Sold Them: We Needed the Money"

Several women realized that they lacked the knowledge to invest the vouchers wisely and the time to conduct the necessary market research, or simply couldn't be bothered with anything so abstract when their lives were focused on feeding their children and coping with the challenges of daily life. They therefore sold their vouchers for cash.

> We sold them and bought an outfit for our daughter.... And we bought something else, but I don't remember what. We never believed that the vouchers would work and provide income, so we sold them right away. [Marta, 45]

> For the value of my voucher we bought jeans for my son. That's how much it was worth at that time. [Maria, 65]

As these recollections imply, it was quite easy to sell one's vouchers instead of investing them. A brisk market sprang up, unregulated and often highly exploitative. One of the commonly told stories—perhaps an urban legend, but probably true—is of people trading their vouchers for a bottle of vodka. It was difficult for many to believe that these bits of paper, with a face value of 10,000 rubles (at the time worth roughly USD 84) for which they had been asked to pay the government a token sum of 25 rubles, actually represented anything worthwhile. Given how few of my respondents in fact ended up benefitting in any significant way from the program, this mistrust was well-founded. One woman contrasted the vouchers with the savings bonds that her grandparents had been required to buy from the government in an earlier era, arguing that those bonds seemed valuable in a way the vouchers never did. This is an interesting perception, because it was not actually possible to redeem most of these savings bonds for cash despite the promises the state had made, which means they were actually less valuable than the vouchers of the 1990s.

> There simply had never been such securities [that is, the vouchers] in the country [and so no one understood]. I remember that at one point there were bonds, people gave money for them. My grandmother saved a very large number of them, because my grandfather was some sort of boss. They required them to buy these bonds. You received your pay and they'd already taken part of it for these bonds. As if somehow you were giving the government money for mutual benefit. There were a lot of these bonds. And there was a time, when I was still little, at the beginning of the 1960s, I remember clearly how my grandmother became really upset [with me]…. My grandfather had a huge desk, two pedestals and a sliding drawer…. [There] I found some notebooks and cut out some numbers. For me these were simply numbers but for my grandmother they were money. I remember how upset she was at the time. These bonds were taken off to the attic, away from me. If for [that generation], these were real money and they laid down hard cash for them, for us the vouchers were just paper. [Inessa, 53]

Since the bonds were "taken off to the attic" rather than redeemed, the child's sense that they were "simply numbers" was perhaps more accurate than her grandmother's view.

The widespread confusion about the vouchers in the early 1990s, the sense that they were unlikely to be very valuable, and uncertainty about how best to use them is further illustrated by the following exchange between a pair of women who would have been in their thirties at the time the vouchers were issued. Like the considerably older women quoted earlier, these two recall the claim that the vouchers would enable people to acquire cars.

> *Inessa*: All my relatives gave me their vouchers and…at the last moment, when they were being bought up for Chubais, I could sell them. Because those who invested in things like MMM, all that went up in flames. I managed to sell them. I didn't buy anything with them and couldn't, but we did manage to sell them in time. And what about you? What did you do with yours? You probably don't remember.

*Emilia*: We invested them somewhere, but there was never any result. All we got was paper.

*Inessa*: You could be rich now and not even know it! Back then such organizations as Gazprom didn't exist.[9] Then we could only invest in [things like] MMM. What more was there?

*Emilia*: We invested in something to do with oil. I still have the paper.

*Inessa*: You might have a lot of oil and not even know it. You need to find that paper. But people here didn't get anything with those vouchers.

*Emilia*: My relatives sold theirs, my aunt and uncle sold theirs.

*Inessa*: At first, they were buying them for a lot. But I didn't even register what these vouchers were. We didn't understand that this was valuable paper. When they gave them to us, they said something like one could almost buy a car for a single voucher. But in the end it was impossible to buy anything. And my mom and dad and grandparents and my child and I—that's 6 vouchers and it was nothing.... These vouchers turned to dust for us.

## "We Received Nothing from Them"

Even those who tried to take advantage of the opportunity to use their vouchers to become shareholders in a privatized enterprise tended not to benefit financially from the venture. There were two fundamental problems. The first was that by its design voucher privatization could not result in an infusion of money into the enterprises. Without such funds, it was impossible to carry out the transformation required by the new economic circumstances or take advantage of the long pent-up demand for consumer goods and services. The second was the proliferation of Ponzi schemes, which made payments to early investors from the amounts received from subsequent investors rather than using the funds received to acquire or establish productive businesses.

The following narratives describe two very different approaches—one casual, the other carefully mapped out. Both, however, led ultimately to the same lack of payoff. In the first account, we see some familiar

[9] The gas industry giant did in fact exist at the time, but its shares were among the last to be made available for vouchers.

themes, including the complete novelty of the concept of private investment, the advantages believed to arise from being employed at the right sort of Soviet enterprise, and the unscrupulous behavior of those to whom the vouchers were entrusted.

> Yes, we got vouchers, my parents, my son and I all received a voucher. As I have said, at that time I didn't care. I was leaving [moving abroad with my new husband]. I was getting my documents ready and preparing myself mentally… I was somehow indifferent to all this, I didn't pay attention. And at that time we didn't know anything about how to deal with this, how to handle it so it would be profitable, so it would be to our advantage. Because I know there are some who worked in the chemical industry, for example, in the oil refinery, at the tire plant here, that is, in those businesses that are associated with certain industries…and they received [shares] in their enterprises and they received very good money for these shares….
>
> But I gave these vouchers—my mother's and father's and son's and mine—to someone, put them into some sort of fund or something. There was some kind of fund that took vouchers and somehow we were supposed to get dividends for these vouchers. They invested them in some companies, but we never received any kind of dividend… We had documents for these shares and many years ago, in 2000 and something, I don't remember when, my neighbor said, "You can get money for your voucher." This turned out to be an absolutely ridiculous sum… just pennies. Well, that is nothing…Our vouchers just went nowhere…. Maybe for those who worked in some giant enterprises it was profitable. Or for those who handled it deliberately, purposefully and maybe not always honestly, but they collected shares in some large company or another, one that really paid dividends later. But my mom worked at a small factory, and she received nothing there. She worked at the printing plant… and the enterprise wasn't particularly successful…So in this sense, we didn't become capitalists. [Veronika, 51]

The next recollection makes clear that even "handl[ing] it deliberately, purposefully" did not guarantee good results.

My experience with the vouchers went very badly…We did everything right and it seemed to us that we would get rich. [We did it] with my brother, and he's a military financier…. He received a good economics education…. So we thought that with my brother, who was practically an economist, we would invest them, buy something with them, and would somehow get rich…but nothing happened. All my vouchers lie at my house as a keepsake. [Unlike the woman quoted earlier, for whom this was literally true, this respondent had bought shares with her vouchers and it was these shares that she kept as souvenirs.] …. It seemed to us that we couldn't go wrong if we invested in something called Moscow Real Estate. Imagine, real estate in Moscow! And there was this slogan, 'Moscow real estate—always in fashion!' And we believed that it really was in fashion, but the firm that started this up turned out not to be what it claimed to be. It ended up paying not a single penny and we didn't acquire a single meter of Moscow real estate for the vouchers.

Voucher #2—went to what was called AVVA [the All-Russia Automobile Alliance]. This was a firm started by Boris Berezovskii,[10] and we thought, "Cars, that's so cool!" But basically it turned out that again it was "repurposed," it turned out to be worth nothing. It was simply a soap bubble, a scrap of paper….

And the third one, I think, was Mr. Stirligov, who has now become so strange. He was a millionaire and now he's gone into some Siberian village, or I don't know where, and has turned into such an Orthodox man, he goes around in *valenki* [felt boots, long associated with Russian peasants], bakes his own bread, and so forth. …And I also acquired shares in his business….

So the three members of the family decided that it would be good economically to invest in different places, with the hope that somewhere would be lucky. We weren't lucky anywhere. We received nothing, absolutely. Someone who in this manner invested in Gazprom or so forth

[10]Berezovski was an oligarch, influential during Yeltsin's years, who came into conflict with Putin and ended up living in London until his death in 2013, the British government having refused to extradite him to Russia, where he was charged with various economic crimes.

suddenly became rich. I heard that they received some money. But from this national wealth no one in my family or my parents or my brother's family got anything at all. [Ekaterina, 56]

The brief exchange below also captures this belief that a primary reason so few benefited was the dishonesty of those who did become rich.

*Klara*: There were all kinds of swindles—MMM and all kinds of companies grew up

*Lidia*: They just made fools of the people.

## "We Were Lucky"

Not all my respondents were disenchanted with voucher privatization, however. Several had benefited in a modest way and were pleased with the results. What form this benefit took varied widely and their positive view of the outcome seemed to have at least as much to do with personality as with the actual results.

One woman, currently a sales representative for a Western firm and given to making light of the difficulties she encountered during the transition, offered the following explanation of how she and her family benefited. There seem to be two very different ways in which she claimed to have used the vouchers and no obvious explanation for the connection between them, so I simply present her story as I heard it.

> Vouchers? Many went to the market and sold them for 33 rubles each. We had 5 vouchers—my husband and I and our three children each had one voucher. My husband told me to go buy a fur collar, an arctic fox. I worried about moths, but the fox is still fine. They gave [vouchers] to the whole family and I bought a fur collar for myself....

> We read in books that there were shares that would provide dividends. There is an oil refinery here. I found out the history of the factory, I looked at statistics about the factory. I went with my little girl to the factory. I put four vouchers in the factory...and one voucher in a tannery. We didn't receive any dividends because the plant was undergoing

> reconstruction. Then they invited us to buy more shares. But these weren't preferred shares so with them one didn't receive dividends. There were preferred shares and with those one could buy an apartment, real estate. With ours, no.
>
> After several years my husband said, "At work everyone is selling their vouchers [sic]." I listened to him and we went to sell them. We sold them and for the money we received the whole family went to the south, to Crimea. We sold them in 2000.
>
> I received letters about shareholder meetings, where they had some sort of raffle. I never went. They gave away televisions, but it's just a waste of time. I still have a few shares left, but they don't pay dividends. It's such a long process, probably about 20 years or so. But I think the vouchers turned out well for us. The family enjoyed a summer vacation. [Eva, 55]

Like the others who mentioned having actually benefited from voucher privatization, this woman invested in an energy-related enterprise. Unlike the others, however, she claims to have played an active role—indeed, the primary role—in the decision about how to use the vouchers. In contrast, of those who invested in Gazprom one credited her son for the decision, two credited their husbands, and one credited Chubais.

After mentioning having made poor decisions about what to do with two of the vouchers—"There were two companies, an investment fund and another company like that. And those safely evaporated"—one woman described how she came to invest in Gazprom.

> But the last voucher I had…Well, the truth is I didn't understand this piece of paper. But on my birthday–it was one of the last few days when one could do something with the voucher—and my son took the voucher from me and submitted it to Gazprom. And I am now the owner of a very good number of Gazprom shares…. When I decided three years ago to open a café in Israel with a partner, I sold half of the vouchers [sic] and opened a café in Israel.
>
> So, I am very pleased. As they say, the child is closer to God. [My son] with his own hand went and gave me a gift; he came and said,

> "Mom, here's this piece of paper they gave you. You now have shares of Gazprom." … And after a while there began to be dividends. At first the dividends were once a year and one had to go and collect them. And, by the way, I cursed a lot that I had to go. [Vera, 56]

One woman who benefited from investment in Gazprom made it clear that this was her husband's investment and that she herself had not been so shrewd.

> *Seventy-year-old Klara*: For this voucher I got shares and each year they pay dividends. It was always around 1700 rubles, then 2000. And not until this year did I get 13,000.
>
> *Lidia, also 70*: Well, you see! This isn't bad!
>
> *Klara*: What do you mean, not bad! For ten years, or what, fifteen years, and this is the first time I've received such a sum!
>
> *Lidia*: But you invested them, at least. All she [indicating the third member of the conversation] got was a pair of blue jeans.
>
> *Klara*: Not me. It was my husband who was smarter. He invested in Gazprom. While I, little fool, I put mine and my daughter's in some company called the National Front. There where the wind blows…. And I lost it.

Another woman who credits her husband with the decision to invest in Gazprom described how she and her family benefited, but then noted that they could have done even better with a slightly different strategy.

> As for the vouchers, we were lucky. We were lucky, because I have a very smart husband with an analytical mind. He analyzed the voucher market and said that we would wait until the last day, we would invest only in Gazprom. Gazprom only appeared in the last 3 days…. And we and all our relatives purchased these vouchers and then we decided to wait until the voucher cost one dollar. I mean, until a share cost one dollar…. We waited 15 years, 15 years.
>
> Just as soon as the price reached one dollar, we quickly sold them and that paid for part of the apartment that we bought. Otherwise it is unlikely that we would have been able to [buy the apartment]. But if

> we had waited one more year the shares would have cost 10 dollars. So my husband guessed a bit wrong. But we don't regret it because...Well I don't regret it. We can second guess ourselves today, but that's what we had decided and that's what we did.
>
> That is, we bought a one-bedroom apartment. If we had waited one more year, we could have bought a three-bedroom apartment. But this, you know, we could not have guessed. So it's not [really] that we were lucky with the vouchers; I cannot say that we were lucky. It was all [due to] my husband. It was a calculation. [Liza, 55]

Despite this successful navigation of voucher privatization, they nonetheless fell victim to a Ponzi scheme.

> Oh, I forgot to say that we were involved in various... MMM? You've heard about this? We didn't lose with MMM, but we played different games. It's hard to imagine now how you would go, carrying money; you would go to some basement and they'd put the money in bags. And there was a line to hand over the money, you understand. Nonsense! It was simply nonsense, but we took part in it. Today I look back and I wonder how it could be, because [they promised] an enormous percent [return].

Since they had purchased Gazprom shares with their vouchers, participation in the Ponzi schemes must have involved the use of personal savings; this was certainly the case for the woman's parents and sister. Like many others they lacked the experience to understand that the promised returns were too good to be true. This was not surprising. Russian leaders, trying to sell the population on the benefits of abandoning the Soviet system, tended to paint the market system in unrealistically glowing colors, and many of the Western advisors were neoliberals, also prone to emphasize the potential advantages and say little about any drawbacks.

> [They promised] an enormous percent, and then suddenly, in just a moment, everything collapsed. [My parents] could not survive this; it was hard, very hard. My mother died prematurely...at 73, because she could not become reconciled to this. They wanted to help us–to give some

> presents to their grandsons, not so much to us—when they retired, but all the money was gone. These were the savings of their entire life. But it was all gone. It was—well, I do not remember exactly, 5000 rubles. It wasn't a large amount.... I do not remember exactly, but something like this. And, of course, they were very, very grieved, they suffered greatly from this. It was very painful. And in fact [the money] has never been replaced. And we lost our savings, too. And my sister, for example, lost absolutely all of her savings. She is a very thrifty woman and she lost all of her savings. [Liza]

The last woman to discuss investing in Gazprom surprisingly credited the generally maligned Chubais for her decision.

> With the vouchers? I bought shares in Gazprom. I simply listened to some radio or TV broadcast and the head of the voucher program, Chubais, was on. And he said it would be good to buy shares of Gazprom, so I bought shares of Gazprom. I only bought shares of Gazprom with my vouchers. But then there was a time when my son went to Poland, he was dealing in furniture. It was at the very beginning, he bought furniture and we needed to sell.... Somehow we failed to organize the sale properly and we needed to borrow money. And I had to [sell] my [shares]. It's a pity, isn't it? I still regret it. All my shares, there were a lot of shares, and I handed them over to repay a debt. Even though, really, I didn't know what it was, whether it was profitable, unprofitable, necessary, unnecessary. I just didn't know. [Tamara, 61]

As these stories make clear, all of the women who invested in Gazprom received some real benefit as a result. Sometimes they invested unsuccessfully in other enterprises as well, sometimes they sold their Gazprom shares prematurely, sometimes the proceeds were swallowed up in unexpected expenses, but they nonetheless benefited in ways that the other women did not. Even luckier than the women who chose to invest in Gazprom was the woman who herself worked at an oil company and therefore was able to acquire shares in that company on the special terms available to employees. When the value of these shares increased sharply, she sold them.

> With my vouchers, I purchased shares of the…company. The company's policy is aimed not so much at paying dividends to shareholders as at increasing capitalization. Therefore, the dividend paid on these shares was very small. For one ruble's worth of shares, one receives one kopeck per year, so the main advantage lies in the market value of the stock. We have already sold [our shares]. There was a second wave of privatization in the city.…The company's shares were worth 25-30 rubles per share and were being actively bought up. The value rose very quickly. And then the employees of the company sold their shares. [Ksenia, 48]

This woman benefited in other ways as well from having the good fortune to be working for an energy company. She is the only person with whom I spoke who seemed to have experienced almost no difficulties at all during the early 1990s.

> This was when the company was flourishing. There was a lot of money, really, a lot of money. [It was] when the border was opened, and they began actively selling oil and oil products abroad. They paid wages regularly. Plus all kinds of other possibilities opened up…. This was a period when the enterprise had no problems. The energy sector was flourishing. …I had an apartment [inherited when my parents died]. And we got an interest-free loan from the company and used it to enlarge the apartment. That was the period when there was a lot of money and they gave interest-free loans. And one didn't even need to pay back 25 percent of it. That's the kind of credit there was.

Despite having avoided most of the problems the rest of my respondents experienced, this woman did not seem to be a member of the class of New Russians (discussed more in Chapter 9). She left the energy company in 2009, entered a graduate school program, and is pursuing work in behavioral economics, psychology and education.

## Conclusion

Marxists identify private ownership of the means of production as a key factor in the economic inequality common in capitalist countries. As the post-Soviet Russian reformers considered how best to put state-owned enterprises into the hands of private owners, one of their goals was to create at least the impression of fairness. The voucher privatization phase was intended to achieve that goal. As the comments in this chapter make clear, however, the program categorically failed in this respect. The women I spoke to referred frequently to what they saw as corruption in the privatization process and the illegal appropriation of state property by those in charge. For these women, what privatization signaled was not fairness but rather a sharp increase in economic inequality and they deeply resented this. In general, they spoke with more anger about the new—or at least newly overt—inequality than about the other ways in which their lives had been upended by the transition. This inequality is examined in the next chapter.

## References

Blasi, Joseph R., Maya Kroumova, and Douglas Kruse. 1997. *Kremlin Capitalism: Privatizing the Russian Economy*. Ithaca, NY: Cornell University.
Gaaze, Konstantin. 2016. How the Battle for Russian Privatization Was Fought and Lost. *The Moscow Times*. Accessed online at https://themoscowtimes.com/articles/russias-privatisation-that-wasnt-55563. August 2017.
Klebnikov, Paul. 1994. Russia—The Ultimate Emerging Market. *Forbes* 153 (4): 88–94.
Mobius, Mark. 2012. The Russian Evolution. Accessed online at http://mobius.blog.franklintempleton.com/2012/08/29/the-russian-evolution/. April 2016.
Pyle, William. 1993. Private Car Ownership and Second Economy Activity. Berkeley-Duke Occasional Papers on the Second Economy in the USSR, no. 37.
Siegelbaum, Lewis. 2009. On the Side: Car Culture in the USSR, 1960s–1980s. *Technology and Culture* 50 (1): 1–23.
Sputnik News. 2011. The 1991 Monetary Reform in the Soviet Union. Accessed online at https://sputniknews.com/business/20110202162419049/. March 2019.

# 9

# Economic Inequality: Income and What It Says about You

## Introduction

Although the ultimate goal of Soviet communism was to create a classless society, achieving this proved impossible. Over the decades, the leaders struggled to find the right degree of income differentiation, widening the gap between top and bottom pay scales, then narrowing it, then widening it again. Too much economic inequality was ideologically unacceptable, while too little left economic planners and managers without the ability to use monetary incentives to motivate the labor force. This was especially true in the late Soviet period, when the initial excitement generated by the dream of creating a brave new world had waned and the terror that had characterized the Stalinist period had been relaxed. In addition to experimenting with different wage scales within and between industries, the leaders relied on special wage supplements and non-monetary benefits for those in particularly dangerous jobs or in particularly unattractive locations (Cook 1993: 38–40; Dyker 1984: 41). These aspects of the economic arrangements were deliberately public; had they been kept hidden, they could not have served as effective incentives.


J. McKinney, *Russian Women and the End of Soviet Socialism*,
https://doi.org/10.1007/978-3-030-16226-9_9

At the same time, there was a less overt element of inequality—a world of privilege behind the closed doors of special shops, apartment complexes, hospitals and summer communities accessible to the Party elite. While ordinary Soviet citizens were almost certainly aware that these privileges existed, especially in the later years as elite consumption became more conspicuous (Humphrey 2002: 60), it is unlikely that many fully grasped either their size or their scope. Furthermore, as long as people did not encounter daily glaring reminders of the inequality, its psychological impact was moderated.

All this changed dramatically with the end of the Soviet system. Even under Gorbachev, as modest private endeavors were permitted and the media were allowed to discuss social and economic conditions more openly, economic differences began to lead to considerable resentment. Under Yeltsin, as policy makers openly embraced the idea that inequality was essential for a market economy and cavalierly dismissed the needs and concerns of those who were struggling (Shlapentokh 1999), this resentment grew and was further exacerbated by three phenomena, experienced particularly painfully by those, like many of the women I spoke to, who were members of the *intelligentsia*.

First was the reordering of social strata. As income and possessions (including home ownership) became a key marker for the first time in living memory, some groups—such as teachers—who had been accorded special respect in Soviet society experienced in its collapse not only a drop in real income but also a painful and disorienting loss of status. As Patico (2008) argues, changes in relative economic position forced people to reconsider what they had thought were enduring truths about the relationship between income (or consumption) and socially useful work, and by extension between income (or consumption) and one's value as an individual. A second reason for bitterness was the ostentation and very conspicuous consumption indulged in by the newly rich, which meant that those without significant wealth, often newly poor, were constantly forced to confront the fact that some people could afford things that were far beyond their own means. Finally, as discussed in Chapter 8, the pronounced sense that the privatization of state property was riddled with corruption reinforced the bad taste left by the conspicuous consumption of the "New Russians." Together, these aspects of post-Soviet life led to a widespread belief that the least deserving, least respectable members of society were now faring better than everyone else: their wealth was ill-gotten and their behavior an affront to all decent people.

Along with their clear unhappiness with the privatization process, many of the women I spoke to expressed deep resentment of the "New Russians" in particular. By 2012, several of the most infamous of the oligarchs had been arrested, exiled or imprisoned and had been effectively stripped of their wealth.[1] This, however, had done nothing to lessen the bitterness with which the women I spoke to judged them.[2] By 2012, obvious economic inequality was no longer new; it had become deeply entrenched and, indeed, had continued to increase. That it had become "normal" did nothing to make it more acceptable to those I interviewed, however.

There are very real problems in comparing data on poverty and inequality from the early post-Soviet period with data from the late Soviet period, both because of changes in definitions and because of changes in the role of money in determining levels of consumption and economic well-being. In the Soviet period, as we have seen, money was neither a necessary nor a sufficient means of acquiring consumer goods and services, while in the early post-Soviet period money's role in the new "market" system was seriously complicated by hyperinflation and pervasive wage arrears. Thus, at neither time did data on earnings give an accurate measure of what a person could actually consume.

Further blurring the picture is the failure of official statistics to capture the income from economic activity taking place in the informal

---

[1]Media mogul Boris Berezovsky, for example, died in England in 2013, having lived there for over a decade and having been found guilty in Russian courts *in absentia* and stripped of most of his assets. Mikhail Khodorkovsky, former head of the oil company Yukos, spent nine years in jail—he was in prison in the fall of 2012—before leaving the country; he, too, lost most of his wealth as a result of government action.

[2]Cf. Patico (2008), who found that the Saint Petersburg teachers she interviewed in 1998–1999 had by 2003 become largely indifferent to the New Russians and no longer considered them worth talking (or telling jokes) about (212–213). It is possible that the difference lies in the fact that I was focusing their attention on the earlier period, while Patico was addressing how things had changed since 1998, but I had no sense that the resentment felt by my respondents had softened over time.

sector. In the Soviet period, the informal sector consisted of the "second economy" of black and gray markets. While estimates of its share in total Soviet economic activity ranged widely, there is no question that, at least in certain sectors, it was significant.[3] During the early 1990s, as private economic activity was fully legalized, the informal sector encompassed unofficial and often unregistered business operations; the primary motivation at that time was to avoid paying taxes.

Despite the need for caution in interpreting the statistics, a rough idea of how unevenly the economic hardships of the early 1990s were spread can be gleaned from the following numbers. In 1989, the percent of Russians living below the official poverty line was 11.0; in March 1993, it was 34.7 (Klugman and Braithwaite 1998: 43). Over the same period, the ratio of the share of income going to the richest fifth of the population to the share going to the poorest fifth, which had been only 3.4 when Gorbachev became General Secretary in 1985, rose from 4.1 to 6.4 (Shorrocks and Kolenikov 2000: 16). Twenty years later, at the time of my interviews, the poverty rate had fallen sharply; according to the World Bank it was only 10.7% in 2012, or slightly below the rate in 1989 (World Bank). Although poverty rates were lower, inequality had become even more pronounced. If in 1985 the top 10% of the population received about 22.5% of national income and in 1995 it received about 43%, by 2010 it was receiving almost 48%. The share of total money income going to the top fifth of the population, meanwhile, had grown from 38.3% in 1992 to 47.6% in 2012, while the share of each of the other four quintiles had fallen (Novokmet et al. 2017; Federal State Statistics 2016: 129).

Economic circumstances in Yaroslavl were similar to those in Russia as a whole. Although the city's concentration in heavy industry, especially machine-building and petrochemicals, meant that the shift away from central planning and from the economic priorities of the Party caused a particularly large drop in output in the early 1990s, overall

[3]Much of what was "known" in the West about the size of the second economy came from interviews with Soviet émigrés, whose estimates of its share in total economic activity ranged from 10 to 50% (Sampson 1987: 124).

indicators of economic well-being for the city were not significantly different from national averages (Sergeyev 2001: 118). One survey carried out in 1995 found that of 975 respondents in a "systematic-probability sample of residents of Yaroslavl' eighteen years of age or older" 52.1% received USD 42.46 or less per month per capita, 20.3% received between USD 42.47 and USD 60.47, 11.3% received between USD 60.48 and USD 75.82, 11.5% received between USD 75.83 and USD 109, and 4.5% received over USD 109 (ibid., 118, 125).

These income levels reflected official Russian calculations of what was necessary to achieve particular consumption benchmarks. The lowest figure (USD 42.46) was the estimated cost of the amount of food necessary to meet the "physiological subsistence minimum," clearly a very restrictive measure of poverty—and yet the survey found that over half of the population of Yaroslavl received no more than that, and many received less. The next two figures represented, respectively, the cost of a basic consumer basket of goods and the cost of a basket of goods that included some consumer durables. The 16% of the population receiving more than USD 75.82 per month were thus in a position to buy more than the basics. Because the last category is open-ended, it presumably captured at least a few individuals who would have seemed rich even by Western standards.

## Attitudes Toward Economic Inequality

### New Russians: The Rich

Whether they characterized their own experiences in the early 1990s as relatively easy or extremely difficult, the women I spoke with were unanimous in the contempt and anger they expressed on the subject of the New Russians. Discussion of this phenomenon always made me wish I had a video camera rather than simply an audio recorder. As soon as the talk turned to this group, almost all of the women, without getting out of their seats, puffed up their chests and mimicked strutting like a peacock, flicking imaginary lint from their imaginary red jackets to call attention to their imaginary gold chains. It was clear that this body language had become as much a part of the culture as the flick of finger to cheek or neck to indicate drinking.

As mentioned earlier, much of the wrath arose from the sense that these newly rich and privileged had come by their status dishonestly and at the expense of the rest of society. The widespread belief that those with large sums of money in the early 1990s had acquired this wealth unscrupulously stemmed not only from the woeful shortcomings in the way the privatization of state-owned assets was carried out but also from decades of propaganda and education about the exploitative nature of private business and trade.

> [There was] a motor factory on the territory of the Leninsky district… [It was like] a huge city. 45,000 worked just at the factory. 45,000! It's like a small town. And then they [divided them] into workshops…. Now, one shop belongs to [this person] and another shop belongs to [that person]…. Each shop was bought by someone, probably for these vouchers, you know? And suddenly everyone, excuse me, has so much money that you can buy a whole shop? [Not me!] I have worked all my life and I don't have the kind of money to buy a shop.
>
> And those guys in their red jackets, those fancy New Russians with their gold chains. It all went on at that time. Those who today are rich, I'm sure that most of them received it not by earning it but by stealing it during those hard years of the 1990s. In troubled waters, it's easy to catch fish. …
>
> I don't understand why we had this *perestroika*. What needed to be restructured? They pilfered everything, right? All that they restructured was to give away the oil and gas to private hands. Really, is there any other country like this? Where the natural wealth is controlled by a handful of people? There's not a single [other] country where this is the case. [Zoya, 52]

Adding to the animosity was the tendency of the newly rich to indulge in flagrant displays of wealth at a time when many were struggling just to get by. After decades of Soviet ideology of equality and the largely hidden nature of the privileges of the rich, such ostentation struck many as deeply immoral. Resentment of those who had become rich was intensified for some by the deep pain associated with the loss of the status that "should" have come from working as a teacher and for others by the inability to provide well for their children.

> We had to admit rich idiots [to the school]… because ordinary kids couldn't pay that kind of money…. It cost USD 1300 a month. Imagine! Paying $1300 a month per child, at a time when my salary…was USD 200, 150, something like that. USD 150 was the salary of a teacher, but how the children paid! … Imagine, a child would come and his outfit cost more than my annual salary. And I'm a teacher, you understand. How could it be? When here comes this rich kid…and [his papa basically] bought the school. You understand at that time we had the era of the crimson jackets and gold chains. That's how it was then, when the father would arrive in a car that was bigger than my apartment, for example. One could live in such a car, right? There was a television in it, and the sun was shining in it. [Yulia, 52]

> I wouldn't want to return to that time, to the 1990s, I wouldn't wish that for anyone. My children, especially the older one, right? He was born in 1980, and when *perestroika* began he was an adolescent, with the especially intense feelings of adolescents and there was all this social inequity. At that point, we had bandits in the country, the so-called New Russians, who went around in their gold chains and rings, with their red jackets. This was the brand look of the New Russians. They drove around in fancy foreign cars…. And a 16-year-old boy wants to dress up or simply go to a café or the movies with a girl, and his mom and dad don't receive their salary for 3-4 months at a time. [Zoya, 52]

In contrast to the clear animosity they displayed toward the "New Russians" of the early transition period, none of my respondents spoke resentfully—or, indeed, at all—about the Soviet-era economic privileges of the political elite. Those who were most open in conveying negative views of the old system focused on the lack of freedom and the power of the KGB rather than on economic inequality. Just as the women I spoke to held onto their anger at the New Russians longer than the teachers in Patico's study, so they seemed less bitter about economic privileges enjoyed by Party bureaucrats than the residents of Omsk interviewed by Pesman (2000) in the mid-1990s, who described both Soviet *apparatchiki* and New Russians as lacking in intelligence, morals and culture (Patico 2008: 43). For some of my respondents, this might be because in the Soviet period they had themselves been quite privileged, married to men in upper management at major enterprises. For most, it may simply have been because of my efforts to focus their recollections on the early 1990s.

## The Poor: Broken Families

Despite official silence on the topic within the Soviet Union, there is no question that poverty, both absolute and relative, existed during the Soviet period. Prior to Khrushchev's time as General Secretary, most urban Soviet families lived in communal apartments, sharing kitchen and bath with other families; they had few consumer durables, access to few retail services, and a limited range of foodstuffs in their diet. Nonetheless, some were significantly more deprived than others.

Only two of the women I spoke with experienced Soviet-era poverty directly, although a few others had worked with disadvantaged families in their capacity as teachers. One of these teachers explained that this work was the result of taking on a specially designated role at school, that of "social educator," in addition to her normal teaching responsibilities. The other woman quoted below did not indicate whether the household visits were officially part of her job or simply something she felt she should do as a good Communist and a good teacher. Both women, reflecting Soviet-era authoritative discourse, clearly viewed poverty as the result of inappropriate or socially aberrant behavior such as alcoholism or divorce.

> Badly-off families, troubled families—I worked with troubled families and children there at school. We did not have a lot of them. I was involved with arranging free meals at school and identifying who had some reason to get these free meals. Mostly I worked with such problem

> children and their parents.... At that time, the social educator and the psychologist would step in, the social worker and the psychologist worked closely together. [Klara, 70]

> I always went around to their homes. It's not that I was inspecting anything or said, "Show me your child's workplace, where he does his homework, whether the light comes from the left or the right." That is ridiculous, of course. The families were all so different. Those I could help, I tried to help, because a lot of the families were very poor. Many families were not complete, or they were two-parent families but the fathers were alcoholics. Yet despite this the children—most of the kids, yes all of the kids—were so responsive at the time, they were so trusting. They wanted to study well. [Anna, 56]

This narrative that poverty is explained by broken families and/or alcoholism continued to have power in the post-Soviet period, despite the clear evidence that many in poverty—especially the "new poor"—did not fit the stereotype (and that divorce and family problems also occurred among those with higher income). Speaking of the students she worked with in the early 1990s, one woman resisted the characterization of children from such homes as somehow inferior while nonetheless accepting the standard explanation for their difficulties.

> It's simply that ... people always assumed that after school one had to attend a higher educational institute.... Per capita we in the Soviet Union probably had the highest number of people with higher education. If for some reason you didn't receive [higher education], then people considered you a loser, a shame, who wouldn't go anywhere, who couldn't do anything. Therefore, the bulk of our graduates wanted to go to an institute, it didn't matter what kind, just as long as they got that higher education. But those kids who for various reasons—social, their family situation, the low level of their parents, a broken family, alcoholic dads, alcoholic moms, those kinds of deviant behavior, these people—their kids, as a rule, were abandoned.... [There were] all these so-called leftovers, like "white trash," [she used the English phrase]. There's that concept in America, people who can't make anything of themselves in any way. They then go to these vocational schools....

> These poor, unfortunate children, who—not because they are stupid, idiots, just that they were in such circumstances that they couldn't realize their abilities. When you work with such students, … there are a lot of opportunities to find a common language, to get them interested, to get them motivated, to show them the possibilities—and that's what happened for me…. The children and I loved one another, and they raced to my lessons headlong. Sometimes I even said to them, "if only you sometimes skipped my class, I could rest" and they said, "It would be better to cut some other subject." [Yulia, 52]

Another woman, after describing in moving terms how hard her life had been during the late 1980s and early 1990s and the physical and emotional toll it had taken, went on to contrast her experience with those less fortunate, again stressing the important role played by incomplete families.

> As long as one has one's family, one is strong, like twigs in a single broom. If you take each twig, it's easy to break it, but if it's a broom you can't break it. I have [two grown sons] and now a daughter-in-law…. I say, all for one and one for all. We were a fist, and with this fist [we survived] all the unpleasantness of the 1990s, all these hardships, all this poverty…. [We managed] to experience all these constant shortages of everything and not break and not fall in spirits, and not argue. Many families did fall apart then …so I think that a huge asset of my family is that we were able to preserve the family, not to quarrel, not to fall apart, but rather to come closer together. And not just my immediate family. My mother and father, even though they divorced, they were there for us. [Zoya, 52]

The two women who described their own childhoods as characterized by serious deprivation grew up without a father in the home, not an uncommon experience given the unusually high male death rates over several decades of war and repression. The first, born in 1938, was raised in a very small village; the second, born in 1951, grew up in the city of Yaroslavl.

> I lived with my mother…. My father died in the war. We were very poor, very poor, and then in 1960 I married. This guy from Yaroslavl married

me. He felt sorry for me because of the awful poverty, such poverty. I didn't even have any new panties, nothing good, everything was mended and darned. [Feodosia]

[We were] very poor. Poor isn't even the right word. Very often we had no food, and kind people gave me my clothes. And that's despite the fact that my mother worked. When it was time for me to go to first grade, Mama didn't have the money to buy my notebook and books and school uniform, so she decided that I needed to wait for a year and I started school at the age of eight. When I finally got to school, the teachers pitied me a great deal because I would often faint from hunger, since there was nothing for me to eat before school. [Sofia]

Despite sharing the deprivations of early poverty, these women have experienced very different life trajectories, with one remaining in poverty throughout her life and the other enjoying considerable professional and economic success. The older woman, now in her 70s, sees her entire life as one of hardship. She was poor as a child; she married early to try to escape poverty but chose unwisely so remained poor and was saddled in addition with an alcoholic husband; she was poor under Gorbachev's reforms and Yeltsin's transition; she is poor today.

And that's how I live right up to now, I wear cast-offs.... I got married, I came to Yaroslavl, and understood that my husband was a drunkard. I understood that if I wanted to live I had to take myself in hand, study, work, and then bit by bit stand on my own two feet. I still today stand on my own two feet; one foot is in the grave, but I still stand on my own. We had a very hard life. My husband drank, I gave birth to my daughter right away....

When *perestroika* began, in general it was worse in Russia than after the war. Just like after the war, there was nothing and I just barely survived, I just barely raised my children, I just barely gave them an education. I lived through *perestroika* with great difficulty. There was nowhere to work.... There was nowhere for the young to work and nowhere for pensioners. We lived badly, we were hungry, we saw nothing worthwhile in life, absolutely nothing....

> Years passed, I grew older, I grew poorer and even now I live in horrible poverty. My pension is 7500 rubles (under USD 250, per month). Everything I'm wearing comes from the church. What the rich people bring to the church, what they're tired of, I take.... Up to today my life has been hard. I don't have anything extra.... I don't have extra panties. I just have enough so that I wash them, dry them, put them back on and go. I walk around in tattered socks, I don't have any other socks. My shoes, these ugly shoes that I'm ashamed to wear. And I walk around in such socks, I don't have any others. I just wash them and put them back on and put on these ugly shoes again, which I would throw away somewhere in the trash but I can't....

Although the financial and emotional difficulties she has endured were a major part of the story she shared with me, she did not see herself—or wish to be seen—as only a victim. Along with the poor sufferer, mistreated by her husband, by fate and by the government (both Soviet and post-Soviet), she offered a portrait of a strong, capable, attractive woman, loved by her children, courted by men, sought after by her friends.

> [My son] married very late.... He said, 'Mama, I'm looking for someone like you. You are my ideal.'...

She lives alone, although a man she is seeing has suggested that she move in with him.

> I've become wise, I've become clever... as if some light had turned on. That 3-room apartment [of his] will go to his son, his car, to the other son; he has a dacha with thirty acres and that, too, will go to a son. He's already drawn up the document, and what will I get from him? 7000 [rubles]? I'd be washing the floors for nothing. If you're going to kiss, then pay up. Buy me some perfume. If you want to hug me, perfume. If you want something from me, fine, give me something.

She was, indeed, receiving gifts from this man, and was able to travel a bit with him.

> I was used to not having anything. I even got used to that.... But now, after the death of my husband, a "boyfriend" [she used the English word] has appeared. He's ugly, I can't stand him, but he supports me. This year he bought me a jacket. He supports me, and so things are a little bit easier for me. For one thing, I feel like a woman. The first thing he bought me were these rings—see?—little silver rings. They're inexpensive, they only cost kopecks, but I would never allow myself even such things. And he gave me this cross. I also wouldn't have let myself get one, it's also silver. I had a tin cross that hung on a cord. And now, see, I have a silver one.

> For three years he's taken me to the south.... And I don't pay a penny for this. I do it all at his expense. So ... I pretend that I love him, that he pleases me. It seems that he is honest with me, he treats me well, he's good to me, and I'm hypocritical, I don't love him. He's just, I don't know, not to my taste.... I myself am a very passionate, energetic, strong person and, it seems to me, a very good person... You know, I throw myself into things.... I'm like a tigress.... I would have gotten rid of this guy a long time ago except for being able to have a spare piece of bread. What can I do?

In contrast, she seems sincerely to value her female friends and the time they spend together.

> My friends and I get together and sing songs. We sing really well.... All my friends—forgive my lack of modesty; modesty will never kill me—they all love me. I tell you... I draw people to me, everyone loves me. Every holiday, every birthday is celebrated at my place. The eighth of March, International Woman's Day, is at my place; Easter is at my place. Only New Year's Eve is with their families, but the First is with me. [Feodosia]

The other woman who was poor as a child has fared much better, having received a university education and eventually a doctorate. She was able to acquire this education and escape from poverty thanks to a combination of talent and government policy.

> In school a very important event occurred: my voice was discovered, a gift from God. In truth, I sang really beautifully.... Unfortunately, it didn't last long, my voice began to change and [my gift] disappeared. But in school they noticed my voice while I was in first grade and the director of the school, knowing my situation, began to hunt for a place for me.
>
> The Moscow and Leningrad conservatories had musical boarding schools for children and she really wanted me to go there, but it was very difficult to get admitted. Happily, there was also a special children's home in Yaroslavl, an orphanage for gifted children. They brought talented orphans from all over the Soviet Union there. In the children's home there were two departments, one for musicians and one for artists. I began to study music and played the piano. We had many courses, including choir and ballet. I was there nine years....That home saved me and taught me a lot. [Sofia]

Despite all she has achieved, this woman considers herself not to have made it into the middle class, a category she denies exists yet in Russia. Objective indicators of her actual financial situation today are mixed. On the one hand, she and her husband have been able to afford some international travel, including a two-week trip to China at the end of 2012. On the other hand, they tend to be very frugal. Although they own two cars, at the time I arrived in Yaroslavl both vehicles were extremely old and in poor shape. They acquired one, a foreign make from the mid-1980s, from friends who were emigrating and needed to dispose of it. I didn't learn the provenance of the other, a Russian model, but it was perhaps the most decrepit vehicle I have ever ridden in, despite a lot of experience riding in private "taxis" in South America. At some point during my stay, the couple replaced this latter vehicle with one considerably newer, although still used, a purchase that was clearly a matter of great importance in their lives.

These two women who spoke of childhood poverty were the harshest critics of the government—both Soviet and post-Soviet—I encountered, although the nature of their dissatisfaction was quite different, with one focusing on economic complaints and the other on political ones. The first blames the government for having ignored her plight, and for not adequately rewarding her hard work and sacrifices. After telling a rather garbled account of how her daughter lost her apartment, apparently the victim of an unscrupulous family member and the sort of privatization scam so common in the early post-Soviet period, she continued:

> This is why I am so offended by the government…. People like me, children of the war, we grew up, we lived after the war and during the war with nothing …
>
> [My children] very much love their homeland. My son has had many opportunities to leave for France, or even go to America. He knows English perfectly. But he says that nowhere is better than Russia. I disagree with my son in this regard… If they invited me, I'd trade Russia for dollars—I'm speaking honestly about this—so that I could have a worthwhile old age. I would leave Russia. I'd sell Russia, along with Putin. It's a bad trait, but I don't hide it. I want a satisfying, good life, I don't want to walk around in a single pair of socks. I don't want to wash my panties at night and in the morning take them from the line and put them on still damp. I don't want that. I'm fed up going around only in rags, I don't want this. [Feodosia]

For the other woman, raised in a children's home and grateful for the education she received, professionally accomplished and relatively secure economically, the failures of the Soviet and post-Soviet government were primarily political and cultural. Over the course of many conversations (only one of which, and not the most interesting, was recorded), I learned of her gradual disenchantment with the Soviet system, her excitement and optimism in the early days of *glasnost* and democratization, and her deep disappointment with the direction the country was taking in the fall of 2012. Her concerns focused on human rights, civil liberties, freedom of thought, freedom of religion, intercultural tolerance. Although she made it clear that her family was not affluent, she said little about either personal or national economic difficulties and seemed less angry about post-Soviet economic inequality than many of the women I spoke to, perhaps because her own relative position was considerably higher than it had been in her childhood.

## The Middle

Despite Sofia's assertion that she was acquainted with no one who had attained a middle-class lifestyle, almost all of those I spoke to effectively presented themselves as falling somewhere within a broad middle range of the Russian income distribution. Although I never asked anyone directly about family income, several of the women made a point of telling me that they personally had suffered far less during the transition than "many people," thus carefully distinguishing themselves from the poor as well as from the New Russians. With the exception of Feodosia, whose story is highlighted in the preceding section, even those who spoke openly about how hard the early 1990s were for them and their families made it clear that life had become much easier since then. This suggests that they still saw economic well-being as correlated with personal merit and socially productive work and the undeserving New Russians as an unfortunate aberration.

Certainly most of my respondents would have considered themselves part of the middle class during the Soviet period.[4] They would have earned this designation by their status as members of the "mass intelligentsia," which consisted of those working as teachers, doctors, journalists, engineers, and cultural workers (Shlapentokh 1999: 1171; Silverman and Yanowitch 1997: 52–53). This mass intelligentsia, as Patico (2008) and others have argued, struggled during the 1990s to make sense of their new position in society. Not only had they lost their ability to live in relative comfort—which, as noted above, carried the moral implication that they might no longer be seen as performing socially productive labor—their contribution to society was *in fact*

[4]Shlapentokh cites VTsIOM (Russian Center for Public Opinion Research) data indicating that some 43% of the Soviet population identified themselves as middle class (1999: 1171). In fact, even the woman who bemoaned her poverty at length to me initially said she came from a middle-class family (*iz srednezazhitochnoi sem'i*) before saying, "even a poor one."

perceived as significantly less valuable by at least certain segments of the population. When the underlying norms and values of a society are being overturned, the role of the intelligentsia in imparting those values to the masses—and, in particular, the role of teachers in imparting them to young people—is called into question (Lane 1985: 270; Patico 2008: 14). In the early 1990s, not only was it unclear what norms and values should be transmitted, it was also unclear what skills it would be most useful to acquire. As several of my respondents mentioned with sorrow, their children had deliberately turned away from acquiring the kind of education that had been an important marker of membership in the Soviet intelligentsia.

Data on the share of various social groups living in poverty or extreme poverty in 1993 suggest that the mass intelligentsia was doing only marginally better than skilled workers and considerably worse than those in state administration. Overall, 10% of the population were characterized as extremely poor (with a monthly income of less than half of the subsistence minimum) and another 32% were considered poor, while for the mass intelligentsia the corresponding figures were 9 and 40% (Silverman and Yanowitch 1997: 52). Nonetheless, most of my respondents stressed that, however difficult they may have found life during the period of perestroika and transition, they were never actually poor. For some of the women, this was probably an objective description of their circumstances. When a woman said, "I can't complain. We were lucky. My husband earned well, he was head of a department," friends who were present confirmed the statement.

For others, however, my sense is that the same internal attribution was at work here as when talking about wage arrears (see Chapter 4). If one were poor, even at a time when the economy had collapsed and all the old social structures were disappearing, it was somehow a reflection on one's own intelligence, effort and capabilities. Thus, the women were apt to describe their situation in the early 1990s in language like the following.

> I can't say that we considered ourselves poor. No, we lived in a normal apartment. As much as possible I tried to feed my family; as much as possible, we dressed ourselves. [Zoya, 52]

> I wouldn't say that we began to live very poorly, but in general we didn't live well. We all had small wages. …The intelligentsia in Russia has always been a class which no one paid attention to. And, in general, we lived then the way we have continued to live… [My husband and I didn't need to moonlight.] It wasn't that we were completely without money, completely without anything. We received money nonetheless. We never lived luxuriously, so it wasn't hard for us to survive this situation. We got used to it. [Regina, 61]

Just as they attributed the wealth of the New Russians to behavior that violated social norms—they were "bandits" who "pilfered" and "received it not by earning it but by stealing it"—so they stressed that their own appropriate behavior—frugality, ingenuity, levelheadedness, lack of materialism—allowed them to get by even when things were at their worst.

## Axes of Inequality

Wealth acquired through corruption or theft and poverty arising from alcoholism or moral weakness were recurring themes in my conversations with these women. Other possible explanations for economic inequality—gender, ethnicity, disability—were largely ignored in this context, as were other kinds of inequality. Because I generally let my respondents steer the conversation, it would be wrong to conclude that they were unaware of these issues, or had no opinions about them, but they did not in general choose to highlight them when we spoke.

### Gender

There was considerable discussion of the differences between men and women in their ability to adapt to the economic and social changes of the 1990s, but almost nothing about gender when we talked about economic inequality. Based on the frequent assertions that men were less willing than women to work at jobs they considered demeaning or unsuited to their education and experience, one might expect the women to have fared better economically than the men, since even low wages from a demeaning job are larger than no wages at all. Instead, the relative wages of women in Russia declined after the dissolution of the Soviet Union.

According to Elizabeth Brainerd, the mean female wage rate fell from 80.3% of the mean male wage rate "pre-reform" to only 67.9% "post-reform" (2000: 148). Brainerd's findings nonetheless may help to explain the women's silence on the topic. She argues that women earned less relative to men than they had in the Soviet period not because of an increase in gender-specific differences in pay for comparable jobs, but because the difference in wages between the highest-paid and lowest-paid jobs increased dramatically. Those filling the jobs at the upper end of the wage distribution tended to be men, those filling jobs at the lower end tended to be women. As the distance between top and bottom widened, women's relative position deteriorated, but did so in a way that was less noticeable than had they been paid less than someone else performing the same job.

At the same time, women were less likely than men to have occupied the kinds of position that made it possible to appropriate state property for personal benefit during both spontaneous and official privatization. Certainly when my respondents spoke of the New Russians, condemning both the way they had acquired their wealth and what they chose to do with it, they spoke only about the men. Not only was there no mention of any female acquiring undue wealth herself, there was no mention of the behavior of the wives, mistresses or daughters of the men who had done so.[5] One woman did suggest that the greed of some women was responsible for the breakup of families, but she was clearly speaking of those who had not become wealthy.

If the rich were portrayed as exclusively male, the poor the women spoke of were female. They told me stories about women struggling to care for themselves and their children after the death or departure of a husband.

[5]This was not true of the schoolteachers Patico talked to, many of whom spoke at length about the empty lives of the "sit-at-home" wives of wealthy men (2008: 157–162).

> Her dad died when she was 10 and her Mom somehow lost it and began to drink, and this girl didn't see [our] kind of family, you understand? After the death of her husband the mother went out of her mind, probably. [Zoya, 52]

> This family had such a tragic, terrible fate. …The father was a businessman, and the family lived very well. They were prosperous. And then suddenly the father was killed by falling ice. A huge icicle fell from a roof and pierced his head. He died immediately… Then, the daughter's husband abandoned her; she could not endure this and committed suicide. They left a little son. And the mother almost killed herself too, but her friends somehow collected money and bought a small shop of some kind for her, so she'd have some income. [Valentina, age not given]

Although the speakers did not draw the connection explicitly, these stories offer further evidence of the state's failure to provide for women attempting to raise children in the early 1990s. It was the woman's friends, not the state, who made it possible for her to "have some income." For my respondents, it was the children's situation that made the stories important.

## Disability

For Soviet citizens, not only the poor but also the disabled were generally viewed as "other" and kept at a distance, and the topic of disability came up very rarely in my conversations. Only three women mentioned it at all, and in two cases it was to refer to government disability benefits received by a family member after a stroke made holding a job impossible. The third case was a striking exception: for the entire two hours of our conversation, disability was the central topic. The woman was as impressive as the topic was unusual and her story offers both a sense of how Russia has dealt with the disabled and an illustration of entrepreneurial ability in the not-for-profit sphere.

The Soviet approach to children born with physical or mental disability was to institutionalize them. To some extent, this can be seen as simply part of the working mother gender contract, since raising children with special needs, likely to be challenging in any case, would have been even more difficult given Soviet housing conditions and the inadequate quantity and quality of consumer goods and services.

By taking over total responsibility for these children, the state freed their mothers to participate more fully in the paid labor force.

At the same time, institutionalizing those with disabilities was consistent with Soviet ideology. Because an individual's value was seen as depending above all on the contribution he or she could make to society, those who were "invalid" or "disabled"—thereby incapable of performing socially productive labor—were not considered valuable. Furthermore, the existence of these individuals challenged the narrative of the Soviet state's ability to overcome all problems, so they were generally hidden away and, as much as possible, forgotten (Phillips 2011: 49–62).

> Care in [these institutions for the elderly and disabled] was framed as a right accorded to vulnerable citizens by the generous Soviet state, and the collective care of disabled persons in institutions designed especially for that purpose was considered optimal for their quality of life. (Phillips: 62)

A post-Soviet newspaper description of a school for the disabled in Yaroslavl challenges the idea that this approach was "optimal."

> Children don't end up [at Special school N.] voluntarily, of course. Diseases, bad heredity, poor social and living conditions, and a diagnosis of mental retardation lead them to these small classes, where they study under a special curriculum. Seventeen-year-old graduates leave the secondary school with the knowledge of a sixth-grader. Let us add that to be a student in such a school means losing all hope of a normal life after graduating…. It was good if you had parents, or more accurately, if you had healthy and sober parents, but of course for many of the youth it wasn't like that. (*Sem'ia* 1993: 7)

It was in that special school that the woman profiled in this section spent her early career as a teacher. She resisted using the terminology of disability, just as she resisted the common attitude toward the students and the common belief about their limited capabilities.

> At first, I … taught Russian language and literature in a school where children with problems studied. That's how I refer to them, so as not to insult them. I don't like to use the word "invalid" because it limits their possibilities.

> The caregivers there receive bonuses because they work with such children, right? The children have to attend school, like the one I worked in. And the teachers receive bonuses, too, but they don't do anything with the children. You know why? Because they never ask themselves whether a child will enter an institute or not. [Valentina, age not given]

That is, the teachers did not expect the children to continue their education after leaving that school or to become self-supporting. Valentina chose to fight against this norm, first at the school, where she introduced innovative approaches to teaching, and later, when the administration at the school chose not to support her efforts, at a facility she ran to serve the school's graduates. She proved to be a remarkable entrepreneur, drawing on her energy and creativity to bring her vision to fruition against great odds.[6] For more than ten years, she taught students with disabilities that included cerebral palsy, Down's syndrome, and incompletely formed limbs. In all, she estimated that she worked with more than 100 children and adolescents at her facility.

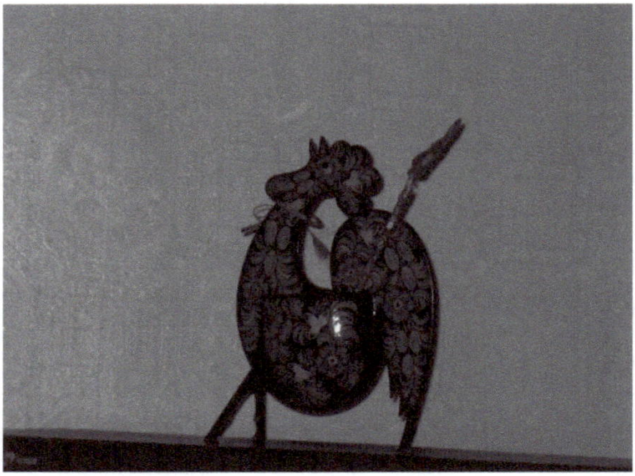

[6]While there is no question that this woman was the driving force behind the success of the initiative, some of the details about its operation—such as the extent to which the government was involved—were unclear and there were some inconsistencies in her recollections. The most striking inconsistency is that she claimed never to have received a salary for her work, but later said the government justified its decision to close the place by saying it could not afford to keep paying her.

Although she was not the only person in Russia carrying out such work—in the 1990s special schools for the disabled had begun to be established (Dunn 2000: 163)—her approach was definitely rare.[7] In her classroom and later at her workshop, the students learned carpentry and decorative arts and put these skills to use producing impressive examples of traditional Russian folk art. Among the many things they learned to make were painted benches, wishing wells, rooster figures, dishes, musical instruments, toys, and samovars. They displayed their handiwork at exhibits throughout the city and offered them for sale at their own shop, the proceeds of which helped to finance the workshop.

The students also helped out by doing daily chores. They learned to prepare food, to clean up afterwards and to perform basic janitorial work. This was necessary, since Valentina had no means to pay others to do these jobs; it was also part of her approach to teaching, since she wanted to ensure that her students could survive on their own. Another part of her pedagogy was what she referred to as a "backwards approach."

> You see, they are like this.... If you read them something, they will not absorb it. But [it is different] if they are working with their hands and turn to me and ask me, 'I don't know this'... and I say, 'Go here, find such and such a book, open it and there you'll find what it is written down.' That is, [I took] a reverse approach, and with this reverse approach they studied history. They painted and saw how many crafts we have scattered all over the country. [They learned] that, let's say, *khokhloma* developed in one place and *gorodets*[8] in another place and why they developed there in particular. When visitors came to visit us, [the students] were like tour guides; they explained everything. They liked it so much that they knew it, that's all it was. And in this way they studied geography, history, and also the Russian language.

---

[7]Dunn cites a 1993 interview in which the deputy minister of social protection described the more typical situation, in which the sort of make-work activities that counted as employment for the disabled "only enhance[d] their sense of hopelessness" (2000: 164).

[8]These refer to two different folk styles of painting wooden objects.

She and her husband also took the students on field trips, giving them the opportunity for new experiences.

> My husband and I even took them on a hike. They could not carry backpacks, so we took them to the upper reaches of some river on boats; we took rubber boats, and we descended. We did not have to carry anything, and we stopped wherever we wanted. That is, some place to eat, to sleep; we camped out and then we went further. And we made it to a bus and rode back home. We went somewhere for a week. It was a lot of fun for them.

She brought the same creativity to bear on keeping the school running on almost no money at all. Initially they were allowed free use of the second floor of a building occupied by an organization devoted to restoration work; later the mayor offered them a better location.

> Of course, they could have shut me down any day. Why? Because I had no sink, no toilet in this workshop. We were on the second floor in the building, which was given to us by [this agency] for free, and we went down to the first floor to use the toilet… We just brought water up from [the first floor]…. We had a few basins and in one we would cook, and in a second wash the dishes and in the third rinse everything to be clean. I was afraid that someone would get poisoned and then they would close it, but that didn't happen.

To get the raw materials for her students to work with, she appealed to local businesses and government offices.

> The machines, the furniture, the tables? Do you know how I did it? I went to some organization, or rather to either the city or regional administration and I asked for furniture they'd written off, so they gave me tables and chairs. Let's say, [if they gave me] an old sideboard…we would make a blackboard out of it….
>
> All the wood we worked with? I never spent a kopeck on it in 10 years…. I'd go to a factory, and there would be a carpenter and there'd be a lot of scrap to burn, so it was best to give it to us, right? We were given

> both plywood and veneer, and different kinds of wood, in general whatever anyone had. The restoration organization helped a lot with paints. [The students] could work only with water-based paints, because they all had different diseases, different allergies, and so on. And the smell would be strong. The only thing we had that had fumes was the varnish; [everything had to be] covered with varnish. But one of the parents made us a small, separate space and made a hood for us, where we painted. When we painted, we turned it on. We made a hood above the stove…so there were no fumes.

Sadly, the undertaking ultimately closed, despite having received international recognition and considerable positive coverage in the local press.[9] Although the official explanation was that it was too expensive, Valentina herself attributes the decision by the regional government to close the place in 1999 to the jealousy of a government official who had long been in love with Valentina's husband. I had no way to corroborate this suspicion, although she did say that the protest was so great when the place was closed that the mayor of the city stepped forward and asked her to re-open it as a project of the city government. (It was originally under the auspices of the regional government.) By this time, she was exhausted, discouraged, and ill with cancer, and she decided against accepting the offer.

That it was a remarkable undertaking and made a great difference in the lives of these young people and their families was clear from the many letters she had received from all over the world praising what she was doing, as well as from local news articles. In the words of one such article:

> The state enterprise 'Larets' does not pride itself on the fact…that it gives work to young people with limited possibilities, but rather on the fact that it expands those possibilities, returning to society healthy and creative people.…It is striking that after three to four years working here, many of the young people are able to put aside their disability. They

[9]In her scrapbook are articles with titles like "A School for One's Entire Life," "Children with Golden Hands," "Like a Fairy Tale" and "They Can Do a Lot; They Just Need Some Help."

> acquire a specialization; they start a family; they lead a normal live, and a few even go into business. (Petrenko 2003)

Valentina herself expressed it this way:

> When they came to me, their parents would…sigh, 'They are all of them vampires; they're all handicapped; they only care for themselves and they think that everyone owes them. They're unhappy and everyone has to help them'…. And when they came to me, I said not a word about their disability. I was alone, right, without any cleaning lady, but you can see in this photo how everything is tidy and clean, right? Here when they went to the toilet…I'd say, 'You cannot leave the toilet until you've cleaned up. How you do it is up to you.' Today many of their parents have died, but I taught them how to cook, how to look after themselves. They can now live independently… And they have at least a little money. They continue to draw. Some of them draw, go to the market and sell [their work].

## Conclusion

While economic inequality existed in the Soviet Union, as a result of both labor policy and differences in the level of economic development in the various republics, it was neither particularly pronounced nor particularly visible. The lessons absorbed by Soviet children were that extreme inequality was one of the great ills of capitalism, that all citizens were entitled to the basic necessities, and that further financial reward and access to consumer goods should reflect the value of one's contribution to society. In the early years it was the contributions of industrial workers that were most heralded. By the time the women I spoke to were growing up, the country had developed and modernized to the point where the contributions of well-educated professionals were being recognized as significant.

These lessons had clearly been internalized by my respondents. In the fall of 2012, they continued to consider it important to tell me that they had not been poor even during the most difficult years. They also continued to feel angry at both the oligarchs and the leaders who had allowed the oligarchs to acquire enormous wealth. Several of the women insisted that the impetus not only for privatization but for the entire attempted economic transition had been the reformers' desire to appropriate the wealth of the state for themselves. Although, as we saw in Chapter 7, many of the women managed over time to find new and interesting ways of benefitting from the greater array of economic opportunities that opened up after 1991, most continued to view those responsible for the economic policies that replaced the Soviet system with anger and contempt.

## References

Brainerd, Elizabeth. 2000. Women in Transition: Changes in Gender Wage Differentials in Eastern Europe and the Former Soviet Union. *ILR Review* 54 (1): 138–162.

Cook, Linda J. 1993. *The Soviet Social Contract and Why It Failed*. Cambridge, MA: Harvard University Press.

Dunn, Ethel. 2000. The Disabled in Russia in the 1990s. In *Russia's Torn Safety Nets: Health and Social Welfare during the Transition*, ed. Mark G. Fielf and Judyth L. Twigg, 153–171. New York: St. Martin's Press.

Dyker, David A. 1984. Planning and the Worker. In *The Soviet Worker: From Lenin to Andropov*, 2nd ed., ed. Leonard Schapiro and Joseph Godson, 39–76. New York: St. Martin's Press.

Federal State Statistics Service. 2016. *Russia in Figures 2016*. Accessed online at http://www.gks.ru/free_doc/doc_2016/rusfig/rus16e.pdf. August 2017.

Humphrey, Caroline. 2002. *The Unmaking of Soviet Life: Everyday Economies After Socialism*. Ithaca, NY: Cornell University.

Klugman, Jeni, and Jeanine Braithwaite. 1998. Poverty in Russia During the Transition: An Overview. *World Bank Research Observer* 13 (1): 37–58.

Lane, David. 1985. *Soviet Economy & Society*. Washington Square, NY: New York University Press.

Novokmet, Filip, Thomas Piketty, and Gabriel Zucman. 2017. From Soviets to Oligarchs: Inequality and Property in Russia, 1905–2016. *VOX CEPR Policy Portal*. Accessed online at https://voxeu.org/article/inequality-and-property-russia-1905-2016. March 2019.

Patico, Jennifer. 2008. *Consumption and Social Change in a Post-Soviet Middle Class*. Washington, DC: Woodrow Wilson Center Press.

Pesman, Dale. 2000. *Russia and Soul: An Exploration*. Ithaca, NY: Cornell University Press.

Petrenko, A. 2003. Volshebnyi Larets [The Magic Box]. *Gorodskie novosti* [City News] (22).

Phillips, Sarah D. 2011. *Disability and Mobile Citizenship in Postsocialist Ukraine*. Bloomington, IN: Indiana University Press.

Sampson, Steven L. 1987. The Second Economy of the Soviet Union and Eastern Europe. *The Annals of the American Academy of Political and Social Science* 493 (September): 120–136.

*Sem'ia* [*Family*]. 1993. Uchitel' otverzhennykh [Teacher of Outcasts]. August 16–22, 7.

Sergeyev, Boris. 2001. Linking the Personal to the National: The Status of Political Trust in Yaroslavl. In *Regional Russia in Transition*, ed. Jeffrey Hahn, 115–137. Washington, DC: Woodrow Wilson Center Press.

Shlapentokh, Vladimir. 1999. Social Inequality in Post-Communist Russia: The Attitudes of the Political Elite and the Masses (1991–1998). *Europe-Asia Studies* 51 (7): 1167–1181.

Shorrocks, Anthony, and Stanislav Kolenikov. 2000. *Poverty Trends in Russia During the Transition*. Accessed online at http://dev3.cepr.org/meets/wkcn/7/745/papers/shorrocks.pdf. September 2014.

Silverman, Bertram, and Murray Yanowitch. 1997. *New Rich, New Poor, New Russia: Winners and Losers on the Russian Road to Capitalism*. Armonk, NY: M.E. Sharpe.

World Bank. Russian Federation Country Profile. Accessed online at http://data.worldbank.org/country/russian-federation. September 2014.

# 10

# Dissolution of a Multinational Empire: Migration Flows and Ethnic Relations

## Introduction

Along with the collapse of the Soviet economic and political system in the late 1980s came deep cracks in the official narrative of a happy multinational union where all lived and worked in harmony. At the time of the Bolshevik Revolution in 1917, Russia was a vast empire, stretching from Eastern Europe across Asia to the Pacific Ocean. Some of the land was populated by nomadic tribes, such as the sheepherders of Central Asia and the reindeer herders of the Far North. Other regions, like Armenia and Georgia in the Caucasus, had a well-established literary, religious and artistic tradition and a strong sense of national identity at the time they were absorbed into the Russian Empire. To address the multinational character of the country, with its more than one hundred ethno-linguistic groups, Soviet leaders adopted a policy of "national in form, socialist in content," deliberately encouraging the development of written local languages and the expression of folk culture while exercising central control over the political and economic spheres. They also created political units—ranging from the fifteen union republics down to small autonomous oblasts within the



J. McKinney, *Russian Women and the End of Soviet Socialism*,
https://doi.org/10.1007/978-3-030-16226-9_10

republics—which were named for a national group living in the area. As has been true with the drawing of political borders everywhere, these units did not (and indeed could not) correspond perfectly to the distribution of the population by national or ethnic identity. As Robert Strayer has put it, "Enshrining nationality as a principle automatically created 'minorities'…in each of [the] constituent republics (1998: 73)."

As time went on, the ethnic homogeneity of the union republics was further diluted by Soviet colonization and modernization policies. Russians were assigned to other republics to assist in economic development, participate in local administration, and serve in the military. It was standard for the First Secretary of the Communist Party of each republic to be a member of the titular nationality, while the Second Secretary, generally responsible for personnel decisions and thus a person of considerable power, was Russian. It was also standard for young men to perform military service in parts of the Soviet Union distant from their native republic, presumably to reduce the likelihood that they would side with the local population against the central authorities if there were ever a conflict (Tsypkin 1988: 107). At the same time, there was some movement from the other union republics into Russia, as many non-Russian Soviet citizens aspired to receive their education at major Russian universities and pursue their careers in major Russian cities.

By the time of the dissolution in 1991, there were therefore a significant number of Soviet citizens living outside of their national "home" republic, and for the first several years after the breakup there were sizeable migration flows among the former republics. The largest of these flows was into the Russian Federation: between 1991 and 1998, of the approximately 25 million ethnic Russians who had been living in other parts of the Former Soviet Union (FSU), over 3 million settled in Russia (Nozhenko 2010: 3).[1] The re-sorting of populations by nationality has remained incomplete, however, in part due to Russian government policy.

[1]Flynn, citing the International Organization of Migration, says that by 2001 estimates put the number of arrivals (that is, gross in-migration) at 8–10 million, of whom about 1.5 million were officially registered as 'forced migrants' or 'refugees' (2004: 1).

Although initially Yeltsin had offered to accept all Russians who wanted to return "home" (Sakwa 2002: 311), by the mid-1990s the government's position had changed. Moya Flynn, in her study of migrant resettlement in the Russian Federation, argues that the policy shift reflected the desire to discourage resettlement and ensure the continued existence of significant numbers of Russians in the former republics (2004: 45). This change in policy had two potential benefits. First, it reduced the costs of absorbing those who moved to Russia—providing housing, medical care, education, and jobs—at a time when the government was already struggling to meet the needs of the resident population.[2] Second, it provided political justification for continuing to treat the "near abroad"—the standard phrase used by the Russian government to refer to the former Soviet republics—as a critical part of Russia's sphere of influence.

## "We Were Afraid"

Several of the ethnically Russian women I spoke to had returned to Russia from other republics before the Soviet Union dissolved, when the move did not involve crossing national borders and was not seen as especially significant. These women mentioned their relocation casually, as a part of their career history. Their stays in the other republics had generally lasted only a few years and were often associated with the military service of husband or father. Although these women sometimes talked about experiences with different climates or food, they did not highlight—or even mention—the fact that the populations of these former republics were of a different nationality.

For those who returned to Russia in the late 1980s or early 1990s, the story was very different. By that time, Gorbachev's reforms of democratization and *glasnost* had unintentionally created opportunities for the expression of nationalism in the non-Russian republics.

[2]Government estimates put the cost of "properly accomodat[ing] each new migrant" at 17,000 USD (Burke 2000: 225).

With the freer expression of national identity and increasing demands for national control came growing ethnic tension. As illustrated by the experiences of a woman who moved to Uzbekistan in 1988 and stayed for two years, life for outsiders became more difficult. Employment became less secure, as calls came for requiring fluency in the local language, and there was fear of ethnic violence.

> I set out for Tashkent really in search of the exotic. After all, this was Asia and I didn't have any friends or even acquaintances there.... I took the step and I don't regret it, I absolutely don't regret it.... I lived there for two years. It was really a fine time, one of the happiest times of my life.... I moved back because of politics. When it was a single government, you understand, priority was given—not necessarily fairly in my opinion, but nonetheless—to the Russian language.... Tashkent—that's the capital of Uzbekistan—it was as if it had been forcibly Russified, even though the language is Uzbek. Tashkent was unique.... There wasn't a single other city [I knew] with such a number of nationalities, who lived amicably, who existed peacefully, without any conflicts—Greeks, Jews, Koreans, Russians, Ukrainians, Belarusians, Poles, Germans—there was a very big German diaspora—Uzbeks, Tadzhiks, Kazakhs, Tatars. It was such a melting pot, you understand, a great big pot, which boiled energetically and very tastily.
>
> Then, when throughout the whole Soviet Union, in all the republics, the national motive was given priority, the situation started to change for the worse. In the [aviation plant] where I worked, for example, they began to compel us...to take exams on our knowledge of the Uzbek language. And the thing is that by itself the Uzbek language...is very primitive, in the sense that it doesn't have the technical terms for building an airplane, blueprints. That is, this is technical terminology and to take Russian terms and make them Uzbek seems to me to make no sense.
>
> And then the national front intensified. There was an incident that sharply turned my consciousness toward taking the decision to go back to Russia. My future husband and I went for a walk through the old town, the old district of Tashkent. Coming out of the subway, when we climbed onto the bridge we saw a demonstration of a very, very large number of people, mostly Uzbeks. They had a National Front, called Birlik.

> And you know, that this chaos, this aggression, [there are] people from whom comes only aggression.... It's like a tsunami, that would destroy everything, everything that comes its way.... I was very scared for my own life. [Renata, 45]

Difficult though this may have been, the challenges were even greater for a woman who migrated from Azerbaijan as a young girl. Her family had lived there for decades and it was the only home she had known. She seemed unaware that some of what she described as an indication of how fully her family belonged there—such as the nice housing they received—could have sparked resentment among the local population.

> And during perestroika, in the 90s, they kicked [us] out, as if they thought [Russia] was a foreign government.... Those years, the first half of the 90s, were, of course, the most difficult and the most hurtful, both for my family and for our friends, the most annoying, because people [like us] who...still considered themselves *Soviet* citizens...weren't [seen as] necessary, either in the republics or in Russia.

> We had a home that had been built by the Caspian Flotilla. That is, in the Soviet period, in the '60s, they gave [housing] to people who, we could say, deserved it. That is, engineers, ship captains, the top staff. And 70-80 percent [of the recipients] were not Azerbaijanis; they were Russians, Jews.... [In] the building where we lived, [the residents] had been almost all Russian....

> We were afraid...There were a few years when there was the National Front. Beginning in 1989, very strong nationalism developed. Besides, it was hard...due to the broken economic situation.... All the [economic] interaction [among the Soviet republics] was broken.... Whatever was in the republic, that's what there was.[3] Already there was nothing from outside, so it was very hard. Even in terms of food, because there wasn't

[3]As output fell in the early 1990s and serious shortages developed, not only entire republics but individual regions and even some cities began to enact measures requiring those making purchases to show proof of residence.

bread, because there was the Karabakh crisis.[4] Russia didn't help, because it was already a separate country…

These were the most terrible days, because there was a curfew, one was forbidden to go out—I can't remember between what hour in the evening and what hour in the morning. There was a curfew. They could simply take you to the police. And since nationalism was so strongly developed, it was simply a mess. They could pick you up, beat you, do this because when there is a mess, anarchy flourishes. Those police officers, who were just young boys, nationalists, they could do anything they wanted. [Oksana, 31]

Both this woman and one who had lived in Estonia from 1982 to 1994 described at length the ways in which the decision to make Russians unwelcome has hurt the economies of the former republics. The woman from Estonia noted the sharp contrast between the Estonians' jubilation in the early 1990s and the struggles she claimed they were experiencing in 2012. She pointed to the lack of fuel with which to keep farm equipment running, the closing of enterprises, the need for young people to leave the country because no jobs were available, and the elimination of cargo trains and regular bus service between the capital, Tallinn, and Moscow. In Azerbaijan, I was told, the leaders were trying to undo some of the damage by inviting foreigners back into the country to increase the supply of educated labor. Although it was never stated explicitly, I received the distinct impression that both women derived some satisfaction from seeing that the departure of the Russians had imposed costs not only on those forced to leave but also on the new nations that had made them feel unwelcome.

Now, our friends [in Azerbaijan] say, that if [you want] a good doctor—where one used to go to the Russian doctors or the Jewish, now one goes

[4]As nationalist sentiments strengthened during the end of the Soviet period, a separatist movement began in the area of Nagorno-Karabakh. This region, which lies within the borders of Azerbaijan, has a majority Armenian population, and both republics (now countries) claimed the area as their own. Despite Oksana's comment that Russia didn't help, the Russian government did assist in the negotiation of a ceasefire in 1994. The underlying issue, however, remains unresolved (BBC News 2016).

> to the Turks. The Turks have replaced this niche of qualified personnel even in the fleet and in the extraction of oil.... [The Azerbaijani] do have their own experts, but they also attract foreigners, they attract them from Turkey, from Iran. That is, their own young generation [of experts] is developing.... They are just beginning to educate their own generation.... Some specialists come from America with their companies, they come from Germany, they come from Turkey to work in Baku because, let's put it this way, it's not easy to find such personnel from the local population. This is why Russians are now valued, because more often than not the Russians who are left are the more educated people, from the educated families, from the supervisors.... They say that in Azerbaijan only 50,000 Russians are left and in the country there are 8 million people in all .... Now they value [Russians] because almost all the educated people left—almost all the doctors, engineers...because they were Russian, Jewish....They almost all left. [Oksana]

## Not Welcome Anywhere

Sadly, the Russians who left the newly independent states in the early 1990s because they no longer felt welcome there often felt unwelcome in Russia as well. As immigrants, despite their ethnicity, they tended to be viewed as outsiders competing with locals for jobs and perhaps for government assistance. In her study of migrants to Saratov, Samara and Novosibirsk, Moya Flynn quotes the following poignant observation by one respondent: "It seems to them that we take their work, their money...We are like competitors for life (2004: 136)." Flynn also offers multiple illustrations of the way ethnically Russian immigrants characterized the local population's view that they were not "truly" Russian: for example, "I am Russian (*russkaia*), my husband is Russian (*russkii*), but everyone treats me as a Kazak (*Kazashka*) at work; if you are from Kazakstan [to them] it means you are a Kazak (2004: 137)."

The sense of being resented was not the only downside to migrating to Russia. The young woman from Azerbaijan spoke at length about the culture shock and feelings of dislocation she and her mother experienced. I found this ironic, given how frequently I was told by others in Yaroslavl that immigrants from the South (the Caucasus and Central Asia) fail to practice the norms of polite behavior.

The most insulting thing is that when the republics [declared independence], people who grew up [in a non-Russian republic] in the Soviet Union,…as citizens of the Soviet Union, were not seen as necessary either to Russia or [in their home republic]. There they said, "You're Russian, get out!" but in Russia, nobody was waiting, because for several generations during Soviet power [they] had been living [in the home republic]; that's where they have friends, acquaintances, some kind of apartment. Well, everything was arranged, their whole life was there….

It was a bit easier for me…. I was young. I was an adolescent, although that too was hard. When you come and there's a completely different mindset, a completely different order, morals, outlook on life. I was an Eastern girl, and here you either had to learn to stand up for yourself or somehow be an "outsider." [She used the English word.] I learned to be more insolent, because here people's temperament was tougher, [with] obscenities [*mat*] and drunkenness.

In Baku, especially in our circle, it wasn't like this at all. But when we moved here… Well, it's only today, after so many years, that my mother and I and even my grandmother, can to some degree answer for ourselves, stand up for ourselves. But when we moved with this Eastern upbringing in the soul—not even Eastern, but the spirit of Baku, which was always to behave with respect, with calm—when we moved to this harsher environment, this crueler mentality, these ruder people—we had a hard time…. I was the first to adapt somewhat…and in a year I learned how to stand up for myself, to answer…, even to be rude to someone. Before that, I couldn't do it.

In this respect, more than any other, it was hard for me…. In Baku… because the school was a good one…all the Azerbaijanis were from very good, educated, intelligent families. That is, the worst that the boys could do would be pull the pigtails of the girls… And I came here in eighth grade…where already the girls were smoking behind the school, already they were meeting boys…. Girls of fourteen were already sleeping with boys and bragging about it in class…. And my mom wouldn't allow me to wear makeup until the 11$^{th}$ class, to say nothing of what would have happened if I'd smoked! [Oksana, 31]

An interesting variation on this theme of cultural differences was offered by another woman, who spoke approvingly of the impact the influx of a more cultured class of Russian speakers had on the city.

> In my opinion, [Yaroslavl became a better place to live] due to the fact that many refugees started to come to Yaroslavl, bringing with them their cultural delights.... Russian speakers arrived, the bearers of the Russian language, people who as a rule had higher education, that is, a seriously cultured class, an intellectual class and naturally this revived the city somewhat, ...changed the dynamics in a positive way. [Renata, 45]

Even these "seriously cultured" Russian immigrants faced considerable difficulties on arrival. Contributing to these difficulties was a state bureaucracy woefully unprepared to deal with the unprecedented inflows. Prior to the dissolution of the Soviet Union there were neither institutions nor laws in place to govern immigration, and at the time of the break-up the authorities scrambled to develop both. This created enormous challenges for those arriving as well as for those employed by the newly-established Federal Migration Services, challenges exacerbated by the upheaval and uncertainty arising from the pervasive systemic changes and made more painful by the relatively privileged status many, like Oksana's family, had previously enjoyed as Russians in the other republics (Flynn 2004: 37).

It was hard to find housing:

> There was no longer a planned economy, there was a market economy. It was clear that no one anywhere was going to give you an apartment the way [they did] in the Soviet Union. It was necessary to sell there [in Baku] and to buy here [in Yaroslavl]. There it was impossible to sell because they said, 'You're Russian and will leave in any case [regardless of how much you receive for the house].' And ...it wasn't just us, but many people were leaving. They were leaving with nothing; all that they had accumulated over the years was reduced virtually to nothing. It turned out to be a very serious financial plight, because...it was impossible to sell the apartment.... We sold it very, very cheap, and here everything was already expensive because it wasn't just us who came. They came from Central Asia; they came from Chechnya.... In Russia—in general

> throughout Central Russia—everything had become very expensive. If you take the example of my family, we ended up in poorer housing conditions. [Oksana]

It was hard to find employment:

> In the beginning, when we arrived, it turned out again because so many people came that the labor market had changed. There were so many people, the influx of people from different social strata, that is, from different spheres of activity… When my mother went to arrange a job, she was told, 'if [you had come] five years ago, three years ago, we would have had vacancies.' She is a rhythmic gymnastics teacher. She graduated from the Institute of Physical Education and worked in a conservatory as the coach for rhythmic gymnastics. And here she was not in demand, because a huge number of people came and there were five people for every one position. And everyone said that five years ago we had five places for every one person, people were snapped up like hot cakes, it was possible to get better wages, better conditions, closer to home, it was possible to choose. But [when we came] it was just if you found any job, in any school, if you found a job at all, that was good. [Oksana]

Many of the difficulties arose from lack of documents—either because they had been left behind in the hasty flight from ethnic violence or because they could be acquired only with the expenditure of large amounts of both time and money. Lack of documents impeded receiving one's pension, getting a job, finding a place to stay—and even, during the period of greatest shortages, acquiring particularly scarce goods.

> If you come today, you are protected from a legal point of view…. But in the early 1990s nothing had yet been developed, so there were no regularly prepared documents, there was nothing….
>
> Before we came my grandfather didn't receive his pension, and neither did my grandmother, because we took the wrong certificates. They had changed the law and we took the wrong certificates. My grandfather, who was a veteran, didn't receive his pension for half a year and he began to receive it only thanks to the fact that the military archives were here in

> Russia. This [problem] has somehow now disappeared. It's already been 20 years and the countries have somehow passed through the period of the collapse.... It's [now] possible to get certain certificates from Azerbaijan, certain certificates in the archives. But in the 1990s, when we arrived there was such disorder that it was impossible even to find a document...The archives were ruined....
>
> Russian citizenship cost 135 USD.[5] In 1994 it was very expensive to obtain Russian citizenship. And you need to consider not just that it was expensive but that when we left they hadn't paid wages for eight months. Even if it had not been expensive... there was nothing from which to pay. And there were four of us....

Unwilling to wait until they had citizenship and afraid to leave without some sort of documentation, people paid for whatever they could get.

> It wasn't official, there was a fee.... If you wanted to process things quickly then there was a set rate. Again, there was such chaos in the legal rules of registration. It wasn't like now, there wasn't the rule of law, it was impossible to go and complain, it was impossible to write up a complaint and sue. Departure—it was like a bazaar. [You were told] either to pay or to go away. So...people paid. Everyone paid, because they were afraid that they'd be checking at the border.... They put a stamp [on our documents] that we were Russian citizens. [Oksana]

Although these recollections emphasize the challenges of migrating at a time of enormous uncertainty and lack of relevant legislation, laws don't always make things easier. In the words of a woman who recently retired from the migration service:

> Everything has become stricter, you might say, with all these rules for citizenship papers... It seems to me that this policy is correct, because there isn't a single civilized country where a person can just arrive, write a form

---

[5]Although extremely high inflation meant that both wages and exchange rates varied greatly over the course of the year, in 1994 the average monthly wage was 220,400 rubles, very roughly equivalent to USD 110 (Federal'naia sluzhba).

> and receive citizenship within a month. That isn't the case anywhere. Very many people came from the republics, from the Caucasus,[6] very many came…in the 1990s up to 2002, when they could receive citizenship within a month. And if the father came, then the mother would come to join him, then all the children, the grandmothers and grandfathers, the whole family. And only in 2002 did they get around to making new laws on citizenship.
>
> Today in order to obtain citizenship it's necessary to pass an exam on the Russian language. They introduced this, I believe, in 2009. Now to receive citizenship you have to take [this exam]. And Putin has said that beginning in 2013 there will be an exam on the history of Russia, and I just don't know how anyone is going to receive citizenship then. The goal is to prevent an excessively large stream of foreigners who want to receive Russian citizenship. Why Russian citizenship? It's all the social services, which the government provides to Russian citizens—pensions, free medical services. [Zoya, 52]

If things were difficult for those migrating to Russia, they were not much easier for those who, like the woman quoted above, worked for the Russian Migration Services. Trained as a history teacher, she had held a job at a school in Kazakhstan for four years, but when she and her husband returned to Yaroslavl, she was unable to find a teaching job close to home and ended up working at Migration Services until she retired.[7] Ironically, given her profession, her own move from Kazakhstan back to Russia occurred in 1989 and so did not entail crossing a national border.

---

[6]Her emphasis on those from the Caucasus is interesting, since much of that territory lies within the Russian Federation and people from there, including those from Chechnya, should already have had Russian citizenship. Chechnya's attempt to break away from Russia led to two extremely destructive wars, the first from 1994 to 1996 and the second, which began with an invasion by Russia in 1999, until 2009, although Russia reestablished direct rule in May 2000. The intense animosity between Chechens and Russians and the devastation of the local economy prompted many to flee the region. The conflict is also notable because authorizing the 1999 invasion was Putin's first significant act as Prime Minister and may have strengthened Yeltsin's decision to resign as President and appoint Putin as Acting President.

[7]Although she did not mention this, her job with the Migration Service probably gave her higher pay and better benefits than teaching would have. In addition, it gave her the right to an early pension.

Her move also predated most of the political unrest and she explained that she returned "because I missed Yaroslavl, I missed my parents… Not for political reasons, I just wanted to be closer to my family."

The heavy inflow of migrants meant difficult work for the department, made harder by the frequently changing rules and by the anxiety of those the office served.

> What does the Passport-Visa Service do? We receive people dealing with questions of registration, filling out documents, passports, citizenship, the whole process. And when the Soviet Union fell apart very many people began to come to Russia, to return to their historical homeland, because it was hard to live in the former republics. They came here to Russia, they became citizens, they stayed here and then brought their families. I had a lot of work at that time. Because we were… tied to the Ministry of Internal Affairs,[8] we worked just the way the men in the police worked, with no fixed work hours. It wasn't a case of coming to work at 9:00 and leaving at 4:00. It wasn't like that, it was long hours, and what time you would get home from work only God knew…. I'd crawl home in the evening at 7:00, 8:00, 9:00 and along the way you'd still be running to collect one child from the nursery, and at home you'd do lessons with the other or check to see what he'd done, what he hadn't done…. There absolutely wasn't any time….
>
> You [would] go home broken, broken not even from being physically tired but from moral exhaustion. In one day, up to 100 stressed people might come and you have to listen to each of them, you have to explain to each of them, understand them and help them. ….
>
> Every year work got harder…. From 1998 to 2004 there was passport reform. They changed the Soviet passports for Russian ones. Then, beginning in 2002, they changed the citizenship law. If earlier a foreigner could

[8]Although since 2002 the Federal Migration Service has been under the Ministry of Internal Affairs, it was initially an independent organization. Its responsibilities were then shifted into a short-lived Ministry of Federation Affairs, National and Migration Policy before it was reestablished in its current position. It appears that these reorganizations had little impact on the conditions of work.

> come and immediately submit his citizenship documents, now he has to receive permission for temporary residency, receive a residence permit and only after that can he submit citizenship documents. There are so many intermediate steps that have been inserted.... Before they came to find work and, after that, they got a work permit, right? Today only those from Belarus and Kazakhstan can come here to work without a work permit.[9] [People from] all the other states must register for permission to work. This, too, means additional processing of documents.... They don't let us get bored; they don't give us a chance to get bored! [Zoya]

As this discussion of immigration restrictions and regulations makes clear, however difficult ethnic Russians may have found it to (re)assimilate to Russia after years (or a lifetime) spent elsewhere, those of other ethnicities who tried to immigrate faced additional challenges.

## One Big Happy Family?

Many of the non-Russians in Yaroslavl have come relatively recently, escaping conflict, economic hardship, or both. Some come from territories within the Russian Federation—most notably Chechnya and the surrounding area. Others come, often illegally, from former Soviet republics to the south of Russia, responding to deceptive advertising about the attractive working conditions and generous pay that await them. Many who arrive without documents see themselves as temporary migrants, driven by the desire to earn some money but not intending to make a new home. Family members stay in the source country; the migrants concentrate in ethnic enclaves and may make little effort to assimilate.

Several of my respondents criticized this unwillingness or inability to assimilate—couched usually in terms of the immigrants' clinging to "inappropriate" customs, as in "It's fine to shoot off rifles to celebrate

[9]These two countries created the Eurasian Economic Union with Russia in 2010. In 2015, it was expanded to include Armenia and Kyrgyzstan, so presumably people from the latter two are also now exempt from the work permit requirement.

weddings in your own country, but that's not how we behave here." They also complained about a lack of civility and high level of corruption. Although these criticisms were frequently leveled at society more broadly, they were often expressed especially harshly when directed at immigrants. Even while voicing these unflattering opinions of many non-Russian groups, my respondents often expressed regret over the decline in amity among the different nationalities. This is consistent with the findings of a number of Russian sociologists that broad support for ethnic tolerance as an abstraction coexists with a willingness to acknowledge "a *personal* feeling of dislike toward one or several nationalities" (Sikevich 1999: 105, as quoted in Kagarlitsky 2003: 66).

Although most of my respondents focused on the individual failings or lack of culture of the immigrants themselves, one woman clearly blamed changes in government policy. In her mid-forties and younger than many I spoke with, she was one of the most clearly nostalgic for the Soviet era and, perhaps not coincidentally, was the only one to request that I not record her comments, although she was willing for me to take notes and to share what she said. She blamed Gorbachev for what had happened in the country, and offered as an example the situation of non-Russian immigrants: "They used to be people, but now they are slaves." Because the government no longer provides them with an education, she claimed, they are relegated to working as janitors and street sweepers.

Other women shared this speaker's sense that ethnic relations had been better in the Soviet period, although one clearly disagreed, stating bluntly, "The story that the Soviet Union was one big unified family—that was just a fairy tale [Renata, 45]." Many expressed regret at the open friction among ethnic groups, and a few were actively engaged in attempts to bring about better understanding and cooperation. Most of the latter were themselves non-Russians (though not necessarily newcomers) and worked together through the Yaroslavl branch of the Assembly of Peoples of Russia,[10] created in 1999 to serve as an umbrella

[10]Although established by the Russian government, this organization is generally referred to as a "public" or "social" body, part of Russia's civil society.

organization for a large number of groups with ethnic identities. According to its website, in 2011 the Assembly consisted of twenty-two national culture groups and about 100 individuals. It sees its mission as

> ensur[ing] a constructive dialogue between the authorities and the public aimed at improving and harmonizing interethnic relations in the city of Yaroslavl and the region, strengthening mutual understanding and friendship among representatives of all peoples living in our region.... It pays attention to solving social and economic problems of those of different nationalities, protecting citizens from discrimination based on ethnicity, promoting the preservation and development of cultures and languages, disseminating knowledge about the history, traditions, customs of all nationalities, and expanding ethno-cultural interaction among the peoples of the region. (Anr76.ru)

The non-Russian population in the city of Yaroslavl, which according to the 2010 census constituted roughly 8% of the 1.27 million people living in the entire Yaroslavl region, is diverse and includes Greeks, Vietnamese, French, Finns (and a lone American). Slightly less than 1% of those not identifying as Russian are other Slavs, mostly Belarusians and Ukrainians. Of the remainder, the largest groups are Armenians (7158), Azerbaijanis (5327), Tatars (4982), Uzbeks (1397), Gypsies [the census designation] (1348) and Tadzhiks (1219), with a mix of other nationalities from the Caucasus and Central Asia constituting another several thousand (*Vserossiiskaya perepis' 2010*).[11]

According to a 2006 report by a European group focused on combating nationalism and racism, the prevailing image of Yaroslavl was that it was the "most tolerant" region in Russia. While the authors of that report contested the characterization, describing the region as one "in which students [who have] arrived to study from FSU republics of Caucasus and Asia constantly face problems with fellow students

[11]The Soviet internal passport included information about nationality. When the passport was introduced in the 1930s, each citizen simply chose what national identity to enter. Later, nationality was derived from that of one's parents; if they were of different official nationalities, one could choose which to claim. With the 1997 introduction of the Russian internal passport, information about nationality was no longer included. See Simonsen (1999).

and teachers and where natives from Caucasus cannot rent [an] apartment without being humiliated," a later report by the group praises the city for "the extensive work carried out by both the local community and local authorities ... to ensure tolerant interethnic attitudes."[12] Information from the SOVA Center for Information and Analysis, a Moscow-based organization focused on human rights, also suggests a city with relatively little serious ethnic conflict: for the period 1 January 2004 to 31 October 2006, of the 1084 total incidents of "racist and neo-Nazi attacks" in Russia documented by the Center, there were 5 in Yaroslavl Oblast, all occurring in 2006. None of the attacks in Yaroslavl led to the death of the victim, compared to 123 Federation-wide deaths from such attacks over the same period. In 2018, SOVA reported no incidents of "racially-motivated" attacks in Yaroslavl.[13] My own observations in Yaroslavl in 2012 suggest a fair amount of frustration, intolerance and ethnic and racial stereotyping by Russians, but also significant efforts to improve the situation. I did witness one small rally on November 4, the Day of National Unity, at which speakers called for a policy of "Russia for Russians!" but it was a very modest affair and passed largely unnoticed.

Two of the women I met—one a Tatar and the other of mixed Russian and Jewish ethnicity—were deeply engaged in efforts to support various ethnic groups in the city and to encourage inter-ethnic cooperation through both governmental and non-government initiatives. A third, a Russian who introduced me to the two activists, was beginning a small-scale personal project, not connected to any organization.

I was unfortunately never able to interview the Tatar woman, despite meeting her several times and accompanying her to a couple of events. She was always immensely busy, juggling multiple conversations in

[12]The first report was accessed online in June 2014 at www.unitedagainstracism.org, but no longer seems to be available. The second report, which is undated, was accessed at http://www.unitedagainstracism.org/pdfs/report_Yaroslavl.pdf in February 2019.

[13]The earlier data were found at tandis.odihr.pl/documents/02977.pdf, accessed June 2014. The 2018 information is from https://www.sova-center.ru/en/xenophobia/reports-analyses/2019/02/d40603/#_Toc536536356 and was accessed February 2019.

person and by phone, and finding an hour to sit and talk with me without interruption proved impossible. My interview with the Jewish woman, though shorter than many, was quite rich. Employed as a teacher in the Soviet period, Polina found it natural to become involved in teaching Russian Jews about their heritage as soon as *glasnost* made it possible. In order to teach others, she first had to learn the history and culture herself.

> When the "iron curtain" fell and people could speak openly about everything and everyone, I started to organize a Jewish community.... I am Jewish on my mother's side.... I began a Jewish school for children on Sundays, not knowing a thing about it myself, not understanding a word of the language. [I didn't know] what things were, what one ate with what. I knew only one thing, that in order to gather Jewish people I should start with the children. Children have older brothers, of school age; they have mothers and fathers, grandmothers and grandfathers. And that is how this community was developed, beginning in 1991. It is officially one of the leading national-cultural associations in Yaroslavl.... Today this community is still alive and we have somehow become sort of teachers for the new national and cultural communities being created ....
>
> We didn't know anything. We learned something new every day. We created something new; there wasn't anything like it before. I like doing something that has never been done before me.... Of course, it was hard. I needed to study a lot, to read and travel, but it was interesting to me because it was interesting for other people. It was interesting for grandmothers, for parents, for children. It was very interesting, because a new world of Jewish traditions, Jewish history, opened up for them. Here I had been living and thinking of myself as Russian. Well, my mother was Jewish, but so what? I was thinking about my father; I didn't know then that you can be Jewish according to your mother. Such concepts as diaspora, *halakha, galut*[14] were very fuzzy for us, because we had never thought about our nationality.... That is why it was difficult; but it was interesting, too, not just difficult. [Polina, 64]

---

[14] *Galut* is the Hebrew word for exile; *halakha* refers to Jewish religious law.

While still active in the school she founded, this woman has now expanded her efforts far beyond the local Jewish community to nurture greater tolerance among all the different ethnic groups in Yaroslavl. I met her, in fact, when I attended an event celebrating the Tajik culture and the accomplishments of local Tajik schoolchildren. It was clear that she is a leader in the ethnic communities and that she takes this work extremely seriously. In both her formal job and her volunteer activity, she focuses on the challenges of multiculturalism in Yaroslavl.

> This is my main job, where I get a salary. This is…the City Methodological Center, which develops city programs, projects, and analytics. I have my own project – the School of Tolerance. This is my project. I lead it. It is for teenagers, high school students, university students, for youth. Universities, schools, colleges, and vocational schools are involved.

> As you've already learned, there is the Assembly of Russian Peoples in Yaroslavl, right? … And I am the co-chair [of that], the deputy president of the Assembly. This is volunteer work. For 20 years I have been doing this volunteer work.

During my stay in Yaroslavl, I attended three events sponsored by the Assembly or by a specific group belonging to it—an evening devoted to Lermontov in the Caucasus,[15] the Tajik awards ceremony and cultural demonstration, and a beauty pageant to name "Miss Assembly of the Peoples of Russia—Yaroslavl." The events were interesting as much for the behavior and interaction of those in attendance as for the official program.

The program for the Lermontov evening included poems, dances, singing, and a couple of speeches, one by a Chechen and the other by a descendant of Lermontov. While the dances and much of the singing highlighted the culture of the Caucasus, the speech by the Lermontov

[15]Mikhail Lermontov, a nineteenth-century Russian writer, was exiled to the Caucasus for writing verses critical of the aristocracy. His novel *Hero of Our Times* and many of his poems were greatly influenced by his time in the region.

descendant was notable for the assertion that Russia would never give up its claim to the Caucasus. Since much of that area consists of the now independent countries of Georgia, Armenia and Azerbaijan, this was almost certainly a reference to Chechnya and its unsuccessful wars for secession. There was also a third speech—though it was not part of the official program. Several younger members of the audience had been talking and laughing quite loudly during the performances, and eventually a man in the audience stood up in the middle of a piece and told them to stop. When the piece was over, he stood again, got up on stage and gave an impassioned lecture about the damage they were doing to attempts to bridge the cultures and live in harmony.

The awards ceremony/cultural celebration, held to honor the tenth anniversary of the establishment of the Tajik cultural organization in Yaroslavl, seemed poorly organized. It began late, lasted a very long time, and failed to hold the attention of most of the scattered audience. Although eventually there were folk dances and an exhibition of martial arts, most of the time was devoted to handing out awards to students and taking photographs of each of them with various dignitaries. A couple of days later, when I interviewed the Jewish woman I met at the event, she expressed considerable dissatisfaction with the experience. It is striking that despite her commitment to interethnic cooperation she quickly moved from criticism of the man in charge of the event to a statement about "them"—that is, about Tajiks—in general.

> For example, [the man] from the Tajik community [who was responsible for the event] …didn't ask my advice. He didn't think about logistics. For them, logistics is an abstract concept; they don't understand what logistics is. In contrast to them, we were taught a lot; we visited a lot of seminars in Israel and Moscow, and a lot of Israeli and American teachers came and taught us how to work with youth, with children. [Polina]

The most elaborate of the three events I attended was the "Miss Assembly of the Peoples of Yaroslavl 2012." (They transliterated the English word "Miss", although the rest of the title was in Russian.) This was the pageant's fifth year. There were eleven contestants in their late teens or early 20s—two Germans, one Russian, two Tatars, one Pole, one Armenian, one Azerbaijani, one Chechen, one Ossetian and one Ingushetian. (The last five nationalities are all from the Caucasus region; of these the last three are from within the Russian Federation.) The categories in which the young women competed were:

- Wearing and briefly describing their national (folk) dress and speaking briefly about themselves.
- Speaking about a "neighboring" culture. I was told that in the past each contestant was asked to speak about her own culture, but that this time they drew names out of a hat.
- Preparing a national dish (which the judges sampled).
- Demonstrating a talent. (These were not necessarily solo acts. Several performed folk dances with male partners, and the winner had half a dozen other people singing and dancing with her.)
- Modeling an evening gown.

The criteria for judging were not clear to me, although those of us in the audience were given the opportunity to vote. In addition to bestowing the title, the judges handed out a very large number of awards, so that every contestant received at least one and thus no nationality was slighted.

## Leaving Russia

Not all the migration flows have been from the former republics into Russia. Some were from Russia to Europe (primarily Germany), Israel, or the United States, and several of my respondents spoke of friends or relatives who had moved abroad. During the Soviet period, emigration was extremely rare, although there were a few high-profile cases of defection (such as the ballet dancers Rudolf Nureyev in 1961 and Mikhail Baryshnikov in 1974). Legal emigration was possible only to join a relative; most of those allowed to emigrate were of either German or Jewish background. In the twenty-four-year period from 1967 to the end of 1990, about 500,000 Jews left the Soviet Union; more than this left in just the subsequent five years, after reform and then dissolution made emigration easier (Buwalda 1997: xv).[16] Those who left in the Soviet period were often dissidents, openly opposing the Soviet system and eager to leave for Israel to help build a Zionist state; those who left after 1990 were much more likely to be driven by the economic difficulties at home than by their political views (Remennick 2009: 44).

Although several women mentioned in passing that they had friends or relatives in Europe or North America, the topic of emigration to Israel elicited lengthier comments. What was said supported the idea that the primary reasons for leaving in the 1990s were economic, rather than religious or cultural. One woman shared this recollection of a conversation she had with a Jewish friend as she was searching for a public protest to join on the first day of the August 1991 coup.

> I basically couldn't think of anything except that we might be returning to communism. I was so anxious about this. And I kept thinking, how can we all unite, how do we begin to protest? I met a classmate who has Jewish roots. And to my question, 'Mila, what should we do?… [We] need to save democracy from these threats!'…she reacted strangely, I can tell you. She said, 'Calm down, I made a decision for myself. I am freeing myself of this country.'… She went to Germany… She lives in Germany. Yes, yes, yes, yes, yes. That is, for some people there was such an exit.
>
> But I did not have any desire to leave. Do you understand? Maybe at that time we could have been accepted as political refugees, I don't know, but I did not think about it. I thought about where to protest. [Ekaterina, 56]

While this woman was not Jewish herself, others who chose not to leave were. They offered various explanations for their decision to stay. The woman who has spent her post-Soviet life committed to teaching Jews

---

[16]Buwalda points out that the 500,000 who left between 1967 and 1990 constituted "more than a quarter of the Jews who, according to the census of 1959, had lived in what was then the Soviet Union." It should be kept in mind, however, that the exact number of Soviet Jews cannot be known. Those designated as Jewish in the census were those so identified in their internal passports. As indicated in Footnote 11, however, marriages between people of different nationalities meant there was some latitude in how one identified and those with one Jewish parent might have chosen the nationality of the other parent for himself or herself to avoid problems or advance a career.

in Yaroslavl about their religious and cultural heritage finds enormous satisfaction in that work, but also feels a deep connection to Russia in general and Yaroslavl in particular, honoring both her father's Russian roots and her mother's Jewish roots.

> So here I am, if you please, although many have left, of course.... I do believe that a person has the right to live where he wants. I did not want to [leave]; I never even thought of it. I like my city, I like my job, I love what I'm doing [at my job] and in public life. I just like that my roots—my dad is Russian—my roots are very deep here, so to speak. I went and studied [in Israel] and I go to visit. My sister is there, my older sister. Well, probably, you know, for each vegetable there is a ripening time. I have not yet matured. [I interpreted this to mean that she might change her mind and decide to emigrate in a few years.] [Polina, 64]

Another woman initially explained her decision not to emigrate by saying she was concerned about her Russian husband.

> This was the time of stagnation,[17] when our friends—my husband's and mine—all left. They all left. Some live in America, ... some live in Germany, our closest friend lives in Israel.... They all left, they scattered to different countries. My husband—he was such a Russian man, so much a Russian *intelligent*.... There's this work of Kuprin called *The Garnet Bracelet*, and a film too. There's this character from this story and that's my husband. The hero and he are one and the same. He so loves, so praises women, he's so patient and so meek. Such was his character. He said, 'if you say that we should go'—everyone had already left—'if you say that we must go to Israel, I will go. I don't know what I will do there, but if you say that we need to go, I will go.' I understood that he would be lost. He simply was a Russian person.... I simply understood that he wouldn't [be able to] find himself there. [Vera, 56]

Then, aware of the contradiction, she suggested that it was actually more difficult for émigrés of Jewish heritage to adapt to life in Israel

---

[17]Although the term usually refers to the later years of Brezhnev's time in office, this woman was talking about the late 1980s and early 1990s.

than it was for the ethnic Russians who moved there. If true, this is ironic, since, as Larissa Remennick argues, one of the reasons the post-1990 immigrants in Israel struggled more than earlier arrivals did was that they often were part of ethnically-mixed families and thus had weaker commitment to the Zionist state (2009: 55–56).

> When I look at our friends it is precisely those of European heritage who cope much better than those with Jewish roots. Much better. Let me explain. The thing is that if a person arrives with Jewish roots he is going to the Promised Land, about which he's been told even in childhood and he thinks that they're awaiting him there, right there at the ramp after the flight. You come to the Holy Land, but it's nothing like that. You come, and no one is waiting for you. There's very high unemployment there, it's very hard to get settled in your specialty, and so for Jews a terrible disappointment begins. So much so that people are returning.
>
> But when a member of a Russian family arrives, he understands that no one is waiting for him, that he must teach himself the language, that he must prove that he can work as well as a Jew and in the end he likes it there because it has a wonderful climate, and the food—well! They say that in Israel one eats only once a day, but from morning to evening. And the state is pretty democratic.

She then returned to her family's story. Although her husband had urged her to leave and take the children with her if he should die, she chose not to follow this advice. Soon after her husband's death, however, their adolescent son did go to Israel, choosing to study and serve in the military there rather than to stay in Russia, where it was hard for his mother to support him financially.

> My son is 31 years old.... He left to study under a program [that provides]...full state support for high school students. That is, he graduated from school in Israel, served in the army and this program gave him the opportunity to study free of charge at the university. So he went with this program.... He left for Israel when he was 15 years old. No one [he knew] was there.... But he went with a group of boys and this program... It's like in America, where there is a campus. There is a closed territory

> and there are educators: they lived there, they studied there, and he studied there in the *kibbutz* in the territory. They even have their own zoo, a rich *kibbutz*, which took children from all over the world to study. There were guys from America, from England, from Russia, from Hungary.... Then after this school the children could go back to their home or stay and [serve in] the army [and attend] the university there and so on.... He understood that it was hard for me.... He understood that he had to stay and stand on his own two feet.

Her parents, too, are now in Israel.

> Twice a year I go to Israel now, twice a year I go, because my parents went. My parents left for two reasons. The first is that my son went into the Israeli army and Mama said, 'This is my beloved grandson and here I won't sleep or eat knowing that he's there serving in the army. If you're not going to go,' said Mama, 'then I will go.' The second reason was purely economic.... In the 1990s, Germany agreed with Russia that it would pay a lifetime pension to all prisoners of concentration camps and ghettos. Our government—Soviet, not Russian, but Soviet—decided that it would take a state fee out of the sum of money that the Germans would pay for life for one's ruined fate. And Mama said, 'They still want to earn money for nothing!' So now she lives in Israel and receives the money Germany grants her, right down to the last mark. It hasn't come into Israel's head to put money in its pocket. But the Soviet Union decided to make money even off the old people. Also, of course, I am grateful to Israel for the way it takes care of their health.... If they lived in Russia, they would already be lying in their graves, because in our country there isn't anybody to look after the elderly.

As noted in Chapter 6, in addition to having friends and relatives in Israel, some of the women I talked to have children living and working in Europe and North America. The woman whose son and parents are living in Haifa, Israel, has a grown daughter living in Paris; another has a daughter who studied in Paris and lived there for several years before moving to Moscow. One woman has a daughter who moved first to Israel with her husband and is now residing in Canada; another has a daughter in St. Louis. Although all of these mothers took obvious pride in their daughters' accomplishments, as we shall see in Chapter 11 the general attitude expressed toward the West was not always positive.

Attitudes toward emigration were also mixed. Below I offer quotes from two women, of roughly similar age, both holding advanced degrees and working in education, both having been true and committed believers in Soviet communism in their youth, both having fared moderately well in the post-Soviet system and both having embraced the new freedom to travel—but with very different thoughts about emigration.

> If I were younger, I would certainly leave here.... If there were such an opportunity now, I would go somewhere, where... there would be no... I don't know how to express it. One can say that we have freedom, right? But I understand very well, and I see it now, completely from my own experience. I do not want to live here. And my husband feels the same way. [Sofia, 61]

> This is what I wanted to say. The bad is forgotten, the good is stored in the memory.... I am glad that I live in our country, I would never want to change it. Well, I think that it is very difficult in the first, even in the second generation, to feel like a second-rate person, being in another country. This is my opinion. Why would anyone do this? But everyone has the right [to decide]. [Liza, 55]

## References


Assembly of Peoples of Russia Website. Accessed online at Anr76.ru. March 2019.

BBC News. 2016. Nagorno-Karabakh Profile. Accessed online at http://www.bbc.com/news/world-europe-18270325. August 2017.

Burke, Justin. 2000. Internal Migration: A Civil Society Challenge. In *Russia's Torn Safety Nets: Health and Social Welfare During the Transition*, ed. Mark G. Field and Judyth L. Twigg, 213–230. New York: St. Martin's Press.

Buwalda, Petrus. 1997. *They Did Not Dwell Alone: Jewish Immigration from the Soviet Union, 1967–1990*. Washington, DC: Woodrow Wilson Center Press.

Federal'naia sluzhba gosudarstvennoi statistiki. Srednemesiachnaia nominal'naia nachislennaia zarabotnaia plata rabotnikov v tselom po ekonomike Rossiiskoi Federatsii v 1991–2018 gg [The Federal Government Statistical Service: Average Monthly Nominal Accrued Wages of Workers in the Economy of the Russian Federation, 1991–2018]. Available online at http://www.gks.ru/wps/wcm/connect/rosstat_main/rosstat/ru/statistics/wages/. Accessed through Elena's models at https://blogs.elenasmodels.com/en/average-salaries-in-russia/. February 2019.

Flynn, Moya. 2004. *Migrant Resettlement in the Russian Federation: Restructuring Homes and Homelands*. London: Anthem Press.

Kagarlitsky, Boris. 2003. Ethnic Problems and National Issues in Contemporary Russian Society. In *Social Capital and Social Cohesion in Post-Soviet Russia*, ed. Judyth L. Twigg and Kate Schecter, 55–73. Armonk, NY/London: M.E. Sharpe.

Nozhenko, Maria. 2010. *Focus Migration: Russian Federation*. Osnabrück, Germany: The Institute for Migration Research and Intercultural Studies. Accessed online at http://focus-migration.hwwi.de/Russian-Federation.6337.0.html?&L=1. February 2019.

Remennick, Larissa. 2009. The Two Waves of Russian-Jewish Migration from the USSR/FSU to Israel: Dissidents of the 1970s and Pragmatics of the 1990s. *Diaspora: A Journal of Transnational Studies* 18 (1/2): 44–66.

Sakwa, Richard. 2002. *Russian Politics and Society*, 3rd ed. London and New York: Routledge.

Sikevich, Zinaida. 1999. Ethnic Hostility in the Mass Consciousness of Russians. In *Intolerance in Russia: Phobias, Old and New*, ed. G. Vitkovskaya and A. Malashenko. Moscow: Moscow Carnegie Center.

Simonsen, Sven Gunnar. 1999. Inheriting the Soviet Policy Toolbox: Russia's Dilemma Over Ascriptive Nationality. *Europe-Asia Studies* 51 (6): 1069–1087.

SOVA Center for Information and Analysis. Accessible on-line at https://www.sova-center.ru/en/xenophobia/reports-analyses/2019/02/d40603/#_Toc536536356. February 2019.

Strayer, Robert. 1998. *Why Did the Soviet Union Collapse? Understanding Historical Change*. Armonk, NY: M.E. Sharpe.

Tsypkin, Mikhail. 1988. The Conscripts. In *The Soviet Union Today: An Interpretive Guide*, 2nd ed., ed. James Cracraft, 105–113. Chicago: University of Chicago Press.

UNITED for Intercultural Action. n.d. Yaroslavl—Real Russian Hospitality: Workshops for Young People in Central Russia. Accessed online at http://www.unitedagainstracism.org/pdfs/report_Yaroslavl.pdf. February 2019.
*Vserossiiskaya perepis' naseleniia 2010 goda, Tom 4. Natsional'nyi sostav i vladenie iazykami grazhdanstva* [All-Russian Census of the Population 2010, Vol. 4. The National Composition and Command of Languages of the Population]. Accessed online at http://www.gks.ru/free_doc/new_site/perepis2010/croc/perepis_itogi1612.htm. February 2014.

# 11

# New Freedoms

## Introduction

In addition to greater freedom in the economic realm, the end of the Soviet Union brought greater freedom in many other aspects of life as well. For some of the women I interviewed, the pleasure provided by greater freedom to travel, to practice religion and to participate in political debate was profound, leading them to view the late 1980s and early 1990s with nostalgia despite the economic difficulties of the period. The sense of nostalgia underscored how much they felt things had changed for the worse by the fall of 2012. While daily life had become far easier and more of them were in a financial position to take advantage of the freedom to travel, no one spoke favorably of the political situation. Some expressed disappointment, others expressed apathy, none—even those who had participated eagerly in political life in the earlier period—seemed actively engaged. Below I explore how the women experienced the greater interaction with the rest of the world, especially the West, made possible by the reforms of the late 1980s and 1990s, and then turn to the role of religion and politics in their lives, then and in 2012.



J. McKinney, *Russian Women and the End of Soviet Socialism*,
https://doi.org/10.1007/978-3-030-16226-9_11

## Encounters with the West

One of the consequences of the decision to move from a centrally planned economic system toward a market-based economy and from single-party rule toward a democracy was the proliferation of contacts with foreigners, both as individuals and as representatives of a wide variety of organizations and companies. Westerners flocked to Russia to give advice, to explore business opportunities, to conduct research, and to proselytize. Russians were invited to Western countries to study, to work, and to observe alternative ways of arranging political and civic life. Once economic conditions improved, Russians also began to travel abroad for pleasure, spending vacations in destinations throughout Europe and Asia.

Although the attempt by the Soviet authorities to limit contact with foreigners and to control information about life in other countries had been only partially successful, it nonetheless meant that most Soviet citizens had little first-hand experience of the rest of the world, especially that beyond the Soviet bloc.[1] Those living in Moscow and Leningrad did occasionally encounter foreign tourists or students, but what most of the population knew of other countries came through official channels—the schools, approved translations of literary works, and state-controlled media. As one of a group of college students in Leningrad in the early 1970s I was an object of intense curiosity. Those individuals brave, naïve, or well-positioned enough to interact with me invariably stressed that they liked and felt kinship with the American people (even though I might be the first they had ever encountered) and that it was only the American government they distrusted. As more and more Russians met with more and more foreigners in more and more kinds of situations, the range of reactions naturally broadened and people shared with me stories of both positive and disappointing—even hurtful—interactions.

[1]See Yurchak (2006: 158–206) for an analysis of the "internal paradox" of late Soviet policy toward Western culture.

It is sometimes difficult to know how to interpret what is said by Russians talking about America with Americans. All of the women I interviewed received their education during the Soviet period, when they would have been constantly reminded of the US–Soviet rivalry and the dangers of interaction with foreigners. Although my interviews preceded the conflict in Ukraine, the accusations of Russian meddling in the 2016 US elections, and the serious deterioration in US–Russia relations that have resulted, they occurred after any hope that the end of the Soviet Union would lead the USA and Russia to become close allies had faded.[2]

In 2012, the fraught history between the countries manifested itself mostly in subtle ways. I encountered no one who was deliberately confrontational.[3] It was simply that there were situations in which it seemed that both the woman I was talking to and I were conscious of serving, unavoidably, as representatives of some larger entity, whether of a people, a culture, or a state. I frequently sensed an underlying belief that our countries remained in clear competition with one another. Usually, comments to this effect were tossed out as if in jest, offered with a laugh that could have meant, "Can you believe we once thought this way?" or "This is what some misguided people think," but could just as plausibly have meant, "You and I both know this is true, but I'm trying to be polite."

At one point, for example, a woman who had visited the Air Force Space and Missile Museum in Cape Canaveral said, "I was very pleased that it said in English that Gagarin was the first cosmonaut." She then noted, "Well, then America decided that it should not concede to Russia in this area. We think the first astronaut who walked on the

---

[2]As an example of the initial optimism, consider the speech by Boris Yeltsin to a joint session of the US Congress in June 1992: "We realize our great responsibility for the success of our changes, not only toward the people of Russia, but also toward the citizens of America, and of the entire world. Today the freedom of America is being upheld in Russia" (*New York Times* 1992: A18).

[3]In 2005, some of my Russian friends clearly expected that I might indeed meet with hostility. In an interesting inversion of our time together more than 30 years earlier, they again asked me not to speak during a short train ride we took together in the environs of St. Petersburg. This time, rather than to protect themselves against charges of unacceptable interaction with foreigners, the goal was to protect me from unpleasantness if I were recognized as American.

moon was an American, Armstrong." At this point, her husband, who had joined us, interjected with a laugh, "If indeed he really did walk." Later, in response to a question about whether she had noticed a change in the quality of her students since the dissolution of the Soviet Union, this woman said she had not, then laughed and added

> But I think that if they are as capable and talented as our son, for example, then Russia will beat America. I think so. If we had not had these disasters, which in our life have befallen us, befallen our country, then we would be a rich, a very clever nation. But unfortunately [there have been] wars, so many wars in our history. Unfortunately, that's how it is. Well, and it also hasn't been the case that the best people in all countries flocked to us, as they do to America. [Liza, 55]

There were also occasional suggestions that Russia's problems had been caused—or at least exacerbated—by the USA.

> But we have such data—I think that you probably know this—that the leaders [of Russian reform efforts in the 1990s] were Americans, that the prompting came from America, how to fool Russia, how to weaken Russia. The political scientists, the political experts, were from there.... It is not a secret, and I think you know that there [in the US] there are lots of detractors of Russia, because Russia has always been a counterbalance. All the time there is this battle, this rivalry. And they undertook everything in order to weaken Russia. [Klara, 70]

Although this particular comment was not softened in any way, it was more typical for even such accusations to be accompanied by laughter, as in the case of a comment made by a woman in response to a reference to the Russian financial crisis of 1998. I had been invited to interview the woman in her office, and a considerably younger woman was working at a desk nearby. She had a much better sense of what I was interested in than did the older woman, who spoke in almost entirely theoretical terms and told me nothing at all about her personal experience. The younger woman would occasionally offer her own observations and had been describing the gradual improvement that had taken place after the very difficult period of the early 1990s. "There were already [by the late 1990s] these positive tendencies and then later it somehow got a little better. Well, of course, if you don't count the '98 crisis, which we also had." At this point, the older woman, who had sprinkled her conversation with mild jokes at the expense of America, said, laughing, "Again the Americans sent us a crisis!"

These pointed jokes reminded me of an experience seven years earlier, when I spent several months volunteering with an organization funded by a Western NGO. The young Russian women working as interpreters and guides for the organization, who would have been in their late teens or early twenties at the time the USSR dissolved, occasionally accused me of being a spy. They would laugh as they said it, but I was struck that this would arise even humorously so many years after the end of the Cold War.[4]

While none of my respondents expressed overt hostility to the USA, the subtext thus often suggested the lingering influence of attitudes developed in the earlier period. Furthermore, there must have been some women who declined to be interviewed because they held strong negative views of America. Most of those who chose not to speak to me were approached by someone else on my behalf, so I received their responses to the request at second hand. These responses, which may have been edited or softened by the intermediary, included: "I have neither the time nor the inclination." "I really don't want to relive such a difficult period of my life." "I would be uncomfortable." One refusal, however, took place over the phone while I was in the room and it was clear in that case that the woman at the other end of the line had little use for nosy Americans.

## Foreign Training

Yeltsin's assertion that he was committed to transforming Russia into a market economy was greeted with enthusiasm by many American neoliberal economists, who saw this as an opportunity for the

[4]This was almost a decade before the revelations by Edward Snowden, so international espionage was not at the time the focus of media attention.

creation of a free-enterprise capitalist system much closer to the textbook models and less tainted by government interference than any actually existing country. Eager to participate in the endeavor, they applied for grants, submitted proposals to international organizations, Western government agencies and NGOs, and set off to Moscow to provide advice and help draft legislation. As noted above, this has made it possible for some Russians to blame the USA for the hardships they endured and for the fall in international stature of their country.[5] Much of the advice provided by Western consultants was indeed ill-suited to the Russian situation, given, as it was, with almost willful disregard of the particularities of Soviet history and society.[6] At the same time, however, for individual Russians some of the advice and training proved enormously helpful and offered hitherto undreamed-of possibilities.

Three women in particular were able to embark on entirely new paths thanks at least in part to foreign training. One, featured in Chapter 10, received advice and support as she developed a Jewish educational program that has continued for many years; she has used what she learned to become a leader in the broader diaspora community in the city as well, and is active in organizing events to celebrate various ethnic communities and to increase ethnic tolerance. Another woman received training in local government and civic engagement on a trip to the USA in 2006, while the third received training in small business administration in the Urals in the early 1990s.

The trip to the USA was sponsored by the League of Women Voters, which at the end of the Cold War established several international programs intended to work for women's rights and to help women develop

---

[5]A different interpretation—that the advisors benefited financially from their support of particular reforms—is offered by Wedel (1998). While she accuses the US government of failure to monitor the administration of its aid program, and many of the advisors of venality, she does not suggest that they were deliberately attempting to weaken Russia.

[6]An entertaining presentation of the debate over whether it was necessary to shape the reform measures to reflect Russian history and existing institutions—and whether it was really best to eliminate all government intervention in the economy—is offered in Adams and Brock (1993).

as leaders.[7] The woman who participated in this LWV program has had a long and varied career and achieved considerable success. During our interview, after describing her many accomplishments, she brought out a box of diplomas, certificates and awards of various sorts—and a mug commemorating her participation in the League program.

It was clear that she was extremely proud of having taken this trip and that she learned a lot from it, although what she remembered most vividly was not part of the official program. Rather, it was that her hosts in the various cities, all of them members of local chapters of the League and most of them women of middle age or older, were entirely comfortable behind the wheel of a car, driving her around their cities with confidence. For a woman who had spent her formative years in a country where the waiting lists to buy a car were years long (Siegelbaum 2009)—and where the very unscientific and casual count of Yaroslavl drivers I carried out in 2005 suggested that even then the ratio of male to female drivers of automobiles was on the order of 10:1[8]—this was a startling and empowering realization.

She also seemed to have absorbed a sense of the power of political engagement and lobbying. Although she did not explicitly link her activism to her experience in the League program, it certainly reflects much of what the program tried to instill.

> In 2006, I wrote a letter to the mayor. I disagreed with some project… so I wrote this letter… I compiled documents… in the first place to criticize the mayor's deputies, and secondly, to show the mayor that it's wrong to focus on this thing, it would be better to focus on this other, and third, that I am ready to help him in the development of this idea. You know, to say to the mayor, 'Look, right here you're a little bit wrong, your deputies are all enemies in this particular matter, and I'm a person who has no ties to any structure anywhere, not in the party and not in any of the city administrations. I'm simply here as a small entrepreneur, a representative of small business, and I see that this is what needs to be done.'…

---

[7]http://library.lwv.org/content/league-women-voters-through-decades-1990s, accessed 26 September 2014.

[8]In 2012, a similarly casual survey suggested that the gender disparity among drivers had largely vanished.

I didn't allow it to go through official channels. In keeping with Russian custom, the mayor's assistant brought it to him, having agreed to deliver it in person. Otherwise, it would never have reached him.... And when the mayor read the letter, he wrote his comments on the letter, and later they showed me the letter with his remarks: 'I agree, I agree, absolutely, absolutely, give a resolution... to carry out.'...

I thought the deputy mayor, about whom I complained, was a smart woman and would take note of what the mayor wrote and simply carry it out. But no, not that one. She smiled at him, nodded as if it would be carried out, and all the same she was lying, she warped the whole idea. I then refused to do it, I said, 'I won't do it in that way.' And I'd be a fool, excuse the expression, to remain silent, to pretend nothing was happening. So at the meeting, I'm sitting there, there are representatives of regional administrations, there are directors of our regions, there are some other people, other departments of city hall.... There were twenty of us. And she couldn't resist, she started to shake this letter, 'You're so smart, you write a letter to the mayor.' ... I said, 'Yes. So what? I have expressed my point of view.' And here they all nineteen sit and vote as she told them to because they are all dependent on her. But she's not my boss, I vote against it. And she started every meeting with the words, 'So, Baba Yaga, voting no again?' I say, 'Yes, Baba Yaga votes no.' They all sit with their eyes lowered, because they cannot contradict her. When we go out into the corridor, they all apologize to me for how they have voted and say, 'But you must understand us.' I said, 'I have no grievance against you.' ...All the same, she did as she wanted– not what the mayor wrote, she still just did as she wanted.

... That's why I sort of drew the curtain for myself and said I was no longer interested. I will work in a different direction, be involved with business. [Yulia, 52]

This decision to retreat did not last, however, and at the time of our interview she had recently started a job in an administrative position at City Hall.

When it came down to [a mayoral race] between [Yakov] Yakushev or [Yevgeny] Urlashov, I said, 'Now is my chance, I have to take part in this.'[9] I called the staff and said, 'Here I am, this is who I am, and I want to help.' And here I am. You understand how everything in this life works out. If you had told me three months ago that I would be [in charge of] some kind of methodological center, some kind of institute, I would have said you had lost your mind. You're crazy to think that I will be in command in city hall, in this position. …

And then when I ended up here, I realized what a perspective, what opportunities, how much we can do in the city! That's the only reason I'm here. Otherwise, I would have said, 'Thank you, but please get along somehow without me.'

In an interesting twist of fate, her grown daughter now lives in the American Midwest and works for a local government there.

If these first two examples of potential unleashed by encounters with Western ideas and approaches had largely to do with civil society, the third example was rooted in market economics.

At that time, there was a wonderful assistant division commander [at a military base in the Urals]…. He said to me: 'Some Americans have arrived…. They would like to meet with the women's committee.' My mom taught me that I should always be a part of the women's organization…. Of course, they were not allowed to come to the military town. Our meeting was on neutral territory in [a nearby] village… They came

[9]The mayoral race to which she refers was a critical event not only for this woman, but also for many observers of Russian politics. Urlashov, an independent candidate, won against the candidate of United Russia, Putin's party, by a very large margin. Following the protests in Moscow challenging the December 2011 elections to the Duma, this victory was hailed by some as a sign that the political opposition in Russia was gaining real leverage. Anna Arutunyan (2012), writing in the English-language paper *Moscow News*, for example, opened her article on the election with the comment, "With an independent candidate winning a mayoral run-off election in Yaroslavl, a historic city about 280 kilometers north-east of Moscow, the opposition seems to be slowly but steadily gaining political weight" and later quoted another journalist who said, "There was a colossal emotional uplift among the residents and the other observers I talked to. There was a sense that something could be done, that a candidate who sincerely meant to change things could win." This "emotional uplift" turned out to be unfounded, however, since in early July of 2013, Urlashov and several members of his administration were arrested by federal authorities and charged with extortion and bribe-taking (Herszenhorn 2013). Alexander Nechayev, who had been deputy mayor for social policy and culture, then began serving as acting mayor.

> with training, they came with help.... [She showed me the business card of the American woman who organized the meeting.] She was in the US military. And this organization had the purpose of supporting military people and their families. The first thing that they did – they organized training, psychological support and I attended this training.
>
> For us it was all very unusual.... We had a trainer, a business coach. At that time, of course, it sounded simply impossible. But they brainwashed us [apparently not meant pejoratively in this context] to believe that we too could do it, that we could create these plans, I mean. If in Europe, after the unification, women could start their own business and all the rest, why shouldn't we try to earn some money and not just by developing private schools and laundries? And it was very useful. The next seminar they organized was at the American center of business in Ekaterinburg and I was there, too. They gave us a lecture "Women in business: The new reality." It was in February 1995. [Vasilisa, 56]

While her initial plans were thwarted by opposition from the local authorities, this woman found other ways to channel her entrepreneurial spirit, and has continued to find or create opportunities ever since. Recounting the initial plans and opposition, she said:

> [The American woman] said maybe we could open a bakery, [since] we didn't have bread on the territory of the military town.... For one thing, this would mean there would be jobs, and a lot of the women weren't employed. For another, the whole post would be provided with bread. They carried out a project like this in the military town in Zelenogorsk. ...But I was prohibited from having these contacts. And I wasn't the one who suffered because of this, you know. My husband did.... He was supposed to go to Germany..., he was supposed to go as a military specialist.... And he was refused. Refused! After that, of course, I started to be more careful.

Her decision to be more careful did not mean, however, that she abandoned all ideas of engaging in business. Since she and her husband were both experiencing serious wage arrears, she devised a successful plan, described in Chapter 5, to earn money through a kind of shuttle trade involving socks and military shirts. Later, after her husband was reassigned and they ended up in Yaroslavl, the ideas instilled by the initial seminar continued to influence her.

> I had been taught [at that seminar], 'You should do something and gather information.' I didn't know how I would work. There were no jobs at the university and my husband said, 'I will not use my influence and responsibility. I've just come to a new position, so I can't help you, I'm not going to request [a job] for you'… So I started to study, I graduated from [a private business and technology institute founded in 1992]. In my group, there were mostly men. It was in 1998. I didn't want to leave the teaching profession because I like that profession very much. As it's turned out, during my life I have had to change jobs many times and go back to school to retrain. I got this diploma "Organization of the small and medium enterprise" only because I earlier attended courses held by American trainers, who instilled in me the foundation, the idea that no matter what the circumstances were I could achieve something in life by myself if I wanted to. Americans were not connected with [the business institute]. It's just that they had taught me the basics of how to act and which steps to take to reach the goal.
>
> I got this diploma, I was taught to develop business projects. I wanted to open a private school very much, some center for little kids, but [this niche] was already occupied, … the field was tilled. I didn't have any friends here to invite to form a team. And I understood that it was pointless. I tried teaching a group of preschoolers [at the business institute]…. Then I found a position in the department of foreign language in the aircraft college….
>
> But this diploma led us to the point where when my husband retired we set up a small private enterprise—a transportation company. We had four cars…. We took out a loan. The Americans taught me how to get a loan, how to talk with bankers, how to charm them, what to tell them about myself. That is why we got a loan and we bought four routes and four route taxis…. But we didn't buy four at once. At first, we had one, then two, then three, then four and now we again have three.

The contrast between Vasilisa's clear sense of indebtedness to Americans for the training she received, on the one hand, and the suspicion (or certainty) of other women that Americans had deliberately undermined Russia by encouraging it to undertake inappropriate reforms, on the other, is reminiscent of the messages I heard in the early 1970s that American people were good, even though the American government was bad. This dichotomy between individuals and government, however, is far from perfect, since a number of the women I spoke to had very disappointing experiences with individual Westerners.

## Joint Ventures

Because a large share of my respondents were teachers, it is not surprising that their primary type of collaboration with foreigners involved language instruction. In some cases, this collaboration proved enduring; in others, it led to disappointment. Some of the disappointment was no doubt due to unrealistic expectations about what was possible under the new system, some the result of cultural misunderstanding, and some simply the inevitable failure of a significant portion of new businesses in any economy.

The most successful of the collaborations I learned of involved that between the German language program at a private higher-education institution in Yaroslavl and the Goethe Institute in Germany. While I was there, they celebrated the anniversary of this association, awarding prizes to a number of high school students who had performed well in a language competition (with food provided by a large German food chain with a store in Yaroslavl). This collaboration has made it possible for the woman who directs the German program to travel repeatedly to Germany, to flourish professionally, and to offer her students a kind of education that was impossible when she herself was studying the language in the 1970s and 1980s. She made one trip to the German Democratic Republic (East Germany) as a student, and then, in spring of 1990, was able to travel as part of a delegation to the Federal Republic of Germany (West Germany).

Upon her return from that trip, still over a year before the dissolution of the Soviet Union, she tried to share some of her experiences and impressions with her students but found it extremely difficult to do so.

> I tried to show them the video [we made]. This wasn't very pleasant for the students. I understood that the students were upset. And they posed a question to me: 'Tell us, what is it that they don't have there?' Do you understand? They asked me, 'What don't they have there?' That is, the Russian people simply could not understand that there could be countries where everything was available. Let's say, so maybe there isn't enough chocolate there? All my videos showed that there was more than enough of everything. I said, 'I didn't discover anything they lacked.' And I remember the very sad eyes of the student who had asked me that question. He was sad. [Ekaterina, 56]

Today, this woman visits Germany frequently, she and others use multimedia presentations showing life there as a routine part of language instruction, and her students are able to enroll in courses there. When they travel to Germany for the first time, they experience nothing like the unsettling culture shock she did on her first trip (recounted in Chapter 3).

In contrast, another woman, who teaches Russian to foreigners and is based at the same private institute, has found her repeated attempts to form ties with Western organizations or individuals frustrating and unsatisfactory. Her first such endeavor took place in the early 1990s, when she spent several months in England.

> In 1989, I met a man from England. He taught Russian and issued an invitation through the British Council for me to go to England to write a book with him, a Russian language textbook for British students. In 1990, I went to England and was there for the academic year. We wrote this book together, but something went wrong. I of course don't want to speak ill of him, but he was a little strange. I wouldn't [normally] say this to anyone, but I need to explain it to you. He was a bit strange and it didn't work out. It was his fault that we didn't finish the book, and I left, though it seemed to me that it would have been very interesting to continue this work and to continue teaching. I was teaching just at a linguistic center

> for those interested in Russian [that is, not part of a formal educational program.] I went to England on the Council's invitation only to write the book [so did not have permission to teach formally]. [Sofia, 61]

After returning to Yaroslavl in the spring of 1991, she began working at a language school with a Russian partner. This collaboration, which had begun before she left for England and is described in Chapter 7, was also a source of disappointment. Her next experience, working with American missionaries, was far more satisfying, but eventually ran its course. When it ended, she again tried to collaborate with foreigners in language instruction and, again, it began auspiciously. She had been working with the study abroad program of an American college but believed that the Russian partner was too interested in making money so had embarked on discussions with one of the representatives of the college to develop a new program. Everything seemed to be going well, but the association ended abruptly and without explanation. Struggling to make sense of it, she has decided that she may have unintentionally offended a young woman of color associated with the program by rebuking her for disrespectful behavior.

She describes the incident this way:

> At first, I got along very well with [the young woman who served as a resident advisor for the American students on the program]. She was African-American… I always thought that our relationship was normal, kind-hearted, very, very friendly. But once…I was walking along the corridor at the university there, and she was sitting on the table. There was a chair in the corridor, but she was sitting on the table, chatting, kicking her legs like this. And she did this [shows me beckoning with a crooked finger]. This of course affected me a little, and I thought, 'Mm-hmmm, I can't just keep quiet about this and say nothing,' so I said, 'Excuse me, please, but here [*u nas*] we don't summon teachers this way.' And for that I heard such fireworks, fireworks, it was such a terrible reaction, completely unexpected.
>
> Since then I've tried hard to analyze it. Maybe the reaction was so painful because she had felt so much. She had very often complained to me that here in Yaroslavl people looked at her and laughed, pointed at her and laughed… I told her, 'Cultured people would never do that, educated

people, normal people are tolerant, they wouldn't do that. Why pay attention to stupid people?' And I would comfort her. … We were friends, right? And then I reacted to her gesture.… I think that it all played a role…a very important role. I don't know what this young woman said about me… about our relationship.… I really would like to know what went wrong.

Whether this explanation is accurate, the plans for cooperation ended.

For a few months, I met with Madame N and [her male colleague]. They even came to our home, and we talked, we made plans.… We had such good, interesting plans for making a really good center… and we even corresponded about it for a while until the episode. I do not know what this young woman said about me, but I think that she must have said.. something about…my attitude to her somehow.… I cannot explain it otherwise. Madame N stopped writing to me, just stopped, even though we had a lot of interesting plans.… I tried to talk with [the male colleague]. We met in Moscow, but … he did not answer questions. He invited me to a café… but he would not talk to me about this. And I wondered what this woman could have said or what else could have happened. Here I was, the only specialist in Russian as a foreign language, and everyone acted as if I had the plague.… I thought, what could it be? I still wonder.… If there is any possibility, I would like to know what it was, what they said, that I work with the KGB, or that I don't treat African-Americans well? I just don't know what. I really want to know by the end of my life, I'd like to know.… It was such a dark spot, a blot, in my life.

Much happier associations were described by two respondents working as representatives for direct sales companies. One worked for an American cosmetic firm, the other for a Japanese business with a broad range of products related to a holistic approach to health. Neither woman seemed to have encountered any of the disappointments or problems arising from cultural misunderstanding described above. I was never sure, however, to what extent they were simply tapping into their usual sales pitch and to what extent they were seriously reflecting on their experiences. For one of the women, the work had clearly been very profitable; for the other, many of the promised prizes and other incentives remained attractive goals and she seemed undeterred by the fact that she had yet to achieve them.

## Travel

Among the women I interviewed formally and others with whom I conversed more casually, several had some experience traveling or living abroad during the Soviet period, but this was almost entirely in the countries of Eastern Europe, the former Soviet bloc. The most frequently mentioned country was Germany, and most of the women who had spent time there did so in connection with military postings of father or husband. The standard of living in the German Democratic Republic—and, indeed, in several of the countries of Eastern Europe—in the 1970s and 1980s was significantly higher than that in the Soviet Union, which meant that this experience could be eye-opening.

One woman, whose husband was posted to the GDR after being stationed in a closed city in the Russian Far East, was struck by the higher quality of both food and books available. (Given the geographical hierarchy of the distribution of goods in the Soviet Union described in Chapter 2, she would probably have been struck as well by the higher quality of both food and books available in Moscow, had she ended up there.) In addition to appreciating the better consumer goods, this woman appreciated differences in social norms. She vividly recalled her first train ride in Germany, describing the sense of calm, quiet, and order, the fact that people weren't shouting, and there wasn't an unpleasant smell. Another woman said that when she visited the GDR she thought it was paradise—an impression that lasted until she later had the opportunity to travel to the western part of divided Germany.

These visits to other countries were unusual experiences. Travel abroad was a privilege, especially travel outside the Soviet bloc, the latter reserved for the well-connected—for top members of the Communist Party or for leading scholars and artists. In contrast, since the dissolution of the Soviet Union the ability to travel internationally has been open to all who can afford it. Since January 1, 1993, all Russian citizens except those "on trial, doing military service or privy to state secrets" can acquire passports for foreign travel and can use them for several years, without applying for a separate exit visa for each trip (Sakwa 2002: 312). Almost all the women I spoke to had taken vacations in Western Europe or Asia, something which distinguished them from the majority of the population. According to a survey carried out in 2014 by the Levada Center, two thirds of those in Russia over the age of 55 had never traveled outside of the former Soviet Union; among younger people, the share not yet having traveled was somewhat higher (Manaev 2018).[10] In striking contrast, one woman I encountered at a gathering for pensioners at a Municipal Center for Social Services noted proudly that she had visited 17 different countries. Another, an academic who traveled in connection with her work, mentioned having been in Germany 58 or 59 times.

Although for many of my respondents foreign travel had become quite routine, several of the women wove amusing (and sometimes poignant) anecdotes about their stunned reactions on their first such visits. (See, for example, the description of shopping for shoes in Chapter 3.) One woman recalled traveling to the USA in 1987 (earlier than most) as part of a delegation of teachers, when Presidents Mikhail Gorbachev and Ronald Reagan were cautiously encouraging cultural exchanges.

> And it was very interesting. I was in Pennsylvania, in Philadelphia, at the University of Pennsylvania. Life was very different then.... I think that nothing has ever surprised me as much as I was surprised then. [Liza, 55]

The woman who considered Germany to be a paradise justified her use of that term.

> It's not a metaphor; it's true. Suddenly with surprise you find out that the colors are not the same, and the houses are not the same, and the entire infrastructure is not the same, and the stores are not the same, everything is different, and [even] the people are a little bit different, which is very important. [Ekaterina, 56]

[10] In comparison, 37% of European Union citizens have never traveled outside their home country, despite the common currency and absence of border controls. https://www.europeandatajournalism.eu/News/Data-news/190-million-Europeans-have-never-been-abroad.

Not everyone viewed the countries they visited so favorably, however. One woman, during an unrecorded conversation, talked about a trip to the USA in the 1990s and her eager anticipation of a gathering at which she was to be the guest speaker. She was excited to be in the USA, still finding it hard to believe that such a thing was possible, and looked forward to sharing her delight at the improved relations between the countries with the women in attendance. What she encountered instead seemed to her to be hostility and suspicion. Because she has a number of close American friends and a deep admiration for the democratic system, she was still struggling, almost two decades after the event, to make sense of the experience.

Even if some trips proved disappointing, for many of the women, especially those who born in the 1950s, this greater freedom to travel was the first thing to come to mind when I asked if there were changes since the late 1980s that they found positive.

A woman in Astrakhan said:

> Even at that time [the very difficult years of the early 1990s], I saw many plusses. A great many plusses. For example, the opportunity to travel abroad, as a tourist, to any country, not just Bulgaria or Czechoslovakia, let's say. To any country. And the opportunity to watch films, read books—that for me was the biggest advantage. And, naturally, to be able to speak freely.

A professor in Yaroslavl, after indicating that she would have been better off financially in the Soviet system than she was when we talked, continued:

> but I wouldn't have been able, like now, to order a ticket, order a hotel room and travel to Madrid. Or if I'd wanted to go to Norway, to the fjords, or to Portugal, I couldn't have done that. Now [my husband and I] work, day and night, in order to be able to enjoy our hobby. Our hobby is travel…. We love to travel, and we wanted to go to Paris…. From 1991 to 1996 we had to save up so that we could go for a week, for ten days, the three of us, to Paris. For ten days in Paris, we had to save for five years. And then we wanted to travel to Italy, and we had to devote two years to that. [Liza, 55]

As is clear from this comment, for the second woman even the positive changes carried a downside. Now they are allowed to travel, but they have to "work day and night" to be able to afford it. This sense that even the greater freedoms brought by the end of the Soviet period were a mixed blessing ran throughout her reminiscences, as it did through the reminiscences of most.

## Religion

Although the Soviet Union was officially an atheist state, neither religious organizations nor religious beliefs were entirely eliminated under communism. At the time of the Bolshevik Revolution, the overwhelming majority of the Russian population belonged to the Orthodox Church and, despite anti-religious propaganda, the arrest of many religious leaders, and the practice of converting church buildings for any number of strictly secular uses—including municipal swimming pools and granaries—some people continued to worship. Of the 54,000 Orthodox churches in operation in 1914, 4200 were still functioning on the eve of World War II. The number grew to 16,000 by 1945, as Joseph Stalin turned to traditional Russian culture, including Orthodoxy, to heighten patriotism during the war, but fell again once the war was over, reaching 7500 in 1966 (Froese 2004: 42).

As freedom of expression increased under Gorbachev in the late 1980s, more people turned to the open practice—or exploration of—religious faith and spiritualism in a wide range of forms, some imported and some home-grown. By 1993, according to one source, some one thousand foreign missionaries affiliated with fifty different organizations had traveled to the former Soviet Union to share their faith (Schmemann 1993). This was, surprisingly, not the first time people from outside the Orthodox faith had proselytized in the country. In fact, in 1970 almost one third of professing Christians in the Soviet Union were not Orthodox believers (Froese 2004: 38–39). There are also parts of the country that have traditionally followed other faith traditions, especially Buddhism and Islam, with the latter second only to Orthodoxy in the number of adherents.

After the dissolution of the USSR and Russia's formal separation from the other former republics, the Orthodox Church reasserted its primacy, growing in both political and symbolic stature. Russian leaders appeared, frequently awkwardly, at church services, and Orthodoxy was officially distinguished from other religions as uniquely Russian. This distinction is embodied, for example, in the preamble to the law *On Freedom of Conscience and on Religious Associations* adopted in 1997, which reads, in part, "Recognizing the special contribution of Orthodoxy to the history of Russia and to the establishment and development of Russia's spirituality and culture" before adding the conciliatory phrase, "Respecting Christianity, Islam, Buddhism, Judaism and other religions which constitute an inseparable part of the historical heritage of Russia's peoples" (Cesnur).

The apparent turn to religion by Russian leaders was the subject of considerable mockery by some of my respondents.

> All our Communists, starting with Yeltsin or thereabouts...all suddenly became believers. And look at them, they don't know how to cross themselves, they don't know the words to the prayers. Svetlana Medvedeva[11] stood there at a Christmas service or some such occasion, I don't remember exactly, in the cathedral. They showed them [on television]. When it came to the choral reading of the prayers...well, if you're a parishioner, if you're a Christian and you go to church and aspire to be seen as a civilized person, well then, you learn [the prayers], at least the most basic ones. You'll somehow remember some of the prayers. She just stood there and moved her lips, out of synch. They showed her on the camera, she opened her mouth like a singer who is lip-synching. Well, how is this possible? This causes me a feeling of some sort of regret. It makes me sad. It's annoying that this takes place, that there's this kind of artificial, manipulative insincerity. I feel this insincerity in my skin. [Yulia, 52]

Religion—Orthodox, Jewish, and Protestant—played an important role in the lives of several of the women I talked to. In some cases, this involved active participation in regular worship services, while in others it was limited to particular rituals, like those marking the death of a family member. One woman, who had been baptized as a child in the 1950s but did not practice openly, told me that praying was what helped her get through the difficult times of the early 1990s. For other women, connection to religion was a post-Soviet development, in some cases directly the result of contact with foreigners.

As discussed in Chapter 10, one woman with a Jewish mother and a Russian father used the new freedom of religion to establish a program to teach Jewish customs. As she makes clear, foreigners were essential in providing her with information and explaining the fundamentals of Jewish religion and culture.

> [In 1991] I started to organize Jewish school on Sundays. But I didn't know anything about it, I didn't understand a word.... We were taught a lot, I visited a lot of seminars in Israel and Moscow, a lot of Israel and

[11]Wife of Dmitri Medvedev, Putin's Prime Minister, who served as placeholder president at the end of Putin's second full term in office and returned to the position of Prime Minister when Putin was re-elected as President in 2012.

American teachers came and taught us how to work with youth, with children. But they didn't ask us to move to Israel… There was always freedom of choice…. [In our] weekend school … we study Hebrew language, traditions, the basics of the Torah, the history of the Jewish people, the music, songs and dances. [Polina, 64]

One woman I met but did not formally interview was eager to talk with me about the way her life had been transformed by her conversion. She attended the Yaroslavl Church of God, an evangelical Pentecostal Church celebrating its twenty-first anniversary in the fall of 2012. Although I was unable to learn the history of the church in any detail, it almost certainly was established as a result of American involvement, first with missionaries teaching Russians about this branch of Christianity and later probably with financial assistance. She joined the church in 1994 at the invitation of a friend and credited it with her decision to pursue more education (a degree in psychology), her choice of career (working with the Department of Social Services), and the transformation of her personal relationships.

A Russian Orthodox believer, who has found great comfort in her faith as she deals with a number of difficulties in her life, traveled to a small town outside of Yaroslavl in 1989 so she could be secretly baptized. Although she did not suggest that there was any connection, 1989 was also the year she survived a serious medical problem. American missionaries did not lead her to her faith, but did give her an opportunity for interesting work, meaningful friendships and, eventually, travel to the USA. After suffering a professional setback, she needed to find employment.

When one door shuts, another opens, yes, another opens—and suddenly I received an invitation from a group of American Christians, who had come to Yaroslavl with a Christian mission. …Their task was to teach Russian teachers [who would be] teaching the Bible in Russian schools… And this great team came [at the invitation of a school whose teachers knew me and recommended me]…. And this was a very happy time for me, because I had a wonderful group of friends, a group of friends who are still with me, with whom I still correspond actively, and in 2000, I

> visited them. I went to America at their invitation and spent a month traveling to various states. It was simply wonderful. These are my friends who still support me, who supported me then.... Unfortunately, the mission ended sometime around 1996, I think. It ended in 1996, then a few of them stayed, but then it closed completely. [Sofia, 61]

She sees the faith of her Protestant missionary friends as compatible with rather than challenging her own Orthodox beliefs. Her openness to other faiths is evident as well in her decision while I was in Yaroslavl to offer Russian language classes to immigrants at a mosque in the city. This endeavor, begun in the fall of 2012, has flourished and led to many close friendships.

Religion, in Russia as elsewhere, has been both a source of divisiveness and a source of comfort and community. The government's decision to allow people to worship openly soon evolved into an effort to use religion as a political tool. Many of my respondents ignored (or criticized) the more manipulative elements of this strategy, while appreciating the opportunity to develop a meaningful, personal relationship with a faith tradition.

## Political Engagement

Although the Soviet system was initially envisioned as a "dictatorship of the proletariat," by the time the 1936 Constitution was adopted this formulation had been replaced and the Communist Party was acknowledged as the "leading and guiding force" of Soviet society. Although about 10% of the population belonged to the Party, by the 1980s this membership was almost entirely instrumental—one became a member to gain access to better education and employment opportunities, not because one espoused the ideology. As one woman said:

> In the past, I belonged to the Komosomol. This was natural, because all people of my age were members of the Komsomol organization, otherwise it was simply impossible, you see? It's natural, natural. You probably know something about our education system. You know that all of us,

> no matter what we were studying—a foreign language, sports, geography, mathematics—we all had to study the history of the Communist Party of the Soviet Union…[and] Marxism-Leninism… and … scientific communism. We all studied this. Therefore, on my diploma all these items are of course listed. It is all listed. Otherwise, I could not [have graduated]. We were required to do it. [Ekaterina, 56]

Another woman of about the same age, on the other hand, stressed that her own membership was sincere and that she was saddened in 1991 when the Party was (as it turned out only temporarily) made illegal. She did not rejoin when the Party was resurrected, however, nor does she have any interest in joining any other political party.

> At one time, I was a member of the Communist Party. Why was I a member? I was someone who held the idea sacred, who believed in the idea. That is, not for a career, not for something else. I joined the Party not for my career, but because I believed….

When I asked at what point she had left the Party, she responded:

> I did not leave. It's just that the Party disappeared. I never left. But I swore to myself that I would never again participate in any political party. Not in the party, not in any religion. Nothing like that can, I don't know, swallow me up. This is what I swear to myself, [I will not commit] to any other idea, because I experienced a very great disappointment when the new period arrived. [Liza, 55]

After Gorbachev assumed power in 1985, political engagement became increasingly real. Not only were controls on public speech and the press gradually loosened, there was the possibility of genuinely contested elections. Voting suddenly mattered, and people began to pay serious attention to the speeches and votes in legislative sessions. In fact, people apparently paid so much attention to live broadcasts of the sessions of the Congress of Peoples' Deputies in 1989 and 1990 that they were distracted from work and industrial output fell during the periods the Congress was meeting (Richter 1995). In addition to closely following discussions in the legislative bodies and voting in elections, people began to participate in street protests and demonstrations. This was particularly true in the non-Russian republics, where the protests tended to be directed against Russian control at least as much as against Soviet policies. Within Russia itself, the most significant protest occurred in August of 1991, in response to the attempted coup by a handful of the old guard. It was the success of this protest, during which Boris Yeltsin stood defiantly atop a tank in Moscow while the vacationing Mikhail Gorbachev was held under house arrest in Crimea, that effectively ended the Soviet Union, although the official dissolution did not take place for another few months.

One of my respondents was actually in Moscow during the coup attempt. Having been granted the opportunity to travel to Germany later in the year, she went to Moscow on August 20, the day after the takeover was announced, to take care of some necessary paperwork. While there, she encountered protests against the seizure of power.

> The whole of the horror that occurred there I saw with my own eyes. I saw the blood… where tanks crushed the people. And I also saw the barricades. You understand, I considered it necessary to visit all these places. [Ekaterina, 56]

That she was able to travel by train from Yaroslavl to Moscow that day suggests just how ill-prepared and disorganized the leaders of the coup were and how little control they were actually exercising over the channels of communication and transportation.

This woman contrasts her own political activism with the apathy of others, describing her experiences on August 19, while she was still in Yaroslavl.

> I set out…to find some barricades…. I thought that something would have begun, that people would be protesting, and I searched for a place where I could protest. But there was nothing like that in Yaroslavl. I'm trying to paint a picture of that day for you. I could think of nothing at all except that we might again return to communism. And this worried me. I kept thinking, how do we all gather, how do we start to protest?… And suddenly I saw that there was a line—and the line was for acquiring

mayonnaise. You know, it just made no sense to me. I thought, what mayonnaise? We should be thinking about democracy, we should be protesting, not standing in some line, waiting for mayonnaise of all things!

Other women admitted to the kind of apathy disparaged above—or to fear—and described deliberately staying away from the protests, and encouraging loved ones to stay away as well.

I was very apolitical. …I was only interested in my family, my child…. My husband was very active and in 1991… he planned to go to Moscow, to defend things there…. He called me and said, 'I'm going to Moscow.' I said, 'How can you say that? What if something happens? What about me? What would happen to me?' So he didn't go…. All that politics just didn't interest me. What was going on in the White House,[12] it was far away, in Moscow, and I was here. [Marta, 45]

On August 19 my son called me and …said, 'Mom, I'm going to Moscow.' I said, 'What are you doing? Don't go.' 'Mom, if not us, then who?' Those were my son's words. And my husband and I—it's hard even to say this—wrote his last name on a piece of paper and put it in his pocket, in case something happened. You understand, the people believed and stood up for this. And some of the young people died.[13] [Lidia, 70]

Watching first the rise in political engagement by Soviet citizens and then the actual dissolution of the Soviet Union, many American observers anticipated the establishment of American-style democracy, even though something akin to the parliamentary systems of much of Western Europe was more likely. In fact, of course, what has emerged in post-Soviet Russia bears little resemblance in substance to either of these models. While officially a parliamentary system is in place, Boris Yeltsin worked successfully to curb the power of the parliament and Vladimir Putin has taken the consolidation of power in the President's office even further.

[12]This is a reference to the Russian White House, the seat of the Russian government and the building housing the office of the Russian Prime Minister.

[13]There were three fatalities.

At the time of my interviews, the country was preparing for a number of regional and local elections, including those for the Yaroslavl city council. There were campaign posters (often defaced) everywhere, and video screens on trolleys repeatedly ran advertisements for political parties, although I never saw any for specific candidates. Most of the women I spoke to planned to vote but displayed little enthusiasm for any particular candidate. Any excitement generated by the surprise success of the independent candidate in the mayoral election earlier that year (see Note 9) seemed to have been dampened by Putin's return to the presidency[14] and the adoption of legislation seriously curtailing political protests (Herszenhorn 2012). One woman had not been aware

[14]Putin was appointed President when Yeltsin resigned on December 31, 1999, and then elected to continue in that position in March of 2000. He was re-elected four years later to a second full term. Since there is a limit of two consecutive terms, he then stepped down, effectively trading places with his Prime Minister, Dmitri Medvedev. After this four-year break he was again eligible to serve as president. He was elected to a (now six-year) term in 2012 and re-elected in 2018.

that municipal elections were about to take place until I mentioned it. Although she assured me that she would vote in them, she expressed no confidence in either her ability to choose among the candidates or in its mattering who ultimately won.

> I will take part. But, you know, it's very complicated, choosing people whom you don't know at all. And it all turns out the same. I don't know where people get information about how to vote, because they're all the same, they're almost all the same, and it all turns out the same, and not at all what we wanted. So there's a choice, but is it really a choice? [Regina, 61]

This sense of resignation was echoed by the husband of one of the women when he told me that he thought there would be no real chance for democracy until an entirely new generation came of political age. A dissenting note, however, came from 55-year-old Liza, self-identified true believer in the Communist Party of the Soviet Union, now determined not to let any idea "swallow her up":

> I am a very law-abiding citizen, and without fail I always vote. We have an election, elections are necessary. I am a respectable citizen, I am a law-abiding citizen, and I think that I definitely need to vote, since my vote can change some decisions. I believe in this. I always vote.

## References

Adams, Walter, and James W. Brock. 1993. *Adam Smith Goes to Moscow: A Dialogue on Radical Reform*. Princeton: Princeton University Press.

Arutunyan, Anna. 2012. An Independent Mayor in Yaroslavl. *Moscow News*, April 3, 2012. Accessed online at http://themoscownews.com/politics/20120402/189583873.html. October 2014.

CESNUR, Center for Studies on New Religions. Keston Institute's Translation of New Russian Law on Religion. Accessed online at https://www.cesnur.org/testi/Russia.htm. February 2019.

Froese, Paul. 2004. Forced Secularization in Soviet Russia: Why an Atheistic Monopoly Failed. *Journal for the Scientific Study of Religion* 43 (1): 35–50.

Herszenhorn, David. 2012. New Russian Law Assesses Heavy Fines on Protesters. *New York Times*, June 9, p. A5.
Herszenhorn, David. 2013. Russian Mayor, an Opposition Figure, Is Arrested. *New York Times*, July 3. Accessed online at http://www.nytimes.com/2013/07/04/world/europe/russian-mayor-an-opposition-figure-is-arrested.html?_r=0. October 2014.
League of Women Voters. *The League of Women Voters Through the Decades—The 1990s*. Accessed online at http://library.lwv.org/content/league-women-voters-through-decades-1990s. February 2019.
Manaev, Georgy. 2018. Why Russians Have 2 Passports. *Russia Behind the Headlines*. Accessed online at https://www.rbth.com/lifestyle/328576-why-russians-have-2-passports. February 2019.
*New York Times*. 1992. Summit in Washington: There Will Be No More Lies, June 18.
Richter, Andrei G. 1995. The Russian Press After Perestroika. *Canadian Journal of Communication* 20 (1). Accessed online at http://cjc-online.ca/index.php/journal/article/view/842/748. January 2018.
Sakwa, Richard. 2002. *Russian Politics and Society* (3rd ed.). London and New York: Routledge.
Schmemann, Serge. 1993. Religion Returns to Russia, with a Vengeance. *New York Times*, July 28, p. A1.
Siegelbaum, Lewis. 2009. On the Side: Car Culture in the USSR, 1960s–1980s. *Technology and Culture* 50 (1): 1–23.
Wedel, Janine R. 1998. The Harvard Boys Do Russia. *The Nation*, May 14.
Yurchak, Alexei. 2006. *Everything Was Forever, Until It Was No More: The Last Soviet Generation*. Princeton: Princeton University Press.

# 12
# Conclusion

Four months talking with women in Yaroslavl about their lives before, during and after the Russian government's introduction of economic "shock therapy" led me to appreciate more fully the insight offered by a woman in Astrakhan in 2010: "For you in the West, the transition is still in the front of your minds, but for us, it's a long time ago and we've gone on with our lives."

One of the consequences of the fact that it was "a long time ago" is that many of the details had blurred and experiences had been reinterpreted in light of subsequent events. What I have presented is therefore a collection of very personal "truths" rather than a strictly accurate account of what happened. In addition to frequently confusing dates and disagreeing about the specifics of particular policies, the women clearly shaped their narratives to reflect their preferred self-images. Often after making a comment they went on to tell me how I should interpret it. This was especially true when the conversation dealt with wage arrears or poverty, but also occurred when they spoke of political engagement and of interaction with non-Russians.

There is a limit to how much one can generalize from the stories I have presented here. These were the experiences of a very particular


J. McKinney, *Russian Women and the End of Soviet Socialism*,
https://doi.org/10.1007/978-3-030-16226-9_12

group of Russians—female, urban, mostly middle-aged, middle-class educated members of the *intelligentsia*, mothers of young children or adolescents during the difficult years of the late 1980s and early 1990s. Despite differences in emphasis loosely correlated with age, these women held largely similar attitudes and expressed largely similar emotions—sorrow that they had been unable to provide as well for their children as they would have liked (and could have expected), regret for the uncertainties the new economic, political and social arrangements had introduced into their children's lives, a complex mix of emotions when those children had chosen unfamiliar paths in order to navigate this new environment, and considerable pride when the children had achieved significant success. There was also pride in their own accomplishments, especially for those who had established their own businesses—pride in their ability to cope when things were particularly difficult and pride in their ability to take advantage of the new economic opportunities to support themselves in ways that avoided behaving like the New Russians and remained consistent with their core values.

Just as their experiences and narratives were colored in important ways by their identities, the recollections they offered were no doubt also colored by my own identities—as an American, an academic, a woman older than several of my respondents, a wife, and the mother of a grown daughter. My American identity led many of the women to compare their own experiences and their country's accomplishments with what they assumed to be true in the USA.[1] My age and education meant that they expected me to be knowledgeable about many of the topics we discussed and to be able to put their experiences in context on my own. My roles as wife and mother almost certainly influenced the content of many of the conversations, since it was taken for granted that I would share their concerns about how their children were faring.

[1]One humorous example involved a woman's embarrassed description of washing, drying and reusing plastic bags because they were so rare, finding it impossible to believe my comment that I have always done the same, if for different reasons.

Overall, the pictures the women painted were of difficult times overcome with intelligence, strength, and above all character—frugality, resilience, lack of ostentation, "culturedness". They did not suffer from wage arrears, they assured me, because they knew how to make do and were content to live modestly. They resented the "New Russians" for vulgar displays of wealth as much as for the ways in which that wealth had been acquired. One of the greatest losses they identified with the collapse of the Soviet Union was that of culture, civility and concern for the well-being of others.

Although talking about their lives in the late 1980s and early 1990s clearly stirred up unhappy memories—a few women were on the brink of tears at some points in our conversations—most of those I spoke with indicated how much they appreciated the opportunity to think back on all that had happened. Those years had indeed been very difficult, but they were "a long time ago" and the women were proud of what they had made of their lives since then. While recognizing that many of their accomplishments were possible precisely because of the changes that had made those times so difficult, they did not generally view present success as justifying past hardships, and clearly believed that the difficulties had been far greater than necessary. The fault for this, in their eyes, lay squarely with the reformers (and their Western advisors). The women might enjoy running their own successful businesses, travelling freely to other countries, being able to acquire a wide array of consumer goods and services with little inconvenience, and being able to talk openly with an American about their lives—but they did not forgive those who had overseen the changes that made this possible. While part of this had to do with regret for the loss of those things about the Soviet system they admired—job security, greater equality, confidence that their children would receive a good education and lead a decent life, better relations among the republics, greater international status—much of it was the result of their conviction that the leaders' focus on enriching themselves caused a great deal of unnecessary pain for the rest of the population.

When I conducted my interviews in the fall of 2012, for most of the women that pain was largely a thing of the past. Unfortunately, in the years since those interviews there has been a dramatic deterioration in

Russian–US relations and, as a result, considerable difficulties in the Russian economy. Although designed to target Putin's inner circle and a particular group of business leaders, sanctions imposed by the West in 2013 in response to Russia's re-appropriation of Crimea and continued involvement in Ukraine have inevitably imposed costs on ordinary Russian citizens as well.

Russians are again facing inflation, although certainly not the hyperinflation of the early 1990s. Some of the increase in prices is attributable to Putin's decision to respond to the Western sanctions by imposing a ban on food imports from the USA and the European Union. This ban, introduced in August of 2014 and extended in the summer of 2018, means that Russians must spend an increasing share of their income on food, leaving less for the purchase of other kinds of consumer goods and services. An April 2016 article in the Russian newspaper *Kommersant* reported that in February of that year over half of retail turnover consisted of food, alcohol and tobacco products "for the first time in eight years" (Ryumin 2016). With wages and pensions rising less than consumer prices, more Russians are also experiencing poverty again. In his addresses to the Federal Assembly in 2018 and 2019, Putin cited a poverty figure of 19–20 million, a bit less than 14% of the population (Putin 2018, 2019). While higher than the 10.7% that held in 2012, this is still far below the 42% living in poverty or extreme poverty in 1993 (Silverman and Yanowitch 1997: 52).

I was unsuccessful in eliciting many responses to an e-mail request for an update on the lives of the women I had interviewed, and most of those I received were friendly but uninformative, so I cannot be sure whether they have been seriously affected by the rising inflation and rising poverty. The one e-mail answer that provided any details or offered any opinion of the current situation was quite negative:

> It seems to me that the situation in Russia is getting worse. People are becoming poorer. Democracy has died. There is very poor health care. I had to have a minor operation in the summer and it was terrible!!! I ran into a lot of problems and realized that we have no social guarantees of any kind. I am thinking about emigrating. [Marta, 45]

In 2012, this woman had said "I would like it very much if my daughter left Russia for somewhere where she could use her mind," but had not indicated any desire to emigrate herself. (She did not mention in her e-mail where her daughter is currently living.) Marta is now, as in 2012, supplementing her income from teaching at the post-secondary level by working a couple of days a week in a school with young children. She is as disenchanted with the situation in education as with the situation in health care:

> I see that only in prestigious schools can one receive an education. In an ordinary public school, no.

In contrast, I know from social media that at least two of the women I interviewed continue to take trips to Europe and Asia—one has also traveled to Africa—which suggests that they are still comfortably well-off.

Recent international developments offer both encouraging and discouraging signs. In the summer of 2018, the US State Department proposed new sanctions against Russia, driving the value of the ruble down by several percent and raising the price of imported goods. Charges that Russia was responsible for the poisoning of a former agent in Britain and for meddling in the 2016 elections in the USA continue to cast a shadow over relations between Russia and the West, as does the political situation in a number of countries where Russia and the USA support opposing sides. At the same time, increased trade tensions between the USA and China may offer Russia the opportunity to strengthen its own economic ties to the East and secure new markets for its energy exports.

Domestically, too, the picture is mixed. In October 2018, Putin signed a law raising the age at which people can begin to receive pensions. While generally considered by economists to be long overdue, this pension reform will nonetheless make it harder for those in their late fifties to get by. Response to the proposed changes was so negative, in fact, that the government back-pedaled a bit, setting the new retirement age for women at 60, rather than at 63, as initially announced. (For men, the age was raised from 60 to 65.) Because most Russian women continue to work for several years after qualifying for pensions, this change will primarily mean a reduction in income for women between 55 and 60 rather than a longer working life. It will also, of course, result in significant savings for the government.

In contrast to the pension reform, some recent policy initiatives would, if implemented, make life easier for many Russians. In 2018, Putin called for expanding a program granting low-interest loans to small businesses and in 2019 he proposed a number of measures aimed at making it easier for families to buy houses, raise children, and get good health care (Putin 2018, 2019). What will come of these proposals is unclear, and the population could be forgiven for a certain amount of cynicism as they listened to Putin's promise of a brighter future.

> Allow me to underscore: thanks to years of common work and the results achieved, we can now direct and concentrate enormous financial resources – at least enormous for our country – on development goals. These resources have not come as a rainfall. We have not borrowed them. These funds have been earned by millions of our citizens – by the entire country. They need to be applied to increase the wealth of Russia and the wellbeing of Russian families. Very soon, this year people should feel real changes for the better. (Putin 2019)

This is a promise Russians heard for years from Soviet leaders and heard again from those overseeing the end of the Soviet system. Unlike earlier leaders, however, Putin is claiming that the sacrifices have already been made and the promised benefits will be realized "this year."

In 2012 one of my respondents told me her favorite expression about her country: "In Russia, everything changes in five years, but nothing changes in 200 years." Having visited and studied this fascinating and frustrating place for almost fifty years, my perspective is considerably longer than the five-year short term and considerably shorter than the 200-year long term. It is therefore perhaps not surprising that what I learned from my interviews in 2012 and have seen happening in the years since then has given me a picture showing both impressive changes from the country I first encountered and disconcerting signs that some of the more positive of those changes are at risk today. I cannot predict what Russia will be like in 150 years, but I know that, for now, the ingenuity, adaptability, resilience and courage my respondents exhibited as the Soviet experiment with socialism came to an end will continue to serve them well.

## References

Putin, Vladimir. 2018. *Presidential Address to the Federal Assembly*. Accessed online at http://en.kremlin.ru/events/president/news/copy/56957. March 2019.

Putin, Vladimir. 2019. *Presidential Address to the Federal Assembly*. Accessed online at http://en.kremlin.ru/events/president/transcripts/messages/59863. March 2019.

Ryumin, Alexander. 2016. *Kommersant*. Accessed online at https://www.rbth.com/politics_and_society/2016/04/21/russians-now-spending-half-of-their-income-on-food_586753. March 2019.

Silverman, Bertram, and Murray Yanowitch. 1997. *New Rich, New Poor, New Russia: Winners and Losers on the Russian Road to Capitalism*. Armonk, NY: M.E. Sharpe.

# Index

A
Alcohol/alcoholism 9, 41, 43, 45, 46, 69, 133, 145, 194, 195, 197, 204, 276
America 5, 47, 97, 131, 195, 200, 201, 221, 236–239, 245–247, 265. *See also* USA
Apartment 7, 21, 22, 25, 37, 38, 43, 63, 73, 90–92, 97, 109, 119, 121, 132, 142, 150, 157, 158, 169, 181–183, 185, 188, 193, 194, 198, 201, 203, 222, 223, 231. *See also* Housing
Astrakhan 58, 70, 84, 104, 109, 260, 273
Authoritative discourse 31, 194

B
Birth rate 24, 41
Bolshevik 15, 23, 26, 28, 67, 126, 164, 167, 215, 261
Brezhnev, Leonid 2, 14, 16, 19, 21, 27, 28, 31, 63, 64, 115, 237

C
Central planning 5, 14, 15, 22, 78, 113, 118, 164, 190
Chechnya 223, 226, 228, 234
Childcare 23, 25, 35, 93, 95, 111, 119, 149
Children 4, 7, 9–11, 17, 24, 25, 36, 39–43, 45, 48, 49, 55–57, 65–68, 72, 82, 91–94, 99, 105, 110, 116, 118, 119, 125,


J. McKinney, *Russian Women and the End of Soviet Socialism*,
https://doi.org/10.1007/978-3-030-16226-9

127–129, 131, 132, 135, 136, 160, 171, 175, 180, 193–198, 200, 201, 203, 205–208, 211, 212, 226, 232–234, 238, 239, 264, 274, 275, 277, 278
Chubais, Anatoly 166, 167, 174, 176, 181, 184
Communist Party of the Soviet Union (CPSU) 26, 126, 266, 270
Consumer goods 17, 18, 20, 25, 35, 57, 64, 74, 75, 177, 189, 206, 212, 258, 275, 276
Coup 7, 236, 267
Coupons 17, 20, 64, 66–72, 109. *See also Talony*

D

Dacha 69, 70, 98–101, 198. *See also* Garden
Democratization 1, 201, 217
Disability 7, 40, 47, 81, 204, 206–208, 211, 212
Divorce 6, 8, 46, 55, 91, 106, 154, 194–196

E

Education 4, 10, 17–19, 23, 31, 37, 40, 43, 44, 46, 49, 51, 56, 96, 117, 119, 126, 127, 129–131, 133, 134, 136, 147, 149, 150, 154, 156, 160, 179, 185, 192, 195, 197, 199, 201, 203, 204, 208, 216, 217, 223, 224, 229, 240, 245, 254, 264, 265, 274, 275, 277
Election 1, 26, 36, 129, 245, 251, 266, 269, 270, 277
Employment 6, 8, 10, 11, 18, 19, 24, 25, 28, 44–46, 55, 67, 83, 84, 89, 91, 93, 98, 102, 111, 114, 116, 122, 123, 126, 131, 133, 139, 147, 149, 173, 218, 224, 264, 265
Entrepreneur 8, 36, 45, 89, 103, 107, 123, 124, 134, 139, 140, 144, 148, 152, 153, 155, 156, 159–162, 206, 208, 249, 252. *See also* Private enterprise; Small business
Ethnicity 11, 121, 204, 216, 218, 221, 230, 231
Extensive mothering 93

G

Garden 25, 83, 98–101
GDR 54, 55, 258. *See also* Germany
Gender contract 13, 23, 24, 42, 206
Germany 8, 20, 54, 58, 172, 221, 235–237, 239, 252, 254, 255, 258, 259, 267. *See also* GDR
*Glasnost* 1, 201, 217, 232
Gorbachev, Mikhail 1, 2, 9, 14, 27–29, 31, 45, 64, 68, 74, 81, 100, 102, 107, 126, 139, 159, 188, 190, 197, 217, 229, 259, 261, 266, 267

H

Housing 19–21, 23, 25, 35, 38, 40, 55, 83, 90–92, 111, 116, 119, 149, 206, 217, 219, 223, 224, 268. *See also* Apartment

I

Inequality 5, 11, 14, 20, 22, 149, 186, 188–190, 204, 212
 economic 11, 22, 186, 187, 189, 191, 193, 201, 204, 212
Inflation 1, 76, 78, 85, 165, 225, 276
Intelligentsia 6, 7, 20, 43, 101, 103, 129, 133, 188, 202–204, 274
Israel 131, 136, 153, 181, 234–239, 263

J

Jews/Jewish 121, 148, 153, 218–221, 231–238, 243, 263
Joint venture 254

K

KGB 8, 36, 51, 52, 193, 257
Khrushchev, Nikita 14, 21, 25, 27–29, 85, 194
Kindergartens 95, 116–119, 128, 149, 150
Komsomol 8, 57, 150, 166, 265

L

Life expectancy 41, 98
Loans for shares 170

M

Market
 farmers 102
 labor 11, 111, 115, 116, 121, 122, 125, 131, 224
 prices 75, 76
 system 16, 23, 110, 183
Marriage 6, 7, 9, 10, 24, 45, 47, 50, 91, 92, 96, 154, 156, 236
Marx, Karl 20, 26, 75
Maternity capital 41
Mavrodi, Sergey 169. *See also* MMM
Men 13, 24, 25, 28, 39, 44–48, 83, 123, 124, 126, 160, 173, 194, 198, 204, 205, 216, 227, 253, 277
Migration
 Services 8, 48, 161, 171, 172, 223, 225–227
MMM 168, 176, 177, 180, 183. *See also* Mavrodi, Sergey
Money, role of 189
Moscow 2–4, 6, 7, 17, 22, 23, 28, 36, 47, 55, 58, 59, 65, 66, 70, 77, 82, 84, 94, 96, 110, 118, 121, 131–136, 144, 160, 174, 179, 200, 220, 231, 234, 239, 244, 248, 257, 258, 265, 267, 268

N

Nationalism 121, 217, 219, 220, 230
Neoliberalism 110, 183, 247
New Russians 3, 140, 149, 152, 167, 185, 188, 189, 191–194, 202, 204, 205, 274, 275

O

Oligarchs 2, 78, 167, 169, 189, 212, 213

P

Pension 6, 7, 40, 78, 81, 95, 96, 98, 99, 106, 107, 124, 128, 160, 198, 224, 226, 239, 276–278
Perestroika 2, 10, 40, 42, 46, 48, 49, 54, 64, 68, 98, 100, 107, 110, 119, 139, 159, 192, 193, 197, 203, 219
Poverty 36, 48, 49, 189–191, 194–200, 203, 204, 273, 276
Prices 1, 2, 11, 16–19, 35, 44, 64, 65, 68, 73–79, 85, 86, 89, 97, 109, 163–166, 168, 170, 175, 182, 276, 277
  liberalization 1, 2, 64, 65, 75, 76, 97
  market 75, 76
Private enterprise 139, 161, 253
  registration of 158
  taxes and 158
Privatization 1, 2, 11, 38, 64, 124, 140, 153, 164, 166–170, 172–174, 177, 180, 181, 183, 185, 186, 188, 189, 192, 201, 205, 213. *See also* Voucher
Propiska 22. *See also* Residence permit
Protests 211, 236, 267–269
Putin, Vladimir 36, 40, 41, 49, 55, 86, 142, 201, 226, 268, 269, 276–278

R

Rationing 2, 17, 20, 67, 174
Residence permit 23, 67, 114, 228. *See also* Propiska

S

Shock therapy 64, 68, 273
Shopping 2, 64, 65, 72, 74, 75, 158, 259
Shortages 9, 35, 64, 73, 74, 78, 196, 224
Shuttle trade 46, 106, 252
Small business 6, 140, 147, 148, 159, 161, 167, 248, 249, 278
Social contract 13, 31, 37
Social network 25, 45, 49, 66, 90, 111, 131, 171
Stalin, Joseph 16, 19, 20, 26, 27, 35, 103, 114, 261

T

*Talony* 66, 67, 70. *See also* Coupons
Travel 6, 10, 11, 17, 23, 30, 36, 54, 55, 57, 59, 103, 105, 107, 119, 135, 136, 158, 173, 198, 200, 232, 240, 243, 244, 254, 255, 258–261, 264, 265, 267, 275, 277

U

Unemployment 1, 83, 113–116, 122, 238
USA 29, 54, 86, 90, 97, 131, 161, 245–248, 259, 260, 264, 274, 276, 277. *See also* America
Uzbekistan 130, 154, 218

V

Voting 29, 30, 235, 248, 250, 266, 269, 270. *See also* Election

Voucher 2, 3, 11, 38, 153, 164, 167–186, 192. *See also* Privatization

W

Wages
  arrears of 3, 9, 78, 79, 100, 124, 189, 203, 252, 273, 275

Y

Yeltsin, Boris 1, 64, 74, 107, 188, 197, 217, 247, 263, 267, 268

Kolibri 360 GmbH
Ferdinand-Jühlke-Straße 7
99095 Erfurt, Deutschland
produktsicherheit@kolibri360.de

Ralph J. Panos, William L. Eschenbacher
**A COPD Primer**

Ralph J. Panos,
William L. Eschenbacher

# A COPD Primer

Managing Editor: Magdalena Wierzchowiecka

Language Editor: Dylan Richards

DE GRUYTER
OPEN

Published by De Gruyter Open Ltd, Warsaw/Berlin
Part of Walter de Gruyter GmbH, Berlin/Munich/Boston



ISBN: 978-3-11-046799-4
e-ISBN: 978-3-11-046800-7

Bibliographic information published by the Deutsche Nationalbibliothek. The Deutsche National-bibliothek lists this publication in the Deutsche Nationalbibliografie; detailed bibliographic data are available in the Internet at http://dnb.dnb.de.

Managing Editor: Magdalena Wierzchowiecka
Language Editor: Dylan Richards

www.degruyteropen.com

Cover illustration: is an original work by Mohammad Ahsan Zafar, MD.

# Contents

**Preface —— xvii**

Ralph J. Panos, MD

**1 Introduction and Definition of Chronic Obstructive Pulmonary Disease COPD —— 1**

1.1 Definition of Chronic Obstructive Pulmonary Disease (COPD) —— **2**
1.1.1 Preventable —— **2**
1.1.2 Progressive —— **2**
1.1.3 Treatable —— **3**
1.1.4 Airflow Obstruction That Is Not Reversible [Persistent] —— **4**
1.1.5 Major Point of Confusion: "Reversibility" —— **4**
1.1.6 Inflammation —— **5**
1.1.7 Lung/Pulmonary —— **6**
1.1.8 Exacerbation —— **6**
1.2 Diagnostic Criteria —— **6**
1.3 Staging Disease Severity —— **7**
1.4 COPD Is a Syndrome —— **8**
1.5 Genetic Factors —— **8**
1.6 Clinical Symptoms and Differential Diagnosis —— **9**
1.7 Imaging —— **10**
1.8 Treatment —— **10**
1.9 Conclusion —— **11**
1.10 Summary Points —— **11**
References —— **11**

Ralph J. Panos, MD

**2 Epidemiology and Economic Consequences of COPD —— 14**

2.1 Introduction —— **14**
2.2 Epidemiology —— **15**
2.2.1 Risk Factors for COPD Development —— **15**
2.2.1.1 Tobacco Smoke —— **15**
2.2.1.2 Passive or Environmental Tobacco Smoke Exposure —— **16**
2.2.1.3 Non-tobacco Smoke Factors —— **16**
2.2.1.4 Occupational Exposures —— **16**
2.2.1.5 Air Pollution —— **17**
2.2.1.6 Sex —— **18**
2.2.1.7 Infections —— **18**
2.2.2 Prevalence —— **18**
2.2.2.2 United States —— **19**
2.3 Economics —— **21**

2.3.1 Direct Costs — **21**
2.3.2 Indirect Costs — **22**
2.3.3 Effect of Treatment — **22**
2.4 Conclusion — **23**
2.5 Summary Points — **24**
References — **24**

William L. Eschenbacher, MD
**3 COPD Recognition and Diagnosis: Approach to the Patient with Respiratory Symptoms — 31**
3.1 Introduction — **31**
3.2 Patient Presenting with Respiratory Symptoms — **31**
3.2.1 Further Discussion of Dyspnea/Shortness of Breath — **33**
3.3 Initial Screening Evaluation for a Patient Presenting with Respiratory Symptoms Including Dyspnea — **35**
3.3.1 Exclude Causes of Symptoms Other than Lung Disease — **36**
3.3.2 Respiratory Causes for Symptoms — **36**
3.3.2.1 Initial Evaluation of Respiratory Processes — **36**
3.3.2.2 Further Evaluation of Causes of Respiratory Symptoms After Spirometry Test Results — **37**
3.4 COPD — **38**
3.4.1 Definition of COPD — **38**
3.4.2 Other Diagnostic Tests to Help Confirm the Presence of COPD — **40**
3.5 Asthma — **41**
3.6 Interstitial Lung Disease — **42**
3.7 Summary Points — **43**
References — **43**

William L. Eschenbacher, MD
**4 Pulmonary Function Testing: Spirometry: Presence and Severity of Airflow Limitation/Obstruction — 45**
4.1 Introduction — **45**
4.2 Reasons for Spirometry Testing — **46**
4.3 Spirometry Screening for COPD — **47**
4.4 Limitations of Spirometry — **47**
4.5 Three Phases of a Spirometry Test — **48**
4.6 Displaying the Results of Spirometry Testing — **49**
4.7 Acceptability and Repeatability Criteria of Spirometry Testing — **51**
4.8 Measurements from Spirometry Testing — **52**
4.9 Patterns of Spirometry Impairment or Limitation — **52**
4.9.1 Airflow Obstruction Pattern — **52**
4.9.2 Restrictive Lung Defect Pattern — **54**

4.9.3 Mixed Impairment with Both Airflow Obstruction and Lung Restriction — **54**
4.10 Interpretation of Spirometry Results — **54**
4.10.1 Reference Equations — **54**
4.10.2 Racial Differences in Reference Equations — **58**
4.10.3 The Lower Limit of the Normal (LLN) Range — **59**
4.10.4 What is Considered to Be Abnormal? — **60**
4.10.5 Determine Predicted Values and % of Predicted Values — **60**
4.10.6 Interpretation of Spirometry Test Results for Impairment Patterns — **60**
4.10.7 Airflow Obstruction — **60**
4.10.7.1 Possible Restrictive Lung Defect — **61**
4.10.7.2 Mixed Impairment Pattern — **62**
4.10.7.3 Controversy for Determination of Airflow Limitation/Obstruction — **62**
4.10.7.4 Bronchodilator Response — **63**
4.11 Summary Points — **64**
References — **64**

William L. Eschenbacher, MD
**5 Radiology: Use of Lung Imaging to Help in the Identification of Patients with COPD — 66**
5.1 Introduction — **66**
5.2 Chest Radiographs — **66**
5.3 Computed Tomography (CT) Scans — **67**
5.3.1 CT Scans and Emphysema — **67**
5.3.2 CT Scans and Air-trapping — **68**
5.3.3 CT Evaluation of Airway Changes in COPD — **69**
5.3.4 CT Scans for COPD Phenotypes — **70**
5.3.5 Lack of Correlation Between CT Findings and Spirometric Results for COPD — **70**
5.3.6 CT Scans for Smoking-related Interstitial Lung Diseases — **71**
5.3.7 Use of Low Dose CT Scans for Surveillance for Lung Cancer — **72**
5.4 Other Advanced Imaging Techniques in COPD — **72**
5.4.1 PET Scans — **72**
5.4.2 MRI Scans — **73**
5.5 Summary Points — **73**
References — **74**

Michael T. Borchers, PhD, Gregory Motz, PhD
**6 Pathogenesis of COPD — 76**
6.1 Introduction — **76**
6.2 Chronic Bronchitis — **77**
6.3 Emphysema — **77**

6.4 Smooth Muscle — **77**
6.5 Fibrosis — **78**
6.6 Pathogenesis of COPD — **78**
6.6.1 Genetics: Gene-association Studies — **78**
6.6.2 Epigenetics — **79**
6.6.3 Protease: Antiprotease Imbalance — **79**
6.6.4 Oxidative Stress — **80**
6.7 Airway Inflammation in COPD — **82**
6.7.1 Epithelium — **83**
6.7.2 Neutrophils — **83**
6.7.3 Macrophages — **84**
6.7.4 Eosinophils — **84**
6.7.5 Mast Cells — **85**
6.7.6 γδ T Cells — **85**
6.7.7 Natural Killer (NK) Cells — **86**
6.7.8 Natural Killer T (NKT) Cells — **86**
6.7.9 T Cells — **87**
6.7.10 B Cells — **88**
6.7.11 Dendritic Cells — **89**
6.8 Cytokines and Chemokines in COPD — **89**
6.9 COPD as an Autoimmune Disease — **90**
6.10 Systemic Inflammation — **91**
6.10.1 Cardiovascular Disease — **91**
6.10.2 Nutritional Abnormalities — **92**
6.10.3 Skeletal Muscle Dysfunction — **92**
6.10.4 Osteoporosis — **93**
6.10.5 Neurological Disorders — **93**
6.11 COPD Exacerbations — **93**
6.12 Summary Points — **94**
References — **94**

Shari Altum, Ph.D., Katherine Butler, Psy.D., Rachel Juran, Psy.D.
**7 Smoking Cessation — 104**
7.1 Introduction — **104**
7.2 Smoking Risks — **105**
7.3 Factors Associated with Cessation — **105**
7.4 Screening Recommendations — **106**
7.5 Using Physiological Data When Addressing Smoking — **110**
7.6 How to Present Spirometry Results to Promote Smoking Cessation — **110**
7.7 Readiness for Change — **111**
7.7.1 Precontemplation — **112**

7.7.2 Contemplation — **113**
7.7.3 Preparation — **114**
7.7.4 Action — **114**
7.7.5 Maintenance — **115**
7.8 The 5 A's Model — **116**
7.8.1 Step 1: ASK — **116**
7.8.2 Step 2: ADVISE — **117**
7.8.3 Step 3: ASSESS — **117**
7.8.4 Step 4: ASSIST — **117**
7.8.5 Step 5: ARRANGE — **117**
7.9 Motivational Interviewing — **121**
7.9.1 Clinical Effectiveness of Motivational Interviewing for Treating Tobacco Use Disorder — **123**
7.9.2 Developing Competency in the Use of Motivational Interviewing — **123**
7.10 Interventions — **123**
7.10.1 Nicotine Replacement Therapies and Medications — **125**
7.11 Other Nicotine Sources — **125**
7.12 Conclusion — **128**
7.13 Summary Points — **128**
References — **129**

Shari Altum, Ph.D., Rachel Juran, Psy.D., Katherine Butler, Psy.D.
**8 Fostering Patient Self-Management of COPD — 131**
8.1 Introduction — **131**
8.2 Clinician Skills — **131**
8.3 Stages of Change — **133**
8.4 Patient Self-Management Skills — **134**
8.5 Self-Management Tasks — **135**
8.5.1 Medication Adherence — **136**
8.5.2 Exacerbation Action Plans — **139**
8.5.3 Coping with Breathlessness — **140**
8.5.4 Exercise — **141**
8.5.5 Nutrition — **142**
8.6 Self-Management Programs — **142**
8.6.1 Pulmonary Rehabilitation — **143**
8.6.2 Living Well with COPD — **144**
8.6.3 Chronic Disease Self-Management Program — **145**
8.7 Shared Decision-Making — **146**
8.8 End-of-Life Discussions — **149**
8.9 Integrated Care Teams — **150**
8.10 Conclusion — **150**

8.11 Summary Points —— **153**
References —— **154**

Muhammad Ahsan Zafar, MD
**9 Natural History, Phenotypes, and Gender Differences in COPD —— 159**
9.1 Natural History of COPD —— **159**
9.2 Factors Influencing Lung Function in COPD —— **160**
9.2.1 Lung Growth and Early Life Events —— **161**
9.2.2 Cigarette Smoking —— **162**
9.2.3 Genetic Susceptibility —— **163**
9.2.4 Advancing Age —— **163**
9.2.5 Emphysema —— **163**
9.2.6 Bronchodilator Responsiveness —— **164**
9.2.7 Early Disease —— **164**
9.2.8 Biomarkers —— **165**
9.3 Role of COPD Exacerbations and Progression of Disease —— **165**
9.3.1 Lung Function Decline —— **165**
9.3.2 Quality of Life —— **166**
9.3.3 Mortality —— **166**
9.3.4 Factors Associated with COPD Exacerbations —— **166**
9.4 COPD Phenotypes —— **168**
9.4.1 Different Phenotypes of COPD —— **168**
9.4.2 Genetic: Alpha 1-antitrypsin Deficiency —— **168**
9.4.2.1 Therapeutic Implications —— **171**
9.4.3 Anatomic: Emphysema-Hyperinflation Phenotype —— **171**
9.4.3.1 Therapeutic Implications —— **171**
9.4.4 Physiologic: Bronchodilator Responsive/COPD-Asthma Overlap Syndrome —— **172**
9.4.4.1 Therapeutic Implications —— **172**
9.4.5 Clinical Frequent Exacerbator —— **173**
9.4.5.1 Therapeutic Implications —— **173**
9.4.6 Clinical: Chronic Bronchitis/Mucous Producer —— **176**
9.4.6.1 Therapeutic Implications —— **176**
9.5 Gender Differences in COPD —— **176**
9.5.1 Reasons for Gender Differences in COPD —— **177**
9.5.1.1 Change in Tobacco Consumption Trend —— **177**
9.5.1.2 Tobacco Susceptibility —— **177**
9.5.1.3 Biologic Differences —— **177**
9.5.2 Epidemiology —— **178**
9.5.3 Clinical Features and Phenotypic Differences —— **178**
9.5.4 Comorbidities —— **179**
9.5.5 Treatment Disparities —— **179**

9.5.6 Health Care Delivery — 180
9.6 Conclusion — 180
9.7 Summary Points — 181
References — 181

Ralph J. Panos, MD
**10 COPD Is a Multi-Organ Disorder: Systemic Manifestations — 189**
10.1 Introduction — 189
10.2 Inflammation in COPD — 189
10.3 COPD Mortality — 189
10.4 Cardio- and Cerebral-vascular Disease — 190
10.4.1 Heart Failure — 191
10.5 Lung Cancer — 192
10.5.1 Pathogenetic Links Between COPD and Lung Cancer — 193
10.5.2 Lung Cancer Screening — 193
10.5.3 Management of Lung Cancer — 194
10.6 Pulmonary Fibrosis — 195
10.7 Hematologic Manifestations — 198
10.8 Musculoskeletal — 200
10.8.1 Risk Factors for Fractures in Individuals with COPD — 201
10.8.2 Osteoporosis — 201
10.8.3 Falls — 201
10.8.4 Muscle Weakness — 202
10.9 Diabetes — 203
10.10 Conclusion — 203
10.11 Summary Points — 204
References — 204

Ralph J. Panos, MD
**11 Sleep and COPD: The Overlap Syndrome — 212**
11.1 Introduction — 212
11.2 Smoking, Sleep, and COPD — 213
11.3 Prevalence of Overlap Syndrome — 214
11.4 Predictors of Overlap Syndrome — 215
11.5 Screening and Diagnosis — 216
11.5.1 Normal Sleep Physiology — 217
11.5.2 Sleep Physiology and OSA — 218
11.5.3 Sleep Physiology and COPD — 219
11.5.4 Sleep Physiology and Overlap Syndrome — 219
11.6 Ventilation and Ventilation Perfusion Matching — 220
11.7 Polysomnography — 220
11.7.1 Consequences of Overlap Syndrome — 221

11.7.2 Pulmonary Hypertension — **221**
11.7.3 Atrial fibrillation — **221**
11.7.4 Cognitive Dysfunction — **222**
11.8 Mortality and COPD Exacerbations — **222**
11.8.1 Treatment — **222**
11.8.2 Respiratory Medications — **222**
11.8.3 Oxygen — **223**
11.8.4 Lung Volume Reduction Surgery (LVRS) — **224**
11.8.5 Noninvasive Positive Pressure Ventilation — **224**
11.9 Conclusion — **225**
11.10 Summary Points — **226**
References — **226**

Jean M. Elwing, MD
**12 COPD and Pulmonary Vasculature — 232**
12.1 Introduction — **232**
12.2 COPD Associated Pulmonary Hypertension — **233**
12.2.1 Epidemiology — **233**
12.2.2 Diagnostic Evaluation — **234**
12.2.2.1 Clinical Evaluation for Pulmonary Hypertension — **234**
12.2.2.2 Noninvasive Testing for Pulmonary Hypertension — **234**
12.2.2.3 Invasive Testing for Pulmonary Hypertension — **236**
12.2.3 Histopathology — **237**
12.2.4 Pathophysiology — **237**
12.2.5 Pathogenesis — **237**
12.2.6 Management of Pulmonary Hypertension — **239**
12.3 COPD Associated Venous Thromboembolic Disease — **240**
12.3.1 Epidemiology of Venous Thromboembolism in COPD — **240**
12.3.2 Diagnostic Evaluation of Venous Thromboembolism in COPD — **240**
12.3.3 Management of Venous Thromboembolism in COPD — **241**
12.4 Summary — **241**
12.5 Summary Points — **242**
References — **243**

Mary E. Panos, Ralph J. Panos, MD
**13 COPD's Effects on Psychosocial Functioning and Familial Interactions — 249**
13.1 Introduction — **249**
13.2 Depression — **249**
13.2.1 Prevalence — **250**
13.2.2 Manifestations — **251**
13.2.3 Mortality — **252**

13.2.4 Healthcare Utilization — 252
13.2.5 Management — 253
13.2.5.1 Pharmacologic Treatment — 253
13.2.5.2 Pulmonary Rehabilitation — 253
13.3 Anxiety — 254
13.3.1 Prevalence — 255
13.3.2 Manifestations — 256
13.3.3 Management of Anxiety — 256
13.3.3.1 Pharmacotherapy — 256
13.3.3.2 Nonpharmacotherapy — 256
13.4 Panic Attacks — 257
13.4.1 Prevalence — 257
13.4.2 Treatment of Panic Disorder — 258
13.5 Cognitive Impairment — 259
13.5.1 Prevalence — 259
13.5.2 Manifestations — 260
13.5.3 Management — 261
13.6 Social Interactions — 261
13.7 Effect of COPD on Caregivers — 262
13.8 Conclusion — 263
13.9 Summary Points — 263
References — 264

Ralph J. Panos, MD
**14 Management of Stable Chronic Obstructive Pulmonary Disease — 275**
14.1 Management of Stable COPD — 275
14.1.1 Breathlessness — 276
14.1.2 Cough — 278
14.1.3 Sputum Production — 279
14.2 Guidelines for the Management of COPD — 280
14.2.1 GOLD Guidelines for the Management of COPD — 281
14.3 Pharmacologic Treatment of COPD — 283
14.3.1 Phosphodiesterase Inhibitors — 284
14.3.2 Macrolides — 284
14.3.3 Mucolytics — 286
14.3.4 Supplemental Oxygen — 286
14.4 Nonpharmacologic Treatment of COPD — 286
14.5 Management of COPD-related Nonpulmonary Co-morbidities — 288
14.6 Summary Points — 288
References — 288

Aaron M Mulhall MD
**15 Practical Guide to Correct Inhaler Use —— 292**
15.1 Introduction —— **292**
15.2 Inhaler Education and Errors in Inhaler Technique —— **293**
15.3 Inhalation Delivery Systems —— **295**
15.3.1 Pressurized Metered-Dose Inhalers (pMDIs) —— **295**
15.3.2 Spacer Utilization —— **297**
15.3.3 Multidose Dry Powder Inhalers (DPIs) —— **298**
15.3.4 Respimat® Soft Mist Inhaler® (SMI®) —— **301**
15.3.5 Nebulized Solutions —— **302**
15.4 Reminders to Increase Adherence —— **305**
15.5 Conclusions —— **306**
15.6 Summary Points —— **306**
References —— **307**

Folarin Sogbetun, MD
**16 Management of Outpatient COPD Exacerbations —— 312**
16.1 Introduction —— **312**
16.2 Definition and Differential Diagnosis —— **313**
16.3 Prevalence —— **313**
16.4 Etiology —— **314**
16.5 Presentation —— **315**
16.6 Natural History —— **315**
16.7 Consequences —— **316**
16.8 Outpatient Management of COPD Exacerbations —— **316**
16.8.1 Indications for Home Care —— **316**
16.8.2 Indications for a Healthcare Encounter —— **318**
16.9 Management —— **318**
16.9.1 Home Care —— **318**
16.9.2 Bronchodilators —— **320**
16.9.2.1 Short Acting Bronchodilators —— **320**
16.9.3 Corticosteroid Therapy —— **321**
16.9.4 Antibiotic Therapy —— **322**
16.9.5 Chronic Antibiotic Treatment —— **322**
16.9.6 Phosphodiesterase 4 (PDE 4) Inhibitors —— **322**
16.9.7 Oxygen Therapy —— **323**
16.9.8 Educational Programs —— **324**
16.9.9 Hospital at Home —— **324**
16.9.10 Respiratory Stimulants —— **325**
16.10 Prevention of COPD Exacerbations —— **325**
16.10.1 Pulmonary Rehabilitation —— **325**

16.10.2 Smoking Cessation — **325**
16.10.3 Nutritional Support — **326**
16.10.4 Lung Volume Reduction Surgery (LVRS) — **326**
16.10.5 Telehealth — **326**
16.11 Risk Factors for Relapse — **326**
16.12 Conclusion — **327**
16.13 Summary Points — **328**
References — **328**

Nishant Gupta, MD
**17 Inpatient Management of Acute COPD Exacerbations — 335**
17.1 Introduction — **335**
17.2 Definition and Risk Factors — **336**
17.3 Risk Factors for COPD Exacerbations — **336**
17.4 Etiology of COPD Exacerbations — **337**
17.5 Triage to Home Versus Hospital for Management of Exacerbations — **338**
17.6 Hospital Management of COPD Exacerbations — **340**
17.6.1 Pharmacologic Therapies for the Management of COPD Exacerbations — **341**
17.6.1.1 Supplemental Oxygen — **341**
17.6.1.2 β adrenergic Agonists — **341**
17.6.1.3 Anticholinergic Agents — **342**
17.6.1.4 Glucocorticoids — **342**
17.6.1.5 Antibiotics — **343**
17.6.1.6 Other Therapies — **344**
17.6.2 Mechanical Ventilation for Acute Exacerbations of COPD — **346**
17.6.2.1 Noninvasive Positive Pressure Ventilation *(NIPPV)*: — **346**
17.6.2.2 Invasive Mechanical Ventilation — **347**
17.7 Hospital Discharge and Follow Up — **349**
17.8 Conclusion — **350**
17.9 Summary Points — **350**
References — **351**

Sara M. Krzywkowski-Mohn Ed.D, FNP
**18 Primary Care and Interaction with Specialty Care for the COPD Patient — 357**
18.1 Introduction: A Healthcare System in Crisis and New Models of Care — **357**
18.2 The Patient Centered Family Medical Home Model — **358**
18.3 How Does the PACT Team Differ from Traditional Roles/ Responsibilities? — **359**

18.4 General Roles of the PACT Team —— **361**
18.5 Care Management of the COPD Patient PACT Roles and Responsibilities —— **361**
18.5.1 The Patient —— **361**
18.5.2 Clerical Associate (CA) —— **362**
18.5.3 The Clinical Associate —— **362**
18.5.4 Nurse Case Manager —— **363**
18.5.5 The Provider —— **363**
18.6 COPD and PACT —— **364**
18.7 Summary Points —— **366**
References —— **367**

Ralph J. Panos, MD
**19 Integrating Supportive, Palliative, and End of Life Care for COPD —— 369**
19.1 Introduction —— **369**
19.2 COPD Disease Course and Management —— **370**
19.3 Patient and Caregiver Burden —— **371**
19.4 Prognostication of Duration and Quality of Life in COPD —— **373**
19.5 Advanced Care Planning Discussions Between Providers and Patients with COPD and Their Families —— **374**
19.6 Timing and Content of Discussions —— **376**
19.6.1 Early Stage COPD —— **376**
19.6.2 Later Stage COPD —— **377**
19.7 Symptom Management —— **379**
19.7.1 Dyspnea —— **379**
19.7.2 Anxiety and Depression —— **380**
19.7.3 Other Symptoms —— **380**
19.8 Bereavement —— **381**
19.9 Effectiveness of Palliative Care —— **381**
19.10 Conclusion —— **382**
19.11 Summary Points —— **382**
References —— **383**

**Index —— 389**

# Preface

On February 1, 2012, they came, and they came, and they came until it was standing room only. The word had gone out to providers at the Cincinnati Veterans Administration Medical Center that there was a meeting for everyone involved in the care of Veterans with Chronic Obstructive Pulmonary Disease (COPD). We had just been awarded a grant from the Office of Specialty Care entitled, "Patient-Centered Model for the Management of Chronic Obstructive Pulmonary Disease." The goals for that proposal were to enhance the recognition and diagnosis of COPD and implement a Patient-Centered Model for the Management of COPD. We invited providers who we knew were interested in COPD to an inaugural planning and organizational meeting and asked them to spread the word and encourage others to attend – and they did. We planned to meet in a conference room with a capacity of 10–15 people but over thirty people attended that first meeting and we had to move to a larger room. Participants included respiratory therapists, primary care providers, pharmacists, tele-health providers, nurse practitioners, researchers, hospitalists, patient-aligned care team (PACT) members, psychologists, smoking cessation counselors, and pulmonologists. In subsequent meetings, we were joined by University of Cincinnati researchers and Jack Kues, the Dean for Continuous Professional Development.

For the next three years, we met nearly every other Wednesday morning to review what and how care was being provided to Veterans with COPD; always asking what tools, new initiatives, or process changes were needed to improve that care. We traced the course of a Veteran with unrecognized, undiagnosed airflow limitation to initial COPD diagnosis including physiologic, radiographic, and laboratory testing. We identified the most appropriate next steps for starting treatment and management of outpatient and inpatient exacerbations. We recognized that optimal management of these patients would require transitions of care between primary care and subspecialists in both outpatient and inpatient settings. Best care also included the identification of pulmonary and nonpulmonary COPD manifestations and complications that in some cases would lead to palliative and end of life care. At each step, we asked how this care could be more patient-centric. Along that journey, Folarin Sogbetun developed a Veteran-specific COPD screening questionnaire that was tested, validated, and compared with other COPD screening surveys; Bill Eschenbacher created a telespirometry program with teaching modules, quality assurance reviews, and interpretation algorithms whose success triggered funding for the purchase of spirometers for every Community Based Outpatient Clinic (CBOC) nationally; we participated in a design course at the University of Cincinnati College of Design, Architecture, Art, and Planning during which students created projects to enhance patients' management of COPD including the visual pill box designed by Siyuan Fan and presented in Figure 8.3.

During this process, we realized that providers did not have an up-to-date, comprehensive, easily read, "how to" manual for the management of COPD despite all the advances in COPD care that have occurred over the past 5 years. Consensus documents such as the VA-DOD Guidelines were abbreviated summaries that were rarely used. From those discussions, the concept for this volume, a COPD Primer, developed. The goal was to develop a practical book that concisely presented COPD to providers with sufficient background and explanation of the physiologic and scientific rationale for various management strategies without becoming an esoteric academic work. We hope that this COPD Primer has achieved that goal and will be a useful, practical text for practitioners and medical trainees alike.

The COPD Primer begins with an examination of what COPD is; it is really a syndrome, a constellation of historical features and clinical, physiologic, and radiographic findings. However, those elements come together in many different ways to create multiple different COPD phenotypes that are only now being recognized and used to define specific management strategies. COPD research has progressed beyond the simple classification of "blue bloaters" and "pink puffers." Next, the epidemiology and economic consequences of COPD are reviewed. Bill Eschenbacher presents an approach to the patient with respiratory symptoms with detailed discussions of pulmonary function testing and how airflow limitation/obstruction is identified by spirometry and the use of lung imaging to identify individuals with COPD. Michael Borchers and Gregory Motz summarize current evidence implicating genetics, proteolytic imbalance, oxidative stress, inflammation, occupational and environmental exposures, and innate and adaptive immune function in the pathogenesis of COPD and the implication of these findings to future treatments. The single most important intervention in the prevention and treatment of COPD is smoking cessation. Shari Altum, Katherine Butler, and Rachel Juran present a practical approach to smoking cessation utilizing motivational interviewing in combination with pharmacologic interventions. Then, they expand upon these concepts to provide practitioners with convenient, realistic suggestions to encourage patient self-management in all aspects of COPD care and overall health. Ahsan Zafar reviews the natural history, recently described COPD phenotypes, and gender differences that clearly illustrate the broad spectrum of disease that comprises the term, COPD. The cover illustration highlights Dr. Zafar's creative and artistic talents. The extensive nonpulmonary aspects of COPD are reviewed by Ralph Panos in an examination of COPD's multi-organ manifestations. Next, the effect of COPD on sleep and the overlap syndrome, the concurrence of COPD and obstructive sleep apnea, and its consequences are presented. Jean Elwing examines the effect of COPD on the pulmonary vasculature with a detailed discussion of the evaluation and management of pulmonary hypertension associated with COPD. COPD's effects on psychosocial functioning and familial interactions are presented by Mary Panos and Ralph Panos.

The focus of the Primer then shifts from manifestations to treatment with a discussion of stable COPD management. With the current plethora of devices for delivering respiratory medications, it is difficult for both patients and providers to sustain knowledge of their proper use. Aaron Mulhall presents a practical guide to correct inhaler use that reviews all the current devices. Folarin Sogbetun then reviews the management of outpatient COPD exacerbations and Nishant Gupta discusses the approach to the patient hospitalized with COPD. Because patients with COPD often see multiple subspecialty physicians in addition to their primary care providers, interdisciplinary communication and coordination of care is essential for their management; Sara Krzywkowski-Mohn reviews the interactions between primary and specialty care for the patient with COPD with suggestions for improved communication and care coordination. Finally, advance care planning including palliative care and hospice is reviewed with a discussion of how end stage COPD affects not only the patient but also their family and social network.

This COPD Primer incorporates the knowledge that we have learned over the past several years during the development and implementation of a patient-centered model for the management of COPD. It was written with an explicit goal of assisting both the practicing provider and medical trainee in the care of patients with COPD.

We thank Magdalena Wierzchowiecka, PhD, Managing Editor, Medicine, at De Gruyter Open, Ltd. for her assistance in editing and producing this work. We are grateful for all of the collaborating authors; their energy, work, and willingness to meet deadlines and quick responses to revisions and suggestions made this COPD Primer possible. We thank all the COPD working group members who participated in three years of Wednesday morning discussions that covered the spectrum of health care from the specifics of COPD to evolving national healthcare reform. The ultimate goal of this program and this book is the improvement of care for individuals with COPD and we thank all of our patients who motivate us to improve and continually strive to provide the best possible care.

We are very appreciative and thankful for the patience and encouragement of our wives, Jean and Judy, for tolerating all these months of writing, revising, and editing. Without your forbearance, this COPD Primer would never have made it to print.

Ralph J. Panos
William L. Eschenbacher

May 2, 2015

Ralph J. Panos, MD

# 1 Introduction and Definition of Chronic Obstructive Pulmonary Disease COPD

Key Points

1. Chronic obstructive pulmonary disease (COPD) is a syndrome, a constellation of historical findings, clinical signs and symptoms, physiologic derangements, and radiologic abnormalities.
2. There is not a single test that can establish a diagnosis of COPD or exclude other similar processes.
3. Recent findings suggest multiple different COPD phenotypes which may have different clinical courses and responses to treatment.
4. COPD is usually characterized by airflow obstruction that does not fully normalize (return to predicted levels) with diverse pulmonary and extra-pulmonary manifestations including variable clinical symptoms, natural history and longevity, physiology, imaging, and responses to therapy.
5. Most commonly, airflow obstruction/limitation is measured by spirometry by demonstrating a reduced $FEV_1$:FVC ratio (Forced Expiratory Volume in one second : Forced Vital Capacity) [GOLD (Global initiative for chronic Obstructive Lung Disease) advocates a fixed ratio < 0.7, whereas others utilize a ratio < LLN (lower limit of normal, the 5$^{th}$ percentile of the population distribution of $FEV_1$/FVC among nonsmokers with no clinical lung disease)].
6. Occasionally, COPD is diagnosed based upon radiographic findings of emphysema in the absence of airflow obstruction.
7. Definitions of COPD include:
   - GOLD Definition: COPD, a common, preventable, and treatable disease, is characterized by persistent airflow limitation that is usually progressive and associated with an enhanced chronic inflammatory response in the airways and the lung to noxious particles or gases. Exacerbations and comorbidities contribute to the overall severity in individual patients.
   - ATS/ERS (American Thoracic Society/European Respiratory Society) Definition: Chronic obstructive pulmonary disease (COPD) is a preventable and treatable disease characterized by airflow limitation that is not fully reversible. The airflow limitation is usually progressive and is associated with an abnormal inflammatory response of the lungs to noxious particles or gases, primarily caused by cigarette smoking. Although COPD affects the lungs, it also produces significant systemic consequences.

## 1.1 Definition of Chronic Obstructive Pulmonary Disease (COPD)

The definition of COPD has evolved over the past several years. The most recent definitions of COPD by national and international groups are presented in Table 1.1. Key words in each of these definitions include: *preventable, progressive, treatable, airflow obstruction that is not reversible [persistent], inflammation, lung/pulmonary, and exacerbation.*

### 1.1.1 Preventable

As presented in Chapter 2, Epidemiology and Economic Consequences of COPD, and Chapter 9, Natural History, Phenotypes, and Gender Differences in COPD, tobacco smoke inhalation is the greatest risk factor for the development of COPD; approximately 75–90% of all individuals with COPD have been or are smokers, but only 20–50% of all smokers develop COPD. The factor(s) that place this subgroup of smokers at risk for the development of COPD are not known. Up to one quarter of individuals with COPD are non-smokers (Zeng, 2012). Other risk factors for the development of COPD include history of asthma or tuberculosis, exposure to traffic, outdoor pollution, and biomass smoke. Refraining from or quitting smoking (see Chapter 7, Smoking Cessation), and mitigating or avoiding chemical, dust, and fume exposure will prevent many individuals from developing COPD.

### 1.1.2 Progressive

Chapter 9, Natural History, Phenotypes, and Gender Differences in COPD, presents the longitudinal time course of lung function from birth to death. In healthy individuals, maximal physiologic function is achieved in the early 20's and is followed by a slow reduction in flow rates measured by spirometry. COPD is characterized by an increased rate of decline in airflow. Although this accelerated decline is marked by parenchymal and airway derangements (including loss of lung tissue in emphysema, excessive airway mucous and inflammatory cell accumulation in chronic bronchitis), COPD can also be considered pulmonary physiologic progeria. This concept is captured by the term "lung age" (Reviewed in Chapter 4, Pulmonary Function Testing: Presence and Severity of Airflow Limitation/Obstruction). Lung age is the physiologic age of the lungs extrapolated from the normal predicted values of lung function based upon age and is compared with an individual's chronologic age to illustrate the accelerated decline in lung function that occurs with COPD. For example, a 60 year old individual with significant airflow limitation might have spirometry (forced expiratory volume in one second ($FEV_1$) and forced vital capacity (FVC)) that would be normal for a 90 year old; thus, this person has a lung (physiologic) age of 90 but is only 60 years old chronologically. The progressive loss of lung function is heterogeneous and the

**Table 1.1:** Recent Definitions of COPD (words common to different definitions are italicized)

**Definitions of COPD**

| Source | Reference | Definition |
|---|---|---|
| GOLD | www.goldcopd.org | a common *preventable* and *treatable* disease, is characterized by *airflow limitation* that is usually *progressive* and associated with an enhanced chronic *inflammatory* response in the airways and the *lung* to noxious particles or gases. *Exacerbations* and comorbidities contribute to the overall severity in individual patients |
| WHO | www.who.int/respiratory/COPD/definition/en/ | a lung disease characterized by chronic obstruction of *lung airflow* that interferes with normal breathing and is not fully *reversible* |
| ATS/ERS | www.thoracic.org/clinical/copd-guidelines | a *preventable* and *treatable* disease state characterized by airflow limitation that is not ful*ly reversi*ble |
| ACP/ACCP/ATS/ERS | (Qaseem, 2011) | a slowly *progressive* disease involving the airways or *pulmonary* parenchyma (or both) that results in *airflow obstruction* |

rate of decline is variable (Vestbo, 2014). (See Chapter 9, Natural History, Phenotypes, and Gender Differences in COPD for a discussion of lung development and the natural history of COPD.) Some interventions, especially early smoking cessation, may be associated with improvement in lung function and a reduction of the loss in years of life that occurs with persistent smoking (Jha, 2013). The effect of exacerbations on lung function decline appears to be less than previously thought, only 2 ml/yr/exacerbation in the ECLIPSE (Evaluation of COPD Longitudinally to Identify Predictive Surrogate Endpoints) study, whereas the mean rate of decline in the $FEV_1$ among participants with COPD was 33 ml/yr (Vestbo, 2011). In addition, ECLIPSE showed that not everyone with COPD experiences progressive decline in lung function measured by $FEV_1$; approximately 15% of participants with COPD had improvements in $FEV_1$ averaged over 3 years. All ECLIPSE participants were treated for COPD so it remains unclear whether the disease management affected the measured rate of decline or contributed to the improvement in lung function in these patients.

### 1.1.3 Treatable

As reviewed in Chapters 14, 15, and 17 Management of Stable COPD, Outpatient Management of COPD Exacerbations, and Inpatient Management of COPD Exacerbations, COPD is a treatable disorder. Current treatments have significant salubrious benefits and reduce the frequency and severity of exacerbations, improve the quantity and quality of life by reducing mortality, decreasing healthcare utilization, and improving health related quality of life. Previously many clinicians and patients had a nihilistic approach to COPD and considered it a self-inflicted, untreatable condition; this approach to COPD has changed dramatically in recent years. Individuals with COPD who receive optimal management can and do live longer with better quality of life.

### 1.1.4 Airflow Obstruction That Is Not Reversible [Persistent]

Airflow limitation is a reduction in expiratory airflow that occurs due to increased resistance to flow and reduced lung parenchymal elastic recoil. Airflow limitation is measured by spirometry (see Chapter 4, Pulmonary Function Testing: Presence and Severity of Airflow Limitation/Obstruction).

### 1.1.5 Major Point of Confusion: "Reversibility"

The term reversible has caused significant confusion among clinicians and has muddled the distinction between asthma and COPD. During pulmonary function testing, a response to bronchodilators is often termed "reversible airflow obstruction". Bronchodilator responsiveness is determined by a ≥12% and ≥200 ml increase in either the $FEV_1$ or the FVC (ATS criteria, see Table 1.2). The intraday variation in $FEV_1$ and FVC is minimal in individuals with no lung disease and a change greater than 5–10% is considered significant (Dawson, 1965; Rozas, 1982). In patients with obstructive lung disease, the daily variation is greater and a significant change is 8–17% (Rozas, 1982; Pennock, 1981; Nickerson, 1980). [Interestingly, although the minimal clinically important difference for a change in $FEV_1$ in individuals with COPD is not known, a $FEV_1$ change of 100 ml can be perceived by most patients with COPD (Donohue, 2005).]

"Reversibility" is not a normalization or return to predicted levels of either the $FEV_1$ or FVC but simply a measured response (an increase in either $FEV_1$ or FVC) to a bronchodilator that exceeds the defined threshold. In individuals with COPD, airflow obstruction may improve after treatment with a bronchodilator but measures of airflow, $FEV_1$ and FVC, do not improve to a normal or predicted level. Depending upon the definition of bronchodilator responsiveness or "reversibility", underlying lung function, the dose, type, and route of bronchodilator administration, between 38% and 73% of individuals with COPD may respond to bronchodilators with increases in $FEV_1$ or FVC (Hanania, 2011). Thus, COPD is characterized by airflow limitation that may improve after treatment with a bronchodilator but does not improve to a normal or predicted level. In contrast, in asthma, one expects measures of airflow to return to normal or predicted levels in all patients except for that subset of asthmatics who have developed fixed airflow limitation. Spirometry testing in this group of asthmatics is indistinguishable from patients with COPD. A response to a bronchodilator should not be equated with normalization of lung function.

**Table 1.2:** Key terms related to the response to bronchodilators

| Term | Definition/Clarification |
|---|---|
| Bronchodilator responsiveness | a >12% and >200 ml increase in either the FEV1 or the FVC after inhalation of a bronchodilator (usually a short acting beta agonist) |
| Normalization of airflow limitation | a return to predicted levels of FEV1 or FVC |
| "Reversibility" | a confusing term which should not be used |

Thus, although bronchodilator response has been used in the past to distinguish COPD and asthma, recent evidence and the large proportion of patients with COPD who respond to bronchodilators demonstrate that ***the acute spirometric response to bronchodilators cannot be used to distinguish asthma from COPD (Chhabra, 2005).*** The response to bronchodilators is used to define a subgroup (phenotype) of individuals with COPD who may respond better to inhaled corticosteroids (see Chapter 9, Natural History, Phenotypes, and Gender Differences in COPD).

### 1.1.6 Inflammation

COPD is characterized by an inflammatory reaction within the lung to inhaled particles or gases and this response may be triggered by activation of both innate and adaptive immune responses (Angelis, 2014; Rovina, 2013). Inflammatory markers are present both systemically as well as within the lung. Chapter 6, COPD Pathogenesis: Etiology and Systemic Inflammation, discusses the etiology and pathophysiologic pathways that are activated in COPD. Recent studies have shown that the inflammation in COPD is not limited to the lungs but occurs systemically and may play a role in the multisystemic manifestations of COPD (see Chapter 10, COPD Is a Multi-organ Disorder: Systemic Manifestations). However, the presence of systemic inflammation does not occur universally among individuals with COPD. The ECLIPSE study showed that about one third of participants with COPD never demonstrated systemic inflammation, 16% had persistent elevation of systemic inflammatory markers, and most participants had evidence of variable systemic inflammation (Agusti, 2012). The regulatory mechanisms that control the development of pulmonary and systemic inflammation in individuals with COPD are not well defined presently. These inflammatory processes are the subject of intense study to develop new therapeutics that interdict the development and consequences of inflammation in COPD.

### 1.1.7 Lung/Pulmonary

COPD is classically considered a pulmonary disorder; however, recent evidence over the past 10 years shows that COPD pathophysiology may extend beyond the lungs and affect other organ systems (see Chapter 10, COPD Is a Multi-organ Disorder: Systemic Manifestations). COPD is also associated with significant psychosocial manifestations that may intensify an individual's reaction to the sensation of breathlessness and profoundly influence their disease manifestations and course (Reviewed in Chapter 13, COPD's Effects on Psychosocial Functioning and Familial Interactions). The breathlessness and exertional limitations caused by COPD may increase the reliance upon others while simultaneously restricting and diminishing familial and social interactions for patients with COPD. Finally, COPD affects other systems including the pulmonary vasculature (see Chapter 12, COPD and Pulmonary Vasculature) and sleep (see Chapter 11, COPD and Sleep: Overlap Syndrome).

### 1.1.8 Exacerbation

The clinical course of COPD is punctuated by exacerbations, episodes of symptom worsening beyond their normal day to day variation that occur after a period of recovery from a prior exacerbation (Triqueros, 2013). COPD exacerbations are often triggered by respiratory infections and are the leading cause of healthcare utilization and cost in the management of COPD (see Chapters 16 and 17 on the management of COPD in the outpatient and inpatient settings). One of the major advancements in COPD management over the past two decades has been the development of treatments that reduce the number and severity of COPD exacerbations.

## 1.2 Diagnostic Criteria

Until recently, the *sine quo non* for the diagnosis of COPD has been the presence of airflow limitation, a reduction in the flow of air from the lungs during exhalation due to increased airway resistance and dynamic airway collapse (see Chapter 4, Pulmonary Function Testing: Presence and Severity of Airflow Limitation/Obstruction). How airflow limitation is defined, measured, and quantified have evolved over the past several decades. Airflow limitation is currently measured by the ratio of $FEV_1$ to FVC and is defined when this ratio is less than a threshold value. The two most common thresholds are an absolute value of 0.7 and the lower limit of normal, the $5^{th}$ percentile of the distribution of the $FEV_1$/FVC ratio in a nonsmoking population with no clinical evidence of lung disease. Because the ratio of $FEV_1$:FVC decreases with age, use of an absolute threshold may be overly sensitive and may over-diagnose airflow obstruction in older individuals and under-diagnose younger people (see

Chapter 4, Pulmonary Function Testing: Presence and Severity of Airflow Limitation/Obstruction.) More individuals with airflow obstruction defined by fixed ratio have emphysema and gas trapping than those who have airflow obstruction defined by the lower limit of normal (Bhatt, 2014).

Recent findings suggest that some individuals with radiographic evidence of emphysema, gas trapping, regional ventilation derangements, and airway alterations may not have airflow limitation on physiologic testing (Coxson, 2014), (see Chapter 5, Radiology: Use of lung imaging to help in the identification of patients with COPD.) Recently developed advanced pulmonary imaging techniques such as x-ray computed tomography, magnetic resonance imaging, and use of hyperpolarized noble gases provide structural as well as functional assessments of the lungs that may detect earlier and more subtle changes than can be measured by spirometry. Thus, although the presence of physiologic airflow limitation is currently a critical criterion for the diagnosis of COPD, it may not be essential as newer lung imaging techniques are developed and become more universally available.

## 1.3 Staging Disease Severity

Traditionally COPD has been categorized and staged based upon spirometry measurements. Airflow severity is determined by the comparison between the measured $FEV_1$ and the predicted $FEV_1$, the $FEV_1$% of predicted value, and is segregated into several categories ranging from mild to very severe (see Chapter 4, Pulmonary Function Testing: Spirometry: Presence and Severity of Airflow Limitation/Obstruction). These divisions are artificial as the reduction in lung function is a continuum from normal to severely deranged.

Previous COPD staging schemes were based solely upon airflow severity. With the realization that airflow severity does not correlate well with disease course, clinical outcomes, health status, or disease management, multivariate staging methods have been proposed (Jones, 2009). One of the more recent and widely adopted schemes is the GOLD staging classification which utilizes three variables: airflow severity, respiratory symptoms measured by the COPD Activity Test or mMRC (modified Medical Research Council) dyspnea scale, and the number of COPD exacerbations within the previous year (see Chapter 14, Management of Stable COPD). Other multifactorial indices include BODE (Body mass index, airflow Obstruction, Dyspnea, and Exercise capacity), ADO (Age, Dyspnea, and airflow Obstruction), and DOSE (Dyspnea, Obstruction, Smoking, and Exacerbation) (Celli, 2004; Puhan, 2009; Jones, 2009). The goals of these multivariate staging classifications are to provide COPD categories that are more clinically useful and assist with disease management and prognostication (see Chapter 19, Integrating Supportive, Palliative, and End of Life Care for COPD).

## 1.4 COPD is a Syndrome

Historically, COPD has been considered an overlapping dyad of pulmonary disorders characterized by airflow obstruction and different clinical, radiographic, and physiologic manifestations: chronic bronchitis and emphysema, that are distinguished from asthma, the other major cause of airflow obstruction (Table 1.3).

**Table 1.3:** Definitions of Chronic Bronchitis and Emphysema

| Term | Definition |
|---|---|
| Chronic bronchitis | the presence of a productive cough for at least 3 consecutive months in 2 consecutive years |
| Emphysema | an abnormal enlargement of the air spaces distal to the terminal bronchioles accompanied by destruction of their wall and without obvious fibrosis pathologically or radiographically |

More recent COPD studies have focused on further refinement and definition of COPD categories or phenotypes (see Chapter 9, Natural History, Phenotypes, and Gender Differences in COPD). The ECLIPSE study is a 3 year prospective investigation of 2,164 patients with clinically stable COPD, 337 smokers with normal lung function, and 245 never smokers that has provided valuable insights into the heterogeneity of COPD and its variable and not always progressive course. Among the COPD phenotypes identified in ECLIPSE are frequent (≥ 2 yearly) exacerbators and infrequent (<2 yearly) exacerbators, those experiencing a more rapid decline in $FEV_1$ (continued smokers, CT defined emphysema, and bronchodilator responsiveness), greater loss of lung density/parenchyma (smokers and women), bronchodilator responsiveness (more frequent exacerbators, although bronchodilator responsiveness was variable throughout the study), and systemic inflammation (approximately one third of patients with COPD never demonstrated evidence of systemic inflammation and 16% had persistent systemic inflammation with a 6-fold increase in overall mortality) (Augusti, 2012; Vestbo, 2014).

## 1.5 Genetic Factors

Only a minority of tobacco smokers develop COPD and the genetic risk factors for the development of COPD are not known. Mutations in the alpha-1-antitrypsin gene are associated with the development of emphysema and have been well characterized and replacement therapy is available. More recently, large multicenter investigations have used genome-wide association studies of populations that are clinically,

**Table 1.4:** Distinguishing features between COPD and asthma

| Characteristic | Asthma | COPD |
|---|---|---|
| Anatomic Distribution | Small airways | Small airways |
| | | Parenchyma |
| Cells | Eosinophil predominant | Neutrophil predominant |
| Cytokines | CD4 Th2: IL-4, IL-5, IL-9, IL-13 | CD8 Th1: IFN g |

physiologically, and radiographically well characterized to identify potential genetic loci associated with the development of COPD and with different COPD phenotypes (Chen, 2013; Cho, 2012; Bosse, 2012; Berndt, 2012). Other studies have focused on epigenetics (heritable variations that alter gene expression but do not change the DNA sequence) such as DNA methylation, histone alteration, and RNA-associated silencing, and their role in the development of COPD (Mortaz, 2011).

## 1.6 Clinical Symptoms and Differential Diagnosis

The three major symptoms associated with COPD are breathlessness, cough, and sputum production (see Chapter 3, COPD Recognition and Diagnosis: Approach to the Patient with Respiratory Symptoms, and Chapter 14, Management of Stable COPD.) Breathlessness is a subjective sensation of shortness of air that is normally experienced by everyone during vigorous or strenuous activity. With COPD, the initial manifestations may be subtle; an inability to maintain the pace when walking with peers or increased sensation of breathing while doing routine activities to overt wheezing and gasping for breath during activities. Cough is the forceful exhalation of air to clear the airways from irritating or obstructing material. Cough may be nonproductive or productive of phlegm. These symptoms are neither sensitive nor specific for the diagnosis of COPD and must be interpreted in conjunction with the clinical history and laboratory and radiographic findings (see Chapter 5, Radiology: Use of lung imaging to help in the identification of patients with COPD).

The differential diagnosis of COPD includes asthma, congestive heart failure, bronchiolitis, pulmonary infections, and bronchiectasis. Some distinguishing features between COPD and asthma are presented in Table 1.4. ***Thus, even though COPD and asthma are characterized by airflow limitation, they are distinct disorders with very different pathophysiologic mechanisms that lead to different and distinct treatment regimens.*** *Nevertheless, in some patients it may not be possible to distinguish asthma and COPD despite extensive evaluation and this undifferentiated group is now classified as asthma COPD overlap syndrome.* Many other disorders may occur concurrently with COPD and it may be difficult to discern the primary process. See Chapter 3, COPD Recognition and Diagnosis: Approach to the Patient with Respiratory Symptoms, for a detailed discussion of the differential diagnosis of COPD and assessment of patients presenting with breathlessness, cough, and sputum production.

## 1.7 Imaging

The chest x-ray may demonstrate hyperinflation with reduced peripheral vascular markings, flattening of the diaphragms, and a central and narrowed cardiac silhouette in individuals with emphysema. Although these findings are sensitive for the presence of COPD, they are not specific (Washko, 2012). Chest CT provides more detailed images of the lung parenchyma, airways, and vasculature. Chest CT imaging is commonly used for the diagnosis of emphysema and may be quantified by various densitometric analyses that demonstrate the loss of lung parenchyma. In addition, chest CTs may be used to measure central and peripheral small airway wall thickness, caliber, and number. More recent studies using micro-CT techniques have demonstrated that COPD is associated with reduced numbers of airways as well as pulmonary vessels in the lung parenchyma (Washko, 2012). Chapter 3 presents a more detailed review of the radiographic findings in COPD.

## 1.8 Treatment

Recent advances in the management of COPD have led to reductions in respiratory symptoms, improvements in quality of life, fewer exacerbations and less hospitalizations, and better survival for individuals with COPD. Chapter 8, Fostering Patient Self-Management of COPD reviews how providers may approach patients with COPD and encourage them to participate actively in their disease management; Chapter 7, Smoking Cessation, discusses smoking cessation, the single most important intervention for the prevention and management of COPD; treatment of stable COPD and exacerbations are reviewed in Chapters 14, 16, and 17, Management of Stable COPD, Management of Outpatient COPD Exacerbations, and Management of Inpatient COPD Exacerbations. Optimal COPD management is interdisciplinary and the role of primary care providers and their interaction with other providers is discussed in Chapter 18, Primary Care and Interaction with Specialty Care for the COPD Patient. Finally, advanced care planning is presented in Chapter 19, Integrating Supportive, Palliative, and End of Life Care for COPD.

## 1.9 Conclusion

COPD is a complex disorder with protean manifestations that are not limited to the lungs. Although, COPD has been classified historically as chronic bronchitis, emphysema, or a combination of these two processes, more recent research has identified a plethora of COPD phenotypes with varying clinical, radiographic, genetic, and biochemical characteristics with distinct prognostic and therapeutic implications. Thus, COPD is clearly a universe of different disorders that we are just beginning to understand and differentiate. The clinical application of these phenotypes and their use in management has begun with the utilization of classification and management guidelines that extend beyond the physiologic characterization of patients to include symptom severity and exacerbation risk. Further studies will identify other clinical, biochemical, physiologic, and radiographic variables that are critical to the characterization and classification of COPD and to better and more precisely directed management strategies.

## 1.10 Summary Points

1. The definition of COPD has evolved and continues to change with further clinical, genetic, biochemical, and radiologic studies.
2. Although COPD has historically been defined by airflow obstruction measured by spirometry, physiologic impairment is only one aspect of this disorder and does not correlate perfectly with disease severity, quality of life, or management.
3. COPD is a plethora of diverse phenotypes that are becoming better defined and characterized; these phenotypes are beginning to define more specific treatment regimens.

## References

Agusti A., Edwards L.D., Rennard S.I., MacNee W., Tal-Singer R., Miller B.E., Vestbo J., Lomas D.A., Calverley P.M.A., Wouters E., Crim C., Yates J.C., Silverman E.K., Coxson H.O., Bakke P, Mayer R.J., & Celli B. (2012) Evaluation of COPD Longitudinally to Identify Predictive Surrogate Endpoints (ECLIPSE) Investigators. Persistent systemic inflammation is associated with poor clinical outcomes in COPD: a novel phenotype. *PLoS One*, *7*, e37483.

Angelis N., Porpodis K., Zarogoulidis P., Spyratos D., Kioumis I., Papaiwannou A., Pitsiou G., Tsakiridis K., Mpakas A., Arikas S., Tsiouda T., Katsikogiannis N., Kougioumtzi I., Machairiotis N., Argyriou M., Kessisis G., & Zarogoulidis K. (2014). Airway inflammation in chronic obstructive pulmonary disease. *J Thorac Dis*, *6* Suppl 1, S167–72.

Berndt A., Leme A.S., & Shapiro S.D. (2012) Emerging genetics of COPD. *EMBO Mol Med*, *4*(11), 1144–55.

Bhatt S.P., Washko G.R., Dransfield M.T., Sieren J.C., Newell J.D. Jr., Hoffman E.A. & COPD Gene Investigators. (2014) Comparison of spirometric thresholds in diagnosing smoking-related airflow obstruction. *Thorax*, *69*(5), 409–14.

Bossé Y. (2012) Updates on the COPD gene list. *Int J Chron Obstruct Pulmon Dis*, *7*, 607–31

Celli B.R., Cote C.G., Marin J.M., Casanova C., Montes de Oca M., Mendez R.A., Pinto Plata V., & Cabral H.J. (2004) The body-mass index, airflow obstruction, dyspnea, and exercise capacity index in chronic obstructive pulmonary disease. *N Engl J Med*, *350*, 1005–1012.

Chen X., Xu X., & Xiao F. (2013). Heterogeneity of chronic obstructive pulmonary disease: from phenotype to genotype. *Front Med*, *7*(4), 425–32.

Chhabra S.K. (2005) Acute bronchodilator response has limited value in differentiating bronchial asthma from COPD. *J Asthma*, *42*(5), 367–372.

Cho M.H., Castaldi P.J., Wan E.S., Siedlinski M., Hersh C.P., Demeo D.L., Himes B.E., Sylvia J.S., Klanderman B.J., Ziniti J.P., Lange C., Litonjua A.A., Sparrow D., Regan E.A., Make B.J., Hokanson J.E., Murray T., Hetmanski J.B., Pillai S.G., Kong X., Anderson W.H., Tal-Singer R., Lomas D.A., Coxson H.O., Edwards L.D., MacNee W., Vestbo J., Yates J.C., Agusti A., Calverley P.M., Celli B., Crim C., Rennard S., Wouters E., Bakke P., Gulsvik A., Crapo J.D., Beaty T.H., Silverman E.K.& ICGN Investigators; ECLIPSE Investigators; COPD Gene Investigators. (2012). A genome-wide association study of COPD identifies a susceptibility locus on chromosome 19q13. *Hum Mol Genet*, *21*(4), 947–957.

Coxson H.O., Leipsic J., Parraga G., & Sin D.D. (2014). Using pulmonary imaging to move chronic obstructive pulmonary disease beyond FEV1. *Am J Respir Crit Care Med*, *190*(2), 135–44.

Dawson A. (1965). Reproducibility of spirometric measurements in normal subjects. *Am Rev Respir Dis*, *93*, 264–268.

Donohue J.F. (2005). Minimal clinically important differences in COPD lung function. *COPD*, *1*, 111–124. Global strategy for the diagnosis, management, and prevention of chronic obstructive pulmonary disease: Revised 2014. Global Initiative for Chronic Obstructive Lung Disease (GOLD). www.goldcopd.org (Accessed on January 23, 2014).

Hanania N.A., Celli B.R., Donohue J.F., & Martin U.J. (2011). Bronchodilator reversibility in COPD. *Chest*, *140*(4), 1055–63.

http://www.thoracic.org/clinical/copd-guidelines/resources/copddoc.pdf. (Accessed on January 23, 2014).

http://www.who.int/respiratory/copd/definition/en/ (Accessed on January 23, 2014).

Jha P., Ramasundarahettige C., Landsman V., Rostron B., Thun M., Anderson R.N., McAfee T., & Peto R. (2013). 21st-century hazards of smoking and benefits of cessation in the United States. *N Engl J Med*, *368*(4), 341–50.

Jones P.W. (2009). Health status and the spiral of decline. *COPD*, *6*, 59–63.

Jones R.C., Donaldson G.C., Chavannes N.H., Kida K., Dickson-Spillmann M., Harding S., Wedzicha J.A., Price D., & Hyland M.E. (2009). Derivation and validation of a composite index of severity in chronic obstructive pulmonary disease: the DOSE index. *Am J Respir Crit Care Med*, *180*, 1189–1195.

Mortaz E., Masjedi M.R., Barnes P.J., & Adcock I.M., (2011). Epigenetics and chromatin remodeling play a role in lung disease. *Tanaffos*, *10*(4), 7–16.

Nickerson B.G., Lemen R.J., Gerdes C.B., Wegmann M.J., & Robertson G: (1980). Within-subject variability and percent change for significance of spirometry in normal subjects and in patients with cystic fibrosis. *Am Rev Respir Dis*, *122*, 859–866.

Pennock B.E., Rogers R.M., & McCaffree D.R: (1981). Changes in measured spirometric indices. What is significant? *Chest*, *80*, 97–99.

Puhan M.A., Garcia-Aymerich J., Frey M., ter Riet G., Anto J.M., Agustı A.G., Gomez F.P., Rodrıguez--Roisın R., Moons K.G.M., Kessels A.G., & Held U. (2009). Expansion of the prognostic

assessment of patients with chronic obstructive pulmonary disease: the updated BODE index and the ADO index. *Lancet*, *374*, 704–711.
Qaseem A., Wilt T.J., Weinberger S.E., Hanania N.A., Criner G., van der Molen T., Marciniuk D.D., Denberg T., Schünemann H., Wedzicha W., MacDonald R., Shekelle P.; American College of Physicians; American College of Chest Physicians; American Thoracic Society; European Respiratory Society. (2011). Diagnosis and management of stable chronic obstructive pulmonary disease: a clinical practice guideline update from the American College of Physicians, American College of Chest Physicians, American Thoracic Society, and European Respiratory Society. *Ann Intern Med*, *155*(3), 179–91.
Rozas, C.J., & Goldman, A.L. (1982). Daily Spirometric Variability Normal subjects and subjects with chronic bronchitis with and without airflow obstruction. *Arch Intern Med*, 1287–1291.
Rovina N., Koutsoukou A., & Koulouris N.G. (2013). Inflammation and immune response in COPD: where do we stand? *Mediators Inflamm*, 413735.
Trigueros Carrero J.A. (2013). How should we define and classify exacerbations in chronic obstructive pulmonary disease? *Expert Rev Respir Med*, *7*(2 Suppl), 33–41.
Vestbo J., Agusti A., Wouters E.F., Bakke P., Calverley P.M., Celli B., Coxson H., Crim C., Edwards L.D., Locantore N., Lomas D.A., MacNee W., Miller B., Rennard S.I., Silverman E.K., Yates J.C., & Tal-Singer R. (2014). Evaluation of COPD Longitudinally to Identify Predictive Surrogate Endpoints Study Investigators. Should we view chronic obstructive pulmonary disease differently after ECLIPSE? A clinical perspective from the study team. *Am J Respir Crit Care Med*, *189*(9), 1022–1030.
Vestbo J., Edwards L.D., Scanlon P.D., Yates J.C., Agusti A., Bakke P., Calverley P.M.A., Celli B., Coxson H.O., Crim C., Lomas D.A., MacNee W., Miller D.E., Silverman E.K., Tal-Singer R., Wouters E., Rennard S.I. for the ECLIPSE Investigators. (2011). Changes in forced expiratory volume in 1 second over time in COPD. *N Engl J Med*, *365*, 1184–1192.
Washko G.R. (2012). The role and potential of imaging in COPD. *Med Clin North Am*, *96*(4), 729–43.
Zeng G., Sun B., & Zhong N. (2012). Non-smoking-related chronic obstructive pulmonary disease: a neglected entity? *Respirology*, *17*(6), 908–12.

Ralph J. Panos, MD

# 2 Epidemiology and Economic Consequences of COPD

Key Points

1. Tobacco smoke inhalation is the major risk factor for the development of COPD.
2. Secondhand, passive, or environmental tobacco smoke exposure may also have a potentially important role in the development of chronic lung disease.
3. Approximately one quarter of individuals with COPD are not smokers; nontobacco smoke risk factors for COPD development include indoor and outdoor air pollutants, workplace dust and fumes, childhood lower respiratory disorders including asthma, and pulmonary infections (tuberculosis and human immunodeficiency virus).
4. Chronic lower respiratory disease (COPD and asthma) is the third leading cause of death in the US.
5. In 2010, the total cost of COPD in the US was estimated to be $36 billion and is projected to rise to $49 billion in 2020.
6. The majority of COPD medical costs are related to healthcare visits (emergency department and hospitalizations) for exacerbations.
7. COPD impairs workers and is a significant contributor to sick and disability leave and employer healthcare costs.

## 2.1 Introduction

Studies of the epidemiology of COPD provide critical associations between environmental risk factors and the development of airflow limitation and other disease manifestations in vulnerable individuals. Obstructive lung disease does not develop in all individuals exposed to known potential risk factors which suggests that, in addition to environmental exposures, a genetic predisposition or susceptibility is required for the development of COPD. Because the hereditary factors (other than alpha 1 antitrypsin mutations) are poorly characterized, these epidemiologic associations provide the best current opportunity to prevent the development of COPD by identifying potentially avoidable exposures and decreasing their detrimental effects.

COPD may be the single most underdiagnosed and misdiagnosed chronic disorder with the greatest economic consequences (Mannino, 2002; Mannino, 2007; Diaz-Guzman, 2014). COPD is the third leading cause of death in the US and accounts for nearly $40 billion dollars in direct healthcare costs with approximately additional $4 billion dollars in indirect costs due to lost or impaired work (Ford, 2014). An analysis of the National Health and Nutrition Examination Survey 2007–2009 revealed COPD under-diagnosis (failure to diagnose COPD in individuals with respiratory symptoms and airflow limitation measured by spirometry) of 82.9% (95% confidence interval (CI) 75.2, 88.6) and over-diagnosis (diagnosis of COPD in individuals who did not have airflow limitation) of 61.1% (95% CI, 49.0, 72.0) (Munson, 2013). Other studies suggest that the under-diagnosis of COPD ranges from 63.3–71.1% (Murphy, 2011; Mannino, 2000; Petty, 2000).

COPD exacerbations including emergency room visits and hospitalizations are the major factors contributing to direct medical costs of COPD (Darnell, 2013). Nearly three quarters of individuals diagnosed with COPD are under 65 years old and employers spend about $17,000 per year on employees with COPD which is three times more than for those who do not have COPD (Bunn, 2008).

Despite COPD's significant economic costs and prevalence, research support for COPD basic science, translational, and clinical studies is severely underfunded. An analysis of National Institutes of Health research funding for 29 common conditions found that COPD was the most underfunded disorder based upon disease burden (Gillum, 2011).

## 2.2 Epidemiology

### 2.2.1 Risk Factors for COPD Development

#### 2.2.1.1 Tobacco Smoke

Although tobacco smoke inhalation is the major factor associated with the development of COPD globally, smoking is the predominant risk factor in the developed world and other factors dominate in the developing world currently. A large meta-analysis of 218 studies examining the relationship between smoking and COPD, chronic bronchitis, and emphysema revealed a relative risk (RR) of ever smoking and developing COPD of 2.89 (95% CI 2.63, 3.17), chronic bronchitis 2.69 (95% CI 2.50, 2.90), and emphysema 4.51 (95% CI 3.38, 6.02) (Forey, 2011). For current smokers, the RR increases to 3.51 (95% CI 3.08, 3.99) for COPD, to 3.41 (95% CI 3.13, 3.72) for chronic bronchitis, and to 4.87 (95% CI 2.83, 8.41) for emphysema. The risk for lung disease increased with the amount and the duration of smoking, and decreased with increasing age of starting to smoke and duration of smoking cessation (Forey, 2011). The effect is greater for cigarette smokers and less for pipe and cigar smokers. In addition, the age of smoking cessation significantly influences the effect of smoking on longevity (Jha, 2013). Quitting smoking by the age of 35 neutralizes most of the excess mortality due to smoking (Jha, 2013). Smoking cessation reduces the rate of lung function decline at all stages of COPD but has the greatest effect in early disease (Welte, 2014). Thus, the amount, duration, age of starting smoking, age of quitting smoking, duration of smoking abstinence, and type of tobacco product all contribute to the development of COPD.

#### 2.2.1.2 Passive or Environmental Tobacco Smoke Exposure

The 2006 Surgeon General's report concluded that secondhand, passive, or environmental tobacco smoke exposure is associated with multiple disorders including COPD, asthma, respiratory infections, cardiovascular disease, and cancer but the evidence was insufficient to establish a causal relationship (U.S. Department of Health and Human Services, 2006). Environmental tobacco smoke exposure includes 85% sidestream smoke from the burning tip of a cigarette and 15% mainstream smoke that is exhaled by an active smoker (Manuel, 1999). Sidestream smoke is unfiltered and contains smaller particles than mainstream smoke but both sources contain multiple toxic and carcinogenic agents (Reardon, 2007).

Passive smoke exposure in utero or during early childhood may adversely affect lung development and predispose to the subsequent development of COPD (Stocks, 2013), (discussed in Chapter 9, Natural History, Phenotypes, and Gender Differences in COPD.) Among nonsmoking adults over the age of 40 in China, over 78% had environmental tobacco smoke exposure and the odds of COPD among those with home or work environmental tobacco smoke exposure is 1.48 (95% CI, 1.18, 1.85) (Regional COPD Working Group, 2003; Yin, 2007). A meta-analysis of the effect of second hand smoke exposure and the development of COPD shows an increased odds ratio (OR) of 1.56 (95% CI 1.40, 1.74) (Eisner, 2010). Workers in environments where laws have been enacted prohibiting smoking experience less cough and phlegm production and their lung function improves after smoking has been banned from their workplace (Goodman, 2007; Menzies, 2006; Eagan, 2006).

#### 2.2.1.3 Non-tobacco Smoke Factors

The attributable risk for the development of COPD due to tobacco smoke ranges from 9.7 to 97.9% but is generally less than 80%, which suggests that other exposures contribute to 20% or more of COPD cases (Eisner, 2010). Approximately one quarter of individuals with COPD in the US, UK, and Spain were never smokers (Salvi, 2009). Factors other than tobacco smoke that have been associated with the development of COPD include indoor and outdoor air pollutants, workplace dust and fumes, childhood lower respiratory infections, pulmonary tuberculosis, chronic asthma, intrauterine growth retardation, poor nutrition, and lower socioeconomic status (Salvi, 2009; Eisner, 2010; Diaz-Guzman, 2012). Depending upon the level of these exposures, between 25 and 45% of individuals with COPD may be never smokers (less than 100 cigarettes in their lifetime) (Salvi, 2009).

#### 2.2.1.4 Occupational Exposures

Combined tobacco smoke and occupational exposures to dusts, gases, fumes, and smoke significantly increase the risk of developing COPD (Blanc, 2009; Salvi, 2009; Eisner, 2010; Doney, 2014; Omland, 2014). In the US, approximately 15% of cases of

COPD may be due to environmental exposures in the workplace when controlling for tobacco smoke exposure (Balmes, 2003; Blanc, 2007). Between 30–40% of farmers have COPD and lung disease is associated with ammonia and dust inhalation (Lamprecht, 2007; Eduard, 2009). Dust exposure, especially from silica, is associated with COPD among construction workers, miners, and foundry and concrete workers (Salvi, 2009). Other industries with increased risk of COPD include plastics, textile, rubber, leather, trucking (especially with diesel exhaust exposure), and food products (Salvi, 2009; Hnizdo, 2002; Weinmann, 2008).

#### 2.2.1.5 Air Pollution

##### 2.2.1.5.1 Indoor

Exposure to biomass fuels (wood, dung, and coal) that are used in open fire stoves throughout the developing world is a significant risk for the development of lung disease, especially among nonsmoking women and children (Regalado, 2006; Rinne, 2006; Grigg, 2009). Worldwide, approximately 50% of all and 90% of rural households use biomass fuels for heating and cooking (Zeng, 2012). Biomass smoke exposure increases the odds for developing COPD by two to three fold (Sood, 2012). A systemic review of the association between solid fuels and COPD and chronic bronchitis demonstrated OR's of 2.80 (95% CI 1.85, 4.0) and 2.32 (95% CI 1.92, 2.80), respectively (Kurmi, 2010). In addition, solid fuel smoke is associated with increased lung infections, especially among women and children, higher risk for asthma, interstitial lung disease, and lung cancer (Sood, 2012).

##### 2.2.1.5.2 Outdoor

Outdoor air pollution is associated with impaired development of lung function in childhood and adolescence which may reduce peak lung function or decrease the duration of the plateau phase of maximal lung function (see Chapter 9. Natural History, Phenotypes, and Gender Differences in COPD.) (Gauderman, 2004; Gauderman, 2007; Rojas-Martinez, 2007; Ko, 2012). The Study on the Influence of Air Pollution on Lung Function, Inflammation, and Aging (SALIA) showed that increasing exposure to aerosolized particulate matter was associated with reductions in $FEV_1$, FVC, and $FEV_1$/FVC and increased risk for COPD in 4,575 German women (Schikowski, 2005). The Swiss Study on Air Pollution and Lung Diseases in Adults demonstrated a reduction in the decline in lung function as air quality improved (Downs, 2007). In the UK, the lung function of postmen working in cities with worse air pollution is reduced compared to those working in areas with better air quality (Fairbairn, 1958; Holland, 1965). In addition, worse air pollution is associated with increased COPD exacerbations; for every 10 microgram/m$^3$ increase in the annual mean particulate matter 10, (PM10 >100 microgram/m$^3$), the hospitalization rate for acute COPD exacerbations increases by 2.4% (Ko, 2007).

#### 2.2.1.6 Sex

Women appear to be more susceptible to the development of smoking related COPD (Aryal, 2014). They develop greater airflow limitation at younger ages and with less tobacco smoke exposure, experience a faster rate of lung function decline than men, and have a higher risk of hospitalization for acute exacerbations of COPD (Aryal, 2014; Gan, 2006, Tam, 2013). Potential explanations for the gender differences in COPD manifestations include dysanapsis (airway size disproportionate to lung size; women's airways are smaller than men's even controlling for differences in lung size), elevated susceptibility to inflammation and mucus hypersecretion, differential effects of hormones, differences in pulmonary particle deposition, and greater and longer cigarette smoke inhalation by women compared with men (Tam, 2013).

#### 2.2.1.7 Infections

Review of epidemiologic studies of tuberculosis (TB) and COPD demonstrate an increased risk of obstructive lung disease in individuals who previously had pulmonary tuberculosis with OR between 1.37 and 2.94 (Allwood, 2013; Ehrlich, 2011). The prevalence of COPD among individuals previously treated for tuberculosis ranges from 28–68% and increases with the time after tuberculosis treatment completion (Jordan, 2010). Prior tuberculosis infection is associated with accelerated lung function decline but it is unclear if the pathophysiology of this reduction is related to the processes that cause lung function decline in tobacco-related COPD (Hnizdo, 2000). Conversely, smoking doubles the risk of TB infection, active disease, and mortality (van Zyl-Smit, 2010).

Human immunodeficiency virus (HIV) infection is another risk factor for COPD, especially emphysema (Raynaud, 2011; Gingo, 2013). Early reports associated HIV infection with air trapping, reduced diffusing capacity, and CT scan evidence of emphysema (Diaz, 1992; Diaz, 2000). When controlling for smoking, HIV infected individuals older than 50 years have an 11% higher incidence of COPD than those who are not infected and, among those less than 50 years old, the incidence is 25% greater (Crothers, 2011). HIV infected injection drug users are 3.4 fold more likely to have obstructive lung disease than non-infected users (Drummond, 2012). Smoking further increases the risk of COPD among HIV infected individuals (Crothers, 2005).

### 2.2.2 Prevalence

#### 2.2.2.1

The measurement of COPD prevalence is extremely dependent upon the criteria used to define COPD, use of spirometry, and the threshold for airflow limitation. Many epidemiologic studies utilize a clinical definition of COPD asking participants if they have ever been told by a healthcare provider that they have COPD, chronic bronchitis, or emphysema. In the absence of physiologic measurement, the clinical diagnosis of COPD may be inaccurate in 25% of patients (Murray, 2011). Even when spirometry is used, the measured prevalence will depend upon whether pre-bronchodilator or post-bronchodilator values are used to determine the presence of airflow limitation. The threshold for the definition of airflow limitation significantly alters the measured prevalence of airflow limitation (discussed in Chapter 4, Pulmonary Function Testing: Presence and Severity of Airflow Limitation/Obstruction). Even studies that used very standardized and uniform methodologies such as the Burden of Obstructive Lung Disease (BOLD) and the Latin American Project for the Investigation of Obstructive Lung Disease (PLATINO) found dramatic variability in COPD prevalence across countries and regions (Buist, 2007; Menezes, 2005). Therefore, when reviewing studies of COPD epidemiology, one should be careful to assess study methodology and disease definitions.

Because tobacco smoke inhalation is the predominant cause of COPD, the prevalence of COPD corresponds closely with smoking rates but with a lag of several decades. In the US, smoking rates for men peaked in the 1950s and 1960s and COPD prevalence and mortality rates have stabilized or begun to decline (http://www.tobaccoatlas.org/products/male_tobacco_use/prevalence/; http://www.cdc.gov/copd/data.htm). For women, smoking rates peaked in the 1970s and 1980s and the prevalence and mortality rates of COPD in women more than doubled from 1980 to 2000 and have stabilized from 1999 to 2010 (http://www.tobaccoatlas.org/products/female_tobacco_use/prevalence/; http://www.cdc.gov/copd/data.htm). Thus, where cigarette smoke inhalation is the predominant cause of COPD, the prevalence of COPD lags smoking rates by several decades.

### 2.2.2.2 United States

#### 2.2.2.2.1 Prevalence

Based upon the National Health Interview Survey, 5.1% of US adults over the age of 18 had COPD in 2007–2009 and the prevalence of COPD was greater in women, 6.1%, than in men, 4.1% (Akinbami, 2011). The overall prevalence of COPD was stable from 1998 through 2009. COPD prevalence increased with age and was higher in women than in men throughout most age groups.

The Third National Health and Nutrition Examination Survey (NHANES III) estimated that the prevalence of COPD was 6.8–8.5% within the general US population (Mannino, 2000). COPD prevalence was estimated to be greater in current (12.5%) and former (9.4%) smokers than in never smokers (5.8%) (Mannino, 2000). In 2011, 6.8% of US adults older than 25 years reported that a caregiver had told them that they had COPD (Ford, 2013). The age adjusted prevalence was higher in American Indian/Alaska natives, 11.0%, than in non-Hispanic whites, 6.9%, non-Hispanic blacks, 5.7%, Hispanics, 4.1%, and Asian/Pacific Islanders, 2.5%. COPD prevalence was also greater in women, 7.3%, than in men, 5.7% (Ford, 2013). Geographically, COPD prevalence was greatest in the states bordering the Ohio and Mississippi Rivers (Ford, 2013).

#### 2.2.2.2.2 Gender Distribution

Over the past decade several dramatic changes in the gender distribution of COPD have occurred in the US (Ohar, 2011). For the first time in 2000, more women than men died from COPD in the US (Arias, 2003). Female smokers are 13 times more likely to die from COPD than nonsmoking women whereas male smokers are 12 times more likely to die from COPD than nonsmoking men (U.S. Department of Health and Human Services, 2014). Women are twice as likely to be diagnosed with chronic bronchitis as men; in 2011, 56.7 women per 1,000 population were diagnosed with chronic bronchitis compared with 29.6 per 1,000 population among men (http://www.lung.org/lung-disease/copd/resources/facts-figures/COPD-Fact-Sheet.html). Also, in 2011, the prevalence of diagnosed emphysema was greater in women than in men, 21.4 per 1,000 compared to 19.0 per 1,000. (http://www.lung.org/lung-disease/copd/resources/facts-figures/COPD-Fact-Sheet.html).

#### 2.2.2.2.3 Healthcare Utilization and Occupational Consequences

In the 2011 Behavioral Risk Factor Surveillance System survey, 6.3% of US had a self-reported caregiver diagnosis of COPD (Centers for Disease Control and Prevention, 2012). Of those with COPD, 76.0% had undergone pulmonary function testing, 64.2% felt their quality of life was impaired by breathlessness, and 55.6% were taking at least one breathing medication. In the year before the survey, 43.2% had seen a physician and 17.7% had been seen in an emergency room or hospitalized for respiratory-related symptoms. In 2010, there were 495 physician office visits, 72 emergency department visits, and 34 hospitalizations with a primary diagnosis of COPD per 10,000 US population (Ford, 2013).

Analysis of data from the National Health and Wellness Survey of over 20,000 employed US adults between 40 and 64 years old revealed that 5.5% self reported a diagnosis of COPD (DiBonaventura, 2012). Those with COPD reported greater presenteeism (the percentage of impairment while at work due to health in the past 7 days), and overall work and daily activity impairment.

#### 2.2.2.2.4 Mortality

In 2007, nearly 60,000 men (63.5 per 100,000 population) and nearly 65,000 women (46.8 per 100,000 population) died from COPD. The death rates from COPD declined for men but did not change for women from 1999 through 2007. Lower respiratory disease (COPD and asthma) was the third leading cause of death in the US in 2008 (Minino, 2010). COPD was the primary cause of approximately one in every 20 deaths in the US in 2005 (CDC, 2008).

## 2.3 Economics

### 2.3.1 Direct Costs

Direct costs are the expenses incurred by the healthcare system, community, and patients and their families due to illness. The total US costs related to COPD and its comorbidities in 2010 are estimated to be $36 billion with $32.1 billion due to direct medical expenditures and $3.9 billion in indirect or absenteeism costs (Ford, 2014). By 2020 the national direct medical costs of COPD are predicted to rise to $49 billion (Ford, 2014). COPD exacerbations and their management account for 45–75% of direct costs (Toy, 2010). A summary of the costs of COPD in 2006 estimated the per-patient direct costs to be $2,700-$5,900 annually with excess costs ranging from $6,100 to $6,600 annually (Foster, 2006). In 2008, hospitalization costs for COPD exacerbations were estimated to range from $7,242 for an uncomplicated admission to $44,909 for a complex admission requiring mechanical ventilation and critical care (Dalal, 2011). Medicare beneficiaries with COPD have annual healthcare costs $20,500 greater than those without COPD (Menzin, 2008). Overall healthcare costs are greater for those with COPD compared to individuals who do not have COPD.

Among 8554 patients with COPD, mean annual COPD related healthcare costs were $4069 overall but $6381 for patients with two or more exacerbations and mean all cause healthcare costs were $18,976 overall and $23,901 for those with two or more exacerbations (Pasquale, 2012). Higher costs occurred among those with more severe exacerbations, comorbid cardiovascular disease, diabetes, and supplemental oxygen use. A review of 58,589 patients with COPD in the United Kingdom showed that the annual cost of COPD care was 1,523, 2,405, and 3,396 pounds (approximately, $2303, $3637, and $5135, US dollars, respectively) for patients with 0, 1, and 2 or more exacerbations (Punekar, 2014).

Hospitalization costs for COPD increase with the severity of the exacerbation. Analysis of administrative data from 602 hospitals in 2008 revealed that hospitalizations requiring intensive care and intubation cost $44909 whereas ward hospitalization cost $7242; complex hospitalizations requiring either intubation or intensive care accounted for only 5.8% of COPD hospitalizations but 20.9% of hospitalization costs (Dalal, 2011). Other factors that may increase the cost of COPD hospitalizations include hospital acquired pneumonia, chronic renal failure, and anemia (Ornek, 2012).

Severity of disease measured by airflow obstruction correlates very positively with the cost of COPD-related healthcare costs (de Miguel diez, 2008). Analysis of direct healthcare costs due to COPD among 160 patients with COPD in Taiwan showed that annual costs increased with airflow obstruction severity, 38,203, 149,031, and 288,825 new Taiwan dollars (approximately $1193, $4657, and $9026 US dollars, respectively for individuals with mild (FEV1% predicted >50%), moderate (FEV1% predicted <30% and <50%), and severe (FEV1% predicted <30%) disease and the greatest contributor to cost was hospitalization (Chiang, 2008). A Swedish review confirmed the strong positive correlation between COPD severity and costs but suggested that over the past decade, costs have decreased for those with more severe disease and increased for individuals with more mild to moderate COPD (Jansson, 2013).

Comorbid conditions increase the healthcare cost for individuals with COPD (de Miguel diez, 2008; Dalal, 2011; Perera, 2012; Nielsen, 2011). Acute coronary syndrome, congestive heart failure, cerebrovascular disease, bronchogenic cancer, cardiac dysrhythmias, pulmonary vascular disease, and weight loss are associated with greater costs and mortality (Perera, 2012). Patients with COPD and cardiovascular disease have more ED visits (OR 1.47), more respiratory-related hospitalizations (OR 1.95), and any hospitalization or ED visit (OR 1.62). The annual total healthcare costs were nearly three-fold greater for those with COPD and cardiovascular disease compared with COPD alone, $22,755 and $8036 (2008 US dollars), respectively (Dalal, 2011).

### 2.3.2 Indirect Costs

Indirect costs are the economic output losses caused by illness. COPD is estimated to cause 16.4 million days of lost work annually (Ford, 2014). Estimated mean annual number of sick leave or disability days taken by employed individuals with COPD due to respiratory symptoms range from 1.3 to 19.4 days with estimated costs of $893-$2,234 per person (Patel, 2014). The type or amount of work performed by approximately 13–18% of individuals with COPD is limited and over one third experience reductions in their general activities (Patel, 2014). The number of days with diminished activity ranges from 27–63 days and employed individuals with COPD utilize between 1.3 and 19.4 days of sick or disability leave and may be bed bound for 13–32 days yearly (Patel, 2014). The annual indirect costs of COPD ranged from $1,521–3,348 per person in 2012 US dollars and comprised 27–61% of the total costs related to COPD (Patel, 2014).

### 2.3.3 Effect of Treatment

Prescription and adherence with respiratory medications correlate inversely with healthcare utilization for individuals with COPD. Yearly hospitalizations and emergency department visits decreased by 2.5% and 1.8%, respectively, for every 5% increase in proportion of days covered (a measure of the percentage of days during which an individual filed claims for respiratory medications; it is an indirect epidemiologic measure of medication adherence) whereas outpatient visits only increased by 0.2% (Toy, 2011). A retrospective analysis of over 55,000 patients with COPD showed that medication adherence increased with less frequent dosing interval of respiratory medications; the proportion of days covered was 43.3%, 37.0%, 30.2%, and 23.0% for once, twice, thrice, and four times daily regimens (Toy, 2011). The annual cost of care for 1000 patients with COPD decreased by $300,000 for every 5% increase in adherence (Toy, 2011). In a retrospective review of 33,816 Medicare beneficiaries with COPD, medication adherence measured by medication continuity or proportion of days covered was associated with lower hospitalization rates (RR, 0.88) and less Medicare cost (-$3764) (Simoni-Wastila, 2012). In addition, patients with a proportion of days covered greater than 80% had less hospitalizations (RR 0.90) and lower cost (-$2185) than those with less than 80% of days covered (Simoni-Wastila, 2012). An analysis of maintenance medication use versus no maintenance medication use among 6322 Medicare beneficiaries demonstrated that the users had fewer hospitalizations (OR 0.70, 95% CI, 0.61–9.79), rehospitalizations (OR 0.74, 95% CI 0.63–0.87) and lower Medicare costs (-S3916, 95% CI, -$4977,-$2854) (Stuart, 2010).

Integrated disease management programs for COPD that incorporate two or more interdisciplinary healthcare providers and two or more treatment components reduce respiratory-related hospitalizations and length of stay and improve respiratory quality of life and exercise capacity (Kruis, 2013). A VHA COPD disease management program produced an average cost savings of $593 per patient mainly by reducing ED visits and hospitalizations (Dewan, 2011). However, another VHA study of a comprehensive COPD care management program was prematurely stopped due to excess mortality in the intervention group (Fan, 2012).

Pulmonary rehabilitation is associated with reduced direct healthcare costs and an analysis of 592 pulmonary rehabilitation participants revealed an annual $344 (Canadian; approximately $291 US) per person decrease in overall healthcare costs (Golmohammadi, 2004). Hospital at home also reduces COPD related healthcare costs (Nicholson, 2001; Puig-Junoy, 2007; Steinel, 2003). A Spanish program found that among 180 patients presenting to the ED with a COPD exacerbation, home care by a specialized respiratory nurse reduced the average direct healthcare cost per patient by euro 810 (95% CI, euro 418–1,169) (approximately $955, US dollars) compared with hospitalization (Puig-Junoy, 2007). In-home healthcare by a pulmonary specialty team reduces hospitalizations, ED visits, and skilled nursing facility utilization, and decreases overall costs by $13,000 per patient annually (Steinel, 2003).

## 2.4 Conclusion

Epidemiology studies have demonstrated strong associations between tobacco smoke inhalation and the development of COPD. However, in the US and developed world, only 70–80% of individuals with COPD have a history of smoking. Other factors contributing to the development of COPD include indoor and outdoor air pollutants, workplace dust and fumes, childhood lower respiratory disorders including asthma, and pulmonary infections (tuberculosis and human immunodeficiency virus).

Although COPD prevalence is about 5–10% of the adult US population, these estimates may significantly underestimate COPD and up to three quarters of individuals with evidence of airflow obstruction may not have a diagnosis. Further, clinical diagnosis of COPD based only upon respiratory symptoms is often incorrect.

The economic costs of COPD due to direct medical care and indirect effects due to work impairment or total disability are approaching $40 billion annually in the US and may reach $50 billion by 2020. Appropriate COPD management with medications and nonpharmacologic measures can reduce the cost of COPD.

## 2.5 Summary Points

1. Tobacco smoke inhalation is the major cause of COPD in the US but nearly one fifth of COPD cases are due to other exposures such as indoor and outdoor air pollutants, workplace dust and fumes, childhood lower respiratory disorders, and pulmonary infections.
2. COPD is under- and mis-diagnosed making accurate measurement of COPD prevalence difficult. Current estimates of COPD prevalence in the US are 5–10%.
3. COPD is a significant contributor to direct and indirect medical care and its cost is estimated to increase by nearly 50% by 2020.

## References

Akinbami L.J., & Liu X. (2011). Chronic obstructive pulmonary disease among adults aged 18 and over in the United States, 1998–2009. *NCHS Data Brief*, *63*, 1–8.

Allwood B.W., Myer L., & Bateman E.D. (2013). A systematic review of the association between pulmonary tuberculosis and the development of chronic airflow obstruction in adults. *Respiration*, *86*(1), 76–85.

Arias E., Anderson R.N., Hsiang-Ching K., Murphy S.L., & Kochanek K.D. (2003). Deaths: Final data for 2001. *National vital statistics report*, 2003, 52 <http://www.cdc.gov/nchs/products/pubs/pubd/nvsr/52/52-23.htm> (Accessed November, 2014).

Aryal S., Diaz-Guzman E., & Mannino D.M. (2014). Influence of sex on chronic obstructive pulmonary disease risk and treatment outcomes. *Int J Chron Obstruct Pulmon Dis*, *9*, 1145–1154.

Balmes J., Becklake M., Blanc P., Henneberger P., Kreiss K., Mapp C., Milton D., Schwartz D., Toren K., Viegi G.; & Environmental and Occupational Health Assembly, American Thoracic Society. (2003). Environmental and Occupational Health Assembly, American Thoracic Society. American Thoracic Society statement: occupational contribution to the burden of airway disease. *Am J Respir Crit Care Med*, *167*, 787–97.

Blanc P.D., Iribarren C., Trupin L., Earnest G., Katz P.P., Balmes J., Sidney S., & Eisner M.D. (2009). Occupational exposures and the risk of COPD: dusty trades revisited. *Thorax*, *64*, 6–12.

Blanc P.D., & Toren K. (2007). Occupation in chronic obstructive pulmonary disease and chronic bronchitis: an update. *Int J Tuberc Lung Dis*, *11*, 251–57.

Blanc P.D. (2012). Occupation and COPD: a brief review. *J Asthma*, *49*(1), 2–4.

Buist A.S., McBurnie M.A., Vollmer W.M., Gillespie S., Burney P., Mannino D.M., Menezes A.M., Sullivan S.D., Lee T.A., Weiss K.B., Jensen R.L., Marks G.B., Gulsvik A., Nizankowska-Mogilnicka E.; & BOLD Collaborative Research Group. (2007). International variation in the prevalence of COPD (The BOLD Study): a population-based prevalence study. *Lancet*, *370*, 741–49.

Bunn W., Pikelny D., Vogenberg F.R., Berger J., Lichtig L.K., Liebeskind D., & Font J.A. (2008). Validation of employer focused actuarial model for measuring the economic burden of chronic obstructive pulmonary disease. *J Health Productiv*, *3*, 3–8.

Centers for Disease Control and Prevention (CDC). (2012). Chronic obstructive pulmonary disease among adults--United States, 2011. *MMWR Morb Mortal Wkly Rep*, *61*(46), 938–43.

Centers for Disease Control and Prevention (CDC). (2008). Deaths from chronic obstructive pulmonary disease--United States, 2000–2005. *MMWR Morb Mortal Wkly Rep*, *57*(45), 1229–32.

Chiang C.H. (2008). Cost analysis of chronic obstructive pulmonary disease in a tertiary care setting in Taiwan. *Respirology*, *13*(5), 689–94.

Crothers K., Griffith T.A., McGinnis K.A., Rodriguez-Barradas M.C., Leaf D.A., Weissman S., Gibert C.L., Butt A.A., & Justice A.C. (2005). The impact of cigarette smoking on mortality, quality of life, and comorbid illness among HIV-positive veterans. *J Gen Intern Med*, *20*(12), 1142–1145.

Crothers K., Huang L., Goulet J.L., Rodriguez-Barradas M.C., Leaf D.A., Weissman S., Gibert C.L., Butt A.A., & Justice A.C. (2011). HIV infection and risk for incident pulmonary diseases in the combination antiretroviral therapy era. *Am J Respir Crit Care Med*, *183*(3), 388–395.

Dalal A.A., Shah M., D'Souza A.O., & Rane P. (2011). Costs of COPD in the exacerbations in the emergency department and inpatient setting. *Respir Med*, *105*(3), 454–460.

Dalal A.A., Shah M., Lunacsek O., & Hanania N.A. (2011). Clinical and economic burden of patients diagnosed with COPD with comorbid cardiovascular disease. *Respir Med*, *105*(10), 1516–22.

Darnell K., Dwivedi A.K., Weng Z., & Panos R.J. (2013). Disproportionate utilization of healthcare resources among veterans with COPD: a retrospective analysis of factors associated with COPD healthcare cost. Cost Eff Resour Alloc, *11*, 13.

de Miguel Diez J., Carrasco Garrido P., García Carballo M., Gil de Miguel A., Rejas Gutierrez J., Bellón Cano J.M., Hernández Barrera V., & Jimenez García R. (2008). Determinants and predictors of the cost of COPD in primary care: a Spanish perspective. *Int J Chron Obstruct Pulmon Dis*, *3*(4), 701–12.

Dewan N.A., Rice K.L., Caldwell M., & Hilleman D.E. (2011). Economic evaluation of a disease management program for chronic obstructive pulmonary disease. *COPD*, *8*(3), 153–9.

Diaz P.T., Clanton T.L., & Pacht E.R. (1992). Emphysema-like pulmonary disease associated with human immunodeficiency virus infection. *Ann Intern Med*, *116*(2), 124–128.

Diaz P.T., King M.A., Pacht E.R., Wewers M.D., Gadek J.E., Nagaraja H.N., Drake J., & Clanton T.L. (2000). Increased susceptibility to pulmonary emphysema among HIV-seropositive smokers. *Ann Intern Med*, *132*(5), 369–372.

Diaz-Guzman E., & Mannino D.M. (2014). Epidemiology and prevalence of chronic obstructive pulmonary disease. *Clin Chest Med*, *35*(1), 7–16.

Diaz-Guzman E., Aryal S., & Mannino D.M. (2012). Occupational chronic obstructive pulmonary disease: an update. *Clin Chest Med*, *33*(4), 625–36.

DiBonaventura M.D., Paulose-Ram R., Su J., McDonald M., Zou K.H., Wagner J.S., & Shah H. (2012). The burden of chronic obstructive pulmonary disease among employed adults. *Int J Chron Obstruct Pulmon Dis*, *7*, 211–9.

Doney B., Hnizdo E., Syamlal G., Kullman G., Burchfiel C., Martin C.J., & Mujuru P. (2014). Prevalence of Chronic Obstructive Pulmonary Disease Among US Working Adults Aged 40 to 70 Years: National Health Interview Survey Data 2004 to 2011. *J Occup Environ Med*, *56*(10), 1088–93.

Donner C.F., Virchow J.C., & Lusuardi M. (2011). Pharmacoeconomics in COPD and in appropriateness of diagnostics, management and treatment. *Respir Med*, *105*(6), 828–37.

Downs S.H., Schindler C., Liu L.J., Keidel D., Bayer-Oglesby L., Brutsche M.H., Gerbase M.W., Keller R., Kunzli N., Leuenberger P., Probst-Hensch N.M., Tschopp J.M., Zellweger J.P., Rochat T., Schwartz J., Ackermann-Liebrich U.; & SAPALDIA Team. (2007). Reduced exposure to PM10 and attenuated age-related decline in lung function. *N Engl J Med*, *357*, 2338–2347.

Drummond M.B., Kirk G.D., Astemborski J., Marshall M.M., Mehta S.H., McDyer J.F., Brown R.H., Wise R.A., & Merlo C.A. (2012). Association between obstructive lung disease and markers of HIV infection in a high-risk cohort. *Thorax*, *67*(4), 309–314.

Eagan T.M., Hetland J., & Aaro L.E. (2006). Decline in respiratory symptoms in service workers five months after a public smoking ban. *Tob Control*, *15*, 242–246.

Eduard W., Pearce N., & Douwes J. (2009). Chronic bronchitis, COPD, and lung function in farmers: the role of biological agents. *Chest*, *136*(3), 716–25

Ehrlich R.I., Adams S., Baatjies R., & Jeebhay M.F. (2011). Chronic airflow obstruction and respiratory symptoms following tuberculosis: a review of South African studies. *Int J Tuberc Lung Dis*, *15*(7), 886–91.

Eisner M.D., Anthonisen N., Coultas D., Kuenzli N., Perez-Padilla R., Postma D., Romieu I., Silverman E.K., Balmes J.R.;& Committee on Nonsmoking COPD, Environmental and Occupational Health Assembly. (2010). An official American Thoracic Society public policy statement: Novel risk factors and the global burden of chronic obstructive pulmonary disease. *Am J Respir Crit Care Med*, *182*(5), 693–718.

Eisner M.D. (2010). Secondhand smoke at work. *Curr Opin Allergy Clin Immunol*, *10*(2), 121–6.

Fairbairn A.S., & Reid D.D. (1958). Air pollution and other local factors in respiratory disease. *Br J Prev Soc Med*, *12*, 94–103.

Fan V.S., Gaziano J.M., Lew R., Bourbeau J., Adams S.G., Leatherman S., Thwin S.S., Huang G.D., Robbins R., Sriram P.S., Sharafkhaneh A., Mador M.J., Sarosi G., Panos R.J., Rastogi P., Wagner T.H., Mazzuca S.A., Shannon C., Colling C., Liang M.H., Stoller J.K., Fiore L., & Niewoehner D.E. (2012). A comprehensive care management program to prevent chronic obstructive pulmonary disease hospitalizations: a randomized, controlled trial. *Ann Intern Med*, *156*(10), 673–83.

Ford E.S., Croft J.B., Mannino D.M., Wheaton A.G., Zhang X., & Giles W.H. (2013). COPD surveillance--United States, 1999–2011. *Chest*, *144*(1), 284–305

Ford E.S., Murphy L.B., Khavjou O., Giles W.H., Holt J.B., & Croft J.B. (2014). Total and state-specific medical and absenteeism costs of chronic obstructive pulmonary disease among adults aged ≥18 years in the United States for 2010 and projections through 2020. *Chest*, *147*(1), 31–45.

Forey B.A., Thornton A.J., & Lee P.N. (2011). Systematic review with meta-analysis of the epidemiological evidence relating smoking to COPD, chronic bronchitis and emphysema. *BMC Pulm Med*, *11*, 36.

Foster T.S., Miller J.D., Marton J.P., Caloyeras J.P., Russell M.W., & Menzin J. (2006). Assessment of the economic burden of COPD in the U.S.: a review and synthesis of the literature. *COPD*, *3*(4), 211–8.

Gan W.Q., Man S.F., Postma D.S., Camp P., & Sin D.D. (2006). Female smokers beyond the perimenopausal period are at increased risk of chronic obstructive pulmonary disease: a systematic review and meta-analysis. *Respir Res*, *7*, 52.

Gauderman W.J., Avol E., Gilliland F., Vora H., Thomas D., Berhane K., McConnell R., Kuenzli N., Lurmann F., Rappaport E., Margolis H., Bates D., & Peters J. (2004). The effect of air pollution on lung development from 10 to 18 years of age. *N Engl J Med*, *351*, 1057–1067.

Gauderman W.J., Vora H., McConnell R., Berhane K., Gilliland F., Thomas D., Lurmann F., Avol E., Kunzli N., Jerrett M., & Peters J. (2007). Effect of exposure to traffic on lung development from 10 to 18 years of age: a cohort study. *Lancet*, *369*, 571–577.

Gillum L.A., Gouveia C., Dorsey E.R., Pletcher M., Mathers C.D., McCulloch C.E., & Johnston S.C. (2011). NIH disease funding levels and burden of disease. *PLoS One*, *6*(2), e16837.

Gingo M.R., Morris A., & Crothers K. (2013). Human immunodeficiency virus-associated obstructive lung diseases. *Clin Chest Med*, *34*(2), 273–82.

Golmohammadi K., Jacobs P., & Sin D.D. (2004). Economic evaluation of a community-based pulmonary rehabilitation program for chronic obstructive pulmonary disease. *Lung*, *182*(3), 187–96.

Goodman P., Agnew M., McCaffrey M., Paul G., & Clancy L. (2007). Effects of the Irish smoking ban on respiratory health of bar workers and air quality in Dublin pubs. *Am J Respir Crit Care Med*, *175*, 840–845.

Grigg J. (2009). Particulate matter exposure in children: relevance to chronic obstructive pulmonary disease. *Proc Am Thorac Soc*, *6*(7), 564–9.

Hnizdo E., Singh T., & Churchyard G. (2000). Chronic pulmonary function impairment caused by initial and recurrent pulmonary tuberculosis following treatment. *Thorax*, *55*, 32–38.

Hnizdo E., Sullivan P.A., Bang K.M., & Wagner G. (2002). Association between chronic obstructive pulmonary disease and employment by industry and occupation in the US population: a study of data from the Third National Health and Nutrition Examination Survey. *Am J Epidemiol*, *156*, 738–46.

Holland W.W., & Reid D.D. (1965). The urban factor in chronic bronchitis. *Lancet*; *285*, 445–48.

http://www.cdc.gov/copd/data.htm (Accessed November, 2014).

http://www.lung.org/lung-disease/copd/resources/facts-figures/COPD-Fact-Sheet.html (Accessed November, 2014).

http://www.tobaccoatlas.org/products/female_tobacco_use/prevalence/ (Accessed November, 2014).

http://www.tobaccoatlas.org/products/male_tobacco_use/prevalence/ (Accessed November, 2014).

Jansson S.A., Backman H., Stenling A., Lindberg A., Rönmark E., & Lundbäck B. (2013). Health economic costs of COPD in Sweden by disease severity--has it changed during a ten years period? *Respir Med*, *107*(12), 1931–8.

Jensen M.B., Fenger-Grøn M., Fonager K., Omland Ø., Vinding A.L., & Hansen J.G. (2013). Chronic obstructive pulmonary disease involves substantial health-care service and social benefit costs. *Dan Med J*, *60*(1), A4557.

Jha P., Ramasundarahettige C., Landsman V., Rostron B., Thun M., Anderson R.N., McAfee T., & Peto R. (2013). 21st-century hazards of smoking and benefits of cessation in the United States. *N Engl J Med*, *368*(4), 341–50

Jordan T.S., Spencer E.M., & Davies P. (2010). Tuberculosis, bronchiectasis and chronic airflow obstruction. *Respirology*, *15*(4), 623–8.

Kaprio J. (2009). Genetic epidemiology of smoking behavior and nicotine dependence. *COPD*, *6*(4), 304–6.

Ko F.W., & Hui D.S. (2012). Air pollution and chronic obstructive pulmonary disease. *Respirology*, *17*(3), 395–401.

Ko F.W., Tam W., Wong T.W., Chan D.P., Tung A.H., Lai C.K., & Hui D.S. (2007). Temporal relationship between air pollutants and hospital admissions for chronic obstructive pulmonary disease in Hong Kong. *Thorax*, *62*, 780–5.

Kruis A.L., Smidt N., Assendelft W.J., Gussekloo J., Boland M.R., Rutten-van Mölken M., & Chavannes N.H. (2013). Integrated disease management interventions for patients with chronic obstructive pulmonary disease. *Cochrane Database Syst Rev*, *10*, CD009437.

Kurmi O.P., Semple S., Simkhada P., Smith W.C., & Ayres J.G. (2010). COPD and chronic bronchitis risk of indoor air pollution from solid fuel: a systematic review and meta-analysis. *Thorax*, *65*(3), 221–8.

Lamprecht B., Schirnhofer L., Kaiser B., Studnicka M., & Buist A.S. (2007). Farming and the prevalence of non-reversible airways obstruction: results from a population-based study. *Am J Ind Med*, *50*, 421–26.

Lareau S.C., & Yawn B.P. (2010). Improving adherence with inhaler therapy in COPD. *Int J Chron Obstruct Pulmon Dis*, *5*, 401–6.

Lee M.H., & Hancox R.J. (2011). Effects of smoking cannabis on lung function. *Expert Rev Respir Med*, *5*(4), 537–546.

Mannino D.M., Gagnon R.C., Petty T.L., & Lydick E. (2000). Obstructive lung disease and low lung function in adults in the United States: data from the National Health and Nutrition Examination Survey, 1984–1994. *Arch Intern Med, 160*, 1683–1689.

Mannino D.M. (2002). COPD: epidemiology, prevalence, morbidity and mortality, and disease heterogeneity. *Chest, 121*(5 Suppl), 121S-126S.

Mannino D.M., & Buist A.S. (2007). Global burden of COPD: risk factors, prevalence, and future trends. *Lancet, 370*(9589), 765–73.

Manuel J. (1999). Double exposure. *Environ Health Perspect*, 107(4), A197–201.

Menezes A.M., Perez-Padilla R., Jardim J.R., Muiño A., Lopez M.V., Valdivia G., Montes de Oca M., Talamo C., Hallal P.C., Victora C.G.; & PLATINO Team. (2005). Chronic obstructive pulmonary disease in five Latin American cities (the PLATINO study): a prevalence study. *Lancet, 366*, 1875–81.

Menzies D., Nair A., Williamson P.A., Schembri S., Al-Khairalla M.Z.H., Barnes M., Fardon T.C., McFarlane L., Magee G.J., & Lipworth B.J. (2006). Respiratory symptoms, pulmonary function, and markers of inflammation among bar workers before and after a legislative ban on smoking in public places. *JAMA, 296*, 1742–1748.

Menzin J., Boulanger L., Marton J., Guadagno L., Dastani H., Dirani R., Phillips A., & Shah H. (2008). The economic burden of chronic obstructive pulmonary disease (COPD) in a U.S. Medicare population. *Respir Med, 102*(9), 1248–56.

Miniño A.M., Xu J.Q., & Kochanek K.D. (2010). Deaths: Preliminary data for 2008. *National Vital Statistics Reports*; vol 59 no 2. Hyattsville, MD: National Center for Health Statistics.

Munson, J.C., Mahler D.A., Schwartz L., & Woloshin S. (2013). Over-diagnosis and under-diagnosis of Chronic Obstructive Pulmonary Disease in the US Population. *Am J Respir Crit Care Med, 187*, A2832

Murphy D.E., Chaudhry Z., Almoosa K.F., & Panos R.J. (2011). High prevalence of chronic obstructive pulmonary disease among veterans in the urban midwest. *Mil Med, 176*(5), 552–60.

Murphy S.L., Xu J., & Kochanek, K.D., (2013). Deaths: Final Data for 2010. *Natl Vital Stat Rep, 61*(4), 1–117.

Nicholson C., Bowler S., Jackson C., Schollay D., Tweeddale M., & O'Rourke P. (2001). Cost comparison of hospital- and home-based treatment models for acute chronic obstructive pulmonary disease. *Aust Health Rev, 24*(4), 181–187.

Nielsen R., Johannessen A., Omenaas E.R., Bakke P.S., Askildsen J.E., & Gulsvik A. (2011). Excessive costs of COPD in ever-smokers. A longitudinal community study. *Respir Med, 105*(3), 485–93.

Ohar J., Fromer L., & Donohue J.F. (2011). Reconsidering sex-based stereotypes of COPD. *Prim Care Respir J, 20*(4), 370–378.

Omland O., Würtz E.T., Aasen T.B., Blanc P., Brisman J.B., Miller M.R., Pedersen O.F., Schlünssen V., Sigsgaard T., Ulrik C.S., & Viskum S. (2014). Occupational chronic obstructive pulmonary disease: a systematic literature review. *Scand J Work Environ Health, 40*(1), 19–35.

Ornek T., Tor M., Altın R., Atalay F., Geredeli E., Soylu O., & Erboy F. (2012). Clinical factors affecting the direct cost of patients hospitalized with acute exacerbation of chronic obstructive pulmonary disease. *Int J Med Sci, 9*(4), 285–290.

Pasquale M.K., Sun S.X., Song F., Hartnett H.J., & Stemkowski S.A. (2012). Impact of exacerbations on health care cost and resource utilization in chronic obstructive pulmonary disease patients with chronic bronchitis from a predominantly Medicare population. *Int J Chron Obstruct Pulmon Dis, 7*, 757–64.

Patel J.G., Nagar S.P., & Dalal A.A. (2014). Indirect costs in chronic obstructive pulmonary disease: a review of the economic burden on employers and individuals in the United States. *Int J Chron Obstruct Pulmon Dis, 19*(9), 289–300.

Perera P.N., Armstrong E.P., Sherrill D.L., & Skrepnek G.H. (2012). Acute exacerbations of COPD in the United States: inpatient burden and predictors of costs and mortality. *COPD, 9*(2), 131–41.

Petty T.L. (2000). Scope of the COPD problem in North America. *Chest,* 117, 326S-331S.
Postma D.S., Bush A., & van den Berge M. (2014). Risk factors and early origins of chronic obstructive pulmonary disease. *Lancet*, Pii, S0140–6736(14), 60446–3.
Puig-Junoy J., Casas A., Font-Planells J., Escarrabill J., Hernández C, Alonso J., Farrero E., Vilagut G., & Roca J. (2007). The impact of home hospitalization on healthcare costs of exacerbations in COPD patients. *Eur J Health Econ*, *8*(4), 325–32.
Punekar Y.S., Shukla A., & Müllerova H. (2014). COPD management costs according to the frequency of COPD exacerbations in UK primary care. *Int J Chron Obstruct Pulmon Dis*, *9*, 65–73.
Raherison C., & Girodet P.O. (2009). Epidemiology of COPD. *Eur Respir Rev*, 18(114), 213–21.
Raynaud C., Roche N., & Chouaid C. (2014). Interactions between HIV infection and chronic obstructive pulmonary disease: Clinical and epidemiological aspects. *Int J Chron Obstruct Pulmon Dis*, *9*, 1145–1154.
Reardon J.Z. (2007). Environmental tobacco smoke: respiratory and other health effects. *Clin Chest Med*, *28*(3), 559–73.
Regalado J., Perez-Padilla R., Sansores R., Paramo Ramirez J.I., Brauer M., Pare P., & Vedal S. (2006). The effect of biomass burning on respiratory symptoms and lung function in rural Mexican women. *Am J Respir Crit Care Med*, *174*, 901–905.
Regional COPD Working Group. (2003). COPD prevalence in 12 Asia-Pacific countries and regions: projections based on the COPD prevalence estimation model. *Respirology, 8*, 192–8.
Rinne S.T., Rodas E.J., Bender B.S., Rinne M.L., Simpson J.M., Galer-Unti R., & Glickman L.T. (2006). Relationship of pulmonary function among women and children to indoor air pollution from biomass use in rural Ecuador. *Respir Med*, *100*, 1208–1215.
Rojas-Martinez R., Perez-Padilla R., Olaiz-Fernandez G., Mendoza-Alvarado L., Moreno-Macias H., Fortoul T., McDonnell W., Loomis D., & Romieu I. (2007). Lung function growth in children with long-term exposure to air pollutants in Mexico City. *Am J Respir Crit Care Med*, *176*, 377–384.
Rycroft C.E., Heyes A., Lanza L., & Becker K. (2012). Epidemiology of chronic obstructive pulmonary disease: a literature review. *Int J Chron Obstruct Pulmon Dis*, *7*, 457–94.
Salvi S. (2014). Tobacco smoking and environmental risk factors for chronic obstructive pulmonary disease. *Clin Chest Med*, *35*(1), 17–27.
Salvi S.S., & Barnes P.J. (2009). Chronic obstructive pulmonary disease in non-smokers. *Lancet*, *374*(9691), 733–43.
Santo Tomas L.H. (2011). Emphysema and chronic obstructive pulmonary disease in coal miners. *Curr Opin Pulm Med*, *17*(2), 123–5.
Schikowski T., Sugiri D., Ranft U., Gehring U., Heinrich J., Wichmann H.E., & Kramer U. (2005). Long-term air pollution exposure and living close to busy roads are associated with COPD in women. *Respir Res*, *6*, 152.
Simoni-Wastila L., Wei Y.J., Qian J., Zuckerman I.H., Stuart B., Shaffer T., Dalal A.A., & Bryant-Comstock L. (2012). Association of chronic obstructive pulmonary disease maintenance medication adherence with all-cause hospitalization and spending in a Medicare population. *Am J Geriatr Pharmacother*, *10*(3), 201–10.
Sood A. (2012). Indoor fuel exposure and the lung in both developing and developed countries: an update. *Clin Chest Med*, *33*(4), 649–65.
Soriano J.B., & Rodríguez-Roisin R. (2011). Chronic obstructive pulmonary disease overview epidemiology, risk factors, and clinical presentation. *Proc Am Thorac Soc*, *8*(4), 363–367.
Soriano J.B., & Lamprecht B. (2012). Chronic obstructive pulmonary disease: a worldwide problem. *Med Clin North Am*, *96*(4), 671–80.
Steinel J.A., & Madigan E.A. (2003). Resource utilization in home health chronic obstructive pulmonary disease management. *Outcomes Manag*, *7*(1), 23–7.
Stocks J., & Sonnappa S. (2013). Early life influences on the development of chronic obstructive pulmonary disease. *Ther Adv Respir Dis*, *7*(3), 161–73.

Stone I.S., Barnes N.C., & Petersen S.E. (2012). Chronic obstructive pulmonary disease: a modifiable risk factor for cardiovascular disease? *Heart, 98*(14), 1055–1062.

Stuart B.C., Simoni-Wastila L., Zuckerman I.H., Davidoff A., Shaffer T., Yang H.W., Qian J., Dalal A.A., Mapel D.W., & Bryant-Comstock L. (2010). Impact of maintenance therapy on hospitalization and expenditures for Medicare beneficiaries with chronic obstructive pulmonary disease. *Am J Geriatr Pharmacother, 8*(5), 441–53.

Stuart B.C., Simoni-Wastila L., Zuckerman I.H., Davidoff A., Shaffer T., Yang H.W., Qian J., Dalal A.A., Mapel D.W., & Bryant-Comstock L. (2010). Impact of maintenance therapy on hospitalization and expenditures for Medicare beneficiaries with chronic obstructive pulmonary disease. *Am J Geriatr Pharmacother, 8*(5), 441–53.

Szczyrek M., Krawczyk P., Milanowski J., Jastrzębska I., Zwolak A., & Daniluk J. (2011). Chronic obstructive pulmonary disease in farmers and agricultural workers - an overview. *Ann Agric Environ Med, 18*(2), 310–3.

Tam A., & Sin D.D. (2013). Why are women more vulnerable to chronic obstructive pulmonary disease? *Expert Rev Respir Med, 7*(3), 197–9.

Tan W.C. (2011). Trends in chronic obstructive pulmonary disease in the Asia-Pacific regions. *Curr Opin Pulm Med*, 17(2), 56–61.

Toy E.L., Gallagher K.F., Stanley E.L., Swensen A.R., & Duh M.S. (2010). The economic impact of exacerbations of chronic obstructive pulmonary disease and exacerbation definition: a review. *COPD, 7*(3), 214–228.

Toy E.L., Beaulieu N.U., McHale J.M., Welland T.R., Plauschinat C.A., Swensen A., & Duh MS. (2011). Treatment of COPD: relationships between daily dosing frequency, adherence, resource use, and costs. *Respir Med, 105*(3), 435–41.

U.S. Department of Health and Human Services. (2014). *The Health Consequences of Smoking—50 Years of Progress: A Report of the Surgeon General.*

U.S. Department of Health and Human Services. (2006). *The health consequences of involuntary exposure to tobacco smoke: a report of the surgeon general.U.S. Department of Health and Human Services,Centers for Disease Control and Prevention, National Center for Chronic Disease Prevention and Health Promotion, Office on Smoking and Health*; Available at: http://www.surgeongeneral.gov/library/secondhandsmoke/factsheets. Accessed November, 2014.

van Zyl Smit R.N., Pai M., Yew W.W., Leung C.C., Zumla A., Bateman E.D., & Dheda K. (2010). Global lung health: the colliding epidemics of tuberculosis, tobacco smoking, HIV and COPD. *Eur Respir J, 35*(1), 27–33.

van Zyl-Smit R.N., Brunet L., Pai M., & Yew W.W. (2010). The convergence of the global smoking, COPD, tuberculosis, HIV, and respiratory infection epidemics. *Infect Dis Clin North Am*, 24(3), 693–703.

Weinmann S., Vollmer W.M., Breen V., Heumann M., Hnizdo E., Villnave J., Doney B., Graziani M., McBurnie M.A., & Buist A.S. (2008). COPD and occupational exposures: a case-control study. *J Occup Environ Med, 50*, 561–69.

Welte T., Vogelmeier C., & Papi A. (2015). COPD: early diagnosis and treatment to slow disease progression. *Int J Clin Pract. 69*(3), 336–349.

Yin P., Jiang C.Q., Cheng K.K. Lam T.H., Lam K.H., Miller M.R., Zhang W.S., Thomas G.N., & Adab P. (2007). Passive smoking exposure and risk of COPD among adults in China: the Guangzhou Biobank Cohort Study. *Lancet, 370*, 751–7.

Zeng G., Sun B., & Zhong N. (2012). Non-smoking-related chronic obstructive pulmonary disease: a neglected entity? *Respirology, 17*(6), 908–12.

William L. Eschenbacher, MD

# 3 COPD Recognition and Diagnosis: Approach to the Patient with Respiratory Symptoms

Key Points

1. Patients who present with respiratory symptoms such as cough, sputum production, wheezing, or breathlessness may have COPD, non-respiratory illnesses, or respiratory conditions other than COPD.
2. The initial evaluation of a patient who presents with respiratory symptoms includes a history, physical examination, spirometry testing, and a chest radiograph.
3. The diagnosis of COPD depends on the findings of appropriate symptoms in the right clinical context with airflow obstruction noted on spirometry testing.

## 3.1 Introduction

Patients who are seen in health care settings often present with respiratory symptoms including shortness of breath, cough, sputum production and chest discomfort or chest tightness. Although the focus of this primer is COPD, not every individual who has these respiratory symptoms and a history of smoking tobacco products has COPD. It is the task for the health care provider to be able to interview individuals who present with these symptoms and perform basic diagnostic tests to determine whether the cause for these symptoms is COPD or another respiratory or non-respiratory condition. This chapter will focus on the approach to a patient who presents with these respiratory symptoms. By obtaining the appropriate history and test results, the provider can determine the cause for the symptoms and, if it is COPD, initiate further management and treatment.

## 3.2 Patient Presenting with Respiratory Symptoms

An individual may present in a clinical setting with one of the following respiratory symptoms:

- Dyspnea or shortness of breath with activity or at rest
- Cough
- Sputum Production
- Chest Discomfort or Chest Tightness
- Wheezes or Rhonchi

**Table 3.1:** Examples of Conditions other than COPD that may present with Respiratory Symptoms

| **Condition** | |
|---|---|
| **Non-respiratory** | |
| Cardiac Disease | Congestive Heart Failure<br>Valvular Heart Disease<br>Restrictive Cardiomyopathy |
| Systemic Disease | Collagen Vascular Disease |
| Neuromuscular Disease | Myasthenia Gravis<br>Amyotrophic Lateral Sclerosis<br>Multiple Sclerosis |
| Infectious Disease | Epstein Barr Virus infection leading to Chronic Fatigue Syndrome |
| Hematologic Disease | Myelodysplastic Syndrome<br>Lymphoma, leukemia or anemia |
| Deconditioning | |
| Weight Gain/Obesity | |
| Adverse Reaction to Medication | |
| **Respiratory Conditions other than COPD** | |
| Airway Diseases | Asthma<br>Bronchiectasis<br>Bronchiolitis Obliterans |
| Interstitial Diseases | Idiopathic Pulmonary Fibrosis<br>Non-specific Interstitial Pneumonitis<br>Sarcoidosis<br>Pneumoconiosis |
| Other Respiratory Conditions | Pulmonary Emboli<br>Pulmonary Hypertension |

These symptoms are not specific to COPD or even to other respiratory illnesses and can be seen in other conditions that will require further investigation. Table 3.1 includes other conditions or causes of these respiratory symptoms other than COPD.

### 3.2.1 Further Discussion of Dyspnea/Shortness of Breath

Of the respiratory symptoms that individuals with COPD may have, dyspnea or breathlessness is a very common presenting symptom. Fifty percent of patients seen in acute care clinical settings present with the symptom of dyspnea (Parshall, 2012). The various descriptors of dyspnea can include: shortness of breath, air hunger, labored breathing, can't get a deep breath, chest tightness, or heavy breathing. The American Thoracic Society's definition of dyspnea is as follows: ***Dyspnea is a subjective experience of breathing discomfort that consists of qualitatively distinct sensations that vary in intensity*** (Parshall, 2012). Like other symptoms that an individual may experience (pain, hunger, thirst, etc.), dyspnea is actually comprised of two separate but interacting elements: sensation and perception.

1. Sensation: the neural activation resulting from stimulation of peripheral neural receptors that varies based on the load, intensity and duration of the stimulation. Also, there are differences among the responses of different peripheral neural receptors.
2. Perception: the reaction of the individual to the neural activation that includes processing of that neural information along with other input including psychological, cultural, and behavioral factors.

In other words, dyspnea, like pain, is comprised of sensory and affective components. The sensory elements are the peripheral neural receptors as shown in Table 3.2.

In normal physiological states (e.g., exercise) and in disease states, stimulation of these peripheral receptors results in neural activation that is transmitted from the thorax to the central nervous system through pathways such as the vagus nerve and spinal cord afferents.

The neural traffic is then received in nuclei in the pons of the brainstem such as the nucleus of the tractus solitarius and in the medulla oblongata. From these locations, there are neural connections to the cortical sensory centers where this neural input is processed in the cortex along with other input depending on behavioral and cultural influences with the resulting sensation being noted as dyspnea or breathlessness. The latter processing is the affective component of the sensation of dyspnea.

Although an individual with disease may note breathlessness as a symptom of hypoxemia and hypercarbia, the input from chemoreceptors is only one signal that can cause the sense of dyspnea. In other scenarios, it is the input from other peripheral receptors that is noted as shortness of breath. As a result, for those individuals who do not exhibit hypoxemia but still note dyspnea, addition of supplemental oxygen will not relieve their dyspnea unless there is some placebo effect that is part of the behavioral input for the perception of dyspnea.

Dyspnea can be scored by different scales noted in Table 3.3. Dyspnea can be an alarming and distressing symptom for many individuals; it is influenced by both the sensory input from peripheral neural receptors; and it can be the result of disease

**Table 3.2:** Sensory: Pulmonary Afferent Neural Receptors and other Afferent Neural Input

| **Sensory: Pulmonary Afferent Neural Receptors and other Afferent Neural Input** | |
|---|---|
| Airway Irritant Receptors | |
| Within Lung Parenchyma/Interstitium | |
| | Slowly Adapting Stretch Receptors |
| | Rapidly Adapting Stretch Receptors |
| | C-Fibers (bronchial and pulmonary) |
| Respiratory Muscles/Chest Wall | |
| | Muscle spindles |
| | Golgi tendon organs |
| Carotid Bodies, aortic bodies, central medullary chemoreceptors | |
| Vascular receptors | |
| | Right Atrial and Left Atrial mechanoreceptors |
| | Pulmonary Artery baroreceptors |
| | Right Ventricular strain receptors |

**Table 3.3:** Scales for scoring Dyspnea

| **Scales for Scoring Dyspnea** |
|---|
| Questionnaires |
| Borg Score: 6 to 20 |
| Visual Analog Scale (VAS): 100 mm |
| Oxygen Cost Diagram (OCD): 13 activities with increasing oxygen requirements |

states in the lungs (airways and interstitium), the respiratory muscles, the chest wall, or the central vasculature.

As dyspnea is often distressing and anxiety-provoking and can lead to overall limitation in activities, the use of anxiolytics for patients with COPD is often a useful adjunctive therapy. Respiratory depression is a potential complication of the medications used to relieve anxiety (such as benzodiazepines).

For patients with COPD, the greater the impairment as determined by clinical scores such as the BODE Index (BMI, airflow obstruction, dyspnea and exercise capac-

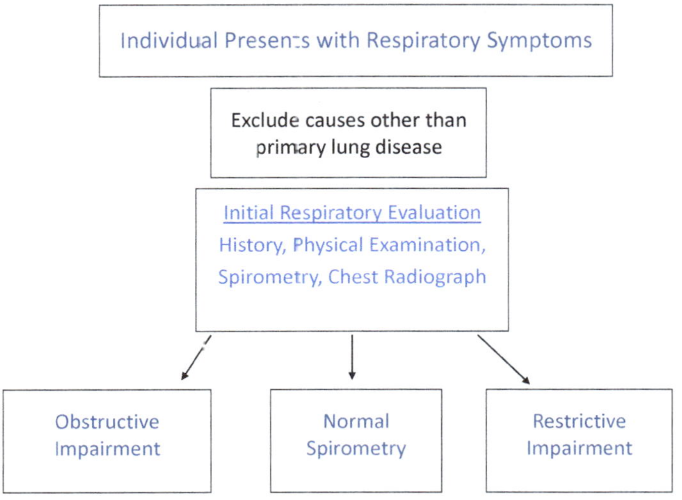


**Figure 3.1:** Approach to the Evaluation of an Individual who Presents with Respiratory Symptoms
This figure presents a basic algorithm for the evaluation of an individual who presents with respiratory symptoms such as shortness of breath, cough, wheezing, and / or phlegm production. Once non-respiratory causes are excluded, a respiratory evaluation including history, physical examination, imaging studies, and physiologic testing is initiated. Based upon spirometry, the respiratory physiology can be classified as normal, restrictive, or obstructive. (Recognition of a mixed restrictive and obstructive pattern requires additional lung function testing as discussed in Chapter 4, Pulmonary Function Testing.)

ity index), the increased use of more extreme affective descriptors such as frightening and awful for the symptom of dyspnea (Williams, 2010).

## 3.3 Initial Screening Evaluation for a Patient Presenting with Respiratory Symptoms including Dyspnea

The presence of a respiratory symptom such as dyspnea does not necessarily indicate the disease process is in the lungs but could be in the heart, the circulation, the respiratory muscles or the chest wall. When a patient presents with respiratory symptoms such as dyspnea, the approach to determining the cause for these symptoms is described in Figure 3.1.

### 3.3.1 Exclude Causes of Symptoms other than Lung Disease

Based upon the initial presentation, relevant medical history and initial evaluation, it may be determined that the cause for the symptoms of dyspnea, chest discomfort, etc. is due to disease processes such as cardiac disease (see Table 3.1). For example, if the cause for these symptoms is cardiac, then the following would be useful: medical history especially relating to cardiac disease, diagnostic testing including electrocardiogram, echocardiogram, and stress testing. Once non-respiratory diseases are excluded or are not considered to be the prime reason for the current symptoms, then evaluation of respiratory causes can be initiated.

### 3.3.2 Respiratory Causes for Symptoms

The respiratory causes for symptoms of dyspnea, cough, sputum production, and chest tightness or discomfort can be divided into primarily airways diseases (such as COPD, asthma, bronchiectasis) or interstitial/parenchymal diseases (interstitial lung disease, pneumoconiosis, alveolar filling disease). Other possible respiratory diseases such as pulmonary vascular disease, pleural disease, or neuromuscular disease involving the respiratory muscles may also be considered.

#### 3.3.2.1 Initial Evaluation of Respiratory Processes

The first steps for the evaluation of possible respiratory disease include history, physical examination, spirometry testing and chest radiograph.

**History**: Detailed respiratory, environmental and occupational history will need to be performed, including all personal habits such as smoking.

**Physical Examination**: focusing on the respiratory system for signs of respiratory insufficiency including use of accessory muscles, chest wall abnormalities, and auscultation for adventitial sounds.

**Spirometry Testing:** The technical details for the performance of spirometry testing will be discussed in greater detail in Chapter 4 of this primer. The interpretation of spirometry test results to help identify the type of respiratory condition will be discussed in greater detail in Chapter 4.

**Chest Radiograph:** A standard PA and lateral chest radiograph can be performed as part of the initial evaluation for any individual who presents with respiratory symptoms. It may not show any specific findings (not sensitive for some airways diseases or mild involvement with interstitial lung disease (ILD) or pulmonary vascular disease). However, there may be findings that will help identify certain patterns of disease presentations such as emphysematous changes in patients with COPD or interstitial markings in patients with ILD. Further description of the radiographic images for patients with COPD can be found in Chapter 5 of this COPD Primer.

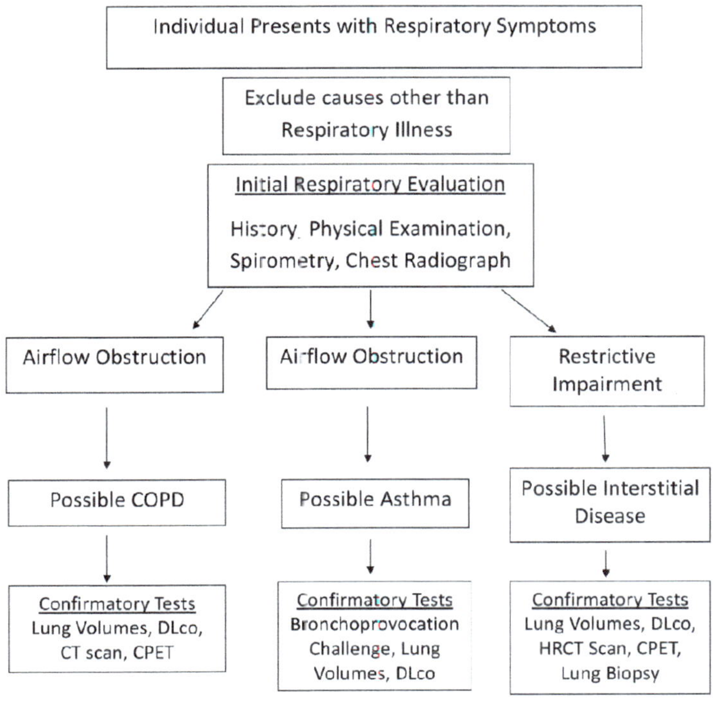


**Figure 3.2:** Further evaluation of patients who present with respiratory symptoms. This figure expands upon the basic approach presented in Figure 3.1 for the evaluation of a patient presenting with respiratory symptoms. Abbreviations: DLco: diffusing capacity measurement of the lung; CPET: Cardiopulmonary exercise test; HRCT: High-resolution CT scan of the chest.

### 3.3.2.2 Further evaluation of Causes of Respiratory Symptoms after Spirometry Test Results

If the initial evaluation suggests that the patient's respiratory symptoms are most likely due to a respiratory condition/disease, then the initial spirometry test results can provide information as to the type of impairment and in turn the type of disease that is being considered. Figure 3.2 is an algorithmic approach based on the results of the spirometry testing.

After excluding non-pulmonary causes of the symptoms and performing the initial screening tests including spirometry, the interpretation of spirometry can reveal normal results, airflow obstruction, or possible restriction (as mentioned, further explanation for the performance and interpretation of spirometry testing will be discussed in Chapter 4).

If airflow obstruction is found on the screening spirometry, possible conditions include COPD or asthma; other airways diseases could also present with airflow obstruction and asthma may present with a normal spirometry.

## 3.4 COPD

As the algorithm indicates, if the spirometry test results show airflow obstruction and the most likely disorder is COPD, then other clinical information and further diagnostic test results can help establish that COPD is present. Recent research indicates that COPD is not a single disease with a common pathogenesis but a syndrome composed of symptoms and findings in the presence of known risk factors.

### 3.4.1 Definition of COPD

As stated in the Key Points at the beginning of this chapter, the diagnosis of COPD depends on the findings of appropriate symptoms in the right clinical context with airflow obstruction noted on spirometry testing.

The following factors are considered when determining whether a patient has COPD:

- COPD is a syndrome related to the appropriate history, clinical signs and symptoms, physiologic and radiographic findings including the presence of airflow obstruction by spirometry (ATS, 2004).
- The airflow obstruction does not normalize or is not fully reversible.
- Various organizations define airflow obstruction differently. The American Thoracic Society/European Respiratory Society (ATS/ERS) definition uses the lower limit of normal (LLN) for the ratio of $FEV_1$/FVC based on reference equations, primarily NHANES III reference equations for spirometry (Hankinson, 1999) whereas the Global initiative for chronic Obstructive Lung Disease (GOLD, 2013) criterion uses a fixed cutoff of 70% for the ratio of $FEV_1$/FVC. In either case, airflow obstruction is considered to be a reduced $FEV_1$/FVC ratio (either below LLN or 70%). However, just like the syndrome of COPD is a continuum from no disease to severe disease, the presence of airflow obstruction itself can be a continuum from no airflow obstruction to very severe airflow obstruction. There are instances with borderline airflow obstruction with values of $FEV_1$/FVC above the threshold value (whether it is the LLN or 70%) that still may have some likelihood of abnormality of airways disease that would be consistent with a clinical diagnosis of COPD. For these borderline cases, the use of reduced mid-expiratory flow values would be helpful to identify instances where there would be intermediate probability or likelihood of airflow obstruction that would be consistent with COPD. The mid-expiratory flow ratio (MEFR) can be useful in these circumstances. When this ratio (actual $FEF_{25-75\%}$/actual FVC)/(predicted $FEF_{25-75\%}$/predicted FVC) is $< 0.70$, at a time when the $FEV_1$/FVC ratio is above the lower cutoff for airflow obstruction, there is an intermediate probability that there is airflow obstruction that would be consistent with COPD.
- Clinical manifestations of COPD and asthma can overlap.

- Historically, COPD was considered to be composed of two disorders: chronic bronchitis and emphysema. More recent information suggest that as a syndrome, COPD is a heterogeneous disorder that is actually composed of several phenotypes. (See further discussion of COPD phenotypes in Chapter 5 on Radiology).
- The history that is usually associated with the development of COPD is related to tobacco smoking with or without environmental or occupational risk factors. There may also be genetic predisposition or susceptibility for the development of COPD combined with exposure to personal or environmental/occupational risk factors.
- The deficiency of the enzyme α-1 antitrypsin is seen in about 1% of patients with COPD.

When COPD is considered a syndrome, there may be a different approach to establish the presence or diagnosis of COPD. As with other clinical conditions or disorders (e.g., pulmonary embolus, obstructive sleep apnea), there may be a degree of certainty or likelihood for the establishment of the diagnosis that in turn is dependent on physiological, historical, and clinical factors. Stated differently, we use Bayes Theorem for the determination of the likelihood for the presence of a disorder that is dependent upon the context or the pre-test probability of the disorder or condition.

The factors used for the diagnosis of COPD are:

1. Physiological:
   - Presence of airflow obstruction defined primarily by a reduced $FEV_1/FVC$ but may include other spirometric parameters as well (e.g., reduced mid-expiratory flow rates).
   - Other physiological factors as described below that may be confirmatory for the presence of COPD (e.g., air-trapping, hyperinflation, increased airways resistance, reduced diffusing capacity).
2. Historical:
   - Smoking history that is considered substantive (e.g., greater than 20–40 pk-yrs).
   - Previous clinical diagnosis of COPD by a health care provider.
   - Other environmental or occupational exposures that are associated with the development of airways diseases.
3. Clinical:
   - Appropriate respiratory symptoms: dyspnea, cough, sputum production, chest tightness, wheezing.
   - Other clinical diagnostic testing: CT scans or chest radiographs showing emphysematous changes.
   - Use of medications for airways diseases including inhaled bronchodilators, inhaled and/or oral corticosteroids.

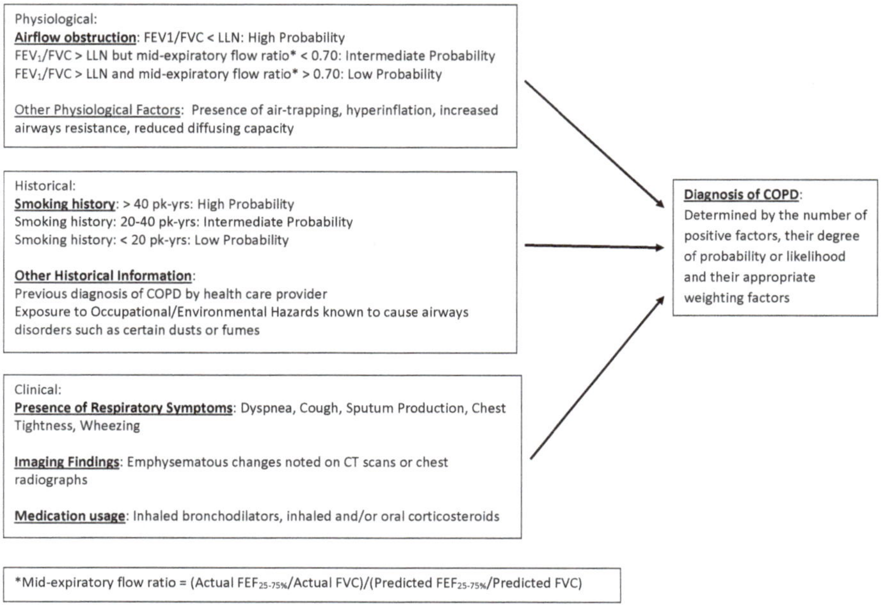


**Figure 3.3:** Factors that are Useful for the Diagnosis of COPD. COPD is best considered a syndrome because there is no single definitive test for its diagnosis. As with other syndromes, the presence of COPD is supported or refuted by multiple historical, physical examination, physiological, and imaging factors that are assessed in determining the presence of COPD. This figure presents an approach to evaluating and prioritizing the most common variables that are assessed in the diagnosis of COPD.

The weighting of these factors for the determination of the likelihood of COPD is not entirely clear but some of these factors are probably more significant than others (airflow obstruction, smoking history, previous diagnosis of COPD, presence of respiratory symptoms). See Figure 3.3 for illustration of this approach to the diagnosis of COPD.

### 3.4.2 Other Diagnostic Tests to Help Confirm the Presence of COPD

As mentioned above, there are other physiological test results that support the diagnosis of COPD. These confirmatory diagnostic tests include more complete pulmonary function testing such as measurement of lung volumes by body plethysmography or nitrogen washout testing. In some patients with COPD, the lung volume measurements show hyperinflation (a total lung capacity that is greater than the upper limits of normal for that parameter) or air-trapping (a residual volume values that is greater than the upper limits of normal for that parameter).

**Table 3.4:** Distinguishing Asthma and COPD

| Distinguishing Asthma and COPD | | |
|---|---|---|
| | **Asthma** | **COPD** |
| Predominant Inflammatory Cells | Eosinophils | Neutrophils |
| Cytokines | Th2: IL-4,5,9,13 | Th1: IFN-γ |
| Air Flow Limitation | Can normalize | Does not normalize |
| Age of onset | Younger | Older |
| Atopy/allergies | More likely | Less likely |
| Variability | Varies day-to-day | Less likely to vary |
| Medication | Inhaled corticosteroid initially | Inhaled corticosteroid after bronchodilators are used |

Diffusing capacity measurement could also be performed. Diffusing capacity values give an indication of the lungs ability to take up oxygen (using carbon monoxide as the surrogate gas for oxygen). Patients with COPD who have emphysematous changes may have a reduced diffusing capacity since there is a loss of pulmonary capillary surface area.

As will be discussed in Chapter 5, radiographic imaging beyond chest radiographs can be useful for patients with COPD. A CT scan of the chest is a more sensitive approach to identify the presence of emphysematous changes as well as any interstitial changes that may be present that are not obvious by a standard chest radiograph.

Cardiopulmonary exercise testing may also be useful for the determination of exercise performance for these patients and, if there is limitation to exercise performance, whether the cause of the limitation is due to COPD (Eschenbacher, 1990).

If the confirmatory tests indicate that the disease process is COPD, then the severity of the disease and recommendations for management can be found in other chapters in this COPD Primer (e.g. Chapter 14).

## 3.5 Asthma

If airflow obstruction is interpreted from the screening spirometry and the disease is thought to be asthma instead of COPD, then confirmatory testing can also be done. Although there may be clinical overlap between these two obstructive airways diseases, there can be differences that help distinguish one condition from the other as shown in Table 3.4.

For asthma, the inflammatory component found in the airways can be eosinophilic or neutrophilic but for COPD, it is usually neutrophilic. Other aspects of the inflammation found in asthma include t-helper type-2 lymphocytes with mediators that can include IL-4, 5, 9 and 13. For COPD, the inflammation may be more of t-helper type-1 lymphocytes with Interferon-γ (IFN-γ). The airflow obstruction with asthma can return to within normal limits at baseline or as a result of medication but this normalization usually does not occur with COPD. Asthma is clinically seen as developing in younger individuals who have an allergic component to their disease. There is usually more day-to-day variability in asthma as a result of exposure to different triggering agents such as environmental antigens. Finally, the management of these two airways diseases differs: inhaled corticosteroids are used as the primary controller medication for asthma and bronchodilators such as long-acting anticholinergic agents are more useful in COPD.

Confirmatory tests to identify asthma include standard lung function tests such as lung volume measurements and diffusing capacity and bronchoprovocation challenge test such as methacholine testing. The usefulness of such a bronchoprovocation challenge test for asthma was described in the NHLBI Guidelines for the Diagnosis and Management of Asthma EPR-3:

"Bronchoprovocation with methacholine, histamine, cold air or exercise challenge may be useful when asthma is suspected and spirometry is normal or near normal. A positive test is diagnostic for the presence of airway hyperresponsiveness, a feature of asthma but can be present in other conditions. A positive test is consistent with asthma; a negative test may be more helpful to rule out asthma" (NHLBI, 2007).

In patients with asthma, lung volume measurements may reveal hyperinflation and air-trapping but may also be within normal limits. For diffusing capacity measurements in asthma, the values can be normal or even elevated as compared to many patients with COPD where the diffusing capacity measurement is reduced (especially if emphysema is present).

## 3.6 Interstitial Lung Disease

If the screening spirometry for individuals who present with respiratory symptoms (including dyspnea and cough) reveals a possible restrictive impairment pattern instead of airflow obstruction and the chest radiograph shows interstitial markings, then the disease process could be an interstitial lung disease. Confirmatory testing to help establish the diagnosis of an interstitial lung disease includes further lung function testing with lung volume measurement and diffusing capacity. Lung volume values would be expected to confirm the presence of a restrictive lung defect that had been suggested by spirometry. Both total lung capacity and residual volume results might be below their respective lower limits of normal (LLN). Diffusing capacity measurement may also be reduced as the interstitial disease process has reduced the pulmonary capillary surface area and reduced the ability of the lungs to take up oxygen.

CT scans of the chest, especially high-resolution CT scans, are useful in the diagnosis of interstitial lung diseases by showing specific patterns that may be associated with certain ILD classifications (Webb, 2009).

Cardiopulmonary exercise testing may reveal pulmonary or ventilatory limitation as well as possible pulmonary vascular limitation. The latter may be seen if there is associated pulmonary hypertension as a result of reduced pulmonary vascular compliance due to the interstitial disease process involving the pulmonary vasculature.

Finally, in some instances, a lung biopsy may be needed. This histopathologic diagnosis would not only help establish the specific type of ILD but may also be useful for prognosis and for disease management.

## 3.7 Summary Points

1. Patients who present with respiratory symptoms require a standardized approach to determine the cause for their symptoms.
2. Not all patients who experience respiratory symptoms and have a significant smoking history have COPD.
3. Other conditions that could explain the presence of symptoms of dyspnea, cough, and chest discomfort include other respiratory diseases (airways diseases such as asthma and bronchiectasis; or restrictive lung diseases including interstitial lung diseases) and non-pulmonary processes such as heart failure.
4. History, physical examination, chest radiograph and spirometry are part of the initial screening evaluation needed to help determine the type of disease process but more advanced testing may be needed subsequently.

## References

ATS/ERS (2004) American Thoracic Society and European Respiratory Society: Standards for the diagnosis and management of patients with COPD. http://www.thoracic.org/clinical/copd-guidelines/resources/copddoc.pdf

Eschenbacher W.L., Mannina A. (1990) An algorithm for the interpretation of cardiopulmonary exercise tests. Chest 97:263–267.

Ferguson G.T., Enright P.L., Buist A.S., Higgins M.W. (2000) Office spirometry for lung health assessment in adults: A consensus statement from the National Lung Health Education Program. Chest, 117:1146–1161.

GOLD (2013) Global Strategy for the Diagnosis, Management, and Prevention of Chronic Obstructive Pulmonary Disease. Global Initiative for Chronic Obstructive Lung Disease. http://www.goldcopd.org/uploads/users/files/GOLD_Report_2013_Feb20.pdf

Hankinson J.L., Odencrantz J.R., Fedan K.B. (1999) Spirometric Reference Values from a Sample of the General U.S. Population. Am J Respir Crit Care Med 159:179–187.

National Heart, Lung, and Blood Institute (2007) National Asthma Education and Prevention Program. Expert Panel Report 3: Guidelines for the Diagnosis and Management of Asthma

Parshall M.B., Schwartzstein R.M., Adams L., Banzett R.B., Manning H.L. et al. (2012) An Official American Thoracic Society Statement: Update on the Mechanisms, Assessment, and Management of Dyspnea. Am J Respir Crit Care Med 185:435–452.

Webb W.R., Muller N.L., Naidich D.P. (2009) High-Resolution CT of the Lung. $4^{th}$ edition. Lippincott Williams & Wilkins, Philadelphia PA.

Williams M., Cafarella P., Olds T., Petkov J., Firth P. (2010) Affective descriptors of sensation of breathlessness are more highly associated with severity of impairment than physical descriptors in people with COPD. Chest 138:315–322.

William L. Eschenbacher, MD

# 4 Pulmonary Function Testing: Spirometry: Presence and Severity of Airflow Limitation/Obstruction

Key Points

1. Spirometry is used to detect airflow limitation which is a key component for the diagnosis of COPD.
2. Spirometry testing must be done correctly to obtain acceptable and repeatable results.
3. Airflow limitation is present when the ratio of the post-bronchodilator forced expiratory volume in one second divided by the forced vital capacity ($FEV_1/FVC$) is less than the lower limit of normal or < 0.70.

## 4.1 Introduction

COPD is characterized by airflow limitation that does not normalize after the use of a bronchodilator. Spirometry is the diagnostic test that is used to confirm the presence of airflow limitation. However, the clinical diagnosis of COPD requires more than the establishment of spirometry-determined airflow limitation. There should also be the presence of appropriate symptoms and known risk factors. As discussed in Chapter 3 on the recognition and diagnosis of COPD, this condition is more of a syndrome than a disease, with the diagnosis depending on the findings of appropriate symptoms in the right clinical context with airflow obstruction noted on spirometry testing. Once a screening questionnaire has identified an individual who may have COPD (by symptoms and history), spirometry is then performed. See Figure 4.1 for an example of a patient undergoing spirometry testing.

Spirometry is a test of respiratory function that measures the volume of air that an individual can inhale and exhale, usually in a forceful manner. After the individual fills his or her lungs to maximal capacity, he or she is asked to exhale forcefully while the exhaled volume is measured over time until the expiration is complete. When graphed, this volume–time relationship is known as a *spirogram*. The device used for the measurement is a spirometer. The important parameters determined by this test include:

- the total volume that is exhaled forcefully; the forced vital capacity (FVC);
- the volume of air that is exhaled in the first second of time; the forced expiratory volume in 1 second ($FEV_1$);
- the ratio between these two values: $FEV_1/FVC$.

Spirometry is useful in the evaluation of a patient who presents with respiratory symptoms (e.g., dyspnea, cough, sputum production, chest tightness, and wheezing).

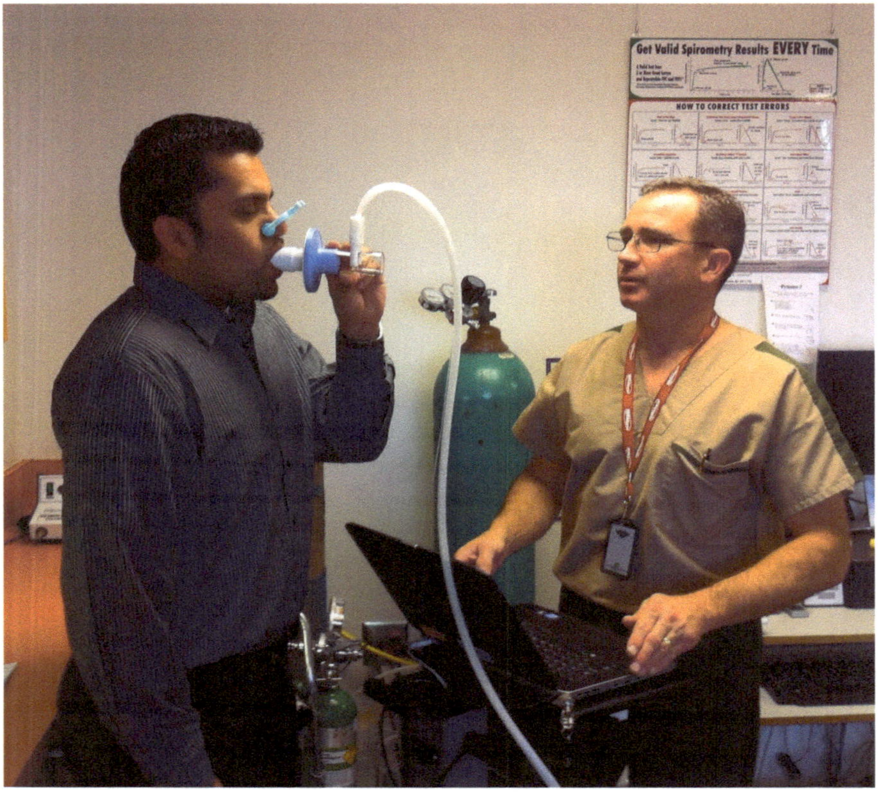


**Figure 4.1:** An individual performing spirometry with a technician coaching him.

Thus, the results of spirometry can be interpreted according to specific patterns of normality or abnormality, including airflow obstruction, possible lung restriction, or a mixed pattern of obstruction and possible restriction. If the spirometry test results are interpreted as abnormal, the individual may then be referred for more complete pulmonary function testing and further evaluation.

## 4.2 Reasons for Spirometry Testing

Reasons for performing spirometry in a clinical setting include:

- Evaluate dyspnea or shortness of breath in an individual
- Determine the presence and type and severity of pulmonary impairment or limitation
- Pre-operative assessment to determine the respiratory risk of a patient being considered for surgery

- Detect if there are changes in lung function over time that may indicate development or worsening of a pulmonary disease
- Determine the benefits or worsening effects of treatment
- Identification of a patient with chronic obstructive pulmonary disease or COPD

It is this last reason that is the focus of this chapter and this primer.

## 4.3 Spirometry Screening for COPD

Although it has been previously suggested that spirometry should be performed in any individual over 45 years of age who is a smoker for the identification of patients with COPD (Ferguson, 2000), the U.S. Preventive Services Task Force in March of 2008 released a recommendation that spirometry was not indicated as a screening test for COPD unless the individual presented with respiratory symptoms including chronic cough, increased sputum production, wheezing or dyspnea (USPSTF, 2008). More recently, the US Preventive Services Task Force is re-examining its position for spirometry screening for COPD asking the question whether screening asymptomatic adults age 40 years and older for COPD could improve health-related quality of life or reduce morbidity or mortality (USPSTF, 2014). However, there may also be selected populations such as U.S. Veterans who have a high rate of smoking and both an increased prevalence of COPD as well as undiagnosed COPD (Murphy, 2013). It is in this population that efforts are being focused to use a specifically designed questionnaire (Sogbetun, 2014) followed by spirometry to screen for airflow obstruction and COPD.

## 4.4 Limitations of Spirometry

Although spirometry can provide useful diagnostic and screening information, it has a few limitations. As a screening test, the results of spirometry can show normal results or restrictive or obstructive disease patterns, but the results cannot identify a specific disease. For example, a person's spirogram may show a low $FEV_1$, but a physician may not be able to determine whether the cause is from asthma, emphysema, or some other obstructive or restrictive lung disease. Additional information, including health and exposures histories, physical examination, chest imaging, and other pulmonary function testing such as lung volumes and diffusing capacity may be needed to make a diagnosis.

Spirometry often can detect obstructive diseases in its early stages, but for some of the restrictive diseases, it may not be sensitive enough to show abnormalities before extensive, and in some cases, irreversible damage has been done. For example, presence of interstitial markings may be found on chest radiographs or CT scans of the chest while spirometry results are still within normal limits.

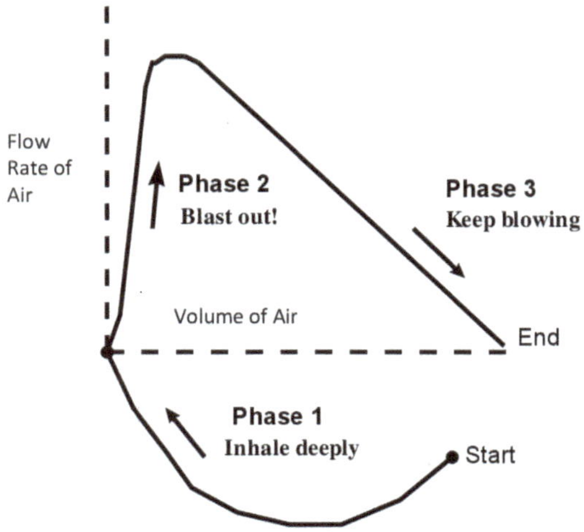


**#1 Phase 1: DEEP Inhalation**

**#2 Phase 2: BLAST the Air Out**

**#3 Phase 3: Keep blowing for > 6 seconds or until told to stop**

**Figure 4.2:** Three Phases of a Spirometry Maneuver: 1) Deep inhalation; 2) Blast the air out; 3) Keep blowing for at least 6 seconds.

## 4.5 Three Phases of a Spirometry Test

The actual performance of a spirometry test is made up of three separate but critical phases:

1. The subject must take in as deep of breath as possible filling his or her lungs to total lung capacity
2. Then without hesitation, the subject must blast out or exhale the air forcefully
3. The subject should then continue to exhale until told to stop or unable to continue

See Figure 4.2 for an image showing the three phases of a spirometry test.

As will be discussed later, the performance of spirometry must meet certain criteria of acceptability and repeatability that depend on the ability of the subject to perform successfully each of these three phases of the test.

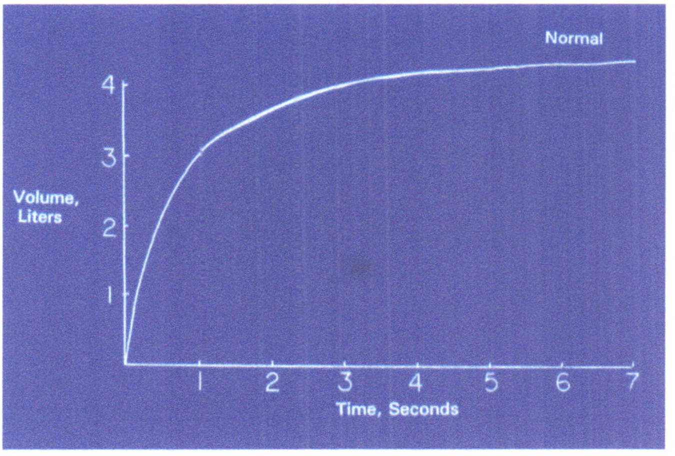


**Figure 4.3:** Volume-time graph. In this graph, the volume of air that is exhaled forcefully is plotted against the exhalation time.

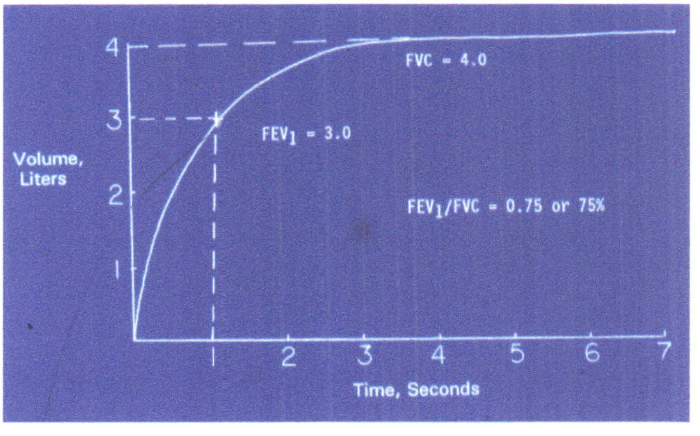


**Figure 4.4:** Volume-time graph showing measurements of $FEV_1$ and FVC and the ratio of $FEV_1$ to FVC ($FEV_1$/FVC)

## 4.6 Displaying the Results of Spirometry Testing

When a spirometry test is performed, the technician coaches the subject or patient to take in a deep inspiration to completely fill their lungs and then without hesitation to exhale forcefully into the spirometer. The resulting exhaled volume of air and the flow rate of the exhaled air are measured and plotted on two different graphs (see Figure 4.3 and 4.4 for one form of the display of spirometry testing: volume of exhaled air against the time of exhalation).

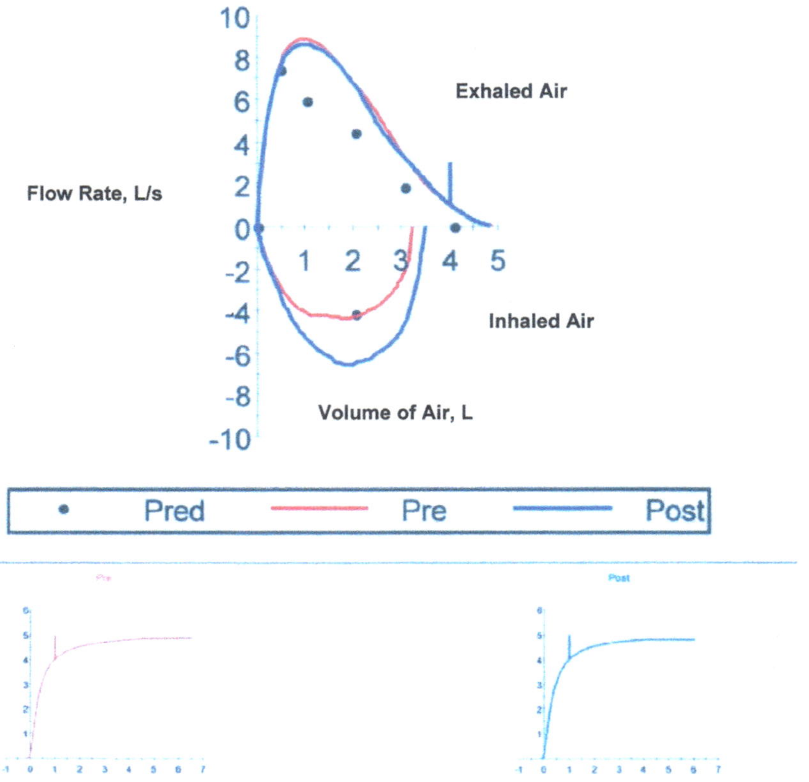


**Figure 4.5:** Flow-Volume Loop. In this type of graph, the flow rate of air in liters per second that is exhaled (or inhaled) is plotted against the volume of air in liters that is exhaled (or inhaled).

Three spirometric measurements are particularly useful: **forced vital capacity (FVC)**, **forced expiratory volume at one second ($FEV_1$)**, and the **ratio of the $FEV_1$ to the FVC ($FEV_1$/FVC)**. Computerized spirometers frequently print out six or more measures of flow or volume. However, for most purposes, the FVC and $FEV_1$ suffice. The FVC is the total volume of air exhaled after a **Forced Expiratory Maneuver** (the act of exhaling as hard and fast as possible after maximal inspiration). The $FEV_1$ is the amount of air that a person breathes out during the first second of a forced expiratory maneuver.

Figure 4.5 is a different presentation of the data obtained with spirometry: the display of the flow rate of exhaled and inhaled air against the volume of air exhaled. This type of graphical representation (flow-volume curve) is quite useful in assessing the quality of spirometry testing especially for the first second of exhalation. The different colored lines refer to the baseline measurement of spirometry (red line) and repeat spirometry after the administration of a bronchodilator (blue line). Also, the dots refer to the predicted values for flow rates for this individual. The volume-time graphs are also shown in this figure for pre- and post-bronchodilator spirometry. The FVC is the greatest point of the curve on the x-axis (in this example, it is 4.7 liters). However, the $FEV_1$ is not obvious since the time of exhalation is not shown. Instead, the spirometer has marked the location of the $FEV_1$ by a vertical line on the exhalation limb of the flow volume loop (in this example, the $FEV_1$ is 3.9 liters).

Spirometry test results can include many more parameters of exhaled flow including the peak expiratory flow rate (FEFmax) and mid-expiratory flow rates (FEF25–75%) as well as other instantaneous flow rates (FEF50%). However, for practical and clinical purposes, the three parameters mentioned below are the most important:
- Forced Vital Capacity (FVC) expressed in liters
- Forced Expiratory Volume in One Second ($FEV_1$) also expressed in liters
- The ratio of $FEV_1$/FVC expressed in percentage (%)

## 4.7 Acceptability and Repeatability Criteria of Spirometry Testing

Spirometry testing must be done in a high quality manner to obtain accurate information about the lung health of each patient. To ensure that the test results provide us with truly representative information, each forced maneuver must be examined for acceptability and each test session must be examined for repeatability. These criteria of acceptability and repeatability are described in detail in the American Thoracic Society/European Respiratory Society (ATS/ERS) recommended guidelines for spirometry testing (Miller, 2005). Spirogram results are used to detect possible conditions that affect the subject's ability to exhale as fully and forcefully as possible. The results are compared either to the subject's previous spirogram results if they are available or to established reference or predicted results that would be expected for a person with his/her characteristics (e.g., sex, age, height, etc.). If inaccurate results are obtained, the information from the comparisons will not be correct, creating the potential for not detecting serious lung diseases, or, diagnosing *disease* where none exists. Therefore, the goal of each testing session is to obtain **acceptable** maneuvers and a **repeatable** test session. That said, patients with lung disease may have a harder time producing acceptable and repeatable results. Acceptable tests are free from artifacts such as cough or glottis closure during the first second of exhalation, early termination (exhalation should be at least 6 seconds), variable effort, leak, or obstruction of the mouthpiece (Miller, 2005). There should be a quick start to the exhalation with the back extrapolated volume <5% of the FVC or 0.150 liters, whichever is greater. After three acceptable maneuvers the maximal two $FEV_1$'s and FVC's should be within 150 ml of each other for the results to be repeatable (Miller, 2005). No more than 8 maneuvers should be attempted due to patient fatigue.

## 4.8 Measurements from Spirometry Testing

Once testing is completed, the spirometry test results for that individual (specifically the forced expiratory volume in one-second ($FEV_1$), forced vital capacity (FVC) and the ratio of those two values $FEV_1$/FVC) are compared to predicted values based on established reference equations e.g. the third National Health and Nutrition Examination Survey (NHANES III) reference equations for spirometry (Hankinson, 1999).

## 4.9 Patterns of Spirometry Impairment or Limitation

In addition to a normal pattern of spirometry test results, different impairments produce distinct spirometry patterns:

- Obstructive Defect Pattern or Airflow Limitation or Obstruction
- Restrictive Lung Defect Pattern
- Mixed Impairment with both Airflow Obstruction/Limitation and Lung Restriction.

### 4.9.1 Airflow Obstruction Pattern

In this pattern, the rate of airflow is reduced due to either narrowing of the airways in the lung (as in asthma or chronic bronchitis) or loss of elastic recoil (as in emphysema) reducing the rate of exhaled airflow. See Figure 4.6 and 4.7 for volume time displays of the airflow obstruction pattern.

With airflow obstruction, there is a reduction in the amount of air that is exhaled in the first second ($FEV_1$) as well a reduction in the ratio of $FEV_1$ to FVC. **In fact, it is the reduced ratio of $FEV_1$ to FVC or $FEV_1$/FVC % that is the hallmark of airflow obstruction.** In this example, the normal spirometry results show a $FEV_1$ of 3.0 liters and a FVC of 4.0 liters; therefore, the ratio of $FEV_1$/FVC is 3.0/4.0 or 75%. For the spirometry showing airflow obstruction or limitation, the $FEV_1$ is 1.0 liters, the FVC is 3.7 liters, and the ratio of $FEV_1$/FVC is 1.0/3.7 or 27%.

See Figure 4.8 for an example of moderately severe airflow obstruction with a flow-volume display. At baseline, the FVC is 2.8 liters, the $FEV_1$ (by the vertical mark) is 1.3 liters, and the ratio of $FEV_1$/FVC is 1.3/2.8 or 46%. After the bronchodilator, the FVC is now 3.7 liters, the $FEV_1$ is 1.9 liters and the $FEV_1$/FVC is 1.9/3.7 or 51%.

Figure 4.9 is an example of severe airflow obstruction with a flow-volume display.

Examples of lung diseases with airflow obstruction are COPD including chronic bronchitis and emphysema, asthma, bronchiectasis, and bronchiolitis obliterans.

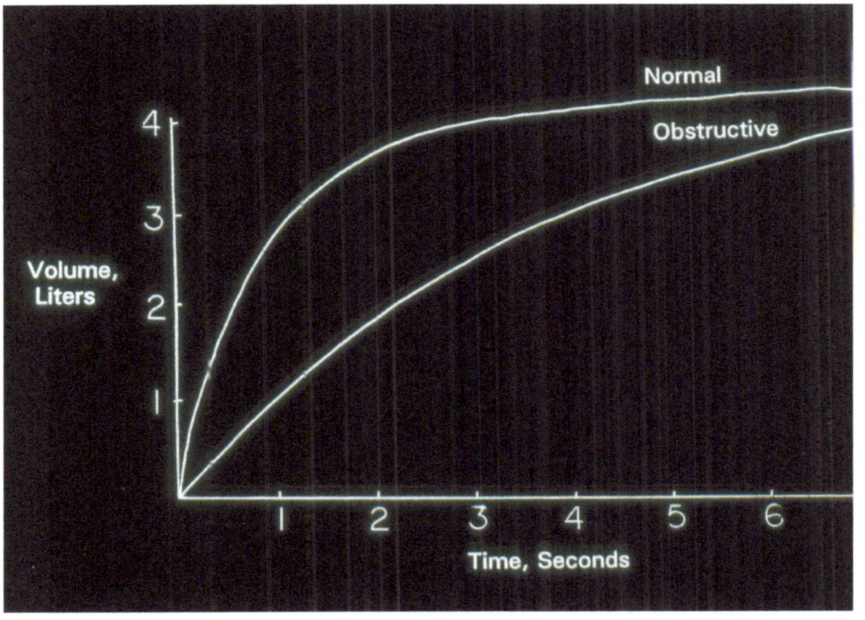


**Figure 4.6:** Volume-time graph of Airflow Obstruction. In this case, as compared to a normal pattern of exhaled volume of air, there is a decreased volume of exhaled air in the first second of exhalation.

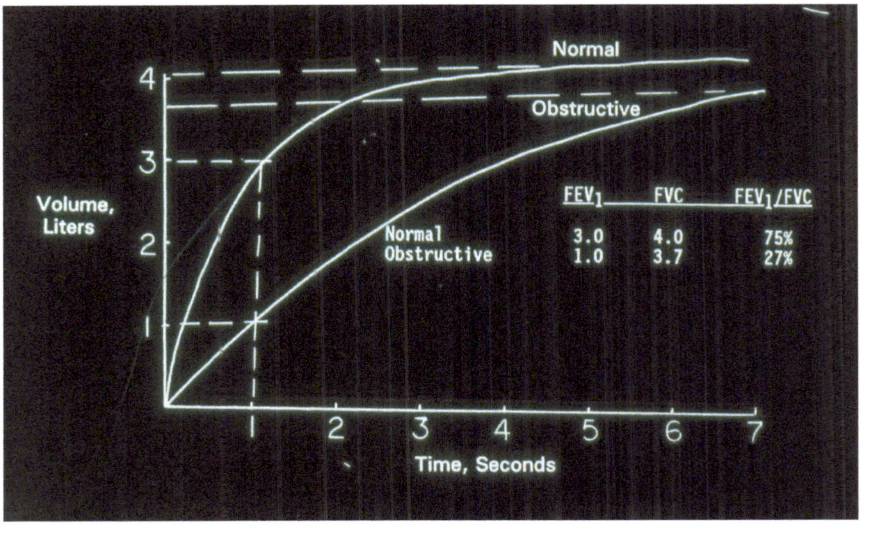


**Figure 4.7:** Volume-time graph of airflow obstruction showing measurements of $FEV_1$ and FVC and the ratio of $FEV_1$ to FVC ($FEV_1$/FVC)

### 4.9.2 Restrictive Lung Defect Pattern

In the case of a restrictive lung defect pattern, the total amount of exhaled air is reduced. This means the Vital Capacity or FVC is reduced. See Figure 4.10 and 4.11 as examples of volume-time displays of a restrictive lung defect.

In a restrictive lung defect, the rate of emptying of the air from the lung may not be reduced so the relationship between $FEV_1$ and FVC is normal. That said, because the FVC is reduced, the $FEV_1$ will be reduced proportionally with the $FEV_1$/FVC ratio being maintained and not reduced or, even on occasions, increased. In this particular case, the FVC is reduced as is the $FEV_1$ but the ratio of $FEV_1$/FVC is maintained or even increased compared to normal. **For a restrictive lung defect, the hallmark is the reduced FVC.** In this example, the normal spirometry results show an $FEV_1$ of 3.0 liters and FVC of 4.0 liters for a ratio of $FEV_1$/FVC of 3.0/4.0 or 75%. For the spirometry showing restriction, the $FEV_1$ is 1.8 liters, the FVC is 2.2 liters and the ratio of $FEV_1$/FVC is 1.8/2.2 or 82%.

See Figure 4.12 and 4.13 as examples of flow-volume displays of restrictive lung disease.

Since spirometry cannot measure the residual volume and, in turn, cannot determine the total lung capacity, spirometry can only suggest the presence of an actual restrictive lung defect. Further testing with lung volume measurements would be needed to confirm the presence of restriction.

Examples of lung diseases that can have a restrictive lung defect include interstitial fibrosis, hypersensitivity pneumonitis, pleural disease, chest wall deformities, pulmonary edema, and obesity.

### 4.9.3 Mixed Impairment with both Airflow Obstruction and Lung Restriction

Mixed impairment may be seen with combined lung diseases: a patient with a long smoking history who has COPD as well as the development of severe obesity leading to a restrictive lung defect. See Figure 4.14, 4.15 and 4.16 as examples of a volume time tracing and flow-volume displays for a mixed impairment result.

## 4.10 Interpretation of Spirometry Results

### 4.10.1 Reference Equations

There have been many studies published in the medical literature which have determined spirometry reference values from groups of relatively healthy persons. At this time, the American Thoracic Society (ATS) recommends using the reference values based on the third National Health and Nutrition Examination Survey (NHANES III) (Hankinson, 1999).

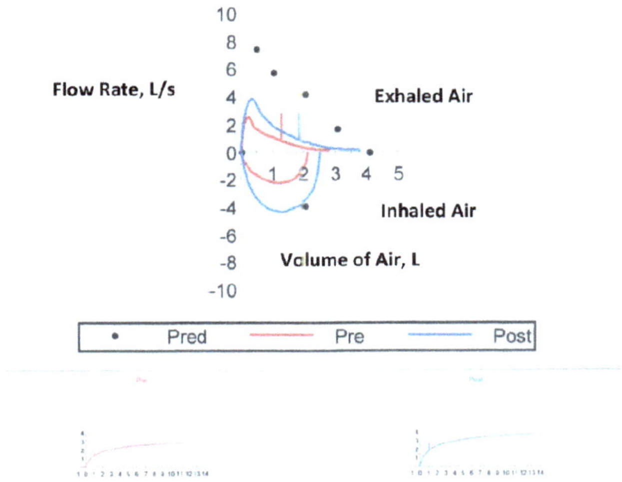


**Figure 4.8:** Flow-volume loop of Moderate Severity Airflow Obstruction. As can be seen in this graphical representation, the flow rate of air during exhalation is reduced throughout exhalation. This gives increased curvature or a greater concave shape to the expiratory limb of the flow volume loop which is another hallmark of airflow obstruction. Again, the different colored lines refer to pre-bronchodilator or baseline spirometry testing (red line) and post-bronchodilator testing (blue line).

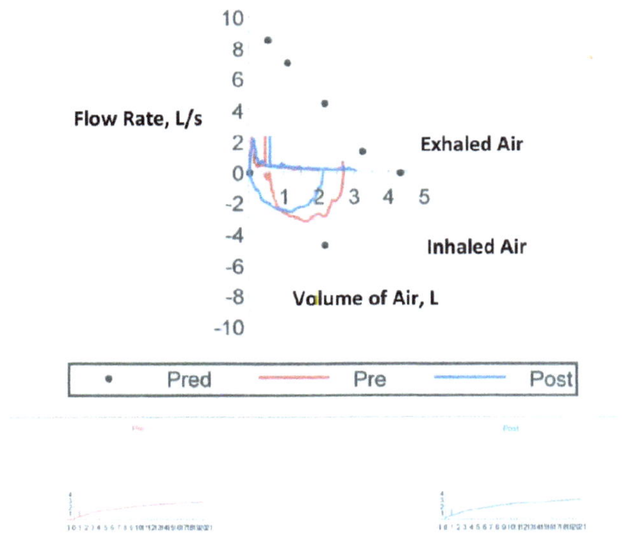


**Figure 4.9:** Flow-volume loop of Severe Airflow Obstruction In this example, there is more severe airflow obstruction which can be seen by even more severely decreased expiratory flow rates. At baseline, the FVC is 2.7 liters and the $FEV_1$ is 0.4 liters for a ratio for $FEV_1$/FVC of 15%. After the bronchodilator, the FVC is 3.1 liters and the $FEV_1$ is 0.6 liters for a ratio for $FEV_1$/FVC of 19%.

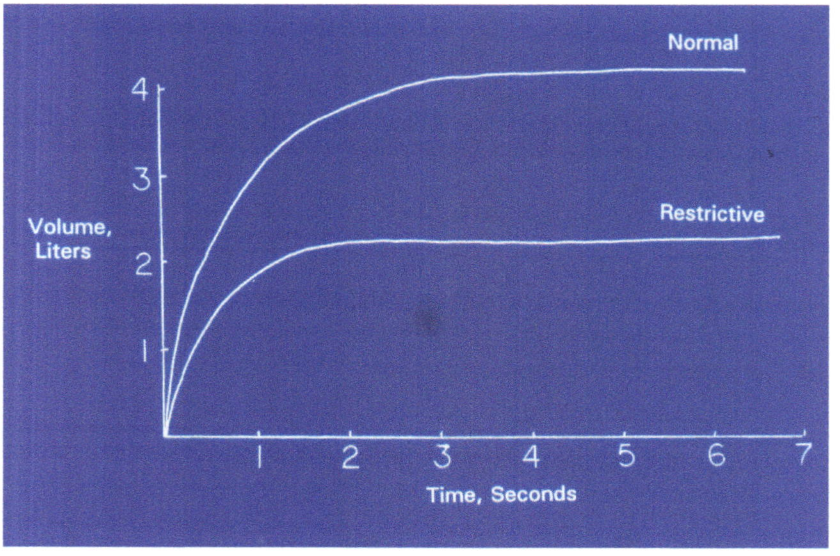


**Figure 4.10:** Volume-time graph of Restrictive Lung Defect Pattern. In the case of a restrictive lung defect pattern, the total amount of air exhaled is reduced. This means the Vital Capacity or FVC is reduced.

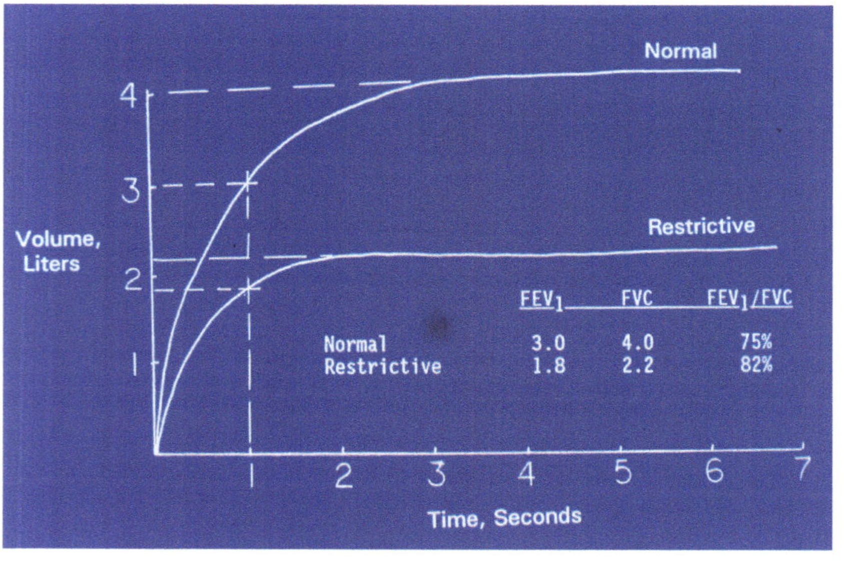


**Figure 4.11:** Volume-time graph of Restrictive Lung Defect showing measurements of $FEV_1$ and FVC and the ratio of $FEV_1$ to FVC ($FEV_1$/FVC).

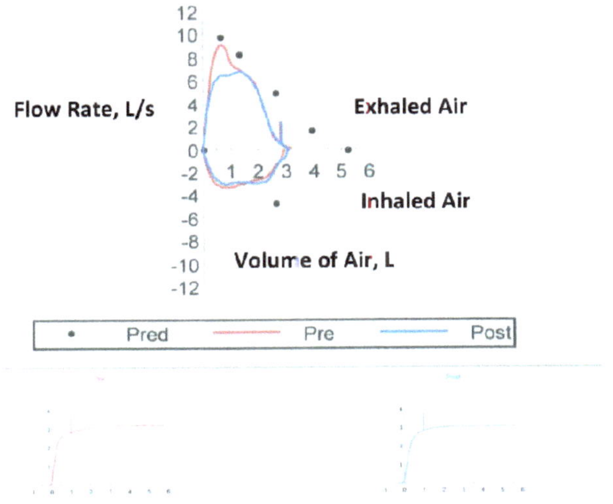


**Figure 4.12:** Flow-volume loop of a Restrictive Lung Defect. In a restrictive lung defect, the flow rates are maintained but the vital capacity (FVC) is reduced. This gives the appearance of a more vertical or upright flow-volume loop. In this case at baseline, the FVC is 3.2 liters and the $FEV_1$ is 2.9 liters for a ratio of $FEV_1$/FVC of 91%. There is really not much change after the use of a bronchodilator.

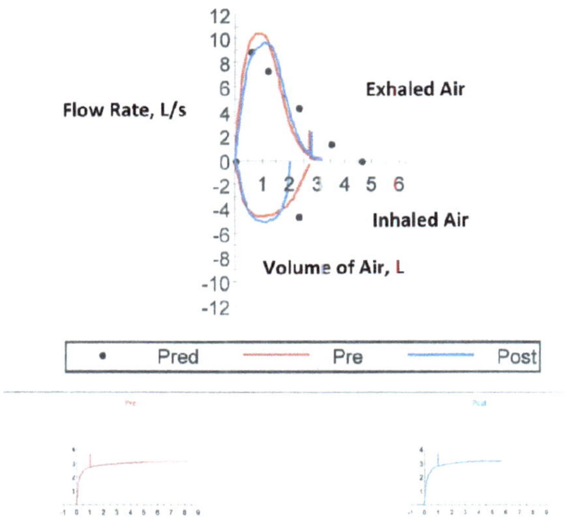


**Figure 4.13:** Another example of a Flow-volume loop for a Restrictive Lung Defect. Again note the more vertical appearance of the flow-volume loop in contrast to the horizontal appearance of the flow-volume loop for the patient with severe airflow obstruction. At baseline, the FVC is 3.2 liters and the FEV1 is 2.7 liters for a ratio of FEV1/FVC of 84%.

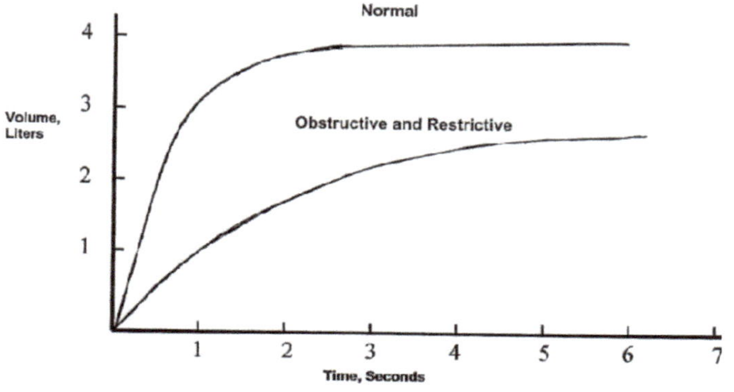


**Figure 4.14:** Volume-time graph of a Mixed Impairment. There is evidence for a reduced vital capacity (FVC) that is the hallmark of a restrictive lung defect as well as reduced rate of volume exhaled over the first second indicating airflow obstruction.

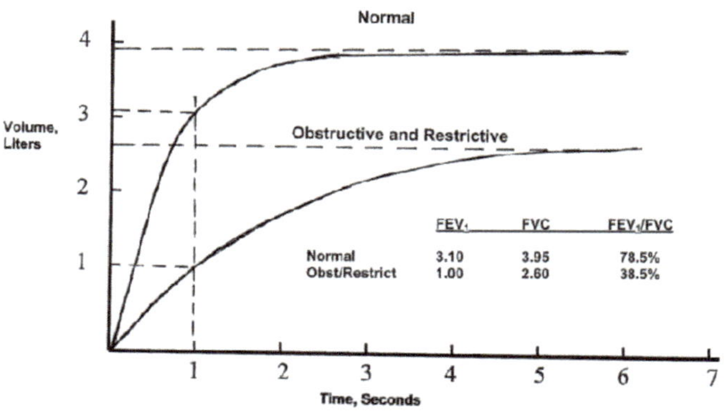


**Figure 4.15:** Volume-time graph of Mixed Impairment showing measurements of $FEV_1$ and FVC and the ratio of $FEV_1$ to FVC ($FEV_1$/FVC). By the numbers, the reduced FVC of 2.0 liters is suggestive of a Restrictive Lung Defect (would require complete lung function testing including lung volume measurements to confirm an actual Restrictive Lung Defect). The reduced $FEV_1$/FVC ratio of 38.5% indicates airflow obstruction.

### 4.10.2 Racial Differences in Reference Equations

The NHANES III study provides a separate set of spirometry reference equations for men and women of African-American, Caucasian, and Mexican-American ethnic groups. The NHANES III study did not provide spirometry reference equations for Asian-Americans, American Indians, East Indians, or other ethnic groups. Other investigations suggest that spirometry results are not substantially different for American

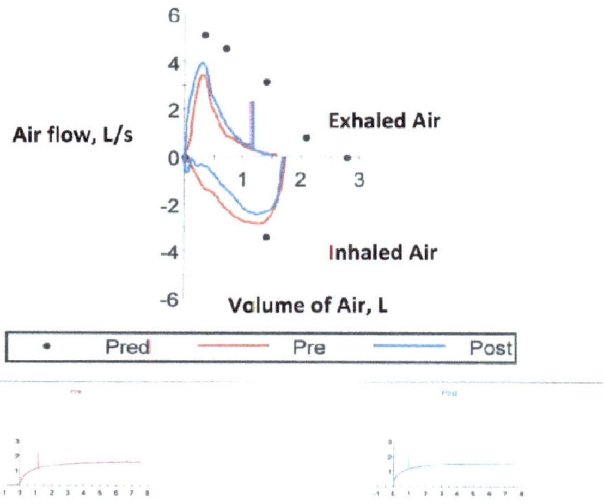


**Figure 4.16:** Flow-volume Loop of a Mixed Impairment. In this case, at baseline, the FVC is 1.7 liters with a predicted value of FVC of 2.8 liters. The $FEV_1$ is 1.1 liters for a ratio of $FEV_1$/FVC of 65%. The predicted value for the ratio of $FEV_1$/FVC for this individual is 70%. Thus, there is evidence for airflow obstruction as well as possible restrictive lung defect.

Indians when compared to Caucasians living in the United States; therefore, NIOSH recommends that when testing American Indian patients, the reference equations for Caucasians be used. For Asian-Americans, until separate reference equations are published and accepted for Asian-American and East Indian ethnic groups, the NHANES III reference equations for Caucasians should be used, but a correction factor of 0.88 should then be applied to the predicted values for FVC and $FEV_1$ (Redlich, 2014).

### 4.10.3 The Lower Limit of the Normal (LLN) Range

The predicted value calculated from spirometry reference equations is the average or mean value observed from many healthy persons of the same age, gender, height, and race as the patient being tested. The predicted value is actually in the middle of a rather wide, bell-shaped distribution (range) of normal values. For instance, some healthy persons may have FVC values as much as 20% lower than the predicted value. The lower limit of the normal range (LLN) is the threshold below which a value is considered abnormal - usually the value is set so that 95% of a “normal” population will have values above the LLN value and, correspondingly, 5% of a “normal” population will have values below the LLN. The LLN is about 80% of the predicted value for $FEV_1$ and for FVC, but about 90% of the predicted value for the $FEV_1$/FVC ratio, and about 60% of the predicted value for the FEF25–75%. However, these are only rough “rules of thumb” and the exact LLN should be determined using the reference equations.

### 4.10.4 What is Considered to Be Abnormal?

Abnormalities detected by spirometry may show one of three patterns: obstructive, restrictive, or mixed impairment (both obstructive and restrictive). Patients with obstructive lung diseases, such as emphysema or chronic asthma, often have an abnormally low $FEV_1/FVC$ and a low $FEV_1$ (below the LLN). Patients with fibrotic lung diseases, such as asbestosis, often have an abnormally low FVC, but their $FEV_1/FVC$ will generally be above the LLN. Persons exposed to certain dusts, such as silica or coal mine dust, can develop either pattern of abnormality, or a mixed pattern with reductions of both the $FEV_1/FVC$ ratio and the FVC below the LLN. Occasionally, spirometry results from a patient without any apparent health problems are found to be slightly below the LLN. In contrast, it is not unusual to have high FVC or high $FEV_1$ spirometry values. Young adults who were competitive athletes in high school, trade school, or college (while their lungs were still growing) may have a percent predicted FVC above 120%.

### 4.10.5 Determine Predicted Values and % of Predicted Values

Spirometry reference or predicted values, percent predicted values, and the LLN's for an individual can be reported from the automated spirometry system that has already been programmed with the appropriate reference equations. The percent of predicted values refers to the actual measured value of the spirometric parameter (e.g., $FEV_1$ or FVC) divided by the predicted or reference value for that individual times 100 for %, or:

$$\%\text{Pred FEV}_1 = 100.0\text{X}\frac{\text{Observed FEV}_1}{\text{Predicted FEV}_1}$$

### 4.10.6 Interpretation of Spirometry Test Results for Impairment Patterns

As mentioned above, lower limits of normal (LLN) for the spirometric parameters are used to determine whether the results are normal or abnormal. The primary impairment patterns of airflow obstruction, a restrictive lung defect and mixed impairment are then determined by interpretation using these LLNs.

### 4.10.7 Airflow Obstruction

The criterion for the interpretation of the presence of airflow obstruction is the finding of a reduced $FEV_1/FVC$ or the numerical value of $FEV_1/FVC$ below the LLN for that value. Some providers may decide to use the guidelines from the Global initiative for Chronic Obstructive Lung Disease: GOLD criteria for airflow obstruction (GOLD, 2013), when interpreting the results of spirometry. Those guidelines define an absolute cutoff for FEV1/FVC of 70% to determine the presence of airflow obstruction. The American Thoracic Society and European Respiratory Society recommend using the LLN from the reference equations chosen for the interpretation of spirometry test results (Pelligrino, 2005), (see "Controversy for Determination of Airflow Limitation/Obstruction" below).

The primary determinant of airflow obstruction is the $FEV_1$/FVC ratio measured by spirometry: If $FEV_1$/FVC < LLN, then airflow obstruction is present

Once airflow limitation is determined to be present, the severity of limitation is then assessed based upon the $FEV_1$ % of predicted value. Using the ATS/ERS guidelines for Interpretative Strategies for Lung Function Tests (Pelligrino, 2005), the following severity categories are used:

- Mild obstruction: $FEV_1$% predicted > 70% (which means the actual value measured is greater than 70% of the predicted value which in turn is based on the patient's age, height and gender with correction for race as appropriate).
- Moderate obstruction: $FEV_1$% predicted <69% but > 60%
- Moderately severe obstruction: $FEV_1$% predicted <59% but > 50%
- Severe obstruction: $FEV_1$% predicted <49% but > 35%
- Very severe obstruction: $FEV_1$% predicted <34%

There may be patients whose results from spirometry testing or from complete pulmonary function testing (if available) may be equivocal for the presence of airflow limitation or COPD. As discussed in Chapter 3 on the Recognition and Diagnosis of COPD, just as the syndrome of COPD may range from no evidence of airways disease to severe COPD, the presence of airflow obstruction is also a continuum from no airflow obstruction to very severe airflow obstruction. In the case of possible borderline airflow obstruction when the $FEV_1$/FVC is above the LLN, the use of reduced mid-expiratory flow rates adjusted for the FVC (the mid-expiratory flow ratio or MEFR) may be helpful (see Chapter 3).

#### 4.10.7.1 Possible Restrictive Lung Defect

Because spirometry cannot measure residual volume (RV) and in turn total lung capacity (TLC), the test cannot determine the presence of an actual restrictive lung defect where the total lung capacity is reduced below its LLN. Instead if the FVC is reduced below its LLN, then the presence of a restrictive lung defect can be suggested. However, it should be stated that further testing including the use of lung volumes will be needed to confirm the presence of an actual restrictive lung defect.

– **If only spirometry results are available, then the presence of restriction *would be suggested* if the FVC is < LLN (especially if the $FEV_1$/FVC ratio is > LLN); however the comment should be made that lung volumes would be recommended for confirmation of the presence of a restrictive lung defect.**

#### 4.10.7.2 Mixed Impairment Pattern

It is possible that there might be both the presence of airflow obstruction and the presence of a possible restrictive lung defect. In that case, a mixed impairment pattern may be interpreted.

– **Mixed impairment will be interpreted if there is both the presence of airflow obstruction and the suggestion of a restrictive lung defect.**

#### 4.10.7.3 Controversy for Determination of Airflow Limitation/Obstruction

As mentioned previously, the determination of the presence of airflow limitation or obstruction is in most cases the finding of a reduced $FEV_1$/FVC ratio. The controversy has been deciding below what value the $FEV_1$/FVC is considered to be reduced. The definition of airflow limitation or airflow obstruction has been a point of discussion based upon different statements from professional groups. Clinical guidelines for COPD disease management include the Global Initiative for Chronic Obstructive Lung Disease (GOLD, 2013), the VA/DoD Clinical Practice Guideline for Management of Outpatient Chronic Obstructive Pulmonary Disease (VA/DoD, 2007), and the American Thoracic Society/European Respiratory Society Standards for the Diagnosis and Management of Patients with COPD (ATS, 2004). These three guidance documents have recommended being more inclusive for identifying individuals who may have COPD and have proposed that the presence of airflow limitation exists when the post-bronchodilator $FEV_1$/FVC ratio is < 0.70. These guidelines acknowledge that this approach may be overly sensitive and include older individuals who are normal but who have an $FEV_1$/FVC ratio that is < 0.70. Other guidance documents are based on a statistical approach for the interpretation of airflow limitation using reference equations which in turn are based on population studies. The ATS/ERS document on Interpretative Strategies for Lung Function Tests states that the presence of an obstructive ventilatory defect exists when the $FEV_1$/FVC ratio is below the $5^{th}$ percentile of its predicted value, a value referred to as the lower limit of normal or LLN for that ratio based on the chosen reference values (Pelligrino, 2005). The most recent revised GOLD guidance (GOLD, 2013) acknowledges that the LLN values are based on a normal distribution and that the use of a fixed ratio of 0.70 will result in more frequent diagnosis of COPD in the elderly.

These different thresholds for the definition of airflow limitation or obstruction, a fixed cutoff of 70% for the ratio of $FEV_1$/FVC or the LLN for this ratio, can yield very different diagnoses as is illustrated in Figure 4.17. As we age, the normal values

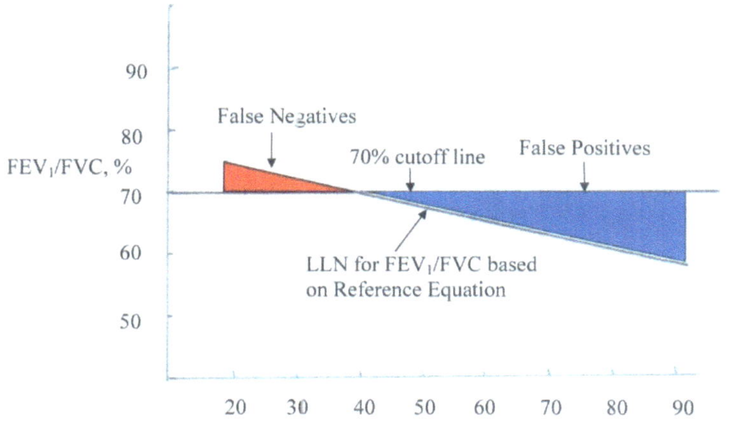


**Figure 4.17:** Comparison of the use of the LLN vs. 70% cutoff for the ratio of $FEV_1$/FVC for the determination of airflow obstruction.

for $FEV_1$/FVC decrease and, in turn, the values for the LLN for the ratio of $FEV_1$/FVC also decrease. The regression line for the decline in the LLN for the $FEV_1$/FVC ratio with increasing age based upon the NHANES III reference equation is shown in this figure. As a result, younger individuals with an $FEV_1$/FVC above 70% but below the LLN would be classified as no airflow obstruction by use of a 70% cutoff but would be interpreted as airflow obstruction by use of the LLN (false negatives). On the other hand, older individuals with $FEV_1$/FVC ratios below 70% but above the LLN would be classified as having airflow obstruction by the use of a 70% cutoff but would have no airflow obstruction by use of the LLN (false positives).

#### 4.10.7.4 Bronchodilator Response

There are times when clinicians want to assess a patient's spirometric response to the one-time use of a bronchodilator. In those instances, the % change and absolute change in volume of $FEV_1$ and FVC is determined comparing the post-bronchodilator spirometry results to the baseline or pre-bronchodilator results.

- **A significant response to the one-time use of a bronchodilator is a 12% increase in $FEV_1$ or in FVC with at least a 200 ml increase in that measurement.**

There needs to be both the 12% increase as well as the 200 ml change in absolute volume for a significant bronchodilator response to be interpreted. This definition of a significant bronchodilator response has been recommended by ATS/ERS in their 2005 statement of the interpretation of lung function testing (Pelligrino, 2005). As is also stated in this report, there may be other definitions of a significant bronchodilator response. As an example, the topic of bronchodilator response was discussed in a recent point and counterpoint series of articles (Pelligrino, 2014; Hansen, 2014). The counterpoint argument to using a 12% and 200 ml increase in FEV1, and FVC is that depending on the quality and precision of the spirometry data, much lower values of an increase may be statistically significant.

Both the ATS/ERS and GOLD spirometry guidelines recommend the use of post-bronchodilator $FEV_1$, FVC, and $FEV_1$/FVC to determine the presence of airflow obstruction. Spirometry after bronchodilators is believed to reduce variability in the measurement of $FEV_1$ and FVC and improve testing repeatability (GOLD, 2014). In addition, post-bronchodilator measurements should provide maximal flow rates and, therefore, represent an individual's "best" or greatest lung function. Even among individuals with normal lung function, the $FEV_1$, FVC, and $FEV_1$/FVC generally increase slightly after administration of a short acting beta-agonist and this effect diminishes with increasing age (Johannessen, 2006).

## 4.11 Summary Points

1. The identification of a patient with COPD has required the demonstration of airflow obstruction or airflow limitation as determined by spirometry testing.
2. If spirometry is performed, the testing must be done according to criteria of acceptability and repeatability as recommended by the American Thoracic Society and the European Respiratory Society.
3. The interpretation of spirometry test results involves the comparison of the actual measured values with predicted or reference values with normal vs abnormal results determined by the use of lower limits of normal (LLN) for the measured parameter.
4. Spirometry test results can be interpreted as different patterns: normal, airflow obstruction, possible restrictive lung defect or a mixed impairment pattern.
5. Airflow obstruction is present when the $FEV_1$/FVC ratio is below the LLN or a value of 0.70 for that parameter. Borderline airflow obstruction may be present when there is a reduction in the mid-expiratory flow ratio.

## References

ATS/ERS (2004) American Thoracic Society and European Respiratory Society: Standards for the diagnosis and management of patients with COPD. http://www.thoracic.org/clinical/copd-guidelines/resources/copddoc.pdf

Ferguson G.T., Enright P.L., Buist A.S., Higgins M.W. (2000) Office spirometry for lung health assessment in adults: A consensus statement from the National Lung Health Education Program. *Chest*, 117, 1146–1161.

GOLD (2013) Global Strategy for the Diagnosis, Management, and Prevention of Chronic Obstructive Pulmonary Disease. Global Initiative for Chronic Obstructive Lung Disease. http://www.goldcopd.org/uploads/users/files/GOLD_Report_2013_Feb20.pdf

Hankinson J.L., Odencrantz J.R., Fedan K.B. (1999) Spirometric Reference Values from a Sample of the General U.S. Population. *Am J Respir Crit Care Med,* 159, 179–187.

Hansen J.E., Porszasz J. (2014) Counterpoint: Is an Increase in $FEV_1$ and/or FVC > 12% and >200 mL the Best Way to Assess Positive Bronchodilator Response? No. *Chest,* 146(3), 538–541.

Johannessen A., Lehmann S., Omenaas E.R., Eide G.E., Bakke P.S., Gulsvik A. (2006). Post-bronchodilator spirometry reference values in adults and implications for disease management. *Am J Respir Crit Care Med*, 173, 1316–1325.

Miller M.R., Hankinson J., Brusasco V., Burgos F., Casaburi R., et al. (2005) Standardization of Spirometry: Series "ATS/ERS Task Force: Standardization of Lung Function Testing". *Eur Respir J*, 26, 319–338.

Murphy D.E., Panos R.J. (2013) Diagnosis of COPD and clinical course in patients with unrecognized airflow limitation. *Int J Chron Obstruct Pulmon Dis*, 8, 199–208.

Pelligrino R., Viegi G., Brusasco V., Crapo R.O., Burgos F., et al. (2005) Interpretative Strategies for Lung Function Tests: Series "ATS/ERS Task Force: Standardization of Lung Function Testing". *Eur Respir J*, 26, 948–968.

Pelligrino R., Brusasco V. (2014) Point: Is an Increase in $FEV_1$ and/or FVC > 12% and > 200 mL the Best Way to Assess Positive Bronchodilator Response? Yes. *Chest*, 146(3), 536–537.

Redlich C.A., Tarlo S.M., Hankinson J.L., Townsend M.C., Eschenbacher W.L., et al. (2014) Official American Thoracic Society Technical Standards: Spirometry in the Occupational Setting. Am J Respir Crit Care Med, 189, 984–994.

Sogbetun F.K., Eschenbacher W.L., Welge J.A., Panos R.J. (2014) Development of a Veterans Health Administration Specific COPD Screening Questionnaire. *Am J Respir Crit Care Med*, 189, A2984.

U.S. Preventive Services Task Force. (2008) Screening for Chronic Obstructive Pulmonary Disease Using Spirometry. http://www.uspreventiveservicestaskforce.org/uspstf08/copd/copdrs.htm Most recently accessed 8/19/2014.

U.S. Preventive Services Task Force. (2014) Final Research Plan: Screening for Chronic Obstructive Pulmonary Disease using Spirometry. http://www.uspreventiveservicestaskforce.org/uspstf14/copd/copdfinalresplan.htm

Most recently accessed 8/19/2014.

VA/DoD (2007) Clinical Practice Guideline for Management of Outpatient Chronic Obstructive Pulmonary Disease. Department of Veteran Affairs/Department of Defense. Version 2.0 –2007. http://www.healthquality.va.gov/copd/copd_20.pdf

William L. Eschenbacher, MD

# 5 Radiology: Use of Lung Imaging to Help in the Identification of Patients with COPD

Key Points
1. Radiographic imaging can be complementary to lung function testing in the identification of patients with COPD.
2. Chest radiographs are useful as part of the initial evaluation of patients with respiratory symptoms but CT scans especially high-resolution CT scans (HRCT) can provide more information for the evaluation of the presence of emphysema, air-trapping, or smoking-related interstitial lung diseases.
3. PET Scans can discriminate malignant vs. benign lesions in patients with smoking histories who are found to have lung nodules by chest radiographs or CT scans.
4. Newer imaging techniques using MRI scans are being evaluated in research settings for functional analysis of smaller airways including airway wall size and distribution of air flow in patients with COPD.

## 5.1 Introduction

The use of radiographic imaging of the lungs is complementary to the use of lung function testing in the identification of patients with COPD. As part of the initial evaluation of patients who present with respiratory symptoms (dyspnea, cough, sputum production, chest tightness, wheezing, etc.), a routine chest radiograph is usually obtained. For most patients with COPD, this may be the only imaging study that is needed. For further evaluation of the presence and severity of the changes seen in patients with COPD, CT imaging can also be performed. This more advanced imaging is useful if abnormalities are identified by the chest radiograph or if other conditions related to smoking are being considered in the evaluation of the patient's symptoms. Other advanced imaging techniques such as PET scanning or MRI scanning have some utility in COPD but are limited by cost and technical capabilities. However, ongoing research in these areas may ultimately provide a better understanding of relationships between distribution of ventilation and structure-function in patients with all severities of COPD including better estimation of disease progression and response to therapy (Coxson, 2014).

## 5.2 Chest Radiographs

Routine posterior-anterior (PA) and lateral views of the chest are standard images that can be ordered for patients who present with respiratory symptoms that may

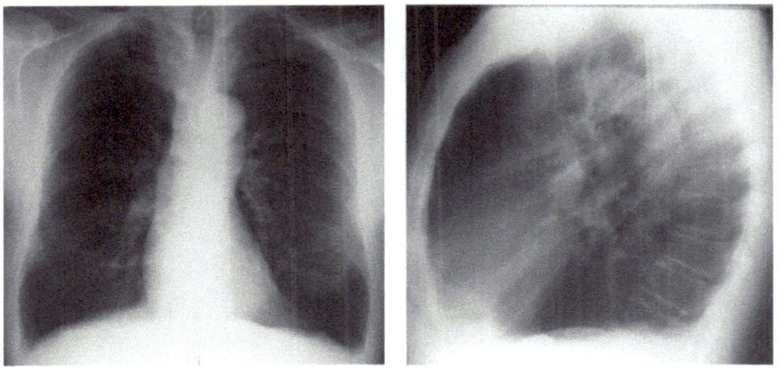

**Figure 5.1:** Posterior-Anterior (PA) (left) and lateral (right) chest radiograph images of a patient with COPD. The size of the heart shadow may appear decreased in patients with COPD unless there is accompanying cardiomegaly as seen in cardiomyopathy or right ventricular failure with COPD (cor pulmonale). Other common chest radiographic findings in COPD include increased lung volumes, flattened diaphragms, and reduced vascular markings.

represent COPD. Besides identifying features of the lung that can be seen with COPD, the routine chest radiograph can be helpful to exclude other conditions such as lung cancer, heart failure and pneumonia.

Features of COPD that can be seen on routine posterior-anterior (PA) and lateral chest radiographs include 1) hyperinflation as noted by flattening of the diaphragms (especially noted on the lateral view) and increase in the retrosternal airspace (also seen on the lateral view) along with widening of the costophrenic angles (on the PA view), 2) presence of bullae that can be detected on standard images, and 3) tapering and reduction of the number of pulmonary vessels especially as they are seen in the lung periphery. An example of a standard chest radiograph for a patient with COPD is seen in Figure 5.1.

Other conditions that may be identified by chest radiographs in patients with COPD that present with acute symptoms include pleural effusions and pneumonia. Other smoking-related lung diseases (such as smoking-related interstitial lung diseases) may be suggested by chest radiographs but in most instances, further evaluation with more advanced imaging including CT scans is indicated.

## 5.3 Computed Tomography (CT) Scans

### 5.3.1 CT Scans and Emphysema

The value of CT scans in the further evaluation of patients with COPD has been well documented (Webb, 2009). This is especially true for the identification of the presence of emphysema (one of the two elements of COPD along with the clinical definition of

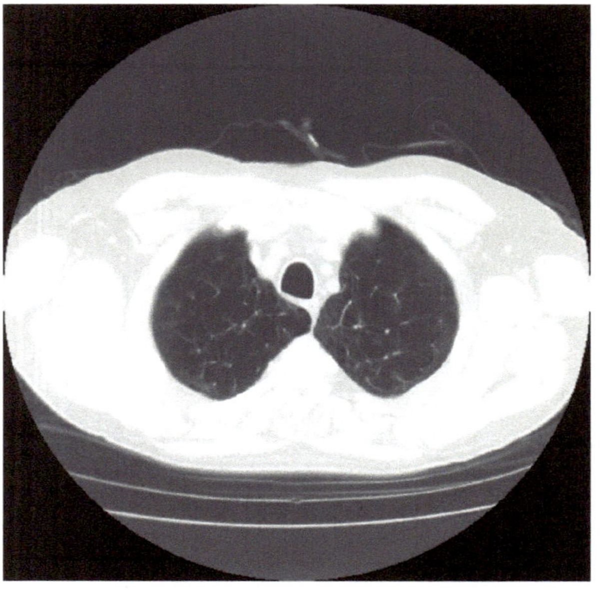

**Figure 5.2:** High-resolution CT scan imaging of a patient with severe emphysema. A hallmark of emphysema on high resolution CT scan imaging is the paucity of parenchymal and vascular markings that is often referred to as “holes without walls.”

chronic bronchitis) (Friedman, 2008; Takahashi, 2008). Emphysematous regions of the lung are defined as those areas that are 2 standard deviations below normal lung parenchymal density (-750 to -850 Hounsfield Units (HU) with a threshold value of -900 to -910 HU. In some studies, a threshold value of -950 HU is used. The presence and extent of emphysema can then be categorized as: 1) less than 25% of the area, 2) 26 to 50% of the area, 3) 51 to 75% of the area or 4) 76 to 100% of the area examined.

Of the different forms of CT imaging, HRCT is the most sensitive method for identifying emphysematous changes. An example of emphysematous changes on a HRCT is shown in Figure 5.2.

### 5.3.2 CT Scans and Air-trapping

Air-trapping is a pathophysiological term indicating the retention of excess gas in all or part of the lungs at any stage of expiration. Air-trapping is a finding characteristic of obstruction of the airways and is found in all forms of obstructive lung diseases including asthma and COPD. There may be other associated pathological conditions associated with air-trapping including bronchiectasis (which also may be seen in a phenotype of COPD: see below) and interstitial lung disease (Miller, 2014).

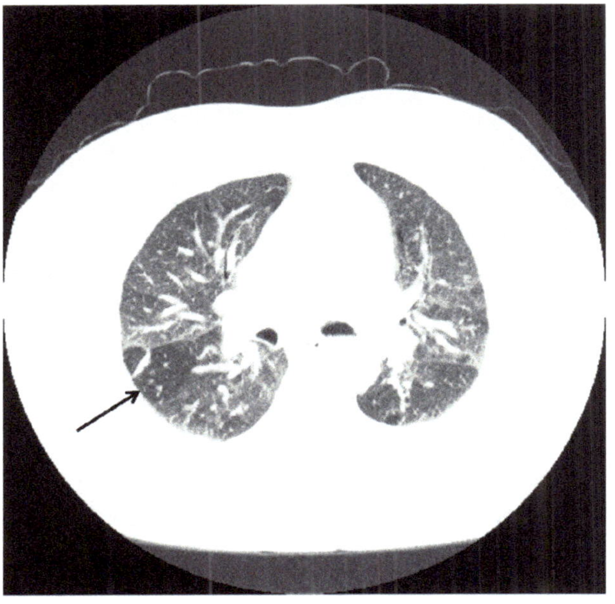

**Figure 5.3:** Expiratory phase of CT scan showing area of air-trapping as identified by arrow. In normal lungs during expiration, each pulmonary lobule deflates to the same extent; however, in individuals with COPD, obstruction to airflow causes lobules to deflate unequally. This ventilatory derangement causes air trapping that produces mosaicism on CT scans of the lung: deflated lobules have increased attenuation whereas obstructed lobules with air trapping retain air and have reduced attenuation (arrow).

In pulmonary function testing, air-trapping is the increase in residual volume (RV) or RV/TLC measurement compared to the predicted value. Radiographically, air-trapping is noted with CT scans with inspiratory and expiratory phases of imaging with the expiratory phase compared to the inspiratory images showing patchy areas of decreased lung attenuation consistent with air that has not been exhaled (Stern,1994; Matsuoka, 2008). The Fleischner Society defines air-trapping as "parenchymal areas with less than normal increase in attenuation and lack of volume reduction" as seen on end-expiration CT scans" (Hansell, 2008). An example of the presence of air-trapping seen with an expiratory phase of a CT scan is shown in Figure 5.3.

### 5.3.3 CT Evaluation of Airway Changes in COPD

In addition to identifying the presence of emphysema, CT scans can identify other characteristics of COPD including airway luminal and airway wall changes that are characteristic of chronic bronchitis and bronchiectasis.

More recent techniques using CT scans have been able to measure airway luminal internal diameter and airway wall thickness in patients with COPD (Nakano, 2005; Patel, 2008). These methods require quantitative measurements of cross-sectional airway dimensions using transverse CT images (Lutey, 2013). Airways less than 2–3 mm in diameter are thought to be the location where the greatest changes occur for patients with COPD and the major site of airflow obstruction. Algorithms have been developed to take into consideration the oblique sectioning of airways on transverse images to arrive at better estimates of luminal diameter and airway wall thickness for these smaller airways. Further studies have shown good correlations between the airway changes and respiratory symptoms (Grydeland, 2010). In addition newer studies using MRI imaging with hyperpolarized helium-3 ($He^3$) demonstrate regional gas distribution changes that correlate with the CT findings of the changes in these smaller airways (see later discussion regarding MRI imaging).

### 5.3.4 CT Scans for COPD Phenotypes

COPD might be best described by different phenotypes of presentation and illness (Vestbo, 2014). For example, there are the phenotypes of the frequent exacerbator (two or more exacerbations in the previous year), the overlap COPD-asthma phenotype, the emphysema-hyperinflation phenotype, and the bronchiectasis phenotype (Miravitlles, 2012; Martinez-Garcia, 2011). Several of these phenotypes are best described using CT scan results such as the emphysema and bronchiectasis phenotype presentations (Shah, 2014). The identification of bronchiectasis by CT scan has been defined previously by Naidich et al: air-fluid levels in distended bronchi, a linear array or cluster of cysts, dilated bronchi in the periphery of the lung and bronchial wall thickening due to peribronchial fibrosis (Naidich,1982). An example of bronchiectasis as noted by CT scan is shown in Figure 5.4.

### 5.3.5 Lack of Correlation Between CT Findings and Spirometric Results for COPD

COPD is composed of two separate conditions: emphysema and airways disease represented by chronic bronchitis. Most patients with COPD will have some combination of these two pathological processes. The hallmark of airflow limitation in COPD is reduced maximal expiratory flow rates measured by spirometry. The pathological changes in the lungs that result in the reduced expiratory flow rates are 1) increased flow resistive properties of the airways (as in chronic bronchitis) and 2) reduced elastic recoil of the lung (as in emphysema). In COPD, the airways can be narrowed as a result of inflammatory changes and smooth muscle hypertrophy in the airway wall and increased amount of mucous and inflammatory material within the airway lumen. There is increased resistance to airflow as a result of the narrowed airway leading to

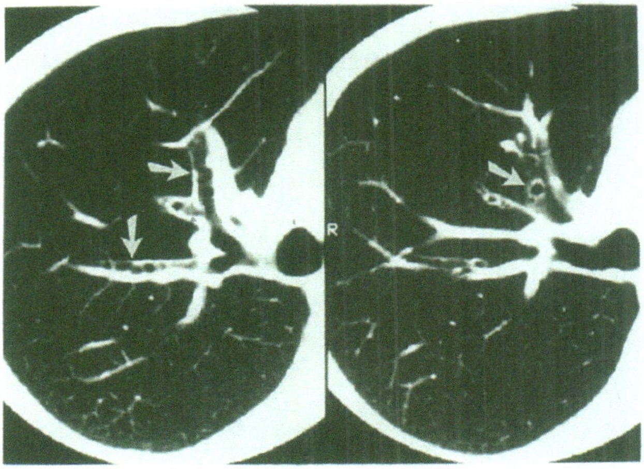


B

**Figure 5.4:** Chest CT scan demonstrating cylindrical bronchiectasis in a patient with COPD. Approximately 30–60% of individuals with COPD have chest CT evidence of bronchiectasis. Different forms of bronchiectasis include cylindrical or tubular, dilated airways alone, varicose, focal areas of constriction in the dilated airways, and saccular or cystic, progressive airway dilation into grape-like clusters. This CT scan demonstrates cylindrical or tubular bronchiectasis (arrows).

reduced flow rates for the same driving pressure that is generated to cause expiratory flow. In addition, loss of parenchymal tissue with emphysematous changes can reduce the support of airway walls contributing to airway narrowing and increased airway resistance. Also, the emphysematous changes reduce the elastic recoil and in turn the pressure gradient that is in part responsible for the generation of the expiratory flow rates.

However, recent studies suggest that the presence of airflow limitation noted by spirometry may not correlate well with the anatomic presence of emphysematous changes as noted on CT scans. In an editorial referring to this disconnect, Dr. James Hogg (Hogg, 2012) noted that the pathological process that leads to emphysema "in which the destructive process rapidly extends along surviving distal conducting airways to initiate emphysematous destruction of the alveolar surface...can account for the appearance of emphysema before a sufficient number of small airways have been destroyed to cause a reduction in $FEV_1$."

### 5.3.6 CT Scans for Smoking-related Interstitial Lung Diseases

As mentioned above, CT scans are also useful when there may be other smoking-related changes in the lungs. These other abnormalities can include smoking-related interstitial lung disease (ILD) and lung cancer.

An example of the usefulness of CT scans in identifying the presence of smoking-related ILD is the finding of Smoking-related Respiratory Bronchiolitis with Fibrosis as described by Reddy and Churg (Reddy, 2013). They described a CT pattern of patchy areas of reticular changes about upper zone emphysematous spaces in individuals who do not have evidence of a diffuse ILD.

Other smoking related ILDs that have been defined using CT scan findings include Desquamative Interstitial Pneumonia (DIP), Respiratory Bronchiolitis-Interstitial Lung Disease (RB-ILD), Pulmonary Langerhans Cell Histiocytosis (PLCH) and even Idiopathic Pulmonary Fibrosis (IPF) which may occur more frequently in current and former smokers (Webb, 2009).

### 5.3.7 Use of Low Dose CT Scans for Surveillance for Lung Cancer

As also mentioned, CT scans can be used for the identification of other lung abnormalities in smokers especially the finding of bronchogenic carcinoma. The U.S. Preventive Services Task Force (among other professional societies) has recommended annual screening for lung cancer with low-dose CT scans in adults ages 55 to 80 years who have a 30 pack-year smoking history and who currently smoke or have quit within the past 15 years (Moyer, 2014).

## 5.4 Other Advanced Imaging Techniques in COPD

### 5.4.1 PET Scans

Positive emission tomography or PET scan is an imaging technique that examines the metabolic activity of lesions throughout the body that have been identified by other imaging techniques. A radiotracer such as fluorodeoxyglucose (FDG) that contains both sugar and radioactive elements is injected into the individual who is then scanned to detect those areas that have taken up and metabolized the sugar moiety and are radioactive. PET scans can differentiate malignant lesions (which are highly metabolically active) and benign lesions such as scars or fibrotic areas that are not active. If the lesion is an inflammatory process such as an active infection, it may also take up the radiotracer and be PET scan positive. The role of PET scanning in COPD is mostly for those patients who have a smoking history and have had nodules or other abnormalities identified by routine chest radiographs or CT scans. The PET scan can then be helpful in discriminating a malignant lesion from a benign lesion in these patients.

### 5.4.2 MRI Scans

1. As mentioned above in the section on CT Evaluation of Airway Changes in COPD, there are newer imaging techniques being evaluated in research settings using magnetic resonance imaging (MRI) scanning. Helium-3 (He3) and xenon-129 (Xe129) are gaseous magnetic resonance (MR) contrast agents that can be inhaled, permitting visualization of lung airspaces in an MR image (Salerno, 2001; Moller, 2002; van Beek, 2004). The MR signal from these *hyperpolarized* gases is easily detected using an MR scanner tuned to the appropriate resonance frequency.
2. MRI of hyperpolarized gases has led to the development of unique strategies for evaluating the structure and function of the lung (Salerno, 2001; Moller, 2002; van Beek, 2004). In particular, the relatively high solubility of xenon in biological tissues (Abraham, 1985), and an exquisite sensitivity to its environment that results in an enormous range (~200 ppm) of chemical shifts upon solution (Miller, 1981), make hypXe129 particularly attractive for exploring certain characteristics of lung function, such as gas exchange and uptake (Sakai, 1996). The quantitative characteristics of exchange and uptake are determined by physiologic parameters, including the surface-to-volume ratio and the thickness of the blood-gas barrier (Driehuys, 2006).
3. Since the primary function of the lung is gas exchange, impaired gas transport or exchange in subjects with pulmonary disease such as COPD can cause symptomatic shortness of breath. Non-equilibrium xenon uptake spectroscopy (NEXUS) can quantify the gas transport from the major airways all the way down to the alveolar gas exchange sites with high temporal resolution. In addition, chemical shift saturation recovery (CSSR) MR spectroscopy can be employed to measure the alveolar septal wall thickness and surface-to-volume ratio, both potentially highly relevant physiological parameters for the characterization of lung function in these patients with obstructive airways disease.

## 5.5 Summary Points

1. To better understand the pathophysiology of COPD including the impact of the disease for the patient and response to therapy requires more information than lung function test results. This additional information can be obtained with currently available imaging technology and other techniques now being developed.
2. Screening chest radiographs have limited usefulness but more advanced techniques such as CT scans (and in the future MRI scanning using polarized gases) can provide more helpful information including insight into the development and progression of COPD. Also, newer imaging techniques may inform us about the patient's response to therapy that cannot be measured by standard pulmonary function testing.

## References

Abraham M.H., Kamlet M.J., Taft R.W., Doherty R.M., Weathersby P.K. (1985). Solubility properties in polymers and biological media. 2. The correlation and prediction of the solubilities of nonelectrolytes in biological tissues and fluids. *J Med Chem*, 28(7), 865–870.

Coxson H.O., Liepsic J., Parraga G., Sin D.D. (2014). Using pulmonary imaging to move chronic obstructive pulmonary disease beyond $FEV_1$. *Am J Respir Crit Care Med*. 190, 135–144.

Driehuys B., Cofer G.P., Pollaro J., Mackel J.B., Hedlund L.W., Johnson G.A. (2006). Imaging alveolar-capillary gas transfer using hyperpolarized 129Xe MRI. *Proc Natl Acad Sci USA*, 103(48), 18278–18283.

Friedman P.J. (2008). Imaging studies in emphysema. *Proc Am Thorac Soc*, 5(4), 494–500.

Grydeland T.B., Dirksen A., Coxson H.O., Eagan T.M.L., Thorsen E., Pillai S.G., Sharma S., et al. (2010). Quantitative computed tomography measures of emphysema and airway wall thickness are related to respiratory symptoms. *Am J Respir Crit Care Med*, 181,353–359.

Hansell D.M., Bankier A.A., MacMahon H., McLoud T.C., Muller N.L., Remy J. (2008). Fleischner Society: Glossary of terms for thoracic imaging. *Radiology*, 246, 697–722.

Hogg J.C. (2012). A pathologist's view of airway obstruction in chronic obstructive pulmonary disease. *Am J Respir Crit Care Med,* 186, v-vii.

Lutey B.A., Conradi S.H., Atkinson J.J., Zheng J., Schechtman K.B., Senior R.B., Gierada D.S. (2013). Accurate measurement of small airways on low-dose thoracic CT scans in smokers. *Chest*, 143, 1321–1329.

Martinez-Garcia M.A., Soler-Cataluna J.J., Sanz Y.D., Serra P.C., Lerma M.A., Vicente J.B., Perpina-Tordera M. (2011). Factors associated with bronchiectasis in patients with COPD. *Chest*, 140, 1130–1137.

Matsuoka S., Kurihara Y., Yagihashi K., Hoshino M., Watanabe N., Nakajima Y. (2008). Quantitative assessment of air trapping in chronic obstructive pulmonary disease using inspiratory and expiratory volumetric MDCT. *AJR Am J Roentgenol*, 190, 762–769.

Miller K.W., Reo N.V., Schoot Uiterkamp A.J., Stengle D.P., Stengle T.R., Williamson K.L. (1981). Xenon NMR: chemical shifts of a general anesthetic in common solvents, proteins, and membranes. *Proc Natl Acad Sci USA*, 78(8), 4946–4949.

Miller W.T., Chatzkel J., Hewitt M.G. (2014). Expiratory air trapping on thoracic CT: A diagnostic subclassification. *Annals ATS*, published on-line 23 June 2014.

Miravitlles M., Calle M., Soler-Cataluna J.J. (2012). Clinical phenotypes of COPD: Identification, definition and implications for guidelines. *Arch Bronconeumol*, 48, 86–98.

Möller H.E., Chen X.J., Saam B., Hagspiel K.D., Johnson G.A., Altes T.A., de Lange E.E., Kauczor H.U. (2002). MRI of the lungs using hyperpolarized noble gases. *Magn Reson Med*, 47(6), 1029–1051.

Moyer V.A. on behalf of the U.S. Preventive Services Task Force (2014). Screening for lung cancer: U.S. Preventive Services Task Force Recommendation Statement. *Ann Int Med*, 160, 330–338.

Naidich D.P., McCauley D.I., Khouri N.F., Stitik F.P., Siegelman S.S. (1982). Computed tomography of bronchiectasis. *J Comput Assist Tomogr*, 6, 437–444.

Nakano Y., Wong J.C., de Jong P.A., Buzatu L., Nagao T., Coxson H.O., Elliott W.M., Hogg J.C., Pare P.D. (2005). The prediction of small airway dimensions using computed tomography. *Am J Respir Crit Care Med*, 171, 142–146.

Patel B.D., Coxson H.O., Sreekumar G.P., Agusti A.G.N., Calverley P.M.A., Donner C.F. et al. (2008). Airway wall thickening and emphysema show independent familial aggregation in chronic obstructive pulmonary disease. *Am J Respir Crit Care Med*, 178, 500–505.

Reddy T.L., Mayo J., Churg A. (2013). Respiratory bronchiolitis with fibrosis: High-resolution computed tomography findings and correlation with pathology. *Annals ATS*, 10, 590–601.

Sakai K., Bilek A.M., Oteiza E., Walsworth R.L., Balamore D., Jolesz F.A., Albert M.S. (1996). Temporal dynamics of hyperpolarized 129Xe resonances in living rats. *J Magn Reson*, 111(3), 300–304.

Salerno M., Altes T.A., Mugler J.P., 3rd, Nakatsu M., Hatabu H., de Lange E.E. (2001). Hyperpolarized noble gas MR imaging of the lung: potential clinical applications. *Eur J Radiol*, 40(1), 33–44.

Shah U., Mirchandani L., Iyer A., Uppe A., Nair G. (2014). COPD phenotypes according to HRCT findings. *DY Patil Journal of Health Sciences*, 1, 1–6.

Stern E.J., Frank M.S. (1994). Small-airway diseases of the lungs: Findings at expiratory CT. *AJR Am J Roentgenol*, 163, 37–41

Takahashi M., Fukuoka J., Nitta N., Takazakura R., Nagatani Y., Murakami Y., Otani H., Murata K. (2008). Imaging of pulmonary emphysema: A pictorial review. *Int J COPD 3(2)*, 193–204.

van Beek E.J., Wild J.M., Kauczor H.U., Schreiber W., Mugler J.P., 3rd, de Lange E.E. (2004). Functional MRI of the lung using hyperpolarized 3-helium gas. *J Magn Reson Imaging*, 20(4), 540–554.

Vestbo J., Agusti A., Wouters E.F.M., Bakke P., Calverley P.M.A., Celli B., Coxson H., Crim C., et al. (2014). Should we view chronic obstructive pulmonary disease differently after ECLIPSE? A clinical perspective from the study team. *Am J Respir Crit Care Med*, 189, 1022–1030.

Webb W.R., Muller N.L., Naidich D.P. (2009). High-Resolution CT of the Lung. 4th edition. Lippincott Williams & Wilkins, Philadelphia PA.

Michael T. Borchers, PhD, Gregory Motz, PhD

# 6 Pathogenesis of COPD

Key Points
1. The pathogenesis of COPD is a complex, multifactorial process that includes genetics, proteolytic imbalance, oxidative stress, inflammation, occupational and environmental exposures, and innate and adaptive immune function.
2. Excessive secretion of proteases and inhibition of antiproteases contribute to the degradation of lung extracellular matrix.
3. Oxidative stress can directly injure alveolar epithelial cells and induce mucus secretion of airway epithelial cells.
4. The chronic inflammation that defines COPD is a strong correlate of disease severity in patients and is critically involved in disease development experimentally.
5. The pathogenesis of COPD includes extrapulmonary manifestations including systemic inflammation, cardiovascular disease, nutritional abnormalities and skeletal muscle dysfunction.

## 6.1 Introduction

Pathologically, COPD is defined as a combination of emphysema, small airway disease (fibrosis, scarring, increases in smooth muscle surrounding the airways), and chronic bronchitis (inflammation and mucus hypersecretion). The extent of each condition varies within individual patients (Barnes, 2003; Chung, 2008; Cosio, 2009). These pathological conditions affect both the large and small airways, as well as the lung parenchyma. The reduction in lung elasticity caused by the destruction of alveoli (emphysema) produces a loss of support and closure of the small airways during expiration (Barnes, 2004). Additionally, the small airways are physically narrowed by fibrotic scarring and an increase in the surrounding smooth muscle mass. This obstruction to airflow diminishes expiratory alveolar emptying and produces air trapping and hyperinflation (Barnes, 2004). Finally, a mucus-rich inflammatory exudate clogs the airways augmenting airflow resistance (Barnes, 2004). Together, these changes contribute to airflow obstruction that causes a reduction in normal lung function, measured as $FEV_1$ (forced expiratory volume in 1 second). In addition, COPD is associated with multiple other pulmonary diseases such as fibrosis, asthma, and lung cancer.

## 6.2 Chronic Bronchitis

Chronic bronchitis is defined clinically as a productive cough of greater than 3 months duration for more than two successive years, and is characterized by inflammation and excessive mucus production. The role of airway inflammation in COPD forms the basis of our current understanding of the pathogenesis of COPD and is elaborated upon in detail below. In COPD, mucus overproduction can physically plug the airways, and mucus hypersecretion is associated with a decline in $FEV_1$ (Prescott, 1995; Vestbo, 1996). Further, a role for mucus production in COPD is supported by the specific observation that accumulation of inflammatory exudates and mucus in the small airways increases with disease severity (Hogg, 2004). Mechanistically, it is believed that mucus/goblet cell hyperplasia and cellular phenotype alterations caused by cigarette smoking are the major causes of mucus hypersecretion in COPD (Innes, 2006).

## 6.3 Emphysema

Emphysema is characterized by a loss of lung elasticity (increased pulmonary compliance) caused by parenchymal lung destruction. Smoking causes both panacinar (destruction of parenchymal alveoli) and centriacinar (destruction around respiratory bronchioles) emphysema (Kim, 1991). Emphysema is a significant contributor to airflow obstruction in COPD and several studies have demonstrated correlations between the severity of macroscopic emphysema and measurable lung function decline (Hogg, 1994; Nakano, 2000). The causes of emphysema are multifactorial, but the best studied hypothesis for the development of emphysema is a protease:antiprotease imbalance leading to the destruction of lung tissue (Chung, 2008). Another major mechanism causing emphysema is lung epithelial and endothelial cell apoptosis. Apoptosis may by caused by oxidative stress or the cytotoxic functions of activated lymphocytes (e.g. CD8+ T cells, NK cells) that release perforin and granzymes directly killing lung epithelial cells. Finally, increased cellular senescence and a failure of lung maintenance and repair after chronic cigarette smoke exposure may also contribute to the development of emphysema (Chung, 2008).

## 6.4 Smooth Muscle

The amount of smooth muscle surrounding the airways, defined by total area, is increased in COPD patients and the amount of smooth muscle inversely correlates with lung function ($FEV_1$) (Bosken, 1990; Cosio, 1980; Saetta, 1998). In patients with severe COPD (GOLD stages 3 and 4), the amount of smooth muscle may be increased as much as 50% (Hogg, 2004). It is not entirely known how, or whether, increases in smooth muscle contribute to the development of COPD. However, it has been speculated that the release of smooth muscle-derived inflammatory mediators in response to cigarette smoke or increased contractility may be involved (Chung, 2008).

## 6.5 Fibrosis

In addition to increases in peri-airway smooth muscle mass in COPD patients, there is also a significant increase in collagen deposition and fibrotic scarring around the small airways (Chung, 2008; Hogg, 2004). The fibrotic process is believed to further restrict proper contractility of the airways during breathing, thus contributing to airflow obstruction (Hogg, 2004). It is not entirely known how the development of fibrosis proceeds, both transforming growth factor β (TGFβ) and connective tissue growth factor (CTGF) levels are elevated in the airways of COPD patients (de Boer, 1998; Takizawa, 2001). TGFβ may cause fibrosis by inducing the expression of CTGF, which in turn drives the production and deposition of collagen (Ihn, 2002).

## 6.6 Pathogenesis of COPD

### 6.6.1 Genetics: Gene-association Studies

Early studies estimated that only 10 to 15% of smokers develop COPD (Rennard, 2006). However, as early COPD is often asymptomatic, it is believed that COPD is significantly underdiagnosed (Coultas, 2001). More recent studies estimate the prevalence of COPD is as high as 20% and that up to 50% of smokers may have spirometric evidence of airflow obstruction (Buist, 2008; Halbert, 2006; Stang, 2000). Most lifelong smokers will develop COPD eventually, provided they do not die from nonpulmonary smoking-related diseases first (e.g. cardiovascular disease, metabolic disease, cancer) (Rennard, 2006). However, a small proportion of individuals will develop very severe COPD even after only smoking for a relatively short period of time (or as lifelong never smokers). The appreciation that the development of COPD in individuals with similar smoking histories is heterogenious has led to fervent investigation into genetic risk factors that contribute to disease development. The first gene associated with the development of COPD was the α1-antitrypsin gene. Individuals who smoke and are homozygous for mutations of this gene develop severe COPD at a very early age. However, only about 1–2% of all COPD patients have this particular deficiency (Wan & Silverman, 2009). Studies involved in the identification of additional genes that confer susceptibility to COPD have been difficult due to the extreme phenotypic heterogeneity among COPD patients (Wan, 2009). Therefore, nonreplication of genetic association studies is extremely commonplace in COPD studies (Wan, 2009). However, there are a number of genetic associations that have been sufficiently replicated across several labs. Replicated gene-association studies have identified proteases (MMP9, MMP12), detoxification/oxidative stress genes (EPHX1, HMOX1, GSTP1), genes involved in the immune response (TNFα, GC), and genes regulating apoptosis (TGFβ) as genes associated with development of COPD (Wan, 2009).

### 6.6.2 Epigenetics

In addition to classical gene-association studies, epigenetic control of gene expression is thought to be involved in COPD. However, as the field itself is relatively new, there are few studies that address this issue in COPD. Histone acetylation typically enhances gene transcriptional activity, and acetylation status is controlled by an enzyme that removes acetyl groups called histone deacetylase. With increasing disease severity, there is a corresponding decrease in overall histone deacetylase activity (increased histone acetylation) in the lungs of COPD patients (Ito, 2005). Therefore, this increased acetylation is believed to increase the transcriptional activity of proinflammatory genes in COPD patients. Supporting this hypothesis, COPD patients exhibit increased levels of histone acetylation and IL-8 expression (Ito, 2005). These observations are supported by animal studies in smoke exposed rats that demonstrate decreased histone deacetylase activity, increased histone acetylation, and enhanced NF-κB binding (Marwick, 2004). It is believed that histone deacetylase activity is reduced due to ubiquitination and subsequent degradation after cigarette smoke exposure (Adenuga, 2009).

### 6.6.3 Protease: Antiprotease Imbalance

The most well-studied mechanism of COPD pathogenesis is an imbalance in pulmonary protease and antiprotease levels. This hypothesis developed from the observation that some smokers with reduced levels of α1-antitrypsin develop emphysema at a very early age. However, these individuals only represent a very small minority of COPD patients (1–2%). Many COPD patients develop a protease:antiprotease imbalance through the overproduction of proteases by activated neutrophils and macrophages (Barnes, 2003). Proteases are important for the development of emphysema because these enzymes, particularly elastin, physically digest the extracellular matrix. A role for proteases in COPD development is supported by the demonstration that the instillation of a number of different proteases into the lungs of animals produces significant emphysema (Barnes, 2003). Elastase derived from neutrophils has received significant attention because it is the molecular target of α1-antitrypsin. Levels of neutrophil elastase are increased in COPD patients and instillation of neutrophil elastase into rodent lungs induces emphysema (Barnes, 2003). In addition to physical destruction of the airways, neutrophil elastase is also believed to be involved in inflammatory cell recruitment and mucus production (Barnes, 2003). Further, chemical inhibition of neutrophil elastase prevents inflammation and emphysema in guinea pigs exposed to cigarette smoke (Table 6.1) (Wright, 2002). Although neutrophil elastase has received a significant amount of attention, a broad range of proteases are activated in COPD. Increased concentrations of cysteine proteases (cathepsins) have been observed in COPD patients, and chemical inhibition in rodent models prevents the development of a number of COPD phenotypes (Table 6.1) (Barnes, 2003). Further, matrix metalloproteinases (MMPs) may also be involved in disease development as a number of MMPs are upregulated in COPD patients and MMP knockout mice exposed to cigarette smoke are protected from the development of COPD phenotypes (Table 6.1) (Barnes, 2003).

### 6.6.4 Oxidative Stress

Cigarette smoke contains $10^{17}$ oxidant molecules per puff and is a significant source of reactive oxygen and reactive nitrogen species (ROS and RNS) (MacNee, 2000). There is considerable evidence of elevated oxidative stress in the lungs of cigarette smokers and there is an even greater increase in individuals with COPD (MacNee, 2005). The evidence in COPD patients includes increased levels of exhaled $H_2O_2$, 8-isopostane, and NO, all indirect measures of oxidative stress (MacNee, 2005). Additionally, COPD patients exhibit a decrease in plasma antioxidants, and an increase of oxidized lipids and proteins in plasma and tissues (MacNee, 2005). Based upon this evidence, it has been proposed that oxidative stress may be critical to the development and progression of COPD. Mechanistically, oxidative stress is believed to contribute to a number of important COPD phenotypes. Inactivation of α1-antitrypsin occurs by oxidation and a decrease in antiprotease activity is observed in bronchoalveolar lavage (BAL) fluid obtained after smoke exposure. Therefore, it is believed that physical inactivation of antiproteases by oxidative stress may significantly contribute to the protease:antiprotease imbalance in COPD patients (MacNee, 2005). Oxidative metabolites can induce the secretion of mucus from airway epithelial cells, and therefore, may be involved in mucus hypersecretion in COPD (Adler, 1990). Also, direct cell death of alveolar epithelial cells induced by oxidative stress has been proposed as a significant mechanism in the development of emphysema (MacNee, 2005; Petrache, 2005). Because oxidative stress can induce the expression of pro-inflammatory cytokines as well as chemotactic proteins, oxidative stress caused by cigarette smoke exposure may also be involved in the inflammatory response in COPD patients (MacNee, 2005).

A role for oxidative stress in COPD is strongly supported by animal models of COPD (Table 6.2). Therapeutic administration of antioxidants or transgenic overexpression of antioxidant genes decreases both the inflammatory response as well as the development of emphysema following cigarette smoke exposure (Foronjy, 2006;

**Table 6.1:** Role of protease:antiprotease imbalance in mouse models of COPD.

| **Species** | **Manipulation** | **Cigarette Smoke Exposure** | **Inflammatory Response** | **Development of Emphysema** | **Comments** | **Reference** |
|---|---|---|---|---|---|---|
| Guinea Pig | serine protease inhibitor | 6 months | decreased vs. untreated | Partial Protection(~50%) vs. untreated | decreased matrix breakdown products in BAL | (Wright et al., 2002) |
| mouse (C57BL/6) | α1-antitrypsin injection | 6 months | decreased vs. untreated | Partial Protection(~70%) vs. untreated | decreased matrix breakdown products in BAL | (Churg, Wang, Xie, & Wright, 2003) |
| mouse (C57BL/6) | NE-/- | 6 months | decreased vs. WT | Partial Protection(~60%) vs. WT | | (Shapiro et al., 2003) |
| mouse (C57BL/6) | MMP-12-/- | 6 months | decreased macrophages, but not neutrophils vs. WT | complete protection vs. WT | | (Hautamaki, Kobayashi, Senior, & Shapiro, 1997) |
| Pallid Mouse | α1-antitrypsin deficient | 6 months | CD4+ increased | Significant Increase vs. WT at 4 months | | (Takubo et al., 2002) |
| Pallid Mouse | α1-antitrypsin deficient | 6 months | not reported | Significant Increase vs. WT at 4 months | | (Cavarra et al., 2001) |
| Guinea Pig | broad spectrum MMP inhibitor | 6 months | decreased vs. untreated | Partial Protection(~30%) vs. untreated | | (Selman et al., 2003) |
| Guinea Pig | MMP-9 and -12 inhibitor | 6 months | decreased vs. untreated | Partial Protection (~70%) vs. untreated | decreased matrix breakdown products in BAL and airway remodeling | (Churg et al., 2007) |
| mouse (C57BL/6) | MMP-9 overexpression | n/a | not reported | Significant Increase vs. WT at 1 year | loss of elastin associated with emphysema | (R. Foronjy et al., 2008) |
| mouse (C57BL/6) | Lung MMP-12 overexpression | n/a | Increased | Significant Increase vs. WT | tumors developed over time | (Qu, Du, Wang, & Yan, 2009) |

continued **Table 6.1:** Role of protease:antiprotease imbalance in mouse models of COPD.

| Species | Manipulation | Cigarette Smoke Exposure | Inflammatory Response | Development of Emphysema | Comments | Reference |
|---|---|---|---|---|---|---|
| mouse (C57BL/6) | cathepsin S inhibitor used on lung IFNγ overexpressing mouse | n/a | not reported | decreased vs. untreated | reduced apoptosis | (Zheng et al., 2005) |

Nishikawa, 1999; Smith, 2002). In mice, cigarette smoke exposure activates the NRF2 protein, a redox sensitive protein critical to the expression of detoxification and antioxidant genes (Rangasamy, 2004). In addition, a broad panoply of antioxidant genes is activated in a NRF2 dependent manner after cigarette smoke exposure (Rangasamy, 2004). Important to the pathogenesis of COPD, NRF2 deficient mice exposed to cigarette smoke have a significantly enhanced inflammatory response, develop more severe emphysema and increased lung apoptosis, and have significantly enhanced levels of oxidative stress relative to wild-type mice (Iizuka, 2005; Rangasamy, 2004). In agreement with this observation, lung specific deletion of KEAP1, an inhibitor of NRF2 activation, leads to an increased basal antioxidant status and decreased pulmonary inflammation after cigarette smoke exposure (Blake, 2009). In conclusion, oxidative stress likely contributes to the development of COPD through multiple mechanisms.

## 6.7 Airway Inflammation in COPD

The significance of chronic inflammation observed in COPD has been demonstrated experimentally (Table 6.3) (Cosio, 2009; Hogg, 2004; Rennard, 2006). Increased inflammation occurs throughout the lungs in the large and small airways, as well as in the parenchyma (Hogg, 2004). It is believed that the inflammation surrounding the small airways is the most significant contributor to airflow limitation (Hogg, 2004). Additionally, patients with severe disease who quit smoking exhibit sustained inflammation and lung function decline, further implicating inflammation as a critical process in COPD development and progression (Gamble, 2007; Turato, 1995). Detailed below are the known functions of specific inflammatory cells in the development of COPD. Although individual cell types contribute to disease development in a number of ways, numerous types of immune cells likely act in a collective, reciprocal manner to cause disease. In addition, identification of the specific functions and roles of each cell type in the pathogenesis of COPD will provide new therapeutic targets.

**Table 6.2:** Role of oxidative stress in mouse models of COPD.

| Species | Manipulation | Cigarette Smoke Exposure | Inflammatory Response | Development of Emphysema | Comments | Reference |
|---|---|---|---|---|---|---|
| Guinea Pig | recombinant superoxide dismutase (SOD) | acute | significantly decreased vs. untreated | not measured | decreased IL-8 and NK-κB activation | (Nishikawa et al., 1999) |
| Rat | catalytic antioxidant | acute | significantly decreased vs. untreated | not measured | decreased MIP-2, airway metaplasia | (Smith et al., 2002) |
| Mouse (C57BL/6xCBA/J) | Transgenic overexpression of CuZnSOD (antioxidant) | 12 months | decreased vs. WT | complete protection vs. WT | protects against lipid peroxidation | (R. F. Foronjy et al., 2006) |
| Mouse (ICR) | NRF2-/- | 6 months | significantly increased vs. WT | earlier and more severe | decreased apoptosis | (Rangasamy et al., 2004) |
| Mouse (BALB/c) | NRF2-/- | 4 months | significantly increased vs. WT | earlier and more severe | decreased TNFα | (Iizuka et al., 2005) |
| Mouse (C57BL/6) | Lung specific KEAP1-/- | acute | significantly decreased vs. WT | not measured | Increased basal antioxidant genes | (Blake et al., 2009) |

### 6.7.1 Epithelium

Alveolar and airway epithelial cells are important in the pathogenesis of COPD. Epithelial cells exposed to cigarette smoke produce a diverse array of inflammatory mediators including TNFα, IL-1β, GM-CSF, IL-8, MCP-1, and LTB4 (Masubuchi, 1998; Mio, 1997). Emphysema develops partly due to apoptotic cell death of the lung epithelial cells, possibly through the actions of cytotoxic lymphocytes or oxidative stress (Chung, 2008; Majo, 2001).

### 6.7.2 Neutrophils

The numbers of activated neutrophils, characterized by increased respiratory burst and granule enzyme release, are greatly increased in the sputum and BAL of COPD patients and smaller increases are detectable in the airways and parenchyma (Finkelstein, 1995; Keatings, 1996; Lacoste, 1993; Pettersen, 2002). The number of circulating and lung neutrophils correlates with the decline in $FEV_1$ and neutrophil numbers in induced sputum correlate with COPD severity, thus implicating them in disease progression (Baraldo, 2004; Keatings, 1996; Sparrow, 1984). It is likely these changes are induced by IL-8. IL-8 is chemotactic for neutrophils, activates neutrophils, and expression is increased in COPD patients (Barnes, 2003; Pettersen, 2002). It is unknown how neutrophils specifically contribute to disease progression, but neutrophils secrete a number of proteases important in COPD pathogenesis such as neutrophil elastase, cathepsin G, proteinase-3, as well as matrix metalloproteinase MMP-8 and MMP-9 (Barnes, 2003). Thus, neutrophils are believed to be crucially involved in tipping the protease:antiprotease balance to a more proteolytic environment within the lungs of individuals with COPD. This hypothesis is further supported by the observation that neutrophil elastase knockout mice are partially protected from disease development after cigarette smoke exposure (Table 6.1) (Shapiro, 2003). Interestingly, although neutrophils can cause an increase in proteases that can cause experimental emphysema, similar emphysematous destruction is not observed in other chronic pulmonary diseases dominated by neutrophils like cystic fibrosis and bronchiectasis (Barnes, 2003).

### 6.7.3 Macrophages

Macrophages are significant contributors to the pathogenesis of COPD. There is an overwhelming increase in the number of macrophages in the BAL and sputum, airways, and parenchyma in COPD patients (Barnes, 2003). Further, macrophages are localized to sites of tissue destruction in COPD (Finkelstein, 1995; Meshi, 2002) and there is a correlation of macrophages with the severity of disease (Di Stefano, 1998). Macrophages secrete a number of inflammatory mediators after exposure to cigarette smoke that may activate and recruit additional cell types (Barnes, 2003). Additionally, alveolar macrophages taken from COPD patients are intrinsically altered, and secrete more inflammatory mediators and have more proteolytic activity at baseline (Barnes, 2003). Macrophages are also significant sources of destructive proteases MMP-2, -9, and -12, and cathepsin K, L, and S, that have key functions in the development of COPD in various mouse models (Table 6.1).

### 6.7.4 Eosinophils

In COPD patients, the number of eosinophils is increased in the sputum, BAL, and airway walls and there are elevated levels of eosinophil cationic protein in the BAL and sputum (Fujimoto, 1999; Lacoste, 1993; Lams, 1998; Linden, 1993; Panzner, 2003). Cytokines that are associated with eosinophilia in asthma, IL-4 and IL-5, are also upregulated in COPD (Zhu, 2007). During COPD exacerbations, the number of eosinophils is increased and IL-5 production is enhanced (Saetta, 1996; Zhu, 2001). It is unclear whether these increases in eosinophil numbers in COPD represents a distinct subgroup of patients with concomitant COPD and asthma, and it is equally unclear whether eosinophilia in COPD correlates to severity of disease. However, patients with enhanced numbers of eosinophils typically respond well to inhaled corticosteroids (Chanez, 1997; Pizzichini, 1998).

### 6.7.5 Mast Cells

Mast cells are present in the airways and alveoli of healthy individuals (Andersson, 2009b; Carroll, 2002) and have critical roles in innate immunity, T cell regulation, and antigen presentation. Despite the fact that these essential functions suggest that mast cells might have a pivotal role in COPD pathogenesis (Dawicki, 2007; Jawdat, 2006; Metz, 2008), very few studies have examined mast cell function in the context of COPD. Although increases in mast cells have been reported in the airways of COPD patients (Grashoff, 1997; Pesci, 1994), a more recent study demonstrated a reduction in mast cells in COPD patients, and that fewer numbers of mast cells correlated with worse lung function suggesting a protective, regulatory role for mast cells in COPD (Gosman, 2008). An additional study corroborates this finding and demonstrated that mast cell numbers decreased with increasing disease severity (Andersson, 2009a). In addition, these authors found that as COPD worsened, the mast cell populations in the lung underwent changes in density, distribution, and molecular phenotype implicating them in COPD pathogenesis (Andersson, 2009a).

### 6.7.6 γδ T Cells

Very little is known about the function of γδ T cells in COPD. γδ T cells are increased in the airways, bronchoalveolar lavage, and peripheral blood of smokers, regardless of whether they have emphysema (Ekberg-Jansson, 2000; Majo, 2001; Pons, 2005; Richmond, 1993). In some cases, the number of γδ T cells is reduced in patients with COPD compared with their levels in smokers (Pons, 2005). γδ T cells are important regulators of tissue repair and mucosal homeostasis (Jameson, 2003). Consistent with this role, the absence of γδ T cells caused enhanced caspase-dependent epithelial cell death in a mouse model of COPD, although inflammation was not affected (Borchers, 2008). Based upon these observations, not only are γδ T cell numbers reduced in COPD but their function may also be impaired.

### 6.7.7 Natural Killer (NK) Cells

There are few studies examining NK cells in COPD, and therefore the role of NK cells in COPD is relatively unknown. One study has shown no increases in NK cells in the lung parenchyma in COPD patients relative to controls, but this study was limited by small sample sizes (Majo, 2001). In contrast, two additional studies using a greater number of samples demonstrated an increase of NK cells in the lungs of COPD patients (Di Stefano, 1998; Elliott, 2009). Importantly, NK cell numbers correlated with disease severity (Di Stefano, 1998; Elliott, 2009). A major function of NK cells is their capacity for cell specific, directed cytotoxicity mediated through the release of perforin and granzymes that induce target apoptosis. Localized inflammatory sites in the lungs of COPD patients are rich with granzyme A+ and granzyme B+ NK cells (Vernooy, 2007). Additionally, the expression of NK cell perforin and granzyme B, as well as functional NK cell cytotoxic effector function, was shown to be increased in the sputum of COPD patients (Urbanowicz, 2009). In a corollary study, perforin and granzyme B expression was increased in peripheral blood NK cells of COPD patients and smokers (n=60) (Hodge, 2006), but this observation was not reproduced by two separate groups using a small number of patients (n=10) (Morissette, 2007). Therefore, it is likely that NK cells contribute to apoptotic cell death and the development of emphysema in COPD. Recent data demonstrate an additional role for NK cells in COPD. In COPD patients, there is increased expression of MICA on the lung epithelium, a stress-inducible ligand for the NK cell activating receptor NKG2D (Borchers, 2009). Importantly, expression of MICA on the lung epithelium correlates with disease severity. Experimentally, chronic cigarette smoke exposure also induced expression of NKG2D ligands on the mouse airway and alveolar epithelium. These observations provide strong support for a role of NKG2D activation and NK cells, in particular, in the development of COPD. In contrast, there is some data suggesting that NK cells may be functionally suppressed in COPD.

### 6.7.8 Natural Killer T (NKT) Cells

A role for NKT cells in COPD is ill-defined and is limited by the overall paucity of studies. CD56+CD3+ NKT-like cell number and function is reduced in the peripheral blood of COPD patients (Urbanowicz, 2009). However, this report is severely limited by the use of very few patients (n=10), the majority of whom were using inhaled corticosteroids, a variable known to interfere with functional assays. In one study, no differences in the numbers of Type-1, invariant NKT (iNKT) cells were detected in the sputum of COPD patients with stable disease or during COPD exacerbations (Vijayanand, 2007). However, in a more recent study using immunohistochemistry, increased numbers of iNKT cells were found in the lungs of COPD patients. iNKT cells stimulate the production of IL-13 which drives alternative activation of macrophages and leads to macrophage generated IL-13 in a feed-forward loop. Persistent IL-13 production is believed to contribute to protease activation, mucus hypersecretion, and mucus cell hyperplasia, all important phenotypic changes in COPD.

### 6.7.9 T Cells

In COPD patients, there are increased numbers of T cells in the lung parenchyma and peripheral and central airways, and, in severe COPD, T cells are located within lymphoid follicles adjacent to airways (Cosio, 2002; Finkelstein, 1995; Hogg, 2004; Majo, 2001; O'Shaughnessy, 1997; Retamales, 2001; Saetta, 1999; Saetta, 1998). Similar to COPD patients, CD3+ T cells are organized in lymphoid follicles in mice chronically exposed to cigarette smoke, suggesting a common mechanism (Bracke, 2006). Although both CD4+ and CD8+ T cell numbers increase, the greatest elevation is in the CD8+ T cell population (Hogg, 2004; Majo, 2001; Saetta, 1999; Saetta, 1998). Significantly, the increase in CD8+ T cells directly correlates with lung function decline (Saetta, 1999; Saetta, 1998). There is also an increase in the number of CD8+ T cells in the peripheral blood of COPD patients who don't smoke (de Jong, 1997; Kim, 2002). Further, peripheral T cells are more activated in COPD patients, and activation correlates with the loss of lung function (Zhu, 2009). Mouse models exhibit the hallmark features of COPD including mucus cell metaplasia, airspace enlargement and peribronchial/perivascular infiltration of neutrophils, macrophages, and T cells. In these models, CD8-deficient mice (but not CD4-deficient mice) fail to develop these key features of COPD, including macrophage accumulation and airspace enlargement (Borchers, 2007; Maeno, 2007). While evidence mounts supporting a causal role for T cells in COPD, the initial stimulus remains to be identified. The most likely mechanism driving T cell-mediated pathology is antigen-specific clonal expansion. In support of this theory, oligoclonal expansions of CD4+ and CD8+ T cells are detected in the lungs of COPD patients (Korn, 2005; Sullivan, 2005). Although the antigen specificity or function of T cells in COPD remains wholly uninvestigated, it is probable that oligoclonal expansions reflect recognition of self antigens. In support of this idea, T cells reactive with elastin have recently been demonstrated in COPD patients. It is unclear what role autoreactive T cells may play, but T cell recognition of antigens present on the lung epithelium may cause robust inflammation and the production of cytokines and chemokines in COPD (Enelow, 1998; Zhao, 2000). Presently, mechanistic data supporting a causal role for T cells in the development or progression of COPD are limited. Derangement of the alveolar architecture may be caused by multiple processes including matrix breakdown as well as epithelial and endothelial cell destruction. The prevailing theory is that T cells are aberrantly activated in COPD patients and contribute to tissue destruction through both direct and indirect effector mechanisms. The direct mechanisms likely involve CD8+ T cell-mediated apoptosis of alveolar cells via the elaboration of cytotoxic granules (perforin-granzyme) or Fas molecules (Henkart, 1994). Along these lines, alveolar epithelial cell apoptosis correlates with CD8+ T cell numbers in emphysema (Majo, 2001) and this theory is supported by evidence that CD8+ T cells in patients with COPD express high levels of perforin with a concomitant enhanced lytic capacity (Chrysofakis, 2004). Indirect mechanisms whereby lymphocyte activation contributes to COPD are more complex and difficult to assess. However, a role for the broad inflammatory cell recruitment and activation in COPD patients and experimental models seems likely. For example, many studies indicate that the production of Th1 cytokines such as IFNγ (Di Stefano, 2004; Grumelli, 2004; Hodge, 2007) and TNFα (Aaron, 2001; Keatings, 1996) are increased in T cells of COPD patients. Di Stefano *et al.* reported that the number of STAT4-positive cells (a transcription factor critical fohr the development of Th1 lineage cytotoxic T cells and IFNγ production) are increased compared to healthy smokers and non-smokers (Di Stefano, 2004). Furthermore, the number of STAT4+ lymphocytes correlated with increased airflow obstruction and IFNγ+ lymphocytes. In a more detailed study, Grumelli *et al.* demonstrated that lung function decline in patients with COPD correlated with Th1 cell markers on both CD4+ and CD8+ T cells, and these cells secreted increased amounts of IFNγ, but not IL-4, relative to control patients (Grumelli, 2004). IFNγ induction may amplify inflammation and increase macrophage metalloproteinase secretion which can lead to matrix degradation and alveolar destruction (Grumelli, 2004; Wang, 2000). Grumelli *et al.* (Grumelli, 2004) also provided a mechanistic link between increased T cell activation and emphysema by demonstrating enhanced production of CXCR3 ligands (*i.e.*, IP-10) which leads to increased MMP-12 activation (elastin-degrading protease linked to emphysema) by alveolar macrophages. In addition to their pro-inflammatory effector function, subpopulations of CD4+ T cells (*i.e.*, regulatory T cells) may also serve to limit the adaptive immune responses. In the context of COPD, a breakdown in the function of these cells may lead to increased expansion of pathogenic T cells.

### 6.7.10 B Cells

CD20+ B cells are increased in the lungs of COPD patients (Gosman, 2006; Hogg, 2004). Importantly, the number or presence of CD20+ B cells in airways and periphery correlates with disease severity (Gosman, 2006; Hogg, 2004). Most often, B cells are organized in lymphoid follicles in COPD patients that are interspersed with CD4+ and CD8+ T cells (Hogg, 2004; Kelsen, 2009; van der Strate, 2006). Interestingly, lymphoid follicles containing high numbers of B cells also develop in mice chronically exposed to cigarette smoke (Bracke, 2006; D'Hulst, 2005; van der Strate, 2006). Currently, it is unknown whether B cells are specifically required for the development of COPD. A primary function of B cells is the generation of antigen-specific antibodies. Differentiated antibody producing B cells, known as plasma B cells, also are increased in the lungs of COPD patients (J. Zhu, 2007), and B cells organized in lymphoid follicles were identified as being oligoclonal, suggesting specific, antigen-directed antibody production (van der Strate, 2006). B cells are likely responding to self-antigens because, in addition to elastin-reactive T cells, elastin-reactive antibodies are present in COPD patients (Lee, 2007). Further evidence for a self-antigen comes from the observation that COPD patients have pulmonary epithelial cell-reactive antibodies (Feghali-Bostwick, 2008).

### 6.7.11 Dendritic Cells

Dendritic cells (DCs) are key cells in antigen presentation and bridge the gap between the innate and adaptive immune system. Increases in DCs occur in patients and mouse models of COPD (D'Hulst, 2005; Demedts, 2007; Freeman, 2009) and the DCs frequently have an activated phenotype (D'Hulst, 2005; Freeman, 2009). Maturation of DCs correlates with disease severity, strongly suggesting a mechanistic role for DCs in COPD (Freeman, 2009). Further, the expression of maturation markers correlates with the activation of CD4+ T cells in COPD patients (Freeman, 2009). However, evidence has accumulated for roles of DCs in COPD independent of their antigen presentation capabilities. Myeloid dendritic cells isolated from the lungs of COPD patients were able to induce Th1 and Th17 responses in the absence of antigen presentation (Shan, 2009). Additionally, *in vitro* exposure of dendritic cells to cigarette smoke extract induced the expression of inflammatory mediators leading to the activation and proliferation of co-cultured CD8+ T cells, providing a potential link between DCs and CD8+ T cell accumulation in COPD (Mortaz, 2009).

## 6.8 Cytokines and Chemokines in COPD

Cytokines and chemokines are involved in a diverse array of COPD phenotypes including the recruitment and activation of macrophages, neutrophils, T cells, B cells, and other immune cells. Cytokines and chemokines are also believed to be involved in the processes of airway remodeling, mucus cell hyperplasia, and emphysema. Therefore, the roles of cytokines and chemokines in COPD are multitudinous. CCL1/I-309, CCL2/MCP-1, CCL3/MIP-1α, CCL4/MIP-1β, CCL11/eotaxin, CXCL1/GROα, CXCL5/ENA-78, CXCL8/IL-8, IL-1β, IL-6, IL-18, IFNγ, IP-10, GM-CSF, and TNFα are among the many cytokines and chemokines that are increased in individuals with COPD (Chung, 2008). These increases are detected in the lung tissue, sputum, or the BAL fluid, and the levels of cytokines and chemokines frequently correlate with disease severity (Chung, 2008). These cytokines and chemokines are frequently derived from a number of resident inflammatory cells as well as the airway epithelium (Chung, 2008). In addition to the cytokines mentioned here, a number of additional cytokines and chemokines are undoubtedly increased in COPD but have yet to be studied. The study of cytokine and chemokines in the development of COPD phenotypes has been aided using mouse models of COPD. Studies utilizing mice that have had either cytokines/chemokines or their receptors knocked out are almost always protected from the development of emphysema, and have reduced inflammation after smoke exposure. Conversely, a number of studies have utilized mice that overexpress proinflammatory cytokines/chemokines explicitly in the lung, and these mice develop COPD-like disease (emphysema and inflammation).

## 6.9 COPD as an Autoimmune Disease

Autoimmune diseases are chronic inflammatory conditions caused by failure of self-tolerance mechanisms. Although it is not completely understood how this breakdown occurs, it likely results from a complex interplay of genetics, failure of natural tolerance, and environmental triggers. The defining criteria for autoimmune diseases are classically defined by Witebsky's postulates (Rose, 1993) a) circumstantial evidence consisting of lymphocytic infiltration of the target organ or association of the disease with a particular MHC haplotype, b) indirect evidence consisting of the isolation of autoantibodies or self-reactive T cells from the organ or identification of human antigen and using immunization processes to reproduce the disease in animals, and finally, c) direct proof consisting of reproducing the disease in a normal recipient by the direct transfer of autoantibodies or T cells. Based on the associations of T cell numbers with declining lung function in COPD patients and evidence that inflammation persists in COPD patients upon smoking cessation (Gamble, 2007; Turato, 1995), Cosio and colleagues proposed the existence of an autoimmune component in COPD (Cosio, 2002; Cosio, 2009). Since then, multiple lines of evidence have accumulated supporting this hypothesis. As mentioned above, oligoclonal T cells and B cells that can react with self-antigens have been identified. Recent evidence that maturation of dendritic cells correlates with T cell activation COPD further supports this hypothesis (Freeman, 2009). In addition, single nucleotide polymorphisms in multiple HLA loci associate with the severity of COPD (DeMeo, 2008). Therefore, since the early hypothesis, a significant body of evidence has accumulated suggesting that COPD has an autoimmune component. Moreover, the possibility exists that the cigarette smoke-induced autoreactivity may have broader implications for systemic manifestations of COPD as cigarette smoking has been identified as a risk factor for established autoimmune diseases such as rheumatoid arthritis (Papadopoulos, 2005), Graves disease (Prummel, 1993), and biliary cirrhosis (Gershwin, 2005).

## 6.10 Systemic Inflammation

The presence of low-grade systemic inflammation is a well-known characteristic of COPD (Agusti, 2003; Gan, 2004). Patients with stable COPD have an increased numbers of circulating leukocytes occasionally present with an activated phenotype (Noguera, 2001; Noguera, 1998). Further, activation of circulating lymphocytes correlates with lung function (Zhu, 2009). Further, COPD patients have increased circulating levels of inflammatory mediators such as C-reactive protein, fibrinogen, IL-6, and TNFa (Agusti, 2003). Additionally, the severity of this inflammation is increased during exacerbations of COPD (Hurst, 2006). Because COPD is overwhelmingly associated with an abnormal inflammatory response in the lungs, it has been proposed that the systemic inflammatory response is simply the result of a spilling over effect from the lungs (Agusti, 2007). However, several investigators were unable to find relationships between inflammation using specific measured variables in the lungs and blood of individual patients (Hurst, 2005; Vernooy, 2002). Therefore, it's really unknown whether a spillover is really a sufficient explanation. Interestingly, several extrapulmonary diseases frequently associated with COPD are also associated with a systemic inflammatory response (Agusti, 2007).

### 6.10.1 Cardiovascular Disease

COPD and cardiovascular disease (CVD) share the common risk factor of cigarette smoking. Additionally, COPD and CVD patients share commonalities such as advanced age and decrease in physical activity. However, several lines of evidence have established that, independent of known risk factors including smoking, COPD correlates as an independent risk factor for CVD (Rodriguez-Roisin, 2008; Sin, 2006). COPD is a significant risk factor for a broad spectrum of CVD manifestations such as atherosclerosis, ischemic heart disease, stroke and sudden cardiac death (Sin, 2006). In patients with mild COPD, complications from CVD are overwhelming the cause (42%) for first time hospitalization (Rodriguez-Roisin, 2008; Sin, 2006). In contrast, respiratory complications are the cause for only 14% of hospitilzations. Most important, CVD is extremely important in COPD as between 25–50% (depending on the study) of all COPD deaths are due to complications of cardiovascular disease (Rodriguez-Roisin, 2008; Sin, 2006). The exact mechanisms involved in cardiac disease in COPD patients are unknown. As described above, patients with COPD have significant levels of systemic inflammation. Systemic inflammation is a key risk factor for the development of CVD (Buffon, 2002). Because systemic inflammation is a common feature in patients with COPD, even in mild to moderate stages, it has been suggested by multiple investigators as a key component of CVD risk. Particularly, increased levels of C-reactive protein is significant risk factor for combined COPD and CVD (Sin, 2003). More work is needed in this area.

### 6.10.2 Nutritional Abnormalities

Divergent Weight Loss and Obesity in COPD. Numerous nutritional abnormalities have been detected in patients with COPD (Nici, 2006; Schols, 2000). Changes in the basal metabolic rate, caloric intake, and body composition are common in patients with COPD (Nici, 2006; Schols, 2000). Weight loss with no apparent explanation occurs in about half of patients with severe COPD, but is also detected in about 15% of COPD patients with mild to modeate disease (Creutzberg, 1998; Nici, 2006). It is believed that weight loss is not due to loss of fat, rather the majority of loss is in skeletal muslcle mass (Schols, 2000). Further, recent weight loss is a significant predictor of future mortality and morbidity (Nici, 2006). Although these changes may be responsible for changes in caloric intake, increases in basal metabolic rate from medications, systemic inflammation, and/or tissue hypoxia have been proposed (Agusti, 2005).

Briefly, metabolic syndrome is characterized by a multitude of factors including abdominal obesity, atherogenic dyslipidemia, hypertension, and insulin resistance (Watz, 2009). In contrast to the description of weight loss above, a signicant number of COPD patients have coexisting metabolic syndrome or obesity (Watz, 2009; Franssen, 2008). Further, obesity is more prevalent in patients with COPD than in the general population (Franssen, 2008). Interestingly, the metabolic syndrome and obesity in COPD patients was associated with increases in markers of systemic inflammation CRP and IL-6 (Watz, 2009). Further, in this study there was a correlation between an increase in severity of COPD and a lower BMI (Watz, 2009). Studies have demonstrated that patients with a predominance of chronic bronchitis are more likely to have a higher BMI, whereas patients with predominantly emphysema will have a lower BMI (Ogawa, 2009). Whatever the mechanism behind the obsesity-COPD relationship, obesity nonetheless is a major problem for COPD patients as obese patients are frequently exercise intolerant, a major problem for exercise-based pulmonary rehabilitation therapies (Franssen, 2008).

### 6.10.3 Skeletal Muscle Dysfunction

Skeletal muscle dysfunction is extremely common in COPD patients (Nici, 2006). There are specific anatomic changes as well as functional changes (Nici, 2006). The precise mechanism underlying muscle wasting is unknown, but could be due to inactivity-induced deconditioning, systemic inflammation, use of medications, oxidative stress or reductions in muscle mass (Nici, 2006). Although little is known in on this topic, these changes significantly contribute to loss of exercise capacity critical for pulmonary rehabilitation and a reduction in the quality of life (Nici, 2006).

### 6.10.4 Osteoporosis

The incidence of osteoporosis is also increased in patients with COPD. The specific causes are unknown, but have been speculated to caused by malnutrition, smoking, steroid use, lack of exercise, and systemic inflammation (Agusti, 2003). However, little is known about osteoporosis in COPD beyond that.

### 6.10.5 Neurological Disorders

There are significant alterations in the nervous system in patients with COPD. The actual bioenergeentic metabolism of the brain is altered in patients with COPD (Mathur, 1999). Importantly, COPD patients frequently suffer depression (Light, 1985; Xu, 2008; Maurer, 2008). The depression and anxiety in COPD have been found to be important and serious risk factors for disease progression (Xu, 2008). It's likely that depression develops in response to having a chronic disease. However, it's been proposed that systemic inflammation may also be involved (Agusti, 2003).

## 6.11 COPD Exacerbations

The underlying COPD pathologies are punctuated by exacerbations of symptoms. Standard criteria for COPD exacerbations do not exist, but they are generally characterized by increased dyspnea, enhanced sputum, enhanced inflammation, and decline in lung function (Bhowmik, 2000; Sapey, 2006), (see Chapters 16, COPD Exacerbations Outpatient Management, and 17, COPD Exacerbations Inpatient Management). Consequently, exacerbations accelerate disease progression and are an integral part of disease pathogenesis. The toll of COPD exacerbations is also psychologically destructive; patients with frequent exacerbations have a lower quality of life and decreased mobility, leading to increased depression (Quint, 2008). Most importantly, exacerbations that require hospitalization result in death 8–11% of the time, and the remaining patients have a mortality rate of 23–43% one year following admission (Connors, 1996; Groenewegen, 2003). Between 40 and 60% of exacerbations are believed to be caused by viral infections (Celli, 2007; Sapey, 2006). The remaining exacerbations are likely the result of non-viral infections and pollution, although roughly 20% have an unknown etiology (Celli, 2007). Exacerbations associated with viral infections are severe; viral exacerbations lead to hospitalization more often than other causes, and have a longer recovery time (Wedzicha, 2004). The connection between viruses and COPD exacerbations remained mostly associative until, in a recent landmark study, Kang *et al.* experimentally demonstrated that exacerbations of symptoms following cigarette smoke (CS) exposure can be caused by viral infection (Kang, 2008). Key to the progression of COPD, viral infection following CS exposure led to enhanced pulmonary inflammation, increased alveolar apoptosis, accelerated emphysema, and airway fibrosis (Kang, 2008). However, the underlying cellular mechanisms responsible for these effects remain undiscovered.

## 6.12 Summary Points

1. The pathophysiology of COPD is incompletely understood, but is thought to involve chronic inflammation, oxidative stress, and increased elastolytic potential in the lung
2. Increased numbers of macrophages, neutrophils, lymphocytes and eosinophils in and around the airways, parenchyma, and vasculature characterize the inflammation. Pathogenesis of COPD is examined mechanistically. Current and future research into the pathways that lead to COPD will provide insight into much needed therapeutic targets.
3. COPD also manifests systemically including systemic inflammation, skeletal muscle dysfunction, metabolic syndrome, cardiovascular disease, osteoporosis, and neurological defects
4. Enhanced understanding of the role of the immune system in acute exacerbations in COPD is critical in the future identification of susceptible patients and the development of new therapeutic strategies.

## References

Aaron, S.D., Angel, J.B., Lunau, M., Wright, K., Fex, C., Le Saux, N., & Dales, R.E. (2001). Granulocyte inflammatory markers and airway infection during acute exacerbation of chronic obstructive pulmonary disease. *Am J Respir Crit Care Med, 163*(2), 349–355.

Adenuga, D., Yao, H., March, T.H., Seagrave, J., & Rahman, I. (2009). Histone deacetylase 2 is phosphorylated, ubiquitinated, and degraded by cigarette smoke. *Am J Respir Cell Mol Biol, 40*(4), 464–473.

Adler, K.B., Holden-Stauffer, W.J., & Repine, J.E. (1990). Oxygen metabolites stimulate release of high-molecular-weight glycoconjugates by cell and organ cultures of rodent respiratory epithelium via an arachidonic acid-dependent mechanism. *J Clin Invest, 85*(1), 75–85.

Agusti, A. (2007). Systemic effects of chronic obstructive pulmonary disease: what we know and what we don't know (but should). *Proc Am Thorac Soc, 4*(7), 522–525.

Agusti, A.G. (2005). Systemic effects of chronic obstructive pulmonary disease. *Proc Am Thorac Soc, 2*(4), 367–370; discussion 371–362.

Agusti, A.G., Noguera, A., Sauleda, J., Sala, E., Pons, J., & Busquets, X. (2003). Systemic effects of chronic obstructive pulmonary disease. *Eur Respir J, 21*(2), 347–360.

Andersson, C.K., Mori, M., Bjermer, L., Lofdahl, C.G., & Erjefalt, J.S. (2009a). Alterations in Lung Mast Cell Populations in Patients with COPD. *Am J Respir Crit Care Med.*

Andersson, C.K., Mori, M., Bjermer, L., Lofdahl, C.G., & Erjefalt, J.S. (2009b). Novel site-specific mast cell subpopulations in the human lung. *Thorax, 64*(4), 297–305.

Baraldo, S., Turato, G., Badin, C., Bazzan, E., Beghe, B., Zuin, R., Saetta, M. (2004). Neutrophilic infiltration within the airway smooth muscle in patients with COPD. *Thorax, 59*(4), 308–312.

Barnes, P.J. (2004). Small airways in COPD. *N Engl J Med, 350*(26), 2635–2637.

Barnes, P.J., Shapiro, S.D., & Pauwels, R.A. (2003). Chronic obstructive pulmonary disease: molecular and cellular mechanisms. *Eur Respir J, 22*(4), 672–688.

Bhowmik, A., Seemungal, T.A. R., Sapsford, R.J., & Wedzicha, J.A. (2000). Relation of sputum inflammatory markers to symptoms and lung function changes in COPD exacerbations. *Thorax, 55*(2), 114–120.

Blake, D.J., Singh, A., Kombairaju, P., Malhotra, D., Mariani, T.J., Tuder, R.M., Biswal, S. (2009). Deletion of Keap1 in the Lung Attenuates Acute Cigarette Smoke-induced Oxidative Stress and Inflammation. *Am J Respir Cell Mol Biol.*

Borchers, M.T., Wesselkamper, S.C., Curull, V., Ramirez-Sarmiento, A., Sánchez-Font, A., Garcia-Aymerich, J., Orozco-Levi, M. (2009). Sustained CTL activation by murine pulmonary epithelial cells promotes the development of COPD-like disease. *J Clin Invest, 119*(3), 636–649.

Borchers, M.T., Wesselkamper, S.C., Eppert, B.L., Motz, G.T., Sartor, M.A., Tomlinson, C.R., Tichelaar, J.W. (2008). Nonredundant Functions of {alpha}{beta} and {gamma}{delta} T Cells in Acrolein-Induced Pulmonary Pathology. *Toxicol Sci, 105*(1), 188–199.

Borchers, M.T., Wesselkamper, S.C., Harris, N.L., Deshmukh, H., Beckman, E., Vitucci, M., Leikauf, G.D. (2007). CD8+ T cells contribute to macrophage accumulation and airspace enlargement following repeated irritant exposure. *Exp Mol Pathol, 83*(3), 301–310.

Bosken, C.H., Wiggs, B.R., Pare, P.D., & Hogg, J.C. (1990). Small airway dimensions in smokers with obstruction to airflow. *Am Rev Respir Dis, 142*(3), 563–570.

Bracke, K.R., D'Hulst, A I., Maes, T., Moerloose, K.B., Demedts, I.K., Lebecque, S., Brusselle, G.G. (2006). Cigarette Smoke-Induced Pulmonary Inflammation and Emphysema Are Attenuated in CCR6-Deficient Mice. *J Immunol, 177*(7), 4350–4359.

Buffon, A., Biasucci, L.M., Liuzzo, G., D'Onofrio, G., Crea, F., & Maseri, A. (2002). Widespread coronary inflammation in unstable angina. *N Engl J Med, 347*(1), 5–12.

Buist, A.S., Vollmer, W.M., & McBurnie, M.A. (2008). Worldwide burden of COPD in high- and low-income countries. Part I. The burden of obstructive lung disease (BOLD) initiative. *Int J Tuberc Lung Dis, 12*(7), 703–708.

Carroll, N.G., Mutavdzic, S., & James, A.L. (2002). Distribution and degranulation of airway mast cells in normal and asthmatic subjects. *Eur Respir J, 19*(5), 879–885.

Cavarra, E., Bartalesi, B , Lucattelli, M., Fineschi, S., Lunghi, B., Gambelli, F., Lungarella, G. (2001). Effects of cigarette smoke in mice with different levels of alpha(1)-proteinase inhibitor and sensitivity to oxidants. *Am J Respir Crit Care Med, 164*(5), 886–890.

Celli, B.R., & Barnes, P.J (2007). Exacerbations of chronic obstructive pulmonary disease. *Eur Respir J, 29*(6), 1224–1238.

Chanez, P., Vignola, A.M., O'Shaugnessy, T., Enander, I., Li, D., Jeffery, P.K., & Bousquet, J. (1997). Corticosteroid reversibility in COPD is related to features of asthma. *Am J Respir Crit Care Med, 155*(5), 1529–1534.

Chrysofakis, G., Tzanakis, N., Kyriakoy, D., Tsoumakidou, M., Tsiligianni, I., Klimathianaki, M., & Siafakas, N.M. (2004). Perforin expression and cytotoxic activity of sputum CD8+ lymphocytes in patients with COPD. *Chest, 125*(1), 71–76.

Chung, K.F., & Adcock, I.M. (2008) Multifaceted mechanisms in COPD: inflammation, immunity, and tissue repair and destruction. *Eur Respir J, 31*(6), 1334–1356.

Churg, A., Wang, R., Wang, X., Onnervik, P.O., Thim, K., & Wright, J.L. (2007). Effect of an MMP-9/MMP-12 inhibitor on smoke-induced emphysema and airway remodelling in guinea pigs. *Thorax, 62*(8), 706–713.

Churg, A., Wang, R.D., Xie, C., & Wright, J.L. (2003). alpha-1-Antitrypsin ameliorates cigarette smoke-induced emphysema in the mouse. *Am J Respir Crit Care Med, 168*(2), 199–207.

Connors, A.F., Jr., Dawson, N.V., Thomas, C., Harrell, F.E., Jr., Desbiens, N., Fulkerson, W.J., Knaus, W.A. (1996). Outcomes following acute exacerbation of severe chronic obstructive lung disease. The SUPPORT investigators (Study to Understand Prognoses and Preferences for Outcomes and Risks of Treatments). *Am J Respir Crit Care Med, 154*(4 Pt 1), 959–967.

Cosio, M.G., Hale, K.A., & Niewoehner, D.E. (1980). Morphologic and morphometric effects of prolonged cigarette smoking on the small airways. *Am Rev Respir Dis, 122*(2), 265–221.

Cosio, M.G., Majo, J., & Cosio, M.G. (2002). Inflammation of the Airways and Lung Parenchyma in COPD. *Chest, 121*(5 suppl), 160S-165S.

Cosio, M.G., Saetta, M., & Agusti, A. (2009). Immunologic Aspects of Chronic Obstructive Pulmonary Disease. *N Engl J Med, 360*(23), 2445–2454.

Coultas, D.B., Mapel, D., Gagnon, R., & Lydick, E. (2001). The health impact of undiagnosed airflow obstruction in a national sample of United States adults. *Am J Respir Crit Care Med, 164*(3), 372–377.

Creutzberg, E.C., Schols, A.M., Bothmer-Quaedvlieg, F.C., & Wouters, E.F. (1998). Prevalence of an elevated resting energy expenditure in patients with chronic obstructive pulmonary disease in relation to body composition and lung function. *Eur J Clin Nutr, 52*(6), 396–401.

D'Hulst A, I., Maes, T., Bracke, K.R., Demedts, I.K., Tournoy, K.G., Joos, G.F., & Brusselle, G.G. (2005). Cigarette smoke-induced pulmonary emphysema in scid-mice. Is the acquired immune system required? *Respir Res, 6*, 147.

D'Hulst, A.I., Vermaelen, K.Y., Brusselle, G.G., Joos, G.F., & Pauwels, R.A. (2005). Time course of cigarette smoke-induced pulmonary inflammation in mice. *Eur Respir J, 26*(2), 204–213.

Dawicki, W., & Marshall, J.S. (2007). New and emerging roles for mast cells in host defence. *Curr Opin Immunol, 19*(1), 31–38.

de Boer, W.I., van Schadewijk, A., Sont, J.K., Sharma, H.S., Stolk, J., Hiemstra, P.S., & van Krieken, J.H. (1998). Transforming growth factor beta1 and recruitment of macrophages and mast cells in airways in chronic obstructive pulmonary disease. *Am J Respir Crit Care Med, 158*(6), 1951–1957.

de Jong, J.W., van der Belt-Gritter, B., Koeter, G.H., & Postma, D.S. (1997). Peripheral blood lymphocyte cell subsets in subjects with chronic obstructive pulmonary disease: association with smoking, IgE and lung function. *Respir Med, 91*(2), 67–76.

Demedts, I.K., Bracke, K.R., Van Pottelberge, G., Testelmans, D., Verleden, G.M., Vermassen, F.E., Brusselle, G.G. (2007). Accumulation of Dendritic Cells and Increased CCL20 Levels in the Airways of Patients with Chronic Obstructive Pulmonary Disease. *Am J Respir Crit Care Med, 175*(10), 998–1005.

DeMeo, D., Campbell, E.J., Rennard, S.I., Delorey, T.M., Barker, A.F., Brantly, M.L., Silverman, E.K. (2008). *Association of MHC region SNPs with airflow obstruction in severe Alpha 1-Antitrypsin Deficiency*, Philadelphia, PA.

Di Stefano, A., Capelli, A., Lusuardi, M., Balbo, P., Vecchio, C., Maestrelli, P., Saetta, M. (1998). Severity of airflow limitation is associated with severity of airway inflammation in smokers. *Am J Respir Crit Care Med, 158*(4), 1277–1285.

Di Stefano, A., Caramori, G., Capelli, A., Gnemmi, I., Ricciardolo, F.L., Oates, T., Adcock, I.M. (2004). STAT4 activation in smokers and patients with chronic obstructive pulmonary disease. *Eur Respir J, 24*(1), 78–85.

Ekberg-Jansson, A., Andersson, B., Avra, E., Nilsson, O., & Lofdahl, C.G. (2000). The expression of lymphocyte surface antigens in bronchial biopsies, bronchoalveolar lavage cells and blood cells in healthy smoking and never-smoking men, 60 years old. *Respir Med, 94*(3), 264–272.

Elliott, W., McDonough, J., Wladichuck, A., Buzatu, L., Utokaparch, S., Javadifard, A., Hogg, J. (2009). The Nature of the Mucosal Immune Response in COPD. *Am. J. Respir. Crit. Care Med., 179*(1_MeetingAbstracts), A2837-.

Enelow, R.I., Mohammed, A.Z., Stoler, M.H., Liu, A.N., Young, J.S., Lou, Y.H., & Braciale, T.J. (1998). Structural and functional consequences of alveolar cell recognition by CD8(+) T lymphocytes in experimental lung disease. *J Clin Invest, 102*(9), 1653–1661.

Feghali-Bostwick, C.A., Gadgil, A.S., Otterbein, L.E., Pilewski, J.M., Stoner, M.W., Csizmadia, E., Duncan, S.R. (2008). Autoantibodies in patients with chronic obstructive pulmonary disease. *Am J Respir Crit Care Med, 177*(2), 156–163.

Finkelstein, R., Fraser, R.S., Ghezzo, H., & Cosio, M.G. (1995). Alveolar inflammation and its relation to emphysema in smokers. *Am J Respir Crit Care Med, 152*(5 Pt 1), 1666–1672.

Foronjy, R., Nkyimbeng, T., Wallace, A., Thankachen, J., Okada, Y., Lemaitre, V., & D'Armiento, J. (2008). Transgenic expression of matrix metalloproteinase-9 causes adult-onset emphysema in mice associated with the loss of alveolar elastin. *Am J Physiol Lung Cell Mol Physiol, 294*(6), L1149–1157.

Foronjy, R.F., Mirochnitchenko, O., Propokenko, O., Lemaitre, V., Jia, Y., Inouye, M., D'Armiento, J.M. (2006). Superoxide dismutase expression attenuates cigarette smoke- or elastase-generated emphysema in mice. *Am J Respir Crit Care Med, 173*(6), 623–631.

Franssen, F.M., O'Donnell, D.E., Goossens, G.H., Blaak, E.E., & Schols, A.M. (2008). Obesity and the lung: 5. Obesity and COPD. *Thorax, 63*(12), 1110–1117.

Freeman, C.M., Martinez, F.J., Han, M.K., Ames, T.M., Chensue, S.W., Todt, J.C., Curtis, J.L. (2009). Lung Dendritic Cell Expression of Maturation Molecules Increases with Worsening COPD. *Am J Respir Crit Care Med, 180*, 1179–1188.

Fujimoto, K., Kubo, K., Yamamoto, H., Yamaguchi, S., & Matsuzawa, Y. (1999). Eosinophilic inflammation in the airway is related to glucocorticoid reversibility in patients with pulmonary emphysema. *Chest, 115*(3), 697–702.

Gamble, E., Grootendorst, D.C., Hattotuwa, K., O'Shaughnessy, T., Ram, F.S., Qiu, Y., Barnes, N.C. (2007). Airway mucosal inflammation in COPD is similar in smokers and ex-smokers: a pooled analysis. *Eur Respir J*.

Gan, W.Q., Man, S.F., Senthilselvan, A., & Sin, D.D. (2004). Association between chronic obstructive pulmonary disease and systemic inflammation: a systematic review and a meta-analysis. *Thorax, 59*(7), 574–580.

Gershwin, M.E., Selmi, C., Worman, H.J., Gold, E.B., Watnik, M., Utts, J., Vierling, J.M. (2005). Risk factors and comorbidities in primary biliary cirrhosis: a controlled interview-based study of 1032 patients. *Hepatology, 42*(5), 1194–1202.

Gosman, M.M., Postma, D.S., Vonk, J.M., Rutgers, B., Lodewijk, M., Smith, M., Timens, W. (2008). Association of mast cells with lung function in chronic obstructive pulmonary disease. *Respir Res, 9*, 64.

Gosman, M.M., Willemse, B.W., Jansen, D.F., Lapperre, T.S., van Schadewijk, A., Hiemstra, P.S., Kerstjens, H.A. (2006). Increased number of B-cells in bronchial biopsies in COPD. *Eur Respir J, 27*(1), 60–64.

Grashoff, W.F., Sont, J.K., Sterk, P.J., Hiemstra, P.S., de Boer, W.I., Stolk, J., van Krieken, J.M. (1997). Chronic obstructive pulmonary disease: role of bronchiolar mast cells and macrophages. *Am J Pathol, 151*(6), 1785–1790.

Groenewegen, K.H., Schols, A.M. W.J., & Wouters, E.F. M. (2003). Mortality and Mortality-Related Factors After Hospitalization for Acute Exacerbation of COPD. *Chest, 124*(2), 459–467.

Grumelli, S., Corry, D.B., Song, L.Z., Song, L., Green, L., Huh, J., Kheradmand, F. (2004). An Immune Basis for Lung Parenchymal Destruction in Chronic Obstructive Pulmonary Disease and Emphysema. *Plos Med, 1*(1), e8.

Halbert, R.J., Natoli, J.L., Gano, A., Badamgarav, E., Buist, A.S., & Mannino, D.M. (2006). Global burden of COPD: systematic review and meta-analysis. *Eur Respir J, 28*(3), 523–532.

Hautamaki, R.D., Kobayashi, D.K., Senior, R.M., & Shapiro, S.D. (1997). Requirement for macrophage elastase for cigarette smoke-induced emphysema in mice. *Science, 277*(5334), 2002–2004.

Henkart, P.A. (1994). Lymphocyte-mediated cytotoxicity: two pathways and multiple effector molecules. *Immunity, 1*(5), 343–346.

Hodge, G., Nairn, J., Holmes, M., Reynolds, P.N., & Hodge, S. (2007). Increased intracellular T helper 1 proinflammatory cytokine production in peripheral blood, bronchoalveolar lavage and intraepithelial T cells of COPD subjects. *Clin Exp Immunol, 150*(1), 22–29.

Hogg, J.C., Chu, F., Utokaparch, S., Woods, R., Elliott, W.M., Buzatu, L., Pare, P.D. (2004). The Nature of Small-Airway Obstruction in Chronic Obstructive Pulmonary Disease. *N Engl J Med, 350*(26), 2645–2653.

Hogg, J.C., Wright, J.L., Wiggs, B.R., Coxson, H.O., Opazo Saez, A., & Pare, P.D. (1994). Lung structure and function in cigarette smokers. *Thorax, 49*(5), 473–478.

Hurst, J.R., Perera, W.R., Wilkinson, T.M., Donaldson, G.C., & Wedzicha, J.A. (2006). Systemic and upper and lower airway inflammation at exacerbation of chronic obstructive pulmonary disease. *Am J Respir Crit Care Med, 173*(1), 71–78.

Hurst, J.R., Wilkinson, T.M., Perera, W.R., Donaldson, G.C., & Wedzicha, J.A. (2005). Relationships among bacteria, upper airway, lower airway, and systemic inflammation in COPD. *Chest, 127*(4), 1219–1226.

Ihn, H. (2002). Pathogenesis of fibrosis: role of TGF-beta and CTGF. *Curr Opin Rheumatol, 14*(6), 681–685.

Iizuka, T., Ishii, Y., Itoh, K., Kiwamoto, T., Kimura, T., Matsuno, Y., Sekizawa, K. (2005). Nrf2-deficient mice are highly susceptible to cigarette smoke-induced emphysema. *Genes Cells, 10*(12), 1113–1125.

Innes, A.L., Woodruff, P.G., Ferrando, R.E., Donnelly, S., Dolganov, G.M., Lazarus, S.C., & Fahy, J.V. (2006). Epithelial mucin stores are increased in the large airways of smokers with airflow obstruction. *Chest, 130*(4), 1102–1108.

Ito, K., Ito, M., Elliott, W.M., Cosio, B., Caramori, G., Kon, O.M., Barnes, P.J. (2005). Decreased histone deacetylase activity in chronic obstructive pulmonary disease. *N Engl J Med, 352*(19), 1967–1976.

Jameson, J., Witherden, D., & Havran, W.L. (2003). T-cell effector mechanisms: gammadelta and CD1d-restricted subsets. *Curr Opin Immunol, 15*(3), 349–353.

Jawdat, D.M., Rowden, G., & Marshall, J.S. (2006). Mast cells have a pivotal role in TNF-independent lymph node hypertrophy and the mobilization of Langerhans cells in response to bacterial peptidoglycan. *J Immunol, 177*(3), 1755–1762.

Kang, M.J., Lee, C.G., Lee, J.Y., Dela Cruz, C.S., Chen, Z.J., Enelow, R., & Elias, J.A. (2008). Cigarette smoke selectively enhances viral PAMP- and virus-induced pulmonary innate immune and remodeling responses in mice. *J Clin Invest, 118*(8), 2771–2784.

Keatings, V.M., Collins, P.D., Scott, D.M., & Barnes, P.J. (1996). Differences in interleukin-8 and tumor necrosis factor-alpha in induced sputum from patients with chronic obstructive pulmonary disease or asthma. *Am J Respir Crit Care Med, 153*(2), 530–534.

Kelsen, S.G., Aksoy, M.O., Georgy, M., Hershman, R., Ji, R., Li, X., Kim, V. (2009). Lymphoid follicle cells in chronic obstructive pulmonary disease overexpress the chemokine receptor CXCR3. *Am J Respir Crit Care Med, 179*(9), 799–805.

Kim, W.D., Eidelman, D.H., Izquierdo, J.L., Ghezzo, H., Saetta, M.P., & Cosio, M.G. (1991). Centrilobular and panlobular emphysema in smokers. Two distinct morphologic and functional entities. *Am Rev Respir Dis, 144*(6), 1385–1390.

Kim, W.D., Kim, W.S., Koh, Y., Lee, S.D., Lim, C.M., Kim, D.S., & Cho, Y.J. (2002). Abnormal peripheral blood T-lymphocyte subsets in a subgroup of patients with COPD. *Chest, 122*(2), 437–444.

Korn, S., Wiewrodt, R., Walz, Y.C., Becker, K., Mayer, E., Krummenauer, F., & Buhl, R. (2005). Characterization of the interstitial lung and peripheral blood T cell receptor repertoire in cigarette smokers. *Am J Respir Cell Mol Biol, 32*(2), 142–148.

Lacoste, J.Y., Bousquet, J., Chanez, P., Van Vyve, T., Simony-Lafontaine, J., Lequeu, N., Michel, F.B. (1993). Eosinophilic and neutrophilic inflammation in asthma, chronic bronchitis, and chronic obstructive pulmonary disease. *J Allergy Clin Immunol, 92*(4), 537–548.

Lams, B.E., Sousa, A.R., Rees, P.J., & Lee, T.H. (1998). Immunopathology of the small-airway submucosa in smokers with and without chronic obstructive pulmonary disease. *Am J Respir Crit Care Med, 158*(5 Pt 1), 1518–1523.

Lee, S.H., Goswami, S., Grudo, A., Song, L.Z., Bandi, V., Goodnight-White, S., Kheradmand, F. (2007). Antielastin autoimmunity in tobacco smoking-induced emphysema. *Nat Med, 13*(5), 567–569.

Linden, M., Rasmussen, J.B., Piitulainen, E., Tunek, A., Larson, M., Tegner, H., Brattsand, R. (1993). Airway inflammation in smokers with nonobstructive and obstructive chronic bronchitis. *Am Rev Respir Dis, 148*(5), 1226–1232.

MacNee, W. (2000). Oxidants/antioxidants and COPD. *Chest, 117*(5 Suppl 1), 303S-317S.

MacNee, W. (2005). Pulmonary and systemic oxidant/antioxidant imbalance in chronic obstructive pulmonary disease. *Proc Am Thorac Soc, 2*(1), 50–60.

Maeno, T., Houghton, A.M., Quintero, P.A., Grumelli, S., Owen, C.A., & Shapiro, S.D. (2007). CD8+ T Cells are required for inflammation and destruction in cigarette smoke-induced emphysema in mice. *J Immunol, 178*(12), 8090–8096.

Majo, J., Ghezzo, H., & Cosio, M.G. (2001). Lymphocyte population and apoptosis in the lungs of smokers and their relation to emphysema. *Eur Respir J, 17*(5), 946–953.

Marwick, J.A., Kirkham, P.A., Stevenson, C.S., Danahay, H., Giddings, J., Butler, K., Rahman, I. (2004). Cigarette smoke alters chromatin remodeling and induces proinflammatory genes in rat lungs. *Am J Respir Cell Mol Biol, 31*(6), 633–642.

Masubuchi, T., Koyama, S., Sato, E., Takamizawa, A., Kubo, K., Sekiguchi, M., Izumi, T. (1998). Smoke extract stimulates lung epithelial cells to release neutrophil and monocyte chemotactic activity. *Am J Pathol, 153*(6), 1903–1912.

Mathur, R., Cox, I.J., Oatridge, A., Shephard, D.T., Shaw, R.J., & Taylor-Robinson, S.D. (1999). Cerebral bioenergetics in stable chronic obstructive pulmonary disease. *Am J Respir Crit Care Med, 160*(6), 1994–1999.

Maurer, J., Rebbapragada, V., Borson, S., Goldstein, R., Kunik, M.E., Yohannes, A.M., & Hanania, N.A. (2008). Anxiety and depression in COPD: current understanding, unanswered questions, and research needs. *Chest, 134*(4 Suppl), 43S-56S.

Meshi, B., Vitalis, T.Z., Ionescu, D., Elliott, W.M., Liu, C., Wang, X.D., Hogg, J.C. (2002). Emphysematous lung destruction by cigarette smoke. The effects of latent adenoviral infection on the lung inflammatory response. *Am J Respir Cell Mol Biol, 26*(1), 52–57.

Metz, M., Siebenhaar, F., & Maurer, M. (2008). Mast cell functions in the innate skin immune system. *Immunobiology, 213*(3–4), 251–260.

Mio, T., Romberger, D.J., Thompson, A.B., Robbins, R.A., Heires, A., & Rennard, S.I. (1997). Cigarette smoke induces interleukin-8 release from human bronchial epithelial cells. *Am J Respir Crit Care Med, 155*(5), 1770–1776.

Morissette, M.C., Parent, J., & Milot, J. (2007). Perforin, granzyme B, and FasL expression by peripheral blood T lymphocytes in emphysema. *Respir Res, 8*, 62.

Mortaz, E., Kraneveld, A.D., Smit, J.J., Kool, M., Lambrecht, B.N., Kunkel, S.L., Folkerts, G. (2009). Effect of cigarette smoke extract on dendritic cells and their impact on T-cell proliferation. *PLoS ONE, 4*(3), e4946.

Nakano, Y., Muro, S., Sakai, H., Hirai, T., Chin, K., Tsukino, M., Mishima, M. (2000). Computed tomographic measurements of airway dimensions and emphysema in smokers. Correlation with lung function. *Am J Respir Crit Care Med, 162*(3 Pt 1), 1102–1108.

Nici, L., Donner, C., Wouters, E., Zuwallack, R., Ambrosino, N., Bourbeau, J., Troosters, T. (2006). American Thoracic Society/European Respiratory Society statement on pulmonary rehabilitation. *Am J Respir Crit Care Med, 173*(12), 1390–1413.

Nishikawa, M., Kakemizu, N., Ito, T., Kudo, M., Kaneko, T., Suzuki, M., Okubo, T. (1999). Superoxide mediates cigarette smoke-induced infiltration of neutrophils into the airways through nuclear factor-kappaB activation and IL-8 mRNA expression in guinea pigs in vivo. *Am J Respir Cell Mol Biol, 20*(2), 189–198.

Noguera, A., Batle, S., Miralles, C., Iglesias, J., Busquets, X., MacNee, W., & Agusti, A.G. (2001). Enhanced neutrophil response in chronic obstructive pulmonary disease. *Thorax, 56*(6), 432–437.

Noguera, A., Busquets, X., Sauleda, J., Villaverde, J.M., MacNee, W., & Agusti, A.G. (1998). Expression of adhesion molecules and G proteins in circulating neutrophils in chronic obstructive pulmonary disease. *Am J Respir Crit Care Med, 158*(5 Pt 1), 1664–1668.

O'Shaughnessy, T.C., Ansari, T.W., Barnes, N.C., & Jeffery, P.K. (1997). Inflammation in bronchial biopsies of subjects with chronic bronchitis: inverse relationship of CD8+ T lymphocytes with FEV1. *Am J Respir Crit Care Med, 155*(3), 852–857.

Ogawa, E., Nakano, Y., Ohara, T., Muro, S., Hirai, T., Sato, S., Mishima, M. (2009). Body mass index in male patients with COPD: correlation with low attenuation areas on CT. *Thorax, 64*(1), 20–25.

Panzner, P., Lafitte, J.J., Tsicopoulos, A., Hamid, Q., & Tulic, M.K. (2003). Marked up-regulation of T lymphocytes and expression of interleukin-9 in bronchial biopsies from patients With chronic bronchitis with obstruction. *Chest, 124*(5), 1909–1915.

Papadopoulos, N.G., Alamanos, Y., Voulgari, P.V., Epagelis, E.K., Tsifetaki, N., & Drosos, A.A. (2005). Does cigarette smoking influence disease expression, activity and severity in early rheumatoid arthritis patients? *Clin Exp Rheumatol, 23*(6), 861–866.

Pesci, A., Rossi, G.A., Bertorelli, G., Aufiero, A., Zanon, P., & Olivieri, D. (1994). Mast cells in the airway lumen and bronchial mucosa of patients with chronic bronchitis. *Am J Respir Crit Care Med, 149*(5), 1311–1316.

Petrache, I., Natarajan, V., Zhen, L., Medler, T.R., Richter, A.T., Cho, C., Tuder, R.M. (2005). Ceramide upregulation causes pulmonary cell apoptosis and emphysema-like disease in mice. *Nat Med, 11*(5), 491–498.

Pettersen, C.A., & Adler, K.B. (2002). Airways inflammation and COPD: epithelial-neutrophil interactions. *Chest, 121*(5 Suppl), 142S-150S.

Pizzichini, E., Pizzichini, M.M., Gibson, P., Parameswaran, K., Gleich, G.J., Berman, L., Hargreave, F.E. (1998). Sputum eosinophilia predicts benefit from prednisone in smokers with chronic obstructive bronchitis. *Am J Respir Crit Care Med, 158*(5 Pt 1), 1511–1517.

Pons, J., Sauleda, J., Ferrer, J.M., Barcelo, B., Fuster, A., Regueiro, V., Agusti, A.G. N. (2005). Blunted {gamma}{delta} T-lymphocyte response in chronic obstructive pulmonary disease. *Eur Respir J, 25*(3), 441–446.

Prescott, E., Lange, P., & Vestbo, J. (1995). Chronic mucus hypersecretion in COPD and death from pulmonary infection. *Eur Respir J, 8*(8), 1333–1338.

Prummel, M.F., & Wiersinga, W.M. (1993). Smoking and risk of Graves' disease. *Jama, 269*(4), 479–482.

Qu, P., Du, H., Wang, X., & Yan, C. (2009). Matrix metalloproteinase 12 overexpression in lung epithelial cells plays a key role in emphysema to lung bronchioalveolar adenocarcinoma transition. *Cancer Res, 69*(18), 7252–7261.

Quint, J.K., Baghai-Ravary, R., Donaldson, G.C., & Wedzicha, J.A. (2008). Relationship between depression and exacerbations in COPD. *Eur Respir J, 32*(1), 53–60. doi: 10.1183/09031936.00120107

Rangasamy, T., Cho, C.Y., Thimmulappa, R.K., Zhen, L., Srisuma, S.S., Kensler, T.W., Biswal, S. (2004). Genetic ablation of Nrf2 enhances susceptibility to cigarette smoke-induced emphysema in mice. *J Clin Invest, 114*(9), 1248–1259.

Rennard, S.I., & Vestbo, J. (2006). COPD: the dangerous underestimate of 15%. *Lancet, 367*(9518), 1216–1219.

Retamales, I., Elliott, W.M., Meshi, B., Coxson, H.O., Pare, P.D., Sciurba, F.C., Hogg, J.C. (2001). Amplification of inflammation in emphysema and its association with latent adenoviral infection. *Am J Respir Crit Care Med, 164*(3), 469–473.

Richmond, I., Pritchard, G.E., Ashcroft, T., Corris, P.A., & Walters, E.H. (1993). Distribution of gamma delta T-cells in the bronchial tree of smokers and non-smokers. *J Clin Pathol, 46*(10), 926–930.

Rodriguez-Roisin, R., & Soriano, J.B. (2008). Chronic obstructive pulmonary disease with lung cancer and/or cardiovascular disease. *Proc Am Thorac Soc, 5*(8), 842–847.

Rose, N.R., & Bona, C. (1993). Defining criteria for autoimmune diseases (Witebsky's postulates revisited). *Immunol Today, 14*(9), 426–430.

Saetta, M., Baraldo, S., Corbino, L., Turato, G., Braccioni, F., Rea, F., Fabbri, L.M. (1999). CD8+ve cells in the lungs of smokers with chronic obstructive pulmonary disease. *Am J Respir Crit Care Med, 160*(2), 711–717.

Saetta, M., Di Stefano, A., Maestrelli, P., Turato, G., Mapp, C.E., Pieno, M., Fabbri, L.M. (1996). Airway eosinophilia and expression of interleukin-5 protein in asthma and in exacerbations of chronic bronchitis. *Clin Exp Allergy, 26*(7), 766–774.

Saetta, M., Di Stefano, A., Turato, G., Facchini, F.M., Corbino, L., Mapp, C.E., Fabbri, L.M. (1998). CD8+ T-lymphocytes in peripheral airways of smokers with chronic obstructive pulmonary disease. *Am J Respir Crit Care Med, 157*(3 Pt 1), 822–826.

Sapey, E., & Stockley, R.A. (2006). COPD exacerbations . 2: aetiology. *Thorax, 61*(3), 250–258.

Schols, A.M. (2000). Nutrition in chronic obstructive pulmonary disease. *Curr Opin Pulm Med, 6*(2), 110–115.

Selman, M., Cisneros-Lira, J., Gaxiola, M., Ramirez, R., Kudlacz, E.M., Mitchell, P.G., & Pardo, A. (2003). Matrix metalloproteinases inhibition attenuates tobacco smoke-induced emphysema in Guinea pigs. *Chest, 123*(5), 1633–1641.

Shan, M., Cheng, H.-F., Song, L.-z., Roberts, L., Green, L., Hacken-Bitar, J., Kheradmand, F. (2009). Lung Myeloid Dendritic Cells Coordinately Induce TH1 and TH17 Responses in Human Emphysema. *Science Translational Medicine, 1*(4), 4ra10–14ra10.

Shapiro, S.D., Goldstein, N.M., Houghton, A.M., Kobayashi, D.K., Kelley, D., & Belaaouaj, A. (2003). Neutrophil elastase contributes to cigarette smoke-induced emphysema in mice. *Am J Pathol, 163*(6), 2329–2335.

Sin, D.D., Anthonisen, N.R., Soriano, J.B., & Agusti, A.G. (2006). Mortality in COPD: Role of comorbidities. *Eur Respir J, 28*(6), 1245–1257.

Sin, D.D., & Man, S.F. (2003). Why are patients with chronic obstructive pulmonary disease at increased risk of cardiovascular diseases? The potential role of systemic inflammation in chronic obstructive pulmonary disease. *Circulation, 107*(11), 1514–1519.

Smith, K.R., Uyeminami, D.L., Kodavanti, U.P., Crapo, J.D., Chang, L.Y., & Pinkerton, K.E. (2002). Inhibition of tobacco smoke-induced lung inflammation by a catalytic antioxidant. *Free Radic Biol Med, 33*(8), 1106–1114.

Sparrow, D., Glynn, R.J., Cohen, M., & Weiss, S.T. (1984). The relationship of the peripheral leukocyte count and cigarette smoking to pulmonary function among adult men. *Chest, 86*(3), 383–386.

Stang, P., Lydick, E., Silberman, C., Kempel, A., & Keating, E.T. (2000). The prevalence of COPD: using smoking rates to estimate disease frequency in the general population. *Chest, 117*(5 Suppl 2), 354S-359S.

Sullivan, A.K., Simonian, P.L., Falta, M.T., Mitchell, J.D., Cosgrove, G.P., Brown, K.K., Fontenot, A.P. (2005). Oligoclonal CD4+ T Cells in the Lungs of Patients with Severe Emphysema. *Am J Respir Crit Care Med, 172*(5), 590–596.

Takizawa, H., Tanaka, M., Takami, K., Ohtoshi, T., Ito, K., Satoh, M., Umeda, A. (2001). Increased expression of transforming growth factor-beta1 in small airway epithelium from tobacco smokers and patients with chronic obstructive pulmonary disease (COPD). *Am J Respir Crit Care Med, 163*(6), 1476–1483.

Takubo, Y., Guerassimov, A., Ghezzo, H., Triantafillopoulos, A., Bates, J.H., Hoidal, J.R., & Cosio, M.G. (2002). Alpha1-antitrypsin determines the pattern of emphysema and function in tobacco smoke-exposed mice: parallels with human disease. *Am J Respir Crit Care Med, 166*(12 Pt 1), 1596–1603.

Turato, G., Di Stefano, A., Maestrelli, P., Mapp, C.E., Ruggieri, M.P., Roggeri, A., Saetta, M. (1995). Effect of smoking cessation on airway inflammation in chronic bronchitis. *Am J Respir Crit Care Med, 152*(4 Pt 1), 1262–1267.

Urbanowicz, R., Lamb, J., Corne, J., & Fairclough, L. (2009). Cytotoxic Cells in the Induced Sputum of Smokers with COPD. *Am. J. Respir. Crit. Care Med., 179*(1_MeetingAbstracts), A4297-.

Urbanowicz, R., Lamb, J., Todd, I., Corne, J., & Fairclough, L. (2009). Altered effector function of peripheral cytotoxic cells in COPD. *Respiratory Research, 10*(1), 53.

van der Strate, B.W., Postma, D.S., Brandsma, C.A., Melgert, B.N., Luinge, M.A., Geerlings, M., Kerstjens, H.A. (2006). Cigarette smoke-induced emphysema: A role for the B cell? *Am J Respir Crit Care Med, 173*(7), 751–758.

Vernooy, J.H., Kucukaycan, M., Jacobs, J.A., Chavannes, N.H., Buurman, W.A., Dentener, M.A., & Wouters, E.F. (2002). Local and systemic inflammation in patients with chronic obstructive pulmonary disease: soluble tumor necrosis factor receptors are increased in sputum. *Am J Respir Crit Care Med, 166*(9), 1218–1224.

Vernooy, J.H., Moller, G.M., van Suylen, R.J., van Spijk, M.P., Cloots, R.H., Hoet, P.H., Wouters, E.F. (2007). Increased granzyme A expression in type II pneumocytes of patients with severe chronic obstructive pulmonary disease. *Am J Respir Crit Care Med, 175*(5), 464–472.

Vestbo, J., Prescott, E., & Lange, P. (1996). Association of chronic mucus hypersecretion with FEV1 decline and chronic obstructive pulmonary disease morbidity. Copenhagen City Heart Study Group. *Am J Respir Crit Care Med, 153*(5), 1530–1535.

Vijayanand, P., Seumois, G., Pickard, C., Powell, R.M., Angco, G., Sammut, D., Djukanovic, R. (2007). Invariant natural killer T cells in asthma and chronic obstructive pulmonary disease. *N Engl J Med, 356*(14), 1410–1422.

Wan, E.S., & Silverman, E.K. (2009). Genetics of COPD and emphysema. *Chest, 136*(3), 859–866.

Wang, Z., Zheng, T., Zhu, Z., Homer, R.J., Riese, R.J., Chapman, H.A., Jr., Elias, J.A. (2000). Interferon gamma induction of pulmonary emphysema in the adult murine lung. *J Exp Med, 192*(11), 1587–1600.

Watz, H., Waschki, B., Kirsten, A., Muller, K.C., Kretschmar, G., Meyer, T., Magnussen, H. (2009). The metabolic syndrome in patients with chronic bronchitis and COPD: frequency and associated consequences for systemic inflammation and physical inactivity. *Chest, 136*(4), 1039–1046.

Wedzicha, J.A. (2004). Role of Viruses in Exacerbations of Chronic Obstructive Pulmonary Disease. *Proc Am Thorac Soc, 1*(2), 115–120.

Wright, J.L., Farmer, S.G., & Churg, A. (2002). Synthetic serine elastase inhibitor reduces cigarette smoke-induced emphysema in guinea pigs. *Am J Respir Crit Care Med, 166*(7), 954–960.

Xu, W., Collet, J.P., Shapiro, S., Lin, Y., Yang, T., Platt, R.W., Bourbeau, J. (2008). Independent effect of depression and anxiety on chronic obstructive pulmonary disease exacerbations and hospitalizations. *Am J Respir Crit Care Med, 178*(9), 913–920.

Zhao, M.Q., Stoler, M.H., Liu, A.N., Wei, B., Soguero, C., Hahn, Y.S., & Enelow, R.I. (2000). Alveolar epithelial cell chemokine expression triggered by antigen-specific cytolytic CD8(+) T cell recognition. *J Clin Invest, 106*(6), R49–58.

Zheng, T., Kang, M.J., Crothers, K., Zhu, Z., Liu, W., Lee, C.G., Elias, J.A. (2005). Role of Cathepsin S-Dependent Epithelial Cell Apoptosis in IFN-{gamma}-Induced Alveolar Remodeling and Pulmonary Emphysema. *J Immunol, 174*(12), 8106–8115.

Zhu, J., Qiu, Y., Valobra, M., Qiu, S., Majumdar, S., Matin, D., Jeffery, P.K. (2007). Plasma cells and IL-4 in chronic bronchitis and chronic obstructive pulmonary disease. *Am J Respir Crit Care Med, 175*(11), 1125–1133.

Zhu, X., Gadgil, A.S., Givelber, R., George, M.P., Stoner, M.W., Sciurba, F.C., & Duncan, S.R. (2009). Peripheral T Cell Functions Correlate with the Severity of Chronic Obstructive Pulmonary Disease. *J Immunol, 182*(5), 3270–3277.

Zhu, Z., Lee, C.G., Zheng, T., Chupp, G., Wang, J., Homer, R.J., Elias, J.A. (2001). Airway inflammation and remodeling in asthma. Lessons from interleukin 11 and interleukin 13 transgenic mice. *Am J Respir Crit Care Med, 164*(10 Pt 2), S67–70.

Shari Altum, Ph.D., Katherine Butler, Psy.D., Rachel Juran, Psy.D.

# 7 Smoking Cessation

Key Points:
1. Smoking cessation is the single most important approach to preventing and treating COPD.
2. Abstinence from smoking tobacco is associated with a variety of health improvements, including decreased mortality and reduced risk of developing lung cancer, myocardial infarction, and stroke.
3. Patients should be screened for tobacco use at every visit; patients who do use tobacco products should be asked about any smoking-related concerns and desire to stop smoking.
4. It is important to investigate a patient's stage-of-change when discussing smoking cessation and ask questions that are appropriate to the patient's current stage.
5. Nicotine replacement therapies and other tobacco treatment medications, used either alone or in combination with counseling, lead to the highest cessation rates.

## 7.1 Introduction

Smoking-related deaths and diseases are preventable but continue to affect a considerable number of individuals. Tobacco use is thought to be responsible for more than 438,000 premature deaths each year in the United States and is considered to be one of the main risk factors responsible for the development of Chronic Obstructive Pulmonary Disease (COPD). Although there are other causes of COPD, 80–90% of those (in the United States and the developed world) who have been diagnosed with COPD are current or past smokers (Rabe, 2007). Parker and Eaton (2012) suggest that the most important approach to preventing and treating COPD in current smokers is smoking cessation. They also suggest that smoking cessation is the only evidenced-based treatment that makes impactful physical changes in multiple areas of functioning (i.e., reduces the accelerated rate of lung function decline, decreases symptoms of cough and sputum, and reduces COPD exacerbations). Their research also indicates that smoking cessation is associated with a short-term increase in lung function (up to 50 mL increase in the forced expiratory volume in one second, FEV1), which lasts approximately one year, followed by a continued decline in lung functioning at the rate of a nonsmoker.

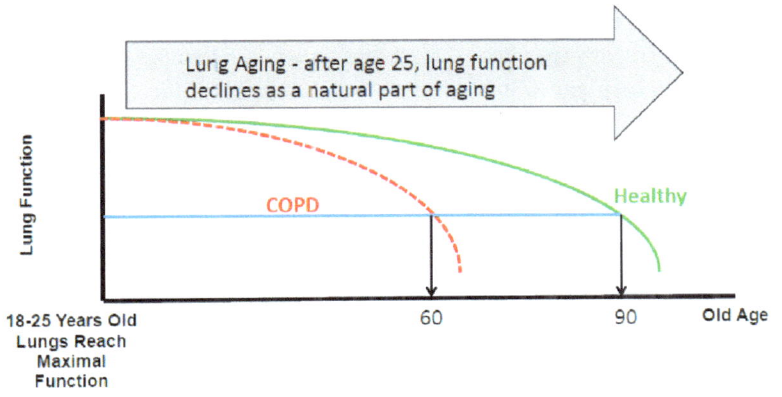


**Figure 7.1:** Lung Age. Lung function reaches a maximal level between 18 and 25 years of age and then naturally declines. In individuals with COPD, the rate of decline of lung function is accelerated. Hence, COPD can be considered pulmonary physiologic progeria which is captured by the term "lung age". Lung age is the physiologic age of the lungs extrapolated from the normal predicted values of lung function based upon age and is compared with an individual's chronologic age to illustrate the accelerated decline in lung function that occurs with COPD. For example, a 60 year old individual with significant airflow imitation might have spirometry ($FEV_1$ and FVC) that would be normal for a 90 year old; thus, this person has a lung (physiologic) age of 90 but is only 60 years old chronologically. This level of lung function is illustrated by the horizontal blue line. An individual with COPD might reach this level of lung function at age 60 but this level is what is expected for a healthy individual who is 90 years old, the two vertical black arrows.

## 7.2 Smoking Risks

The risks of increased disability and premature death for smokers who have COPD is reflected in Figure 7.1 (Lung Age Graph; Panos, 2014). The graph also depicts improvements in longevity and health that might be gained when one stops smoking. Research indicates that complete abstinence from tobacco decreases mortality and reduces the risks of developing lung cancer, myocardial infarction, and stroke (Anthonisen, 2005). Non-smokers who have COPD can experience disease exacerbations, including increased cough and sputum production, if exposed to passive smoke (Leuenberger, 1994). Complete elimination of exposure to tobacco smoke, whether active or passive, is recommended.

## 7.3 Factors Associated with Cessation

COPD develops after years of tobacco use. Approximately 50% of current smokers over the age of 75 have COPD (Lundback, 2003). Older age, along with the duration and severity of nicotine dependence, add to the challenges of quitting (Tashkin, 2001).

A chronic illness model is often used to conceptualize tobacco use (Burke, 2008). Smoking cessation is a process that occurs across a series of attempts that finally culminate in permanent abstinence. Smokers often relapse after quitting; half of the patients who reach six months of abstinence will smoke again within eight years (Yudkin, 2003). Thus, ongoing assessment and relapse prevention are important even after a patient successfully quits. It is recommended that health care providers continue to engage with patients who have experienced a smoking relapse, similar to how patients who have poorly-controlled hypertension or diabetes are treated.

## 7.4 Screening Recommendations

The Clinical Practice Guideline for Treating Tobacco Use and Dependence (henceforth known as Clinical Practice Guideline; U.S. Department of Health and Human Services, 2008) recommends that all patients be screened for tobacco use at every visit. Screening is especially critical for patients who are at risk for or have been diagnosed with COPD. This recommendation applies to all healthcare professionals (e.g., primary care providers, specialty physicians, nurses, dentists, psychologists, pharmacists). A team approach, in which each health care provider with whom the patient has contact explores the patient's concerns and readiness for change, is optimal.

More than 70% of the 45 million smokers in the United States report that they would like to quit, and approximately 44% of these smokers attempt to quit each year (Centers for Disease Control and Prevention, 2006). However, whereas smokers might view quitting as desirable or important, they might also lack the skills, abilities, resources, and/or coping strategies needed to feel confident in their ability to succeed. The distinction between how *important* it is to quit and how *confident* the patient is in his/her ability to quit is critical. Health care providers might erroneously assume that smokers are not concerned or do not care about the negative effects of smoking on their health when the actual barrier to quitting might actually be a patient's lack of confidence in their ability to succeed.

A patient's stance on smoking cessation can be quickly and easily assessed with the *Importance and Confidence Rulers* (Miller, 2013). After determining that the patient is a current smoker, the provider might ask a few exploratory questions:

- "What are your thoughts about quitting?"
- "What concerns you the most about continuing to smoke?"
- "What would be the benefits of quitting?"
- "On a scale from 1 to 10, with 1 being 'not at all important' and 10 being 'the most important thing in your life,' how important is it for you to stop smoking?"

With regard to the last question, the health care provider should follow-up on the patient's response by asking why the patient chose that number and not a lower number (e.g., "Why is it a seven and not a three?"). Ideally, the patient will verbalize desires, reasons, and needs for quitting, which reinforces the likelihood that the patient will quit. These questions provide a relatively quick (i.e., three to five minutes) way for the provider to clarify the patient's knowledge and concerns about tobacco use which can then be used to tailor the rest of the discussion to the patient's individual needs. Further, the act of verbalizing how important it is to quit is associated with increased behavioral change (Miller, 2009). Patients who report an importance level of seven or higher tend to be more motivated to make a change.

If a patient indicates an importance level of seven or higher, a few questions about how he or she would quit smoking should follow:

- "What are your thoughts about how you might quit?"
- "What resources or supports will you need to help you quit?"
- "What might get in the way?"
- "On a scale from 1 to 10, with 1 being 'not at all confident' and 10 being 'completely confident,' how confident are you that you can stop smoking?"

Once again, with regard to the last question, the health care provider should follow-up on the patient's response by asking why the patient chose that number and not a lower number. A confidence level of seven or higher is again associated with higher likelihood of making a change. Exploring these questions with patients is necessary, as patients might not be aware of many of the resources available to assist with tobacco cessation, or they may feel ambivalent about whether the resources will actually help them. Patients might benefit from receiving information from providers about effective strategies for smoking cessation, which will be addressed later in this chapter. Refer to *The Five R's – Strategies to Enhance Motivation to Quit* (Table 7.1) for more detailed information about exploring importance and confidence levels.

For patients who are not ready to attempt smoking cessation, the Clinical Practice Guideline (2008) suggests making a professional recommendation that the patient quit. Approximately 5–10% of patients quit smoking based upon a clinical recommendation from their healthcare provider alone (Wilson, 1990). Some possible statements might include, "As your provider, it is important for me to tell you that quitting tobacco is the single most important thing you can do to improve your health" or "I am not sure if you realize, but quitting tobacco is the most effective treatment for COPD. It can slow the progression of the disease and improve breathlessness. I would like to help you quit whenever you are ready."

For those who have successfully quit, screening for current use and risks for relapse remains important, as tobacco dependence is a chronic condition and may require multiple quit attempts and treatment interventions.

**Table 7.1:** The Five R's: Strategies to Enhance Motivation to Quit

| R's | Motivational Factors | Sample Open-Ended Questions | Possible Patient Responses |
|---|---|---|---|
| **R**elevance | Importance | "What are your thoughts about quitting smoking?" | Patient offers specific personal concerns that might include:<br>– prior quitting experiences<br>– desires and reasons to quit<br>– perceived ability to quit<br>– personal barriers to cessation |
| **R**isks | Importance | "What concerns you the most about continuing to smoke?" | Provider reflects patients concerns and may probe for concern in three specific areas:<br>– Acute risks: Shortness of breath, chronic cough, respiratory infections, harm to pregnancy, impotence, infertility, loss of smell and taste.<br>*e.g., "What symptoms are you experiencing that seem related to smoking?"*<br>– Long-term risks: Increased risk for heart attacks, strokes, vascular disease, lung and other cancers; increased likelihood of long-term disability and need for extended care.<br>*e.g., "How do you think your smoking affects your COPD and overall health?"*<br>– Environmental risks: Increased risk of lung cancer and heart disease in household family members; higher rates of smoking in children of tobacco users; increased risk of low birth weight, sudden infant death syndrome (SIDS), asthma, middle ear disease, and respiratory infections in children of smokers; fires.<br>*e.g., "What concerns you about the affect your smoking has on your family?"* |

continued **Table 7.1:** The Five R's: Strategies to Enhance Motivation to Quit

| R's | Motivational Factors | Sample Open-Ended Questions | Possible Patient Responses |
|---|---|---|---|
| Rewards | Importance | "What would be the benefits of quitting?" | The specific rewards identified by the patient should be reflected and emphasized several times throughout the conversation. Rewards include:<br>– Improved personal and family health<br>– Breathe more easily<br>– Food tastes better<br>– Improved sense of smell<br>– Significant financial savings<br>– Feel better about self<br>– Home, car, clothing, breath will smell better<br>– Stop worrying about quitting - free from addiction<br>– Set a good example for children<br>– Stop worrying about exposing others to smoke<br>– Feel better physically<br>– Improved performance at work and in physical activities<br>– Reduced wrinkling/aging of skin |
| Road-blocks | Confidence | "What might get in the way of quitting?" | Provider could ask permission to share information about tobacco resources to address barriers. Typical barriers might include:<br>– Withdrawal symptoms<br>– Fear of failure<br>– Weight gain<br>– Managing stress<br>– Lack of support<br>– Enjoyment of Tobacco |
| Repetition | Importance and/or Confidence | "What are your thoughts about quitting today?" | Repeat the process at every visit for patients who continue to smoke. Reassure them that the average smoker has seven to nine quit attempts before achieving success. Offer to share strategies that will maximize their likelihood of success. |

## 7.5 Using Physiological Data When Addressing Smoking

Medical providers might use physiological data to encourage patients to consider smoking cessation. In the case of COPD, spirometry results that confirm the diagnosis and/or indicate the severity of the disease might increase patients' concerns about smoking. Research supports the combination of providing spirometry results, supportive counseling, and nicotine replacement products to promote smoking cessation (Anthonisen, 1994; Toljamo, 2010). The manner in which a health care provider presents the information (e.g., physiological results, counseling) has a significant impact on effectiveness. Kotz and colleagues (2009) found that patients made more quit attempts but did not achieve sustained abstinence in response to health care providers who used a confrontational style to provide education about the consequences of smoking and prognosis with continued smoking.

Motivational interviewing (described later in this chapter) and the explanation of spirometry results in terms of "lung age" improve abstinence rates (Parkes, 2008). "Lung age" is the translation of $FEV_1$ values into a concept that is easier for patients to understand and internalize. Providing information about "lung age," or the age that the lungs would appear to be if the spirometry test had been completed on a healthy person who never smoked, demonstrates premature aging in the lungs that is caused by smoking and/or other environmental irritants. For example, telling a 55-year-old smoker that his lung function is comparable to that of a 95-year-old who has never smoked might be more meaningful and effective than telling him that his $FEV_1$ is 77% of predicted. (See Chapter 4, Pulmonary Function Testing: Spirometry: Presence and Severity of Airflow Limitation/Obstruction for more information.)

Researchers have identified specific populations who seem to benefit from receiving spirometry results as part of the smoking cessation intervention. Patients who are diagnosed with moderate to severe airflow obstruction experience more success with smoking cessation when spirometry results are provided (Gorecka, 2003). Additionally, patients who are motivated to quit, are receiving pharmacotherapy, are of older age, and have a higher body mass index demonstrate more success with tobacco cessation when spirometry results are provided (Toljamo, 2010).

## 7.6 How to Present Spirometry Results to Promote Smoking Cessation

Motivational interviewing (MI), a collaborative approach that elicits patients' reasons for change, offers an effective strategy when sharing spirometry results with patients. In keeping with the patient-focused spirit of MI, it is critical to ask for the patient's permission before providing information. Asking the patient before sharing results demonstrates respect for the patient's autonomy and the patient's ability to choose whether he/she wants to hear the information. After gaining permission to

**Table 7.2:** A Sample Conversation Between a Provider and a Patient Illustrating the Four-Step Ask-Elicit-Tell-Elicit Process

| Step | Role | Sample Conversation |
|---|---|---|
| Ask | Provider | "I would like to go over your spirometry results with you today. Is that okay?" |
| | Patient | "Sure." |
| Elicit | Provider | "First, can you tell me what you already know about the lung function test?" |
| | Patient | "Well, I guess it will say whether I have lung disease or not." |
| Tell | Provider | "Yes, that's right. Actually, it helps me determine if you have a lung disease, how severe it is, and to some extent, what type of lung disease. Your results show that you have moderate airflow obstruction characteristic of Chronic Obstructive Pulmonary Disease. To help you understand how your lungs are doing, I've calculated your lung age. Lung age is the age your lungs appear to be if you were a healthy person who never smoked. So, even though you are 55, your lungs are functioning like a 95-year-old. What do you make of that?" |
| | Patient | "Are you kidding? Is there anything I can do to reverse it?" |
| Elicit | Provider | "The most important thing you can do to preserve your lung function is to stop smoking. I would like to talk to more about that, but, first, can you tell me what you think it means to have the lung age of a 95-year-old? |
| | Patient | "I guess it means that smoking has aged my lungs by about 40 years!" |

discuss spirometry results, a four-step process of *Ask–Elicit–Tell–Elicit* is recommended. Table 7.2 depicts each step in a sample conversation between a provider and patient.

The *Ask–Elicit–Tell–Elicit* sequence supports patient autonomy by offering a small amount of information in easy-to-understand terms and then probing for the patient's reaction and understanding. It is essential that the provider seeks the patient's reaction without imposing his/her own opinions so that the patient will feel free to articulate his/her experience and concerns.

## 7.7 Readiness for Change

The Transtheoretical Model of Change (Prochaska, 1983) is a theoretical model of behavior change that was originally drafted by examining the attributes and strategies of self-changers who successfully quit smoking without professional assistance. This temporal model is based on the assumption that behavior change is not a discrete event, but rather a process that occurs in stages across time. Rather than assuming that the decision to quit smoking happens on one specific day, the model acknowledges that people are more likely to go through an extended process that may include the following: spend a few months questioning whether to quit or not, seek help from a PCP, weigh the pros and cons for another month, set a quit date, buy nicotine replacement products, change daily routines, seek support from a friend, stop smoking on the quit date, call a telephone quit line for support, relapse after two weeks, seek additional support, etc.

According to this model, there are five stages through which people progress, often in a non-linear fashion. In general, a person moves from being uninterested, unaware, or unwilling to make a change (precontemplation), to considering a change (contemplation), to deciding and preparing to make a change (preparation), to taking steps and problem-solving challenges or barriers (action), to incorporating the change into a daily routine (maintenance). Relapses are almost inevitable and become part of the process of working toward permanent change. The following descriptions of each stage were adapted from Velicer and colleagues (1998):

### 7.7.1 Precontemplation

Precontemplation, the initial stage, is characterized by people who have no intention of quitting in the next six months. Smokers in this stage are likely to deny that smoking causes any problems in their lives. Patients in this stage are uninformed or under informed. When information is presented, they may try to avoid or deny it. People in this stage might have tried to change and failed, leaving them feeling hopeless and demoralized. Tobacco treatment programs are often not designed for people in the precontemplation stage. It is estimated that 40% of current smokers are in the precontemplation stage (Velicer, 1995).

Clinician Goals During the Precontemplation Stage:

1. Validate the patient's experience.
2. Encourage further self-exploration through smoking self-assessment tools (e.g., Fagerstrom Test for Nicotine Dependence (Heatherton, 1991)).
3. Offer factual written information about the risks of smoking and the benefits of quitting. The Centers for Disease Control offers free booklets, "A Report of the Surgeon General, How Tobacco Smoke Causes Disease" through their website: www.surgeongeneral.gov.
4. Offer websites where patients can go to learn more (e.g., www.smokefree.gov).
5. Leave the door open for future conversations.

Open-Ended Questions to Facilitate Change During the Precontemplation Stage:

1. "What would have to happen to let you know that smoking is a problem?"
2. "What warning signs would let you know that smoking is a problem?"
3. "Tell me about times when you have tried to quit in the past."

4. "How might smoking cause problems for you in the future?"
5. "If you do nothing to change the way you take care of your health, what is the worst thing that might happen in 10 years?"

### 7.7.2 Contemplation

Contemplation, the second stage, is characterized by patients who intend to change in the next six months. They are more likely to acknowledge that smoking is a problem and consider reasons for quitting. Unresolved ambivalence is a hallmark of this stage, as patients consider the costs and benefits of continuing to smoke. The importance of quitting might rise, but a lack of confidence and a fear of failure interferes with quit attempts. Patients who are attempting to stop smoking spend an average of two years in contemplation, searching for a feasible, simple, quick solution. They are often not ready for traditional, action-oriented programs. Forty percent of current smokers tend to be in the contemplation stage.

Clinician Goals During the Contemplation Stage:
1. Validate the patient's experience.
2. Explore the patient's perceptions of the barriers and benefits of quitting smoking.
3. Help the patient clarify values that are inconsistent with smoking, such as being a good role model for children.
4. Encourage further self-exploration through smoking self-assessment tools (Fagerstrom Test for Nicotine Dependence (Heatherton, 1991)).
5. Offer factual written information about the risks of smoking and the benefits of quitting.
6. Educate about the resources available and their efficacy, including nicotine replacement treatments (NRTs), medications, quit lines, text support, mobile apps
7. Leave the door open for moving to preparation.

Open-Ended Questions to Facilitate Change During Contemplation Stage:
1. "Why do you want to stop smoking now?"
2. "What are the reasons for not quitting?"
3. "What concerns you the most about your smoking?"
4. "What might keep you from quitting right now?"
5. "What might help you overcome the barriers to quitting?"
6. "What people, programs or behaviors might help you quit?"
7. "What do you think you need to learn about the effects of smoking or how to quit?"

### 7.7.3 Preparation

Preparation, the third stage, occurs when patients plan to make a behavioral change in the next month. They have taken steps to prepare, like researching tools and programs that they might use to quit. Ambivalence may still be present, but the pros tend to outweigh the cons. Patients in the preparation stage may spend a considerable amount of time thinking about and planning the strategies they will use. Small steps leading toward behavior change might be attempted (e.g., cutting back on the number of cigarettes smoked, making their intentions to quit public). These patients are ready for traditional tobacco treatment programs and are likely to follow through with treatment. About 20% of current smokers are in the preparation stage.

Clinician Goals During the Preparation Stage:

1. Praise the decision to change behavior.
2. Offer a variety of resources to quit, including NRTs, medications, tobacco treatment groups, quit lines, text support, and mobile apps.
3. Identify and assist in problem-solving obstacles.
4. Encourage small initial steps.
5. Encourage identification of social supports.

Open-Ended Questions to Facilitate Change During the Preparation Stage:

1. (Pick one of the patient's barriers to quitting) "What are some things you could do to overcome this barrier?"
2. "What additional steps can you take to feel certain that you will succeed?"
3. "How will you feel about yourself when you are able to quit for good?
4. "Who will support you in your first few months of quitting?
5. "How will you change your environment to help you quit?
6. "What will you do to distract yourself when you have a craving?

### 7.7.4 Action

Action involves an actual smoking cessation attempt and includes the first six months after quitting. Patients in the action stage move from thinking and planning to doing. The strategies used in the action stage involve stimulus control, substitution, and rewards. Behaviors that support stimulus control include disposing of cigarettes and paraphernalia (e.g., lighters, ash trays) before the quit date, avoiding the gas station or other location where cigarettes were typically purchased, and choosing not to drink alcohol during the first three months of quitting (because of the strong association between smoking and consuming alcohol). Behaviors that support substitution involve planning an alternate activity or action to replace smoking or smoking related behaviors. Patients might drink water or use a nicotine replacement therapy when a craving arises. Some patients substitute a cinnamon stick or flavored toothpick for a cigarette to satisfy the familiar hand-to-mouth action that is involved in smoking. Rewards that are obtained during this stage can be internal or external. Positive self-statements and a sense of accomplishment and pride can offer powerful reinforcement. Tangible rewards, such as using the money saved from cigarettes to invest in a desired item or activity, are concrete benefits of quitting. Recognition of positive changes from other members and providers in a tobacco treatment program can also be reinforcing.

Clinician Goals During the Action Stage:

1. Affirm steps to change.
2. Explore and highlight successful strategies and benefits.
3. Probe for cravings and struggles, and problem-solve ways to manage them.
4. Encourage continued use of a variety of support options, including NRTs, medications, tobacco treatment groups, quit lines, text support, and mobile apps.

Open-Ended Questions to Facilitate Change During the Action Stage:

5. "What has worked in taking this step?"
6. "What could help it work even better?"
7. "What else would help?"
8. "How do you reward yourself for not smoking?"
9. "How committed are you to remaining a non-smoker?"

### 7.7.5 Maintenance

Maintenance generally begins six months after quitting and can last indefinitely. Cravings tend to dwindle for most patients and less vigilance and effort is required to remain smoke-free. However, relapse is common during this stage. The average smoker makes seven to nine quit attempts before becoming fully successful. The most frequently cited reason for relapse is the emersion of an emotional stressor. The patient in the maintenance stage should be encouraged to consider and plan for how he or she might manage stressful situations without resuming smoking. Weight gain is a second reason people (particularly women) cite for a relapse. It is important for the patient to incorporate healthy strategies that will address managing both emotional stressors and cravings during the maintenance stage. Examples of these strategies include using nicotine replacement therapies, participating in exercise, and engaging in relaxation. While relapse potential is high (95% in some samples), research suggests that the majority of smokers who relapse (85%) do not return to the beginning of the change process (i.e., the precontemplation stage) (Prochaska, 2006). Rather, patients are much more likely to return to the contemplation stage.

Clinician Goals During Maintenance Stage:

1. Praise continued success.
2. Review and highlight successful strategies and benefits.
3. Explore risks for relapse and problem-solve ways to manage them.

Open-Ended Questions to Facilitate Change During the Maintenance Stage:

4. “Congratulations! What's helping you?”
5. “What else will help?”
6. “What are your high risk situations and how do you prepare for them?”
7. “What is the best part about being a non-smoker?”

## 7.8 The 5 A's Model

The 2008 Clinical Practice Guideline (U.S. Department of Health and Human Services) recommend providers use a five-step process (Ask, Advise, Assess, Assist, Arrange) for identifying current smokers and assisting them in quitting.

### 7.8.1 Step 1: ASK

The best practice for identifying current tobacco users is to ask every patient about his or her smoking habits at every visit. Some may view this approach as “badgering” the patient. However, assessing smoking habits at every visit can have a significant impact across time if the questions are asked in a non-judgmental way that takes into account the patient's readiness to change. System changes can be used to standardize this approach by implementing a reminder system within an electronic medical record or incorporating tobacco screening in the collection of vitals, although the effectiveness of reminders systems has been mixed. A review of seven randomized control trials found that reminder systems alone increased the number of patients advised to quit by 13% and the patients who were successful in quitting by 4% (Zaza, 2005). However, the Clinical Practice Guideline (2008) reviewed three studies and found that reminder systems did not have a significant impact on smoking cessation rates. Reminders sometimes prompt health care professionals to address smoking cessation in an ineffective way (e.g., “You meet this criteria. Do you want this service?”). While asking is an important first step, evidenced-based approaches should then be used to motivate and prepare smokers to quit. Caplan and colleagues (2011) indicate that two-thirds of patients are asked about smoking status, yet only about 20% of those identified as smokers are offered support for quitting. As such, appropriate clinical follow-up with strategies discussed in this chapter should also be used to improve the effectiveness of these systems.

### 7.8.2 Step 2: ADVISE

As reviewed earlier in this chapter, a personalized statement recommending that the patient consider quitting can have an impact on those who are ambivalent. Including a message of support and assistance can help to create a sense of collaboration.

### 7.8.3 Step 3: ASSESS

Assess whether current smokers are ready to quit. Use open-ended questions to explore readiness for change. Use the importance and confidence rulers (Table 7.1) to gauge investment and potential barriers. See the Screening and Readiness for Change sections earlier in this chapter for more specific strategies.

### 7.8.4 Step 4: ASSIST

Assist patients who are willing to quit by offering nicotine replacement therapy (NRT), medications, and more intensive services. Offer the full array of options available and allow the patients to select the ones that suit them the best. Share information about success rates for each form of treatment and the most effective combinations of treatments. Honor whatever choice they select without judgment. Specific options and more detailed information about NRTs and medication will be discussed in the Interventions section of this chapter.

Patients who elect to take NRTs or medication without additional services, as well as those who decline to receive any services, should be invited to consider some strategies to help them prepare to quit, if they are ready to do so. Written patient education materials can be useful and effective, especially fill-in-the-blank-style handouts that patients can use to personalize their quit plans (see Figure 7.2 for an example; “Tobacco Cessation: How to Change?” Handout (Altum, 2013)). Table 7.3 identifies key ingredients of a quit plan to review when a patient decides to quit. Table 7.4 lists potential barriers to quitting, triggers for smoking, and strategies that patients can use to overcome these challenges (Himstreet, 2013).

### 7.8.5 Step 5: ARRANGE

Ideally, the provider or a nurse on the Primary Care team offers follow-up either in-person or by phone. Secure email may be another option. Clinical Practice Guideline (2008) recommend contact at one week and one month after the quit date. Issues to address in the follow-up contacts include:

Department of Veterans Affairs Medical Center
Cincinnati – Fort Thomas Divisions

VA HEALTH CARE | Defining EXCELLENCE in the 21st Century

Primary Care

## Tobacco Cessation: How to Change?

**Do you want to change your tobacco use?**
If you answer yes, the best way is to take into account all the factors that contribute to your use. It can help to think of these factors as falling into one of these 3 main groups:

- Physical Factors
- Behavioral Factors (habits)
- Psychological Factors (feelings)

**Physical Factors**
Nicotine is the most addictive substance on the planet. But, there is help. Your doctor will help you decide if you can use a nicotine replacement product, such as the patch or gum. These products are shown to help people quit and are often the key to success.

- Most often there is a better success rate when a medication type of product is used.
- Some medications, like Zyban, are very helpful to some people. But for others, they don't seem to offer enough help with nicotine cravings.
- For some people, using two types of products will work better to relieve cravings and withdrawal symptoms than just using one.

Work closely with your doctor to find the best replacement product(s) for you.

**Behavioral Factors**
You need to change your habits and the situations where you most often use tobacco. There are some times when you have greater cravings for tobacco. Counseling and support are helpful to those trying to quit. You can learn skills to help you make other choices at these times.

- Be more aware of the situations when you are most tempted to use nicotine
- Learn problem-solving skills to better cope with these situations

**What does the VA offer to help?**

- Tobacco cessation groups/classes
- Individual counseling through tobacco cessation clinics.

If you would find telephone counseling helpful, you can call **1-800-QUIT-NOW** (1-800-784-8669). You will be connected to your state's phone support staff.

**Behavioral Factors**
*Your feelings (thoughts and emotions)* are some of the hardest aspects of tobacco use to change. Often, people think that they need tobacco to get through their tough times. Changing these thoughts to cope with stress is a vital aspect of beating this habit.

One helpful strategy is to list your top 3 reasons for quitting, and remind yourself of them as a way to stay strong if you need a boost along the way. Take a moment to list *your* main reasons for quitting:

1. ____________________
2. ____________________
3. ____________________

**Figure 7.2:** How to Change Handout. This How to Change Handout for Smoking Cessation uses the 5 A's Approach: Avoid, Alter, Alternatives, Action, and Appointment to assist providers in helping their patients stop smoking.

## Preparing to Quit

**Your Quit Date**

When is the last day and time that you are going to use tobacco?

Month______ Day_______ Year_______ Time________

**Prepare Your Surroundings**

What are the things that remind you to use tobacco? It is important to change these things so you won't be reminded about tobacco use as often.

Before your quit date consider the following:

- Don't buy tobacco in bulk (e.g., don't buy cartons).
- Find all of your hidden stashes of tobacco. Check in the couch, the car, in your drawers at home and at work. It is unwise to keep an emergency stash once you quit.
- Get rid of tobacco-related materials—things like ashtrays and lighters. Don't carry lighters or matches in your pockets or purse.
- Prepare family and friends. Let them know that you are planning to quit. Ask for their help. If you have friends and family who do use tobacco, ask them to avoid using it around you.
- Prepare a plan for to cope with your cravings and withdrawal symptoms. Use the combination of strategies that works for you.
- Choose a method to quit. There are many ways to think about quitting. But one of the most important considerations is to avoid thinking favorably about your last tobacco use. If you remember your tobacco fondly, then you are more likely to go back to using it when you think you need it.

Quitting is difficult. Many people feel it's a challenge. Preparing for difficult situations as you quit can help you succeed. What do you expect to be the hardest challenge for you as you quit?

- Will it be going without a cigarette with your morning coffee?
- Will it be not smoking when your spouse or friends light up?

Anticipating and having a plan for how to handle these challenges will increase your success.

As you prepare to quit there are other things in your life that you can change that will help you to be successful. Think about the places you should avoid or things you should do differently.

- **Avoid:** What situations (e.g., bars, sporting events, smoking areas) do you need to **avoid** during the next month to limit your urges to use tobacco?
- **Alter:** How can you change situations that you can't avoid so that you'll be more successful with your quit attempt?
- **Alternatives:** "When you feel the urge to put tobacco in your mouth what could you use instead" (e.g. gum, hard candies or mints, toothpicks, cinnamon sticks)?
- **Activities:** "Are there things you can do (e.g., going for a walk) or ways to keep you busy if you feel an urge to use tobacco?"

continued **Figure 7.2:** How to Change Handout. This How to Change Handout for Smoking Cessation uses the 5 A's Approach: Avoid, Alter, Alternatives, Action, and Appointment to assist providers in helping their patients stop smoking.

## Using the Four A's to Outsmart Tobacco Urges

***Avoid.*** What are the situations or places that you need to avoid over the next month?

1. ______________________________
2. ______________________________
3. ______________________________

***Alter.*** What situations will you need to change to help you be more successful?

1. ______________________________
2. ______________________________
3. ______________________________

***Alternatives.*** What can you put in your mouth or hands instead of using tobacco?

1. ______________________________
2. ______________________________
3. ______________________________

***Action.*** When you get an urge to use tobacco, what can you do to be active or busy?

1. ______________________________
2. ______________________________
3. ______________________________

**Follow-Up Appointment Plan:**

______________________________________________________________

______________________________________________________________

______________________________________________________________

Adapted from: Hunter, C.L., Goodie, J.L., Oordt, M.S., & Dobmeyer, A.C. (2009). Integrated *Behavioral Health in Primary Care: Step-by-step Guidance for Assessment and Intervention.* Washington, DC: American Psychological Association

continued **Figure 7.2:** How to Change Handout. This How to Change Handout for Smoking Cessation uses the 5 A's Approach: Avoid, Alter, Alternatives, Action, and Appointment to assist providers in helping their patients stop smoking.

**Table 7.3:** Key Elements of a Quit Plan

| |
|---|
| – Set a quit date. Some time to prepare is often indicated but long delays may preclude action. |
| – Share the quit plan with others and ask for their understanding and support. |
| – Identify potential challenges and triggers and how they will be overcome. These might include withdrawal symptoms, daily routines that are heavily associated with smoking, alternative strategies for coping with stress and cravings, etc. Each patient may have a different perspective of challenges. It may be useful to offer a list (see Tab. 7.4) and ask them to select the top three or four items to address. |
| – Remove tobacco products from home, work, and car. |
| – Consider making the home smoke-free. |
| – Identify and plan for challenging triggers by altering or avoiding them (e.g., avoid spending time with others who smoke, go for a walk in the morning instead of smoking a cigarette and taking a shower first thing). |
| – Consider avoiding alcohol because alcohol use is associated with tobacco relapse. |
| – Offer information about additional supports such as telephone quit lines, text support, mobile apps, and websites. |
| – Have tobacco treatment education materials in every exam room to offer when patients are preparing to quit. |

1. Congratulating them if they remain abstinent. Probing for strategies that have led to their success.
2. Exploring medication use and side effects.
3. Problem-solving ways to address any slips or challenges to managing cravings.
4. Asking about use of additional supports and reviewing available resources as needed.
5. Plan to review again at the next clinic visit.

## 7.9 Motivational Interviewing

Motivational Interviewing (MI) is an evidenced-based interviewing style that seeks to draw out a patient's own reasons for change. MI is a collaborative approach that recognizes and supports the patient's struggles, values, beliefs, and desires. Skilled clinicians move the interview towards change while respecting the patient's autonomy and personal choice.

**Table 7.4:** Barriers to Quitting, Triggers for Smoking, and Strategies to Overcome Both Barriers and Triggers

| | | |
|---|---|---|
| **Barriers** | | |
| I have not been able to quit in the past. | I do not know what to do without a cigarette. | I am afraid it will make my stress, anxiety, or mood worse. |
| I live with others who still smoke. | How will I socialize with my friends who still smoke? | I cannot get back to sleep unless I smoke a cigarette. |
| I am concerned about weight gain. | I am worried about how I will handle stress. | It is the only vice I have left; I quit everything else. |
| I smoke when I am bored. | I always have a cigarette with my coffee/beer. | I do not know how to say "no." |
| **Triggers** | | |
| Waking up in the morning | Drinking coffee | Stress |
| Before bedtime | Drinking alcohol | After meals |
| Driving | After sex | During breaks |
| Working on the computer | Talking on the phone | Waking during the night |
| Feeling bored | After completing a task | Having nightmares |
| Feeling anxious, angry, impatient | Seeing and/or smelling someone else smoke | Watching TV |
| **Behavioral Strategies** | | |
| Avoid stressful situations whenever possible. | Remove triggers (e.g., ashtrays, lighters) from home, car, clothing, etc. | Exercise. Go for a walk. |
| Fill your time with enjoyable hobbies and interests that are not associated with tobacco use. | Stock up on tobacco substitutes (e.g., sugar-free chewing gum and candy, carrot and celery sticks, toothpicks, straws, cinnamon sticks). | Keep track of the number of cigarettes smoked to make the behavior less automatic. |
| Practice relaxation techniques (e.g., deep breathing exercises). | Move your tobacco to a different location that is less convenient to access. | Wait to smoke after waking, eating, etc. Slowly increase the amount of time daily - wait 10 minutes today, 20 minutes tomorrow, etc. |
| Drink water. | Read a book. | Play computer games. |
| Brush your teeth. | Talk to a friend or family member. | Do a crossword puzzle or Sudoku. |

### 7.9.1 Clinical Effectiveness of Motivational Interviewing for Treating Tobacco Use Disorder

A randomized, controlled trial conducted in Spain found that three 20-minute physician interventions using MI were five times more effective than three minutes of advice and guidance to quit smoking offered by the same physician (Raimundo, 2006). In a review of four meta-analyses of the clinical effectiveness of MI for tobacco cessation, Lundahl and Burke (2009) found that MI success rates ranged from 5% to 17% above no treatment at all, with mixed findings when MI was compared with other evidence-based treatments. Ideally, MI should be incorporated into a package of treatment approaches that complement one another. This interviewing skill might be most effective in Primary Care or Pulmonary Specialty Care clinics, where patients are most likely to be in the precontemplation or contemplation stages of change. Denial and ambivalence are prominent features of these stages, and MI strategies are well-suited to promoting movement and investment in change.

### 7.9.2 Developing Competency in the Use of Motivational Interviewing

There are currently no established standards for developing competency in MI. However, MI experts tend to agree that 14 to 28 hours of training followed by audio-taped practice and supervision are generally needed to achieve proficiency in several critical and quantifiable skill domains. Efraimsson and colleagues (2011) addressed the question of whether four days of MI training impacted nurses' use of MI communication for smoking cessation with COPD patients. The nurses' interventions were more instructive (e.g., provided information, closed questions, simple reflections) and rarely expressed empathy using complex reflections, collaborated with patients, or supported the patients' choices, thereby making them less likely to support motivation for change. This study suggests that follow-up practice and supervision are necessary to gain proficiency in MI. The authors propose that training in MI needs to be integrated into nursing education, at the basic and advanced levels, with audio- or video-taped supervision needed to achieve proficiency. Annual training and proficiency evaluations would ensure competence is maintained. These recommendations would be advisable for all healthcare professions who address health behavior change, such as physicians, nurses, dieticians, clinical pharmacists, social workers, psychologists, physical and occupational therapists, and speech pathologists.

## 7.10 Interventions

Smoking cessation intervention options that are provided to patients should be numerous and varied. Patients should be encouraged to use multiple strategies rather

**Table 7.5:** Success Rates of Different Smoking Cessation Methods

| Intervention | Success Rate |
|---|---|
| Counseling + NRT/medication | 22% – 32%* |
| Medication alone | 24% – 33%* |
| NRT's alone | 19% – 27%* |
| Counselling alone | 12% – 25%* |
| Brief interventions in Primary Care | 8% – 12%* |
| Self-Initiated Strategies | 8% – 10%* |

* consolidated data from 2008 Clinical Practice Guidelines

than selecting only one at a time. Tobacco treatment options might include group or individual counseling (in outpatient mental health or in specialty medical clinics), nicotine replacement therapy (NRT), medications (e.g., bupropion [Wellbutrin] or varenicline [Chantix®] ), telephone quit lines, home telehealth programs, Nicotine Anonymous, mobile apps, websites and text support. Daily support strategies like home telehealth, a daily home monitoring system, or a mobile app with daily log-in, can support the frequency of cravings in the first month of quitting. Telephone quit lines might be especially useful in the maintenance stage, when there is a higher likelihood of emotional stressors that may lead to relapse.

Brief interventions (3–10 minutes) for smoking cessation that occur in the Primary Care setting have been associated with smoking cessation rates of 5–10% (Wilson, 1990). More intense interventions lead to a greater likelihood of success. Interventions can be made more intense by increasing the number of sessions, the length of the sessions, or the follow-up period. Having at least 4 individual brief (10–15 minute) appointments substantially improves abstinence rates (2–3 sessions: 16%; 4–8 sessions: 21%; Clinical Practice Guidelines, 2008). Additionally, a multidisciplinary team approach in a primary care setting might allow for more frequent review of the patient's efforts to quit.

In general, studies of successful tobacco treatment confirm that a structured counseling program combined with an NRT and/or medication is the most successful (see Table 7.4). This result was replicated in a review of randomized controlled clinical trials of tobacco treatment for COPD patients (Parker, 2012). Table 7.5 identifies success rates by type of intervention.

### 7.10.1 Nicotine Replacement Therapies and Medications

As indicated, nicotine replacement therapies and medications – either used individually or in combination with counseling – lead to the highest cessation rates. Nicotine replacement therapies and medications are considered to be critical for any patient who wants to quit smoking and should be offered to everyone engaging in smoking cessation. If a patient is not having success with smoking cessation while using a particular NRT or medication regimen, the provider should adjust the types and/or dosages of NRTs and/or medications, or try a combination of therapies (Ebbert, 2007). Nicotine cravings and unmanageable withdrawal symptoms are common reasons for relapse when NRT's or medications are not used or used in insufficient dosages. Burke et al. (2008) suggested monotherapy with an NRT for patients who smoke 10 cigarettes per day or less. Relapse after monotherapy usually suggests the need to add additional agents. Patients who smoke more than 10 cigarettes per day are encouraged to try a combination of NRTs; this might include wearing a nicotine patch that provides steady dosing, and choosing nicotine gum, spray, lozenge, or inhaler for breakthrough cravings or withdrawal symptoms. The researchers note that while the FDA has not approved combination therapy, their evidence supports the practice of NRT combination therapy.

Tobacco treatment literature describes tobacco dependence as a chronic condition, and, as such, the effectiveness and the type and dosage of the NRT and/or medication needs to be regularly evaluated. Recommendations and doses for NRTs and tobacco cessation medications should be adjusted with each quit attempt, much the same way medications and doses are adjusted over time for hypertension or diabetes (Burke, 2008). Table 7.6 offers a summary of NRT's and medications for tobacco dependence. See medication package inserts for complete information.

Unfortunately, only 22% of smokers who attempt smoking cessation use a nicotine replacement product or medication (Clinical Practice Guideline, 2008). Additionally, many smokers have unrealistic expectations about the quitting process and stop using NRTs or medications prematurely, which leads to relapse. Discussing these misconceptions and sharing information about the most effective smoking cessation strategies might help patients succeed.

## 7.11 Other Nicotine Sources

Although outside of the scope of this chapter, smokeless tobacco (e.g., chewing tobacco, snuff, and dissolvable tobacco) also has deleterious effects. While smokeless tobacco does not directly cause or contribute to symptoms of COPD, it has been shown to cause a variety of negative health effects, including mouth, tongue, cheek, gum and throat cancer, esophagus cancer, stomach cancer, and pancreatic cancer (American Cancer Society, 2013). Additionally, while smokeless tobacco products are

**Table 7.6:** Pharmacologic Treatments for Smoking Cessation

| Medication | Features | Dosing | Side Effects |
|---|---|---|---|
| Nicotine Patch | – OTC<br>– 24 hour delivery<br>– Slow to build up<br>– Rotate patch site; anywhere on the upper body | For <10 cigarettes/day<br>– 14 mg for 6 wks<br>– 7 mg for 2 wks<br>For >10 cigarettes/day<br>– 21 mg for 4–6 wks<br>– 14 mg for 2–4 wks<br>– 7 mg for 2–4 wks | – Skin irritation<br>– Sleep disturbance or vivid dreams<br>– Require additional adhesive with sweat-ing |
| Nicotine Gum | – OTC<br>– Delivers nicotine through the mouth while gum is parked between cheek and gum<br>– Quick delivery<br>– Avoid eating or drinking 15 min before or during use<br>– Chew 15–30 times then park between cheek and gum until tingle fades | <20 cigarettes/day:<br>– 2 mg gum<br>>20 cigarettes/day:<br>– 4 mg gum<br>Dosing:<br>– 1–2 pieces per 1–2 hrs for 6 wks<br>– 1 piece per 2–4 hrs for 3 wks<br>– 1 piece per 4–8 hrs for 3 weeks | – Improper "chewing" leads to less nicotine absorbed & stomach upset<br>– Mouth soreness |
| Nicotine Lozenge | – OTC<br>– Delivers nicotine through the mouth while lozenge dissolves; 25% more nicotine than gum<br>– Quick delivery<br>– Avoid eating or drinking 15 min before or during use<br>– Should not be chewed or swallowed | < 20 cigarettes/day:<br>– 2 mg<br>> 20 cigarettes/day:<br>– 4 mg<br>Dosing:<br>– 1–2 pieces per 1–2 hrs for 6 wks<br>– 1 piece per 2–4 hrs for 3 wks<br>– 1 piece per 4–8 hrs for 3 weeks | – Throat irritation<br>– Nausea (12–15%)<br>– Hiccups<br>– Heartburn |
| Nicotine Nasal Spray | – Prescription only<br>– Delivers nicotine through the oral mucosa but is NOT sniffed<br>– Fastest NRT delivery system | – 1 spray in each nostril 1–2x/hr<br>– Average 14–15 doses/day initially; 40 doses/day max | – Nose and eye irritation in 1st week especially |
| Nicotine Inhaler | – Prescription only<br>– Delivers nicotine through the mouth<br>– Quick delivery; need to puff more frequently than a cigarette | – Minimum 6 car-tridges/day; Max 16/day<br>– Each cartridge designed for 80 puffs in 20 min. | – Few reported |

continued **Table 7.6:** Pharmacologic Treatments for Smoking Cessation

| Medication | Features | Dosing | Side Effects |
|---|---|---|---|
| Bupropion SR (Well-butrin®) | – Non-nicotine prescription<br>– May be used in combination with NRT's<br>– Start 1 week before quit date<br>– Beneficial for smokers with depression | – 150 mg 1x/day for 3 days<br>– 150 mg BID for 4 days before quit date<br>– Continue 150 mg BID for 8 wks – 6 mo. | – Increased risk of seizures (1:1000)<br>– Insomnia (daytime dosing suggested, 8 hours apart)<br>– Use with caution in patients with liver disease<br>– Dry mouth |
| Varenicline (Chantix®) | – Non-nicotine prescription<br>– Not recommended with NRT's<br>– Start 1 week before quit date<br>– May stop abruptly without taper | – 0.5 mg 1x/day for 3 days<br>– 0.5 mg BID for 4 days<br>– 1.0 mg BID for 11 weeks<br>– May continue up to 24 weeks total | – Nausea, take with food<br>– Adjust dose if kidney function is impaired<br>– Monitor for irritability and suicidality<br>– Avoid use with serious psychiatric illness |

* Adapted from Fiore, 2008; vaww.publichealth.va.gov/smoking/index.asp.

less lethal than cigarettes, they are not recommended as a cigarette substitute as they have not been proven to help smokers quit.

The electronic cigarette (e-cigarette) has become another popular nicotine delivery system. Research about the e-cigarette's potential negative health effects is still sparse. Questions about the safety of inhaling the substances found in e-cigarettes into the lungs have been raised (The American Cancer Society, 2014). The limited available research indicates that e-cigarettes cause short-term lung changes. The long-term effects are still unclear. Additionally, the ingredients in e-cigarettes are not identified, making the substances and nicotine levels contained within them unclear. As the safety and effectiveness of e-cigarettes is currently unknown, The American Cancer Society indicates that they cannot recommend the e-cigarette as a nicotine replacement therapy. With regard to both smokeless tobacco and the e-cigarette, it is important to discuss the potentially harmful health effects that these tobacco and nicotine products can cause.

## 7.12 Conclusion

Eighty to 90% percent of patients diagnosed with COPD are current or past smokers. Thus, the single most important approach to treating and preventing COPD is smoking cessation.

More than 70% of the 45 million smokers in the United States report that they would like to quit, and approximately 44% of those people attempt to quit each year. NRT's and medications – either used individually or in combination with counseling – lead to the highest cessation rates. Unfortunately, only 22% of smokers who attempt smoking cessation use a nicotine replacement product or medication. Smokers should be offered multiple resources to help them quit and be encouraged to use more than one. The role of Primary Care in tobacco treatment is to (1) assess the patient's readiness for change, (2) match the intervention strategy to the patient's stage of change, (3) ask open-ended questions that explore the risks, roadblocks, rewards, and relevance of quitting, and (4) use the five A's process: Ask about smoking status at every visit; Advise smokers to quit; Assess readiness for change; Assist patients with a variety of resources; and Arrange follow-up.

## 7.13 Summary Points

1. Up to 90% of those diagnosed with COPD are or were smokers; therefore, addressing smoking cessation is important to prevent and treat COPD.
2. Abstinence from tobacco is associated with a variety of health improvements, including decreased mortality and reduced risk of developing lung cancer, myocardial infarction, and stroke.
3. Providers should screen patients for tobacco use at each visit; Providers can use the five A's process (Ask about smoking status at every visit; Advise smokers to quit; Assess readiness for change; Assist patients with a variety of resources; and Arrange follow-up).
4. Providers can use a variety of data to encourage patients to consider and follow through with smoking cessation, including lung age to explore the patient's perceived need to quit and statistics about effective treatments to consider methods to assist with quitting.
5. Providers should use Motivational Interviewing (MI) techniques to assess a patient's stage of change when discussing smoking cessation; Motivational Interviewing questions might also help a patient explore the costs and benefits of smoking cessation.

## References


Altum, S. & Seltzer, J. (2013). *Tobacco Cessation: How to Change?*. Cincinnati Veterans Affairs Medical Center, Cincinnati, OH.

Anthonisen, N.R., Connett, J.E., Kiley, J.P., et al. (1994). Effects of smoking intervention and the use of an inhaled anticholinergic bronchodilator on the rate of decline of FEV1. The Lung Health Study. *JAMA*, *272*(19), 1497–505.

Anthonisen, N.R., Skeans, M.A., Wise, R.A., et al. (2005). The effects of a smoking cessation intervention on 14.5 year mortality: A randomized clinical trial. *Annals of Internal Medicine*, *142*(4), 233–239.

Burke, M.V., Ebbert, J.O., & Hays, J.T. (2008). Treatment of Tobacco Dependence. *Mayo Clinic Proceedings*, *83*(84), 479–484.

Caplan, L., Stout, C., & Blumenthal, D.S. (2011). Training physicians to do office-based smoking cessation increases adherence to PHS guidelines. *J Community Health*, *36*(2), 238–43.

Centers for Disease Control and Prevention. (2007). Cigarette smoking among adults—United States, 2006. *MMWR*, *56*, 1157–1161.

Ebbert, J.O., Sood, A., Hays, T., et al. (2007). Treating Tobacco Dependence: Review of the best and latest treatment options. *Journal of Thoracic Oncology*, *2*(3), 249–256.

Efraimsson, E.O., Fossum, B., Ehrenberg, A., et al. (2011). Use of motivational interviewing in smoking cessation at nurse-led chronic obstructive pulmonary disease clinic. *Journal of Advanced Nursing*, *68*(4), 767–782.

Fiore, M.C., Jaén, C.R., Baker, T.B., et al. (2008). Treating tobacco use and dependence: 2008 update. *Clinical Practice Guideline*. Rockville, MD: U.S. Department of Health and Human Services. Public Health Service.

Gorecka, D., Bednarek, M., Nowinski, A., et al. (2003). Diagnosis of airflow limitation combined with smoking cessation advice increase stop-smoking rate. *Chest*, *123*(6), 1916–23.

Heatherton, T.F., Kozlowski, L.T., Frecker, R.C., et al. (1991). The fragerstrom test for nicotine dependence: a revision of the Fagerstrom Tolerance Questionnaire. *British Journal of Addiction*, *86*(9), 1119–27.

Himstreet, J. (2013, September). My tobacco cessation workbook: A resource for veterans. Published by U.S. Department of Veterans Affairs, Veterans Health Administration. Washington, D.C.

Kotz, D., Wesseling, G., Hulbers, M.J.H., & van Schayck, O.C.P. (2009). Efficacy of confronting smokers with airflow limitation for smoking cessation. *European Respiratory Journal*, *33*(4), 754–762.

Leuenberger, P., Schwartz, J., Ackermann-Liebrich, U., et al. (1994) Passive smoking exposure in adults and chronic respiratory symptoms (SAPALDIA Study). *Am J Respir Crit Care Med 150*, 1222–1228.

Lundbäck, B., Lindberg, A., Lindström, M., et al. (2003). Not 15 but 50% of smokers develop COPD? Report from the Obstructive Lung Disease in North Sweden Studies. *Respir Med*, *97*(2), 115–122.

Lundahl, B. & Burke, B.L. (2009) The effectiveness and applicability of motivational interviewing: a practice-friendly review of four meta-analyses. *Journal of Clinical Psychology*, *65*, 1232–1245.

Miller, W.R & Rollnick, S. (2013). *Motivational Interviewing: Helping People Change* (3rd ed.). New York, NY: Guilford Press.

Miller, W.R., & Rose, G.S. (2009). Toward a Theory of Motivational Interviewing. *American Psychologist*, *64*(6), 527–537.

Miller, W.R., Yahne, C.E., Moyers T.B., et al. (2004) A randomized trial of methods to help clinicians learn motivational interviewing. *Journal of Consulting and Clinical Psychology*, *72*, 1050–1062.

Panos, R. (2014). *Lung Age Graph*. (Unpublished.) Cincinnati Veterans Affairs Medical Center, Cincinnati, OH.

Parkes, G., Greenhalgh, T., Griffin, M., et al. (2008). Effect on smoking quit rate of telling patients their lung age: The Step2quit randomized controlled trial. *BMJ, 336*(7644), 598–600.

Parker, D.R., & Eaton, C.B. (2012). Chronic obstructive pulmonary disease and smoking cessation. *American Journal of Lifestyle Medicine, 6*, 159–166.

Prochaska, J., & DiClemente, C. (1983). Stages of processes of self-change of smoking: Toward an integrative model of change. *Journal of Consulting and Clinical Psychology, 51*(3), 390–395.

Prochaska, J., DiClemente, C., & Norcross, J. (1992). In search of how people change: Applications to addictive behaviors. *American Psychologist, 47*(9), 1002–1114.

Prochaska, J., Norcross, J., & DiClemente, C. (1994). Changing for Good. Harper Collins.

Raimundo, S., Almudena, L., Concepión, E. et al. (2006). A randomised controlled trial of motivational interviewing for smoking cessation, *British Journal of General Practice, 56*, 768–774.

Rabe, K.F., Hurd, S., Anzueto, A., et al. (2007) Global strategy for the diagnosis, management, and prevention of chronic obstructive pulmonary disease: GOLD executive summary. *American Journal of Respiratory and Critical Care Medicine, 176*, 532–555.

Tashkin, D.P., Kanner, R., Bailey, W., et al. (2001). Smoking cessation in patients with chronic obstructive pulmonary disease: A double-blind, placebo-controlled, randomized trial. *Lancet, 357*, 1571–1575.

The American Cancer Society. (2013). *Smokeless Tobacco.* http://www.cancer.org/cancer/cancercauses/tobaccocancer/smokeless-tobacco

The American Cancer Society. (2014). *What about electronic cigarettes? Aren't they safe?* http://www.cancer.org/cancer/cancercauses/tobaccocancer/questionsaboutsmokingtobaccoandhealth/questions-about-smoking-tobacco-and-health-e-cigarettes

Tobacco Control Research Branch of the National Cancer Institute. (2014). www.smokefree.gov

Toljamo, T., Hamari, A., Nieminen, P., et al. (2012). Young male daily smokers are nicotine dependent and experience several unsuccessful quit attempts. *Scandinavian Journal of Primary Health Care, 30*(3), 183–188.

Toljamo, T., Kaukonen, M., Nieminen, P., & Kinnula, V.L. (2010). Early detection of COPD combined with individualized counseling for smoking cessation: A two-year prospective study. *Scandinavian Journal of Primary Health Care, 28*, 41–46.

Velicer, W.F., Fava, J.L., Prochaska, J.O., et al. (1995). Distribution of smokers by stage in three representative samples. *Preventive Medicine, 24*, 401–411.

Velicer, W.F., Prochaska, J.O., Fava, J.L., et al. (1998). Smoking cessation and stress management: Applications of the Transtheoretical Model of behavior change. *Homeostasis, 38*, 216–233.

Wilson, D.H., Wakefield, M.A., Steven, I.D., et al., (1990). Sick of smoking: evaluation of a minimal smoking cessation intervention in general practice. *Medical Journal of Australia*, 518–521.

Yudkin, P., Hey, K., Roberts, S., et al. (2003). Abstinence from smoking eight years after participation in randomized controlled trial of nicotine patch. *British Medical Journal, 327*, 28–29.

Zaza, S., Briss, P.A., & Harris, K.W., (eds.) (2005). *The Guide to Community Preventive Services: What Works to Promote Health?* Atlanta, GA: Oxford University Press, 3–79.

Shari Altum, Ph.D., Rachel Juran, Psy.D., Katherine Butler, Psy.D.

# 8 Fostering Patient Self-Management of COPD

Key Points

1. Healthcare providers play an important role in helping patients learn to actively self-manage their COPD.
2. The core skills needed to become a good self-manager include problem-solving, decision-making, resource utilization, formation of the patient-provider relationship, and taking action.
3. Self-management tasks that are important to patients with COPD include tobacco cessation, medication adherence, establishing an action plan for exacerbations, learning to cope with breathlessness, eating a healthy diet, and following an exercise plan.
4. Self-management programs offer interventions that not only educate but also empower patients and their families by supporting their efforts toward health improvement.
5. Decision-making should be shared between the clinician and the patient and will vary depending on the stage of disease and the individual focus of the patient (e.g., curative vs. healing).

## 8.1 Introduction

Chronic Obstructive Pulmonary Disease (COPD), like most other long-term health problems, requires more from medical providers than medication management alone. It necessitates a collaborative partnership between patient and provider. Patient understanding of and investment in efforts to manage symptoms can impact disease burden, quality of life, and healthcare utilization. Although the most challenging aspect of chronic disease management is the art of engaging patients in active self-management, many primary care and pulmonary providers receive little training in these skills and feel least prepared for this aspect of their practice.

## 8.2 Clinician Skills

Clinician skills that foster behavior change are quite important to the overall management of COPD, but are often ignored. Orleans (1988, cited in Prochaska, 1994, p. 62) reported that 66% of medical providers are pessimistic about their patients' ability to change. This negativism can easily become the biggest obstacle to helping patients change. Patients and medical providers often feel hopeless about their circumstances and their ability to make improvements, which leads to a vicious cycle of poor health

**Table 8.1:** Key Concepts to Stimulate Behavior Change in Patients with COPD

| |
|---|
| – Knowledge does not equal motivation. |
| – Non-adherence to a treatment plan does not mean the patient does not care. |
| – It is the patient's agenda. |
| – Spend more time focusing on the positive effects of adaptive behaviors than on the negative effects of poor health choices. |
| – Stimulate patient responsibility by asking open-ended questions instead of giving advice or solving the problem for the patient. |
| – Help patients formulate action plans that are action-oriented, time-limited and measurable. |
| – Highlight patient self-efficacy by asking them how confident they are on a scale from 1 to 10 (with 10 being the most confident) that they can accomplish their action plan. |

outcomes. Clinicians need a basic understanding of the stages of change, as well as training in strategies such as motivational interviewing, to engage patients in efforts to improve their health. Interventions that are matched to the patients' readiness for change and help the patients explore their reasons, needs, and ability to change are much more likely to be effective.

In a comprehensive review of COPD self-management, Effing et al. (2012) offer practical tips for stimulating behavior change. Durdock (2010) also provides tips for affecting behavior change in patients with chronic diseases. The following list incorporates their recommendations, which are also summarized in Table 8.1:

1. **Knowledge does not equal motivation**. Knowledge can be a useful tool in helping patients identify a need to change. However, the process of changing behavior happens over time and involves several other key ingredients. Patients need to consider their ability to make a change, how it will impact the lives of others, how they will cope with any losses associated with the change, and where and how the new behavior might fit into their daily lives.
2. **Non-adherence to a treatment plan does not mean the patient does not care**. There may be a number of barriers to accomplishing behavioral goals. Teaching patients to brainstorm alternative strategies and resources is an important skill-building task to address barriers. The skilled clinician will ask open-ended questions to help explore and resolve ambivalence about making a change. Fight the urge to think negatively about a patient who does not seem to put effort towards behavior change. It may be that the patient feels helpless or depressed. The clinician's attitude can have a profound impact in either reinforcing the patient's negatively skewed view or providing hope and compassion.
3. **It is the patient's agenda**. The first question to ask might be, is this the patient's goal that he or she created? The patient must be the one to set priorities and iden-

tify what is most important for him/her to change. The clinician may feel that quitting smoking is a priority but the patient may select to invest in pulmonary rehabilitation instead. Often success with a smaller, more feasible goal will eventually lead to approaching larger, more challenging goals in the future. Alternatively, the patient may feel overwhelmed and depressed by the debility of the disease and select to invest in psychotherapy first before any other behavior change is feasible. It is important to offer options to patients and to honor their choices.

4. **Spend more time focusing on the positive effects of adaptive behaviors than on the negative effects of poor health choices**. It is tempting to share information about all the dangers of smoking or inactivity. If this is a strong urge, ask the patient what they know about the negative effects first. For many patients, a lack of knowledge is not the problem (see Tip #1). It is more important for the patient to verbalize how life will be better if he/she is able to make the behavior change. The more the patient states his/her reasons, abilities, desires and needs to change, the greater the likelihood that change will occur (Miller, 2013).
5. **Stimulate patient responsibility by asking open-ended questions instead of giving advice or solving the problem for the patient**. Patients are more engaged and activated when asked, "What concerns you the most about COPD and your health in the next five years?" or "What might you do differently to prevent another hospitalization?" It may actually take less clinician time and energy to ask these open-ended questions than to think of two or three ideas for the patient to try, only to hear the response, "No, that's not feasible for me."
6. **Help patients formulate action plans that are action-oriented, time-limited and measurable**. Patients just starting to make self-management goals should focus on weekly action plans and would benefit from weekly support. As patients successfully complete weekly action plans, they may be ready to create monthly or quarterly plans. Self-management classes like the Chronic Disease Self-Management Program, Living Well with COPD, Tobacco Treatment classes, and weight management classes are ideal for building this skill and generating success.
7. **Highlight patient self-efficacy by asking them how confident they are on a scale from 1 to 10 (with 10 being the most confident) that they can accomplish their action plan.** Ask what makes it the number given and not a LOWER number. This leads the patient to again vocalize the reasons, abilities, desires, and needs for completing the plan. This repetition may seem like a waste of precious time. However, stating the reasons for change is the most critical factor associated with behavior change (Miller, 2013).

## 8.3 Stages of Change

A patient's readiness for change is a crucial factor in all health behavior changes. Prochaska and DiClemente (1983) outlined the stages of change in their investigations of self-changers. They delineated five distinct stages in the Transtheoretical Model of Change (also known as the Stages of Change Model) that all self-changers progress through as they attempt to make a behavioral change. Generally, a person moves from being uninterested, unaware or unwilling to make a change (precontemplation), to considering making a change (contemplation), to deciding and preparing to make a change (preparation), to taking steps and problem-solving challenges or barriers (action), and to incorporating the change into a daily routine (maintenance). Relapses are usually inevitable and become part of the process of working toward permanent change. No matter what behavior is targeted for change, each stage is progressed through. No stage is skipped, although progress is often non-linear. Ambivalence about changes leads people to "recycle" through some stages several times. The Stages of Change model is discussed in more detail in Chapter 7.

## 8.4 Patient Self-Management Skills

Engaging patients in active self-management starts with Primary Care and often requires more intensive support and guidance from a variety of services to address a number of tasks. Self-management is generally understood as "the day-to-day tasks an individual must undertake to control or reduce the impact of disease on physical health status" (Clark, 1991, p. 5). Healthcare providers work with their patients to help them develop and sustain self-management. Self-management involves coping with direct physical symptoms and reduced ability as well as the psychosocial problems that may accompany COPD. Clark and colleagues (Clark, 1991) defined three tasks of good self-managers:

1. Have knowledge about the disease and treatment options in order to make informed decisions;
2. Complete tasks aimed at managing the condition;
3. Apply skills to manage psychosocial distress associated with the chronic illness.

The Social Cognitive Theory of self-management emphasizes the development of core skills needed to become a good self-manager (Lorig, 2003). These skills include: problem solving, decision-making, resource utilization, formation of the patient-provider relationship, and taking action. Workbooks and exercises lead patients to build these skills, often in individual case management visits or in patient education classes. Skill mastery is accomplished through completion of short-term action plans. This new competence leads to increased confidence and *self-efficacy*, which is the belief that one can successfully complete the desired task/behavior (Bandura, 1977). Improved self-efficacy is predictive of lasting behavior change.

**Table 8.2:** Prevalence of Tasks in COPD Self-Management Curricula

| Self-Management Task | Prevalence |
|---|---|
| Medication Adherence | 87% |
| Action Plan for Exacerbations | 74% |
| Tobacco Cessation | 74% |
| Coping with Breathlessness | 57% |
| Healthy Diet | 57% |
| Exercise Plan | 48% |

## 8.5 Self-Management Tasks

COPD-specific self-management tasks are a significant part of successful treatment. Zwerink and colleagues (Zwerink, 2014) completed a comprehensive review of COPD self-management studies and identified six tasks that are common to the various self-management curricula: 1) medication adherence, 2) exacerbation action plans, 3) smoking cessation, 4) coping with breathlessness, 5) healthy diet, and 6) exercise plan. A workgroup of COPD self-management experts concurred that all of these tasks except for medication adherence are essential to successful self-management of COPD (Effing, 2012). Table 8.2 depicts the prevalence of each task in the studies reviewed.

Medication adherence, exacerbation action plans, coping with breathlessness, healthy diet, and exercise plans specific to COPD will be discussed in depth in this chapter. Smoking cessation – perhaps the most important self-management task for patients with COPD – is discussed in detail in Chapter 7. Coping with psychosocial distress related to chronic illness is also an important self-management task that will be discussed further in Chapter 13. Energy conservation strategies (e.g., pacing of activities) will be reviewed briefly in this chapter and will be covered in more detail in Chapter 14.

Benzo et al. (2013) recommend offering patients a choice of a variety of self-management options. Graphic representations and worksheets may facilitate the selection process and serve to:

1. Educate the patient about all of the tasks involved in successful COPD self-management;
2. Allow the patient to explore and understand each option to make an informed decision;
3. Provide a worksheet to spell out a specific action plan to initiate change; and
4. Act as a reminder of all of the tasks and the behavioral plan.

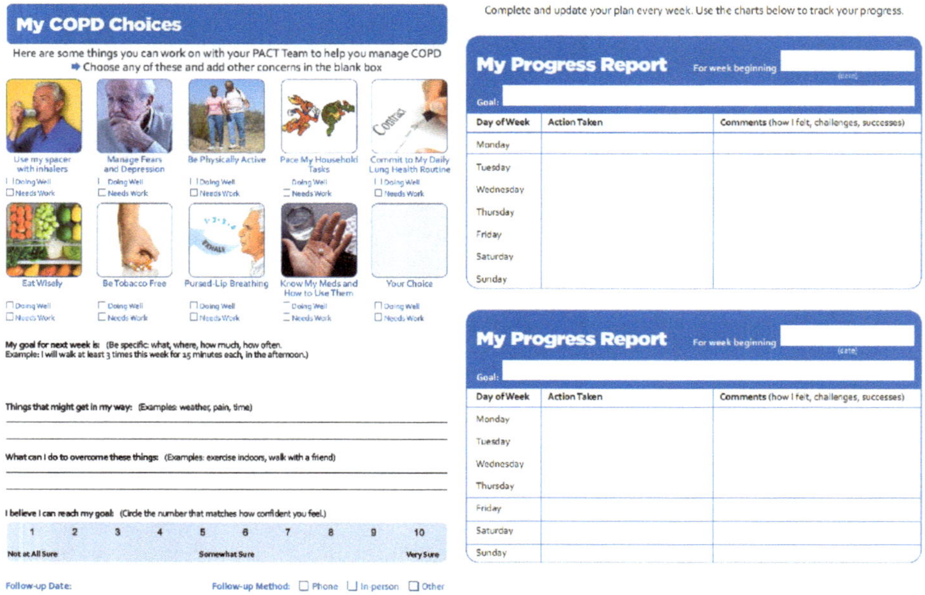


**Figure 8.1:** My COPD Choices. This handout offers the patient with COPD several choices of personal health management that they can work on with their primary care team. The COPD Choices handout is an example of an agenda setting tool that may aid patients in their management of their COPD.

Two examples of these agenda-setting tools are *My COPD Choices* (Figure 8.1) and *COPD Self-Management Choices* (Figure 8.2).

### 8.5.1 Medication Adherence

One specific behavior that is unique to COPD and requires special attention is proper inhaler use (see Chapter 15, *Correct Inhaler Techniques*). Patients are often confused about:

1. Which inhalers to take at what time;
2. The difference between short-acting and long-acting inhalers;
3. Whether a spacer is necessary;
4. How to properly use inhalers to get the most benefit.

Patients' poor compliance with COPD medications has been documented for decades (Windsor, 1980; Kaplan, 1990; Dolce, 1991; George, 2005; Krigsman, 2007a, b). Across studies, an average of 60% of COPD patients do not adhere to inhaler therapy over time (Chryssidis, 1981; Taylor, 1984; Dompeling, 1992; Bosley, 1994; Krigsman, 2007a,

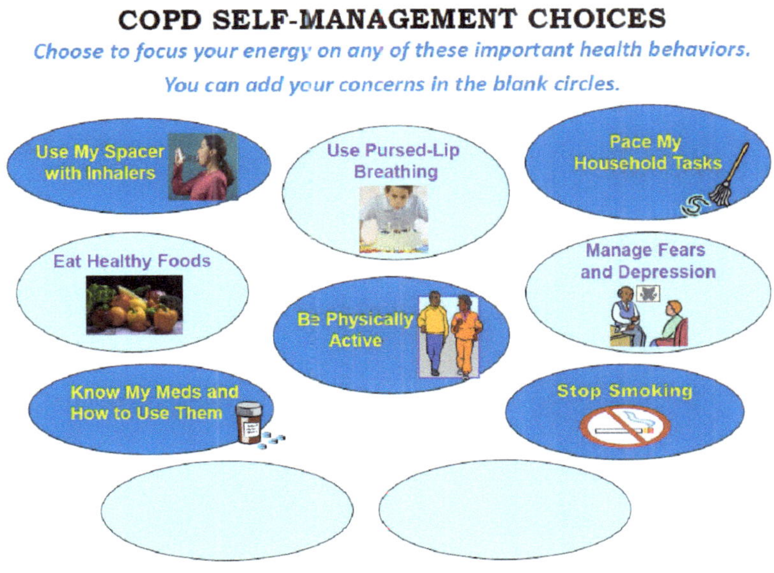


**Figure 8.2:** COPD Self-Management Choices. This handout assists the patient with COPD in the selection of healthy behaviors related to COPD and is another example of an agenda setting tool that might aid patients in their management of their COPD.

b; Haupt, 2008) and up to 85% do not use their inhalers correctly (Crompton, 1990; Thompson, 1994; Van Beerendonk, 1998; van der Palen, 1995, 1998; Hesselink, 2001; Serra-Batlles, 2002). The most common self-reported reasons for poor adherence to inhaler use are forgetting (51%) and consciously deciding not to use it when feeling good (31%; Dolce, 1991).

In a review by Restrepo et al. (2008), regular instruction, supervision, and re-demonstration of proper inhaler technique were recommended to improve inhaler adherence. It is well recognized that demonstration and supervised practice with inhalers are far superior to written instruction alone. Another visual aid that can reduce confusion and improve compliance is the *Cincinnati VAMC Respiratory Medications Visual Pillbox* (Figure 8.3), which displays pictures of all inhalers on the formulary classified by type of inhaler and spacer use if applicable, and denotes dosing schedules. Inhalers prescribed for a particular patient are circled and the dosing times are checked by the provider. The Visual Pillbox is used in conjunction with inhaler demonstrations and practice. To assist with re-teaching, patients waiting to see their provider may be invited to watch videos demonstrating proper inhaler use. Providers can follow up by asking the patient about any differences between their technique and that portrayed in the video. (Correct inhaler use techniques are reviewed in Chapter 15, Practical Guide to Inhaler Use.)

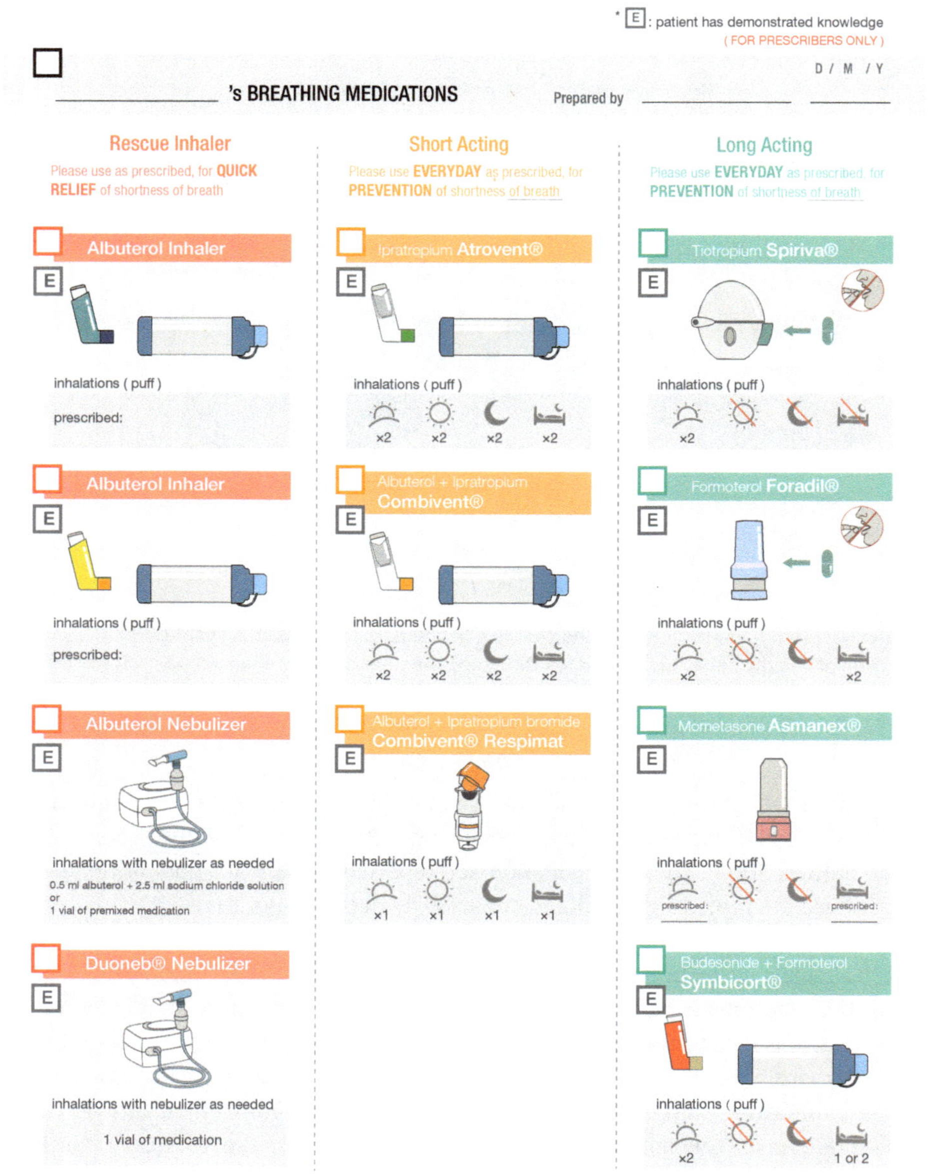


**Figure 8.3:** Visual Pillbox. The Cincinnati VAMC Respiratory Medications Visual Pillbox is a visual medication aid that can reduce confusion and improve medication adherence. Pictures of all inhalers on the formulary are classified by type of inhaler and spacer use (if applicable) and the dosing schedule is pictorially displayed. Inhalers prescribed for a particular patient are circled and the dosing times are checked by the provider. The Visual Pillbox should be used in conjunction with inhaler demonstrations and practice.

Although improving patient comprehension may be helpful for some, other barriers to compliance should be considered as well. Patients with poor medication compliance are less likely to have a strong sense of faith and trust in their provider, they are more likely to rely on natural remedies, and they have low confidence in treatment effectiveness (George, 2005). To a lesser extent, non-adherence is associated with the complexity of the medical regimen, patient concerns about side-effects, the cost of treatment, and the number of medications the patient is prescribed. Underuse, especially in periods of increased symptoms and respiratory distress, is a common problem that might also be related to depression. Depressed patients are three times more likely to be noncompliant with treatment regimens (DiMatteo et al., 2007).

### 8.5.2 Exacerbation Action Plans

Reduced frequency of hospitalizations has been a major focus in COPD self-management studies. The financial burden of hospitalization is considerable given that 34% of patients are readmitted for respiratory issues within 90 days of discharge (Bucknall, 2012). Initial hospitalization and readmittance may occur because patients have trouble identifying exacerbation symptoms. The subsequent delay in seeking treatment (Rice, 2010; Bourbeau, 2003) increases the need for more intensive treatment, such as hospitalization. Researchers have concluded that exacerbation action plans can help patients become better able to identify symptoms and implement appropriate treatment plans, thereby reducing delays in intervention, preventing or reducing hospital stays, and promoting quicker recovery. Exacerbation action plans have also demonstrated effectiveness for asthma, congestive heart failure, and diabetes (Ofman, 2004).

There is evidence that COPD exacerbation action plans improve health-related quality of life (Zwerink, 2014). A meta-analysis of nine studies indicated that when self-management interventions included an exacerbation action plan, the risk of a respiratory hospital admission was reduced (Zwerink, 2014). Bischoff et al. (2011) concluded that exacerbation action plans were associated with a decrease in the number of days to recovery and associated with reduced healthcare utilization. However, exacerbation action plans did not necessarily reduce hospitalizations (Bischoff, 2011; Trappenburg, 2011), particularly when there was limited follow-up or education about the plans (Walters, 2010). While many studies have shown COPD exacerbation plans to be effective, not all have consistently yielded positive results. In fact, one study was terminated before completion because of a higher rate of death in the intervention group (Fan, 2012). The researchers hypothesized that a theory-based comprehensive care management program, an individualized treatment action plan for worsening COPD symptoms, and telephone case management would reduce the risk of COPD-related hospitalizations for patients who have severe COPD and are at risk for hospital admission. The study was stopped after an imbalance in mortality between the usual care group and intervention group was discovered. When the study was terminated, 28 patients in the intervention group had died, compared to 10 patients in the usual care group. Despite extensive data analysis, no individual factors or combination of factors plausibly explained the differences in mortality (Fan, 2012).

There are emerging data that outline more specific characteristics of patients who benefit from exacerbation action plans. Gadoury and colleagues (2005) found several patient characteristics that predicted reduced hospitalizations, including being female, having a higher level of education, and increased walking capacity. Bucknall et al. (2012) identified patient activation or readiness for change, younger age, and living with other people as critical factors for patients to be successful self-managers and have fewer hospitalizations.

In sum, the research to date remains fairly inconclusive about the clinical effectiveness of exacerbation action plans. The proposed Department of Veterans Affairs/ Department of Defense [VA/DoD] Guidelines for COPD (2014) recommend the use of exacerbation action plans only within the context of close monitoring by providers to ensure supported self-management. As such, treatment effectiveness and successful mastery of the action plan must be assessed continuously to ensure comprehension and adherence. Symptom diaries, enlisting caregiver support, and self-report regarding adherence are possible strategies that will allow the provider to better support the patient's treatment adherence.

### 8.5.3 Coping with Breathlessness

Dyspnea, or breathlessness, is a multi-factorial symptom that involves both pathophysiologic and psychosocial factors. A cardinal feature of end-stage COPD, dyspnea can lead to high levels of distress and anxiety. Patients can benefit from having a thorough understanding of the causes of dyspnea (e.g., air trapping) and various self-management strategies they can use to gain a greater sense of control over their breathing. The most effective non-pharmacological treatments for dyspnea include pursed-lip breathing and pulmonary rehabilitation, although other strategies, such as abdominal breathing, yoga, and relaxation techniques, should be discussed to allow patients to decide what works best for them (Allen, 2010; see Chapter 14, Management of Stable COPD). Although a systematic review conducted by Holland et al. (2012) did not find evidence for consistent effects of pursed-lip breathing, abdominal breathing, and yoga on dyspnea or health-related quality of life, participants did experience improvement in exercise capacity.

Among patients with COPD, higher levels of anxiety and depression are associated with increased fatigue, dyspnea, and frequency of respiratory symptoms (Doyle, 2013). Dyspnea may occur in earlier stages of COPD in some patients, usually among females with comorbid anxiety and depression (Di Marco, 2005). Psychotherapy has been found to be useful for the treatment of depression and adjustment to chronic illness but is not directly effective in addressing dyspnea (Marciniuk, 2011). However, patients hospitalized with COPD exacerbations have demonstrated reductions in dyspnea, depression, and anxiety after learning controlled breathing techniques from a respiratory therapist (Valenza, 2014). Thus, learning to manage breathing independently can help to improve overall quality of life for patients with COPD. See Chapter 13, COPD's Effects on Psychosocial Functioning and Familial Interactions, for more information about the relationship between depression, anxiety, and COPD.

### 8.5.4 Exercise

Patients with COPD might find exercise to be too physically difficult to incorporate into their daily routines or they might feel overwhelmed by the amount of time and energy they are already contributing to self-managing COPD. Additionally, dyspnea can limit physical functioning. However, exercise programs, breathing retraining, and breathing exercises have been shown to reduce dyspnea and improve quality of life (VA/DoD, 2014). The proposed VA/DoD Clinical Practice Guideline for the Management of Chronic Obstructive Pulmonary Disease (2014) suggest that supervised exercise programs be provided to patients who have limited physical capabilities due to dyspnea.

Casaburi et al. (1997) investigated the effect of exercise tolerance and physiological responses in patients who have COPD. The researchers found that patients with severe COPD who exercise rigorously and regularly improve exercise breathing patterns and lower ventilation, both of which are associated with improved exercise tolerance. McNamara et al. (2013) suggested aquatic exercise for individuals who feel more comfortable with low-impact exercise. They concluded that aquatic exercise provides as much physical benefit (e.g., improve walking distance) as land-based exercise, and actually improves endurance exercise more than land-based exercise. Leung et al. (2013) determined that Sun-style t'ai chi is an effective moderate exercise for people with COPD, and can result in a number of health benefits (e.g., increased endurance shuttle walk time). For patients who are unable to participate in physical exercise because of dyspnea, the VA/DoD guidelines (2014) recommend offering breathing exercises to patients. One such breathing intervention is inspiratory muscle training (IMT). Inspiratory muscle training focuses on increasing the strength of the inspiratory muscles (e.g., the diaphragm) using a device or pursed lip breathing. Even when used as a stand-alone therapy, IMT is effective in strengthening inspiratory muscles, decreasing symptoms of dyspnea, and improving exercise capacity (Gosselink, 2011; Geddes, 2008). Finally, exercise has been shown to improve mental functioning. Emery et al. (2001) suggest that individuals with COPD have difficulty with fluid intelligence (the ability to take in new material and make sense of it). The researchers determined that just 20 minutes of exercise at peak levels (based on an individual's heart and breathing rates) improves mental functioning.

### 8.5.5 Nutrition

Proper nutrition is particularly important for patients with COPD who require more energy than individuals with normal lung functioning to acquire and utilize oxygen (Allen, 2010). Being underweight increases the risk of mortality for patients with COPD (Schols, 1993). Even patients with stable COPD can experience weight loss due to the disease, which highlights the importance of identifying and addressing weight changes quickly and effectively. Nutritional screening should focus on assessing BMI and weight change, the latter of which is defined as weight loss of more than 10% of one's body weight in the past six months, or more than 5% of one's body weight in the past month (Celli, 2004). Weight loss (i.e., imbalance between energy expenditure and dietary intake) and muscle wasting (i.e., imbalance between protein synthesis and break-down) contribute to the disability and mortality experienced by patients with COPD. As such, nutritional interventions may need to be combined with an exercise regimen in order to provide benefit to the patient (Creutzberg, 2003).

Patients should be educated about ways to obtain adequate caloric intake while choosing foods that do not raise carbon dioxide levels (i.e., choosing complex carbohydrates and healthy fats rather than simple carbohydrates and protein). Nutritional recommendations that might be made to all patients, such as watching salt intake, avoiding overeating, and staying hydrated, become particularly important for patients with COPD, whose ability to breathe and expel mucus are strongly impacted by these behaviors. Meal tips that may be beneficial for patients include sitting at the table while eating to encourage good posture and allow the diaphragm to work properly, taking small bites and chewing slowly to prevent overeating, resting before eating to maintain energy during the meal, and drinking fluids at the end of the meal to allow room for food (Allen, 2010).

## 8.6 Self-Management Programs

There are outstanding resources available to support patients with COPD and the healthcare teams who treat them. Self-management programs specific to COPD include pulmonary rehabilitation and Living Well with COPD (www.livingwellwithcopd.com, 2014). Other self-management programs, including the Chronic Disease Self-Management Program, tobacco treatment, and weight management programs, are also excellent options to empower patients and support their efforts toward health improvement. A few of the above-mentioned programs will be reviewed to address their unique contributions to COPD management.

### 8.6.1 Pulmonary Rehabilitation

Pulmonary rehabilitation (PR) primarily focuses on building physical strength and endurance through a supervised, graded exercise program that occurs several times per week. The American Thoracic Society (ATS) and the European Respiratory Society (ERS) recently updated their definition of pulmonary rehabilitation (Spruit, 2013, p. e14):

> "Pulmonary rehabilitation is a comprehensive intervention based on a thorough patient assessment followed by patient-tailored therapies that include, but are not limited to, exercise training, education, and behavior change, designed to improve the physical and psychological condition of people with chronic respiratory disease and to promote the long-term adherence to health-enhancing behaviors."

Most PR programs are multi-disciplinary and include weekly education and support sessions to address a number of self-management tasks. Topics may include basic education about COPD and how to manage it, proper medication use, nutrition, energy conservation, coping with difficult emotions, and breathing strategies. There are a number of positive outcomes associated with pulmonary rehabilitation, including reduced dyspnea, increased exercise capacity, and improved quality of life (Spruit, 2013). Similar results were found in a systematic review of 18 randomized clinical trials that focused on home-based programs, which suggests that home-based pulmonary rehabilitation is an acceptable alternative to clinic-based programs (Liu, 2014).

Recent research has also added the following new advances (Spruit et al., 2013, p. e14):

- There is increased evidence for use and efficacy of a variety of forms of exercise training as part of pulmonary rehabilitation; these include interval training, strength training, upper limb training, and transcutaneous neuromuscular electrical stimulation.
- Symptomatic individuals with COPD who have lesser degrees of airflow limitation and participate in pulmonary rehabilitation derive similar improvements in symptoms, exercise tolerance, and quality of life as do those with more severe disease.
- Pulmonary rehabilitation initiated shortly after a hospitalization for a COPD exacerbation is clinically effective, safe, and associated with a reduction in subsequent hospital admissions.
- Exercise rehabilitation commenced during acute or critical illness reduces the extent of functional decline and hastens recovery.
- Appropriately resourced home-based exercise training has proven effective in reducing dyspnea and increasing exercise performance in individuals with COPD.
- The scope of outcomes assessment has broadened, allowing for the evaluation of COPD-related knowledge and self-efficacy, lower and upper limb muscle function, balance, and physical activity.
- Symptoms of anxiety and depression are prevalent in individuals referred to pulmonary rehabilitation, may affect outcomes, and can be ameliorated by this intervention

### 8.6.2 Living Well with COPD

Living Well with COPD is a self-management program that teaches patients with COPD the skills necessary to manage their illness in a collaborative environment designed to enhance self-efficacy and motivation for change. The goal of Living Well with COPD is to "develop a partnership between patients and healthcare professionals to facilitate the adoption of healthy lifestyle behaviors and the skills needed to better manage COPD on a day-to-day basis" (Nault, 2006). Drawing from the chronic care model (Wagner, 2001), the Chronic Disease Self-Management Program (Lorig, 2003), and the Precede-Proceed Model (Green, 1999), Living Well with COPD provides educational interventions that are tailored to the learning needs of individual patients and are designed to enhance self-efficacy, increase motivation to create and maintain behavioral change, and facilitate mastery of self-management skills. The objectives of the program are to help patients improve quality of life, maximize autonomy, prevent and manage progression of the disease, and help caregivers support the patients' efforts to achieve behavioral change.

Living Well with COPD can be completed on a weekly basis in individual sessions, a group setting, or as part of a pulmonary rehabilitation program. The program consists of seven skill-oriented modules that provide detailed information related to self-management of various facets of COPD (e.g., medication compliance, controlling breathlessness, prevention and management of exacerbations). The patient education process requires that the educator utilize the following steps:

1. Assessment of readiness and motivation to learn,
2. Setting mutually realistic learning goals and objectives,
3. Use of efficient educational methods,
4. Implementation of educational objectives, and
5. Evaluation of patients' learning outcomes (e.g., direct questioning, problem solving, repetition of key instructions).

Effective provision of the Living Well with COPD program requires that the provider (i.e., any health care professional willing to devote time to this process) have both expertise regarding proper management of COPD as well as empathy and enthusiasm for the patients and their journey toward effective COPD self-management through long-term behavior change. (Patients and providers can learn more about the program at www.livingwellwithcopd.com.)

Utilization of the Living Well with COPD program yields positive outcomes. In a one-year, multi-site, randomized clinical trial, the program improved quality of life, reduced hospitalizations and emergency department visits for COPD exacerbations by 40%, and decreased unscheduled medical visits by nearly 60% (Bourbeau, 2003). Another one-year, multi-site, randomized clinical trial conducted by Gadoury et al. (2005) found that participants of the Living Well with COPD program continued to demonstrate reductions in all-cause hospitalizations (27%) and all-cause emergency visits (21%) at the end of a two-year follow-up period.

### 8.6.3 Chronic Disease Self-Management Program

Disease-specific education is necessary but not sufficient to produce patient actions related to managing the disease (Becker, 1980). Becoming a better self-manager is linked to learning how to set goals, organize resources, and use problem-solving strategies (Clark, 1991). Bodenheimer et al. (2002) indicated that self-management classes that included action planning were more likely to improve health outcomes, particularly for participants with more severe symptoms.

The Chronic Disease Self-Management Program (CDSMP), which was created by Kate Lorig, Virginia Gonzalez, and Diana Laurent, focuses on developing self-management skills needed to manage effectively any chronic health condition by teaching goal-setting, problem-solving, and action planning (Lorig, 2012). This structured treatment, led by healthcare professionals and/or lay leaders, is unique in its ability to address a number of health problems in one group format. Patients with comorbid chronic conditions can benefit from the patient education approach, which focuses on improving breathing, healthy eating, physical activity, medication usage, dealing with difficult emotions, relaxation strategies, positive thinking, and communication skills. However, the true lasting benefit from the program is the skill building that takes place around brainstorming, problem solving, and action planning. Each class incorporates an opportunity to brainstorm, a process where ideas are quickly generated without being questioned or censored to allow for the most creative and extensive list possible. Participants also learn and practice a problem-solving method that encourages them to consider and try alternative strategies, which provides a greater sense of control and improves investment in care.

Action planning in CDSMP helps participants work toward goals of their choice during and between each class. Participants may choose any goal, as long as it meets the criteria listed in Table 8.3 (Lorig, 2001). Initially, participants may struggle to meet all these criteria, perhaps choosing things that will not fit into their schedule, are more strenuous than they can handle, or involve resources they may not have. The group is utilized to brainstorm ways to make the plan more specific or practical and build the participants' confidence in their ability to succeed. The following session involves progress reports and brainstorming by the group to identify strategies that can make the goal more feasible. Through this process, participants learn to make action plans that they can accomplish. They build on small successes and become more confident in their ability to feel in control of their symptoms and their lives.

Lorig et al. (2001) conducted a two-year follow-up study that looked at health status, health care utilization and self-efficacy outcomes for 831 participants 40-years or older with heart disease, lung disease, stroke, or arthritis. Participants who completed at least four of six CDSM sessions had significantly fewer ER and outpatient visits, declines in self-reported health distress, and improvement in perceived self-efficacy. Boedenheimer et al. (2002) reported that patients attending self-management classes had fewer hospitalizations over a six-month period compared to con-

**Table 8.3:** Elements of Patient-Selected Goals During Action Planning in the Chronic Disease Self-Management Program

| |
|---|
| – Something YOU (the patient) want to do |
| – Achievable |
| – Action-specific |
| – Answers the questions: |
| 1. What? |
| 2. How much? |
| 3. When? |
| 4. How often? |
| – Level of confidence in your ability to complete your action plan<br>– GOAL: 7 or more on a scale of 1–10 |

trols. Healthcare utilization cost savings of the program have been estimated between $390–$750 per year per participant (Lorig, 2001; Boedenheimer, 2002).

Ongoing engagement in self-management is critical to maximizing health, wellness, and independence. The Chronic Disease Self-Management Program is one tool that effectively engages patients and helps them recognize and become actively engaged in their care.

## 8.7 Shared Decision-Making

Shared decision-making is the clinical process that occurs when providers share treatment options, including risks and benefits, and patients weigh their options based on their values and beliefs. While shared decision-making might be most critical when considering end-of-life care, it should be a vital part of all stages of chronic disease management. Clinicians provide the expert information about treatment options, risks, and benefits. Patients feel empowered to use the information to make the choices that fit them best.

Shared decision-making is supported by a focus on whole person care (Hutchinson, 2011), which broadens the scope of clinical interactions to include all aspects of the patient's life, including physical, emotional, and spiritual factors. A whole person assessment expands beyond a physical exam to include conversations about supportive relationships, meaningful activities, stable safe housing, physical activity, healthy eating, stress and sleep, and active involvement in medical care. This process offers the opportunity for patients and providers to gain a full picture of all aspects of life and how they interact. Creating this unique perspective of one's life allows the patient to see strengths and areas in which progress is being made. Patients may also start

**Figure 8.4:** Wheel of Health. The *Cincinnati VAMC Personalized Health Plan Wheel of Health* is an example of a patient handout that can be used to facilitate a whole person assessment. The patient is asked to review each area of health and determine whether they are doing well, are working on improvements, or want to work on improvements. The Wheel of Health provides the patient with a self-assessment tool that can also be used by providers to explore those areas that the patient has identified as important and, potentially, those areas that they are interested in improving.

to make connections between areas of difficulty and prioritize areas that still need to be addressed. See Figure 8.4 (*Cincinnati VAMC Personalized Health Plan Wheel of Health*) for an example of a document that can be used to facilitate a whole person assessment.

Chronic disease management calls upon the medical provider and the patient to choose between two areas of focus: curative or healing (Hutchinson, 2011) (Table 8.4). Patients who seek a cure are focused on survival and maintaining all things in life prior to disease onset, which leads to efforts to avoid change, whether adaptive or maladaptive. Patients seeking a cure often have an external locus of control and feel powerless to improve their situation. They look to medical professionals to “fix” the problem. Those seeking a cure are in the precontemplation stage of change and often use defense mechanisms such as externalizing, blame, and denial. Alternatively, patients who are able to shift to a healing perspective are accepting of change. They develop a new identity and are able to recognize that their own actions and efforts can

**Table 8.4:** Curative and Healing/Palliative Areas of Focus for Providers and Patients

| **Curative** | **Healing / Palliative** |
|---|---|
| – Patient:<br>– Is focused on survival<br>– Is focused on maintaining "pre-diagnosis" life<br>– Avoids changes<br>– Feels powerless to improve situation<br>– Looks to health care professionals to fix it<br>– Externalizes, blames, denies | – Patient:<br>– Accepts change<br>– Develops new identity<br>– Recognizes power in situation |
| – Provider:<br>– Uses scientific knowledge to assess symptoms and diagnosis<br>– Focuses on symptom constellations, physical exam and test results<br>– Prescribes treatments | – Provider:<br>– Follows patient's lead<br>– Offers treatments based on patient's preferences<br>– Works within a team<br>– Uses a *whole person approach* |

help them obtain functional improvement and satisfaction. The shift from a curative focus to a healing focus is commonly referred to as *adjustment to chronic illness.*

The role of the provider varies depending on whether the patient is in "curing" mode or "healing" mode. If the patient is focused on finding a cure, the provider can use scientific knowledge to assess symptoms and arrive at a diagnosis. The focus is on the use of algorithms, symptom constellations, physical exam, and test results. Evidenced-based treatments are prescribed. When the patient is focused on "healing" – or palliative care – a collaborative patient-provider relationship is necessary. Rather than directing an assessment using an algorithm, the provider can offer treatment options but follow the patient's wishes as the patient shares what he/she would like to change, how important the change is, and how he/she would like to make it. A team approach is often most effective and fosters an environment of support and guidance that is important for behavioral changes. This whole person approach relieves suffering and promotes healing, particularly in COPD care. The process helps foster a sense of wholeness and balance. Patients identify what really matters in their lives, and clinicians use this information to better align the patients' health goals and behaviors with their priorities.

Of note, as disease severity increases, the treatment often shifts from being patient-driven to provider-driven. In the early stages of COPD, patients are physically able to invest in exercise programs and self-management classes, which reduces disease burden and improves functioning. Having a positive attitude about patients' ability and desire to improve is critical during this phase. Adjustment to disease, readiness for change, anxiety, and depression are all possible complicating factors that may make behavior change more challenging. A perspective of whole person health, including physical, emotional, and spiritual health, can help to identify these potential barriers and lead patients to appropriate resources. As COPD progresses, physical limitations increase, and other comorbid conditions impact health, patients become more reliant on medical providers for direction and support. Again, anxiety and depression may develop as patients develop fears about dying and feel that their situation is hopeless.

## 8.8 End-of-Life Discussions

Advanced stages of COPD require a shift in care choices to address end-of-life issues. The primary care provider is often identified as the most appropriate person on the healthcare team to initiate this discussion. Timing of the discussion may be difficult to gauge. The American Thoracic Society recommends that it take place when the patient is stable rather than during an acute exacerbation or hospitalization (American Thoracic Society, 2014). Lanken et al. (2007) argue that palliative care discussions are appropriate anytime there is an exacerbation of symptoms. Discussions about restorative measures are likely to occur simultaneously with options for palliative care.

Curtis et al. (2004) reported that only about a third of patients with COPD discuss end-of-life choices with their primary care provider. As compared to patients with other life-threatening illnesses like cancer and HIV, COPD patients are less satisfied with the information they receive from their healthcare provider about COPD, its course, and end-of-life planning (Curtis, 2004). One complicating factor for providers is the large variability of decline. Patients with very severe impairment can live an average of three years (Celli, 2004), adding to the challenge of when to initiate the end-of-life discussion.

Au et al. (2011) found that COPD patients want to know how long they have to live and what dying might be like and they would like their providers to ask them about their religious beliefs and their feelings about disease progression. While this discussion is best initiated by the primary care provider, it is clearly a topic about which all members of the integrated care team should be well informed and prepared to address. The discussion is likely to happen over a series of visits with different members of the team. It is worthy of revisiting after acute episodes, whether hospitalization was necessary or not. Au et al. (2011) suggest that providers create a standard statement that might help initiate the end-of-life conversation (e.g., "This is something I talk about with all my patients to make sure I understand their wishes."). Core skills of motivational interviewing, reflections, and open-ended questions are useful to explore and clarify the patient's preferences, values, and wishes. Examples of standard statements and open-ended questions can be found in Table 8.5. (See Chapter 19, Palliative Care and Hospice, for more information about end-of-life issues.)

**Table 8.5:** Examples of Motivational Interviewing Standard Statements and Open-Ended Questions

- "What concerns you the most about dying?"
- "Where would you like to be and who will be with you when you die?"
- (after discussing treatment options) "What treatment options would you prefer?"
- "If you could be assured of one thing about dying, what would it be?"

## 8.9 Integrated Care Teams

All self-management studies of COPD agree that a multifaceted approach from an integrated care team is most effective. Wagner (1998) supports an integrated team approach in his Chronic Care Model. His model focuses on Primary Care as the hub and the patient-provider relationship as critical to health improvement. Across studies, key ingredients of services tend to vary, making it difficult to discern whether an ideal combination exists. Patient preference and disease severity are two factors that might impact the options for integrated team members/services. Table 8.6 outlines possible available options and attempts to categorize the service based upon disease severity and the addressed needs and skills. These suggestions are based on the COPD Specialty Care Neighborhood Project at the Cincinnati VAMC (2011–2014).

## 8.10 Conclusion

Effective self-management of COPD requires active collaboration between the provider and the patient. This alliance will help facilitate patient understanding of and investment in effective disease management which can impact disease burden, quality of life, and healthcare utilization. Self-management strategies should focus on tobacco cessation, medication adherence, establishing an exacerbation action plan (with close monitoring) to intervene early and prevent full-blown exacerbations and hospitalizations, using effective breathing techniques, eating a healthy diet, and following an exercise plan. Patients can benefit from a variety of self-management programs (e.g., pulmonary rehabilitation, Living Well with COPD, Chronic Disease Self-Management Program) that are designed to provide education about COPD, increase motivation to create and maintain behavioral changes, and teach skills necessary to problem-solve when barriers to effective symptom management arise. Providers should utilize strategies to stimulate and support behavior change in patients by maintaining awareness of how a patient's stage of change and approach to managing chronic illness (i.e., curative or healing) are individually and collectively impacting the patient's self-management behaviors. By taking a whole person approach to treatment, providers can help patients feel empowered by their strengths and recognize the areas in which

**Table 8.6:** Effect of COPD Severity on Skills Offered by Integrated Team Members/Services

| Disease Severity | Type of Service | Skill Building Offered |
|---|---|---|
| 1–4 | Primary Care Provider | 1. Diagnoses<br>2. Medication management<br>3. Referral for self-management |
| 1–3 | RN Care Manager in Primary Care | 1. Inhaler teaching<br>2. Individualized self-management training for COPD<br>3. Transitions of care – Inpatient, Primary Care, Pulmonology<br>4. Referral to self-management<br>5. Monitoring of exacerbation action plan |
| 1–3 | Clinical Pharmacist | 1. Initial inhaler teaching<br>2. Individualized self-management training for COPD |
| 1–2 | Chronic Disease Self-Management Classes Ex., Living Well with COPD, Chronic Disease Self-Management Program | 1. Problem-solving<br>2. Action planning<br>3. Decision-making<br>4. Partnering with providers<br>5. Building self-efficacy |
| 1–2 | Other Related Self-Management Programs Tobacco Treatment Weight Management Classes | 1. Action planning<br>2. Building self-efficacy |
| 1–2 | Telephone Support, Text Support, Secure Email and Mobile Apps for Self-Management[a] | 1. Action planning<br>2. Problem-solving<br>3. Building self-efficacy<br>4. Maintaining improvements long-term |
| 1–2 | Shared Medical Appointment for COPD[b] | 1. Medication management<br>2. Inhaler teaching<br>3. Symptom management<br>4. Action planning |
| 2–3 | COPD Case Manager in Pulmonary Clinic | 1. Inhaler teaching<br>2. Individualized self-management training for COPD<br>3. Symptom management<br>4. Transitions of care – Inpatient, Primary Care, Pulmonology<br>5. Monitoring of exacerbation action plan |
| 2–3 | Home Telehealth Nurse for COPD[c] | 1. Adherence to medication<br>2. Problem-solving<br>3. Decision-making<br>4. Action planning<br>5. Symptom management |

continued **Table 8.6:** Effect of COPD Severity on Skills Offered by Integrated Team Members/Services

| Disease Severity | Type of Service | Skill Building Offered |
|---|---|---|
| 1–4 | Primary Care Provider | 1. Diagnoses<br>2. Medication management<br>3. Referral for self-management |
| 1–3 | RN Care Manager in Primary Care | 1. Inhaler teaching<br>2. Individualized self-management training for COPD<br>3. Transitions of care – Inpatient, Primary Care, Pulmonology<br>4. Referral to self-management<br>5. Monitoring of exacerbation action plan |
| 1–3 | Clinical Pharmacist | 1. Initial inhaler teaching<br>2. Individualized self-management training for COPD |
| 1–2 | Chronic Disease Self-Management Classes<br>Ex., Living Well with COPD, Chronic Disease Self-Management Program | 1. Problem-solving<br>2. Action planning<br>3. Decision-making<br>4. Partnering with providers<br>5. Building self-efficacy |
| 1–2 | Other Related Self-Management Programs<br>Tobacco Treatment<br>Weight Management Classes | 1. Action planning<br>2. Building self-efficacy |
| 1–2 | Telephone Support, Text Support, Secure Email and Mobile Apps for Self-Management[a] | 1. Action planning<br>2. Problem-solving<br>3. Building self-efficacy<br>4. Maintaining improvements long-term |
| 1–2 | Shared Medical Appointment for COPD[b] | 1. Medication management<br>2. Inhaler teaching<br>3. Symptom management<br>4. Action planning |
| 2–3 | COPD Case Manager in Pulmonary Clinic | 1. Inhaler teaching<br>2. Individualized self-management training for COPD<br>3. Symptom management<br>4. Transitions of care – Inpatient, Primary Care, Pulmonology<br>5. Monitoring of exacerbation action plan |
| 2–3 | Home Telehealth Nurse for COPD[c] | 1. Adherence to medication<br>2. Problem-solving<br>3. Decision-making<br>4. Action planning<br>5. Symptom management |

continued **Table 8.6:** Effect of COPD Severity on Skills Offered by Integrated Team Members/Services

| Disease Severity | Type of Service | Skill Building Offered |
|---|---|---|
| 2–3 | Pulmonary Rehabilitation | 1. Increased strength and endurance<br>2. Problem-solving<br>3. Decision-making<br>4. Action planning |
| 3 | Home Based Primary Care[d] | 1. Inhaler teaching<br>2. Symptom management<br>3. Medication management<br>4. Monitoring of exacerbation action plan |
| 3 | Hospital at Home[e] | 1. Early intervention to prevent exacerbation<br>2. Intensive treatment to reduce length of hospital stay |
| 3–4 | Inpatient/Palliative Care | 1. Resolve exacerbation<br>2. Symptom Management<br>3. Quality of Life decisions |
| 4 | Hospice | 1. End of life care |

Note: Disease Severity refers to the GOLD standards: 1 = mild; 2 = moderate ; 3 = severe; 4 = terminal
Explanation of select types of service: a = clinical visits by telephone or email to follow-up on self-management goals; patient initiated text message service or mobile app that provides tips, inspirational messages, tracking tools to support self-management; b = a group visit coordinated and led by the Primary Care team that incorporates education, action planning, and individual medical review; c = a home monitoring program that involves daily reporting of vitals and symptoms with follow-up by a nurse if responses indicate support or medical review is needed; d = an interdisciplinary team that provides comprehensive Primary Care services and close monitoring of patients at risk for hospitalization; e = a focused interdisciplinary team that sees patients in the home daily for a brief period of time to prevent or stabilize a COPD exacerbation/hospitalization.

they can take more responsibility for their own well-being. Providers can also engage patients in discussions about end-of-life care to ensure that patients have the opportunity to receive answers to their questions and to express their wishes.

## 8.11 Summary Points

1. Learning specific skills (e.g., problem-solving, resource utilization, taking action) can help patients feel more confident in their ability to initiate and maintain long-term behavioral change.
2. While tobacco cessation is perhaps the most important self-management task, patients who effectively manage COPD also succeed in implementing other self-management strategies (e.g., medication adherence, using an action plan for

exacerbations, learning to cope with breathlessness, eating a healthy diet, and following an exercise plan).

3. Behavior change is a complex process that occurs over time. Self-management programs, such as pulmonary rehabilitation, Living Well with COPD, and the Chronic Disease Self-Management Program offer more intensive support, skill building, and translation of skills to everyday life.
4. Clinicians should have a basic understanding of the stages of change in order to match interventions to the patients' readiness for change which is clarified through exploration of the patient's motivations, needs, and abilities.
5. Collaborative end-of-life discussions involving the patient and family members should be conducted in a way that respects the patient's current stage of acceptance but also calls attention to the importance of making end-of-life decisions as early as possible.

## References

Altum, S. (2014). *My COPD Choices.* (Unpublished.) Cincinnati Veterans Affairs Medical Center, Cincinnati, OH.

Au, D.H., Udis, E.M., Engelberg, R.A., et al. (2011). A randomized trial to improve communication about end-of-life care among patients with COPD. *Chest, 141*(3), 726–735.

Bandura, A. (1977). Analysis of self-efficacy theory of behavioral change. *Cognitive Theory and Research, 1*(4), 287–310.

Becker, M.H., & Maiman, L.A. (1980). Strategies for enhancing patient compliance. *J Community Health, 6*(2), 113–135.

Bischoff, E.W., Hamd, D.H., Sedeno, M., et al. (2011). Effects of written action plan adherence on COPD exacerbation recovery. *Thorax, 66*(26), 26–31.

Bodenheimer, T., Lorig, K., Holman, H., et al. (2002). Patient self-management of chronic disease in primary care. *JAMA, 288*(19). 2469–2475.

Bosley, C.M. Parry, D.T., & Cochrane GM. (1994). Patient compliance with inhaled medication. Does combining beta agonists with corticosteroids improve compliance? *Eur Respir J, 7,* 501–509.

Bourbeau, J., Julien, M., Maltais, F., et al. (2003). Reduction of hospital utilization in patients with chronic obstructive pulmonary disease: A disease-specific self-management intervention. *International Archives of Medicine*, 163, 585–591.

Bucknall, C.E., Miller, G., Lloyd, S.M., et al. (2012). Glasgow supported self-management trial (GSuST) for patients with moderate to severe COPD: randomised control trial. BMJ, 344(e1060).

Celli, B.R., MacNee, W., & Committee Members. (2004). Standards for the diagnosis and treatment of patients with COPD: A summary of the ATS/ERS position paper. *European Respiratory Journal, 23*: 932–946.

Chryssidis, E., Frewin, D.B., Frith, P.A., et al. (1981). Compliance with aerosol therapy in COPD. *NZ Med J, 250,* 122–124.

Cincinnati VAMC. *Respiratory Medications Visual Pillbox.* (Revised 4/2013).

Clark, N.M., Becker, M.H., Janz, N.K., et al. (1991). Self-management of chronic disease by older adults: A review and questions for research. *Journal of Aging and Health,* **3***(1),* 3–27.

Creutzberg, E.L., Wouters, E.F., Mostert, R., et al. (2003). Efficacy of nutritional supplementation therapy in depleted patients with chronic obstructive pulmonary disease. *Nutrition, 19*: 120–127.

Collins, P.F., Elia, M., & Stratton, R.J. (2013). Nutritional support and functional capacity in chronic obstructive pulmonary disease: A systematic review and meta-analysis. *Respirology, 18*(4):616–629.

COPD Working Group (2012). Pulmonary rehabilitation for patients with chronic pulmonary disease (COPD): An evidence-based analysis. *Ontario Health Technology Assessment Series, 12*(6),1–75.

Crompton, G.K. (1990). The adult patient's difficulties with inhalers. *Lung, 168,* (Suppl), 658–662.

Curtis, J.R., Wenrich, M.D., Carline, J.D., et al. (2004). Patients' perspectives on physicians' skills at end-of-life care: Differences between patients with COPD, cancer, and AIDS. *Chest, 122,* 356–362.

Di Marco, F., Verga, M., Reggente, M., et al. (2006). Anxiety and depressionin COPD patients: The roles of gender and disease severity. *Respir Med*, 100, 1767–74.

DiMatteo, M.R., Haskard, K.B., & Williams, S.L. (2007). Health beliefs, disease severity, and patient adherence: A meta-analysis. *Med Care, 45,* 521–528.

Dolce, J.J., Crisp, C., Manzella, B., et al. (1991). Medication adherence patterns in chronic obstructive pulmonary disease. *Chest, 99*, 837–841.

Dompeling, E., Van Grunsven, P.E., Van Schayck, C.P. et al. (1992). Treatment with inhaled steroids in asthma and chronic bronchitis: Longterm compliance and inhaler technique. *Fam Pract, 9, 161–166.*

Doyle, C., Dunt, D., Ames, D., & Selvarajah, S. (2013). Managing mood disorders in patients attending pulmonary rehabilitation clinics. *International Journal of COPD, 2013:*8, 15–20.

Durdock, K. (2010). Top 5 tips for case managers working with chronic disease. Motivational Interviewing: An emerging trend in medical management. Rockville, MD: Access Intelligence. Retrieved from: http://c.ymcdn.com/sites/www.patientadvocatetraining.com/resource/resmgr/files/ppai_specialreport_mi.pdf

Effing, T.W., Bourbeau, J., Vercoulen, J., et al. (2012). Self-management programmes for COPD: Moving forward. *Chronic Respiratory Disease, 9*(1), 27–35.

Fan, V.S., Gaziano, J.M., Lew R., et al. (2012). A comprehensive care management program to prevent chronic obstructive pulmonary disease hospitalizations: A randomized, controlled trial. *Annuals of Internal Medicine, 156*(10), 673–683.

Gadoury, M.A., Schwarzman, K., Rouleau, M., et al. (2005). Self-management reduces both short- and long-term hospitalization in COPD. *European Respiratory Journal, 26*(5), 853–857

Geddes, E.L., O'Brien, K., Reid, W.D., et al. (2008). Inspiratory muscle training in adults with chronic obstructive pulmonary disease: an update of a systematic review. *Respir, 102*, 1715–29.

Gosselink, R., De Vos, J., van den Heuvel, S.P., et al. (2011). Impact of inspiratory muscle training in patients with COPD: What is the evidence? *Eur Respir J, 37*(2), 416–425.

George, J., Kong, D.C., Thomas, R., et al. (2005). Factors associated with medication nonadherence in patients with COPD. *Chest, 128,* 3198–3204.

Haupt, D., Krigsman, K., & Nilsson, J.L. (2008). Medication persistence among patients with asthma COPD drugs. *Pharm World Sci, 30*(5), 509–514.

Hesselink, A.E., Penninx, B.W., Wijnhoven, H.A., et al. (2001). Determinants of an incorrect inhalation technique in patients with asthma or COPD. *Scand J Prim Health Care, 19*, 255–260.

Holland, A.E., Hill, C.J., Jones, A.Y., et al. (2012). Breathing exercises for chronic obstructive pulmonary disease. *Cochrane Database Syst Rev., 10,* Cd008250.

Hutchinson, T.A. (2011). Whole Person Care, in *Whole Person Care: A New Paradigm for the 21st Century*, Tom A. Hutchinson, Editor.

Kaplan, R.M., Toshima, M.T., Atkins, C.J., et al. (1990). Behavioral interventions for patients with COPD. In O'Keene, J.K., Shumaker, S.A. (eds). *Adoption and Maintenance of Behavior for Optimal Health*. New York: Springer Verlag.

Krigsman, K., Nilsson, J.L., et al. (2007a). Refill adherence by the elderly for asthma/chronic obstructive pulmonary disease drugs dispensed over a 10-year period. *J Clin Pharm Ther, 32*, 603–611.

Krigsman, K., Lars, J.G., & Ring, L. (2007b). Refill adherence for patients with asthma and COPD: Comparison of a pharmacy record database with manually collected repeat prescriptions. *Pharmacoepidemiol Drug Saf, 16*, 441–448.

Juran, R. (2014). *COPD Self-Management Choices* (Unpublished). Cincinnati Veterans Affairs Medical Center, Cincinnati, OH.

Lanken, P.N., Terry, P.B., DeLisser, H.M., et al. (2008). An Official American Thoracic Society Clinical Policy Statement: Palliative Care for Patients with Respiratory Diseases and Critical Illnesses. *American Journal of Respiratory Critical Care Medicine, 177*, 912–927.

Lorig, K., Gonzalez, V., & Laurent, D. (2012). *The Chronic Disease Self-Management Workshop: Leader's Manual.* Stanford, CA: The Board of Trustees, Leland Stanford Junior University.

Lorig, K.R., Holman, H. (2003). Self-management education: history, definition, outcomes, and mechanisms. *Annuals of Behavioral Medicine*, *26*, 1–7.

Lorig, K.R., Ritter, P., Stewart, A.L., et al. (2001). Chronic Disease Self-Management Program: 2-Year Health Status and Health Care Utilization Outcomes. *Medical Care*, *39*(11),1217–1223.

Leung, R.W., McKeough, Z.J., Peters, M.J., et al. (2013). Short-form Sun-style t'ai chi as an exercise training modality in people with COPD. *European Respiratory Journal, 41*(5), 1051–1057.

Liu, X.L., Tan, J.Y., Wang, T., et al. (2014). Effectiveness of home-based pulmonary rehabilitation for patients with chronic obstructive pulmonary disease: A meta-analysis of randomized controlled trials. *Rehabil Nurs, 39*(1), 36–59.

Marciniuk, D.D., Goodridge, D., Hernandez, P., et al. (2011). Managing dyspnea in patients with advanced chronic obstructive pulmonary disease: A Canadian Thoracic Society clinical practice guideline. *Can Respir J, 18*(2), 69–78.

McGill University Health Centre & Quebec Asthma and COPD Network. (2014). *Living Well with COPD.* Retrieved from http://www.livingwellwithcopd.com

McLean, S., Nurmatov, U., Liu, J.L., et al. (2011). Telehealthcare for chronic obstructive pulmonary disease. *Cochrane Database Syst Rev,* 7, Cd007718.

McNamara, R.J., McKeough, Z.J., McKenzie, D.K., et al. (2013). Water-based exercise training for chronic obstructive pulmonary disease. *Cochrane Database Syst Rev,* 12:Cd008290.

Miller, W.R & Rollnick, S. (2013). *Motivational Interviewing: Helping People Change* (3rd ed.). New York, NY: Guilford Press.

Nault, D., & Sedeno, M. Reference Guide for Patient Education: Education COPD Patients Using the Self-Management Program "Living Well with COPD." From http://www.livingwellwithcopd.com/DATA/DOCUMENT/70_en~v~introduction-reference-guide-for-patient-education.pdf

Ofman, J.J., Badamgarav, E., Henning, J.M., et al. (2004) Does disease management improve clinical and economic outcomes in patients with chronic diseases? A systematic review. *Am J Med, 117,* 182–92.

Orleans, C.T., et al. (1988, November). *Effectiveness of self-help quit smoking strategies*. Symposium presented at the annual meeting of the Association for the Advancement of Behavior Therapy, New York, N.Y.

Ortega, F., Toral, J., Cejudo, P., et al. (2002). Comparison of effects of strength and endurance training in patients with chronic obstructive pulmonary disease. *American Journal of Respiratory and Critical Care Medicine, 166*, 669–674.

Personalized Health Plan Wheel of Health. (2014). Cincinnati Veterans Affairs Medical Center, Cincinnati, OH.

Peytremann-Bridevaux I., Taffe P., Burnand B., et al. (2014). Mortality of patients with COPD participating in chronic disease management programmes: A happy end? *Thorax, 69*(9), 865–866.

Prochaska, J., & DiClemente, C. (1983). Stages of processes of self-change of smoking: Toward an integrative model of change. *Journal of Consulting and Clinical Psychology, 51*(3), 390–395.

Prochaska, J., DiClemente, C., & Norcross, J. (1992). In search of how people change: Applications to addictive behaviors. *American Psychologist, 47*(9), 1002–1114.

Restrepo, R.D., Alverex, M.T., Wittnebel, L.D., et al. (2008). Medication adherence issues in patients treated for COPD. *International Journal of COPD, 3*(3), 371–384.

Rice K., Bourbeau J., MacDonald R., et al. (2014). Collaborative self-management and behavioral change. *Clin Chest Med,* 35(2), 337–351.

Rice, K.L., Dewan N., Bloomfield, H.E., et al. (2010). Disease management program for chronic obstructive pulmonary disease: A randomized controlled trial. *American Journal of Respiratory and Critical Care Medicine, 182*(7), 890–896.

Siyuan, F. (2013). *Integrating design into interactive personal medicine education experience.* (Electronic Thesis). Retrieved from https://etd.ohiolink.edu/

Schols, A.M., Soeters, P.B., Dingemans, A.M., et al. (1993). Prevalence and characteristics of nutritional depletion in patients with stable COPD eligible for pulmonary rehabilitation. The *American Review of Respiratory Disease, 147*:1151–1156.

Serra-Batlles, J., Plaza, V., Badiola, C., et al. (2002). Patient perception and acceptability of multidose dry powder inhalers: A randomized crossover comparison of Diskus/Accuhaler with Turbuhaler. *J Aerosol Med, 15* 59–64.

*COPD Specialty Care Neighborhood Project*. (2014). (Unpublished). Cincinnati Veterans Affairs Medical Center, Cincinnati, OH.

Spruit, M.A., Singh, S.J., Garvey, C., et al. (2013). An official American Thoracic Society/European Respiratory Society statement: Key concepts and advances in pulmonary rehabilitation. *Am J Respir Crit Care Med, 188*(8), e13–64.

Taylor, D.R., Kinney, C.D., & McDevitt, D.C. (1984). Patient compliance with oral theophylline therapy. *Br J Clin Pharm, 17,* 15–20.

Thompson, J., Irvine, T., Grathwohl, K., et al. (1994). Misuse of metered-dose inhalers in hospitalized patients. *Chest, 105,* 715–717.

Trappenburg, J.C., Monninkhof, E.M., Bourbeau, J., et al. (2011) Effect of an action plan with ongoing support by a case manager on exacerbation-related outcome in patients with COPD: A multicentre randomised controlled trial. *Thorax, 66*(11), 977–984.

Valenza, M.C., Valenza-Peña, G., Torres-Sánchez, I., et al. (2014). Effectiveness of controlled breathing techniques on anxiety and depression in hospitalized patients with COPD: a randomized clinical trial. *Respiratory Care: 59*(2). 209–15. doi: 10.4187/respcare.02565

Van Beerenconk, I., Mesters, I., Mudde, A.N., et al. (1998). Assessment of the inhalation technique in outpatient with asthma or chornic obstructive pulmonary disease using a metered-dose inhaler or dry powder devise. *J Asthma, 35,* 273–279.

van der Palen, J., Klein, J.J., Kerkhoff, A.H., et al. (1995). Evaluation of the effectiveness of four different inhalers in patients with chronic obstructive pulmonary disease. *Thorax, 50,* 1183–1187.

van der Palen, J., Klein, J.J., Schildkamp, A.M. (1998). Comparison of a new multidose powder inhaler (Diskus/Accuhaler) and the Turbuhaler regarding preference and ease of use. *J Asthma, 35,* 147–152.

Wagner, E.H. (1998). Chronic disease management: What will it take to improve care for chronic illness? *Eff Clin Pract, 1,* 2–4.

Wagner, E.H., Glasgow, R.W., Davis, C., et al. (2001). Quality improvement in chronic illness care: A collaborative approach. *The Joint Commission Journal on Quality Improvement, 27*(2), 63–80.

Walters, J.A.E., Turnock, A.C., Walters, E.H., et al. (2010). Action plans with limited patient education only for exacerbation of chronic obstructive pulmonary disease (Review). *The Cochrane Library*, *5*.

Windsor, B.A., Green, L.W., & Roseman, B.M. (1980). Health promotion and maintenance for patients with chronic obstructive pulmonary disease, a review. *J Chronic Dis, 33*, 5–12.

Zwerink, M., Brusse-Keizer, M., van der Valk, P., et al. (2014). Self-management for patients with chronic obstructive pulmonary disease (Review). *The Cochrane Library*, *3*.

Muhammad Ahsan Zafar, MD

# 9 Natural History, Phenotypes, and Gender Differences in COPD

Key Points
1. COPD is a heterogeneous group of diseases characterized by persistent airflow obstruction with a variable rate of decline in lung function.
2. Progression of lung function decline varies and is dependent upon continued smoking, presence of emphysema, responsiveness to bronchodilators, and acute exacerbations of COPD.
3. The single best predictor for a COPD exacerbation is a history of prior exacerbations. Other risk factors include advanced disease, gastro-esophageal reflux, poorer quality of life, and elevated white blood cell count.
4. Different phenotypes of COPD vary in their clinical presentation, exacerbation rates, disease progression, and response to treatment. Current known phenotypes include asthma-COPD overlap syndrome, frequent exacerbation, emphysema predominant, mucus producers, and alpha 1-antitrypsin deficiency.
5. Gender differences in COPD include differential disease presentation, response to therapies, and health care delivery and utilization.

## 9.1 Natural History of COPD

Chronic Obstructive Pulmonary Disease (COPD) is a constellation of heterogeneous lung diseases characterized by persistent expiratory airflow limitation that is non-normalizing (does not return to predicted levels), and an abnormal inflammatory response of the lungs to noxious particles and gases such as cigarette smoking (GOLD, 2014). COPD is a preventable and treatable chronic lung disease with a wide range of systemic manifestations (reviewed in Chapter 10). Contrary to the classic belief (Fletcher, 1976), all patients with COPD do not experience progressive, accelerated decline in lung function; instead, the clinical presentation and disease course can be vastly variable among individuals and are influenced by numerous factors (Vestbo, 2011).

COPD is caused by several different and overlapping etiologies. Tobacco smoking is the leading cause of COPD worldwide. Smoking exposure in the form of cigarettes, cigars, water-pipes, or second hand exposure also increases the risk of disease (Koeverden, 2014; Raad, 2011; Thun, 2013). Occupational and environmental exposures account for 20–30% of COPD cases. In urban areas, environmental air pollution (Tashkin, 1984) and working in dusty places (Melbostad, 1997) play roles in the development of COPD; whereas, in rural areas and developing countries, smoke generated from biomass fuels (Lopez, 2006) is a major risk factor. The risk of occupational and environmental exposures increases geometrically with concomitant tobacco smoke exposure (Blanc, 2009). Significant inter-individual variation to the injury caused by these noxious particles is caused by different genetic susceptibilities that lead to modulation of the inflammatory response. A genome wide search (COPDGene) has identified multiple genes that are associated with COPD development and inter-person variations in disease manifestations (Castaldi, 2014; Cho, 2014).

Our ability to recognize the heterogeneity in pathophysiology and clinical course of COPD has led to the recognition of 'phenotypes' of COPD. The characterization of different phenotypes is essential as they can vary in clinical course, symptoms, response to different treatments, and prognosis (Mannino, 2013). One example of such a phenotype is the "frequent exacerbator" type. These patients experience multiple episodes of acute decompensation in respiratory status related to COPD called acute exacerbations of COPD. The disease course, health care utilization, and therapeutic options for this category of patients are different than for non-frequent exacerbators (Hurst, 2010). The treatment guidelines from the Global Initiative for Obstructive Lung Disease (GOLD, 2014) encourage physicians to identify this phenotype and adjust maintenance therapies accordingly.

It is also important to recognize that COPD is a systemic inflammatory disease with extensive and variable extra-pulmonary involvement (Agusti, 2013). Our understanding of these extra-pulmonary manifestations is evolving and their role in influencing the long term disease course and outcomes is unclear. Most longitudinal studies have used lung function (such as forced expiratory volume in 1 second, $FEV_1$) as a hallmark of disease state. However, $FEV_1$ may not be influenced by the numerous extra-pulmonary manifestations and, hence, may not correctly estimate the disease state or progression. This prognostic limitation of physiologic variables has led to the development of newer multi-dimensional approaches to assess disease severity and progression. One example of a multivariable assessment tool is the BODE index which is comprised of Body mass index, airflow Obstruction, Dyspnea, and Exercise capacity (Celli, 2004). Higher scores on the BODE index correspond to a higher risk of death. Searches for other surrogate markers to monitor disease progression and response to treatments are currently underway (Vestbo, 2008).

## 9.2 Factors Influencing Lung Function in COPD

A natural decline in lung function is observed as part of aging in healthy individuals. After reaching maximal lung growth, a plateau phase of lung function exists between 20 and 30 years of age (Figure 9.1). After this plateau phase, a healthy person may lose 1L of $FEV_1$ in 50 years of adult life at an average rate of decline of 20 ml/year.

The natural history of lung function decline in COPD is influenced by multiple factors occurring over a person's life span. The factors include early life events such as intra-uterine and childhood lung development, childhood-adolescent lung growth, and later life exposures such as smoking, occupational chemical, dust, and fume

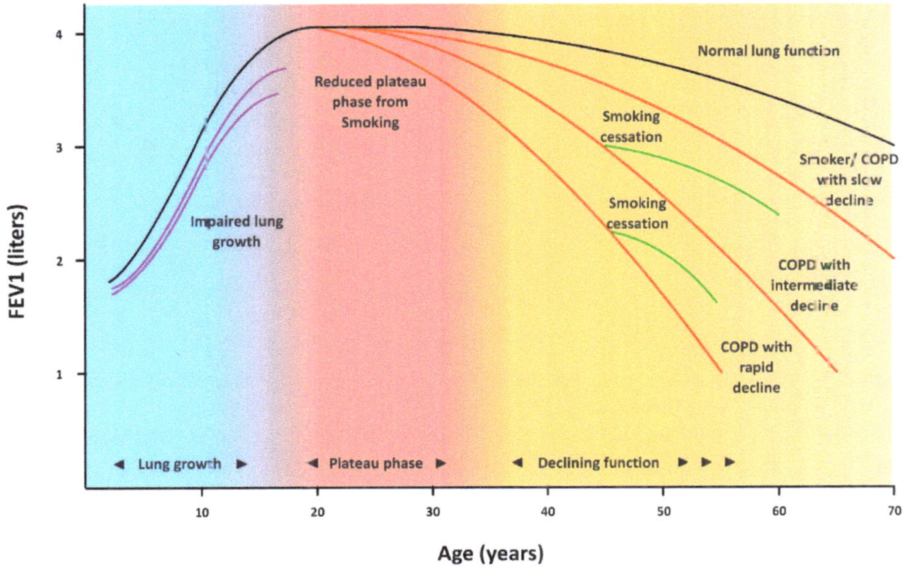


**Figure 9.1:** The course of lung function ($FEV_1$) throughout life. Black line: lung function trend in healthy individuals. **Purple lines:** impaired lung growth due to various factors that influence "maximal lung growth". **Red lines:** trends in lung function decline in patients with COPD. Trends in $FEV_1$ decline have variations based on different factors and phenotypes. The decline may not be a continuous trend as shown in the figure, but can also be a step-wise decline due to acute exacerbations of COPD. **Green lines:** effect of smoking cessation on lung function. The beneficial effect of smoking cessation may be variable at different stages of COPD as shown by different trajectories.

inhalation. In addition, genetic factors are also critically important. Each person may vary in lung function capacity at any given time in life and will experience different trajectories of lung function decline, as shown in Figure 9.1. The roles of factors that influence the lung function in COPD are described here and summarized in Figure 9.2.

### 9.2.1 Lung Growth and Early Life Events

In humans, the conducting airways are developed during intra-uterine life by 16 weeks of gestation (Ten Have-Opbroek, 1981). However, the development of gas exchange units (respiratory bronchioles and alveoli) continues throughout childhood into the early adolescent years. After eight years of life, the alveolar number does not increase any further and lung growth is then achieved by increases in the size of the alveoli and airways. Any significant life event during this period of lung development can reduce the maximum lung function that a person achieves in adulthood (Stern, 2007). Infant onset atopy, maternal asthma, and maternal smoking are associated with low

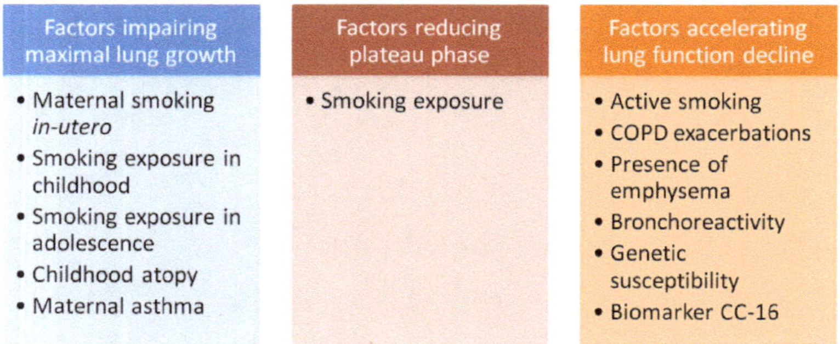


**Figure 9.2:** Factors associated with reduced lung function in different phases of lung life. Lung function in patients with COPD is affected by multiple factors during the lung growth phase, plateau phase and declining lung function phase. Smoking exposure is a major contributor of reduced lung function in all phases of lung life. CC-16: Clara cell secretory protein 16

lung function that is detectable at 1 month of age and persists through 18 years of age (Turner, 2014). Cigarette smoking in adolescence also slows lung growth and reduces the maximally attained lung function (Gold, 1996). Therefore, the maximal lung function achieved by individuals can vary and these differences in "baseline" lung function may affect the onset of COPD in later life.

### 9.2.2 Cigarette Smoking

Smoking is the most influential factor affecting the natural history of COPD. It plays a role in disease development, severity of lung function impairment, frequency of exacerbations, and progression of disease. Maximal lung growth is reduced by maternal smoke exposure and smoking during the adolescent years while the lungs are still growing (Gold, 1996; Turner, 2014). During the 'plateau phase' of maximal lung function, smokers experience a premature onset of lung function decline which reduces the duration of this phase. In severe cases, the plateau phase may even become non-existent (Tager, 1988). Finally, continued smoking most strongly affects the annual rate of lung function decline in patients with COPD. The rate of decline as measured by $FEV_1$ is 21 ml more per year in active smokers than non-smokers or previous smokers. Thus, an average active smoker will lose almost 40 ml/year of lung function compared with a natural 20 ml/year decline in healthy aging adults. The cumulative prior smoke exposure does not influence the annual rate of lung function decline (Vestbo, 2011).

Smoking cessation at any time during adulthood is expected to slow the rate of decline in lung function (Anthonisen, 2002). The magnitude of smoking cessation's effect, however, may be variable at different stages of COPD, with a lesser change noted in advanced stages (Jha, 2013; Kohansal, 2009; Vestbo, 2011).

### 9.2.3 Genetic Susceptibility

COPD presents with heterogeneous clinical features and the smoking related injury to the lungs may vary among individuals (Burrows, 1964; Burrows, 1966). Genetic susceptibilities contribute significantly to the manifestation of these variations (Ingebrigtsen, 2010). Previously, the only proven genetic abnormalities that caused a predisposition to the development of COPD were mutations in the alpha 1-antitrypsin inhibitor gene – a serine proteinase inhibitor (Eriksson, 1964; Laurell, 2013). Concurrent tobacco smoke exposure further accelerates the lung function decline in patients with alpha 1-protease inhibitor mutations (Silverman, 1998). Recent large population based genome wide sequencing studies (COPDGene) have revealed strong genetic associations with development, severity, and phenotypes of COPD (Cho, 2012). Several gene loci such as *CH RNA3, FAM13A, HHIP, RIN3, MMP12 and TGFB2*, have been associated with the development of moderate and severe COPD (Cho, 2014). Genetic associations have been linked to the pattern of distribution of emphysema in smokers. Mild upper zone emphysema is associated with rs1980057 near *HHIP*, and severe emphysema with rs8034191 on chromosome 15q region (Castaldi, 2014).

### 9.2.4 Advancing Age

COPD is associated with advancing age; however, it remains unclear if age itself is a risk for COPD or whether it reflects lung injury related to the cumulative effect of exposures throughout life. Human lung parenchyma loses elasticity with age which results in the development of airflow obstruction. In normal aging, this process is slow and does not lead to clinically significant respiratory impairment (Figure 1). In COPD, however, there is loss of lung parenchymal elasticity leading to air flow limitation and respiratory symptoms. Thus, COPD can be regarded as premature and accelerated aging of the lungs.

### 9.2.5 Emphysema

Emphysema is characterized by destruction of gas-exchanging air spaces. In genetically susceptible individuals, the response to lung injury from smoking or other noxious stimuli may lead to emphysematous changes (Castaldi, 2014). The presence and extent of emphysema can be assessed radiographically using computed tomography (CT) scans (Gietema, 2011). Emphysema is an independent risk factor for rapid decline in lung function. In the 'Evaluation of COPD Longitudinally to Identify Predictive Surrogate Endpoints – ECLIPSE' cohort, patients with emphysema had an additional 13 ml decline in their $FEV_1$ annually compared to those without emphysema (Vestbo, 2011). Similar findings have been seen in other cohorts where emphysema is associated with rapid decline (Nishimura, 2012; Yuan, 2009). The presence of emphysema also independently increases the risk of COPD exacerbations irrespective of the disease severity measured by $FEV_1$. Patients with emphysema that involves more than 35% of the lung parenchyma are at a higher risk for COPD exacerbations. The risk continues to increase by 1.18 fold for every 5% increase in emphysema area (Han, 2011). The rate of increase in the extent of emphysema is variable among individuals and is related to smoking and gender. A more rapid increase is observed in women and in active smokers (Coxson, 2013).

### 9.2.6 Bronchodilator Responsiveness

A subset of patients with COPD has a significant bronchodilator response measured by pulmonary function testing. These individuals experience a more rapid rate of decline in $FEV_1$ and lose an additional 17 ml yearly (Vestbo, 2011). They are at higher risk for exacerbations, hospitalizations, and worse health related quality of life (Hardin, 2011; Menezes, 2014). However, despite these distinct features, the presence and magnitude of bronchodilator responsiveness is not uniformly consistent and changes over time in this subset of COPD patients (Albert, 2012).

### 9.2.7 Early Disease

Diagnosing early stage COPD is essential but remains challenging for multiple reasons (Csikesz, 2014). First, patients do not experience disabling symptoms until the disease has advanced due to high baseline pulmonary reserves. Patients may also adapt their life style by reducing activity to compensate for their symptoms. Secondly, in the past, it was incorrectly thought that early diagnosis of COPD is a fruitless chore as the treatment does not alter the course of disease (Celli, 1995). Patients with early disease actually have a faster rate of lung function decline and an increased mortality primarily related to acute cardiac events (Sin, 2005; Vestbo, 2011). In the ECLIPSE cohort, patients with GOLD stage 2 disease ($FEV_1$ 80–50% of predicted) had a mean rate of $FEV_1$ decline of 35 ml/year, which was significantly higher than 33 ml/year for GOLD stage 3 and 25 ml/year for GOLD stage 4 patients (Vestbo, 2011). This inverse relationship between GOLD stage of airflow severity and rate of $FEV_1$ decline has been consistently noted in other long term studies (Calverley, 2007; Tashkin, 2008). Some patients with early disease have also shown evidence of lung function recovering with appropriate treatment (Galban, 2012; Vestbo, 2011). These findings have sparked interest to identify early COPD to prevent rapid decline, reduce mortality, and institute treatment with goals of complete normalization of lung function.

### 9.2.8 Biomarkers

Numerous biomarkers have been investigated to predict the disease course and identify various phenotypes. Among the few that have shown potential, serum fibrinogen level is most significantly associated with disease severity and exacerbation rate. Elevated serum white blood cell count level is also associated with increased exacerbations. Weak associations are observed with Clara cell secretory protein 16 (CC-16) and the rate of lung function decline (Faner, 2014; Hurst, 2010a; Vestbo, 2011).

## 9.3 Role of COPD Exacerbations and Progression of Disease

The disease course of COPD is punctuated with episodes of acute exacerbations which are associated with significant increases in health care utilizations, cost, and mortality (Miravitlles, 2002; Soler-Cataluna, 2005). Exacerbations are episodes of worsening of respiratory symptoms outside of normal day-to-day variations. They are associated with airway and systemic inflammation and increased dynamic hyperinflation (O'Donnell, 2006).

In the last two decades, the importance of exacerbations in lung function decline and worse patient outcomes has been increasingly recognized. Previously, based upon the work of Fletcher and Petro, exacerbations were thought to have an insignificant role in overall disease course (Fletcher, 1976). Acute exacerbations of COPD are now known to have both short and long term effects on disease course and outcomes. Given their deleterious impact on patients, reducing the rates and severity of COPD exacerbations has now become a widely accepted surrogate marker of treatment success in clinical trials. The following effects of exacerbations are observed in patients with COPD:

### 9.3.1 Lung Function Decline

Exacerbations accelerate the rate of lung function decline. Patients with frequent exacerbations have an almost 25% faster rate of $FEV_1$ decline compared to those who do not have frequent exacerbations (Donaldson, 2002; Kanner, 2001). Larger observational and interventional studies such as the UPLIFT trial and ECLIPSE cohort have confirmed that patients with frequent exacerbations have lower $FEV_1$ at any stage of the disease compared to those who do not have frequent exacerbations (Halpin, 2012; Vestbo, 2011). Frequent exacerbations also accelerate the rate of lung function decline, which increases in a linear fashion as the number of exacerbations per year increase (Halpin, 2012).

### 9.3.2 Quality of Life

Acute exacerbations of COPD significantly impair patients' health status. Different tools have been used to assess the effect of exacerbations on quality of life and all of these instruments show significant deterioration that persists for prolonged periods of time. Major recovery is seen four weeks after the event; however, it may take up to six months to achieve baseline functionality. If patients suffer another exacerbation during this time period, the effects on health status are much more profound (Seemungal, 1998; Spencer, 2003).

An acute fall in outdoor activities is seen after an exacerbation. This reduction is thought to be related to physical inactivity, bed rest, and changes in metabolic, nutritional, and inflammatory states associated with the episode (Donaldson, 2005; Pitta, 2006). Exacerbations also have permanent effects on physical activity of the patients. Patients with frequent exacerbations (>2 per year) have a faster decline in time spent outdoors each day, -0.16 h/year, compared to infrequent exacerbators (Donaldson, 2005).

### 9.3.3 Mortality

Mortality after a severe exacerbation requiring hospitalization increases dramatically to 40 deaths per 10,000 patients per day in the first week after admission. The rate then gradually drops down to 5 deaths per 10,000 patients per day after 3 months (Suissa, 2012). There is a wide range of reported inpatient mortality from COPD exacerbations which is influenced by comorbid conditions and practice variations. Risk factors for inpatient mortality include cor pulmonale, congestive heart failure, low arterial pH, age, $SpO_2$ <86%, mechanical ventilation, and low body mass index (Connors, 1996; Roberts, 2002).

Frequent acute exacerbations are independent risk factors for all-cause mortality in COPD (Soler-Cataluna, 2005). The risk of death increases with each subsequent exacerbation. The mortality risk is five times greater after the tenth admission compared to the first admission (Suissa, 2012).

### 9.3.4 Factors Associated with COPD Exacerbations

It is estimated that COPD patients suffer between one and four exacerbations per year; however, these events are not uniformly distributed among all individuals with COPD. Many factors have been identified to increase the risk and susceptibility to exacerbations. A list of known risk factors associated with repeated exacerbations is provided in Table 9.1. The single best predictor of a future exacerbation is a history of prior exacerbations. Exacerbations tend to occur more frequently as the disease progresses.

**Table 9.1:** Risk Factors associated with frequent exacerbations of COPD (*Modified from: Miravitlles, 2012)*

| **Risk Factors** |
|---|
| History of previous exacerbation<br>– Most predictive risk factor; odds ratio >5 |
| Older age |
| Asthma - COPD overlap syndrome *OR* COPD with bronchodilator responsiveness |
| Lower body mass index (BMI) |
| COPD severity:<br>– Greater baseline dyspnea<br>– Low $FEV_1$<br>– Low $PaO_2$ |
| Inflammation<br>– Greater airway inflammation<br>– Greater systemic inflammation |
| Bacterial load in stable disease phase |
| Chronic bronchial hyper-secretion |
| Comorbidity/ extra pulmonary manifestations<br>– Cardiovascular<br>– Anxiety-depression<br>– Myopathy<br>– Reflux |
| $FEV_1$: Forced expiratory volume in 1 second, $PaO_2$: Partial pressure of oxygen in arterial blood. |

In the ECLIPSE cohort, other factors associated with frequent (≥ 2 per year) exacerbations were gastro-esophageal reflux, poorer quality of life, and elevated serum white blood cell count (Hurst, 2010).

COPD exacerbations tend to occur in clusters and the risk of subsequent exacerbations increases exponentially with each episode. After the 10th episode of exacerbation, the risk of subsequent exacerbations is 24-fold higher relative to the risk after the first episode (Suissa, 2012). A subset of patients experience exacerbations more frequently and are identified as the 'frequent exacerbator' phenotype. See section 9.4.5 for more information about this phenotype.

## 9.4 COPD Phenotypes

A phenotype refers to the physical appearance or biochemical characteristics that result from the expression of genes, environmental influences, and their interactions. In COPD, the causative genes are mainly unknown or poorly characterized; hence, the phenotypes in COPD are synonymous with clinical subgroups. The one exception to this clinical characterization is alpha 1-antitrypsin (A1AT) deficiency where a defined genetic abnormality predisposes to the development and rapid acceleration of COPD. Classification of patients with different COPD phenotypes identifies subgroups of patients with features that impact their outcomes and response to certain treatments. Thus, COPD phenotype is defined as: **"A COPD phenotype is a single or combination of disease attributes that describe differences between individuals with COPD as they relate to clinically meaningful outcomes (symptoms, exacerbations, response to therapy, rate of disease progression or death)."** (Han, 2010)

The concept of COPD phenotypes dates back to the original recognition of smoking associated lung disease with two separate categories: emphysema and chronic bronchitis, which were clinically classified as the "pink puffer" and "blue bloater" (Burrows, 1964; Burrows, 1966). These were considered separate diseases before being unified under the term COPD (Karon, 1960). The heterogeneity in COPD has long been recognized (Warren, 2009) and suggestions of different phenotypes have also been described previously (Snider, 1989). One phenotype is unlikely to be uniquely present in a patient. As described by Snider in 1989, there seems to be significant overlap among subgroups where one patient may have multiple different phenotypic traits. Figure 9.3 shows a non-proportional Venn diagram of different COPD phenotypes.

### 9.4.1 Different Phenotypes of COPD

The phenotypes of COPD can be broadly categorized under the following types: genetic, physiologic, anatomic, and clinical. Table 9.2 is a list of various COPD phenotypes in these respective categories which are distinguished based on their disease manifestations, clinical course, and therapeutics.

### 9.4.2 Genetic: Alpha 1-antitrypsin Deficiency

Alpha 1-antitrypsin (A1AT) deficiency is the most common and most well established genetic cause of emphysema. A1AT is a serine proteinase inhibitor or serpin encoded on the serpin a-1 gene (Pi) on chromosome 14. Expression of two parental alleles determines the protein phenotype. Normal phenotype PiMM is present in 90% of the white population. There are more than 75 know pleomorphic alleles, some of them

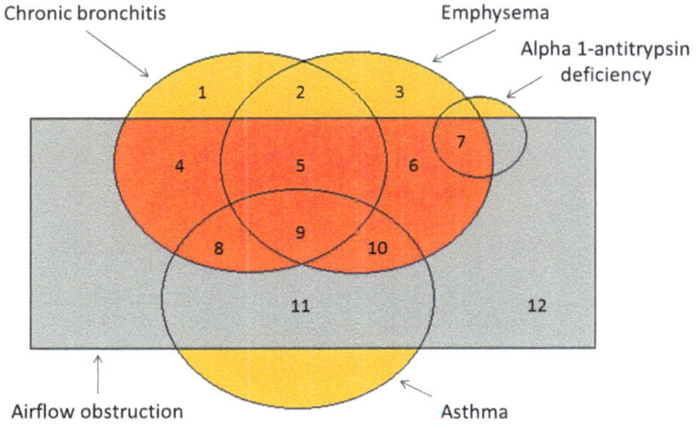


**Figure 9.3:** Non-proportional Venn diagram of COPD phenotypes. The COPD subset is colored red. The grey rectangle represents airflow obstruction. The yellow subsets have features of either chronic bronchitis, emphysema, asthma or alpha 1-antitrypsin deficiency (A1ATD) but do not have airflow obstruction to qualify for COPD. Subset areas are non-proportional to the actual relative subset size. Patients with asthma whose airflow obstruction completely normalizes (subset 11) are not considered to have COPD. Because in many cases it is nearly impossible to differentiate patients with asthma whose airflow obstruction does not remit completely from persons with chronic bronchitis and emphysema who have airflow obstruction with bronchodilator responsiveness, patients with unremitting asthma are classified as having COPD, asthma - COPD overlap syndrome or COPD with bronchodilator responsiveness (subset 8,9 & 10). Chronic bronchitis and emphysema with airflow obstruction usually occur together (subset 5), and some patients may have asthma associated with these two disorders (subset 9). Individuals with asthma who have been exposed to chronic irritation, such as from cigarette smoke, may develop achronic productive cough, which is a feature of chronic bronchitis (subset 8). Persons with chronic bronchitis and /or emphysema without airflow obstruction (subsets 1,2 & 3) are not classified as having COPD. A small proportion of patients with emphysema have A1ATD as a contributing etiology (subset 7). Not all patients with A1ATD develop COPD. Patients with airway obstruction due to disease with known etiology or specific pathology such as cystic fibrosis, bronchiectasis or obliterative bronchiolitis (subset 12) are not included in this definition. *Modified from American thoracic Society (ATS), 1995.*

leading to lower A1AT levels. A1AT is synthesized primarily in the liver and is normally present in serum at concentrations of 27–64 μM. It is an acute phase reactant and A1AT levels are elevated in pregnancy, infections, severe burns, and malignancies. A1AT diffuses into lung connective tissue and airways where it functions to neutralize elastase released by neutrophils. Genetic mutations such as Pi ZZ, Znull and null-null lead to critically low levels of A1AT in serum (< 11 μM) which result in uninhibited action of neutrophil elastase in the lungs leading to airway destruction and subsequent development of emphysema. A1AT deficiency is classically associated with early onset, basal predominant, panacinar emphysema. The clinical manifestations and anatomic distribution can be variable. Concomitant cigarette smoking leads to earlier onset (age 40 vs 53 years in non-smokers) and an accelerated worsening of emphysema in patients with AAT deficiency (Stockley, 2014).

**Table 9.2:** Characteristics and therapeutic implications of different phenotypes of COPD

| | |
|---|---|
| GENETIC : Alpha 1-antitrypsin deficiency | |
| Clinical Course | Early onset COPD<br>Familial tendency with variable penetrance<br>Increased susceptibility to smoking related lung injury<br>Emphysema can have variable anatomic distribution and lower lobe predominance |
| Therapeutic Implications | Augmentation therapy with intra-venous alpha 1-antitrypsin |
| ANATOMIC: Emphysema predominant phenotype | |
| Clinical Course | More dyspnea and exercise intolerance<br>Higher severity of airflow limitation and faster rate of lung function decline<br>Higher risk for exacerbations |
| Therapeutic Implications | Possibly more benefit from dual bronchodilator therapy and pulmonary rehabilitation in symptomatic patients<br>**Lung volume reduction surgery**; consideration for upper zone predominant emphysema in patients with refractory poor function status<br>**Endobronchial valve** (one way valves); consideration for heterogeneous emphysema with no collateral ventilation<br>**Endobronchial coils**; consideration for heterogeneous or homogenous emphysema irrespective of collateral ventilation |
| PHYSIOLOGICAL: Asthma - COPD overlap syndrome *OR* COPD with bronchodilator responsiveness | |
| Clinical Course | Faster rate of lung function decline<br>Higher risk for exacerbations<br>Higher frequency of hospitalizations |
| Therapeutic Implications | More beneficial effects of inhaled corticosteroids |
| CLINICAL: Frequent exacerbator phenotype (> 2 acute exacerbations / year) | |
| Clinical Course | Faster rate of lung function decline<br>More hospitalizations and utilization of health care cost<br>Higher risk of death |
| Therapeutic Implications | Medications to reduce inflammation: inhaled corticosteroids, long term macrolide (Azithromycin), phosphodiesterase 4 inhibitor (Roflumilast) |
| CLINICAL: Chronic bronchitis predominant type *OR* mucous secretor phenotype | |
| Clinical Course | Higher risk and frequency of exacerbations<br>Faster rate of lung function decline |
| Therapeutic Implications | Phosphodiesterase 4 inhibitor (Roflumilast) reduces frequency of exacerbations |

#### 9.4.2.1 Therapeutic Implications

Augmentation therapy with plasma-derived A1AT is widely accepted and recommended in moderate to severe disease (Stockley, 2014). In randomized controlled trials, augmentation therapy slows down the rate of decline of lung density which is a marker of emphysema (Campos, 2014).

### 9.4.3 Anatomic: Emphysema-Hyperinflation Phenotype

Emphysema is the permanent destruction of the air spaces beyond the terminal bronchioles. The loss of elastic recoil and presence of expiratory flow limitation causes air-trapping and hyperinflation. The presence, severity, and distribution of emphysema is variable among individuals with COPD. This clinical phenotype is characterized by physiologic derangements that cause hyperinflation and air-trapping and are measured by low inspiratory capacity/ total lung capacity ratio (IC/ TLC <0.25), presence of emphysema on HRCT, and/or low diffusing capacity (DLCO).

Recently genetic associations have also been identified in the anatomic distribution and severity of emphysema. Mid-upper zone emphysema in smokers is linked with rs1980057 near *HHIP* and severe emphysema with rs8034191 on chromosome 15 (Castaldi, 2014). AAT deficiency is associated with lower zone predominant panacinar emphysema (Stockley, 2014).

Emphysema-hyperinflation rather than the severity of airflow obstruction is more closely associated with clinical symptoms of dyspnea and exercise intolerance (Diaz, 2000; O'Donnell, 2001). Identification of this phenotype is clinically important as dyspnea, exercise intolerance, and hyperinflation are independent predictors of mortality (Casanova, 2005; Martinez, 2006; Nishimura, 2002; O'Donnell, 1993). Patients with IC/TLC <0.25 (markers of hyperinflation) are more than three times more likely to die than those with higher IC/TLC ratios, regardless of $FEV_1$, age, dyspnea, exercise capacity, or comorbidities (Casanova, 2005). The presence of emphysema is also associated with the severity of airflow limitation and a faster rate of $FEV_1$ decline (Nishimura, 2012; Vestbo, 2011) and is an independent risk factor for increased frequency of COPD exacerbations (Han, 2011).

#### 9.4.3.1 Therapeutic Implications

Hyperinflation, to a certain degree, is potentially reversible with appropriate treatments as evidenced by reductions in lung volumes after treatment with bronchodilators (Man, 2004; O'Donnell, 2004a). Dual bronchodilator therapies improve dyspnea and quality of life in symptomatic patients with emphysema-hyperinflation (Rabe, 2008; van Noord, 2005). Since they have more dyspnea and exercise intolerance, these patients are also expected to obtain greater benefit from pulmonary rehabilitation (Casaburi, 2009).

Patients with emphysema who maintain poor functional capacity despite maximal medical treatment and pulmonary rehabilitation can be candidates for lung volume reduction interventions to reduce the residual air trapped in the chest cavity and improve pulmonary mechanics and gas exchange. The National Emphysema Treatment Trial (NETT) showed that lung volume reduction surgery in patients with heterogeneously distributed upper zone predominant emphysema leads to improvement in functional capacity and a reduction in exacerbations and mortality (Fishman, 2003; Washko, 2008). Other less invasive options for lung volume reduction are placement of endo-bronchial coils and one way endo-bronchial valves. Appropriate candidates for endo-bronchial valves are patients with heterogeneous distribution of emphysema with no collateral ventilation to the emphysematous lobe or segment. Endo-bronchial coils, on the other hand, have been used in patients with homogenous and heterogeneous distribution of emphysema irrespective of collateral ventilation (Ninane, 2012; Sciurba, 2010; Shah, 2013).

### 9.4.4 Physiologic: Bronchodilator Responsive/ COPD-Asthma Overlap Syndrome

A subset of patients with COPD manifest significant responses to bronchodilators; however, this responsiveness does not produce normal lung function. The airways of these patients manifest chronic inflammation with both neutrophilic and eosinophilic cell infiltrations. This phenotype has been categorized as mixed asthma-COPD or COPD-asthma overlap syndrome (CAOS). Between 20–40% of COPD patients may have mixed CAOS (Miravitlles, 2012). Patients with CAOS experience a faster rate of decline in $FEV_1$, (Vestbo, 2011), higher risk for exacerbations, increased frequency of hospitalizations, and worse health related quality of life (Hardin, 2011; Menezes, 2014). The response to bronchodilators in patients with COPD is not longitudinally consistent; therefore, it may not be a reliable marker to identify a distinct phenotype (Albert, 2012). Sputum eosinophils and inhaled nitric oxide levels may be some of the features that can help identify CAOS. Other characteristics may include a history of asthma and/or atopy, frequent exacerbations, and wheezing.

#### 9.4.4.1 Therapeutic Implications

Many large clinical trials of COPD and asthma have excluded this subset of patients as they are not exclusively classified as either asthma or COPD (Calverley, 2007). COPD patients that demonstrate even partial responsiveness (less than the American Thoracic Society criteria of >200 ml and > 12% increase in either $FEV_1$ or FVC) have greater eosinophilic bronchial inflammation compared to non-responding patients (Papi, 2000). Several studies have used greater airflow reversibility (Kerstjens, 1993; Lee, 2010), a higher concentration of eosinophils in sputum (Brightling, 2005; Leigh, 2006), or a greater concentration of inhaled nitric oxide (Kunisaki, 2008; Lehtimaki,

2010) as markers of potential benefit in lung function and clinical symptoms after inhaled corticosteroids (ICS) treatment. ICS dose adjustments according to sputum eosinophil count have reduced hospitalizations and exacerbation frequency. When treated with LABA and ICS combination inhalers, CAOS patients have greater short and long term improvement in lung function compared with patients with emphysema who do not respond to bronchodilators (Lee, 2010; Mahler, 2002).

### 9.4.5 Clinical Frequent Exacerbator

In the recent years, much attention has been attracted by a subset of patients having frequent exacerbations of COPD. In longitudinal studies, some patients are more likely to develop exacerbations irrespective of their disease severity. Patients who suffer from two or more exacerbations a year maintain an increased propensity toward frequent exacerbations over the subsequent years, making them a consistent phenotype called 'frequent exacerbators'. In the ECLIPSE study, which included 2138 patients with moderate-severe COPD, 12% of cases had ≥ 2 exacerbations per year over the 3-year course of the study. The frequent exacerbators maintained a notable stability over time. Of the patients suffering ≥ 2 exacerbations in first year, 60% had frequent exacerbations in the second year and 70% of the second year frequent exacerbators had frequent exacerbations in the third year (Hurst, 2010).

COPD exacerbation heterogeneity and susceptibility are likely caused by multiple contributing factors with complex interactions, as shown in Figure 9.4. Potential contributing factors include background airway and systemic inflammation, airway microbial patterns, host immunologic response, comorbid health conditions, genetic predisposition, viral and bacterial infections, and adherence to medications (Wedzicha, 2013).

The 'frequent exacerbator phenotype' has sparked great interest in recent years due to faster lung function decline, poor quality of life, and higher health care utilization and mortality within this group. See section 9.3 for more information on factors associated with frequent exacerbations and role of frequent exacerbations on lung function decline, health quality, and mortality. The current COPD treatment guidelines, therefore, encourage physicians to recognize 'frequent exacerbators', defined as those who have either two of more exacerbations per year or having one severe exacerbation in a year requiring hospitalization (GOLD, 2014).

#### 9.4.5.1 Therapeutic Implications

The therapeutic goal for frequent exacerbators is to reduce the frequency of exacerbations, delay the next acute exacerbation, and minimize health care utilization and cost by reducing the severity of these episodes. Long acting bronchodilators like tiotropium have been shown to reduce the frequency of exacerbations (Vogelmeier,

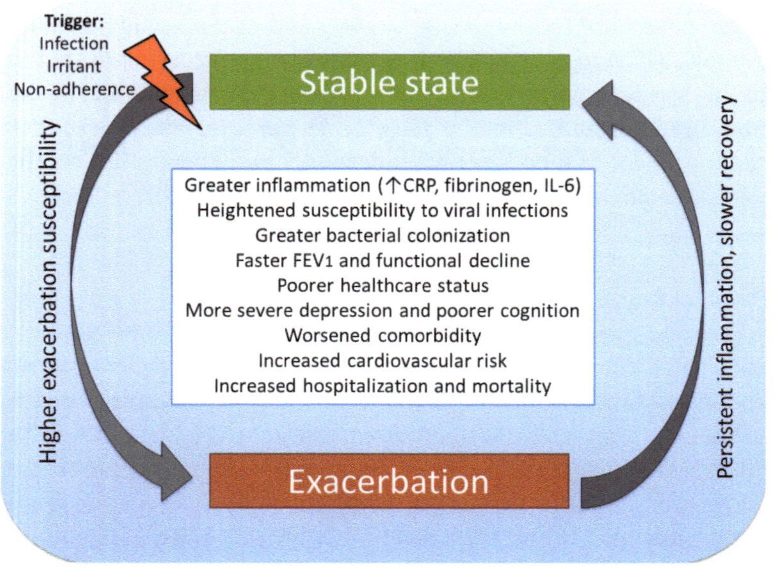


**Figure 9.4:** Schematic illustration of the frequent exacerbation phenotype. While many patients with COPD experience exacerbations, there is a subgroup of patients who enter a destructive cycle of frequent exacerbations with associated poorer outcomes. This phenotype of frequent exacerbators is maintained over time. *Modified from Wedzicha, 2013*

2011). Treatment modalities that reduce airway inflammation and have immune modulatory effects have been used successfully. For recurrent exacerbations, all current practice guidelines recommend addition of inhaled corticosteroids along with the bronchodilators. Inhaled corticosteroids reduce the frequency of exacerbations significantly and also improve health related quality of life in these individuals (ATS, 1995; GOLD, 2014).

Macrolides administered for a prolonged amount of time, such as azithromycin 250 mg daily, can be used as additional therapy to reduce exacerbation frequency (Albert, 2011). The potential for cardiotoxicity and hearing loss have to be cautiously monitored. Also, the risk of possible development of bacterial antibiotic resistance should also be considered. Roflumilast, an orally administered selective phosphodiesterase IV inhibitor, has anti-inflammatory effects. It has been approved for preventing exacerbations in patients with severe COPD and features of chronic bronchitis (mucous producers) (Calverley, 2009). In a recent large clinical trial, long term use of statins (simvastatin) did not reduce the number of acute exacerbations of COPD (Criner, 2014).

### 9.4.6 Clinical: Chronic Bronchitis/Mucous Producer

Another COPD phenotype is chronic bronchitis, which is characterized by chronic cough and sputum expectoration. These patients demonstrate greater airway inflammation and a higher risk of respiratory infections (Prescott, 1995). Patients with this phenotype have a higher risk of COPD exacerbations, independent of other known risk factors (Foreman, 2007; Miravitlles, 2011). Some studies have also described an association with faster $FEV_1$ decline, particularly in younger adults (Guerra, 2009).

#### 9.4.6.1 Therapeutic Implications

The most important clinical characteristic of the chronic bronchitis/mucous producer phenotype is the predisposition to frequent recurrent exacerbations. Phosphodiesterase-4 inhibitors such as roflumilast produce greater reductions in COPD exacerbation frequency in patients with this phenotype compared to those who do not produce mucous (Calverley, 2009).

## 9.5 Gender Differences in COPD

In the past few decades the prevalence and mortality from COPD have increased rapidly in women compared with men which has changed the historic perspective that COPD is predominantly a disease of men. It is thought that the increase in the prevalence of cigarette smoking among women is the major contributor to this epidemiological shift. Gender differences are also observed in susceptibility to the development of COPD from tobacco exposure, clinical features, response to certain treatments, and health care utilization. Table 9.3 provides a summary of the gender differences in COPD.

### 9.5.1 Reasons for Gender Differences in COPD

It is commonly believed that behavioral and environmental factors are responsible for the gender disparities in COPD. However, there is also growing evidence of gender-based genetic and hormonal factors playing an important role in this regard.

#### 9.5.1.1 Change in Tobacco Consumption Trend

As mentioned previously, cigarette smoking is the most influential risk factor for COPD development and progression in the developed world. Trends in COPD mirror the trends in cigarette smoking in populations. The risk of COPD development from cigarette smoking increased throughout last century in the US as successive generations began smoking at earlier ages. Daily cigarette consumption in the US peaked during the 1970s in males, whereas the peak among female smokers did not occur until the 1980s (Burns, 2003). In developing countries, the prevalence of cigarette smoking is still rising. By 2025, the prevalence of smoking among females is predicted to increase to 20% from 9% in the early 2000s (Mackay, 2003).

#### 9.5.1.2 Tobacco Susceptibility

There is mixed evidence suggesting gender differences in the susceptibility to the development of COPD caused by smoking. Women tend to develop severe COPD with lower cumulative cigarette exposure, and at a younger age, than men. They also demonstrate a faster rate of $FEV_1$ decline (Gan, 2006). The gender difference is more profound in earlier disease phases where women seem to have more airflow obstruction with less (<20 pack years) cumulative smoking exposure. With higher smoking exposures and in later phases of the disease, gender disparities become less obvious (Sorheim, 2010). The greater susceptibility to cigarette smoke in women could be due to women having smaller airways; consequently, the same amount of smoking will lead to relatively higher exposure. Other smoking behaviors such as inhalation techniques may also play a role (Han, 2007). Gender related genetic differences also disproportionately increase the risk in women. In one observational study, a smoking female who has first-degree relatives with early-onset COPD is almost twice as likely to experience airflow obstruction, and 3.5 times more likely to have severe obstruction ($FEV_1$ < 40% predicted) than male relatives who smoked (Silverman, 2000).

#### 9.5.1.3 Biologic Differences

Female sex hormones are known to influence airway function, especially in asthma (Han, 2007). The increased susceptibility in women may start in early childhood. A larger reduction in lung function is seen in girls than boys when exposed to tobacco smoke or environmental air pollution (Chen, 2005; Rojas-Martinez, 2007). Based upon epidemiologic studies, up to 23% of all COPD patients have not been exposed to tobacco smoke (Lamprecht, 2011). Nearly 80% of these patients are females, suggesting that women are more vulnerable to non-smoking related COPD risk factors (Birring, 2002). Variations in immune responses are also observed between males and females with COPD. Males tend to have higher levels of interlukin-6 and vascular endothelial growth factor which may suggest higher emphysema predominance in males. Females have relatively higher levels of interlukin-16. It is unclear how these differences play a role in disease course (de Torres, 2011).

**Table 9.3:** Gender differences in Chronic Obstructive Pulmonary Disease (COPD)

| | **Male** | **Female** |
|---|---|---|
| **Epidemiology** | | |
| Prevalence | Higher by administrative data | Higher by self-report; higher than males in developed world; increasing in developing world |
| Mortality | Declining during past few decades | Stable over past few decades |
| **Risk Factors** | | |
| Tobacco use | Peaked during 1970s in USA | Peaked during 1980's in USA; increasing in developing world |
| Tobacco susceptibility | Susceptible | More susceptible |
| Environmental risks | Air pollution; occupational exposures | Increasing occupational exposures; indoor air pollution major risk in developing world |
| Phenotypic factors | More emphysema; bronchial hyperresponsive and correlates with atopy | More chronic bronchitis; more hyperresponsiveness and correlates with smoking |
| **Clinical Features** | | |
| Symptoms | Correlate with disease activity | More and higher intensity dyspnea; less phlegm |
| Comorbidities | IHD, arrhythmias, alcoholism, renal failure, cancers | Depression, anxiety, osteoporosis, reflux, IBD |
| Acute exacerbations | Higher associated mortality; more number of hospitalizations | Lower associated mortality |
| **Treatment options** | | |
| Smoking cessation | More attempts and more sustained quitting; nicotine replacement more effective | Fewer attempts and less sustained quitting; better improvement in $FEV_1$ after quitting |
| Pharmacologic treatment | ICS reduces phlegm; benefits of LTOT may not be as good as women; Inhaler use may be better | ICS may not reduce phlegm but worsened deterioration on stopping; chronic macrolide therapy may be more effective |
| Pulmonary rehabilitation | Effects may be more sustained | More emotional and psychosocial benefits |

continued **Table 9.3:** Gender differences in Chronic Obstructive Pulmonary Disease (COPD)

| | Male | Female |
|---|---|---|
| **Health care delivery and utilizations** | | |
| Bias in diagnosis | More likely to be diagnosed with COPD | More likely to be diagnosed with asthma |
| Perception of COPD care | Less report of diagnostic delay or reaching physician | More diagnostic delay, difficulty reaching physician or having adequate time |

IHD: ischemic heart disease, IBD: inflammatory bowel disease, $FEV_1$: forced expiratory volume in 1 second, ICS: inhaled corticosteroid, LTOT: long-term oxygen therapy. *Modified from; Aryal S, 2013*

### 9.5.2 Epidemiology

The assessment of COPD prevalence has either relied on self-reports of disease, spirometric analysis, or medical billing. Women tend to have a higher prevalence of COPD compared to men by self-report, whereas men have a higher prevalence when medical billing data are used (Camp, 2007). In the US, the prevalence of moderate COPD measured by spirometry increased in women from 50.8 to 58.2 per 1000 from 1975 (NHANES I) to 2000 (NHANES III). The prevalence in men decreased from 108.1 to 74.3 per 1000 during the same period. Self-reported prevalence of COPD from 1999–2008 has remained higher in women than men (Mannino, 2002). Similar trends are noted in other developed countries (Bischoff, 2009; Gershon, 2010). In developing countries, COPD prevalence is still higher in men than women but is expected to rise in women given changes in smoking trends and air pollution (Bhome, 2012; Menezes, 2005; Schirnhofer, 2007).

A recent comprehensive assessment of smoking related mortality in the US showed that in the decade from 2000 to 2010, male and female current smokers had similar relative mortality risks from COPD, 26.6 for males and 22.3 for females. This risk was doubled compared with the period of 1982–1988 (Thun, 2013). For the first time in 2000, the total number of female deaths from COPD surpassed the number of male deaths because the percentage of women in the general U.S population was greater. The age-adjusted COPD death rates for men were 1.3 times more than for women (Mannino, 2002).

### 9.5.3 Clinical Features and Phenotypic Differences

Numerous studies highlight the gender differences in clinical presentation and disease course. Women are more likely to report dyspnea and a higher severity of dyspnea compared to men with comparable smoking exposure and $FEV_1$ (de Torres,

2005; Watson, 2004). Men are more likely to report productive cough than women (Cydulka, 2005; Gershon, 2010). These differences may be due to behavioral and societal influences where women are less likely to report phlegm production or dyspnea than men (Becklake, 1999; Camp, 2007).

In the ECLIPSE study, no difference was seen in the ages of males and females for a given GOLD category. However, for each GOLD category, women had lower BMI, less smoking exposure, and reported more exacerbations than men (Agusti, 2010). Higher exacerbation rates among women also occurred in the TORCH study (Celli, 2011).

Gender differences are also observed in COPD phenotypes. Based on National Health Interview Survey data, chronic bronchitis is more common in women whereas emphysema is more common in men. Radiographic and histological data also suggest that women with COPD tend to have smaller airway lumens with thicker bronchial walls and less severe peripheral emphysema than men (Dransfield, 2007).

### 9.5.4 Comorbidities

Comorbid diseases are commonly present in patients with COPD; however, their prevalence differs in males and females. Cardiovascular comorbidities, arrhythmias, ischemic heart disease, and cancers are more often seen in male patients with COPD compared to females (Agusti, 2010; Almagro, 2010). Women have higher rates of osteoporosis, diabetes, inflammatory bowel disease, anxiety, and depression (Agusti, 2010; Almagro, 2010; Gudmundsson, 2005).

### 9.5.5 Treatment Disparities

Smoking cessation is critical in COPD management. Mixed results have been observed in studies between men and women. Some analyses suggest that women have lower smoking cessation success rates and tend to quit less frequently (Han, 2007). A recent large population study from the US, Canada, and UK found little gender differences in smoking cessation (Jarvis, 2013). Certain pharmacotherapies like bupropion and varenicline seem to have better results in women, whereas, nicotine replacement therapy has shown better success rates in men (Han, 2007). Women experience a 2.5 fold greater improvement in lung function ($FEV_1$) after smoking cessation than men (Scanlon, 2000).

Bronchodilators and inhaled corticosteroids have remained the cornerstone of COPD management for many years. Studies suggest similar efficacy of inhaled salmeterol/fluticasone combination therapy and tiotropium in both genders in terms of $FEV_1$, exacerbation rate, and quality of life (O'Donnell, 2004; Vestbo, 2004). Mixed findings have been noted in medication adherence. In one study with mild-moderate COPD patients, the proportion of females on respiratory medicines was twice that of men. However, in severe COPD, no gender differences in prescriptions were noted (Dales, 2006). Men are reported to be more likely to be on newer dry powder inhalers rather than metered dose inhalers (Sestini, 2006). Disproportionately lower rates of influenza and pneumonia vaccine usage in women have also been reported (Wershof Schwartz, 2013).

### 9.5.6 Health Care Delivery

Despite substantial increases in prevalence and mortality from COPD among females, health care providers remain more likely to diagnose males with COPD than females. In a study done in the US and Canada, physicians were found more likely to diagnose females with asthma and males with COPD in similar hypothetical cases. The bias decreased if spirometry values were provided to the physicians (Chapman, 2001). Similar results were seen in a subsequent study in Spain (Miravitlles, 2006). In another large population study, women were 1.27 times more likely to have underdiagnosed COPD despite spirometric values confirming the presence of airflow limitation (Ancochea, 2013). Women are more likely to report delay in COPD diagnosis, difficulty in reaching physicians, and spending insufficient time with their physician (Martinez, 2012).

## 9.6 Conclusion

The natural disease course of COPD is generally characterized by an accelerated decline in lung function. However the rate of decline remains highly variable among individuals and is influenced by numerous factors. Smoking exposure impairs lung growth, reduces maximal lung function and accelerates the rate of deterioration. Smoking cessation at any stage of the disease slows the rate of decline. Exacerbations punctuate the disease course and increase the risk of mortality, morbidity and health care utilization. COPD can be classified into different phenotypes based on certain features that are responsible for clinical variations in the disease course and outcomes among individuals. Some of the well-recognized phenotypes are frequent exacerbators, alpha 1-antitrypin deficiency, emphysema predominant, COPD-asthma overlap syndrome, and mucous producers. Gender differences in the epidemiology of COPD are primarily implicated to the changing smoking trends. Women also appear to be more susceptible to smoking related lung injury and tend to have slightly different clinical features and outcomes than men.

## 9.7 Summary Points

1. The disease course of COPD is classically characterized by accelerated lung function decline. The rate of this decline, however, is highly variable among individuals.
2. Factors that are associated with a faster rate of decline include active smoking, genetic susceptibility, emphysema, broncho-reactivity and early disease.
3. Acute exacerbations of COPD have short and long term effects on disease course and outcomes. They are associated with increased health care utilization and costs, decline in lung function and life quality and an increase in mortality.
4. Many factors increase the risk and susceptibility to exacerbations. The single most important risk factor is a prior history of a recent exacerbation.
5. COPD phenotypes are disease attributes that describe differences between individuals with COPD as they relate to symptoms, exacerbations, response to therapy and rate of disease progression.
6. Well recognized COPD phenotypes are alpha 1-antitrypsin deficiency, emphysema predominant, COPD-asthma overlap syndrome, frequent exacerbator and chronic bronchitis. Each of these phenotypes has different therapeutic implications in patient management.
7. In the developed world, gender differences in the epidemiologic trends of COPD are primarily attributed to the change in smoking behavior in men and women over the past several decades.
8. Women tend to have an increased susceptibility to smoking related lung damage, report more dyspnea, and experience more diagnostic delays compared with men with COPD.

## References

Agusti, A., Barbera, J.A., Wouters, E.F., et al. (2013). Lungs, bone marrow, and adipose tissue. A network approach to the pathobiology of chronic obstructive pulmonary disease. *American Journal of Respiratory and Critical Care Medicine, 188*(12), 1396–1406.

Agusti, A., Calverley, P.M., Celli, B., et al. (2010). Characterisation of COPD heterogeneity in the ECLIPSE cohort. *Respiratory Research, 11*, 122–9921–11–122.

Albert, P., Agusti, A., Edwards, L., et al. (2012). Bronchodilator responsiveness as a phenotypic characteristic of established chronic obstructive pulmonary disease. *Thorax, 67*(8), 701–708.

Albert, R.K., Connett, J., Bailey, W.C., et al. (2011). Azithromycin for prevention of exacerbations of COPD. *The New England Journal of Medicine, 365*(8), 689–698.

Almagro, P., Lopez Garcia, F., Cabrera, F., et al. (2010). Comorbidity and gender-related differences in patients hospitalized for COPD. the ECCO study. *Respiratory Medicine, 104*(2), 253–259.

Anthonisen, N.R., Connett, J.E., & Murray, R.P. (2002). Smoking and lung function of lung health study participants after 11 years. *American Journal of Respiratory and Critical Care Medicine, 166*(5), 675–679.

ATS (American Thoracic Society). (1995). Standards for the diagnosis and care of patients with chronic obstructive pulmonary disease. american thoracic society. *American Journal of Respiratory and Critical Care Medicine, 152*(5 Pt 2), S77–121.

Becklake, M.R., & Kauffmann, F. (1999). Gender differences in airway behaviour over the human life span. *Thorax, 54*(12), 1119–1138.

Bhome, A.B. (2012). COPD in india: Iceberg or volcano? *Journal of Thoracic Disease, 4*(3), 298–309.

Birring, S.S., Brightling, C.E., Bradding, P., et al. (2002). Clinical, radiologic, and induced sputum features of chronic obstructive pulmonary disease in nonsmokers: A descriptive study. *American Journal of Respiratory and Critical Care Medicine, 166*(8), 1078–1083.

Bischoff, E.W., Schermer, T.R., Bor, H., et al. (2009). Trends in COPD prevalence and exacerbation rates in dutch primary care. *The British Journal of General Practice : The Journal of the Royal College of General Practitioners, 59*(569), 927–933.

Blanc, P.D., Eisner, M.D., Earnest, G., et al. (2009). Further exploration of the links between occupational exposure and chronic obstructive pulmonary disease. *Journal of Occupational and Envirnmental Medicine, 51(7), 804–10*

Brightling, C.E., McKenna, S., Hargadon, B., et al. (2005). Sputum eosinophilia and the short term response to inhaled mometasone in chronic obstructive pulmonary disease. *Thorax, 60*(3), 193–198.

Burns, D., Major, J., & Shanks, T. (2003). *Changes in number of cigarettes smoker per day: Cross-sectional and birth control analyses using NHIS.* In Marcus S. (Ed.) *Tthose who continue to smoke: Is achieving abstinence harder and do we need to change our interventions? smoking and tobacco control monograph* (15th ed.). Bethesda, MD: NIH publication no. 03–5370.

Burrows, B., Fletcher, C.M., Heard, B.E., et al. (1966). The emphysematous and bronchial types of chronic airways obstruction. A clinicopathological study of patients in london and chicago. *Lancet, 1*(7442), 830–835.

Burrows, B., Niden, A.H., Fletcher, C.M., et al. (1964). Clinical types of chronic obstructive lung disease in london and in chicago. a study of one hundred patients. *The American Review of Respiratory Disease, 90*, 14–27.

Calverley, P.M., Anderson, J.A., Celli, B., et al. (2007). Salmeterol and fluticasone propionate and survival in chronic obstructive pulmonary disease. *The New England Journal of Medicine, 356*(8), 775–789.

Calverley, P.M., Rabe, K.F., Goehring, U.M., et al. (2009). Roflumilast in symptomatic chronic obstructive pulmonary disease: Two randomised clinical trials. *Lancet, 374*(9691), 685–694.

Camp, P.G., & Goring, S.M. (2007). Gender and the diagnosis, management, and surveillance of chronic obstructive pulmonary disease. *Proceedings of the American Thoracic Society, 4*(8), 686–691.

Campos, M.A., & Lascano, J. (2014). Alpha1 antitrypsin deficiency: Current best practice in testing and augmentation therapy. *Therapeutic Advances in Respiratory Disease, 8*(5), 150–161.

Casaburi, R., & ZuWallack, R. (2009). Pulmonary rehabilitation for management of chronic obstructive pulmonary disease. *The New England Journal of Medicine, 360*(13), 1329–1335.

Casanova, C., Cote, C., de Torres, J.P., et al. (2005). Inspiratory-to-total lung capacity ratio predicts mortality in patients with chronic obstructive pulmonary disease. *American Journal of Respiratory and Critical Care Medicine, 171*(6), 591–597.

Castaldi, P.J., Dy, J., Ross, J., et al. (2014). Cluster analysis in the COPDGene study identifies subtypes of smokers with distinct patterns of airway disease and emphysema. *Thorax, 69*(5), 415–422.

Celli B, Snider GL, Heffner J. (1995). Standards for the diagnosis and care of patients with chronic obstructive pulmonary disease. american thoracic society. *American Journal of Respiratory and Critical Care Medicine, 152*(5 Pt 2), S77–121.

Celli, B., Vestbo, J., Jenkins, C.R., et al. (2011). Sex differences in mortality and clinical expressions of patients with chronic obstructive pulmonary disease. the TORCH experience. *American Journal of Respiratory and Critical Care Medicine, 183*(3), 317–322.

Celli, B.R., Cote, C.G., Marin, J.M., et al. (2004). The body-mass index, airflow obstruction, dyspnea, and exercise capacity index in chronic obstructive pulmonary disease. *The New England Journal of Medicine, 350*(10), 1005–1012.

Chen, Y., Rennie, D.C., Lockinger, L.A., et al. (2005). Gender, environmental tobacco smoke, and pulmonary function in rural children and adolescents: The humboldt study. *Journal of Agricultural Safety and Health, 11*(2), 167–173.

Cho, M.H., Castaldi, P.J., Wan, E.S., et al. (2012). A genome-wide association study of COPD identifies a susceptibility locus on chromosome 19q13. *Human Molecular Genetics, 21*(4), 947–957.

Cho, M.H., McDonald, M.L., Zhou, X., et al. (2014). Risk loci for chronic obstructive pulmonary disease: A genome-wide association study and meta-analysis. *The Lancet.Respiratory Medicine, 2*(3), 214–225.

Connors, A.F.,Jr, Dawson, N.V., Thomas, C., et al. (1996). Outcomes following acute exacerbation of severe chronic obstructive lung disease. the SUPPORT investigators (study to understand prognoses and preferences for outcomes and risks of treatments). *American Journal of Respiratory and Critical Care Medicine, 154*(4 Pt 1), 959–967.

Coxson, H.O., Dirksen, A., Edwards, L.D., et al. (2013). The presence and progression of emphysema in COPD as determined by CT scanning and biomarker expression: A prospective analysis from the ECLIPSE study. *The Lancet.Respiratory Medicine, 1*(2), 129–136.

Criner, G.J., Connett, J.E., Aaron, S.D., et al. (2014). Simvastatin for the prevention of exacerbations in moderate-to-severe COPD. *The New England Journal of Medicine, 370*(23), 2201–2210.

Csikesz, N.G., & Gartman, E.J. (2014). New developments in the assessment of COPD: Early diagnosis is key. *International Journal of Chronic Obstructive Pulmonary Disease, 9*, 277–286.

Cydulka, R.K., Rowe, B.H., Clark, S., et al. (2005). Gender differences in emergency department patients with chronic obstructive pulmonary disease exacerbation. *Academic Emergency Medicine : Official Journal of the Society for Academic Emergency Medicine, 12*(12), 1173–1179.

Dales, R.E., Mehdizadeh, A., Aaron, S.D., et al. (2006). Sex differences in the clinical presentation and management of airflow obstruction. *The European Respiratory Journal, 28*(2), 319–322.

de Torres, J.P., Casanova, C., Hernandez, C., et al. (2005). Gender and COPD in patients attending a pulmonary clinic. *Chest, 128*(4), 2012–2016.

de Torres, J.P., Casanova, C., Pinto-Plata, V., et al. (2011). Gender differences in plasma biomarker levels in a cohort of COPD patients: A pilot study. *PloS One, 6*(1), e16021.

Diaz, O., Villafranca, C., Ghezzo, H., et al. (2000). Role of inspiratory capacity on exercise tolerance in COPD patients with and without tidal expiratory flow limitation at rest. *The European Respiratory Journal, 16*(2), 269–275.

Donaldson, G.C., Seemungal, T.A., Bhowmik, A., et al. (2002). Relationship between exacerbation frequency and lung function decline in chronic obstructive pulmonary disease. *Thorax, 57*(10), 847–852.

Donaldson, G.C., Wilkinson, T.M., Hurst, J.R., et al. (2005). Exacerbations and time spent outdoors in chronic obstructive pulmonary disease. *American Journal of Respiratory and Critical Care Medicine, 171*(5), 446–452.

Eriksson, S. (1964). Pulmonary emphysema and Alpha1-antitrypsin deficiency. *Acta Medica Scandinavica, 175*, 197–205.

Faner, R., Tal-Singer, R., Riley, J.H., et al. (2014). Lessons from ECLIPSE: A review of COPD biomarkers. *Thorax, 69*(7), 666–672.

Fishman, A., Martinez, F., Naunheim, K., et al. (2003). A randomized trial comparing lung-volume-reduction surgery with medical therapy for severe emphysema. *The New England Journal of Medicine, 348*(21), 2059–2073.

Fletcher, C., Peto, R., Tinker, C., et al. (1976). *The natural history of chronic bronchitis and emphysema*. New York: Oxford University Press.

Foreman, M.G., DeMeo, D.L., Hersh, C.P., et al. (2007). Clinical determinants of exacerbations in severe, early-onset COPD. *The European Respiratory Journal, 30*(6), 1124–1130.

Galban, C.J., Han, M.K., Boes, J.L., et al.(2012). Computed tomography-based biomarker provides unique signature for diagnosis of COPD phenotypes and disease progression. *Nature Medicine, 18*(11), 1711–1715.

Gan, W.Q., Man, S.F., Postma, D.S., et al. (2006). Female smokers beyond the perimenopausal period are at increased risk of chronic obstructive pulmonary disease: A systematic review and meta-analysis. *Respiratory Research, 7*, 52.

Gershon, A.S., Wang, C., Wilton, A.S., et al. (2010). Trends in chronic obstructive pulmonary disease prevalence, incidence, and mortality in ontario, canada, 1996 to 2007: A population-based study. *Archives of Internal Medicine, 170*(6), 560–565.

Gietema, H.A., Muller, N.L., Fauerbach, P.V., et al. (2011). Quantifying the extent of emphysema: Factors associated with radiologists' estimations and quantitative indices of emphysema severity using the ECLIPSE cohort. *Academic Radiology, 18*(6), 661–671.

GOLD. (2014). *Global strategy for the diagnosis, management and prevention of COPD*, global initiative for chronic obstructive lung disease (GOLD) 2014. Retrieved from http://www.goldcopd.org/. Last accessed September 2014.

Gold, D.R., Wang, X., Wypij, D., et al. (1996). Effects of cigarette smoking on lung function in adolescent boys and girls. *The New England Journal of Medicine, 335*(13), 931–937.

Gudmundsson, G., Gislason, T., Janson, C., et al. (2005). Risk factors for rehospitalisation in COPD: Role of health status, anxiety and depression. *The European Respiratory Journal, 26*(3), 414–419.

Guerra, S., Sherrill, D.L., Venker, C., et al. (2009). Chronic bronchitis before age 50 years predicts incident airflow limitation and mortality risk. *Thorax, 64*(10), 894–900.

Halpin, D.M., Decramer, M., Celli, B., et al. (2012). Exacerbation frequency and course of COPD. *International Journal of Chronic Obstructive Pulmonary Disease, 7*, 653–661.

Han, M.K., Agusti, A., Calverley, P.M., et al. (2010). Chronic obstructive pulmonary disease phenotypes: The future of COPD. *American Journal of Respiratory and Critical Care Medicine, 182*(5), 598–604.

Han, M.K., Kazerooni, E.A., Lynch, D.A., et al. (2011). Chronic obstructive pulmonary disease exacerbations in the COPDGene study: Associated radiologic phenotypes. *Radiology, 261*(1), 274–282.

Han, M.K., Postma, D., Mannino, D.M., et al. (2007). Gender and chronic obstructive pulmonary disease: Why it matters. *American Journal of Respiratory and Critical Care Medicine, 176*(12), 1179–1184.

Hardin, M., Silverman, E.K., Barr, R.G., et al. (2011). The clinical features of the overlap between COPD and asthma. *Respiratory Research, 12*, 127–9921–12–127.

Hurst, J.R., Vestbo, J., Anzueto, A., et al. (2010). Susceptibility to exacerbation in chronic obstructive pulmonary disease. *The New England Journal of Medicine, 363*(12), 1128–1138.

Ingebrigtsen, T., Thomsen, S.F., Vestbo, J., et al. (2010). Genetic influences on chronic obstructive pulmonary disease - a twin study. *Respiratory Medicine, 104*(12), 1890–1895.

Jarvis, M.J., Cohen, J.E., Delnevo, C.D., et al. (2013). Dispelling myths about gender differences in smoking cessation: Population data from the USA, canada and britain. *Tobacco Control, 22*(5), 356–360.

Jha, P., Ramasundarahettige, C., Landsman, V., et al. (2013). 21st-century hazards of smoking and benefits of cessation in the united states. *The New England Journal of Medicine, 368*(4), 341–350.

Kanner, R.E., Anthonisen, N.R., Connett, J.E., et al. (2001). Lower respiratory illnesses promote FEV(1) decline in current smokers but not ex-smokers with mild chronic obstructive pulmonary

disease: Results from the lung health study. *American Journal of Respiratory and Critical Care Medicine, 164*(3), 358–364.
Karon, E.H., Koelsche, G.A., & Fowler, W.S. (1960). Chronic obstructive pulmonary disease in young adults. *Proceedings of the Staff Meetings.Mayo Clinic, 35*, 307–316.
Kerstjens, H.A., Overbeek, S.E., Schouten, J.P., et al. (1993). Airways hyperresponsiveness bronchodilator response, allergy and smoking predict improvement in FEV1 during long-term inhaled corticosteroid treatment. dutch CNSLD study group. *The European Respiratory Journal, 6*(6), 868–876.
Koeverden, I.V., Blanc, P.D., Bowler, R.P., et al. (2014). Secondhand tobacco smoke and COPD risk in smokers: A COPDGene study cohort subgroup analysis. *Copd*, doi:10.3109/15412555.2014.922173 [doi]
Kohansal, R., Martinez-Camblor, P., Agusti, A., et al. (2009). The natural history of chronic airflow obstruction revisited: An analysis of the framingham offspring cohort. *American Journal of Respiratory and Critical Care Medicine, 180*(1), 3–10.
Kunisaki, K.M., Rice, K.L., Janoff, E.N., et al. (2008). Exhaled nitric oxide, systemic inflammation, and the spirometric response to inhaled fluticasone propionate in severe chronic obstructive pulmonary disease: A prospective study. *Therapeutic Advances in Respiratory Disease, 2*(2), 55–64.
Lamprecht, B., McBurnie, M.A., Vollmer, W.M., et al. (2011). COPD in never smokers: results from the population-based burden of obstructive lung disease study. Chest, 139, 752–763.
Laurell, C.B., & Eriksson, S. (2013). The electrophoretic alpha1-globulin pattern of serum in alpha1-antitrypsin deficiency. 1963. *Copd, 10 Suppl 1*, 3–8.
Lee, J.H., Lee, Y.K., Kim, E.K., et al. (2010). Responses to inhaled long-acting beta-agonist and corticosteroid according to COPD subtype. *Respiratory Medicine, 104*(4), 542–549.
Lehtimaki, L., Kankaanranta, H., Saarelainen, S., et al. (2010). Bronchial nitric oxide is related to symptom relief during fluticasone treatment in COPD. *The European Respiratory Journal, 35*(1), 72–78.
Leigh, R., Pizzichini, M.M., Morris, M.M., et al. (2006). Stable COPD: Predicting benefit from high-dose inhaled corticosteroid treatment. *The European Respiratory Journal, 27*(5), 964–971.
Lopez, A.D., Mathers, C.D., Ezzati, M., et al. (2006). Global and regional burden of disease and risk factors, 2001: Systematic analysis of population health data. *Lancet, 367*(9524), 1747–1757.
Mackay, J., & Amos, A. (2003). Women and tobacco. *Respirology (Carlton, Vic.), 8*(2), 123–130.
Mahler, D.A., Wire, P., Horstman, D., et al. (2002). Effectiveness of fluticasone propionate and salmeterol combination delivered via the diskus device in the treatment of chronic obstructive pulmonary disease. *American Journal of Respiratory and Critical Care Medicine, 166*(8), 1084–1091.
Man, W.D., Mustfa, N., Nikoletou, D., et al. (2004). Effect of salmeterol on respiratory muscle activity during exercise in poorly reversible COPD. *Thorax, 59*(6), 471–476.
Mannino, D.M., Diaz-Guzman, E., & Pospisil, J. (2013). A new approach to classification of disease severity and progression of COPD. *Chest, 144*(4), 1179–1185.
Mannino, D.M., Homa, D.M., Akinbami, L.J., et al. (2002). Chronic obstructive pulmonary disease surveillance--united states, 1971–2000. *Morbidity and Mortality Weekly Report.Surveillance Summaries (Washington, D.C.: 2002), 51*(6), 1–16.
Martinez, F.J., Foster, G., Curtis, J.L., et al. (2006). Predictors of mortality in patients with emphysema and severe airflow obstruction. *American Journal of Respiratory and Critical Care Medicine, 173*(12), 1326–1334.
Melbostad, E., Eduard, W., & Magnus, P. (1997). Chronic bronchitis in farmers. *Scandinavian Journal of Work, Environment & Health, 23*(4), 271–280.

Menezes, A.M., Montes de Oca, M., Perez-Padilla, R., et al. (2014). Increased risk of exacerbation and hospitalization in subjects with an overlap phenotype: COPD-asthma. *Chest, 145*(2), 297–304.

Menezes, A.M., Perez-Padilla, R., Jardim, J.R., et al. (2005). Chronic obstructive pulmonary disease in five latin american cities (the PLATINO study): A prevalence study. *Lancet, 366*(9500), 1875–1881.

Miravitlles, M. (2011). Cough and sputum production as risk factors for poor outcomes in patients with COPD. *Respiratory Medicine, 105*(8), 1118–1128.

Miravitlles, M., Calle, M., & Soler-Cataluna, J.J. (2012). Clinical phenotypes of COPD: Identification, definition and implications for guidelines. *Archivos De Bronconeumologia, 48*(3), 86–98.

Miravitlles, M., Murio, C., Guerrero, T., et al. (2002). Pharmacoeconomic evaluation of acute exacerbations of chronic bronchitis and COPD. *Chest, 121*(5), 1449–1455.

Ninane, V., Geltner, C., Bezzi, M., et al. (2012). Multicentre european study for the treatment of advanced emphysema with bronchial valves. *The European Respiratory Journal, 39*(6), 1319–1325.

Nishimura, K., Izumi, T., Tsukino, M., et al. (2002). Dyspnea is a better predictor of 5-year survival than airway obstruction in patients with COPD. *Chest, 121*(5), 1434–1440.

Nishimura, M., Makita, H., Nagai, K., et al. (2012). Annual change in pulmonary function and clinical phenotype in chronic obstructive pulmonary disease. *American Journal of Respiratory and Critical Care Medicine, 185*(1), 44–52.

O'Donnell, D.E., Fluge, T., Gerken, F., et al. (2004). Effects of tiotropium on lung hyperinflation, dyspnoea and exercise tolerance in COPD. *The European Respiratory Journal, 23*(6), 832–840.

O'Donnell, D.E., & Parker, C.M. (2006). COPD exacerbations . 3: Pathophysiology. *Thorax, 61*(4), 354–361.

O'Donnell, D.E., Revill, S.M., & Webb, K.A. (2001). Dynamic hyperinflation and exercise intolerance in chronic obstructive pulmonary disease. *American Journal of Respiratory and Critical Care Medicine, 164*(5), 770–777.

O'Donnell, D.E., & Webb, K.A. (1993). Exertional breathlessness in patients with chronic airflow limitation. the role of lung hyperinflation. *The American Review of Respiratory Disease, 148*(5), 1351–1357.

Papi, A., Romagnoli, M., Baraldo, S., et al. (2000). Partial reversibility of airflow limitation and increased exhaled NO and sputum eosinophilia in chronic obstructive pulmonary disease. *American Journal of Respiratory and Critical Care Medicine, 162*(5), 1773–1777.

Pitta, F., Troosters, T., Probst, V.S., et al. (2006). Physical activity and hospitalization for exacerbation of COPD. *Chest, 129*(3), 536–544.

Prescott, E., Lange, P., & Vestbo, J. (1995). Chronic mucus hypersecretion in COPD and death from pulmonary infection. *The European Respiratory Journal, 8*(8), 1333–1338.

Raad, D., Gaddam, S., Schunemann, H.J., et al. (2011). Effects of water-pipe smoking on lung function: A systematic review and meta-analysis. *Chest, 139*(4), 764–774.

Rabe, K.F., Timmer, W., Sagkriotis, A., et al. (2008). Comparison of a combination of tiotropium plus formoterol to salmeterol plus fluticasone in moderate COPD. *Chest, 134*(2), 255–262.

Roberts, C.M., Lowe, D., Bucknall, C.E., et al. (2002). Clinical audit indicators of outcome following admission to hospital with acute exacerbation of chronic obstructive pulmonary disease. *Thorax, 57*(2), 137–141.

Rojas-Martinez, R., Perez-Padilla, R., Olaiz-Fernandez, G., et al. (2007). Lung function growth in children with long-term exposure to air pollutants in mexico city. *American Journal of Respiratory and Critical Care Medicine, 176*(4), 377–384.

Scanlon, P.D., Connett, J.E., Waller, et al. (2000). Smoking cessation and lung function in mild-to-moderate chronic obstructive pulmonary disease. the lung health study. *American Journal of Respiratory and Critical Care Medicine, 161*(2 Pt 1), 381–390.

Schirnhofer, L., Lamprecht, B., Vollmer, W.M., et al. (2007). COPD prevalence in salzburg, austria: Results from the burden of obstructive lung disease (BOLD) study. *Chest, 131*(1), 29–36.

Sciurba, F.C., Ernst, A., Herth, F.J., et al. (2010). A randomized study of endobronchial valves for advanced emphysema. *The New England Journal of Medicine, 363*(13), 1233–1244.

Seemungal, T.A., Donaldson, G.C., Paul, E.A., et al. (1998). Effect of exacerbation on quality of life in patients with chronic obstructive pulmonary disease. *American Journal of Respiratory and Critical Care Medicine, 157*(5 Pt 1), 1418–1422.

Sestini, P., Cappiello, V., Aliani, M., et al. (2006). Prescription bias and factors associated with improper use of inhalers. *Journal of Aerosol Medicine : The Official Journal of the International Society for Aerosols in Medicine, 19*(2), 127–136.

Shah, P.L., Zoumot, Z., Singh, S., et al. (2013). Endobronchial coils for the treatment of severe emphysema with hyperinflation (RESET): A randomised controlled trial. *The Lancet.Respiratory Medicine, 1*(3), 233–240.

Silverman, E.K., Chapman, H.A., Drazen, J.M., et al. (1998). Genetic epidemiology of severe, early-onset chronic obstructive pulmonary disease. risk to relatives for airflow obstruction and chronic bronchitis. *American Journal of Respiratory and Critical Care Medicine, 157*(6 Pt 1), 1770–1778.

Silverman, E.K., Weiss, S.T., Drazen, J.M., et al. (2000). Gender-related differences in severe, early-onset chronic obstructive pulmonary disease. *American Journal of Respiratory and Critical Care Medicine, 162*(6), 2152–2158.

Sin, D.D., Wu, L., & Man, S.F. (2005). The relationship between reduced lung function and cardio-vascular mortality: A population-based study and a systematic review of the literature. *Chest, 127*(6), 1952–1959.

Snider, G.L. (1989). Chronic obstructive pulmonary disease: A definition and implications of structural determinants of airflow obstruction for epidemiology. *The American Review of Respiratory Disease, 140*(3 Pt 2), S3–8.

Soler-Cataluna, J.J., Martinez-Garcia, M.A., Roman Sanchez, P., et al. (2005). Severe acute exacerbations and mortality in patients with chronic obstructive pulmonary disease. *Thorax, 60*(11), 925–931.

Sorheim, I.C., Johannessen, A., Gulsvik, A., et al. (2010). Gender differences in COPD: Are women more susceptible to smoking effects than men? *Thorax, 65*(6), 480–485.

Spencer, S., Jones, P.W., & GLOBE Study Group. (2003). Time course of recovery of health status following an infective exacerbation of chronic bronchitis. *Thorax, 58*(7), 589–593.

Stern, D.A., Morgan, W.J., Wright, A.L., et al. (2007). Poor airway function in early infancy and lung function by age 22 years: A non-selective longitudinal cohort study. *Lancet. 1;370(9589):758–64.*

Stockley, R.A. (2014). Alpha1-antitrypsin review. *Clinics in Chest Medicine, 35*(1), 39–50.

Suissa, S., Dell'Aniello, S., & Ernst, P. (2012). Long-term natural history of chronic obstructive pulmonary disease: Severe exacerbations and mortality. *Thorax, 67*(11), 957–963.

Tager, I.B., Segal, M.R., Speizer, F.E., et al. (1988). The natural history of forced expiratory volumes. effect of cigarette smoking and respiratory symptoms. *The American Review of Respiratory Disease, 138*(4), 837–849.

Tashkin, D.P., Celli, B., Senn, S., et al. (2008). A 4-year trial of tiotropium in chronic obstructive pulmonary disease. *The New England Journal of Medicine, 359*(15), 1543–1554.

Tashkin, D.P., Clark, V.A., Coulson, A.H., et al. (1984). The UCLA population studies of chronic obstructive respiratory disease. VIII. effects of smoking cessation on lung function: A prospective study of a free-living population. *The American Review of Respiratory Disease, 130*(5), 707–715.

Ten Have-Opbroek, A.A. (1981). The development of the lung in mammals: An analysis of concepts and findings. *The American Journal of Anatomy, 162*(3), 201–219.

Thun, M.J., Carter, B.D., Feskanich, D., et al. (2013). 50-year trends in smoking-related mortality in the united states. *The New England Journal of Medicine, 368*(4), 351–364.

Turner, S., Fielding, S., Mullane, D., et al. (2014). A longitudinal study of lung function from 1 month to 18 years of age. *Thorax,* doi:thoraxjnl-2013–204931 [pii]

van Noord, J.A., Aumann, J.L., Janssens, E., et al. (2005). Comparison of tiotropium once daily, formoterol twice daily and both combined once daily in patients with COPD. *The European Respiratory Journal, 26*(2), 214–222.

Vestbo, J., Anderson, W., Coxson, H.O., et al. (2008). Evaluation of COPD longitudinally to identify predictive surrogate end-points (ECLIPSE). *The European Respiratory Journal, 31*(4), 869–873.

Vestbo, J., Edwards, L.D., Scanlon, P.D., et al. (2011). Changes in forced expiratory volume in 1 second over time in COPD. *The New England Journal of Medicine, 365*(13), 1184–1192.

Vestbo, J., Soriano, J.B., Anderson, J.A., et al. (2004). Gender does not influence the response to the combination of salmeterol and fluticasone propionate in COPD. *Respiratory Medicine, 98*(11), 1045–1050.

Vogelmeier, C., Hederer, B., Glaab, T., et al. (2011). Tiotropium versus salmeterol for the prevention of exacerbations of COPD. *The New England Journal of Medicine, 364*(12), 1093–1103.

Warren, C.P. (2009). The nature and causes of chronic obstructive pulmonary disease: A historical perspective. the christie lecture 2007, chicago, USA. *Canadian Respiratory Journal : Journal of the Canadian Thoracic Society, 16*(1), 13–20.

Washko, G.R., Fan, V.S., Ramsey, S.D., et al. (2008). The effect of lung volume reduction surgery on chronic obstructive pulmonary disease exacerbations. *American Journal of Respiratory and Critical Care Medicine, 177*(2), 164–169.

Watson, L., Vestbo, J., Postma, D.S., et al. (2004). Gender differences in the management and experience of chronic obstructive pulmonary disease. *Respiratory Medicine, 98*(12), 1207–1213.

Wedzicha, J.A., Brill, S.E., Allinson, J.P., et al. (2013). Mechanisms and impact of the frequent exacerbator phenotype in chronic obstructive pulmonary disease. *BMC Medicine, 11*, 181–7015–11–181.

Wershof Schwartz, A., Clarfield, A.M., Doucette, J.T., et al. (2013). Disparities in pneumococcal and influenza immunization among older adults in israel: A cross-sectional analysis of socio-demographic barriers to vaccination. *Preventive Medicine, 56*(5), 337–340.

Yuan, R., Hogg, J.C., Pare, P.D., et al. (2009). Prediction of the rate of decline in FEV(1) in smokers using quantitative computed tomography. *Thorax, 64*(11), 944–949.

Ralph J. Panos, MD

# 10 COPD Is a Multi-Organ Disorder: Systemic Manifestations

Key Points

1. COPD is a disorder that affects multiple systems beyond the lungs; these nonpulmonary manifestations include cardio- and cerebrovascular, oncologic, musculoskeletal, hematologic, psychological, and endocrine effects.
2. Much of the early mortality related to COPD is caused by cardiac and oncologic effects of COPD; late mortality is caused by respiratory failure.
3. Significant COPD-related morbidity is due to nonpulmonary manifestations.
4. In general, management of the extra-pulmonary manifestations of COPD is the same as treatment of these processes when they are not associated with COPD.
5. It remains to be determined if treatment of COPD ameliorates its nonpulmonary manifestations and whether management of COPD's extrapulmonary processes improves the health and wellbeing of individuals with COPD.

## 10.1 Introduction

Although COPD is usually defined and managed as a disorder confined to the lungs, numerous investigations over the past decade have demonstrated that COPD is associated with multiple nonpulmonary manifestations that contribute significantly to its morbidity and mortality. These associated processes include cardiac and cerebrovascular, oncologic, musculoskeletal, hematologic, psychological, and endocrine effects (Cavailles, 2013; Albu, 2012; Huertas, 2011; Nussbaumer-Ochsner, 2011; Barnes, 2009; Decramer, 2008; Augusti 2007; Augusti, 2008; Fabbri, 2008).

## 10.2 Inflammation in COPD

The pathophysiologic process linking pulmonary and nonpulmonary manifestations of COPD has been postulated to be inflammation. For a detailed review of the pathogenesis of pulmonary and systemic inflammation in COPD, please see chapter 6, Pathogenesis of COPD.

## 10.3 COPD Mortality

As discussed in Chapter 9, Natural History of COPD, Phenotypes, and Gender Differences in COPD, the major causes of death in individuals with early COPD (measured by severity of airflow limitation (AFL)) are lung cancer and cardiac disease (Sin, 2006; Mannino, 2006). During acute exacerbations of COPD, the leading causes of death are heart failure (37.2%), pneumonia (27.9%), pulmonary (20.9%), and respiratory failure (14%) (Zvezdin, 2009). Even when adjusted for sex and smoking history, individuals with AFL have an increased risk for acute myocardial infarction, hazard ratio (HR) 3.53 [95% confidence interval, 3.02–4.13] and for stroke, HR 2.79 [2.56–3.04] (Feary, 2010). For individuals aged 35–44 years old, the risk is even greater, acute myocardial infarction, HR 10.34 [3.28–32.60] and stroke, HR 3.44 [0.85–13.84] (Feary, 2010).

A 17 year longitudinal study of mortality among patients with COPD from 1987 to 2004 who were started on long term oxygen in Sweden showed that 71% of patients died of respiratory causes, 16% circulatory processes, and 7.6% from cancer (Ekstrom, 2011). However, the adjusted annual change in mortality due to COPD declined by 3.0% annually whereas nonrespiratory causes of death rose by 6.3% annually. Another Swedish longitudinal study of 21,361 patients diagnosed with COPD from 1999 to 2009 showed that the number of COPD exacerbations declined from 3.0 to 1.3 exacerbations/patient/year and the number of hospitalizations decreased from 1.02 to 0.2 per patient per year (Stallberg, 2014). Long acting anti-cholinergic and inhaled corticosteroid/long acting beta agonist prescriptions increased from 0% to 36% and 37% of patients, respectively (Stallberg, 2014). **Thus, respiratory morbidity and mortality among those with COPD are declining but nonrespiratory morbidity and mortality are increasing. These improvements in respiratory mortality may be due to better pharmacologic and nonpharmacologic management of COPD. The increase in nonrespiratory related mortality suggests that greater identification and management of nonpulmonary processes associated with COPD may be warranted to improve the longevity and health of individuals with COPD.**

## 10.4 Cardio- and Cerebral-vascular Disease

The prevalence of cardiovascular (CV) disease in individuals with COPD, 20–22%, is over two-fold greater than in the general population who do not have COPD, 9% (Mannino, 2008). Among patients with AFL, the prevalence of cardiovascular disease is increased over 2 fold (odds ratio (OR) = 2.7, 95% CI 2.3–3.2) (Finkelstein, 2009). Reduced $FEV_1$ is associated with increased CV mortality independent of age, gender, and smoking history (Sin, 2005A). Adjusted CV mortality rises by 28% for every 10% decrease in $FEV_1$ (Sin, 2005B). Coronary artery calcifications detected by CT scanning were increased in individuals with COPD compared with smokers with normal spirometry or nonsmokers and correlated with dyspnea, exercise capacity, all cause mortality, and inflammatory markers (IL6, IL8, CCP 16, SP D, and neutrophils) but not $FEV_1$ or acute exacerbations of COPD (Williams, 2014).

Acute COPD exacerbations are associated with an increased rate of myocardial infarction. Elevated cardiac enzymes occur in 17–27% of patients hospitalized for

COPD exacerbations and MI occurs in 1:12 patients (McAllister, 2012). There is a 2.27 fold increase in MI during the 5 days after onset of a COPD exacerbation (Donaldson, 2010). Acute COPD exacerbations may increase the risk of cardiac ischemia and infarction through demand ischemia, acute coronary syndrome with plaque rupture, peripheral arterial stiffness, interactions between the heart and lungs including increased right and left ventricular afterload due to increased intrathoracic pressures, medication effects, and cardiac muscle mass depletion (Harvey, 2014; Visca, 2013).

β blockers significantly decrease mortality after myocardial infarction in patients with COPD (Quint, 2013). Of 1063 patients with COPD presenting with an initial MI from 2003–2008, the mortality HR was 0.59 [95% confidence interval (CI), 0.44–0.79] for those who were taking β blockers at presentation and 0.50 [95% CI, 0.36–0.69] for those who started β blockers during that admission (Quint, 2013). β blockers are tolerated well by patients with all stages of COPD including individuals who demonstrated bronchodilator responsivity during spirometry testing (Salpeter 2002, 2003, 2004, 2005).

### 10.4.1 Heart Failure

Approximately 19–48% of patients with heart failure have COPD and 9–52% of patients with COPD have heart failure (Hawkins, 2009). The relative risk of developing heart failure among patients with COPD is 4.5 controlling for age and cardiovascular risk factors. Coexistent COPD and heart failure is associated with greater mortality and healthcare utilization than either disorder alone (Hawkins, 2013).

It may be difficult to distinguish COPD and heart failure because the symptoms frequently overlap and include nonspecific features such as exertional dyspnea, fatigue, and reduced activity. The presence of lower extremity edema may be due to cor pulmonale or left ventricular failure. Emphysematous changes may mask the presentation of pulmonary edema on chest radiographs and it may be difficult to determine heart size. Echocardiography may be technically difficult in patients with COPD due to hyperinflation and attenuation of the ultrasound signal. Minor elevations in B-type natriuretic peptide (BNP) may be nonspecific and due to cor pulmonale, pulmonary hypertension, left, right, or biventricular failure. A BNP greater than 400 pg/ml suggests left ventricular failure and warrants evaluation of LV function with an ECHO. Finally, use of inhaled bronchodilators in patients who have heart failure but do not have COPD is associated with a 69% increase in mechanical ventilation and a 40% increase in intravenous vasodilator use (Singer, 2008).

Most pharmacologic treatment trials of respiratory medications for COPD have excluded concomitant heart failure. Chronic β blocker use in individuals with COPD and CHF is considered to be safe and β blockers can be continued during hospitalizations for COPD exacerbations (Stefan, 2012). Statins, ACE inhibitors, and angiotensin receptor blockers reduce respiratory related hospitalizations among individuals with

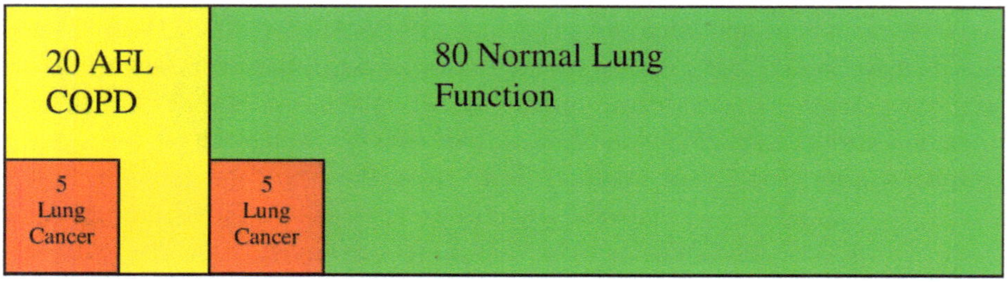


**Figure 10.1:** Prevalence of Lung Cancer Among Smokers with and without COPD. Of 100 cigarette smokers, approximately 20% will develop airflow limitation (AFL) and COPD; 80 will maintain normal lung function. 5 smokers with AFL will develop lung cancer (25%) and 5 smokers with normal lung function will develop lung cancer (6.25%).

COPD (Mancini, 2006) and statin and ACE inhibitor use at the time of admission is associated with a reduction in mortality (Mortenson, 2009). In contrast, patients with left ventricular heart failure who are treated with β agonists have increased mortality and hospitalization (Au, 2003). The use of systemic steroids (more than 20 mg/d of prednisone) increases the risk of heart failure decompensation (Souverein, 2004) and phosphodiesterase inhibitors are associated with an increased risk of dysrhythmias (Barnes, 2013). There is an increasing need to assess and determine the optimal management of COPD in individuals who also have heart failure (Hawkins, 2009, 2011, 2013; Mentz. 2012).

## 10.5 Lung Cancer

Of 100 smokers, approximately 20 will develop COPD, and, of those 20 individuals, 5 will develop lung cancer whereas of the 80 smokers who do not develop COPD, only 5 will develop lung cancer (Young, 2009). Thus, the risk of lung cancer is significantly greater in smokers with COPD, 1:4, compared with smokers who do not have COPD, 1:16. (Figure 10.1) The relative risk of lung cancer in individuals with a diagnosis of COPD is 2.22 [1.66–2.97], chronic bronchitis 1.52 [1.25–1.84], and emphysema 2.04 [1.72–2.41] (Brenner, 2011). The visual detection of emphysema on CT scans increases the odds ratio for lung cancer, 3.5 [2.71–4.51] (Smith, 2012).

Between 50% and 90% of all lung cancer patients have COPD (deTorres, 2007; Turner, 2007; Wilson, 2008; Young, 2009). COPD is associated with a 2 to 6-fold increase in lung cancer risk compared with smokers who do not develop COPD (deTorres, 2007, 2011; Mannino, 2003; Turner, 2007; Wilson, 2008; Young, 2009). AFL increases the risk of lung cancer independent of the smoking history (Wilson, 2008). Several studies have found that the risk of lung cancer is greater in individuals with mild to moderate AFL compared to those with more severe COPD (Young, 2009;

Anthonisen, 2005; deTorres, 2011); whereas others have found that the lung cancer risk increases with the decline in lung function (Mannino, 2003). The presence of COPD portends a worse prognosis for individuals with lung cancer (Kiri, 2010). Thus, not only is the risk for lung cancer greater for smokers who develop AFL, they generally do worse.

### 10.5.1 Pathogenetic Links Between COPD and Lung Cancer

The strong association between lung cancer and COPD has spurred studies to discover common cellular and molecular pathways for these two processes (Houghton, 2013; Adcock, 2011; Yang, 2011; Young, 2011). Inhalation of tobacco smoke in genetically susceptible individuals may generate inflammation and reactive oxygen species within the lungs and systemically (El-Zein, 2012). These inflammatory cytokines and reactive biochemical compounds may induce or repress gene expression and cause alterations in genetic and epigenetic complexes leading to deranged cellular proliferation and altered lung airway and parenchymal anatomy and function (Lee, 2009). Other recently discovered biologic pathways are also common to the development of COPD and lung cancer. MicroRNA's modulate post-translational gene regulation and are critical for lung development, pulmonary inflammation, and the development of bronchogenic carcinoma (Sittka, 2013). The biologic processes maintaining telomeres, the DNA-protein caps on the ends of chromosomes, have also been implicated in the pathogenesis of several pulmonary processes including idiopathic pulmonary fibrosis, COPD, and lung cancer and may be another common pathway that is deranged in these disorders (Ganser, 2013). Unifying pathogenetic processes for COPD and lung cancer are being intensely investigated to identify common pathways and means to interdict the development of both of these disorders.

### 10.5.2 Lung Cancer Screening

Based upon the American National Lung Screening Trial that demonstrated a 20% reduction in lung cancer mortality in the group that underwent low dose CT scan screening examinations, current recommendations advise lung cancer screening for smokers or former smokers with at least 30 pack years smoking history and age between 55 and 74 years (The National Lung Screening Trial Research Team, 2011; Wender, 2013). Although lung cancer screening has not been recommended for individuals with COPD, based upon the results of the NLST, low dose chest CT scanning screening may be beneficial for individuals with COPD, even with moderate AFL. Earlier detection of AFL and diagnosis of COPD may identify individuals with even greater potential benefit from lung cancer screening (Sekine, 2012).

### 10.5.3 Management of Lung Cancer

Multiple clinical practice guidelines for lung cancer have been published (von Dincklage, 2013). Evaluation and management of suspected lung cancer in a patient with COPD begins with radiographic and cardiopulmonary physiologic assessments (Backhus, 2013). In general, once the histopathological diagnosis is confirmed or the clinical suspicion for lung cancer is sufficiently high, the critical decision is to determine whether the patient is a candidate for surgical excision of the cancer. Only 15–25% of lung cancers are operable at the time of diagnosis (Von Groote-Bidlingmaier, 2011). Essential components for the determination of a patient's candidacy for surgical resection of bronchogenic carcinoma include radiographic staging of the cancer and assessment of cardiovascular and pulmonary physiologic function. Because of the high prevalence of coronary artery disease among individuals with COPD, ascertainment of the cardiovascular risk for anesthesia and thoracic surgery should be pursued. If either the $FEV_1$ or DLCO are less than 80% of predicted, the postoperative lung function should be calculated by either quantitative perfusion scans or the anatomic method based upon the number of lung segments to be resected. If either the $FEV_1$ or DLCO % predicted is less than 40%, the patient is at increased risk for perioperative respiratory complications including death, infections, respiratory compromise or failure, and requirement for supplemental oxygen. In patients with marginal pulmonary physiologic function, cardiopulmonary exercise testing demonstrating a maximal oxygen consumption ($VO_2$ max) less than 15 ml/kg/min precludes surgery (Colice, 2007). Combined lung volume reduction surgery and lung cancer surgical resection in a selective population of patients with emphysema in a upper zone predominant distribution and cancer stage amenable to resection may improve postoperative lung function and respiratory symptoms as well as permit resection in patients who might otherwise not be considered for surgery (Choong, 2009; Colice, 2007).

Historically, the most common lung cancer subtype among male smokers was squamous cell carcinoma but more recent studies show that by the mid 1990's adenocarcinoma was the most frequent histopathologic subtype regardless of gender or smoking history (Devesa, 2005).

Surgery is the first line treatment for lung cancer depending upon stage and surgical and operative risk factors. For patients with nonresectable lung cancer, chemotherapy, radiation therapy, or combination therapy may be pursued after referral to oncologists and radiation specialists.

Pulmonary rehabilitation may benefit patients with lung cancer and COPD by improving quality of life, performance status, oxygen consumption, exercise tolerance, chemotherapy-associated fatigue, and perioperative morbidity and mortality (Pasqua, 2013; Shannon, 2010; Nici, 2009). Palliative care improves the quantity and quality of life in individuals with lung cancer (Davis, 2012; see chapter 19, End of Life Issues/Palliative Care).

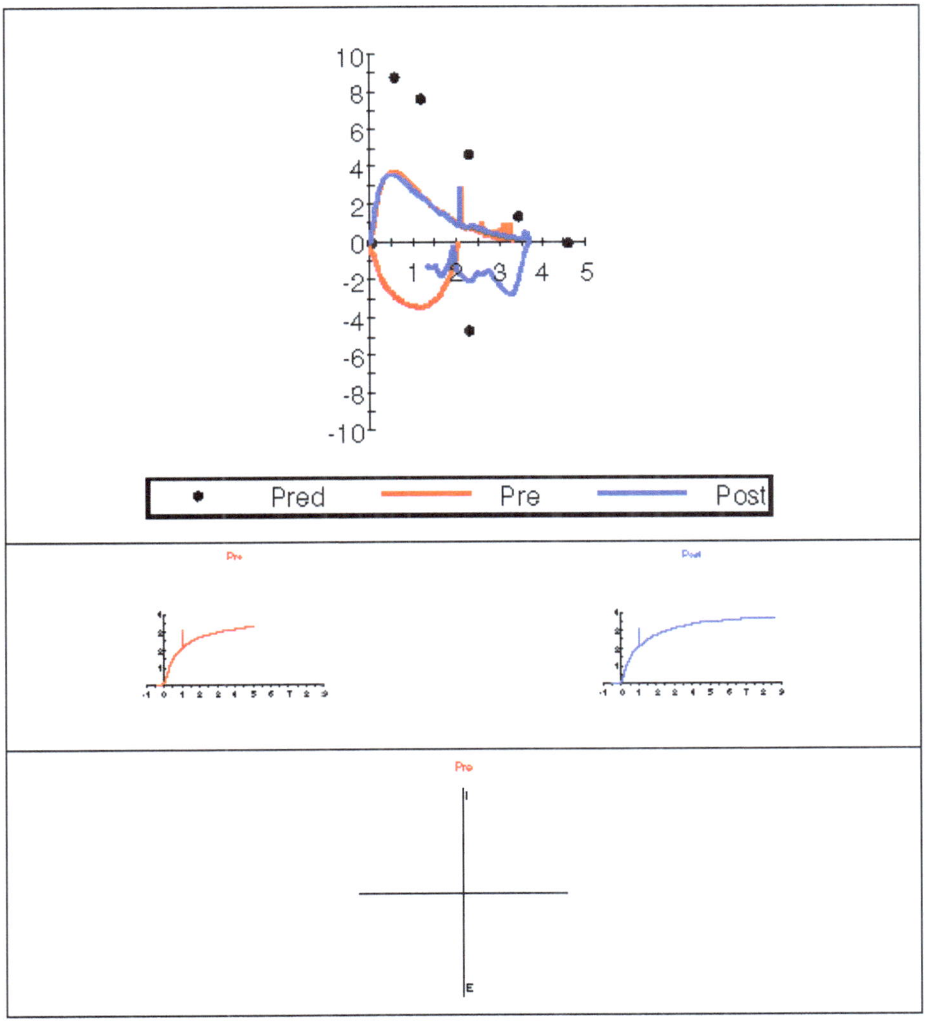


**Figure 10.2:** Flow volume loop from a patient with combined pulmonary fibrosis and emphysema. The flow volume loop demonstrates reduced peak expiratory flow rates and scooping of the expiratory loop.

## 10.6 Pulmonary Fibrosis

The clinical syndrome of combined pulmonary fibrosis and emphysema (CPFE) has recently been defined by the presence of breathlessness, upper lobe emphysema, lower lobe fibrosis, and deranged pulmonary gas exchange (Jankowich, 2012). Nearly all patients with this syndrome have been smokers and 90% are male (Jankowich,

Diagnosis: Chronic Obstructive Pulmonary Disease
Dyspnea: After any exertion Cough: Productive Wheeze: Frequent
Tbco Prod: Cigarette Yrs Smk: 50.0 Pks/Day: 2.0 Yrs Quit:
Medications: Albuterol; Budesonide/Formoter; Tiotropium
Pre Test Comments:
Post Test Comments: PLEASE REFER TO THE COMPUTERIZED RECORD FOR THE ORDER AND INTERPRETATION OF THESE RESULTS. ATTENTION: PFT NOT VERIFIED UNTIL REVIEWED BY ATTENDING. Good patient effort & cooperation. SaO2 on 2 LPM=91/HR=94. 2 puffs of Proventil given via aerochamber with 1 minute between puffs,10 minutes elapsed before post tests. Patient given outpatient medication list. Patient reviewed list and reported no discrepancies. No recent Hgb available. Pt had difficulty exhaling maximally during all tests due to coughing. He used 2 LPM during DLCO manuever(pt only able to complete one test). Extra time given, patient was short of breath during testing.

| | Baseline | | | | Post Bronchodilator | | |
|---|---|---|---|---|---|---|---|
| | **Actual** | **Pred** | **%Pred** | **LLN** | **Actual** | **%Chng** | **%Pred** |
| -- SPIROMETRY --- | | | | | | | |
| FVC (L) | 3.30 | 4.56 | 72 | 3.64 | 3.69 | 12 | 81 |
| FEV1 (L) | 2.14 | 3.41 | 63 | 2.63 | 2.09 | -3 | 61 |
| FEV1/FVC (%) | 65 | 75 | 87 | 65 | 57 | -13 | 75 |
| FEF Max (L/sec) | 3.71 | 8.80 | 42 | 6.51 | 3.60 | -3 | 41 |
| FEF 25-75% (L/sec) | 1.30 | 2.73 | 48 | 1.15 | 1.31 | 0 | 48 |
| -- LUNG VOLUMES -- | | | | | | | |
| TLC (Pleth) (L) | 6.58 | 7.02 | 94 | 5.62 | | | |
| SVC (L) | 3.47 | 4.53 | 77 | | | | |
| ERV (L) | 1.42 | 1.13 | 126 | | | | |
| IC (L) | 2.05 | 3.40 | 60 | | | | |
| RV (Pleth) (L) | 3.10 | 2.49 | 125 | 1.67 | | | |
| RV/TLC (Pleth) (%) | 47 | 39 | 121 | 28 | | | |
| Raw (cmH2O/L/s) | 1.36 | 1.45 | 94 | 0.66 | | | |
| Gaw (L/s/cmH2O) | 0.75 | 1.03 | 73 | | | | |
| -- DIFFUSION --- | | | | | | | |
| DLCOcor (ml/min/mmHg) | | 21.91 | | 12.23 | | | |
| DLCOunc (ml/min/mmHg) | 8.53 | 21.91 | 39 | 13.92 | | | |
| VA (L) | 4.70 | 6.72 | 70 | 5.35 | | | |
| DL/VA (ml/min/mmHg/L) | 1.81 | 4.15 | 44 | 2.69 | | | |
| IVC (L) | 3.12 | | | | | | |

**Figure 10.3:** Pulmonary function tests from a patient with combined pulmonary fibrosis and emphysema. The studies demonstrate normal lung volumes (total lung capacity is 94% of predicted), airflow obstruction with the FEV1/FVC equal to the lower limit of normal and a response to bronchodilators with an increase in the FVC by 12% and 390 ml. The diffusing capacity is markedly and disproportionately reduced to 39% of predicted.

2012). Patients typically present with breathlessness and pulmonary physiologic testing reveals profoundly reduced DLCO but relatively preserved lung volumes due to pseudonormalization. This effect is due to the opposite effects of the fibrosis which reduces lung volumes and emphysema which causes hyperinflation; these two opposing forces result in relatively normal lung volumes whereas both adversely affect DLCO, causing it to be disproportionately reduced. (Figure 10.2 and 10.3). The reduction in DLCO is associated with significant hypoxemia and requirement for supplemental oxygen (Cottin, 2005). The chest radiograph often shows basilar reticulo-linear opacifications with reduced upper zone lung markings (Figure 10.4 and

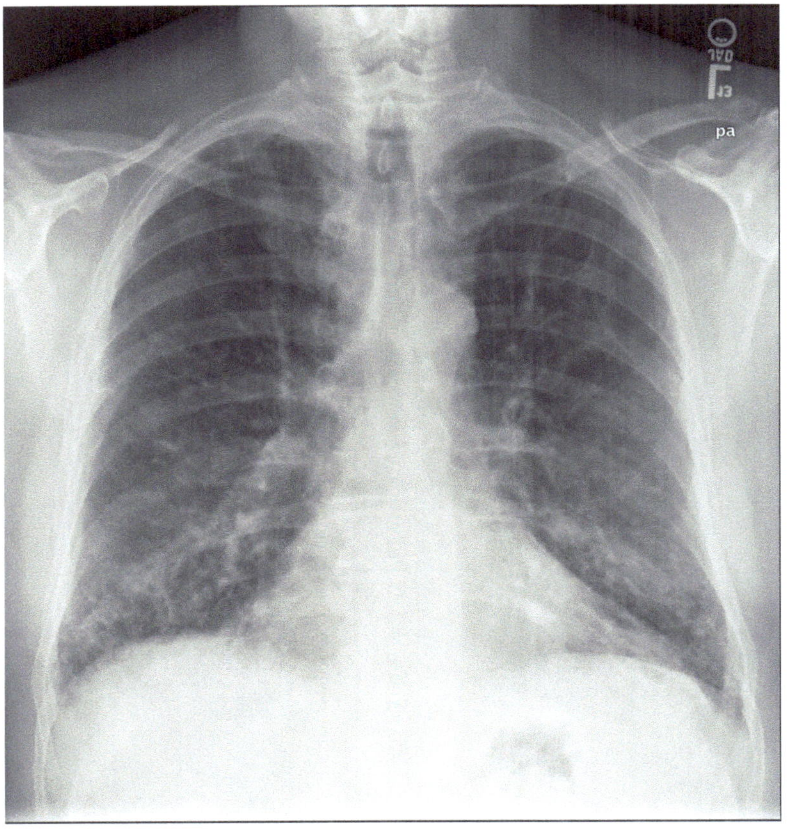


**Figure 10.4:** Posterior-apical chest radiograph demonstrating increased bi-basilar reticulo-linear opacifications with preservation and areas of reduced apical lung markings.

10.5). Chest CT scans demonstrate emphysematous changes in the upper lung zones and reticular opacifications with honeycombing in the lung bases. (Figure 10.6) The median survival is only 2.1–8.8 years and is adversely affected by the development of pulmonary hypertension and lung cancer which occur frequently in association with CPFE.

Treatment of CPFE depends upon early recognition and smoking cessation, institution of supplemental oxygen to prevent desaturation, and management of COPD. It is not yet known whether the recently discovered effective treatments for idiopathic pulmonary fibrosis, pirfenidone or nintedanib, are beneficial in patients with CPFE. It is also not known whether PH treatment modulates the disease course. Lung cancer screening has not been assessed in patients with CPFE but the increased incidence of lung cancer would suggest potential benefit to earlier detection if the patients are candidates for surgical resection.

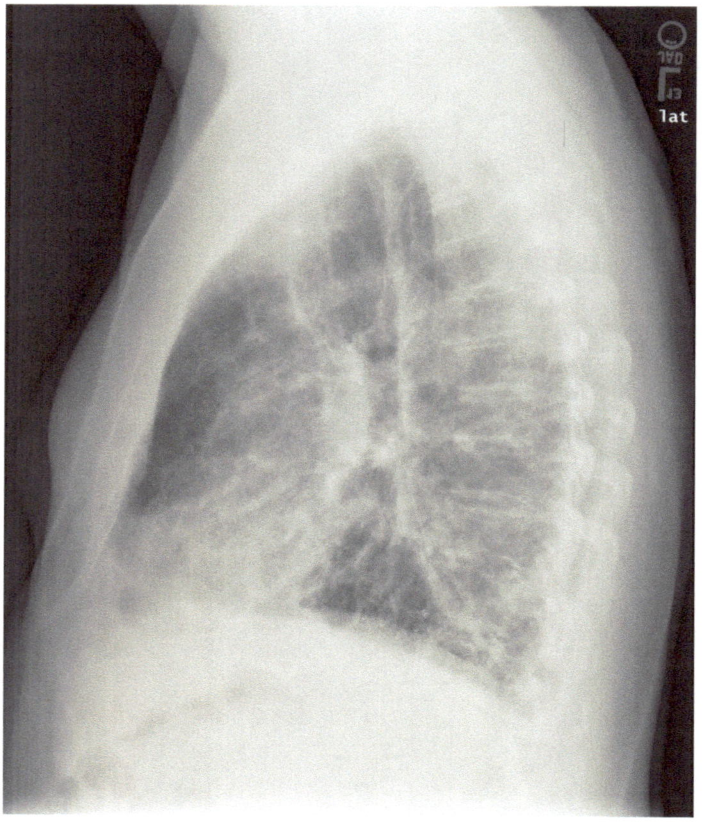


**Figure 10.5:** Lateral chest radiograph from a patient with combined pulmonary fibrosis and emphysema.

## 10.7 Hematologic Manifestations

Although polycythemia associated with hypoxemia is often considered the principle hematologic manifestation of COPD, anemia occurs in 7.5–32.7% of patients with COPD (Yohannes, 2011; Cote, 2007; Chambellan, 2005; Shorr, 2008; Nowinski, 2011; Portillo, 2013). Only 6% of 683 patients with COPD had polycythemia whereas 17% had anemia (Cote, 2007). COPD-related anemia is characterized by a normal to low MCV, low serum iron, and normal to increased ferritin and is associated with higher systemic inflammation (including IL6 and CRP), greater healthcare costs, and mortality (Kollert, 2013). The anemia of COPD is believed to be due to chronic inflammation (anemia of chronic disease). Inflammatory cytokines such as TNF $\alpha$ and IL6 suppress hepcidin synthesis and inhibit erythropoietin which decreases iron availability and decreases erythropoiesis.

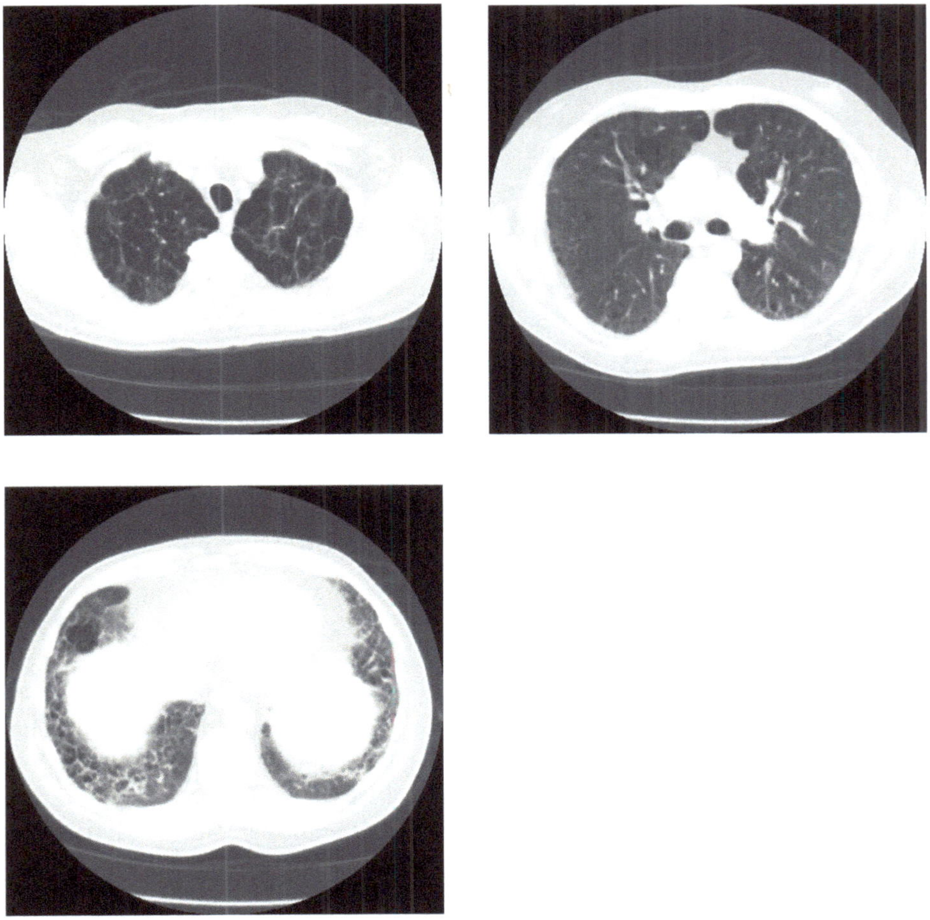

**Figure 10.6:** Chest computed tomography at the level of the lung apices (left upper image), just below the carina (right upper image), and the lung base (left lower image). The apical view shows emphysematous cysts and blebs; at the carina, there are emphysematous changes anteriorly and slight subpleural increased reticular opacifications posteriorly; at the bases, there are extensive linear and reticular opacifications with parenchymal cysts.

Anemia in patients with COPD is associated with higher levels of dyspnea and diminished 6 minute walk distances (Cote, 2007) and anemic individuals with COPD have reduced exercise capability during cardiopulmonary exercise testing with greater breathlessness (Bouton, 2011). Patients with COPD and anemia have worse quality of life measured by the physical functioning and physical component scores on the Short Form-36 survey compared with those with normal hemoglobin levels (Krishnan, 2006). Anemia is associated with increased healthcare utilization, prolonged length of hospital stay, more frequent readmissions, greater healthcare costs, and mortality among individuals with COPD (Chambellan, 2005; Shorr, 2008; Nowinski, 2011; Halpern, 2006; Barba, 2012; Martinez-Rivera, 2012; Martinez-Rivera, 2012; Celli, 2004). The one year mortality after hospitalization for a COPD exacerbation was approximately 40% in anemic individuals but only 10% in those with normal hematocrits (Martinez-Rivera, 2012).

It is not known whether treatment of anemia associated with COPD improves survival, alters respiratory symptoms, reduces healthcare utilization, or COPD related health care costs. Red blood cell transfusions may assist in ventilator liberation and reduce minute ventilation and work of breathing in critically ill patients with COPD who require mechanical ventilator support (Schonhofer, 1998A, 1998B).

The number of circulating bone marrow-derived progenitor cells is reduced in patients with COPD (Huertas 2011, 2010; Palange, 2006; Fadini, 2006)

## 10.8 Musculoskeletal

The prevalence of osteoporosis is greatly increased in individuals with COPD and ranges from 24–69% depending upon the population studied and the severity of AFL (Graat-Verbom, 2009). Vertebral fractures occur in 24%-63% of patients with COPD and predominantly involve T7, T8, and T12 (Jorgensen, 2007; Nuti, 2009; Papioannou, 2003; McEvoy 1998). Approximately 10% of patients admitted with COPD exacerbations have chest radiographs documenting vertebral compression fractures (Majumdar, 2010). These compression fractures may decrease patients' heights affecting the normative equations for predictive values used in the interpretation of pulmonary function testing. Therefore, it may be beneficial to consider using arm span in determining the predicted normal values in patients with COPD who have severe vertebral fracture associated kyphosis. Further, the vertebral fractures may lead to a reduction in lung volumes. Each vertebral fracture is associated with a 9% reduction in the FVC (Leech, 1990).

Osteoporosis is more prevalent in patients with COPD who have emphysema and an increase in the RV to TLC ratio, a lower BMI, are older, have used systemic steroids or chronic supplemental oxygen, and have worse AFL (Graat-Verboom, 2012; Ogura-Tomomatsu, 2012). Systemic inflammation measured by CRP, TNFα and IL 6 is greater in patients with COPD with osteopenia or osteoporosis than in those individuals with normal bone density (Liang, 2011).

Of 12,646 Veterans undergoing hip fracture surgery in the VHA from 1998 to 2005, 5,944 (47%) had COPD and a diagnosis of osteoporosis was known before the hip fracture in only 3% of cases (Regan, 2013). Using the FRAX$^{R}$ tool to estimate the risk of hip fracture in Spanish patients admitted with an acute exacerbation of COPD, 1.8% (95%CI: 0.9–3.6) had a 10 year probability of > 20% for a major osteoporotic fracture and 49.7% (95% CI: 44.8–54.7) had a probability of hip fracture >3% (Diez-Mangiano,

2011). Thus, nearly half of individuals with hip fractures have COPD and the presence of COPD portends a very high likelihood of future hip fracture.

The 3 year fracture rate HR ranged from 5.1–6.3 across the various treatment and placebo groups in the TORCH trial (Ferguson, 2009). Hip fractures occurred most commonly, followed by wrist, spine, and rib fractures.

### 10.8.1 Risk Factors for Fractures in Individuals with COPD

Osteoporosis and falls are major risk factors for fractures and occur commonly in individuals with COPD. In an analysis of 14,828 subjects participating in the National Health and Nutrition Examination Survey (NHANES) from 1999–2008, individuals with physician-diagnosed COPD were more likely than those without physician-diagnosed COPD to have osteoporosis (16.9% vs 8.5%) and more likely to report mobility difficulty (55.6% vs 32.5%) and dizziness/balance problems (41.1% vs. 23.8%) (Schnell, 2012)

### 10.8.2 Osteoporosis

In individuals with COPD, the prevalence of osteoporosis and osteopenia range from 9–69% and 27–67%, respectively (Graat-Verboom, 2009; Lehouck, 2011; Graat-Verboom, 2011; Jorgensen, 2007; Rittayamai, 2012). In a longitudinal cohort study of 102 patients with COPD, 16 of 48 (33%) patients with normal initial bone density developed osteoporosis over 3 years (Graat-Verboom, 2012). In the TORCH trial, 18% of men and 30% of women had osteoporosis and 42% of men and 41% of women had osteopenia at baseline based on bone mineral density measurements (Ferguson, 2009).

Evaluation of bone mineral density in patients with COPD should include a comprehensive history and physical examination to identify risk factors associated with reduced bone mineral density, fractures, and bone loss, determination of vitamin D levels, DEXA, and spine radiographs, especially in individuals with back pain, height loss, or kyphosis (Mazokopakis, 2011). Treatment of osteoporosis in individuals with COPD includes pharmacologic and nonpharmacologic interventions (Table 10.1).

### 10.8.3 Falls

Despite the presence of multiple predisposing factors to falls, the prevalence and incidence of falls in individuals with COPD has not been studied extensively. In a study comparing 36 patients with COPD with 20 normal individuals, hypoxemia, dyspnea, and fatigue were associated with balance impairment and falls (Ozalevli, 2011). In a retrospective study, 46% of 39 participants with COPD (mean FEV1% predicted

**Table 10.1:** Management of Osteoporosis Associated with COPD

| **Management of Osteoporosis** | **Associated with COPD** |
|---|---|
| **Pharmacologic** | **Nonpharmacologic** |
| Calcium and vitamin D | Balanced nutrition |
| Bisphosphonates | Smoking cessation |
| Teriparatide | Exercise, including pulmonary rehabilitation |
| Strontium ranelate | Fall prevention |
| Denosumab | Lung volume reduction surgery (Mineo 2005) |

42%) reported at least one fall in the preceding year. Those with self-reported falls scored lower on the Activity-Specific Balance Confidence (ABC) Scale (66 v 82) and the Berg Balance Scale (BBS) (45 v 49), and had prolonged times on the Time Up and Go Test (TUG) 17 v 14 s. Falls correlated with the use of supplemental oxygen and dyspnea severity (Beauchamp, 2009). Another retrospective study found that 25% of 80 patients with COPD (mean $FEV_1$% predicted 47.5%) reported a fall in the prior year and 29% expressed a fear of falling (Hellstroem, 2009). In a prospective study of 101 patients with COPD (mean $FEV_1$% predicted 46%) for 6 months, 31.7% reported at least one fall and the fall incidence rate was 0.1 (95% CI: 0.06–0.14) falls per person/month. Risk factors for falls included age, sex, oxygen requirement, history of prior falls, co-morbidities, number of medications (Roig, 2011A).

Factors contributing to the increased risk of falling in patients with COPD include alterations in proprioception (Janssens, 2013), impaired postural and balance control mechanisms (Roig, 2011B; Beaucham, 2009; Butcher, 2004; Eisner, 2008; Smith, 2010), slower reaction times, reduced physical activity levels, and skeletal muscle weakness (Beauchamp, 2012).

### 10.8.4 Muscle Weakness

Skeletal muscle dysfunction in patients with COPD is characterized by muscle atrophy (decreased mass and cross-sectional area), deranged distribution of fiber types (fewer oxidative fibers and more glycolytic fibers), altered metabolic capacity (diminished mitochondrial enzyme activities and expression), and reduced vascular supply (loss of capillary density) that cause diminished muscle strength and endurance (Kim, 2008; Gea, 2013). Factors that contribute to skeletal muscle dysfunction include disuse and inactivity, systemic inflammation, malnutrition, corticosteroid use, hypoxemia, senescence, and myocyte biochemical derangements including reactive oxygen and nitrogen species production, and muscle fiber degradation due to increased calpain and caspase activities (Kim, 2008). Quadriceps muscle strength is

20–30% less in individuals with moderate to severe COPD compared with those who do not have COPD (Gosselink, 1996; Bernard, 1998; Franssen, 2005).

## 10.9 Diabetes

Approximately 12.6–14.5% of individuals with COPD have diabetes mellitus (DM) (Mannino, 2008, Laghi, 2009). Patients with COPD have an odds ratio of developing diabetes of 2.04 [1.97–2.12] compared with those who do not have a physician diagnosis of COPD (Feary, 2010). The relative risk of diabetes is 1.8 [1.1–2.8] in patients with COPD compared with those with asthma (Rana, 2004). The presence of both DM and COPD increases the risk of death and the length of hospitalizations for patients with AECOPD and diabetes is 10.3% longer than those who do not have DM (Burt, 2013; Parrapil, 2010; Emerging Risk Factors Collaborative, 2011). In one study, the length of stay increased by 10% for each mmol/L increase in mean glucose level (Burt, 2013).

Treatment with prednisone is associated with afternoon and evening hyperglycemia rather than elevated morning glucose levels (Burt, 2011). Therefore, it may be beneficial to monitor glucose levels later in the day and adjust insulin type and dosing for individuals with COPD and DM who require insulin and are being treated with long term corticosteroids .

Individuals with COPD and metabolic syndrome have more frequent and longer exacerbations than those who do not have metabolic syndrome (Kupeli, 2010).

## 10.10 Conclusion

Over the past decade, COPD has been recognized as a systemic process that extends beyond the lungs to involve nearly all other organs and systems. This widespread involvement is believed to be mediated through systemic inflammation. Respiratory failure is the major cause of mortality in individuals with more severe respiratory impairment whereas cancer and cardiovascular processes predominant in those individuals with more mild airflow limitation. Death due to respiratory causes has been decreasing with improvements in COPD management but mortality due to nonrespiratory causes is increasing. The systemic manifestations of COPD are increasingly being recognized as contributing to the mortality and morbidity caused by COPD. The increase in nonrespiratory related mortality and morbidity suggests that earlier identification and management of nonpulmonary processes associated with COPD may be warranted to improve the longevity and health of individuals with COPD.

## 10.11 Summary Points

1. Comorbidities associated with COPD contribute significantly to COPD mortality and morbidity.
2. In individuals with similar smoking histories, the presence of airflow limitation increases the risk of lung cancer by approximately 3–4 fold.
3. Ischemic heart disease and heart failure contribute significantly to COPD morbidity especially in those with less severe disease (more mild to moderate AFL).
4. Individuals with COPD can be treated safely with β blockers and, with concurrent myocardial ischemia, have lower mortality than those who do not receive β blockers; in contrast, β agonists are associated with increased morbidity and mortality especially in patients with COPD and heart failure.
5. Fractures occur more often in individuals with COPD due to increased prevalence of osteoporosis/penia, muscle weakness, and gait and balance instability.
6. Increased awareness, detection, and treatment of nonpulmonary manifestations of COPD will be critical in improving quality of life and wellbeing of individuals with COPD.

## References

Adcock I.M., Caramori G., & Barnes P.J. (2011). Chronic obstructive pulmonary disease and lung cancer: new molecular insights. *Respiration*, *81*(4), 265–84.

Agustí A. (2007). Systemic effects of chronic obstructive pulmonary disease: what we know and what we don't know (but should). *Proc Am Thorac Soc*, *4*(7), 522–5.

Agusti A., & Soriano J.B. (2008). COPD as a systemic disease. *COPD*, *5*(2), 133–138.

Albu A., Fodor D., Poantă L., & Man M. (2012). Markers of systemic involvement in chronic obstructive pulmonary disease. *Rom J Intern Med*, *250*(2), 129–34.

Anthonisen N.R., Skeans M.A., Wise R.A., Manfreda J., Kanner R.E., Connett J.E.; & Lung Health Study Research Group. (2005). The effects of a smoking cessation intervention on 145-year mortality: a randomized clinical trial. *Ann Intern Med, 142*, 233–39.

Au D.H., Udris E.M., Fan V.S., Curtis J.R., McDonell M.B., & Fihn S.D. (2003). Risk of mortality and heart failure exacerbations associated with inhaled beta-adrenoceptor agonists among patients with known left ventricular systolic dysfunction. *Chest, 123*(6), 1964–1969.

Backhus L., Puneet B., Bastawrous S., Mariam M., Michael M., & Varghese T. Jr. (2013). Radiographic evaluation of the patient with lung cancer: surgical implications of imaging. *Curr Probl Diagn Radiol*, *42*(3), 84–98.

Barba R., de Casasola G.G., Marco J., Emilio Losa J., Plaza S., Canora J., & Zapatero A. (2012). Anemia in chronic obstructive pulmonary disease: a readmission prognosis factor. *Curr Med Res Opin*, *28*, 617–22.

Barnes P.J. Theophylline. (2013). *Am J Respir Crit Care Med*,*188*(8), 901–906.

Barnes P.J., & Celli B.R. (2009). Systemic manifestations and comorbidities of COPD. *Eur Respir J*, *33*(5), 1165–85.

Beauchamp M.K., Hill K., Goldstein R.S., Janaudis-Ferreira T., & Brooks D. (2009). Impairments in balance discriminate fallers from non-fallers in COPD. *Respir Med*, *103*(12), 1885–1891.

Beauchamp M.K., Sibley K.M., Lakhani B., Romano J., Mathur S., Goldstein R.S., & Brooks D. (2012). Impairments in systems underlying control of balance in COPD. *Chest*, 141(6), 1496–503.

Bernard S., LeBlanc P., Whittom F., Carrier G., Jobin J., Belleau R., & Maltais F. (1998). Peripheral muscle weakness in patients with chronic obstructive pulmonary disease. *Am J Respir Crit Care Med*, *158*, 629–634.

Boutou A.K., Stanopoulos I., Pitsiou G.G., Kontakiotis T., Kyriazis G., Sichletidis L., & Argyropoulou P. (2011). Anemia of chronic disease in chronic obstructive pulmonary disease: a case-control study of cardiopulmonary exercise responses. *Respiration*, *82*, 237–45.

Brenner D.R., McLaughlin J.R., & Hung R.J. (2011). Previous lung diseases and lung cancer risk: a systematic review and meta-analysis. *PLoS One*, *6*(3), 17479

Burt M.G., Roberts G.W., Aguilar-Loza N.R., Frith P., & Stranks S.N. (2011). Continuous monitoring of circadian glycemic patterns in patients receiving prednisolone for COPD. *J Clin Endocrinol Metab*, *96*(6), 1789–96.

Burt M.G., Roberts G.W., Aguilar-Loza N.R., Quinn S.J., Frith P.A., & Stranks S.N. (2013). Relationship between glycaemia and length of hospital stay during an acute exacerbation of chronic obstructive pulmonary disease. *Intern Med J*, *43*(6), 721–4.

Butcher S.J., Meshke J.M., & Sheppard M.S. (2004). Reductions in functional balance, coordination, and mobility measures among patients with stable chronic obstructive pulmonary disease. *J Cardiopulm Rehabil*, *24*(4), 274–280.

Cavaillès A., Brinchault-Rabin G., Dixmier A., Goupil F., Gut-Gobert C., Marchand-Adam S., Meurice J.C., Morel H., Person-Tacnet C., Leroyer C., & Diot P. (2013). Comorbidities of COPD. *Eur Respir Rev*, *22*(130), 454–75.

Celli B.R., Cote C.G., Marin J.M., Casanova C., Montes de Oca M., Mendez R.A., Pinto Plata V., & Cabral H.J. (2004). The body-mass index, airflow obstruction, dyspnea, and exercise capacity index in chronic obstructive pulmonary disease. *N Engl J Med*, *350*, 1005–12.

Chambellan A., Chailleux E., & Similowski T. (2005). ANTADIR Observatory Group. Prognostic value of hematocrit in patients with severe COPD receiving long-term oxygen therapy. *Chest*, *128*, 1201–8.

Choong C.K., Mahesh B., Patterson G.A., & Cooper J.D. (2009). Concomitant lung cancer resection and lung volume reduction surgery. *Thorac Surg Clin*, *19*(2), 209–16.

Clini E.M., Beghé B., & Fabbri L.M. (2013). Chronic obstructive pulmonary disease is just one component of the complex multimorbidities in patients with COPD. *Am J Respir Crit Care Med*, *187*(7), 668–71.

Colice G.L., Shafazand S., Griffin J.P., Keenan R., & Bolliger C.T. (2007). American College of Chest Physicians. Physiologic evaluation of the patient with lung cancer being considered for resectional surgery: ACCP evidenced-based clinical practice guidelines (2nd edition). *Chest*, *132*(3 Suppl), 161S-77S.

Cote C., Zilberberg M.D., Mody S.H., Dordelly L.J., & Celli B. (2007). Haemoglobin level and its clinical impact in a cohort of patients with COPD. *Eur Respir J*, *29*, 923–9.

Cottin V., Nunes H., Brillet P.-Y., Delaval P., Devouassoux G., Tillie-Leblond I., Israel-Biet D., Court-Fortune I., Valeyre D., Cordier J.F.; & Groupe d'Etude et de Recherche sur les Maladies Orphelines Pulmonaires (GERM O P) (2005). Combined pulmonary fibrosis and emphysema: a distinct underrecognised entity. *Eur Respir J*, *26*(4), 586–593.

de Torres J.P., Bastarrika G., Wisnivesky J.P., Alcaide A.B., Campo A., Seijo L.M., Pueyo J.C., Villanueva A., Lozano M.D., Montes U., Montuenga L., & Zulueta J.J. (2007). Assessing the relationship between lung cancer risk and emphysema detected on low-dose CT of the chest. *Chest*, *132*, 1932–38.

Davis M.P. (2012). The emerging role of palliative medicine in the treatment of lung cancer patients. *Cleve Clin J Med*, *79* Electronic Suppl 1, eS51–5.

de Torres J.P., Marin J.M., Casanova C., et al. (2010). Lung cancer in patients with chronic obstructive pulmonary disease—incidence and predicting factors. *Am J Respir Crit Care Med* 2011; *184*: 913–919.

Decramer M., Rennard S., Troosters T., Mapel D.W., Giardino N., Mannino D., Wouters E., Sethi S., & Cooper C.B. (2008). COPD as a lung disease with systemic consequences--clinical impact, mechanisms, and potential for early intervention. *COPD*, *5*(4), 235–56.

Devesa S.S., Bray F., Vizcaino A.P., & Parkin D.M., (2005). International lung cancer trends by histologic type: male:female differences diminishing and adenocarcinoma rates rising. *Int. J. Cancer*, *117*(2), 294–299.

Díez-Manglano J., López-García F., Barquero-Romero J., Galofré-Alvaro N., Montero-Rivas L., Almagro-Mena P., Soriano J.B.; & en nombre de los investigadores del estudio ECCO y del Grupo de Enfermedad Pulmonar Obstructiva Crónica de la Sociedad Española de Medicina Interna. (2011). Risk of osteoporotic fracture and hip fracture in patients with chronic obstructive pulmonary disease. *Rev Clin Esp*, *211*(9), 443–9.

Donaldson G.C., Hurst J.R., Smith C.J., Hubbard R.B., & Wedzicha J.A. (2010). Increased risk of myocardial infarction and stroke following exacerbation of COPD. *Chest*, *137*(5), 1091–7.

Eisner M.D. , Blanc P.D., Yelin E.H., Sidney S., Katz P.P., Ackerson .L, Lathon P., Tolstykh I., Omachi T., Byl N., & Iribarren C. (2008). COPD as a systemic disease: impact on physical functional limitations. *Am J Med*, *121*(9), 789–796.

Ekström M.P., Wagner P., & Ström K.E. (2011). Trends in cause-specific mortality in oxygen-dependent chronic obstructive pulmonary disease. *Am J Respir Crit Care Med*, *183*(8), 1032–1036.

El-Zein R.A., Young R.P., Hopkins R.J., & Etzel C.J. (2012). Genetic predisposition to chronic obstructive pulmonary disease and/or lung cancer: important considerations when evaluating risk. *Cancer Prev Res (Phila)*, *5*(4), 522–527.

Emerging Risk Factors Collaboration, Seshasai S.R., Kaptoge S., Thompson A., Di Angelantonio E., Gao P., Sarwar N., Whincup P.H., Mukamal K.J., Gillum R.F., Holme I., Njølstad I., Fletcher A., Nilsson P., Lewington S., Collins R., Gudnason V., Thompson S.G., Sattar N., Selvin E., Hu F.B., & Danesh J. (2011). Diabetes mellitus, fasting glucose, and risk of cause-specific death. *N Engl J Med*, *364*(9), 829–841.

Fabbri L.M., Luppi F., Beghé B., & Rabe K.F. (2008). Complex chronic comorbidities of COPD. *Eur Respir J*, *31*(1), 204–12.

Fadini, G.P., Schiavon, M., Cantini, M., Baesso, I., Facco, M., Miorin, M. Tassinato M., de Kreutzenberg S.V., Avogaro A., & Agostini C. (2006). Circulating progenitor cells are reduced in patients with severe lung disease. *Stem Cells*, *24*, 1806–1810.

Feary J.R., Rodrigues L.C., Smith C.J., Hubbard R.B., & Gibson J.E. (2010). Prevalence of major comorbidities in subjects with COPD and incidence of myocardial infarction and stroke: a comprehensive analysis using data from primary care. *Thorax*, *65*(11), 956–62.

Ferguson G.T., Calverley P.M., Anderson J.A., Jenkins C.R., Jones P.W., Willits L.R., Yates J.C., Vestbo J., & Celli B. (2009). Prevalence and progression of osteoporosis in patients with COPD: results from the TOwards a Revolution in COPD Health study. *Chest*, *136*(6), 1456–65.

Finkelstein J., Cha E., & Scharf S.M. (2009). Chronic obstructive pulmonary disease as an independent risk factor for cardiovascular morbidity. *Int J Chron Obstruct Pulmon Dis*, *4*, 337–49.

Franssen F.M., Broekhuizen R., Janssen P.P., Wouters E.F., & Schols A.M. (2005). Limb muscle dysfunction in COPD: effects of muscle wasting and exercise training. *Med Sci Sports Exerc*, *37*, 2–9.

Gansner J.M., & Rosas I.O. (2013). Telomeres in lung disease. *Transl Res*, *162*(6), 343–52.

Gelberg J., & McIvor R.A. (2010). Overcoming gaps in the management of chronic obstructive pulmonary disease in older patients: new insights. *Drugs Aging*, *27*(5), 367–375.

Gosselink R., Troosters T., & Decramer M. (1996). Peripheral muscle weakness contributes to exercise limitation in COPD. *Am J Respir Crit Care Med*, *153*, 976–980.

Graat-Verboom L., Smeenk F.W., van den Borne B.E., Spruit M.A,, Jansen F.H., van Enschot J.W., & Wouters E.F. (2012). Progression of osteoporosis in patients with COPD: a 3-year follow up study. *Respir Med*, *106*(6), 861–70.

Graat-Verboom L., van den Borne B E., Smeenk F.W., Spruit M.A., & Wouters E.F. (2011). Osteoporosis in COPD outpatients based on bone mineral density and vertebral fractures. *J Bone Miner Res*, *26*(3), 561–8.

Graat-Verboom L., Wouters E.,F, Smeenk F.W., van den Borne B.E., Lunde R., & Spruit M.A. (2009). Current status of research on osteoporosis in COPD: a systematic review. *Eur Respir J*, *34*(1), 209–18.

Halpern M.T., Zilberberg M.D., Schmier J.K., Lau E.C., & Shorr A.F. (2006). Anemia, costs and mortality in chronic obstructive pulmonary disease. *Cost Eff Resour Alloc*, *16*, 17.

Harvey K.L., Hussain A., & Maddock H.L. (2014). Ipratropium bromide-mediated myocardial injury in in vitro models of myocardial ischaemia/reperfusion. *Toxicol Sci*, *138*(2), 457–67.

Hawkins N.M., Petrie M.C., Jhund P.S., Chalmers G.W., Dunn F.G., & McMurray J.J. (2009). Heart failure and chronic obstructive pulmonary disease: diagnostic pitfalls and epidemiology. *Eur J Heart Fail*, *11*(2), 130–9.

Hawkins N.M., Petrie M.C., Macdonald M.R., Jhund P.S., Fabbri L.M., Wikstrand J., & McMurray J.J. (2011). Heart failure and chronic obstructive pulmonary disease the quandary of Beta-blockers and Beta-agonists. *J Am Coll Cardiol*, *57*(21), 2127–38.

Hawkins N.M., Virani S., & Ceconi C. (2013). Heart failure and chronic obstructive pulmonary disease: the challenges facing physicians and health services. *Eur Heart J*, *34*(36), 2795–27803.

Hellström K., Vahlberg B., Urell C. & Emtner M. (2009). Fear of falling, fall-related self-efficacy, anxiety and depression in individuals with chronic obstructive pulmonary disease. *Clin Rehabil*, *23*(12), 1136–44.

Houghton A.M. (2013). Mechanistic links between COPD and lung cancer. *Nat Rev Cancer*, *13*(4), 233–45.

Huertas A., & Palange P. (2011). COPD: a multifactorial systemic disease. *Ther Adv Respir Dis*, *5*(3), 217–24.

Huertas, A., & Palange. P. (2011) Circulating progenitor cells and chronic pulmonary diseases. *Eur Respir J*, *37*, 426–431.

Huertas, A., Testa, U., Riccioni, R., Petrucci, E., Riti,V., Savi, D. Serra P., Bonsignore M.R., & Palange P. (2010) Bone marrow-derived progenitors are greatly reduced in patients with severe COPD and low-BMI. *Respir Physiol Neurobiol*, *170*(1), 23–31.

Jankowich M.D., & Rounds S.I. (2012). Combined pulmonary fibrosis and emphysema syndrome: a review. *Chest*, *141*(1), 222–231.

Janssens L., Brumagne S., McConnell A.K., Claeys K., Pijnenburg M., Burtin C., Janssens W., Decramer M., & Troosters T. (2013). Proprioceptive changes impair balance control in individuals with chronic obstructive pulmonary disease. *PLoS One*, *8*(3), 57949.

Jorgensen N.R., Schwarz P., Holme I., Henriksen B.M., Petersen L.J., & Backer V. (2007). The prevalence of osteoporosis in patients with chronic obstructive pulmonary disease: a cross sectional study. *Respir Med*, *101*, 177–185.

Kim H.C., Mofarrahi M., & Hussain S.N. (2008). Skeletal muscle dysfunction in patients with chronic obstructive pulmonary disease. *Int J Chron Obstruct Pulmon Dis*, *3*(4), 637–58.

Kiri V.A., Soriano J., Visick G., & Fabbri L. (2010). Recent trends in lung cancer and its association with COPD: an analysis using the UK GP Research Database. *Prim Care Respir J*, *19*, 57–61.

Kollert F., Tippelt A., Müller C., Jörres R.A., Porzelius C., Pfeifer M., & Budweiser S. (2013). Hemoglobin levels above anemia thresholds are maximally predictive for long-term survival in COPD with chronic respiratory failure. *Respir Care*, *58*(7), 1204–12.

Krishnan G., Grant B.J., Muti P.C., Mishra A., Ochs-Balcom H.M., Freudenheim J.L., Trevisan M., & Schünemann H.J. (2006). Association between anemia and quality of life in a population sample of individuals with chronic obstructive pulmonary disease. *BMC Pulm Med*, *6*:23.

Küpeli E., Ulubay G., Ulasli S.S., Sahin T., Erayman Z., & Gürsoy A. (2010). Metabolic syndrome is associated with increased risk of acute exacerbation of COPD: a preliminary study. *Endocrine*, *38*(1), 76–82.

Laghi F., Adiguzel N., & Tobin M.J. (2009). Endocrinological derangements in COPD. *Eur Respir J*, *34*(4), 975–96.

Lee G., Walser T.C., & Dubinett S.M. (2009). Chronic inflammation, chronic obstructive pulmonary disease, and lung cancer. *Curr Opin Pulm Med*, *15*(4), 303–7.

Leech J.A., Dulberg C., Kellie S., Pattee L., & Gay J. (1990). Relationship of lung function to severity of osteoporosis in women. *Am Rev Respir Dis*, *141*(1), 68–71.

Lehouck A., Boonen S., Decramer M., & Janssens W. (2011). COPD, bone metabolism, and osteoporosis. *Chest*, *139*(3), 648–57.

LeJemtel T.H., Padeletti M., & Jelic S. (2006). Diagnostic and therapeutic challenges in patients with coexistent chronic obstructive pulmonary disease and chronic heart failure. *J Am Coll Cardiol*, *49*(2), 171–180.

Liang B., & Feng Y. (2012). The association of low bone mineral density with systemic inflammation in clinically stable COPD. *Endocrine*, *42*(1), 190–195.

Majumdar S.R., Villa-Roel C., Lyons K.J.,& Rowe B.H. (2010). Prevalence and predictors of vertebral fracture in patients with chronic obstructive pulmonary disease. *Respir Med*, *104*(2), 260–6.

Mancini G.B., Etminan M., Zhang B., Levesque L.E., FitzGerald J.M., & Brophy J.M. (2006). Reduction of morbidity and mortality by statins, angiotensin-converting enzyme inhibitors, and angiotensin receptor blockers in patients with chronic obstructive pulmonary disease. *J Am Coll Cardiol*, *47*(12), 2554–60.

Mannino D.M., Doherty D.E. & Sonia Buist A. (2006). Global Initiative on Obstructive Lung Disease (GOLD) classification of lung disease and mortality: findings from the Atherosclerosis Risk in Communities (ARIC) study. *Respir Med*, *100*(1), 115–22.

Mannino D.M., Aguayo S.M., Petty T.L. & Redd S.C. (2003). Low lung function and incident lung cancer in the United States: data from the first National Health and Nutrition Examination Survey follow-up. *Arch Intern Med*, *163*, 1475–80.

Mannino D.M., Thorn D., Swensen A. & Holquin F. (2008). Prevalence and outcomes of diabetes, hypertension and cardiovascular disease in COPD. *Eur Respir J*, *32*, 962–69.

Martinez-Rivera C., Portillo K., Munoz-Ferrer A., Martínez-Ortiz M.L., Molins E., Serra P., Ruiz-Manzano J., & Morera J. (2012). Anemia is a mortality predictor in hospitalized patients for COPD exacerbation. *COPD*, *9*, 243–50.

Mazokopakis E.E., & Starakis I.K. (2011). Recommendations for Diagnosis and Management of Osteoporosis in COPD Men. *ISRN Rheumatol*, 2011, 901416.

McAllister D.A., Maclay J.D., Mills N.L., Leitch A., Reid P., Carruthers R., O'Connor J., McAlpine L., Chalmers G., Newby D.E., Clark E., Macfarlane P.W., & Macnee W. (2012). Diagnosis of myocardial infarction following hospitalisation for exacerbation of COPD. *Eur Respir J*, *39*(5), 1097–103.

McEvoy C.E., Ensrud K.E., Bender E., Genant H.K., Yu W., Griffith J.M. & Niewoehner D.E. (1998). Association between corticosteroid use and vertebral fractures in older men with chronic obstructive pulmonary disease. *Am J Respir Crit Care Med*, *157*(3Pt1), 704–709.

Mentz R.J., Fiuzat M., Kraft M, Lindenfeld J. & O'Connor C.M. (2012). Bronchodilators in heart failure patients with COPD: is it time for a clinical trial? *J Card Fail*, *18*(5), 413–22.

Mortensen E.M., Copeland L.A., Pugh M.J., Restrepo M.I., de Molina R.M., Nakashima B., & Anzueto A. (2009). Impact of statins and ACE inhibitors on mortality after COPD exacerbations. *Respir Res*, *10*, 45.

Nici L. (2009). The role of pulmonary rehabilitation in the lung cancer patient. *Semin Respir Crit Care Med*, *30*(6), 670–4.

Nowinski A., Kaminski D., Korzybski D., Stokłosa A. & Gorecka D. (2011). The impact of comorbidities on the length of hospital treatment in patients with chronic obstructive pulmonary disease. *Pneumonol Alergol Pol*, *79*, 383–96.

Nussbaumer-Ochsner Y. & Rabe K.F. (2011). Systemic manifestations of COPD. *Chest*, *139*(1), 165–73.

Nuti R., Siviero P., Maggi S., Guglielmi G., Caffarelli C., Crepaldi G., & Gonnelli S. (2009). Vertebral fractures in patients with chronic obstructive pulmonary disease: the EOLO Study. *Osteoporos Int*, *20*(6), 989–998.

Ogura-Tomomatsu H., Asano K., Tomomatsu K., Miyata J., Ohmori N., Kodama M., Ueda S., Takihara T., Tanaka K., Kamiishi N., Suzuki Y., Fukunaga K., Oguma T., Sayama K., & Betsuyaku T. (2012). Predictors of osteoporosis and vertebral fractures in patients presenting with moderate-to-severe chronic obstructive lung disease. *COPD*, *9*(4), 332–337.

Ozalevli S., Ilgin D., Narin S., & Akkoclu A. (2011). Association between disease-related factors and balance and falls among the elderly with COPD: a cross-sectional study. *Aging Clin Exp Res*, *23*(5–6), 372–7.

Palange P., Testa U., Huertas A., Calabro` L., Antonucci R., Petrucci E., Pelosi E., Pasquini L., Satta A., Morici G., Vignola M.A., & Bonsignore M.R. (2006). Circulating haemopoietic and endothelial progenitor cells are decreased in COPD. *Eur Respir J*, *27*, 529–541.

Papaioannou A., Parkinson W., Ferko N., Probyn L., Ioannidis G., Jurriaans E., Cox G., Cook R.J., Kumbhare D., & Adachi J.D. (2003). Prevalence of vertebral fractures among patients with chronic obstructive pulmonary disease in Canada. *Osteoporos Int*, *14*(11), 913–7.

Parappil A., Depczynski B., Collett P., & Marks G.B. (2010). Effect of comorbid diabetes on length of stay and risk of death in patients admitted with acute exacerbations of COPD. *Respirology*, *15*(6), 918–922.

Pasqua F., Geraneo K., Nardi I., Lococo F., & Cesario A. (2013). Pulmonary rehabilitation in lung cancer. *Monaldi Arch Chest Dis*, *79*(2), 73–80.

Portillo K., Martinez-Rivera C., & Ruiz-Manzano J. (2013). Anaemia in chronic obstructive pulmonary disease. Does it really matter? *Int J Clin Pract*, *67*(6), 558–65.

Quint J.K., Herrett E., Bhaskaran K., Timmis A., Hemingway H., Wedzicha J.A., & Smeeth L. (2013). Effect of β blockers on mortality after myocardial infarction in adults with COPD: population based cohort study of UK electronic healthcare records. *BMJ*, *347*, f6650.

Rana J.S. Mittleman M.A., Sheikh J., Hu F.B., Manson J.E., Colditz G.A., Speizer F.E., Barr R.G., & Camargo C.A. Jr. (2004). Chronic obstructive pulmonary disease, asthma, and risk of type 2 diabetes in women. *Diabetes Care*, *27*(10), 2478–84.

Regan E.A., Radcliff T.A., Henderson W.G., Cowper Ripley D.C., Maciejewski M.L., Vogel W.B. & Hutt E. (2013). Improving hip fractures outcomes for COPD patients. *COPD*, *10*(1), 11–9.

Rittayamai N., Chuaychoo B. & Sriwijitkamol A. (2012). Prevalence of osteoporosis and osteopenia in Thai COPD patients. *J Med Assoc Thai*, *95*(8), 1021–7.

Roig M., Eng J.J., MacIntyre D.L., Road J.D., FitzGerald J.M., Burns J. & Reid W.D. (2011A). Falls in people with chronic obstructive pulmonary disease: an observational cohort study. *Respir Med*, *105*(3), 461–9.

Roig M., Eng J.J., Macintyre D.L., Road J.D. & Reid W.D. (2011B). Postural Control Is Impaired in People with COPD: An Observational Study. *Physiother Can*, *63*(4), 423–31.

Romme E.A., Rutten E.P., Geusens P., de Jong J.J., van Rietbergen B, Smeenk F.W., Wouters E.F. & van den Bergh J.P. (2013) Bone stiffness and failure load are related with clinical parameters in men with chronic obstructive pulmonary disease. *J Bone Miner Res 38*(10), 2186–2193.

Salpeter S., Ormiston T. & Salpeter E. (2005). Cardioselective beta-blockers for chronic obstructive pulmonary disease. *Cochrane Database Syst Rev*, (4), CD003566.

Salpeter S., Ormiston T. & Salpeter E. (2002). Cardioselective beta-blockers for reversible airway disease. *Cochrane Database Syst Rev*, (4), CD002992.

Salpeter S.R., Ormiston T.M., Salpeter E.E., Poole P.J. & Cates C.J. (2003). Cardioselective beta-blockers for chronic obstructive pulmonary disease: a meta-analysis. *Respir Med, 97*(10), 1094–1101

Salpeter S.R., Ormiston T.M. & Salpeter E.E. (2004). Cardiovascular effects of beta-agonists in patients with asthma and COPD: a meta-analysis. *Chest, 125*(6), 2309–21.

Schnell K., Weiss C.O., Lee T., Krishnan J.A., Leff B., Wolff J.L. & Boyd C. (2012). The prevalence of clinically-relevant comorbid conditions in patients with physician-diagnosed COPD: a cross-sectional study using data from NHANES 1999–2008. *BMC Pulm Med, 9*, 12:26.

Schönhofer B., Böhrer H. & Köhler D. (1998A). Blood transfusion facilitating difficult weaning from the ventilator. *Anaesthesia*, 53(2), 181–4.

Schönhofer B., Wenzel M., Geibel M. & Köhler D. (1998B). Blood transfusion and lung function in chronically anemic patients with severe chronic obstructive pulmonary disease. *Crit Care Med, 26*(11), 1824–8.

Sekine Y., Katsura H., Koh E., Hiroshima K. & Fujisawa T. (2012). Early detection of COPD is important for lung cancer surveillance. *Eur Respir J, 39*(5), 1230–1240.

Shannon V.R. (2010). Role of pulmonary rehabilitation in the management of patients with lung cancer. *Curr Opin Pulm Med, 16*(4), 334–339.

Shorr A.F., Doyle J., Stern L., Dolgitser M. & Zilberberg M.D. (2008). Anemia in chronic obstructive pulmonary disease: epidemiology and economic implications. *Curr Med Res Opin, 24*, 1123–30.

Sin D.D., Anthonisen N.R., Soriano J.B. & Agusti A.G. (2006). Mortality in COPD: Role of comorbidities. *Eur Respir J, 28*(6), 1245–57.

Sin D.D, Wu L., & Man S.F, (2005A). The Relationship Between Reduced Lung Function and Cardiovascular Mortality. *Chest, 127*, 1952–1959.

Sin D.D., & Man S.F. (2005B). Chronic obstructive pulmonary disease as a risk factor for cardiovascular morbidity and mortality. *Proc Am Thorac Soc, 2*, 8–11.

Singer A.J., Emerman C., Char D.M., Heywood J.T., Kirk J.D., Hollander J.E., Summers R., Lee C.C., Wynne J., Kellerman L. & Peacock W.F. (2008). Bronchodilator therapy in acute decompensated heart failure patients without a history of chronic obstructive pulmonary disease. *Ann Emerg Med, 51*(1), 25–34.

Sittka A. & Schmeck B. (2013). MicroRNAs in the lung. *Adv Exp Med Biol, 774*, 121–134.

Smith B.M., Pinto L., Ezer N., Sverzellati N., Muro S. & Schwartzman K. (2012). Emphysema detected on computed tomography and risk of lung cancer: a systematic review and meta-analysis. *Lung Cancer, 77*(1), 58–63.

Smith M.D., Chang A.T., Seale H.E., Walsh J.R. & Hodges P.W. (2010). Balance is impaired in people with chronic obstructive pulmonary disease. *Gait Posture, 31*(4), 456–460.

Souverein P.C., Berard A., Van Staa T.P., Cooper C., Egberts A.C., Leufkens H.G. & Walker B.R. (2004). Use of oral glucocorticoids and risk of cardiovascular and cerebrovascular disease in a population based case-control study. *Heart, 90*(8), 859–865.

Ställberg B., Janson C., Johansson G., Larsson K., Stratelis G., Telg G. & Lisspers K.H. (2014). Management, morbidity and mortality of COPD during an 11-year period: an observational retrospective epidemiological register study in Sweden (PATHOS). *Prim Care Respir J, 23*(1), 38–45.

Stefan M.S., Rothberg M.B., Priya A., Pekow P.S., Au D.H. & Lindenauer P.K. (2012). Association between β-blocker therapy and outcomes in patients hospitalised with acute exacerbations of chronic obstructive lung disease with underlying ischaemic heart disease, heart failure or hypertension. *Thorax, 67*(11), 977–984.

The National Lung Screening Trial Research Team (2011). Reduced Lung-Cancer Mortality with Low-Dose Computed Tomographic Screening. *N Engl J Med, 365*, 395–409

Turner M.C., Chen Y., Krewski D., et al. (2007). Chronic obstructive pulmonary disease is associated with lung cancer mortality in a prospective study of never smokers. *Am J Respir Crit Care Med, 176*, 285–90.

Visca D., Aiello M. & Chetta A. (2013). Cardiovascular function in pulmonary emphysema. *Biomed Res Int*, 2013, 184678.

von Dincklage J.J., Ball D. & Silvestri G.A. (2013). A review of clinical practice guidelines for lung cancer. *J Thorac Dis*, *5* Suppl, S607–22.

von Groote-Bidlingmaier F., Koegelenberg C.F. & Bolliger CT. (2011). Functional evaluation before lung resection. *Clin Chest Med*, *32*(4), 773–82.

Wender R., Fontham E.T., Barrera E. Jr, Colditz G.A., Church T.R., Ettinger D.S., Etzioni R., Flowers C.R., Gazelle G.S., Kelsey D.K., LaMonte S.J., Michaelson J.S., Oeffinger K.C., Shih Y.C., Sullivan D.C., Travis W., Walter L., Wolf A.M., Brawley O.W. & Smith R.A., (2013). American Cancer Society lung cancer screening guidelines. *CA Cancer J Clin*, *63*(2), 107–117.

Williams M.C., Murchison J.T., Edwards L.D., Agustí A., Bakke P., Calverley P.M., Celli B., Coxson H.O., Crim C., Lomas D.A., Miller B.E., Rennard S., Silverman E.K., Tal-Singer R., Vestbo J., Wouters E., Yates J.C., van Beek E.J., Newby D.E., MacNee W.; Evaluation of COPD Longitudinally to Identify Predictive Surrogate Endpoints (ECLIPSE) investigators. (2014). Coronary artery calcification is increased in patients with COPD and associated with increased morbidity and mortality. *Thorax*, *69*(8), 718–23.

Wilson D.O., Weissfeld J.L., Balkan A., Schragin J.G., Fuhrman C.R., Fisher S.N., Wilson J., Leader J.K., Siegfried J.M., Shapiro S.D. & Sciurba F.C. (2008). Association of radiographic emphysema and airflow obstruction with lung cancer. *Am J Respir Crit Care Med, 178*, 738–44.

Yang I.A., Relan V., Wright C.M., Davidson M.R., Sriram K.B., Savarimuthu Francis S.M., Clarke B.E., Duhig E.E., Bowman R.V. & Fong K.M. (2011). Common pathogenic mechanisms and pathways in the development of COPD and lung cancer. *Expert Opin Ther Targets*, *15*(4), 439–56.

Yohannes A.M. & Ershler W.B. (2011). Anemia in COPD: a systematic review of the prevalence, quality of life, and mortality. *Respir Care*, *56*(5), 644–52.

Young R.P., Hopkins R.J., Christmas T., Black P.N., Metcalf P. & Gamble G.D. (2009). COPD prevalence is increased in lung cancer, independent of age, sex and smoking history. *Eur Respir J*, *34*, 380–86.

Young R.P. & Hopkins R.J. (2011). How the genetics of lung cancer may overlap with COPD *Respirology*, *16*(7), 1047–55.

Yu W., Ravelo A., Wagner T.H., Phibbs C.S., Bhandari A., Chen S. & Barnett P.G. (2003). Prevalence and costs of chronic conditions in the VA health care system. *Med Care Res Rev, 60*, 146S-67S.

Zvezdin B., Milutinov S., Kojicic M., Hadnadjev M., Hromis S., Markovic M. & Gajic O. (2009). A postmortem analysis of major causes of early death in patients hospitalized with COPD exacerbation. *Chest*, *136*(2), 376–380.

Ralph J. Panos, MD

# 11 Sleep and COPD: The Overlap Syndrome

Key Points

1. Sleep disturbances occur in 34–78% of patients with COPD due to nocturnal respiratory symptoms, intrinsic sleep disordered breathing, or a combination of both processes.
2. The overlap syndrome is the concurrence of COPD and obstructive sleep apnea (OSA).
3. Although the prevalence of OSA among those with COPD was initially thought to be increased, more recent studies suggest that the prevalence of the overlap syndrome is about 1% of the general population which is the predicted prevalence if COPD and OSA are independent processes.
4. The recognition and identification of sleep disordered breathing among patients with COPD requires a strong index of suspicion and a sleep-directed history and physical examination.
5. Overlap syndrome is characterized by more profound nocturnal hypoxemia and deranged sleep architecture than either COPD or OSA alone.
6. The physiologic derangements of COPD accentuate normal sleep-related respiratory changes to cause hypoventilation and ventilation-perfusion mismatching during sleep increasing $PaCO_2$ and decreasing $PaO_2$.
7. Management of the overlap syndrome includes optimal treatment of COPD and use of noninvasive positive pressure ventilation for the OSA.

## 11.1 Introduction

Sleep quality is worse in individuals with COPD compared with those without COPD (Fleetham, 1982; Calverley, 1982; Brezinova, 1982). Between 34 and 78% of individuals with COPD report difficulty initiating or maintaining sleep, nocturnal awakenings, or nonrestorative sleep (Agusti, 2011; Tashkin, 2008; Price, 2013, Weizenblum 2004; Marrone, 2006; Klink, 1994; Rennard, 2002). Sleep efficiency is only 50–70% in patients with COPD and the proportion of sleep time is increased in light sleep and decreased in REM sleep, shifts between sleep stages occur more frequently, and micro-arousals disrupt sleep (McNicholas, 2013). At least half of all patients with COPD experience nocturnal respiratory symptoms (Miravitlles, 2014). Some studies suggest that this proportion increases as lung function worsens whereas other investigations show no relationship between nocturnal respiratory symptoms and COPD severity (Kessler, 2011; Lange, 2014; Miravitlles, 2014).

Nocturnal symptoms are associated with worse sleep quality, greater daytime breathlessness, more frequent COPD exacerbations, and greater number of respiratory medications (Price, 2011; Miravitlles, 2014). In addition, patients with nocturnal respiratory symptoms have greater dyspnea, anxiety, and depression and worse health status (Miravitlles, 2014). Nocturnal breathlessness is associated with daytime respiratory symptoms including dyspnea, phlegm production, and wheezing (Lange, 2014; Miravitlles, 2014; Kessler 2011).

Approximately one third of patients with OSA have chronic cough (Chan, 2010). Those with cough have similar sleep and respiratory symptoms but are more likely to be female and have more rhinitis and nocturnal gastrointestinal reflux symptoms than those without cough. In a group of 75 patients with chronic cough, 44% had OSA and 93% of them had improvement in their cough with optimized CPAP treatment (Sundar, 2010). Thus, OSA may contribute to chronic cough in patients with COPD and the cough may be improved with CPAP.

Physicians greatly underestimate the prevalence of nocturnal symptoms and their effects in patients with COPD (Price, 2011). Conversely, only 11.8% of patients with COPD discuss sleep concerns with their provider (Ohayon, 2014). The Nighttime Symptoms of COPD Instrument is a recently developed and validated patient-reported outcome instrument to document nocturnal symptoms in patients with COPD which may help in the recognition of night-time manifestations of COPD (Hareendran, 2013).

In addition to OSA, other sleep disorders that occur in individuals with COPD can include insomnia, periodic limb movement syndrome, and psychiatric sleep disorders (Ohayon, 2014; Valipour, 2012). Approximately half of all patients with COPD have insomnia symptoms, which is twice the prevalence as in those who do not have COPD (Ohayon, 2014). Concurrent depression or anxiety increases the prevalence of insomnia to 84.4% and 59.7%, respectively (Ohayon, 2014). Insomnia symptoms appear to correlate positively with COPD severity measured by the BODE index, current smoking, and greater sadness/anxiety and negatively with supplemental oxygen use (Hynninen, 2013; Budhiraha, 2012). Periodic limb movement and psychiatric sleep disorder scale scores derived from the Sleep Disorders Questionnaire are greater in patients with mild to moderate COPD compared with those who do not have obstructive lung disease (Valipour, 2012).

## 11.2 Smoking, Sleep, and COPD

Inhalation of tobacco smoke is the major cause of COPD (See Chapter 9, Natural History, Phenotypes, and Gender Differences in COPD and Chapter 6, Pathogenesis of COPD). Many patients with COPD continue to smoke and tobacco smoke inhalation is associated with sleep disturbances including reduced sleep efficiency, increased sleep latency, nonrestorative sleep, and alterations in sleep stages with less REM sleep and more time in lighter sleep (Lan, 2012; Wetter, 1994A; Wetter, 1994B; Zhang, 2006; Zhang, 2008; Jaehne, 2009). Some smokers may experience nocturnal partial nicotine withdrawal which can disrupt sleep by inducing frequent and prolonged awakenings

(Philips, 1995). Former smokers who have completely quit smoking have a similar sleep architecture to never smokers, so the effects of smoking on sleep appear to reverse once smoking cessation is achieved (Zhang, 2006; Soldatos, 1980).

Smoking has also been associated with the development of OSA and some researchers have proposed that OSA may contribute to nicotine addiction (Lin, 2012). In a study of 811 individuals undergoing polysomnography, current smokers were more likely to snore, odds ratio (OR) 2.26 (95% confidence interval (CI), 1.46, 3.49), and to have sleep disordered breathing, OR 1.64 (95% CI, 0.94–2.86), and this risk was greatest among those who smoked more than 2 packs per day, OR 8.39 (95% CI, 1.68–41.94) (Wetter, 1994A). Smoking prevalence is higher in individuals with OSA than in those who do not have sleep disordered breathing, 35% and 18%, respectively (Kashyap, 2001). The period of smoking cessation is associated with sleep alterations including more arousals and worse sleep quality that correlate with poorer smoking cessation rates (Jaehne, 2009). Further, weight gain often accompanies smoking cessation and can either worsen existing OSA or increase the risk of its development (Williamson, 1991; Peppard, 2000).

Nicotine may have beneficial effects in individuals with OSA. It increases the tone of posterior pharyngeal dilator muscles helping to maintain upper airway patency and, thereby, reduces resistance to airflow (Haxhiu, 1984). Nicotine also stimulates the phrenic nerve increasing diaphragmatic activity (Haxhiu, 1984). Because of these potential beneficial effects, nicotine has been evaluated for the treatment of OSA. A small study showed that enteral nicotine reduced the number of apneas during the initial hours of sleep (Gothe, 1985) but a subsequent study showed that transdermal nicotine had no effect on the number of apneas and hypoponeas or snoring intensity in patients with habitual snoring (Davila, 1994). Nicotine delivered locally to the posterior pharynx via a tooth patch increases salivary nicotine levels but has no effect on the number of apneas or hypoponeas in patients with OSA (Zevin, 2003).

## 11.3 Prevalence of Overlap Syndrome

In 1985, David Flenley coined the term overlap syndrome to refer to the co-existence of OSA and any chronic respiratory disorder and, over the past three decades, overlap syndrome has been most commonly used to denote the concurrence of COPD and OSA (Flenley, 1985; Weitzenblum, 2008). Earlier studies suggested that the prevalence of OSA was increased among individuals with COPD. However, these studies sampled populations from sleep or respiratory clinics and their conclusions may be affected by selection bias. The prevalence of the overlap syndrome among men is estimated to be approximately 1% (Chaouat, 1995; Ioachimescu, 2013; Sanders, 2003; Bednarek, 2005; McNicholas, 2009; Owens 2010). If one estimates a prevalence of 10% for both COPD and OSA, the expected prevalence of the overlap syndrome is 1%. However, since both COPD and OSA are under-recognized and under-diagnosed, the actual prevalence of the overlap syndrome is most likely greater than reported or estimated.

The largest epidemiologic study of the overlap syndrome analyzed the 5,954 participants in the Sleep Health Heart Study who underwent unattended home polysomnography testing and spirometry (Sanders, 2003). This study was designed to address the relationship between sleep disordered breathing and hypertension and cardiovascular disease in adults and oversampled individuals younger than 65 years old who snored. The proportion of participants with OSA with or without airflow limitation was similar, 22.32% versus 28.86%, or 13.97% versus 18.63%, using apnea-hypopnea index (AHI) thresholds of either >10 or >15 events/hour to define OSA, respectively (Sanders, 2003). The AHI was positively correlated with the $FEV_1$/FVC ratio, suggesting that among individuals with mild airflow limitation, more severe obstruction was associated with a lower AHI. Participants with both airflow limitation and OSA had greater sleep disturbances and greater nocturnal desaturations than those with either disorder alone. The OR for nocturnal desaturation (defined as $SpO_2$ <90% for more than 5% of total sleep time) was 3.36 (95% CI, 1.98, 5.70) in those with an $FEV_1$/FVC ratio less than 60% and as the $FEV_1$/FVC ratio declined the proportion of participants with nocturnal desaturation increased (Sanders, 2003). Participants with overlap syndrome had higher Epworth Sleepiness Scale scores (a measure of sleepiness), and greater proportions of total sleep time in stage 2 and less time in REM and stage 3/4 sleep than those with either disorder alone (Sanders, 2003). Thus, the Sleep Health Heart Study showed that the prevalence of OSA is not increased among individuals with mild COPD but those with the overlap syndrome do have more deranged sleep architecture and greater nocturnal oxygen desaturation than those with either disorder alone.

The results of the SHHS were corroborated by the Monica II study that showed that the prevalence of airflow limitation in participants with OSA was the same as in the general population, approximately 10–11% (Bednarek, 2005). Those with the overlap syndrome had a lower mean $SpO_2$ and spent more time with a $SpO_2$ <90%.

## 11.4 Predictors of Overlap Syndrome

Among individuals with COPD, the risk of sleep disordered breathing increases with body mass index (BMI), age, smoking status, presence of peripheral edema, and use of systemic steroids (Chaouat, 2005; McNicholas, 2013). A small study of 177 subjects with COPD, 33 of whom had OSA, suggested that BMI and smoking history measured in pack years were associated with the AHI (Steveling, 2014). A recent study of patients with overlap syndrome did not find that they were more obese or had more excessive daytime sleepiness than those who did not have OSA and suggested that a high index of suspicion is needed to recognize and diagnose overlap syndrome (Venkateswaran, 2014).

The GOLD Guidelines recommend screening patients with COPD for OSA if they are experiencing sleep related symptoms or excessive nocturnal awakenings (GOLD). Because of the high association of pulmonary hypertension with the overlap syndrome, screening sleep studies may be indicated in individuals with COPD and elevated pulmonary artery pressures (See Chapter 12, COPD and Pulmonary Vasculature) (Celli, 2004). A small retrospective study found an association between the severity of airflow and the presence of OSA and suggested that sleep studies should be considered in patients with severe COPD (Lopez-Acevedo, 2009). However, another study did not find an association between OSA and severity of airflow limitation among patients with COPD (Sharma, 2011). In patients with the overlap syndrome, lung hyperinflation measured by the inspiratory capacity divided by the total lung capacity (IC/TLC) correlates with worse sleep efficiency independent of the AHI or severity of hypoxemia; therefore, the presence of hyperinflation might be another screening pulmonary physiologic variable to consider in determining which patients to evaluate for overlap syndrome (Kwon, 2009).

## 11.5 Screening and Diagnosis

The recognition and diagnosis of COPD is discussed in Chapter 3, COPD Recognition and Diagnosis. A high level of vigilance and attentiveness are required for the recognition and diagnosis of OSA in patients with COPD.

A comprehensive sleep history is an important first step in the evaluation of patients with COPD and sleep related symptoms. The discrimination of sleep disordered breathing due to intrinsic sleep disorders from disrupted sleep due to nocturnal respiratory symptoms can be difficult. The sleep history and examination may increase the suspicion of obstructive sleep apnea or other sleep disturbance, but polysomnography is required to establish the diagnosis and initiate treatment.

In general, patients who are obese, have highly associated comorbidities such as congestive heart failure, atrial fibrillation, hypertension that is difficult to control, pulmonary hypertension, and who work in potentially high risk occupations (pilot, school bus driver) should be evaluated further (Epstein, 2009). Another key historical feature is previous motor vehicle accidents especially if they are related to sleepiness. Key elements of the sleep history include sleep initiation including insomnia, total sleep time, quality of sleep (restorative versus nonrestorative), presence or absence of recalled dreams, snoring, observed apneas or episodes of choking, gasping, or sputtering, excessive daytime sleepiness, nocturnal awakenings including nocturia, morning headache, excessive daytime sleepiness, reduced memory, and emotional lability (Epstein, 2009). A review of the accuracy of the clinical history in the diagnosis of OSA showed that a history of choking or gasping at night was the most predictive historical finding, summary likelihood ratio (LR), 3.3; (95% CI, 2.1–4.6) when an AHI ≥10/h was used to diagnose OSA (Myers, 2013). Although patients with OSA frequently reported snoring, it was not useful in discriminating OSA (summary LR, 1.1; 95% CI, 1.0–1.1) (Myers, 2013). Thus, in individuals with COPD, these discriminating characteristics may not be as reliable and the clinician should consider a careful sleep history while maintaining a high index of suspicion for sleep disturbances. Finally, it may be difficult to differentiate sleep dysfunction related to respiratory symptoms due to COPD such as cough and sleep symptoms related to OSA.

Several validated surveys are available to assist clinicians in the identification of individuals at risk for sleep disordered breathing. The Epworth sleepiness scale is a measure of sleep propensity and correlates with sleep latency, the apnea hypopnea index, and minimal nocturnal $SpO_2$ in individuals with OSA (Johns, 1991). The Berlin questionnaire is a screening survey for OSA in the general population that has a sensitivity and specificity of 86% and 77%, respectively, in primary care patients (Netzner, 1999). The Nighttime Symptoms of COPD Instrument assists in the identification of nocturnal respiratory symptoms (Hareendran, 2013). The use of these instruments in the overlap syndrome is less well studied.

Elements of the physical examination may also suggest the presence of OSA. Hypertension, especially when it is refractory to treatment, and elevated body mass index are abnormal vital signs that may be associated with OSA. An increased neck circumference, reduced posterior pharyngeal diameter, enlarged tonsils, and retrognathia may also increase the risk of OSA.

There are no elements of the history or physical examination that can conclusively diagnose OSA and further evaluation with a form of sleep diagnostic testing, formal full polysomnographic study in a sleep laboratory or home study, is usually indicated. Overnight pulse oximetry has limited utility in the diagnosis of OSA in patients with COPD and is not reliable for the diagnosis of the overlap syndrome due to the indiscriminant frequency, pattern, and severity of oxygen desaturation events in both disorders (Scott, 2014).

### 11.5.1 Normal Sleep Physiology

Physiologic regulation of respiration during wakefulness is an integrally connected tripartite system of sensors, central control, and effectors. Aortic and carotid body sensors monitor changes in oxygen and carbon dioxide, vagal afferent neurons sense lung parenchymal alterations, and other systems respond to external stimuli and volitional control (Newton, 2014). Within the medullary ventilator center, neurons generate an automated respiratory rhythm that is modulated by these sensory and volitional inputs. The signals from the respiratory center stimulate the diaphragm and other respiratory muscles to generate inspiratory and expiratory airflow and maintain upper airway muscle tone and patency modulating both respiratory frequency and tidal volume. This system is highly regulated to maintain usual $PaO_2$ and $PaCO_2$ levels within narrow ranges.

Respiratory physiology is markedly altered during sleep and the ventilatory changes vary during different stages of sleep. With sleep onset, external stimuli and volitional signals are no longer processed or produced and internal biochemical and biomechanical sensory inputs predominant. The usual change from primarily upright to horizontal posture alters thoracic musculoskeletal and diaphragmatic mechanics and may also affect posterior pharyngeal architecture by reducing the airway lumen. During sleep, respiratory center responses to biochemical stimuli, $PaO_2$ and $PaCO_2$, are blunted. Combined with a lower metabolic rate, the diminished chemosensitivity to oxygen and carbon dioxide levels causes a reduction in minute ventilation mainly through a decrease in tidal volume. Consequently, $PaCO_2$ rises and $PaO_2$ may decline slightly. During REM sleep, skeletal muscle atonia occurs and the diaphragm is the only functioning respiratory muscle which reduces tidal volume and minute ventilation and further accentuates hypoxemic and hypercarbic changes.

### 11.5.2 Sleep Physiology and OSA

OSA is diagnosed by the presence of either cessation (apnea) or reduction (hypopnea) of airflow caused by recurrent upper airway occlusion or blockage during sleep despite maintained central respiratory drive. These events are measured by the apnea-hypopnea index (AHI), the number of apneas and hypopneas per hour, and OSA is usually defined as an AHI greater than 5 events per hour. Central sleep apnea is caused by the absence of central respiratory drive stimuli. Initiation and maintenance of airflow during sleep requires central signaling, activation of respiratory muscles including not only the diaphragm and accessory muscles, but also those controlling the posterior pharyngeal lumen to maintain upper airway patency and counteract the inward negative pressure of inspiration. If the airway aperture is not maintained, airflow is reduced (hypopnea) or stopped (apnea). Depending upon the duration and severity of reduced airflow, $PaCO_2$ levels may rise and $PaO_2$ levels decrease. Apneic or hypopneic events are usually terminated by an arousal followed by augmented minute ventilation to normalize oxygen and carbon dioxide levels. Reduced biochemical sensitivity may derange normal feedback loops causing over or under compensation and wide variation in respiratory patterns. These arousals lead to sleep fragmentation and reduced REM sleep time. Factors that may contribute to the development of OSA include individual anthropomorphic features, upper airway architecture which is determined by anatomic, mechanical, and neuromuscular processes, medications including alcohol, and respiratory center function (Deegan, 1995).

### 11.5.3 Sleep Physiology and COPD

COPD-related respiratory derangements may adversely affect normal sleep physiology. Supine positioning during sleep may reduce the posterior pharyngeal aperture increasing airway resistance. Resistance to airflow is greatest in the posterior pharynx in the region circumscribed by the base of the tongue and the soft palate. The airway in this zone is flexible and potentially collapsible. The base of the tongue may move posteriorly and approach the posterior pharyngeal wall reducing the anterior-posterior aperture and the lateral walls may also encroach upon the lumen due to excessive soft tissue, mucosal edema and inflammation, negative intraluminal pressure during inspiration, and relaxed pharyngeal dilator muscle tone (Mieczkowski, 2014). This increase in upper airway resistance necessitates generation of a greater inspiratory force by the respiratory muscles which may be handicapped due to intrinsic muscle weakness related to COPD and mechanical disadvantages.

Intrinsic muscle dysfunction associated with COPD may affect the upper airway musculature as well as the diaphragm and accessory muscles of respiration diminishing their function. In individuals with hyperinflation and air trapping, the diaphragm may be mechanically disadvantaged due to elongation and distension of diaphragmatic muscle fibers. Hyperinflation is associated with worse sleep efficiency in patients with overlap syndrome (Kwon, 2009). Additionally, the pressure of abdominal contents in the supine positioning further disadvantages the diaphragm by increasing its load due to the additional caudad force required for movement during inspiration. Individuals with COPD and hyperinflation may be more reliant upon accessory muscles of respiration to maintain minute ventilation; the hypotonia of REM sleep may further reduce minute ventilation by eliminating the contribution of accessory muscles to ventilation. These physiologic changes may cause more profound hypoxemia, up to 40% declines in oxygen saturation during REM sleep and 20% reductions during non-REM sleep, in patients with severe COPD (Becker, 1999).

### 11.5.4 Sleep Physiology and Overlap Syndrome

COPD-related respiratory derangements may augment and accentuate many of the physiologic consequences of OSA. Patients with the overlap syndrome generally have more profound sleep-related hypoxemia and hypercarbia than individuals with either disorder alone (McNicholas, 2013). Factors that may contribute to hypoxemia severity in the overlap syndrome include lower baseline oxygen level, ventilation/perfusion mismatching, and blunted oxygen sensing. Worsened ventilation perfusion mismatching due to reductions in functional residual capacity, supine posture, intrinsic parenchymal lung disease, retained secretions occluding or blocking airways, may contribute to nocturnal desaturations in individuals with COPD (McNicholas, 2013).

Although isocapnic hypoxemia is not a usual stimulus for arousal during sleep and desaturations to 70% may not trigger awakenings, individuals with COPD may have resting low normal oxygenation levels that place them on the shoulder of the oxygen-hemoglobin desaturation curve. Thus, even slight declines in oxygenation may precipitate severe desaturation. An increase of approximately 15 mmHg in end tidal carbon dioxide level is the threshold for usual hypercapneic-induced arousals but patients with COPD and hypercarbia may have severely blunted responses to further increases in carbon dioxide levels (Ayas, 2000).

Both COPD and OSA are characterized by systemic inflammation. The pathophysiology and consequences of inflammation in COPD are discussed in Chapter 6, Pathogenesis of COPD and Chapter 10, COPD is a Multi-Organ Disorder: Systemic Manifestations. OSA is categorized by enhanced production of inflammatory cytokines, sympathetic nervous system activation, and abnormal vascular and coagulant function. Recurrent hypoxemic stress and sleep disruption are believed to be primary etiologic factors. The relationship between etiologic processes underlying systemic inflammation in the overlap syndrome and its component disorders, COPD and OSA, is an active area of research.

As discussed below in Comorbidities, the prevalence of comorbidities including COPD exacerbations and cardiovascular events related to inflammation and excessive mortality in the overlap syndrome appears to be greater than can be accounted for by either OSA or COPD alone suggesting a synergistic interaction.

## 11.6 Ventilation and Ventilation Perfusion Matching

During sleep, the cough reflex is diminished and the normal clearance of respiratory secretions (the production of which is increased in chronic bronchitis and bronchiectasis) is reduced (Power, 1984). These secretions may accumulate within the airways causing partial or total occlusion increasing airway resistance and altering ventilation patterns. These perturbations may disrupt ventilation-perfusion matching precipitating lower oxygenation and desaturation.

## 11.7 Polysomnography

Polysomnography (PSG) is the usual diagnostic study to evaluate sleep disordered breathing. PSG tests are multimodality studies that usually include electroencephalographic (EEG), electrooculographic (EOG), electrocardiographic (ECG), and electromyographic (EMG) measurements as well as monitoring pulse oximetry, thoracic and abdominal respiratory efforts, and audiovisual recording. Based upon EEG and EOG tracings, sleep is categorized into wakefulness, N1, N2, N3, and REM sleep (Silber, 2007). Most individuals progress through the nonREM stages to REM several times during the night with more time in deep, N3 sleep during the early cycles and an increasing proportion of time in REM during the later cycles prior to awakening. Normally deep N3 sleep and REM sleep each account for approximately one quarter of sleep time and the remaining half of sleep time is transitional N1 and N2 sleep.

### 11.7.1 Consequences of Overlap Syndrome

In a group of 177 patients with COPD who underwent home sleep studies, 20% had apnea hypopnea indices greater than 10 events/hour, and this group had a higher BMI and greater smoking history and more arterial hypertension and diabetes than the group who did not have OSA (Steveling, 2014). Measures of arterial stiffness are greater in individuals with overlap syndrome compared with those with OSA alone and this increase is independent of nocturnal hypoxemia and systemic inflammatory markers (Shiina, 2012). The elevated arterial stiffness may contribute to increased cardiovascular comorbidities in the overlap syndrome.

Patients with overlap syndrome have higher $PaCO_2$ (44.59 mmHg) compared with those with either OSA (39.22 mmHg) or COPD (39.63 mmHg) which could only be partially explained by weight and airflow limitation (Resta, 2002). Patients with the overlap syndrome and daytime hypercapnia have more profound nocturnal desaturations and greater derangements in sleep quality including more apneas and hypopneas than those with normocapnia (Lopez-Acevedo, 2006).

### 11.7.2 Pulmonary Hypertension

The prevalence of pulmonary hypertension is greater among individuals with overlap syndrome compared with those with either COPD or OSA only (Rizzi, 1997; Bady, 2000; Laks, 1995; Sanner, 1997; Chaouat, 1996; Hawrylkiewicz, 2004). The diagnosis and treatment of pulmonary hypertension are discussed in Chapter 12, COPD and Pulmonary Vasculature.

### 11.7.3 Atrial fibrillation

A retrospective two year study revealed the incidence of new onset atrial fibrillation was 21% in those with the overlap syndrome compared with 10% among patients with COPD, 6% among those with OSA, and 4.9% for those with neither disorder (Ganga, 2013). Even after adjusting for comorbidities, overlap syndrome was associated with new onset atrial fibrillation, OR 3.66, 95% CI 1.056, 6.860. Another study showed that incident AF is associated with OSA and smoking but did not assess airflow (Gami, 2007).

### 11.7.4 Cognitive Dysfunction

Both COPD and OSA are associated with neurocognitive dysfunction including impaired attention, memory and learning, language and higher executive functions, and deranged visuospatial and constructional capacity (Andreou, 2014). Normally, cerebral blood flow (CBF) increases during episodes of arterial hypoxemia to protect the brain from neuronal injury but this compensatory mechanism is lost during non-rapid eye movement sleep (Alexancre, 2014). Thus, this loss of compensatory CBF during sleep may contribute to enhanced hypoxemia-induced neuronal injury and increased cognitive dysfunction in the overlap syndrome. Cognitive function in the overlap syndrome has not been well studied but, since hypoxemia is believed to be the major factor contributing to poor performance, these impairments may be more pronounced in individuals with overlap syndrome.

## 11.8 Mortality and COPD Exacerbations

The leading cause of death among patients with the overlap syndrome is cardiovascular disease (Marin, 2010; McNicholas, 2009). Among patients with OSA, mortality is associated with concurrent COPD, OR, 7.07, 95% CI 2.75–18.16 (Lavie, 2007). Conversely, mortality is increased in individuals with COPD and untreated OSA compared with those with the same severity of COPD and no OSA (Marin, 2010). Patients with overlap syndrome not treated with CPAP have a higher mortality, relative risk (RR) 1.79, 95% CI 1.16, 2.77, and greater risk of a COPD exacerbation requiring hospitalization, RR 1.70, 95% CI 1.21–2.38 compared with patients with COPD after adjusting for age, sex, body mass index, tobacco and alcohol use, comorbidities, COPD severity, AHI, and daytime sleepiness (Marin, 2010).

### 11.8.1 Treatment

In general, there is no specific treatment for the overlap syndrome and management is directed toward the two underlying disorders, COPD and OSA, and associated comorbidities.

### 11.8.2 Respiratory Medications

Therapy for COPD is discussed in Chapter 14, Management of Stable COPD. Both short and long acting anticholinergics improve nocturnal oxygenation and sleep quality in patents with COPD (Martin, 1999; McNicholas, 2004). In patients with OSA alone, the mean $SpO_2$ and duration of time with $SpO_2 \leq 90\%$ are reduced after treatment with salmeterol but total sleep time, quality of sleep, and AHI were unchanged (Rasche, 1998; Rasche, 1999). The proportion of respiratory symptom free nights increase in patients with COPD treated with high dose but not low dose combined LABA/ICS and with LABA alone (Tashkin, 2012). The proportion of patients with stable COPD who have insomnia is less in those treated with a beta agonist, either albuterol or formoterol, or with a long acting inhaler, either tiotropium or formoterol (Budhiraja, 2012).

Some treatments for COPD may reduce sleep quality. Systemic corticosteroids are associated with an increased risk of insomnia in individuals with COPD (Wood-Baker, 2005; Aaron, 2003). In addition, prolonged or recurrent, intermittent use of steroids may cause weight gain, a risk factor for OSA, and steroid myopathy which might reduce respiratory muscle strength further worsening hypoventilation during sleep (Mieczkowski, 2014).

Despite its benefits on physical conditioning, quality of life, anxiety, and depression, the effect of pulmonary rehabilitation on sleep quality in patients with COPD is not clear with some studies demonstrating improvement and others showing no effect (Lan, 2014; McDonnell, 2014).

### 11.8.3 Oxygen

Oxygen improves survival in individuals with COPD and resting hypoxemia despite optimized medical management (reviewed in Chapter 14, Management of Stable COPD). The effect of supplemental oxygen for patients with COPD with resting low normal oxygenation and transient desaturations during exercise or sleep is not known. Similarly, the effect of nocturnal supplemental oxygen in individuals with OSA remains unclear. Earlier studies with small numbers of patients studied for short periods suggested that nocturnal supplemental oxygen improved sleep parameters and nocturnal oxygenation (Martin, 1982; Smith, 1984; Gold, 1986) but a more recent double blind, randomized trial showed that supplemental oxygen did not improve sleep parameters and only increased nocturnal oxygen levels (Loredo, 2006).

A large prospective trial comparing CPAP and oxygen treatment in individuals with OSA and cardiovascular disease or risk factors showed that CPAP but not supplemental oxygen reduced 24 hour mean arterial blood pressure; sleep parameters were not assessed but C reactive protein, a measure of systemic inflammation was only reduced with CPAP (Gottlieb, 2014).

In patients with profound nocturnal hypoxemia that is refractory to CPAP and supplemental oxygen, use of transtracheal oxygen may maintain oxygen levels during sleep (Biscardi, 2014).

### 11.8.4 Lung Volume Reduction Surgery (LVRS)

In patients with emphysema amenable to surgical treatment, LVRS improves sleep quality (increased total sleep time and sleep efficiency and reduced arousal index) and nocturnal oxygenation (Krachman, 2005). These benefits appear to be more related to improvements in lung mechanics, reduced air trapping and hyperinflation, than oxygenation (Krachman, 2008).

### 11.8.5 Noninvasive Positive Pressure Ventilation

For patients with OSA, noninvasive ventilation with positive pressure, usually continuous positive airway pressure (CPAP), is the main treatment (Epstein, 2009). In patients with the overlap syndrome, CPAP improves quality of sleep, reduces complications and mortality, and decreases COPD exacerbations (Stanchina, 2013; Marin, 2010). A retrospective review of 227 patients with overlap syndrome revealed that 17 (7.4%) died over a 3 year period; adherence with CPAP was greater in surviving patients, 65.9±1.8% of nights with > 4 hours use and mean use 5.4±0.1 hr/night, than in patients who died, 21.2±8.1% of nights with >4 hours of use and 1.7±0.2 hr/night (Stanchina, 2013). Patients with overlap syndrome not treated with CPAP have a higher mortality, RR 1.79, 95% CI 1.16, 2.77, and greater risk of a COPD exacerbation requiring hospitalization, RR 1.70, 95% CI 1.21–2.38, compared with patients with COPD after adjusting for age, sex, body mass index, tobacco and alcohol use, comorbidities, COPD severity, AHI, and daytime sleepiness (Marin, 2010). Patients with overlap syndrome treated with CPAP had the same risk of death and hospitalization for COPD exacerbations as those with COPD alone (Marin, 2010). In a study of 271 patients with overlap syndrome treated with CPAP, those with hypercapnia had less mortality than those with normocapnia, hazard ratio (HR) 0.47 (95% CI 0.23–0.89) versus 0.72 (5% CI 0.32–1.63), respectively (Jaoude, 2014). This study suggested that CPAP's mortality benefit in the overlap syndrome occurred only in patients with hypercapnia.

In patients with obesity hypoventilation or overlap syndrome, nocturnal NIV may reduce daytime $PACO_2$ levels and this decrease is associated with less daytime somnolence and EEG activation suggesting that hypercarbia may be a contributing factor to daytime sleepiness (Wang, 2014).

A prospective randomized controlled study comparing standard therapy with or without nocturnal noninvasive ventilation in patients with stable, hypercapneic COPD for 1 year showed that, when NIV was targeted to achieved a 20% reduction in baseline $PaCO_2$ or to achieve a $PaCO_2$ less than 48.1 mmHg, mortality decreased from 33% (NIV+standard therapy) to 12% (standard therapy alone), HR 0.24 (95% CI, 0.11–0.49) (Köhnlein, 2014). A meta-analysis of NIV in patients with stable COPD showed that non-targeted routine use of NIV did not affect sleep efficiency (Struik, 2014). Thus, it appears that CPAP treatment using pressure levels determined by the measured effect on $PaCO_2$ optimizes CPAP's benefits but these studies need to be verified in a population of patients with overlap syndrome. In general, these titration studies are best performed in a monitored setting such as a sleep laboratory, measuring oxygen saturation and end tidal $CO_2$ levels. Bilevel noninvasive ventilation is most frequently used to augment minute ventilation and reduce $PaCO_2$ levels by increasing the difference between the inspiratory and expiratory pressures.

Nocturnal intelligent volume-assured pressure support noninvasive ventilation improves sleep quality and reduces $PACO_2$ more than high-intensity noninvasive positive pressure ventilation in patients with COPD and resting hypercapnea (Ekkemkamp, 2014). These ventilator modes have not yet been evaluated for the overlap syndrome.

Nocturnal noninvasive ventilation may improve exercise capacity in individuals with the overlap syndrome. Walking capacity measured by the incremental shuttle walking test improves after CPAP treatment (Wang, 2013). A small study suggested that exercise tolerance measured by maximal work load during cardiopulmonary exercise testing increased in patients with overlap syndrome treated with CPAP (Nowinski, 2007).

CPAP reduces paroxysmal atrial fibrillation, sinus bradycardia, and sinus pauses among patients with OSA but its effect on these dysrhythmias in the overlap syndrome is not known (Abe, 2010).

## 11.9 Conclusion

Sleep disturbances may occur in up to 75% of individuals with COPD and may be due to nocturnal respiratory symptoms especially cough, sleep disordered breathing mainly OSA, or combinations of these processes. The concurrence of COPD and OSA is known as the overlap syndrome and, although its prevalence is not greater than would be predicted from the prevalence of either disorder alone, the overlap syndrome is associated with significant nocturnal hypoxemia and impaired sleep quality. This profound desaturation is due to the combined effects of COPD's detrimental consequences on ventilation and ventilation-perfusion matching and usual hypoventilation and REM-related skeletal muscle atony. The overlap syndrome is associated with pulmonary hypertension. Treatment of the overlap syndrome includes minimizing nocturnal respiratory symptoms through optimal management of COPD, supplemental oxygen, and noninvasive positive pressure ventilation. CPAP improves sleep quality, and reduces COPD exacerbations, nocturnal desaturation, and mortality. More recent studies suggest that CPAP is mostly, and potentially only, beneficial in individuals with hypercapnia, and that use of noninvasive ventilation targeted to achieve a reduction in hypercarbia is more advantageous than non-targeted therapy.

## 11.10 Summary Points

1. Sleep disturbances due to nocturnal respiratory symptoms, sleep disordered breathing, or both processes occur commonly in patients with COPD.
2. Approximately 10% of individuals with COPD have OSA and the concurrence of COPD and OSA, the overlap syndrome, occurs in approximately 1% of the general population.
3. To identify sleep issues in patients with COPD, a careful and complete sleep history and sleep directed examination should be obtained.
4. Factors associated with the overlap syndrome include pulmonary hypertension, obesity, and possibly worse airflow limitation.
5. The overlap syndrome is characterized by profound nocturnal desaturation due to the combined effects of COPD and sleep on nocturnal ventilation.
6. Treatment of the overlap syndrome includes respiratory medications, supplemental oxygen, and noninvasive positive pressure ventilation.
7. Use of continuous positive airway pressure (CPAP) improves sleep symptoms, decreases COPD exacerbations, and increases survival.
8. CPAP is most beneficial in patients with overlap syndrome and hypercarbia.

## References

Aaron S.D., Vandemheen K.L., Hebert P., Dales R., Stiell I.G., Ahuja J., Dickinson G., Brison R., Rowe B.H., Dreyer J., Yetisir E., Cass D., & Wells G. (2003). Outpatient oral prednisone after emergency treatment of chronic obstructive pulmonary disease. *N Engl J Med*, *348*(26), 2618–2625.

Abe H., Takahashi M., Yaegashi H., Eda S., Tsunemoto H., Kamikozawa M., Koyama J., Yamazaki K., & Ikeda U. (2010). Efficacy of continuous positive airway pressure on arrhythmias in obstructive sleep apnea patients. *Heart Vessels*, *25*(1), 63–69.

Agusti A., Hedner J., Marin J.M., Barbe F., Cazzola M., & Rennard S. (2011). Night-time symptoms: a forgotten dimension of COPD. *Eur Respir Rev*, *20*, 183–194.

Alexandre F., Heraud N., & Varray A. (2015). Is nocturnal desaturation a trigger for neuronal damage in chronic obstructive pulmonary disease? *Med Hypotheses*, *84*(1), 25–30

Andreou G., Vlachos F., & Makanikas K. (2014). Effects of chronic obstructive pulmonary disease and obstructive sleep apnea on cognitive functions: evidence for a common nature, *Sleep Disord*, 2014, 768210.

Ayas N.T., Brown R., & Shea SA. (2000). Hypercapnia can induce arousal from sleep in the absence of altered respiratory mechanoreception. *Am J Respir Crit Care Med*, *162*(3 Pt 1), 1004–8.

Bady E., Achkar A., Pascal S., Orvoen-Frija E., & Laaban J.P. (2000). Pulmonary arterial hypertension in patients with sleep apnoea syndrome. *Thorax*, *55*(11), 934–9.

Becker H.F., Piper A.J., Flynn W.E., McNamara S.G., Grunstein R.R., Peter J.H., & Sullivan C.E. (1999). Breathing during sleep in patients with nocturnal desaturation. *Am J Respir Crit Care Med*, *159*(1), 112–118.

Bednarek M., Plywaczewski R., Jonczak L., Górecka D., & Sliwiñiski P. (2005). There is no relationship between chronic obstructive pulmonary disease and obstructive sleep apnea syndrome: a population study. *Respiration*, *72*, 142–149.

Biscardi F.H., & Rubio E.R. (2014). Transtracheal oxygen and positive airway pressure: A salvage technique in overlap syndrome. *Lung India*, *31*(1), 67–69.

Brezinova V., Catterall J.R., Douglas N.J., Calverley P.M., & Flenley D.C. (1982). Night sleep of patients with chronic ventilatory failure and age matched controls: number and duration of the EEG episodes of intervening wakefulness and drowsiness. *Sleep*, *5*(2), 123–130.

Budhiraja R., Parthasarathy S., Budhiraja P., Habib M.P., Wendel C., & Quan S.F. (2012). Insomnia in patients with COPD. *Sleep*, *35*(3), 369–375.

Calverley P.M., Brezinova V., Douglas N.J., Catterall J.R., & Flenley D.C. (1982). The effect of oxygenation on sleep quality in chronic bronchitis and emphysema. *Am Rev Respir Dis*, *126*(2), 206–210.

Celli B.R., MacNee W., & ATS/ERS Task Force. (2004). Standards for the diagnosis and treatment of patients with COPD: a summary of the ATS/ERS position paper. *Eur Respir J*, *23*(6), 932–946.

Chan K.K.Y., Ing A.J., Laks L., Cossa G., Rogers P., & Birring S.S. (2010). Chronic cough in patients with sleep-disordered breathing. Eur Respir J; *35*, 368–372.

Chaouat A., Bugnet A.S., Kadaoui N., Schott R., Enache I., Ducoloné A., Ehrhart M., Kessler R., & Weitzenblum E., (2005). Severe pulmonary hypertension and chronic obstructive pulmonary disease. *Am J Respir Crit Care Med*, *172*, 189–194.

Chaouat A., Weitzenblum E., Krieger J., Ifoundza T., Oswald M., & Kessler R., (1995). Association of chronic obstructive pulmonary disease and sleep apnea syndrome. *Am. J. Respir. Crit. Care Med*, *151*, 82–86.

Chaouat A., Weitzenblum E., Krieger J., Oswald M., & Kessler R. (1996). Pulmonary hemodynamics in the obstructive sleep apnea syndrome. Results in 220 consecutive patients. *Chest*, *109*(2), 380–386.

Davila D.G., Hurt R.D., Offord K.P., Harris C.D., & Shepard J.W. (1994). Acute effects of transdermal nicotine on sleep architecture, snoring, and sleep-disordered breathing in nonsmokers. *Am J Respir Crit Care Med*, *150*(2), 469–474.

Deegan P.C., & McNicholas W.T. (1995). Pathophysiology of obstructive sleep apnoea. *Eur Respir J*, *8*(7), 1161–1178.

Ekkernkamp E., Storre J.H., Windisch W., & Dreher M. (2014). Impact of intelligent volume-assured pressure support on sleep quality in stable hypercapnic chronic obstructive pulmonary disease patients: a randomized, crossover study. *Respiration*, *88*(4), 270–276.

Epstein L.J., Kristo D., Strollo P.J. Jr., Friedman N., Malhotra A., Patil S.P., Ramar K., Rogers R., Schwab R.J., Weaver E.M., & Weinstein M.D. (2009). Adult Obstructive Sleep Apnea Task Force of the American Academy of Sleep Medicine. Clinical guideline for the evaluation, management and long-term care of obstructive sleep apnea in adults. *J Clin Sleep Med*, *5*(3), 263–276.

Fleetham J., West P., Mezon B., Conway W., Roth T., & Kryger M. (1982). Sleep, arousals, and oxygen desaturation in chronic obstructive pulmonary disease. The effect of oxygen therapy. *Am Rev Respir Dis*, *126*(3), 429–433.

Flenley D.C. (1985). Sleep in chronic obstructive lung disease. *Clin Chest Med*, 6(4), 651–61.

Gami A.S., Hodge D.O., Herges R.M., Olson E.J., Nykodym J., Kara T., & Somers V.K. (2007). Obstructive sleep apnea, obesity, and the risk of incident atrial fibrillation. *J Am Coll Cardiol*, *49*(5), 565–571.

Ganga H.V., Nair S.U., Puppala V.K., & Miller W.L. (2013). Risk of new-onset atrial fibrillation in elderly patients with the overlap syndrome: a retrospective cohort study. *J Geriatr Cardiol*, *10*(2), 129–134.

Global Initiative for Chronic Obstructive Lung Disease (GOLD). *Global Strategy for the Diagnosis, Management and Prevention of COPD, Updated 2014*. http://www.goldcopd.org/. Accessed December, 2014.

Gold A.R., Schwartz A.R., Bleecker E.R., & Smith P.L. (1986). The effect of chronic nocturnal oxygen administration upon sleep apnea. *Am Rev Respir Dis*, *134*(5), 925–929.

Gottlieb D.J., Punjabi N.M., Mehra R., Patel S.R., Quan S.F., Babineau D.C., Tracy R.P., Rueschman M., Blumenthal R.S., Lewis E.F., Bhatt D.L., & Redline S. (2014). CPAP versus oxygen in obstructive sleep apnea. N Engl J Med, *370*(24), 2276–2285.

Gothe B., Strohl K.P., Levin S., & Cherniack N.S. (1985). Nicotine: a different approach to treatment of obstructive sleep apnea. *Chest*, *87*(1), 11–17.

Hareendran A., Palsgrove A.C., Mocarski M., Schaefer M.L., Setyawan J., Carson R., & Make B. (2013). The development of a patient-reported outcome measure for assessing nighttime symptoms of chronic obstructive pulmonary disease. *Health Qual Life Outcomes*, *11*, 104.

Hawryłkiewicz I., Sliwinski P., Górecka D., Pływaczewski R., & Zielinski J. (2004). Pulmonary haemodynamics in patients with OSAS or an overlap syndrome. *Monaldi Arch Chest Dis*, *61*(3), 148–152.

Haxhiu M.A., Van Lunteren E., Van de Graaff W.B., Strohl K.P., Bruce E.N., Mitra J., & Cherniack N.S. (1984). Action of nicotine on the respiratory activity of the diaphragm and genioglossus muscles and the nerves that innervate them. *Respir Physiol*, *57*(2), 153–69

Hynninen M.J., Pallesen S., Hardie J., Eagan T.M., Bjorvatn B., Bakke P., & Nordhus I.H. (2013). Insomnia symptoms, objectively measured sleep, and disease severity in chronic obstructive pulmonary disease outpatients. *Sleep Med*, *14*(12), 1328–33.

Ioachimescu O.C., & Teodorescu M. (2013). Integrating the overlap of obstructive lung disease and obstructive sleep apnoea: OLDOSA syndrome. *Respirology*, *18*(3), 421–431.

Jaehne A., Loessl B., Bárkai Z., Riemann D., & Hornyak M. (2009). Effects of nicotine on sleep during consumption, withdrawal and replacement therapy. *Sleep Med Rev*, *13*(5), 363–77.

Jaoude P., Kufel T., & El-Solh A.A. (2014). Survival benefit of CPAP favors hypercapnic patients with the overlap syndrome. *Lung*, *192*(2), 251–258.

Johns M.W. (1991). A new method for measuring daytime sleepiness: the Epworth sleepiness scale. *Sleep*, *14*(6), 540–5.

Kashyap R., Hock L.M., & Bowman T.J. (2001). Higher prevalence of smoking in patients diagnosed as having obstructive sleep apnea. *Sleep Breath*, *5*, 167–172.

Kessler R., Partridge M.R., Miravitlles M., Cazzola M., Vogelmeier C., Leynaud D., & Ostinelli J., (2011). Symptom variability in patients with severe COPD: a pan-European cross-sectional study. *Eur Respir J*, *37*, 264–272.

Klink M.E., Dodge R., & Quan S.F. (1994). The relation of sleep complaints to respiratory symptoms in a general population. *Chest*, *105*(1), 151–154.

Köhnlein T., Windisch W., Köhler D., Drabik A., Geiseler J., Hartl S., Karg O., Laier-Groeneveld G., Nava S., Schönhofer B., Schucher B., Wegscheider K., Criée C.P., & Welte T. (2014). Non-invasive positive pressure ventilation for the treatment of severe stable chronic obstructive pulmonary disease: a prospective, multicentre, randomised, controlled clinical trial. Lancet Respir Med, *2*(9), 698–705.

Krachman S.L., Chatila W., Martin U.J., Nugent T., Crocetti J., Gaughan J., Criner G.J. & National Emphysema Treatment Trial Research Group. (2005). Effects of lung volume reduction surgery on sleep quality and nocturnal gas exchange in patients with severe emphysema. *Chest*, *128*(5), 3221–3228.

Krachman S., Minai O.A., & Scharf S.M. (2008). Sleep Abnormalities and Treatment in Emphysema. *Proc Am Thorac Soc*, *5*(4), 536–542.

Kwon J.S., Wolfe L.F., Lu B.S., & Kalhan R. (2009). Hyperinflation is associated with lower sleep efficiency in COPD with co-existent obstructive sleep apnea. *COPD*, *6*(6), 441–445.

Laks L., Lehrhaft B., Grunstein R.R., & Sullivan C.E. (1995). Pulmonary hypertension in obstructive sleep apnoea. *Eur Respir J*, *8*(4), 537–541.

Lan C.C., Huang H.C., Yang M.C., Lee C.H., Huang C.Y., & Wu Y.K. (2014). Pulmonary rehabilitation improves subjective sleep quality in COPD. *Respir Care*, *59*(10), 1569–76.

Lange P., Marott J.L., Vestbo J., & Nordestgaard B.G. (2014). Prevalence of night-time dyspnoea in COPD and its implications for prognosis. *Eur Respir J*, *43*(6), 1590–1598.

Lavie P., Herer P., & Lavie L. (2007). Mortality risk factors in sleep apnoea: a matched case-control study. *J Sleep Res*, *16*(1), 128–34.

Lee R., & McNicholas W.T. (2011). Obstructive sleep apnea in chronic obstructive pulmonary disease patients. *Curr Opin Pulm Med*, *17*(2), 79–83.

Lin Y.N., Li Q.Y., & Zhang X.J. (2012). Interaction between smoking and obstructive sleep aprea: not just participants. *Chin Med J (Engl)*, *125*(17), 3150–3156.

López-Acevedo M.N., Torres-Palacios A., Elena Ocasio-Tascón M., Campos-Santiago Z., & Rodríguez-Cintrón W. (2009). Overlap syndrome: an indication for sleep studies? : A pilot study. *Sleep Breath*, *13*(4), 409–413.

Loredo J.S., Ancoli-Israel S., Kim E.J., Lim W.J., & Dimsdale J.E. (2006). Effect of continuous positive airway pressure versus supplemental oxygen on sleep quality in obstructive sleep apnea: a placebo-CPAP-controlled study. *Sleep*, *29*(4), 564–571.

Marin J.M., Soriano J.B., Carrizo S.J., Boldova A., & Celli B.R. (2010). Outcomes in patients with chronic obstructive pulmonary disease and obstructive sleep apnea: the overlap syndrome. *Am J Respir Crit Care Med*, *182*(3), 325–331.

Marrone O., Salvaggio A., & Insalaco G. (2006). Respiratory disorders during sleep in chronic obstructive pulmonary disease. *Int J Chron Obstruct Pulmon Dis*, *1*, 363–372.

Martin R.J., Bartelson B.L., Smith P., Hudgel D.W., Lewis D., Pohl G., Koker P., & Souhrada J.F. (1999). Effect of ipratropium bromide treatment on oxygen saturation and sleep quality in COPD. *Chest*, *115*(5), 1338–1345.

Martin R.J., Sanders M.H., Gray B.A., & Pennock B.E. (1982). Acute and long-term ventilatory effects of hyperoxia in the adult sleep apnea syndrome. *Am Rev Respir Dis*, *125*(2), 175–180.

McDonnell L.M., Hogg L., McDonnell L., & White P. (2014). Pulmonary rehabilitation and sleep quality: a before and after controlled study of patients with chronic obstructive pulmonary disease. NPJ Prim Care Respir Med, *24*, 14028.

McNicholas W.T., Calverley P.M., Lee A., & Edwards J.C. Tiotropium Sleep Study in COPD Investigators. (2004). Long-acting inhaled anticholinergic therapy improves sleeping oxygen saturation in COPD. *Eur Respir J*, *23*(6), 825–831.

McNicholas W.T., Verbraecken J., & Marin J.M. (2013). Sleep disorders in COPD: the forgotten dimension. Eur Respir Rev, *22*(129), 365–75.

McNicholas W.T. (2009). Chronic obstructive pulmonary disease and obstructive sleep apnea: overlaps in pathophysiology, systemic inflammation, and cardiovascular disease. *Am. J. Respir. Crit. Care Med*, *180*, 692–700.

Mieczkowski B., & Ezzie M.E. (2014). Update on obstructive sleep apnea and its relation to COPD. *Int J Chron Obstruct Pulmon Dis*, *9*, 349–62.

Miravitlles M., Worth H., Soler Cataluña J., Price D., de Benedetto F., Roche N., Godtfredsen N., van der Molen T., Löfdahl C.G., Padullés L., & Ribera A. (2014). Observational study to characterise 24-hour COPD symptoms and their relationship with patient-reported outcomes: results from the ASSESS study. *Respir Res*, *15*(1), 122.

Myers K.A., Mrkobrada M., & Simel D.L. (2013). Does this patient have obstructive sleep apnea?: The Rational Clinical Examination systematic review. *JAMA*, *310*(7), 731–741.

Netzer N.C., Stoohs R.A., Netzer C.M., Clark K., & Strohl K.P. (1999). Using the Berlin Questionnaire to identify patients at risk for the sleep apnea syndrome. *Ann Intern Med*, *131*(7), 485–491.

Newton K., Malik V., & Lee-Chiong T. (2014). Sleep and breathing. *Clin Chest Med*, *35*(3), 451–456.

Nowiński A., Bieleń P., Jonczak L., & Sliwiński P. (2007). Influence of treatment with continuous positive airway pressure on respiratory muscle function and physical fitness in patients with obstructive sleep apnoea and overlap syndrome. *Pneumonol Alergol Pol*, *75*(1), 46–56.

Ohayon M.M. (2014). Chronic Obstructive Pulmonary Disease and its association with sleep and mental disorders in the general population. *J Psychiatr Res*, *54*, 79–84.

Owens R.L., & Malhotra A. (2010). Sleep-disordered breathing and COPD: the overlap syndrome. *Respir. Care*, *55*, 1333–1344.

Peppard P.E., Young T., Palta M., Dempsey J., & Skatrud J. (2000). Longitudinal study of moderate weight change and sleep-disordered breathing. *JAMA*, *284*(23), 3015–3021.

Phillips B.A., & Danner F.J. (1995). Cigarette smoking and sleep disturbance. *Arch Intern Med*, *155*(7), 734–737.

Power J.T., Stewart I.C., Connaughton J.J., Brash H.M., Shapiro C.M., Flenley D.C., & Douglas N.J., (1984). Nocturnal cough in patients with chronic bronchitis and emphysema. *Am Rev Respir Dis*, *130*(6), 999–1001.

Price D., Small M., Milligan G., Higgins V., Gil E.G., & Estruch J. (2013). Impact of night-time symptoms in COPD: a real-world study in five European countries. *Int J Chron Obstruct Pulmon Dis*, *8*, 595–603.

Rasche K., Duchna H.W., Lauer J., Orth M., Kotterba S., Bauer T.T., Gillissen A., & Schultze-Werninghaus G. (1999). Obstructive sleep apnea and hypopnea efficacy and safety of a long-acting beta2-agonist. *Sleep Breath*, 3(4), 125–130.

Rasche K., Duchna H.W., Orth M., Bauer T.T., Lauer J., Podbregar D., & Schultze-Werninghaus G. (1998). Effect of salmeterol in obstructive sleep apnea syndrome]. *Pneumologie*, *52*(1), 11–13.

Rennard S., Decramer M., Calverley P.M., Pride N.B., Soriano J.B., Vermeire P.A., & Vestbo J. (2002). Impact of COPD in North America and Europe in 2000: subjects'perspective of Confronting COPD International Survey. *Eur Respir J*, *20*, 799–805.

Resta O., Foschino Barbaro M.P., Brindicci C., Nocerino M.C., Caratozzolo G., & Carbonara M. (2002). Hypercapnia in overlap syndrome: possible determinant factors. *Sleep Breath*. *6*(1), 11–18.

Rizzi M., Palma P., Andreoli A., Greco M., Bamberga M., Antivalle M., & Sergi M. (1997). Prevalence and clinical feature of the “overlap syndrome”, obstructive sleep apnea (OSA) and chronic obstructive pulmonary disease (COPD), in OSA population. *Sleep Breath*, *2*(3), 68–72.

Sanders M.H., Newman A.B., Haggerty C.L., Redline S., Lebowitz M., Samet J., O'Connor G.T., Punjabi N.M., & Shahar E.; Sleep Heart Health Study. (2003). Sleep and sleep-disordered breathing in adults with predominantly mild obstructive airway disease. *Am. J. Respir. Crit. Care Med*, *167*, 7–14.

Sanner B.M., Doberauer C., Konermann M., Sturm A., & Zidek W. (1997). Pulmonary hypertension in patients with obstructive sleep apnea syndrome. *Arch Intern Med*, *157*(21), 2483–2487.

Scott A.S., Baltzan M.A., & Wolkove N. (2014). Examination of pulse oximetry tracings to detect obstructive sleep apnea in patients with advanced chronic obstructive pulmonary disease. *Can Respir J*, *21*(3), 171–175.

Sharma B., Feinsilver S., Owens R.L., Malhotra A., McSharry D., & Karbowitz S. (2011). Obstructive airway disease and obstructive sleep apnea: effect of pulmonary function. *Lung*, *189*(1), 37–41.

Shiina K., Tomiyama H., Takata Y., Yoshida M., Kato K., Nishihata Y., Matsumoto C., Odaira M., Saruhara H., Hashimura Y., Usui Y., & Yamashina A. (2012). Overlap syndrome: additive effects of COPD on the cardiovascular damages in patients with OSA. *Respir Med*, *106*(9), 1335–41.

Silber M.H., Ancoli-Israel S., Bonnet M.H., Chokroverty S., Grigg-Damberger M.M., Hirshkowitz M., Kapen S., Keenan S.A., Kryger M.H., Penzel T., Pressman M.R., & Iber C. (2007). The visual scoring of sleep in adults. *J Clin Sleep Med*, 3(2), 121–31.

Smith P.L., Haponik E.F., & Bleecker E.R. (1984). The effects of oxygen in patients with sleep apnea. *Am Rev Respir Dis*, *130*(6), 958–963.

Soldatos C.R., Kales J.D., Scharf M.B., Bixler E.O., & Kales A. (1980). Cigarette smoking associated with sleep difficulty. *Science*, *207*(4430), 551–553.

Stanchina M.L., Welicky L.M., Donat W., Lee D., Corrao W., & Malhotra A. (2013). Impact of CPAP use and age on mortality in patients with combined COPD and obstructive sleep apnea: the overlap syndrome. *J Clin Sleep Med*, *9*(8), 767–72.

Steveling E.H., Clarenbach C.F., Miedinger D., Enz C., Dürr S., Maier S., Sievi N., Zogg S., Leuppi J.D., & Kohler M. (2014). Predictors of the Overlap Syndrome and Its Association with Comorbidities in Patients with Chronic Obstructive Pulmonary Disease. *Respiration*, *88*(6), 451–457.

Struik F.M., Lacasse Y., Goldstein R.S., Kerstjens H.A., & Wijkstra P.J. (2014). Nocturnal noninvasive positive pressure ventilation in stable COPD: a systematic review and individual patient data meta-analysis. *Respir Med*, *108*(2), 329–337.

Sundar K., Daly S., Pearce M., & Alward W.T. (2010). Chronic cough and obstructive sleep apnea in a community-based pulmonary practice. *Cough*, *6*(1), 2.

Tashkin D.P., Doherty D.E., Kerwin E., Matiz-Bueno C.E., Knorr B., Shekar T., Gates D., & Staudinger H. (2012). Efficacy and safety characteristics of mometasone furoate/formoterol fumarate fixed-dose combination in subjects with moderate to very severe COPD: findings from pooled analysis of two randomized, 52-week placebo-controlled trials. *Int J Chron Obstruct Pulmon Dis*, *7*, 73–86.

Tashkin D.P., Rennard S.I., Martin P., Ramachandran S., Martin U.J., Silkoff P.E., & Goldman M. (2008). Efficacy and safety of budesonide mand formoterol in one pressurized metered-dose inhaler in patients with moderate to very severe chronic obstructive pulmonary disease: results of a 6-month randomized clinical trial. *Drugs, 68*, 1975–2000.

Valipour A., Lavie P., Lothaller H., Mikulic I., & Burghuber O.C. (2011). Sleep profile and symptoms of sleep disorders in patients with stable mild to moderate chronic obstructive pulmonary disease. *Sleep Med*, *12*(4), 367–72.

Venkateswaran S., & Tee A. (2014). Overlap syndrome between chronic obstructive pulmonary disease and obstructive sleep apnoea in a Southeast Asian teaching hospital. *Singapore Med J*, *55*(9), 488–492.

Wang T.Y., Lo Y.L., Lee K.Y., Liu W.T., Lin S.M., Lin T.Y., Ni Y.L., Wang C.Y., Ho S.C., & Kuo H.P. (2013). Nocturnal CPAP improves walking capacity in COPD patients with obstructive sleep apnoea. *Respir Res*, *19*, 14:66.

Wang D., Piper A.J., Yee B.J., Wong K.K., Kim J.W., D'Rozario A., Rowsell L., Dijk D.J., & Grunstein R.R. (2014). Hypercapnia is a key correlate of EEG activation and daytime sleepiness in hypercapnic sleep disordered breathing patients. *J Clin Sleep Med*. *10*(5), 517–522.

Weitzenblum E., & Chaouat A. (2004). Sleep and chronic obstructive pulmonary disease. *Sleep Med Rev*, *8*, 281–294.

Weitzenblum E., Chaouat A., Kessler R., & Canuet M. (2008). Overlap syndrome: obstructive sleep apnea in patients with chronic obstructive pulmonary disease. *Proc Am Thorac Soc*, *5*(2), 237–241.

Wetter D.W., Young T.B., Bidwell T.R., Badr M.S., & Palta M. (1994A). Smoking as a risk factor for sleep-disordered breathing. *Arch Intern Med*, *154*, 2219–2224.

Wetter D.W., & Young T.B. (1994B). The relation between cigarette smoking and sleep disturbance. *Prev Med*, *23*, 328–334.

Williamson D.F., Madans J., Anda R.F., Kleinman J.C., Giovino G.A., & Byers T. (1991). Smoking cessation and severity of weight gain in a national cohort. *N Engl J Med*, *324*(11), 739–745.

Wood-Baker R.R., Gibson P.G., Hannay M., Walters E.H., & Walters J.A. (2005). Systemic corticosteroids for acute exacerbations of chronic obstructive pulmonary disease. *Cochrane Database Syst Rev*, (1), CD001288.

Zevin S., Swed E., & Cahan C. (2003). Clinical effects of locally delivered nicotine in obstructive sleep apnea syndrome. *Am J Ther*, *10*(3), 170–175.

Zhang L., Samet J., Caffo B., Bankman I., & Punjabi N.M. (2008). Power spectral analysis of EEG activity during sleep in cigarette smokers. *Chest*, *133*, 427–432.

Zhang L., Samet J., Caffo B., & Punjabi N.M. (2006). Cigarette smoking and nocturnal sleep architecture. *Am J Epidemiol*, *164*, 529–537.

Jean M. Elwing, MD

# 12 COPD and Pulmonary Vasculature

Key Points

1. Elevated pulmonary pressures are a common finding in patients with advanced COPD and are associated with increased morbidity and mortality.
2. Pulmonary hypertension causes progressive right ventricular hypertrophy, dilation, and dysfunction.
3. Management of COPD related pulmonary hypertension includes treatment of underlying COPD, supplemental oxygen, and smoking cessation. Systemic vasodilators are ineffective. Pulmonary vasodilators require further study to determine their efficacy.
4. Venous thromboembolism frequently complicates COPD exacerbations. 25% of all COPD exacerbation are associated with venous thromboembolism and increase morbidity and mortality in COPD patients.

## 12.1 Introduction

Chronic obstructive pulmonary disease (COPD) is a multisystem chronic illness that is a major worldwide healthcare burden. It is estimated that COPD will be the fourth largest contributor to mortality by 2020 (Murray, 1997). In addition to obstructive airway disease, COPD is frequently associated with progressive pulmonary vascular disease. It is estimated that 20–65% of patients with COPD are affected by elevations in pulmonary pressures (Weitzenblum, 1984; Burrows, 1972; Oswald-Mammosser, 1987; Cuttica, 2010) with a small fraction (< 5%) having severely elevated pulmonary pressures (Thabut, 2005; Chaouat, 2005; Cuttica, 2010). Survival in COPD correlates negatively with pulmonary arterial pressures (PAP) (Oswald-Mammosser, 1995; Cuttica, 2010). Patients with COPD and pulmonary hypertension (PH) have increased morbidity and are at risk for hospitalizations for COPD exacerbations (Weitzenblum, 1984; Burrows, 1972; Barbera, 2003; Kessler, 1999). Additionally, COPD patients with PH have more severe exercise impairment (Sims, 2009; Cuttica, 2010).

COPD patients are also often affected by venous thromboembolic (VTE) disease and have a twofold increased risk of VTE as compared to other chronic medical conditions (Sidney, 2005). A systematic review of the published literature in 2009 revealed that approximately one fourth of hospitalized COPD patients presenting with dyspnea had VTE (Jacques, 2009).

Both progressive pulmonary vascular disease as well as thromboembolic disease increase morbidity and mortality in patients with COPD. This chapter will review the epidemiology of PH associated with COPD including its clinical manifestations, methods of diagnosis, pathophysiology, and treatment strategies. Additionally, this chapter will briefly discuss prevalence, impact and management of VTE in the setting of COPD.

## 12.2 COPD Associated Pulmonary Hypertension

### 12.2.1 Epidemiology

The prevalence of PH in COPD has not been accurately assessed in large epidemiologic studies because of variations in definitions of PH, limitations of accurate measurement of pulmonary pressures by echocardiogram (Fisher, 2009) as well as the risks and expense of invasive pressure measurement by right heart catheterization (RHC). To date, most studies have utilized noninvasive measures with echocardiogram to estimate pulmonary arterial pressures which provides limited insight into this condition. Some estimations of prevalence can be gleaned from limited post-mortem data and small studies evaluating pulmonary pressures by RHC. Prior to the use of supplemental oxygen and modern COPD therapy, at autopsy, approximately two thirds of chronic bronchitic patients (Millard, 1974; Scott, 1976) and one third of emphysematous patients (Leopold, 1957) have evidence of right ventricular hypertrophy supporting the ante-mortem presence of PH. In 1981, Weitzenblum evaluated 175 COPD patients' hemodynamics with RHC and 35% were found to have elevated resting mean pulmonary artery pressures (mPAP ≥ 20 mmHg) (Weitzenblum, 1981). In 2005, hemodynamic data from 215 end-stage disease COPD patients undergoing RHC prior to lung volume reduction surgery or lung transplantation were reviewed. Pulmonary pressures were more significantly elevated in patients with end-stage pulmonary disease with more than half having a resting mPAP > 25 mmHg and approximately 15% had moderately to severely elevated pulmonary pressures (mPAP > 35 mmHg) (Thabut, 2005). Severe elevation in pulmonary pressures (>45 mmHg) is rare and most frequently found in patients with concomitant conditions contributing to PH (Thabut, 2005; Chaouat, 2005). More recently, Cuttica et al (Cuttica, 2010) retrospectively reviewed hemodynamic data from 4930 lung transplant candidates with COPD. In this cohort of patients with advanced COPD, 30.4% (1499/4930) had elevations in pulmonary pressures (mPA ≥25mmHg) of which 4.0% (196/4930) had severe PH (mPA ≥ 35mmHg) and 17% had increased left sided filling pressures. In this group, PH was associated with lower exercise capacity as well as increased mortality despite controlling for confounders such as age, ethnicity, BMI, lung function and NYHA class (Cuttica, 2010).

Resting PH associated with COPD is slowly progressive with an average increase of 0.4 mmHg per year based on data from a cohort of 131 patients followed over 6.8+/-2.9 years (Kessler, 2001). Despite slow progression of resting PH, pulmonary pressures can rise acutely with exercise (Christensen, 2004; Fujimoto, 2002), illness and sleep in COPD patients (Chaouat, 2008). Furthermore, exercise induced PH is estimated to occur in two-thirds of patients with COPD even when pulmonary pressures are normal at rest (Oswald-Mammosser, 1991; Christensen, 2004).

### 12.2.2 Diagnostic Evaluation

#### 12.2.2.1 Clinical Evaluation for Pulmonary Hypertension

A thorough clinical history is important in evaluating patients with COPD and suspected PH. Other coexisting risk factors for pulmonary vascular disease should be carefully evaluated (Chaouat, 2005). History of previous VTE should be explored as a high proportion of patients experiencing COPD exacerbations also have had previous thromboembolic events (Tillie-Leblond, 2006).

Symptoms related to the development of PH in the setting of COPD may be subtle and often masked by dyspnea from obstructive lung disease (Salvaterra, 1993). Although the predictive value of specific symptoms and physical examination findings in detecting pulmonary vascular disease in a patient with COPD is not clearly elucidated, several signs and symptoms suggests the presence of PH (Salvaterra, 1993). Decreasing functional capacity with stable pulmonary function testing suggests pulmonary vascular involvement. Signs of right ventricle enlargement or overload such as the presence of a right ventricular heave, prominent P2, right sided S4 gallop, and the murmur of tricuspid regurgitation suggest the presence of PH (Salvaterra, 1993). Elevated jugular venous pressure, hepatojugular reflux, and a pulsatile liver are often signs of tricuspid insufficiency and right heart failure (Elwing, 2008).

#### 12.2.2.2 Noninvasive Testing for Pulmonary Hypertension

Routine chest radiography may reveal prominence of the pulmonary arteries or evidence of right ventricular enlargement on lateral films. The hilar to thoracic index (distance between the right and left main pulmonary arteries divided by diameter of the chest) of > 0.36 correlates with elevated pulmonary pressures (Chetty, 1982). Additionally, enlargement of the right pulmonary artery > 16 mm or left pulmonary artery > 18 mm has been associated with elevated pulmonary pressures (Matthay, 1981).

CT chest imaging is useful to evaluate the pulmonary parenchyma in the dyspneic patient but also can reveal evidence of pulmonary hypertension. Enlargement of the main pulmonary artery > 2.9 cm correlated well with elevated pulmonary pressures in a small study of 36 patients with pulmonary hypertension due to variable causes (Tan, 1998). Furthermore, a ratio of pulmonary artery (PA) to aortic diameter > 1 was 70% sensitive and 92% specific for PH in a group of 50 patients with various etiologies of RHC proven PH (Ng, 1999). Enlarged PAs are also associated with increased COPD disease activity. In 2012 Wells et al evaluated markers associated with severe COPD exacerbations. Increased PA to aortic diameter ratio (> 1) was associated with a history of severe exacerbations as well as a predictor of future COPD events (Wells 2012). Figure 12.1.

COPD patients with associated PH frequently have electrocardiographic abnormalities consistent with right ventricular hypertrophy or strain. Additional electrocardiographic features consistent with PH include right atrial enlargement, right

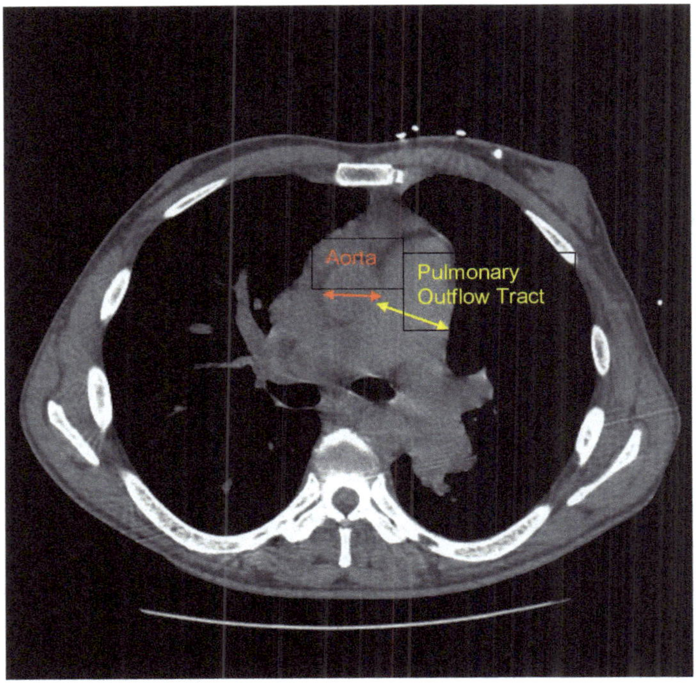


**Figure 12.1:** Chest CT Scan from a Patient with COPD and Pulmonary Hypertension. The pulmonary artery diameter is greater than the aortic diameter. The aorta is labeled in red with a red arrow and the main pulmonary artery (pulmonary outflow tract) is labeled in yellow with a yellow arrow.

axis deviation and right sided conduction abnormalities (Babera, 2003; Harrigan, 2002).

Echocardiography is the most frequent noninvasive test used to assess for PH. Pulmonary artery pressure is most frequently calculated by obtaining a maximum tricuspid regurgitant (TR) flow velocity with continuous wave Doppler and then using this value to calculate an estimated right ventricular (RV) pressure utilizing a modified Bernoulli's equation. The peak TR velocity, v, is used to calculate the trans-tricuspid gradient, $4v^2$. The RV systolic pressure is then calculated as the sum of the trans-tricuspid gradient plus the estimated right atrial pressure (RAP) (Metz, 1987). (Figure 12.2.)

Accurate estimation of pulmonary pressures is limited by several technical factors which may be accentuated in patients with COPD due to chest wall configuration changes, air trapping and cardiac orientation in COPD (Arcasoy, 2003). Doppler echcardiographic success in estimating systolic pulmonary artery pressure in patients with COPD ranges from 26–66% (Arcasoy, 2003; Bach, 1998; Tramarin, 1991; Laaban, 1989) and often requires invasive hemodynamic assessment to confirm diagnosis of PH.

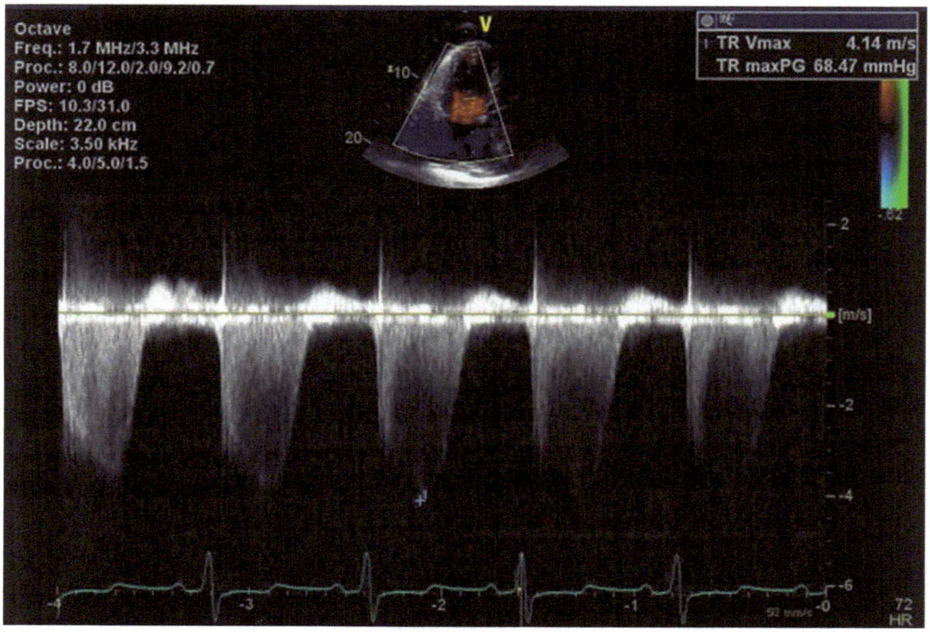


**Figure 12.2:** Echocardiogram showing flow across the tricuspid valve. Pulmonary artery systolic pressure (PASP) estimation is calculated from tricuspid regurgitant (TR) flow velocity utilizing a modified Bernoulli's equation. The peak TR velocity, v, is used to calculate the trans-tricuspid gradient, $4v^2$. The PASP is then calculated as the sum of the trans-tricuspid gradient plus the estimated right atrial pressure (RAP). PASP = TR gradient + RA pressure (RAP) PASP = $(4.14^2 \times 4) + 20 = 88$ mm Hg

### 12.2.2.3 Invasive Testing for Pulmonary Hypertension

Historical data, clinical clues, examination findings, and noninvasive testing may raise concern for the presence of pulmonary hypertension but elevated pulmonary artery pressures can only be formally diagnosed by invasive right heart catheterization with direct measurement of pulmonary pressures of ≥ 25 mmHg. Current guidelines from the Fifth World Health Organization (WHO) meeting on pulmonary hypertension include 5 subgroups of pulmonary hypertension. Pulmonary hypertension related to COPD is included in WHO Group III disease, hypoxic pulmonary hypertension (Simonneau, 2013). Right heart catheterization (RHC) is not routinely required for the evaluation of COPD patients but may be of benefit in patients with worsening dyspnea and progressive right heart failure. RHC may better delineate the etiology of symptoms and help guide management. Additionally, invasive hemodynamic data is beneficial if patients are considering lung volume reduction surgery or pulmonary transplant (Malcolm, 2008).

### 12.2.3 Histopathology

Histopathological changes seen in patients with COPD and associated pulmonary hypertension include pulmonary vascular changes (Hicken, 1965; Wilkinson, 1988) as well as increased RV mass (Millard, 1974; Scott, 1976). Most notable changes in the arterioles include circumferential muscular hyperplasia in the media. Additionally, the arterioles as well as the small pulmonary arteries have increased deposition of longitudinal smooth muscle (Hicken, 1965). These findings are present regardless of the use of supplemental oxygen (Wilkinson, 1988). The media of the normally poorly muscularized arterioles reveal a circular muscular coat bound by a new internal elastic lamina. Luminal narrowing is present with frequent recanalization of the arteriolar lumen (Wilkinson, 1988; Wright, 1983; Hale, 1984; Wright, 1992). In smokers, the density of the fully muscularized (0–300 mu diameter) pulmonary arteries and the thickness of the medial muscle layer is doubled and the depth of intimal fibrosis is tripled (Hale, 1984). This intimal thickening is due to both smooth muscle cell proliferation and increased elastin and collagen deposition (Santos, 2002).

### 12.2.4 Pathophysiology

The pulmonary vasculature of patients with COPD associated PH has abnormal intimal and medial thickening that cause luminal narrowing and obstruction of the small pulmonary arteries (Wright, 1992). These changes lead to decreased elasticity and lack of vascular recruitment (Kubo, 2000). This pulmonary vascular stiffness causes an increase in pulmonary vascular resistance (PVR) and subsequent elevation of pulmonary artery pressures (PAP). The severity of vascular abnormalities does not correlate directly with the pulmonary pressure at rest (Wright, 1992; Wilkinson, 1988). PH is slowly progressive in most patients with COPD increasing by an average of 0.4 mmHg yearly (Kessler, 2001). Eventually, PH leads to pressure overload of the right ventricle (RV). In response to pressure overload, RV muscular hypertrophy occurs (Scott, 1976; Dias, 2002; Fishman, 1976). Hypertrophy precedes contractile dysfunction of the RV (Voelkel, 2006) and is followed by a downward spiral of RV dilation, a decrease in cardiac output, and an increase in right sided filling pressures (Voelkel, 2006). Inevitably, the ability of the RV to compensate is overwhelmed and RV failure ensues.

### 12.2.5 Pathogenesis

The pathogenesis of the vascular abnormalities associated with COPD most likely are combined effects of hypoxia (Burrows, 1974), pulmonary dysfunction with air trapping, (Wright, 1993) and effects of smoking (Santos, 2002; Hale, 1980) leading to inflammation (Peniado, 1999), endothelial dysfunction, (Dinh-Xaun, 1991; Peniado, 1998), and angiogenesis (Santos, 2003).

Acute hypoxemia can lead to transient increases in pulmonary vascular tone in pulmonary vascular resistance (Von-Euler, 1946; Pease, 1972). Intermittent acute hypoxemia may contribute to PH, but chronic hypoxemia likely is playing a significant role (Heath, 1973; Thompson, 1989; Vender, 1994; Reeves, 2005). The pathophysiologic mechanism of hypoxic pulmonary vasoconstriction is not fully elucidated but is likely related in part to direct action on the potassium and calcium channels (Weir, 1995), stimulation of transcription factors, (Yan, 1998; Mechtcheriakova, 1999) and release of endogenous mediators (Morrell, 1995; Chen, 1994; DiCarlo, 1995; Elton, 1992; Hu, 1998) as well as growth factors (Mechtcheriakova, 1999; Santos, 2003) triggering vasoconstriction and vascular remodeling.

Tobacco smoke is known to cause airways disease but also has a significant effect on the pulmonary vasculature. Small arterioles in smokers develop intimal changes with elastin deposition and increased collagen prior to the development of obstructive lung disease (Santos, 2002; Hale, 1980). These changes are likely related to tobacco smoke's effects on gene expression of vasoconstrictors as well as altered nitric oxide production (Santos, 2003; Barbera, 2001; Wright, 2002; Su, 1998).

Endothelial function dysregulation in the setting of hypoxic stress (Chen, 1994; DiCarlo, 2995; Elton, 1992) and toxin exposure (Wright, 2002; Wright, 2004; Santos, 2003) plays a role in COPD associated PH (Clini, 2000; Giaid, 1993). Nitric oxide (NO), a potent vasodilating mediator with antiproliferative effects (Murad, 1997), is decreased in smokers (Barbera, 2001) and patients with COPD (Giaid, 1993). It is postulated that the reduction in NO may play a role in the development of pulmonary vascular changes in COPD related PH. Endothelin-1 (ET-1), a potent vasoconstricting (LaDouceur, 1993) and mitogenic mediator, produced by the endothelium (Dubin, 1989; Boscoe, 2000; Wedgwood, 2001) is increased in COPD (Spiropoulos, 2003) and PH (Giaid, 1993).

Various growth factors are involved in the pathogenesis of pulmonary vascular disease. Vascular endothelial growth factor (VEGF) is a growth factor that stimulates angiogenesis (Papaioannou, 2006), is increased in the pulmonary arteries of patients with COPD (Santos, 2003), and is triggered by hypoxia. Platelet derived growth factor (PDGF), a potent mitogen for smooth muscle cells (Hannink, 1989), has been demonstrated to play a role in animal models with PH (Schermuly, 2005) but no clear role has been delineated in COPD and PH to date.

The role of inflammation in COPD related PH is unclear but the degree of inflammatory infiltrate in the pulmonary vasculature does correlate with severity of intimal thickening in the pulmonary arteries (Peniado, 1999) suggesting a possible association.

### 12.2.6 Management of Pulmonary Hypertension

The treatment of COPD related PH requires a multimodal approach including smoking cessation, COPD management and correction of hypoxemia.

Smoking cessation and elimination of all secondhand smoke exposure is the first step in management of COPD. Because of tobacco smoke's known adverse effect on the pulmonary vasculature (Hale, 1980; Santos, 2002), smoking cessation likely will also have a beneficial effect on pulmonary vascular disease associated with COPD.

Correction of hypoxemia with supplemental oxygen is recommended for patients with COPD as well as COPD related PH. Long-term oxygen therapy (LTOT) improves survival in hypoxic COPD patients and is associated with a mild improvement in pulmonary hemodynamics (Medical Research Council, 1981; Noctural Oxygen Therapy Trial Group, 1980). Furthermore, supplemental oxygen may improve exercise tolerance (Fujimoto, 2002) and may impact RV function (Olvey, 1980). LTOT has been found to slow the progression of COPD associated PH (Weitzenblum, 1985) but did not normalize pulmonary pressures (Abraham, 1968) or reverse histologic change in the pulmonary vasculature (Wilkinson, 1988).

Systemic vasodilators have been evaluated for the treatment of COPD related PH. Calcium channel blockers (CCB) have been associated with acute improvement in hemodynamics but are not effective long-term pulmonary vasodilators (Agostoni, 1989) and do not slow progression of COPD associated PH (Sturani, 1983). Furthermore, CCBs can worsen ventilation/perfusion matching (V/Q) and increase hypoxemia (Melot, 1984). CCBs are not recommended for the treatment of COPD associated PH. Hydralazine, angiotensin-converting enzyme inhibitors (ACE-I) and angiotensin receptor blocking agents have been assessed for the treatment of COPD associated PH. These agents are ineffective (Cerda, 1985; Dal Nogare, 1986; Nong; 1996, Morrell, 2005).

Therapies targeted at pulmonary vasodilatation may play a future role in the treatment of pulmonary vascular disease associated with COPD. Currently there is limited data on the effectiveness of therapies directed at the pulmonary vasculature in COPD-related PH. Inhaled nitric oxide was tested in 2003 for outpatient treatment and it improved hemodynamics (Vonbank, 2003) but was limited by a complex delivery system and risk of worsening V/Q matching (Barbera, 1996). Phosphodiesterase inhibitors (PDEI) have been tested in small numbers of patients with COPD associated PH. PDEI prolongs the effect of NO by inhibiting the degradation of NO's second messenger (cGMP) and promoting smooth muscle relaxation (Rabe, 1994). A study of 20 patients in 2010 revealed improved hemodynamics but worsening hypoxemia associated with the treatment of COPD associated PH with sildenafil (Blanco, 2010). Furthermore, another study of 15 patients in 2008 revealed no improvement in stroke volume or exercise capacity in COPD PH patients (Rietema, 2008). Thus, the use of pulmonary vasodilators in COPD-related PH is an area of ongoing investigation to find treatments that are effective yet safe.

## 12.3 COPD Associated Venous Thromboembolic Disease

### 12.3.1 Epidemiology of Venous Thromboembolism in COPD

COPD exacerbations are not infrequently associated with vague, nonspecific worsening of underlying breathlessness and other respiratory symptoms. 30% of exacerbations do not have a clearly documented cause. A 2009 systematic review of the literature revealed acute venous thromboembolism (VTE) complicates one of every four COPD exacerbations (Rizkallah, 2009). VTE accounts for significant morbidity among patients with COPD. This increased risk of thromboembolic disease is likely multifactorial with immobility, malignancy, and inflammation playing significant roles. In 2006, Tillie-Leblond found 25% of 211 consecutive admissions for COPD exacerbation were associated with VTE. Risk factors for VTE in this group included previous VTE, history of malignancy, and decrease in $pCO_2$ by > 5 mmHg (Tillie-Leblond, 2006). A 2002 French study retrospectively analyzed 50 consecutive COPD admissions with exacerbations and found that 20% had associated VTE without clearly associated risk factors. A prospective analysis at the same center also evaluated hospitalized COPD patients with increased breathlessness, no significant symptoms of infection, and a positive D-dimer. 29% of these patients had VTE. Risk factors for PE in that group were the presence of a deep vein thrombosis (DVT) and a decrease in $PaO_2$ by > 22 mmHg (Mispelaere, 2002)

### 12.3.2 Diagnostic Evaluation of Venous Thromboembolism in COPD

Venous thromboembolic disease can cause significant dyspnea, hypoxemia, and acute elevations in pulmonary pressures. Large thrombus burden or events in patients with advanced cardiopulmonary disease can produce right heart dysfunction, hypotension, shock, and death (Tapson, 2008).

Clinical evaluation of COPD patients presenting with acute onset of dyspnea should begin with a thorough history. Lack of infective symptoms should raise the suspicion for non-infectious causes of the COPD exacerbation. Physical examination should include assessment for findings consistent with obstructive airways disease including wheezing, decreased breath sounds, or prolonged expiratory phase. The lack of these features, should also prompt further assessment of alternative etiologies of dyspnea including VTE. If the examination reveals clinical findings consistent with elevated pulmonary pressures and right heart failure (including RV heave, TR murmur, RV gallop, hepatojugular reflux, jugular venous distention, ascites or edema), concern for VTE should be heightened.

D-dimer may be a useful laboratory test in the outpatient setting to assess patients with COPD with increased dyspnea. D-dimer antigen is a marker of fibrin degradation (Adam, 2009) and is frequently used to evaluate select patients for the presence of VTE (Wells, 2001). Unfortunately, D-dimer positivity can be seen in multiple conditions and is not a reliable tool in patients with other conditions including renal failure, surgery, cancer, sepsis, and normal pregnancy (Rathbun, 2004).

VTE encompasses all thromboembolic diseases including DVT and pulmonary embolism (PE). Currently, multi-detector computed tomography pulmonary angiography (CTPA) is the best imaging study for the diagnosis of acute PE (Mos, 2012; Klok, 2011). This technique has both high sensitivity, 96–100%, and specificity, 97–98% (Remy-Jardin, 2007). Unfortunately, the use of intravenous contrast may be contraindicated in patients with allergies to iodinated contrast and those with renal insufficiency or who are at risk for contrast-induced nephropathy.

In patients are unable to undergo CTPA, ventilation perfusion scintigraphy (V/Q) is the next best imaging procedure for acute PE (Mos, 2012). Results of V/Q scanning require correlation with clinical presentation for interpretation (PIOPED, 1990). Known pulmonary parenchymal and airways disease in patients with advanced COPD may increase the difficulty of interpretation. Up to half of patients with suspected PE may have intermediate scans and require further testing to exclude or establish a diagnosis of PE (Anderson, 2007).

### 12.3.3 Management of Venous Thromboembolism in COPD

VTE should be considered in any COPD patient presenting with dyspnea. If VTE is detected, full dose anticoagulation is indicated as per current guidelines without delay (Guyatt, 2012). Patients who do have VTE with COPD have poor outcomes. In the RIETE registry, an ongoing international multicenter prospective cohort of consecutive patients with symptomatic objectively confirmed acute VTE, COPD patients with concomitant VTE have a threefold increase in mortality (11%) compared with those patients who do not have VTE (Bertoletti, 2013). Patients should be treated with anticoagulation according to the most recent guidelines (Guyatt, 2012). Patient should be monitored closely after discontinuation as affected individuals have higher risk of recurrent disease.

## 12.4 Summary

Pulmonary vascular disease including chronic progressive pulmonary vascular changes leading to pulmonary hypertension as well as acute venous thromboembolic disease has a severe negative effect on the outcomes of patients with COPD. Pulmonary hypertension is a common feature of advanced COPD and is estimated to affect ≥ 20% of patients with advanced COPD (Weitzenblum, 1981; Schraf, 2002; Oswald-Mammosser, 1991). The vast majority of PH associated with COPD is mild to moderate (mPAP 20 – 35 mmHg) with severe PH (mPAP ≥ 40 mmHg) occurring in

<5% of patients with COPD (Chaouat, 2005). Elevated pulmonary pressures correlate with an increased risk of exacerbations and hospitalizations for COPD (Kessler, 1999). Severe PH in patients with COPD reduces median survival by approximately 40 months (Chaouat, 2005). The pathogenesis of PH associated with COPD has not been clearly elucidated but is likely due to the combined effects of inflammation (Peinado, 1999), endothelial cell dysfunction (Dinh-Xaun, 1991; Peinado, 1998), and angiogenesis (Santos, 2003) that lead to intimal thickening, luminal narrowing, and arteriolar muscularization (Barbera, 1994; Peinado, 1998; Magee, 1988; Hale, 1980). Smoking cessation, COPD management and oxygen therapy are recommended for management. Long-term oxygen therapy is a proven therapy for COPD and is associated with slowing progression but not resolution of associated PH (Medical Research Council, 1981; Noctural Oxygen Trial Group, 1980). Systemic vasodilators are not effective therapy in COPD related pulmonary hypertension (Sturani, 1983). Selective pulmonary vasodilators require further study to determine if they may be of benefit to patients with COPD and PH. VTE is another serious pulmonary vascular complication of COPD. It is associated with a three-fold increase in mortality in COPD patients. A high index of suspicion for VTE with prompt evaluation and treatment initiation is recommended. Further study is required to better understand the etiology, pathophysiology, and optimal management of patients with COPD and concomitant VTE.

## 12.5 Summary Points

1. The prevalence of PH among individuals with COPD increases with airflow obstruction severity; approximately 20% of patients with advanced COPD have PH.
2. The vast majority of PH associated with COPD is mild to moderate (mPAP 20–35 mmHg); severe PH (mPAP ≥ 40 mmHg) occurs in <5% of patients with COPD.
3. Elevated pulmonary pressures correlate with increased risk of COPD exacerbations and hospitalizations.
4. Severe PH in patients with COPD reduces median survival by approximately 40 months.
5. Treatment of COPD-related PH includes smoking cessation, COPD management, and supplemental oxygen therapy.
6. Systemic vasodilators are not effective therapy in COPD related PH.
7. Selective pulmonary vasodilators require further study to determine if they may be of benefit to patients with COPD and PH.
8. VTE is another serious pulmonary vascular complication of COPD and occurs in approximately 25% of patients hospitalized for COPD exacerbations.

## References


Abraham, A.S., Cole, R.B., Bishop, J.M. (1968). Reversal of pulmonary hypertension by prolonged oxygen administration to patients with chronic bronchitis. *Circ Res*, 23, 147–57.

Adam, S.S., Key N.S., Greenberg, C.S. (2009). D-dimer antigen, current concepts and future prospects. *Blood*, 113(13), 2878–87.

Agostoni, P., Doria, E., Galli, C., et al. (1989). Nifedipine reduces pulmonary pressure and vascular tone during short- but not long-term treatment of pulmonary hypertension in patients with chronic obstructive pulmonary disease. *Am Rev Respir Dis*, 139, 120–5.

Anderson, D.R., Kahn, S.R., Rodger, M.A., Kovacs, M.J., Morris, T., Hirsch, A., Lang, E., Stiell, I., Kovacs, G., Dreyer, J., Dennie, C., Cartier, Y., Barnes, D., Burton, E., Pleasance, S., Skedgel, C., O'Rouke, K., Wells, P.S. (2007). Computed tomographic pulmonary angiography vs ventilation-perfusion lung scanning in patients with suspected pulmonary embolism, a randomized controlled trial. *JAMA*, 298(23), 2743–53.

Arcasoy, S.M., Christie, J.D., Ferrari, V.A., et al. (2003). Echocardiographic assessment of pulmonary hypertension in patients with advanced lung disease. *Am J Respir Crit Care Med*, 167, 735–740.

Bach, D.S., Curtis, J.L., Christensen, P.J., et al. (1998). Preoperative echocardiographic evaluation of patients referred for lung volume reduction surgery. *Chest*, 114, 972–980.

Barbera, J.A., Peinado, V.I., Santos, S., et al. (2001). Reduced expression of endothelial nitric oxide synthase in pulmonary arteries of smokers. *Am J Respir Crit Care Med*, 164, 709–13.

Barbera, J.A., Peinado, V.I., Santos, S. (2003). Pulmonary hypertension in chronic obstructive pulmonary disease. *Eur Respir J*, 21, 892–905.

Barbera, J.A., Roger, N., Roca, J., et al. (1996). Worsening of pulmonary gas exchange with nitric oxide inhalation in chronic obstructive pulmonary disease. *Lancet*, 347, 436–40.

Barbera, J.A., Riverola, A., Roca, J., et al. (1994). Pulmonary vascular abnormalities and ventilation-perfusion relationships in mild chronic obstructive pulmonary disease. *Am J Respir Crit Care Med*, 149, 423–9.

Bertoletti, L., Quenet ,S., Laporte, S., Sahuquillo, J.C., Conget , F., Pedrajas, J.M., Martin, M., Casado, I., Riera-Mestre, A., Monreal, M.; RIETE Investigators. (2013). Pulmonary embolism and 3-month outcomes in 4036 patients with venous thromboembolism and chronic obstructive pulmonary disease, data from the RIETE registry. *Respir Res*, 14, 75.

Blanco, I., Gimeno, E., Munoz, P.A., et al. (2010). Hemodynamic and gas exchange effects of sildenafil in patients with chronic obstructive pulmonary disease and pulmonary hypertension. *Am J Respir Crit Care Med*, 181, 270–278.

Boscoe, M.J., Goodwin, A.T., Amrani, M., et al. (2000). Endothelins and the lung. *Int J Biochem Cell Biol*, 32, 41–62.

Burrows, B. (1974). Arterial oxygenation and pulmonary hemodynamics in patients with chronic airways obstruction. *Am Rev Respir Dis*, 110, 64–70.

Burrows, B., Kettel, L.J., Niden, A.H., el al. (1972). Patterns of cardiovascular dysfunction in chronic obstructive lung disease. *N Engl J Med*, 286, 912–918.

Cerda, E., Esteban, A., de la Cal, M.A., et al. (1985). Hemodynamic effects of vasodilators on pulmonary hypertension in decompensated chronic obstructive pulmonary disease. *Crit Care Med*, 13, 221–3.

Chaouat, A., Bugnet, A.S., Kadaoui, N., et al. (2005). Severe pulmonary hypertension and chronic obstructive pulmonary disease. *Am J Respir Crit Care Med*, 172, 189–194.

Chaouat, A., Naeije, R., Weitzenblum, E. (2008) Pulmonary hypertension in COPD. *Eur Respir J*, 32(5), 1371–85.

Chen, S.J., Chen, Y.F., Meng, Q.C., et al. (1995). Endothelin-receptor antagonist bosentan prevents and reverses hypoxic pulmonary hypertension in rats. *J Appl Physiol*, 79, 2122–31.

Chetty, K.G., Brown, S.E., Light, R.W. (1982). Identification of pulmonary hypertension in chronic obstructive pulmonary disease form routine chest radiographs. *Am Rev Respir Dis*, 126, 338–341.

Christensen, C.C., Ryg, M.S., Edvardsen, A., et al. (2004). Relationship between exercise desaturation and pulmonary haemodynamics in COPD patients. *Eur Respir J*, 24, 580–586.

Clini, E., Cremona, G., Campana, M., et al. (2000). Production of endogenous nitric oxide in chronic obstructive pulmonary disease and patients with cor pulmonale. Correlates with echo-Doppler assessment. *Am J Respir Crit Care Med*, 162, 446–50.

Cuttica, M.J., Kalhan, R., Shlobin, O.A., et al. (2010). Categorization and impact of pulmonary hypertension in patients with advanced COPD. *Respir Med*, 104, 1877–1882.

Dal Nogare, A.R., Rubin, L.J. (1986). The effects of hydralazine on exercise capacity in pulmonary hypertension secondary to chronic obstructive pulmonary disease. *Am Rev Respir Dis*, 133, 385–9.

DiCarlo, V.S., Chen, S.J., Meng, Q.C, et al. (1995). ETA-receptor antagonist prevents and reverses chronic hypoxia-induced pulmonary hypertension in rat. *Am J Physiol*, 269, L690–7.

Dias, C.A., Assad, R.S., Caneo, L.F., et al. (2002). Reversible pulmonary trunk banding. II. An experimental model for rapid pulmonary ventricular hypertrophy. *J Thorac Cardiovasc Surg*, 124, 999–1006.

Dinh-Xuan, A.T., Higenbottam, T.W., Clelland, C.A., et al. (1991). Impairment of endothelium-dependent pulmonary-artery relaxation in chronic obstructive lung disease. *N Engl J Med*, 324, 1539–47.

Dubin, D., Pratt, R.E., Kooke, J.P., Dzau, V.J. (1989). Endothelin, a potent vasoconstrictor, is a vascular smooth muscle mitogen. *J Vasc Biol Med*, 1, 150–4.

Elton, T.S., Oparil, S., Taylor, G.R., et al. (1992). Normobaric hypoxia stimulates endothelin-1 gene expression in the rat. *Am J Physiol*, 263, R1260–4.

Elwing, J., Panos, R.J. (2008). Pulmonary hypertension associated with COPD. *Int J Chron Obstruct Pulmon Dis*, 3(1), 55–70.

Fisher, M.C., Forfia, P.R., Chamera, E., Housten-Harris, T., Champion, H.C., Girgis, R.E., Corretti, M.C., Hassoun, P.M. (2009). Accuracy of Doppler Echocardiography in the Hemodynamic Assessment of Pulmonary Hypertension. *Am J Respir Crit Care Med*, 179(7), 615–621.

Fishman, A.P. (1976). State of the art, chronic cor pulmonale. *Am Rev Respir Dis*, 114, 775–94.

Fujimoto, K., Matsuzawa, Y., Yamaguchi, S., et al. (2002). Benefits of oxygen on exercise performance and pulmonary hemodynamics in patients with COPD with mild hypoxemia. *Chest*, 122, 457–63.

Harrigan, H.A., Jones, K. (2002). ABC of clinical electrocardiography, Conditions affecting the right side of the heart. *BMJ* , 324, 1201–1204.

Giaid, A., Saleh, D. (1995). Reduced expression of endothelial nitric oxide synthase in the lungs of patients with pulmonary hypertension. *N Engl J Med*, 333, 214–21.

Giaid, A., Yanagisawa, M., Langleben, D., et al. (1993). Expression of endothelin-1 in the lungs of patients with pulmonary hypertension. *N Engl J Med*, 328, 1732–9.

Guyatt, G.H., Akl, E.A., Crowther, M., Gutterman, D.D., Schuünemann, H.J., (2012). Executive summary, Antithrombotic Therapy and Prevention of Thrombosis, 9th ed, American College of Chest Physicians Evidence-Based Clinical Practice Guidelines. American College of Chest Physicians Antithrombotic Therapy and Prevention of Thrombosis Panel. *Chest*, 141 (2 Suppl), 7S–47S.

Hale, K.A., Ewing, S.L., Gosnell, B.A., Niewoehner, et al. (1984). Lung disease in long-term cigarette smokers with and without chronic air-flow obstruction. *Am Rev Respir Dis*, 130, 716–21.

Hale, K.A., Niewoehner, D.E., Cosio, M.G. (1980). Morphologic changes in the muscular pulmonary arteries, relationship to cigarette smoking, airway disease, and emphysema. *Am Rev Respir Dis*, 122, 273–8.

Hannink, M., Donoghue, D.J. (1989). Structure and function of platelet-derived growth factor (PDGF) and related proteins. *Biochim Biophys Acta*, 198, 1–10.

Heath, D., Edwards, C., Winson, M., Smith, P. (1973). Effects on the right ventricle, pulmonary vasculature, and carotid bodies of the rat of exposure to, and recovery from, simulated high altitude. *Thorax* , 28, 24–8.

Hicken, P., Heath, D., Brewer, D.B., et al. (1965). The small pulmonary arteries in emphysema. *J Pathol Bacteriol*, 90, 107–14.

Hu, J., Discher, D.J., Bishopric, N.H., et al. (1998). Hypoxia regulates expression of the endothelin-1 gene through a proximal hypoxia-inducible factor-1 binding site on the antisense strand. *Biochem Biophys Res Commun*, 245, 894–9.

Kessler, R., Faller, M., Fourgaut, G., Mennecier, B., Weitzenblum, E. (1999). Predictive factors of hospitalization for acute exacerbation in a series of 64 patients with chronic obstructive pulmonary disease. *Am J Respir Crit Care Med*, 159(1), 158–64.

Kessler, R., Faller, M., Weitzenblum, E., et al. (2001). "Natural history" of pulmonary hypertension in a series of 131 patients with chronic obstructive lung disease. *Am J Respir Crit Care Med*, 164, 219–24.

Klok, F.A., Mos, I.C., Kroft, L.J., de Roos, A., Huisman, M.V. (2011). Computed tomography pulmonary angiography as a single imaging test to rule out pulmonary embolism. *Curr Opin Pulm Med*, 17(5), 380–6.

Kubo, K., Ge, R.L., Koizumi, T., Fujimoto, K. et al. (2000). Pulmonary artery remodeling modifies pulmonary hypertension during exercise in severe emphysema. *Respir Physiol*, 120, 71–9.

Laaban, J.P., Diebold, B., Zelinski, R., et al. (1989). Noninvasive estimation of systolic pulmonary artery pressure using Doppler echocardiography in patients with chronic obstructive pulmonary disease. *Chest*, 96, 1258–1262.

LaDouceur, D.M., Flynn, M.A., Keiser, J.A., et al. (1993). ETA and ETB receptors coexist on rabbit pulmonary artery vascular smooth muscle mediating contraction. *Biochem Biophys Res Commun*, 196, 209–15.

Leopold, J.G., Gough, J. (1957). The centrilobular form of hypertrophic emphysema and its relation to chronic bronchitis. *Thorax*, 12, 219–235.

Magee, F., Wright, J.L., Wiggs, B.R., et al. (1988). Pulmonary vascular structure and function in chronic obstructive pulmonary disease. *Thorax*, 43, 183–9.

DeCamp, M.,Lipson, D,,Krasna, M., Minai, O., McKenna, R.,Thomashow, B. (2008). The Evaluation and Preparation of the Patient for Lung Volume Reduction Surgery. *Proc Am Thorac Soc*, 5(4), 427–431.

Matthay, R.A., Schwarz, M.I., Ellis, J.H. Jr, et al. (1981). Pulmonary artery hypertension in chronic obstructive pulmonary disease, determination by chest radiography. *Invest Radiol*, 16, 95–100.

Mechtcheriakova, D., Wlachos, A., Holzmuller, H., et al. (1999). Vascular endothelial cell growth factor-induced tissue factor expression in endothelial cells is mediated by EGR-1. *Blood*, 93, 3811–3823.

Melot, C., Hallemans, R., Naeije, R., et al. (1984). Deleterious effect of nifedipine on pulmonary gas exchange in chronic obstructive pulmonary disease. *Am Rev Respir Dis*, 130, 612–6.

Metz, D., Laudinat ,J.M., Beruben, E., Marchal, E., Blaise, C., Deschildre, A., Bajolet, A. (1987). Evaluation of pulmonary systolic arterial pressures by continuous Doppler in tricuspid regurgitation in adults. Apropos of 43 cases. *Arch Mal Coeur Vaiss*, 80(11), 1605–9.

Millard, J., Reid, J. (1974). Right ventricular hypertrophy and its relationship to chronic bronchitis and emphysema. *Brit J Dis Chest*, 68, 103–110.

Mispelaere, D., Glerant, J.C., Audebert ,M., et al. (2002). Pulmonary embolism and sibilant types of chronic obstructive pulmonary disease decompensations. *Rev Mal Respir*, 19, 415–423.

Morrell, N.W., Higham, M.A., Phillips ,P.G., et al. (2005). Pilot study of losartan for pulmonary hypertension in chronic obstructive pulmonary disease. *Respir Res*, 6, 1–10.

Morrell, N.W., Morris, K.G., Stenmark, K.R. (1995). Role of angiotensin-converting enzyme and angiotensin II in development of hypoxic pulmonary hypertension. *Am J Physiol*, 269, H1186–94.

Mos, I.C., Klok, F.A., Kroft, L.J., de Roos, A., Huisman, M.V. (2012). Imaging tests in the diagnosis of pulmonary embolism. *Semin Respir Crit Care Med*, 33(2), 138–43.

Murad, F. (1997). What are the molecular mechanisms for the antiproliferative effects of nitric oxide and cGMP in vascular smooth muscle? *Circulation*, 95, 1101–3.

Murray, C.J., Lopez, A.D. (1997). Mortality by cause for eight regions of the world, Global Burden of Disease Study. *Lancet*, 349, 1269–1276.

Ng, C.S., Wells, A.U., Padley, S.P. (1999). A CT sign of chronic pulmonary arterial hypertension, the ratio of main pulmonary artery to aortic diameter. *J Thoracic Imaging*, 14, 270–278.

Nocturnal Oxygen Therapy Trial Group. (1980). Continuous or nocturnal oxygen therapy in hypoxemic chronic obstructive lung disease, a clinical trial. *Ann Intern Med*, 93, 391–8.

Nong, Z., Stassen, J.M., Moons, L., et al. (1996). Inhibition of Tissue Angiotensin-Converting Enzyme With Quinapril Reduces Hypoxic Pulmonary Hypertension and Pulmonary Vascular Remodeling. *Circulation*, 94, 1941–1947 .

Olvey, S.K., Reduto, L.A., Stevens, P.M., et al. (1980). First pass radionuclide assessment of right and left ventricular ejection fraction in chronic pulmonary disease. Effect of oxygen upon exercise response. *Chest*, 78, 4–9.

Oswald-Mammosser, M., Apprill, M., Bachez, P., et al. (1991). Pulmonary hemodynamics in chronic obstructive pulmonary disease of the emphysematous type. *Respiration*, 58, 304–310.

Oswald-Mammosser, M., Oswald, T., Nyankiye, N., Dickele, M.C., Grange, D., Weitzenblum, E. (1987). Non-invasive diagnosis of pulmonary hypertension in chronic obstructive pulmonary disease. Comparison of ECG, radiological measurement, echocardiography, and myocardial scintigraphy. *Eur Respir J*, 715, 419–429.

Oswald-Mammosser, M., Weitzenblum, E., Quoix, E., et al. (1995) Prognostic factors in COPD patients receiving long-term oxygen therapy. Importance of pulmonary artery pressure. *Chest*, 107(5), 1193e8.

Papaioannou, A.I., Kostikas, K., Kollia, P., et al. (2006). Clinical implications for vascular endothelial growth factor in the lung, friend or foe? *Respir Res*, 7, 128.

Pease, R.D., Benumof ,J.L, Trousdale, F.R. (1982). PAO2 and PVO2 interaction on hypoxic pulmonary vasoconstriction. *J Appl Physiol*, 53, 134–9.

Peinado, V.I., Barbera, J.A., Abate, P., et al. (1999). Inflammatory reaction in pulmonary muscular arteries of patients with mild chronic obstructive pulmonary disease. *Am J Respir Crit Care Med*, 159, 1605–11.

Peinado, V.I., Barbera, J.A., Ramirez, J., et al. (1998). Endothelial dysfunction in pulmonary arteries of patients with mild COPD. *Am J Physiol*, 274, L908–13.

Rabe, K.F., Tenor, H., Dent, G., et al. (1994). Identification of PDE isozymes in human pulmonary artery and effect of selective PDE inhibitors. *Am J Physiol*, 266, 536–43.

Rathbun, S.W., Whitsett ,T.L., Raskob, G.E. (2004). Negative D-dimer result to exclude recurrent deep venous thrombosis, a management trial. *Ann Intern Med*, 141(11), 839–45.

Reeves, J.T., Grover, R.F. (2005). Insights by Peruvian scientists into the pathogenesis of human chronic hypoxic pulmonary hypertension. *J Appl Physiol*, 98, 384–9.

Remy-Jardin, M., Pistolesi, M., Goodman, L.R., et al. (2007). Management of suspected acute pulmonary embolism in the era of CT angiography, a statement from the Fleischner Society. *Radiology*, 245(2), 315–329.

Report of the Medical Research Council Working Party. (1981). Long term domiciliary oxygen therapy in chronic hypoxic cor pulmonale complicating chronic bronchitis and emphysema. *Lancet*, 1, 681–6.

Rietema, H., Holverda, S., Bogaard, H.J., et al. (2008). Sildenafil treatment in COPD does not affect stroke volume or exercise capacity. *Eur Respir J*, 31, 759–764.

Rizkallah, J., Paul Man, S.F. Sin, D.D. (2009). Prevalence of Pulmonary Embolism in Acute Exacerbations of COPD. *CHEST*, 135(3), 786–793.

Salvaterra, C.G., Rubin, L.J. (1993). Investigation and management of pulmonary hypertension in chronic obstructive pulmonary disease. *Am Rev Respir Dis*, 148, 1414–1417.

Santos, S., Peinado, V.I., Ramirez, et al. (2002). Characterization of pulmonary vascular remodeling in smokers and patients with mild COPD. *Eur Respir J*, 19, 632–8.

Santos, S., Peinado, V.I., Ramirez ,J., et al. (2003). Enhanced expression of vascular endothelial growth factor in pulmonary arteries of smokers and patients with moderate chronic obstructive pulmonary disease. *Am J Respir Crit Care Med*, 167, 1250–6.

Scharf, S.M., Iqbal, M., Keller, C. et al. (2002). National Emphysema Treatment Trial (NETT) Group. Hemodynamic characterization of patients with severe emphysema. *Am J Respir Crit Care Med*, 166, 314–22.

Schermuly, R.T., Dony, E., Ghofrani, H.A., et al. (2005). Reversal of experimental pulmonary hypertension by PDGF inhibition. *J Clin Invest*, 115, 2811–21.

Scott, K.W.M. (1976). A clinicopathological study of fatal chronic airways obstruction. *Thorax*, 31, 693–701.

Sidney, S., Sorel, M., Quesenberry, C.P. Jr, et al. (2005). COPD and incident cardiovascular disease hospitalizations and mortality, Kaiser Permanente Medical Care Program. *Chest*, 128, 2068–2075.

Sims, M.W., Margolis, D.J., Localio, A.R., et al. (2009) Impact of pulmonary artery pressure on exercise function in severe COPD. *Chest*, 136, 412– 419.

Simonneau, G., Gatzoulis, M.A., Adatia, I., et al. (2013). Updated Clinical Classification of Pulmonary Hypertension. *J Am Coll Cardiol*, 62(25S), D34–41.

Spiropoulos, K., Trakada, G., Nikolaou, E, et al. (2003). Endothelin-1 levels in the pathophysiology of chronic obstructive pulmonary disease and bronchial asthma. *Respir Med*, 97, 983–9.

Sturani, C. Bassein, L. Schiavina, M., et al. (1983). Oral nifedipine in chronic cor pulmonale secondary to severe chronic obstructive pulmonary disease (COPD). *Chest*, 84, 135–42.

Su, Y., Han, W., Giraldo, C., et al. (1998). Effect of cigarette smoke extract on nitric oxide synthase in pulmonary artery endothelial cells. *Am J Respir Cell Mol Biol*, 19, 819–25.

Tan, R.T., Kuzo, R., Goodman, L.R., et al. (1998). Utility of CT scan evaluation for predicting pulmonary hypertension in patients with parenchymal lung disease. *Chest*, 113, 1250

Tapson, V.F. (2008) Acute Pulmonary Embolism. N Engl J Med, 358, 1037–1052.

Thabut, G., Dauriat, G., Stern J.B., et al. (2005). Pulmonary hemodynamics in advanced COPD candidates for lung volume reduction surgery or lung transplantation. *Chest*, 127, 1531–1536.

The PIOPED Investigators . (1990). Value of the ventilation/perfusion scan in acute pulmonary embolism. Results of the prospective investigation of pulmonary embolism diagnosis (PIOPED). *JAMA*. 263 (20), 2753 – 2759.

Thompson, B.T., Hassoun, P.M., Kradin, RL., et al. (1989). Acute and chronic hypoxic pulmonary hypertension in guinea pigs. *J Appl Physiol*, 66, 920–28.

Tillie-Leblond, I., Marquette, C.H., Perez, T., et al. (2006). Pulmonary embolism in patients with unexplained exacerbation of chronic obstructive pulmonary disease, prevalence and risk factors. *Ann Intern Med*, 144, 390–396.

Tramarin, R., Torbicki, A., Marchandise, B., et al. (1991). Doppler echocardiographic evaluation of pulmonary artery pressure in chronic obstructive pulmonary disease. A European multicentre study. Working Group on Noninvasive Evaluation of Pulmonary Artery Pressure. European Office of the World Health Organization, Copenhagen. *Eur Heart J*, 12, 103–11.

Vender,R.L. (1994). Chronic hypoxic pulmonary hypertension. Cell biology to pathophysiology. *Chest*, 106, 236–43.

Voelkel, N.F., Quaife, R.A., Leinwand, L.A., et al. (2006). Right ventricular function and failure, report of a national heart, lung, and blood institute working group on cellular and molecular mechanisms of right heart failure. *Circulation*, 114, 1883–1891.

Vonbank, K., Ziesche, R., Higenbottam, T.W., et al. (2003). Controlled prospective randomized trial on the effects on pulmonary haemodynamics of the ambulatory long term use of nitric oxide and oxygen in patients with severe COPD. *Thorax*, 58, 289–93.

Von Euler, U., Liljerstrand, G. (1946). Observations on the pulmonary arterial blood pressure in the cat. Act Physiol Scand, 12, 301–320.

Wedgwood, S., Dettman, R.W., Black, S.M. (2001). ET-1 stimulates pulmonary arterial smooth muscle cell proliferation via induction of reactive oxygen species. *Am J Physiol Lung Cell Mol Physiol*, 281, L1058–67.

Wells, J.M., Washko, G.R., Han, M.K., Abbas, N., et al, COPDGene Investigators; ECLIPSE Study Investigators. (2012). Pulmonary arterial enlargement and acute exacerbations of COPD. *N Engl J Med*. 367(10), 913–21.

Wells P.S., Anderson D.R., Rodger M., Stiell I., Dreyer J.F., Barnes D., Forgie M., Kovacs G., Ward J., Kovacs M.J. (2001). Excluding pulmonary embolism at the bedside without diagnostic imaging, management of patients with suspected pulmonary embolism presenting to the emergency department by using a simple clinical model and d-dimer. *Ann Intern Med*, 135(2), 98–107.

Weir, E.K., Archer, S.L. (1995). The mechanism of acute hypoxic pulmonary vasoconstriction, the tale of two channels. *FASEB J*, 9, 183–9.

Weitzenblum, E., Hirth, C., Ducolone, A., et al. (1981). Prognostic value of pulmonary artery pressure in chronic obstructive pulmonary disease. *Thorax*, 36, 752–758.

Weitzenblum, E., Sautegeau, A., Erhart, M., et al. (1984). Long-term course of pulmonary arterial pressure in chronic obstructive pulmonary disease. *Am Rev Respir Dis*, 130, 993–998.

Weitzenblum, E., Sautegeau, A., Ehrhart, M., et al. (1985). Long-term oxygen therapy can reverse the progression of pulmonary hypertension in patients with chronic obstructive pulmonary disease. *Am Rev Respir Dis*, 131, 493–8.

Wilkinson, M., Langhorne, C.A., Heath, D., et al. (1988). A pathophysiological study of 10 cases of hypoxic cor pulmonale. *Q J Med*, 66, 65–85.

Wright, J.L. (1993). Relationship of pulmonary arterial pressure and airflow obstruction to emphysema. *J Appl Physiol*, 74, 1320–4.

Wright, J.L., Lawson, L., Pare, P.D., et al. (1983). The structure and function of the pulmonary vasculature in mild chronic obstructive pulmonary disease. The effect of oxygen and exercise. *Am Rev Respir Dis*, 128, 702–7.

Wright, J.L., Petty, T., Thurlbeck, W.M. (1992). Analysis of the structure of the muscular pulmonary arteries in patients with pulmonary hypertension and COPD, National Institutes of Health nocturnal oxygen therapy trial. *Lung*, 170, 109–24.

Wright ,J.L., Tai, H., Dai, J., et al. (2002). Cigarette smoke induces rapid changes in gene expression in pulmonary arteries. *Lab Invest*, 82, 1391–8.

Wright, J.L., Tai, H., Churg, A., (2004). Cigarette smoke induces persisting increases of vasoactive mediators in pulmonary arteries. *Am J Respir Cell Mol Biol*, 31, 501–9.

Yan, S.F., Zou, Y.S., Gao, Y., Zhai,, et al. (1998). Tissue factor transcription driven by EGR-1 is a critical mechanism of murine pulmonary fibrin deposition in hypoxia. *Proc Natl Acad Sci USA*, 95, 8298–8303.

Mary E. Panos, Ralph J. Panos, MD

# 13 COPD's Effects on Psychosocial Functioning and Familial Interactions

Key Points

1. COPD profoundly affects patients' psychosocial functions and these adverse effects may deleteriously affect a patient's perception and response to COPD's respiratory manifestations.
2. The prevalence of depression, anxiety, and panic disorders is markedly increased in individuals with COPD.
3. Depression and anxiety are associated with increased healthcare utilization and morbidity and mortality.
4. Panic disorders may impair patients' ability to react to and treat acute exacerbations of COPD.
5. Cognitive dysfunction may impair the ability to use or adhere with respiratory treatments, daily function, and interpersonal relationships.
6. The familial and social networks of patients with COPD are frequently reduced and interpersonal relationships are strained, causing stress for all parties.
7. Pulmonary rehabilitation reduces anxiety and depression associated with COPD.

## 13.1 Introduction

COPD is associated with psychosocial disorders including depression, anxiety, panic attacks, and cognitive impairment as well as alterations in interpersonal relationships (Fan, 2014). These psychological comorbidities may worsen the underlying disease, alter the perception of respiratory symptoms, and may affect self-management of COPD (DeJean, 2013). Cognitive impairment may affect a patient's ability to understand or remember medications or appointments. Changes in social interactions may lead to social isolation, spousal or familial conflict, and may affect psychological manifestations of COPD. Although profound psychosocial alterations may accompany COPD, these processes have only recently been comprehensively studied and optimal approaches to treatment are still under evaluation.

## 13.2 Depression

Depression is an altered mood characterized by a loss of interest or pleasure in life's activities (American Psychiatric Association, 2013). The Diagnostic and Statistical Manual (DSM) IV criteria for major depression are presented in Table 13.1. Measures of depression in patients with COPD include the Beck Depression Inventory, the Center

**Table 13.1:** DSM-IV Criteria for Major Depressive Disorder (APA, 2013)

**Criteria for Major Depressive Disorder**

Depressed mood or a loss of interest or pleasure in daily activities for more than two weeks.
- Mood represents a change from the person's baseline.
- Impaired function: social, occupational, educational.
- Specific symptoms, at least 5 of these 9, present nearly every day:
  1. **Depressed mood or irritable** most of the day, nearly every day, as indicated by either subjective report (e.g. feels sad or empty) or observation made by others (e.g. appears tearful).
  2. **Decreased interest or pleasure** in most activities, most of each day
  3. **Significant weight change (5%) or change in appetite**
  4. **Change in sleep**: Insomnia or hypersomnia
  5. **Change in activity**: Psychomotor agitation or retardation
  6. **Fatigue or loss of energy**
  7. **Guilt/worthlessness:** Feelings of worthlessness or excessive or inappropriate guilt
  8. **Concentration**: Diminished ability to think or concentrate, or more indecisiveness
  9. **Suicidality:** Thoughts of death or suicide, or has suicide plan

for Epidemiological Studies Depression Inventory, the Patient Health Questionnaire Depression Scale, and the Hospital Anxiety and Depression Scale (Beck, 1978; Radloff, 1977; Kroenke, 2001; Zigmond, 1983).

### 13.2.1 Prevalence

The prevalence of depression among individuals with COPD ranges from 7–88% and depends upon the sample population of patients with COPD, airflow limitation severity, and the diagnostic tool(s) used to define depression (Yohannes, 2010; Hynninen, 2005; Putman-Casdorph, 2009). COPD increases the risk of concurrent depression, relative risk (RR) 1.69 [95% confidence interval (CI) 1.45–1.96] and depression increases the risk of mortality in those with COPD, RR 1.83 [95% CI 1.00–3.36] (Atlantis, 2013). A meta-analysis revealed an odds ratio (OR) of 2.8 for depression among individuals with COPD compared with healthy controls (Zhang, 2011). A 2013 meta-analysis of 6 studies showed that COPD is associated with an increased risk of depression, RR 1.69 [95% CI 1.45-1.96] (Atlantis, 2013).

Only one third of patients with COPD and high depression scores have been diagnosed with treatment relevant depression and only 22% have been treated (Hanania, 2011). The estimated annual care cost for patients with COPD and associated depression or anxiety is $28,961 versus $22,512 for COPD alone (Dalal, 2011).

A review of 38,010 patients with a new diagnosis of COPD from 2000–2004 compared with matched controls in Taiwan demonstrated that incident depression was 1.88 fold greater in those with COPD (12.2 versus 6.47 per 1000 person years) and that the diagnosis of depression was greatest in the year after COPD diagnosis and declined thereafter (Tsai, 2013). Younger women, lower socioeconomic status, hospitalization, and comorbidities (hypertension, arthritis, cancer, and cardiovascular disease) were associated with an increased diagnosis of depression (Tsai, 2013).

In another group of 245 patients with COPD, 17.6% had depression defined by a Centers for Epidemiologic Studies Depression (CES-D) scale of 24 or higher and the presence of depression increased with the BODE quartile but did not correlate with COPD severity measured by GOLD stage (Kim, 2014). The level of education was inversely correlated with the prevalence of depression (Kim, 2014).

In a group of 307 patients with COPD, 12.4% had anxiety, 9.1% had depression, and 16.3% had both anxiety and depression measured by the Hospital Anxiety and Depression Scale (HADS) (Hilmarsen, 2014). Anxiety and depression scores correlated with COPD Assessment Test (CAT) scores, a disease-specific health status survey, but not with updated GOLD scores (Hilmarsen, 2014). In contrast, others have found a higher prevalence of anxiety and depression in patients with former GOLD stage IV compared with stages I and II (Janssen, 2010) and among patients with greater respiratory symptoms (updated GOLD groups B and D) (Lee, 2013).

### 13.2.2 Manifestations

Manifestations of depression in patients with COPD include poor self-reported health status, feelings of hopelessness and pessimism, poor sleep quality and quantity (see Chapter 11, COPD and Sleep), reduced appetite, concentration, and social interactions, fatigue, and lassitude (Felker, 2001; Emery, 2008). Depression may be associated with increased somatization and heightened awareness and sensitivity to respiratory symptoms. Depression and activities of daily living appear to be more important determinants of quality of life than severity of airflow impairment (Yohannes, 1998). Functional impairment, disability, and health status are worse for depressed patients with COPD compared with those who do not have depression and functional capacity may be more highly correlated with depression than severity of pulmonary physiologic impairment (Graydon, 1995; Yohannes, 1998; Yohannes, 2005; Felker, 2001; Kim, 2000). Individuals with COPD and depression are less likely to utilize self-management strategies or healthy behaviors such as smoking cessation compared with those who are not depressed (Stapleton, 2005; Dowson, 2004; Wagena, 2004).

Higher anxiety and depression levels are associated with greater fatigue, breathlessness, and frequency of respiratory symptoms among patients with COPD (Doyle, 2013). Depression, along with poor health status and COPD severity, is a key predictor of reduced physical activity (a key prognostic indicator in COPD) measured by walking less than 30 minutes daily (Miravitlles, 2014). In contrast, others have shown that depression is associated with poorer quality of life but not reduced activities of daily living (Weldam, 2013). A meta-analysis of studies evaluating depression and quality of life among individuals with COPD and airflow limitation confirmed by spirometry showed that depression significantly correlated with health related quality of life, pooled r=0.48, 95% CI 0.37–0.57 (Blakemore, 2014).

Individuals with COPD have twice the prevalence of insomnia (adjusted odds ratio (aOR), 2.4) compared with the general population and nearly half (48.1%) of individuals with COPD have insomnia (Ohayon, 2014). Most individuals with COPD and depression (84.4%) or anxiety (59.7%) had associated insomnia symptoms (Ohayon, 2014). Co-occurrence of insomnia and depression or anxiety was associated with a five-fold increase of hospitalization for COPD and a reduced quality of life (Ohayon, 2014).

### 13.2.3 Mortality

Depression is a risk factor for mortality in individuals with COPD (Atlantis, 2013; Yohannes, 2005; de Voogd, 2009). A meta-analysis of 16 studies following 28,759 individuals with COPD for 1 to 8 years showed that depression was associated with increased mortality, RR 1.43 [95% CI, 1.00–3.36] (Atlantis, 2013). Among 100 patients hospitalized for acute exacerbations of COPD, 56% had depression, and depression was associated with an increased one year mortality, OR 1.13 [95% CI, 1.02–1.26] (Yohannes, 2005). Depression was associated with a greater mortality, OR 1.93 [95% CI, 1.12–3.33], among 121 patients with COPD who completed inpatient pulmonary rehabilitation and were followed for 8.5 years (de Voogd, 2009).

### 13.2.4 Healthcare Utilization

Anxiety and depression are significant factors associated with admissions and readmissions for COPD exacerbations. Other factors include: reduced quality of life, COPD severity, female sex, lower BODE scores, persistent smoking, increased breathlessness, hypercapnea, hypoxemia, long term oxygen use, sense of loss, inability to cope, decrease in self-efficacy, poor adherence to therapy, lower socioeconomic status, and prior COPD exacerbations (Pooler, 2014). Depression may reduce an individual's motivation to seek assistance either medically or socially.

A 2012 meta-analysis of nine prospective studies showed that, among individuals with COPD, the number of exacerbations requiring hospitalization was increased in those with concurrent depression (RR 1.12, 95% CI 1.02–1.24) and both anxiety and depression (RR 1.18, 95% CI 1.01–1.38) but not with anxiety alone (RR 1.05, 95% CI 0.92–1.19) (Laurin, 2012). A subsequent 2013 meta-analysis of 13 studies showed that anxiety or depression were associated with an increased risk of adverse COPD-related outcomes (RR 1.43, 95% CI 1.22–1.68) and that depression increased the risk of mortality (RR 1.83, 95% CI 1.00–3.36) (Atlantis, 2013).

Anxiety and depression are associated with activation of the hypothalamic-pituitary-adrenal axis and increased systemic inflammation (Cameron, 2004; Ehlert, 2001; Bremmer, 2008; Joynt, 2004). Anxiety and depression are also associated with low self-confidence or self-efficacy which may detrimentally affect a number of health care activities including physical activity, medication adherence, smoking cessation, healthful nutrition, and pulmonary rehabilitation engagement (Laurin, 2012).

### 13.2.5 Management

Increased disease knowledge, self-efficacy, and better perceived social support are associated with fewer depressive symptoms in individuals with COPD (Lee, 2013). Problem-oriented coping strategies that focus on eliminating the source of the stress or learning how to best cope with the stressor may translate into a better understanding of COPD into less depressive symptoms and may provide a mechanism of intervention to alleviate psychological symptoms of COPD (Lee, 2013). Controlled breathing techniques (relaxation exercises, pursed-lip breathing, and active expiration) taught by respiratory therapists may reduce breathlessness, anxiety, and depression in patients hospitalized with COPD exacerbations (Valenza, 2014). Systemic review of randomized controlled trials of psychological and or lifestyle interventions for individuals with COPD showed that exercise training was the only intervention associated with significant treatment effects for depression and anxiety (Coventry, 2013).

#### 13.2.5.1 Pharmacologic Treatment

Antidepressants have not been shown to induce remission of depression or to reduce respiratory symptoms in individuals with COPD (Yohannes, 2014). A review of pharmacologic treatment of depression in COPD analyzed six studies of selective serotonin reuptake inhibitors and four trials of tricyclic antidepressants and concluded that there is no conclusive evidence for the efficacy of any antidepressant in this patient population (Yohannes, 2014). In a retrospective analysis of 17,320 Medicare beneficiaries with COPD, 86.8% of those with concurrent depression were receiving antidepressant treatment, and treatment was associated with lower mortality, hazard ratio (HR) 0.55 [99% CI, 0.44–0.68] (Qian, 2013). Further studies are required to determine the efficacy and optimal class of antidepressant for the management of depression in individuals with COPD.

#### 13.2.5.2 Pulmonary Rehabilitation

Pulmonary rehabilitation reduces levels of anxiety and depression for individuals with all levels of COPD severity (Tselebis, 2013; Emery, 1998; Griffiths, 2000; Guell, 2006; Guell, 2006; Withers, 1999; Hui, 2003). Individuals who do not complete pul-

**Table 13.2:** DSM-IV Criteria for the Diagnosis of Generalized Anxiety Disorder (APA, 2013)

| **Criteria for Generalized Anxiety** |
| --- |
| – At least 6 months of "excessive anxiety and worry" about a variety of events and situations. Generally, "excessive" can be interpreted as more than would be expected for a particular situation or event. Most people become anxious over certain things, but the intensity of the anxiety typically corresponds to the situation. |
| – There is significant difficulty in controlling the anxiety and worry. If someone has a very difficult struggle to regain control, relax, or cope with the anxiety and worry, then this requirement is met. |
| – The presence for most days over the previous six months of 3 or more (only 1 for children) of the following symptoms:<br>1. Feeling wound-up, tense, or restless<br>2. Easily becoming fatigued or worn-out<br>3. Concentration problems<br>4. Irritability<br>5. Significant tension in muscles<br>6. Difficulty with sleep |
| – The symptoms are not part of another mental disorder. |

monary rehabilitation have higher rates of depression and somatization measured by the SCL-90 compared with those who complete rehabilitation (Tselebis, 2014). Pulmonary rehabilitation participants with anxiety and or depression are 10 fold more likely not to achieve the minimal clinically important difference improvement in breathlessness (Hornikx, 2013).

## 13.3 Anxiety

Anxiety is an apprehensive anticipation of danger or stressful situations associated with increased nervousness or worry (APA, 2013). The DSM-IV criteria for the diagnosis of Generalized Anxiety Disorder are presented in Table 13.2. Anxiety disorders associated with COPD include generalized anxiety disorder (6–33%), panic disorder (with or without agoraphobia) (0–41%), specific phobia (10–27%), and social phobia (5–11%) (Willgoss, 2013). The Anxiety Inventory for Respiratory Disease (AIR) is a COPD-specific nonsomatic anxiety scale that can be used to screen for and measure anxiety in individuals with COPD and correlates well with the Hospital Anxiety and Depression-Anxiety subscale (Willgoss, 2013). Other anxiety measures include the Beck Anxiety Inventory, the State-Trait Anxiety Inventory, and the Hospital Anxiety and Depression Scale (Beck, 1988; Spielberger, 1970; Zigmond, 1983). Surveys that include screens for somatic complaints such as shortness of breath and tiredness tend to overestimate the prevalence of anxiety among individuals with COPD because of the overlap of symptoms between anxiety and COPD (Mikkelsen, 2004).

### 13.3.1 Prevalence

The reported prevalence of anxiety among individuals with COPD ranges widely from 2–100% and depends upon the sample population of patients with COPD, airflow limitation severity, and the diagnostic tool(s) used to define anxiety (Brenes, 2003; Mikkelsen, 2004; Yohannes, 2010; Hynninen, 2005; Putman-Casdorph, 2009). The prevalence of anxiety ranges from 10–55% in hospitalized patients to 13–46% among outpatients with COPD and is greater among women than men (Willgoss, 2013).

Anxiety is related to depression in individuals with COPD; 37% of those patients with COPD and depression have anxiety, whereas only 5% of nondepressed individuals have anxiety (Yohannes, 2000). In a study of 45 Veterans with COPD, anxiety and depression scores were highly correlated and all participants with mild or moderate anxiety also had depression (Light, 1985). Greater use of catastrophic coping strategies, higher levels of negative social support, and lower levels of symptom self-management are associated with greater anxiety among men with COPD whereas higher levels of positive social support are associated with less anxiety (McCathie, 2002). Anxiety levels are associated with greater social isolation (Lustig, 1972). A meta-analysis of studies evaluating anxiety and quality of life among individuals with COPD and airflow limitation confirmed by spirometry showed that anxiety significantly correlated with health related quality of life, pooled r=0.36, 95% CI 0.23–0.48 (Blakemore, 2014).

Anxiety levels in individuals with COPD are higher in women than men, current smokers than nonsmokers, and those with marital dissatisfaction (Ashmore, 2005; Gudmundsson, 2006). Most, but not all, studies suggest that anxiety levels do not correlate with levels of resting or exertional breathlessness, airflow limitation severity, or other pulmonary physiologic impairments (Garuti, 2003; Gudmundsson, 2006; Hajiro, 2000; Wagena, 2005; Engstrom, 1996; Dowson, 2001). The relationship between breathlessness and anxiety is unclear but Bailey has proposed a "dyspnea-anxiety-dyspnea" cycle that suggests that anxiety does not cause breathlessness but is a sign of dyspnea (Bailey, 2004).

Levels of anxiety do not correlate with pulmonary physiology or 12 minute walking tests (Light, 1985). Anxious individuals experience more symptoms of nicotine withdrawal upon smoking cessation and, therefore, may have a higher predilection to nicotine addiction due to increased difficulty in stopping smoking (Breslau, 1992; Hill, 2008).

In patients presenting to the emergency department with respiratory exacerbations of asthma or COPD, the presence of anxiety and or depression correlated with hospitalization and relapse within 30 days (Dahlen, 2002). Among patients hospitalized with a COPD exacerbation, greater anxiety is associated with a higher risk of rehospitalization within 12 months, HR 1.07, 95% CI 1.03–1.11, per 4 unit increase in the hospital anxiety and depression scale (Gudmundsson, 2005). In contrast, a study of 43 Veterans showed that anxiety and depression were associated with poor functional status but not with inpatient or outpatient healthcare utilization (Kim, 2000). Poor emotional functioning measured by the chronic respiratory questionnaire portends higher mortality in women with COPD who live alone and are prescribed long-term oxygen (Crockett, 2002).

### 13.3.2 Manifestations

Manifestations of anxiety in patients with COPD include muscle tension, breathlessness, chronic worry, palpitations, feeling on edge, nausea, numbness, and fear of losing control (Emery, 2008). Anxiety correlates with quality of life in patients with COPD (Brenes, 2003). Many individuals with COPD and anxiety experience panic attacks (see Panic Attack section below).

### 13.3.3 Management of Anxiety

#### 13.3.3.1 Pharmacotherapy

Two trials of buspirone, a serotonin receptor agonist, yielded mixed results, whereas citalopram, a selective serotonin reuptake inhibitor, was not effective in treating anxiety in patients with COPD (Argyropoulou, 1993; Singh, 1993; Silvertooth, 2004). Nortriptyline, a tricyclic antidepressant, effectively reduced both anxiety and depression (Borson, 1992). Due to a paucity of studies, a 2011 Cochrane analysis was not able to determine whether pharmacological treatment of anxiety disorders in individuals with COPD was effective (Usmani, 2011).

#### 13.3.3.2 Nonpharmacotherapy

Psychotherapy has yielded mixed results for the treatment of anxiety in pulmonary rehabilitation programs (Lustig, 1972; de Godoy, 2003; Renfroe, 1988). A systemic meta-analysis of psychologically based interventions for the psychological manifestations of COPD showed benefit that was limited to anxiety (Baraniak, 2011). A qualitative study of 14 individuals with COPD and self-reported symptoms of anxiety revealed intense thoughts of fear, hopelessness, and confusion that were associated with anxiety and panic attacks and ameliorated with self-talk coping strategies (Willgoss, 2012). Progressive muscle relaxation techniques do not reduce anxiety in patients with COPD (Renfroe, 1988; Gift, 1992; Sassi-Dambron, 1995). Participation in comprehensive pulmonary rehabilitation reduces anxiety in patients with COPD (Emery, 1991; Griffiths, 2000; Guell, 2006; Kayahan, 2006; Emery, 1998).

**Table 13.3:** DSM-IV Criteria for Panic Attack (APA, 2013)

| Criteria for Panic Attack |
| --- |
| A brief period of intense fear or discomfort in which four or more of these 13 symptoms develop abruptly and reach a peak within 10 minutes: |
| 1. Palpitations, pouncing heart, or accelerated heart rate |
| 2. Sweating |
| 3. Trembling or shaking |
| 4. Sensations of shortness of breath or smothering |
| 5. Feeling of choking |
| 6. Chest pain or discomfort |
| 7. Nausea or abdominal distress |
| 8. Feeling dizzy, unsteady, lightheaded, or faint |
| 9. Derealization (feelings of unreality) or depersonalization (being detached from oneself) |
| 10. Fear of losing control or going crazy |
| 11. Fear of dying |
| 12. Paresthesias (numbness of tingling sensations) |
| 13. Chills or hot flushes |

## 13.4 Panic Attacks

Panic attack is defined as a brief period of intense fear or discomfort in which four or more of 13 symptoms (listed in Table 13.3) develop abruptly and reach a peak within 10 minutes (Craske, 2010).

Panic disorder is defined as recurrent panic attacks, at least one of which has been followed by one month of any or all of persistent concern about having additional attacks or their consequences; worry about the implications of the attack or its consequences or a significant change in behavior related to the attacks; the panic attacks are not due to the direct physiological effects of a substance or a general medical condition; the panic attacks are not better accounted for by another mental disorder (Craske, 2010). In individuals with COPD, panic disorder can only be diagnosed when the panic attacks are not cued by internal stressors such as respiratory infections triggering COPD exacerbations or by external stressors such as exertion (Livermore, 2010).

### 13.4.1 Prevalence

Depending upon the population of COPD patients sampled and the method and threshold for defining and identifying panic attacks and panic disorder, between 6.5 and 67% of patients with COPD have a diagnosis of panic disorder (Weaver, 1997; Kim, 2000; Patten, 2007; Hallas, 2009; Kunik, 2005; Pollack, 1996; Livermore, 2010).

In a study of hospitalized patients with COPD, 73% of those with an anxiety disorder had panic disorder with agoraphobia (Voegele, 2008). Conversely, the lifetime prevalence of respiratory disorders is greater in patients with panic disorder (47%) compared with those with obsessive-compulsive disorder (13%) or eating disorders (13%) (Zanderbergen, 1991) and more patients with panic disorders have respiratory diseases, especially bronchitis, than those with other anxiety disorders, 42.7 versus 16.2% (Verburg, 1995A). Over 12 months, 63% of individuals with COPD experience at least one panic attack and, when surveyed, 37–51% have had a panic attack in the prior 3–4 weeks (Porzelius, 1992; Howard, 2009). Elderly women with COPD report more panic attacks than those without COPD, OR 4.13 [95% CI, 2.65–6.43] (Smoller, 2003). A large European telephone survey of 10,854 adults reported an adjusted odds ratio of 7.1 for panic disorder among those with COPD compared with those who did not have COPD (Ohayon, 2014). Predictors of panic-spectrum psychopathology in individuals with COPD include more severe depressive symptoms, greater catastrophic interpretations of shortness of breath, greater anxiety sensitivity, and degree of recent life stressors, and lower $FEV_1$ (Livermore, 2012). Individuals with COPD and panic disorder have a heightened sensation of breathlessness during inspiratory load testing compared with age-matched individuals with similar levels of airflow limitation and COPD (Livermore, 2008; Giardino, 2010). This increased sensation of dyspnea appears to be due to heightened emotional responses to breathlessness rather than increased interoceptive sensitivity (Giardino, 2010). Patients with panic disorder experience a greater increase in subjective anxiety when exposed to 35% $CO_2$ than individuals with generalized anxiety disorder (Verburg, 1995B).

Individuals with COPD and panic disorder have more frequent and longer respiratory hospital admissions (Yellowlees, 1987; Gudmundsson, 2005) and greater disability and impaired function (Kim, 2000) than those without panic disorder. COPD self management may be impaired in individuals with panic disorders (Dowson, 2004).

### 13.4.2 Treatment of Panic Disorder

Although cognitive behavioral therapy (CBT) has been demonstrated to be effective management of panic disorder in individuals who do not have COPD, its efficacy in those with COPD is less clear (Barrera, 2014; Livermore, 2010). Several studies have shown that CBT may reduce both panic attacks and respiratory hospitalizations in patients with COPD, but these studies have used different therapeutic presentations (group versus individual sessions), concurrent education and or exercise sessions, and varying durations of therapy and follow up (Livermore, 2010; Kunik, 2001; Kunik, 2007; de Godoy, 2003; Emery, 1998).

Benzodiazepines are effective treatments for panic attacks and panic disorder; however, they should be used cautiously in patients with COPD due to the potential to blunt respiratory drive and to cause or worsen hypercapnea (Smoller, 1996). Other pharmacologic treatments for panic disorders in individuals with COPD include selective serotonin reuptake inhibitors and tricyclic antidepressants (Smoller, 1996).

## 13.5 Cognitive Impairment

Neuropsychological impairment may occur in individuals with COPD, especially those with hypoxemia (Dodd, 2010; Klein, 2010). The optimal screening test for cognitive function in individuals with COPD has not been determined. A study of the validity of the Mini-Mental State Examination (MMSE) and the Montreal Cognitive Assessment (MoCA) compared with a comprehensive neuropsychologic assessment in individuals with COPD showed that the MMSE did not have an acceptable cutoff and the optimal MoCA cutoff was 26 (Villeneuve, 2012).

### 13.5.1 Prevalence

The prevalence of cognitive dysfunction among individuals with COPD ranges from 10.4–48.5% depending upon the population studied and the methods used to detect cognitive impairment (Antonelli-Inc, 2006; Incalzi, 1993; Villeneuve, 2012; Schou, 2012). The prevalence of mild cognitive impairment among patients with moderate to severe COPD is 36% compared with 12% among healthy controls and the major impairment was nonamnestic mild cognitive impairment with attention and executive dysfunctions (Villeneuve, 2012). In a survey of 27,106 nursing home residents with COPD, 62% had short-term memory impairment and 43.3% had moderately or severely impaired daily decision making cognitive skills (Zarowitz, 2012).

Cognitive function measured by the MoCA test is more impaired among patients with acute COPD exacerbations than in those with stable COPD (Crisan, 2014). Greater deficits occurred in language abstraction and attention and delayed recall and orientation than in visuospatial and naming functions. Impairment was negatively correlated with pulmonary function and positively associated with measures of inflammation and level of $CO_2$ (Crisan, 2014). A multivariate analysis of factors associated with cognitive impairment among individuals with stable COPD and varying levels of physiologic impairment showed that only the number of COPD exacerbations in the prior year was associated with reduced cognitive function measured by an array of standardized neuropsychological tests (Tulek, 2014).

A longitudinal study of elderly individuals showed that COPD increased the risk for nonamnestic mild cognitive impairment (NA-MCI) by 83% and that those individuals with a diagnosis of COPD for more than 5 years had the greatest risk for NA-MCI, HR 1.58 [95% CI, 1.04–2.40] (Singh, 2013; Singh, 2014). In the Cardiovascular Risk Factors, Aging, and Dementia study, a population-based longitudinal study with

25 years of follow-up, midlife COPD was associated with an increased risk for mild cognitive impairment, HR 1.85 [95% CI, 1.05–3.28] (Rusanen, 2013).

When cognitive function is measured among individuals hospitalized for acute exacerbations of COPD, 57% have impaired function, and 20% have a pathologic loss in processing speed and there was no improvement 3 months after recovery (Dodd, 2013). Cognitive function in patients with acute on chronic respiratory failure requiring mechanical ventilation is worse at hospital discharge compared with healthy controls but improves to comparable levels within six months (Ambrosino, 2002). Cognitive impairment was associated with worse quality of life measured by the St. George's Respiratory Questionnaire and longer length of hospital stay (Dodd, 2013). Among the 432 individuals with COPD in the Cardiovascular Health Study, co-existing COPD and cognitive impairment were associated with increased respiratory-related, aHR 4.10 [95% CI, 1.86–9.05], and all cause hospitalizations, aHR 1.34 [95% CI, 1.00–1.80] and death, aHR2.29 [95% CI, 1.18–4.45] (Chang, 2012). Impaired performance on the copy with landmark test is associated with an increased mortality risk in individuals with severe COPD (Antonelli-Incalzi, 2006).

In patients with hypoxemic respiratory failure treated with supplemental oxygen, worse physiologic function measured by severity of airflow obstruction may predict those individuals who will experience cognitive decline (Incalzi, 1998). Poor adherence to medications is associated with impaired verbal memory measured by the delayed recall test (Incalzi, 1997).

### 13.5.2 Manifestations

Cognitive impairment may be associated with effects on day-to-day function in individuals with COPD. Driving simulation testing demonstrates increased accident frequency among individuals with COPD compared with healthy controls (Orth, 2008). Activities of daily living including self-administration of medications, continence, fiscal responsibility, and dressing correlate better with cognitive function than with lung physiologic function in individuals with COPD (Antonelli-Incalzi, 2008). Further, impaired cognitive function correlates with inability to perform technically acceptable pulmonary function testing (Allen, 2008).

Hippocampal atrophy measured by magnetic resonance imaging is associated with cognitive dysfunction and chronic hypoxemia in individuals with COPD (Li, 2013). Serum S100B levels correlate with cognitive impairment in COPD and may be a useful biomarker (Li, 2013). Among individuals with COPD, hypoxemia, $SpO_2<88\%$, correlates with greater cognitive impairment, OR 5.45 (95% CI, 1.014–29.2) and the use of supplemental oxygen decreases the risk, OR 0.14 (95% CI, 0.07–0.27) (Thakur, 2010). Short term reduction of the $SpO_2$ to 85% by reduction of the inspired oxygen concentration in patients with COPD does not affect cognitive function measured by multiple tests suggesting that chronic rather than transient oxygen desaturation may be critical in the development of cognitive impairment (Martin, 2011). Similarly, acute oxygen treatment does not improve neuropsychological test performance (Vos, 1995; Wilson, 1985). Longer term supplemental oxygen has either no or minimal benefits on cognitive function (Heaton, 1983; Krop, 1973; Incalzi, 1993; Hjalmarsen, 1999; Borak, 1996; Incalzi, 1993). Chronic hypoxemia combined with hypercapnia may be significant etiologic factors in the development of cognitive impairment in individuals with COPD (Zheng, 2008). Cerebral perfusion is diminished in patients with COPD and is more reduced in those with hypoxemia than in those with normoxemia and the reduction in perfusion correlates with cognitive impairment (Ortapamuk, 2006; Antonelli-Incalzi, 2003).

### 13.5.3 Management

Pulmonary rehabilitation and exercise may improve cognitive function among individuals with COPD (Etnier, 2001; Angevaren, 2008; Emery, 2008). Acute and prolonged (10 weeks) exercise improves performance on the Verbal Fluency test (Emery, 2001; Emery, 1998). Individuals who maintain an exercise regimen after pulmonary rehabilitation sustain improvements in cognitive and psychological function, whereas those who stop exercising lose the benefits of rehabilitation (Emery, 2003). Lung volume reduction surgery may be associated with six month improvements in visuomotor speed that are not sustained one or two years after surgery (Kozora, 2008; Kozora, 2011). Cognitive training is not effective in improving cognitive function in individuals with COPD (Incalzi, 2008).

## 13.6 Social Interactions

The effect of COPD on social interactions has only recently been investigated. In older individuals, negative social interactions have greater effects than positive interactions (Newsom, 2005). Perceived negative social support is associated with higher levels of anxiety and depression among patients with COPD, whereas positive social support correlates with less anxiety and depression (McCathie, 2002). Individuals with COPD often experience a shrinking social network and nearly one third of Veterans with COPD felt social and familial isolation due to respiratory limitations on activities and concern for developing respiratory symptoms or distress with activities or interactions (Panos, 2013). Individuals with COPD who are homebound have increased risk of hospitalization during the winter in the United Kingdom (Jordan, 2008) and those with reduced social support have a 50% increased risk of hospital admissions for COPD (Partridge, 2011). Patients with COPD who are single have an 18% higher admission rate for COPD exacerbations than those individuals with a supporting spouse (Wong, 2008). Socio-economic deprivation measured by the Scottish Index of Multiple Deprivation (a weighted index of seven domains: employment, income, crime, housing, health, education, and access) correlates with the frequency of hospital admissions for COPD (McAllister, 2013). Negative social support, perceived insensitive and unsympathetic responses by social network members and perception that their social network let them down when needed, and receipt of instrumental support, receiving aid or assistance from others, are associated with greater anxiety among patients with COPD. Negative social support may foster fears of social isolation and rejection whereas instrumental support may realize an individual's needs and dependence upon others (DiNicola, 2013).

A higher perceived level of social support correlates with better overall functioning in depressed elderly with COPD (Marino, 2008). Positively perceived social support is associated with fewer hospitalizations and COPD exacerbations, improved quality of life, and increased self-efficacy for including participation in health promoting activities such as smoking cessation and physical activity (Harris, 2007; Lee, 1991; Murray, 1995).

## 13.7 Effect of COPD on Caregivers

Until recently, the effect of COPD on caregivers has not been fully examined, interventions to improve COPD management have largely ignored nonhealthcare providers, and economic analyses of COPD's costs usually do not include care provided by family or others (Caress, 2009). Nearly two thirds (63.5%) of caregivers have anxiety, 34% have depression, and 27.1% have both anxiety and depression (Jacome, 2014). Perceived burden and limitation on activities, female gender, and older age were significant predictors of caregivers' anxiety and depression (Jacome, 2014).

The number of tasks that a caregiver must supervise for an individual with COPD correlates with symptoms of depression, anxiety, interpersonal sensitivity, hostility, stress, and psychotropic medication use (Cossette, 1993). Increasing emotional support caused the greatest stress on caregivers (Cossette, 1993). The burden felt by caregivers of individuals with COPD was greater among younger caregivers and did not correlate with gender, education, perceived financial capability, or employment status (Cain, 2000). In interviews of women caring for husbands with COPD, Bergs (Bergs, 2002) found that the women were dissatisfied with their recreation, lack of support from other family members, friends, and the healthcare system; they desired more information and support from healthcare providers, recognition of their caring role, and opportunities for respite care. Less positive and more negative dyadic coping (methods of dealing with stress within a couple) are associated with greater psychological stress including anxiety and depression and lower quality of life, and the higher the patient perceived the imbalance in delegated dyadic coping, the lower the couple's quality of life (Meier, 2011). Patient marital adjustment is associated with patient well-being and partner marital adjustment is associated with patient physical function (Ashmore, 2005). Patients with poor marital adjustment experience greater improvements in psychological functioning after pulmonary rehabilitation than those with better marital adjustment (Ashmore, 2005). Qualitative studies of the effect of COPD on family members identified several themes: restriction in family social life, emotional distress related to COPD exacerbations, tension in couple relationships, financial strain, and coping resources (Gabriel, 2014).

Caregivers of individuals with more advanced COPD have greater subjective burden, more symptoms of depression, and worse self-rated mental health than those caring for individuals with less severe COPD; the subjective burden increased with COPD severity, depression and anxiety comorbidities, caregiver hours per week, and self-rated mental health (Fiqueiredo, 2014). As an individual with COPD's respiratory status declines, caregiver tasks change, their relationship with the patient evolves, and they modify their expectations (Philip, 2014).

The interactions or perceptions of interactions between caregivers and individuals with COPD may affect the anxiety level. Individuals with COPD have greater anxiety levels if they perceive more insensitive and unsympathetic responses or feel that they are not supported when they need assistance or have greater anxiety levels (DiNicola, 2013). Both patients with COPD and their spouses have high and clinically significant levels of anxiety and depression and spouses who perceive patients to have higher levels of breathlessness report greater distress (Al-Gamal, 2014). They often feel powerless to relieve the breathlessness and suffering experienced by the patient (Booth, 2003; Seamark, 2004).

## 13.8 Conclusion

COPD is increasingly being recognized as a systemic process that affects the entire person, not only physiologically but also psychosocially. The psychological manifestations of COPD may severely affect the perception and reaction to respiratory symptoms leading to increased healthcare utilization and morbidity and mortality from COPD. The social and familial networks of individuals with COPD are often reduced and interpersonal relationships strained. Identification and management of the psychosocial manifestations of COPD is increasingly being recognized and optimal treatments are being studied.

## 13.9 Summary Points

1. The prevalence of depression among individuals with COPD ranges from 7–88%.
   - Depression may be associated with increased somatization and heightened awareness and sensitivity to respiratory symptoms.

- Manifestations of depression in patients with COPD include poor self-reported health status, feelings of hopelessness and pessimism, poor sleep quality and quantity, reduced appetite, concentration, and social interactions, fatigue, and lassitude. Anxiety and depression are significant factors associated with admissions and re-admissions for COPD exacerbations.
- Depression may reduce an individual's motivation to seek assistance either medically or socially.

2. Anxiety occurs in 2–100% of individuals with COPD.
   - Most, but not all, studies suggest that anxiety levels do not correlate with levels of resting or exertional breathlessness, airflow limitation severity or other pulmonary physiologic impairments.
   - Manifestations of anxiety in patients with COPD include muscle tension, breathlessness, chronic worry, palpitations, feeling on edge, nausea, numbness, and fear of losing control.
   - Anxiety negatively correlates with quality of life in patients with COPD.
3. Between 6.5 and 43% of patients with COPD have a diagnosis of panic disorder.
   - Individuals with COPD and panic disorder have more frequent and longer respiratory hospital admissions than those without panic disorder, greater disability, and impaired function.
   - COPD self-management may be impaired in individuals with panic disorders.
4. The prevalence of cognitive dysfunction among individuals with COPD ranges from 10.4–48.5%.
   - Co-existing COPD and cognitive impairment is associated with increased respiratory-related and all cause hospitalizations and death.
5. The effect of COPD on social interactions has only recently been investigated.
   - Positively perceived social support is associated with fewer hospitalizations and COPD exacerbations, improved quality of life, and increased self-efficacy including participation in health promoting activities such as smoking cessation and physical activity.

## References

Al-Gamal E. (2014). Quality of life, anxiety and depression among patients with chronic obstructive pulmonary disease and their spouses. *Issues Ment Health Nurs*, *35*(10), 761–7.

Allen S., Yeung P., Janczewski M., & Siddique N. (2008). Predicting inadequate spirometry technique and the use of FEV1/FEV3 as an alternative to FEV1/FVC for patients with mild cognitive impairment. *Clin Respir J*, *2*(4), 208–13.

American Psychiatric Association. (2013). *Diagnostic and statistical manual of mental disorders* (5th ed.).

Ambrosino N., Bruletti G., Scala V., Porta R., & Vitacca M. (2002). Cognitive and perceived health status in patient with chronic obstructive pulmonary disease surviving acute on chronic respiratory failure: a controlled study. *Intensive Care Med, 28*(2), 170–7.

Angevaren M., Aufdemkampe G., Verhaar H.J., Aleman A., & Vanhees L. (2008). Physical activity and enhanced fitness to improve cognitive function in older people without known cognitive impairment. *Cochrane Database Syst Rev*, 2, CD005381.

Antonelli Incalzi R., Marra C., Giordano A., Calcagni M.L., Cappa A., Basso S., Pagliari G., & Fuso L. (2003). Cognitive impairment in chronic obstructive pulmonary disease--a neuropsychological and spect study. *J Neurol*, *250*(3), 325–32.

Antonelli-Incalzi R., Corsonello A., Pedone C., Trojano L., Acanfora D., Spada A., Izzo O., & Rengo F. (2006). Drawing impairment predicts mortality in severe COPD. *Chest*, 2006, *130*(6), 1687–94.

Antonelli-Incalzi R., Corsonello A., Trojano L., Acanfora D., Spada A., Izzo O., & Rengo F. (2008). Correlation between cognitive impairment and dependence in hypoxemic COPD. *J Clin Exp Neuropsychol*, *30*(2), 141–50.

Argyropoulou P., Patakas D., Koukou A., Vasiliadis P., & Georgopoulos D. (1993). Buspirone effect on breathlessness and exercise performance in patients with chronic obstructive pulmonary disease. *Respiration*, *60*, 216–220.

Ashmore J.A., Emery C.F., Hauck E.R., & MacIntyre NR. (2005). Marital adjustment among patients with chronic obstructive pulmonary disease who are participating in pulmonary rehabilitation. *Heart Lung*, *34*(4), 270–8.

Atlantis E., Fahey P., Cochrane B., & Smith S. (2013). Bidirectional associations between clinically relevant depression or anxiety and COPD: a systematic review and meta-analysis. *Chest*, *144*(3), 766–77.

Bailey P.H. (2004) The dyspnea-anxiety-dyspnea cycle COPD patients' stories of breathlessness: "It's scary when you can't breathe". *Qual Health Res*, *14*, 760–78.

Baraniak A., & Sheffield D. (2011). The efficacy of psychologically based interventions to improve anxiety, depression and quality of life in COPD: a systematic review and meta-analysis. *Patient Educ Couns*, *83*(1), 29–36.

Barrera T.L., Grubbs K.M., Kunik M.E., & Teng E.J. (2014). A review of cognitive behavioral therapy for panic disorder in patients with chronic obstructive pulmonary disease: the rationale for interoceptive exposure. *J Clin Psychol Med Settings*, *21*(2), 144–54.

Beck A.T., Epstein N., Brown G., & Steer R.A. (1988). An inventory for measuring clinical anxiety: psychometric properties. *J Consult Clin Psychol*, *56*(6), 893–897.

Beck A.T. (1978) Depression inventory. Philadelphia: Center for CognitiveTherapy.

Bergs D. (2002). 'The hidden client' – women caring for husbands with COPD: their experience of quality of life. *Journal of Clinical Nursing*, *11*, 613–621.

Blakemore A., Dickens C., Guthrie E., Bower P., Kontopantelis E., Afzal C., & Coventry P.A. (2014). Depression and anxiety predict health-related quality of life in chronic obstructive pulmonary disease: systematic review and meta-analysis. *Int J Chron Obstruct Pulmon Dis*, *9*, 501–12.

Booth S., Silvester S., & Todd C. (2003). Breathlessness in cancer and chronic obstructive pulmonary disease: using a qualitative approach to describe the experience of patients and carers. *Palliat Support Care*, *1*(4), 337–44.

Borak J., Sliwinski P., Tobiasz M., Gorecka D., & Zielinski J. (1986). Psychological status of COPD patients before and after one year of long-term oxygen therapy. *Monaldi Arch Chest Dis*, *51*, 7–11.

Borson S., McDonald G.J., Gayle T., Deffebach M., Lakshminaravan S., & VanTuinen C. (1992). Improvement in mood, physical symptoms, and function with nortriptyline for depression in patients with chronic obstructive pulmonary disease. *Psychosomatics*, *33*, 190–201.

Bremmer M.A., Beekman A.T., Deeg D.J., Penninx B.W., Dik M.G., Hack C.E., & Hoogendijk W.J. (2008). Inflammatory markers in late-life depression: results from a population-based study. *J Affect Disord*, *106*, 249–255.

Brenes G.A. (2003). Anxiety and chronic obstructive pulmonary disease: prevalence, impact, and treatment. *PsychosomMed*, *65*, 963–970.

Breslau N., Kilbey M.M., & Andreski P. (1992). Nicotine withdrawal symptoms and psychiatric disorders: findings from anepidemiologic study of young adults. *Am J Psychiatry*, *149*, 464–469.
Cain J.C., & Wicks M.N. (2000). Caregivers attributes as correlates of burden in family caregivers coping with chronic obstructive pulmonary disease. *Journal of Family Nursing*, *6*, 46–68.
Cameron O.G., Abelson J.L., & Young E.A. (2004). Anxious and depressive disorders and their comorbidity: effect on central nervous system noradrenergic function. *Biol Psychiatry*, *56*, 875–883.
Caress A.L., Luker K.A., Chalmers K.I., & Salmon M.P. (2009). A review of the information and support needs of family carers of patients with chronic obstructive pulmonary disease. *J Clin Nurs*, *18*(4), 479–91.
Chang S.S., Chen S., McAvay G.J., & Tinetti M.E. (2012). Effect of coexisting chronic obstructive pulmonary disease and cognitive impairment on health outcomes in older adults. *J Am Geriatr Soc*, *60*(10), 1839–46.
Cossette S., & Levesque L. (1993). Caregiving tasks predictors of mental health of wife caregivers of men with chronic obstructive pulmonary disease. *Research in Nursing and Health*, *16*, 251–263.
Coventry P.A., Bower P., Keyworth C., Kenning C., Knopp J., Garrett C., Hind D., Malpass A., & Dickens C. (2013). The effect of complex interventions on depression and anxiety in chronic obstructive pulmonary disease: systematic review and meta-analysis. *PLoS One*, *8*(4), e60532.
Craske, M.G., Kircanski K., Epstein A., Wittchen H.U., Pine D.S., Lewis-Fernandez R., Hinton D., & DSM V Anxiety, OC Spectrum, Posttraumatic and Dissociative Disorder Work Group. (2010). Panic Disorder: A review of DSM IV Panic disorder and proposals for DSM V *Depress Anxiety*, *27*(2), 93–112.
Crişan A.F., Oancea C., Timar B., Fira-Mladinescu O., Crişan A., & Tudorache V. (2014). Cognitive impairment in chronic obstructive pulmonary disease. *PLoS One*, *9*(7), e102468.
Crockett A.J., Cranston J.M., Moss J.R., & Alpers J.H. (2002). The impact of anxiety, depression and living alone in chronic obstructive pulmonary disease. *Qual Life Res*, *11*, 309–316.
Dahlen I., & Janson C. (2002). Anxiety and depression are related to the outcome of emergency treatment in patients with obstructive pulmonary disease. *Chest*, *122*, 1633–1637.
Dalal A.A., Shah M., Lunacsek O., & Hanania N.A. (2011). Clinical and economic burden of depression/anxiety in chronic obstructive pulmonary disease patients within a managed care population. *COPD*, *8*(4), 293–9.
de Godoy D.V., & de Godoy R.F. (2003). A randomized controlled trial of the effect of psychotherapy on anxiety and depression in chronic obstructive pulmonary disease. *Arch Phys Med Rehabil*, *84*, 1154–1157.
de Voogd J.N., Wempe J.B., Koëter G.H., Postema K., van Sonderen E., Ranchor A.V., Coyne J.C., & Sanderman R. (2009). Depressive symptoms as predictors of mortality in patients with COPD. *Chest*, *135*(3), 619–25.
DeJean D., Giacomini M., Vanstone M., & Brundisini F. (2013). Patient experiences of depression and anxiety with chronic disease: a systematic review and qualitative meta-synthesis. *Ont Health Technol Assess Ser*, *13*(16), 1–33.
Dinicola G., Julian L., Gregorich S.E., Blanc P.D., & Katz P.P. (2013). The role of social support in anxiety for persons with COPD. *J Psychosom Res*, *74*(2), 110–5.
Dodd J.W., Charlton R.A., van den Broek M.D., & Jones P.W. (2013). Cognitive dysfunction in patients hospitalized with acute exacerbation of COPD. *Chest*, *144*(1), 119–27.
Dodd J.W., Getov S.V., & Jones P.W. (2010). Cognitive function in COPD. *Eur Respir J*, *35*(4), 913–22.
Dowson C., Laing R., Barraclough R., Town I., Mulder R., Norris K., & Drennan C. (2001). The use of the Hospital Anxiety and Depression Scale (HADS) in patients with chronic obstructive pulmonary disease: a pilot study. *N Z Med J*, *114*, 447–449.

Dowson C.A., Town G.I., Framptom C., & Mulder C.T. (2004). Psychopathology and illness beliefs influence COPD self-management. *J Psychosom Res*, *56*(3), 333–340.

Ehlert U., Gaab J., & Heinrichs M. (2001). Psychoneuroendocrinological contributions to the etiology of depression, posttraumatic stress disorder, and stress-related bodily disorders: the role of the hypothalamus– pituitary–adrenal axis. *Biol Psychol*, *57*, 141–152.

Emery C., Schein R., Hauck E., & MacIntyre N. (1998). Psychological and cognitive outcomes of a randomised trial of exercise among patients with chronic obstructive pulmonary disease. *Health Psychol*, *17*, 232–40.

Emery C.F., Green M.R., & Suh S. (2008). Neuropsychiatric function in chronic lung disease: the role of pulmonary rehabilitation. *Respir Care*, *53*(9), 1208–16.

Emery C.F., Honn V.J., Frid D.J., Lebowitz K.R., & Diaz P.T. (2001). Acute effects of exercise on cognition in patients with chronic obstructive pulmonary disease. *Am J Respir Crit Care Med*, *164*(9), 1624–7.

Emery C.F., Leatherman N.E., Burker E.J., & MacIntyre N.R. (1991). Psychological outcomes of a pulmonary rehabilitation program. *Chest*, *100*, 613–617.

Emery C.F., Schein R.L., Hauck E.R., & MacIntryre N.R. (1998). Psychological and cognitive outcomes of a randomized trial of exercise among patients with chronic obstructive pulmonary disease. *Health Psychol*, *17*(3), 232–240.

Emery C.F., Shermer R.L., Hauck E.R., Hsiao E.T., & MacIntyre N.R. (2003). Cognitive and psychological outcomes of exercise in a 1-year follow-up study of patients with chronic obstructive pulmonary disease. *Health Psychol*, *22*(6), 598–604.

Engstrom C.P., Persson L.O., Larsson S., Ryden A., & Sullivan M. (1996). Functional status and well being in chronic obstructive pulmonary disease with regard to clinical parameters and smoking: a descriptive and comparative study. *Thorax*, *51*, 825–830.

Etnier J.L., & Berry M. (2001). Fluid intelligence in an older COPD sample after short- or long-term exercise. *Med Sci Sports Exerc*, *33*, 1620–1628.

Fan V.S., & Meek P.M. (2014). Anxiety, depression, and cognitive impairment in patients with chronic respiratory disease. *Clin Chest Med*, *35*(2), 399–409.

Felker B., Katon W., Hedrick S.C., Rasmussen J., McKnight K., McDonnell M.B., & Fihn S.D. (2001). The association between depressive symptoms and health status in patients with chronic pulmonary disease. *Gen Hosp Psychiatry*, *23*(2), 56–61.

Figueiredo D., Gabriel R., Jácome C., Cruz J., & Marques A. (2014). Caring for relatives with chronic obstructive pulmonary disease: how does the disease severity impact on family carers? *Aging Ment Health*, *18*(3), 385–93.

Gabriel R., Figueiredo D., Jácome C., Cruz J., & Marques A. (2014). Day-to-day living with severe chronic obstructive pulmonary disease: Towards a family-based approach to the illness impacts. *Psychol Health*, *29*(8), 967–83.

Garuti G., Cilione C., Dell'Orso D., Gorini P., Lorenzi M.C., Totaro L., Cirelli G., & Clini E. (2003). Impact of comprehensive pulmonary rehabilitation on anxiety and depression in hospitalized COPD patients. *Monaldi Arch Chest Dis*, *59*, 56–61.

Giardino N.D., Curtis J.L., Abelson J.L., King A.P., Pamp B., Liberzon I., & Martinez F.J. (2010). The impact of panic disorder on interoception and dyspnea reports in chronic obstructive pulmonary disease. *Biol Psychol*, *84*(1). 142–6.

Gift A.G., Moore T., & Soeken K. (1992). Relaxation to reduce dyspnea and anxiety in COPD patients. *Nurs Res*, *41*, 242–246.

Griffiths T.L., Burr M.L., Campbell I.A., Lewis-Jenkins V., Mullins J., Shiels K., Turner- Lawlor P.J., Payne N., Newcombe R.G., Ionescu A.A., Thomas J., & Tunbridge J. (2000). Results at 1 year of outpatient multidisciplinary pulmonary rehabilitation: a randomised controlled trial. *Lancet*, *355*, 362–368.

Gudmundsson G., Gislason T., Janson C., Lindberg E., Suppli Ulrik C., Brondum E., Nieminen MM., Aine T., Hallin R., & Bakke P. (2006). Depression, anxiety and health status after hospitalisation for COPD: a multicentre study in the Nordic countries. *Respir Med*, *100*, 87–93.

Gudmundsson G., Gislason T., Janson C., Lindberg E., Hallin R., Ulrik C.S., Brondum E., Nieminen M.M., Aine T., & Bakke P. (2005). Risk factors for rehospitalisation in COPD: role of health status, anxiety and depression. *Eur Respir J*, *26*, 414–419.

Guell R., Resqueti V., Sangenis M., Morante F., Martorell B., Casan P., & Guyatt G.H. (2006). Impact of pulmonary rehabilitation on psychosocial morbidity in patients with severe COPD. *Chest*, *129*, 899–904.

Hajiro T., Nishimura K., Tsukino M., Ikeda O., & Oga T. (2000). Stages of disease severity and factors that affect the health status of patients with chronic obstructive pulmonary disease. *Respir Med*, 94, 841–846.

Hallas C., Howard C., & Wray J. (2009). Understanding panic disorder in chronic respiratory disease. *Br J Nurs*, *18*(9), 527–9.

Hanania N.A., Muellerova H., Locantore N.W., Vestbo J., Watkins M.L., Wouters E.F., Rennard S.I., & Sharafkhaneh A. (2011). Determinants of depression in the ECLIPSE chronic obstructive pulmonary disease cohort. *Am J Respir Crit Care Med*, *183*, 604–611.

Harris S. (2007). COPD and coping with breathlessness at home: a review of the literature. *Br J Community Nurs*, *12*(9), 411–5.

Heaton R.K., Grant I., McSweeny A.J., Adams K.M., & Petty T.L. (1983). Psychologic effects of continuous and nocturnal oxygen therapy in hypoxemic chronic obstructive pulmonary disease. *Arch Intern Med*, *143*, 1941–1947.

Hill K., Geist R., Goldstein R.S., & Lacasse Y. (2008). Anxiety and depression in end-stage COPD. *Eur Respir J*, *31*(3), 667–77.

Hilmarsen C.W., Wilke S., Engan H., Spruit M.A., Rodenburg J., Janssen D.J., Steinshamn S., Jones P.W., Wouters E.F., Oldervoll L., & Franssen F.M. (2014). Impact of symptoms of anxiety and depression on COPD Assessment Test scores. *Eur Respir J*, *43*(3),898–900.

Hjalmarsen A., Waterloo K., Dahl A., Jorde R., & Vitanen M. (1999). Effect of long-term oxygen therapy on cognitive and neurological dysfunction in chronic obstructive pulmonary disease. *Eur Neurol*, *42*, 27–35.

Hornikx M., Van Remoortel H., Demeyer H., Marcal Camillo C.A., Decramer M., Janssens W., & Troosters T. (2013). The influence of comorbidities on outcomes of pulmonary rehabilitation programs in patients with COPD: a systematic review. *Biomed Res Int*, 2013, 146148

Howard C., Hallas C., Wray J., & Carby M. (2009). The relationship between illness perceptions and panic in chronic obstructive pulmonary disease. *Behav Res Ther*, *47*, 71–6.

Hui K.P., & Hewitt A.B. (2003). A simple pulmonary rehabilitation program improveshealth outcomes and reduces hospital utilization in patients with COPD. *Chest*, *124*, 94–97.

Hynninen K.M., Breitve M.H., Wiborg A.B., Pallesen S., & Nordhus N.H. (2005). Psychological characteristics of patients with chronic obstructive pulmonary disease: a review. *J Psychosom Res*, *59*, 429–443.

Incalzi R.A., Chiappini F., Fuso L., Torrice M.P., Gemma A., & Pistelli R. (1998). Predicting cognitive decline in patients with hypoxaemic COPD. *Respir Med*, *92*(3), 527–33.

Incalzi R.A., Corsonello A., Trojano L., Pedone C., Acanfora D., Spada A., Izzo O., & Rengo F. (2008). Cognitive training is ineffective in hypoxemic COPD: a six-month randomized controlled trial. *Rejuvenation Res*, *11*(1), 239–50.

Incalzi R.A., Gemma A., Marra C., Capparella O., Fuso L., & Carbonin P. (1997). Verbal memory impairment in COPD: its mechanisms and clinical relevance. *Chest*, *112*(6), 1506–13.

Incalzi R.A., Gemma A., Marra C., Muzzolon R., Capparella O., & Carbonin P. (1993). Chronic obstructive pulmonary disease. An original model of cognitive decline. *Am Rev Respir Dis*, *148*(2), 418–24.

Jácome C., Figueiredo D., Gabriel R., Cruz J., & Marques A. (2014). Predicting anxiety and depression among family carers of people with Chronic Obstructive Pulmonary Disease. *Int Psychogeriatr*, *13*, 1–9.

Janssen D.J., Spruit M.A., Leue C., Gijsen C., Mameleers H., Schols J.M., Wouters E.F., & Ciro network. (2010). Symptoms of anxiety and depression in COPD patients entering pulmonary rehabilitation. *Chron Respir Dis*, *7*, 147–157.

Jordan R.E., Hawker J.I., Ayres J.G., Adab P., Tunnicliffe W., Olowokure B., Kai J., McManus R.J., Salter R., & Cheng K.K. (2008). Effect of social factors on winter hospital admission for respiratory disease: a case-control study of older people in the UK. *Br J Gen Pract*, *58*, 400–402.

Joynt K., Whellan D.J., & O'Connor C.M. (2004). Why is depression bad for the failing heart? A review of the mechanistic relationship between depression and heart failure. *J Card Fail*, *10*, 258–271.

Kayahan B., Karapolat H., Atyntoprak E., Atasever A., & Ozturk O. (2006). Psychological outcomes of an outpatient pulmonary rehabilitation program in patients with chronic obstructive pulmonary disease. *Respir Med*, *100*, 1050–1057.

Kim F.S., Kunik M.E., Molinari V.A., & Hillman S.L. (2000). Functional impairment in COPD patients. *Psychosomatics*, *41*, 465–71

Kim K.U., Park H.K., Jung H.Y., Ahn J.J., Moon E., Kim Y.S., Lee M.K., & Lee H. (2014). Association of depression with disease severity in patients with chronic obstructive pulmonary disease. *Lung*, *192*(2), 243–9.

Klein M., Gauggel S., Sachs G., & Pohl W. (2010). Impact of chronic obstructive pulmonary disease (COPD) on attention functions. *Respir Med*, *104*(1), 52–60.

Kozora E., Emery C., Kaplan R.M., Wamboldt F.S., Zhang L., & Make B.J. (2008). Cognitive and psychological issues in emphysema. *Proc Am Thorac Soc*, *5*(4), 556–60.

Kozora E., Emery C.F., Zhang L., Hoth K.F., Murphy J., Make B.; & National Emphysema Treatment Trial Research Group. (2011). Sequential cognitive skills in emphysema patients following lung volume reduction surgery: a 2-year longitudinal study. *J Cardiopulm Rehabil Prev*, *31*(6), 386–91.

Kroenke K., Spitzer R.L., & Williams J.B. (2001). The PHQ-9: validity of a brief depression severity measure. *J Gen Intern Med*, *16*(9), 606–613.

Krop H.D., Block A.J., & Cohen E. (1973). Neuropsychologic effects of continuous oxygen therapy in chronic obstructive pulmonary disease. *Chest*, *64*, 317–322.

Kunik M., Braun U., Stanley M., Wristers K., Molinari V., Stoebner D., & Orengo C.A. (2001). One session cognitive behavioural therapy for elderly patients with chronic obstructive pulmonary disease. *Psychol Med*, *31*(4), 717–23.

Kunik M., Roundy K., Veazey C., Souchek J., Richardson P., Wray N.P., & Stanley M.A. (2005). Surprisingly high prevalence of anxiety and depression in chronic breathing disorders. *Chest*, *127*(4), 1205–1211.

Kunik M.E., Veazey C., Cully J., Souchek J., Graham D.P., Hopko D., Carter R., Sharafkhanen A., Goepfert E.J., Wray N., & Stanley M.A. (2008). COPD education and cognitive behavioral therapy group treatment for clinically significant symptoms of depression and anxiety in COPD patients: a randomized controlled trial. *Psychol Med*, *38*(3), 385–396.

Laurin C., Moullec G., Bacon S.L., & Lavoie K.L. (2012). Impact of anxiety and depression on chronic obstructive pulmonary disease exacerbation risk. *Am J Respir Crit Care Med*, *185*(9), 918–23.

Lee R.N., Graydon J.E., & Ross E. (1991). Effects of psychological well-being, physical status, and social support on oxygen-dependent COPD patients' level of functioning. *Res Nurs Health*, *14*(5), 323–8.

Lee Y.S., Park S., Oh Y.M., Lee S.D., Park S.W., Kim Y.S., In K.H., Jung B.H., Lee K.H., Ra S.W., Hwang Y.I., Park Y.B., Jung K.S.; & Korean COPD Study Group. (2013). Chronic obstructive pulmonary disease assessment test can predict depression: a prospective multi-center study. *J Korean Med Sci*, *28*, 1048–1054.

Li J., & Fei G.H. (2013). The unique alterations of hippocampus and cognitive impairment in chronic obstructive pulmonary disease. *Respir Res*, *14*, 140.

Liesker J.J., Postma D.S., Beukema R.J., ten Hacken N.H., van der Molen T., Riemersma R.A., van Zomeren E.H., & Kerstiens H.A. (2004). Cognitive performance in patients with COPD. *Respir Med*, *98*(4), 351–356.

Light R.W., Merrill E.J., Despars J.A., Gordon G.H., & Mutalipassi L.R. (1985). Prevalence of depression and anxiety in patients with COPD. Relationship to functional capacity. *Chest*, *87*, 35–38.

Livermore N., Butler J., Sharpe L., McBain R., Gandevia S., & McKenzie D. (2008). Panic attacks and perception of inspiratory resistive loads in chronic obstructive pulmonary disease. *Am J Respir Crit Care Med*, *178*, 7–12.

Livermore N., Sharpe L., & McKenzie D. (2012). Catastrophic interpretations and anxiety sensitivity as predictors of panic-spectrum psychopathology in chronic obstructive pulmonary disease. *J Psychosom Res*, *72*(5), 388–92.

Livermore N., Sharpe L., & McKenzie D. (2010). Prevention of panic attacks and panic disorder in chronic obstructive pulmonary disease. *Eur Respir J*, *35*, 557–63.

Lustig F.M., Haas A., & Castillo R. (1972). Clinical and rehabilitation regime in patients with chronic obstructive pulmonary diseases. *Arch Phys Med Rehabil*, *53*, 315–322.

Marino P., Sirey J.A., Raue P.J., & Alexopoulos G.S. (2008). Impact of social support and self-efficacy on functioning in depressed older adults with chronic obstructive pulmonary disease. *Int J Chron Obstruct Pulmon Dis*, *3*(4), 713–8.

Martin S.E., Bradley J.M., Buick J.B., Crossan A., & Elborn J.S. (2011). The effect of hypoxia on cognitive performance in patients with chronic obstructive pulmonary disease. *Respir Physiol Neurobiol*, *177*(1), 36–40.

McAllister D.A., Morling J.R., Fischbacher C.M., MacNee W., & Wild S.H. (2013). Socioeconomic deprivation increases the effect of winter on admissions to hospital with COPD: retrospective analysis of 10 years of national hospitalisation data. *Prim Care Respir J*, 22(3), 296–9.

McCathie H.C., Spence S.H., & Tate R.L. (2002). Adjustment to chronic obstructive pulmonary disease: the importance of psychological factors. *Eur Respir J*, *19*, 47–53.

Meier C., Bodenmann G., Mörgeli H., & Jenewein J. (2011). Dyadic coping, quality of life, and psychological distress among chronic obstructive pulmonary disease patients and their partners. *Int J Chron Obstruct Pulmon Dis*, *6*, 583–96.

Mikkelsen R.L., Middelboe T., Pisinger C., & Stage K.B. (2004). Anxiety and depression in patients with chronic obstructive pulmonary disease (COPD). A review. *Nord J Psychiatry*, *58*, 65–70.

Mulhall A.M., Lach L.A., Krzywkowski-Mohn S.M., Welge J.A., & Panos R.J. (2013). Therapeutic paralysis in veterans with COPD. *Respir Med*, *107*(10), 1547–57.

Murray R.P., Johnston J.J., Dolce J.J., Lee W.W., & OHara P. (1995). Social support for smoking cessation and abstinence: the Lung Health Study. Lung Health Study Research Group *Addict Behav*, *20*(2), 159–70.

Newsom J.T., Rook K.S., Nishishiba M., Sorkin D.H., & Mahan T.L. (2005). Understanding the relative importance of positive and negative social exchanges: examining specific domains and appraisals. *J Gerontol B Psychol Sci Soc Sci*, *60*(6), P304–P12.

Ohayon M.M. (2014). Chronic Obstructive Pulmonary Disease and its association with sleep and mental disorders in the general population. *J Psychiatr Res*, *54*, 79–84.

Ortapamuk H., & Naldoken S. (2006). Brain perfusion abnormalities in chronic obstructive pulmonary disease: comparison with cognitive impairment. *Annals of Nuclear Medicine*, *20*(2), 99–106.

Orth M., Diekmann C., Suchan B., Duchna H.W., Widdig W., Schultze-Werninghaus G., Rasche K., & Kotterba S. (2008). Driving performance in patients with chronic obstructive pulmonary disease. *J Physiol Pharmacol*, *59* Suppl 6, 539–47.

Panos R.J., Krywkowski-Mohn S.M., Sherman S.N., & Lach L.A. (2013). Patient reported determinants of health: a qualitative analysis of veterans with chronic obstructive pulmonary disease. *COPD*, *10*(3), 333–47.

Partridge M.R., Dal Negro R.W., & Olivieri D. (2011). Understanding patients with asthma and COPD: insights from a European study. *Primary Care Respiratory Journal*, *20*, 315–323.

Patten S.B., & Williams J.V. (2007). Chronic obstructive lung diseases and prevalence of mood, anxiety, and substance-use disorders in a large population sample. *Psychosomatics*, *48*(6), 496–501.

Philip J., Gold M., Brand C., Miller B., Douglass J., & Sundararajan V. (2014). Facilitating change and adaptation: the experiences of current and bereaved carers of patients with severe chronic obstructive pulmonary disease. *J Palliat Med*, *17*(4), 421–7.

Pollack M., Kradin R., Otto M., Worthington J., Gould R., Sabatino S.A., & Rosenbaum J.F. (1996). Prevalence of panic in patients referred for pulmonary function testing at a major medical centre. *Am J Psychiat*, *153*, 110–3.

Pooler A., & Beech R. (2014). Examining the relationship between anxiety and depression and exacerbations of COPD which result in hospital admission: a systematic review. *Int J Chron Obstruct Pulmon Dis*, *9*, 315–30.

Porzelius J., Vest M., & Nochomovitz M. (1992). Respiratory function, cognitions, and panic in chronic obstructive pulmonary patients. *Behav Res Ther*, *30*, 75–7.

Putman-Casdorph H., & McCrone S. (2009). Chronic obstructive pulmonary disease, anxiety, and depression: state of the science. *Heart Lung*, *38*, 34–47.

Qian J., Simoni-Wastila L., Rattinger G.B., Lehmann S., Langenberg P., Zuckerman I.H., & Terrin M. (2013). Associations of depression diagnosis and antidepressant treatment with mortality among young and disabled Medicare beneficiaries with COPD. *Gen Hosp Psychiatry*, *35*(6), 612–8.

Radloff L.S. (1977). The CES-D scale: a self-report depression scale for research in the general population. *Appl Psychol Measure*, *1*(3), 385–401.

Renfroe K.L. (1988). Effect of progressive relaxation on dyspnea and state anxiety in patients with chronic obstructive pulmonary disease. *Heart Lung*, *17*, 408–413.

Rusanen M., Ngandu T., Laatikainen T., Tuomilehto J., Soininen H., & Kivipelto M. (2013). Chronic obstructive pulmonary disease and asthma and the risk of mild cognitive impairment and dementia: a population based CAIDE study. *Curr Alzheimer Res*, *10*(5), 549–55.

Sandhu H.S. (1986). Psychosocial issues in chronic obstructive pulmonary disease. *Clin Chest Med*, *7*(4), 629–642.

Sassi-Dambron D.E., Eakin E.G., Ries A.L., & Kaplan R.M. (1995). Treatment of dyspnea in COPD. A controlled clinical trial of dyspnea management strategies. *Chest*, *107*, 724–729.

Schou L., Østergaard B., Rasmussen L.S., Rydahl-Hansen S., & Phanareth K. (2012). Cognitive dysfunction in patients with chronic obstructive pulmonary disease--a systematic review. *Respir Med*, *106*(8), 1071–81.

Seamark D.A., Blake S.D., Seamark C.J., & Halpin D.M. (2004). Living with severe chronic obstructive pulmonary disease (COPD): perceptions of patients and their carers. an interpretative phenomenological analysis. *Palliat. Med*, *18*, 619–625.

Silvertooth E.J., Doraiswamy P.M., Clary G.L., Babyak M.A., Wilkerson N., Hellegars C., & Palmer S.M. (2004). Citalopram and quality of life in lung transplant recipients. *Psychosomatics*, *45*, 271–272.

Singh B., Mielke M.M., Parsaik A.K., Cha R.H., Roberts R.O., Scanlon P.D., Geda Y.E., Christianson T.J., Pankratz V.S., & Petersen R.C. (2014). A prospective study of chronic obstructive pulmonary disease and the risk for mild cognitive impairment. *JAMA Neurol*, *71*(5), 581–8.

Singh B., Parsaik A.K., Mielke M.M., Roberts R.O., Scanlon P.D., Geda Y.E., Pankratz V.S., Christianson T., Yawn B.P., & Petersen R.C. (2013). Chronic obstructive pulmonary disease and association with mild cognitive impairment: the Mayo Clinic Study of Aging. *Mayo Clin Proc*, *88*(11), 1222–30.

Singh N.P., Despars J.A., Stansbury D.W., Avalos K., & Light R.W. (1993). Effects of buspirone on anxiety levels and exercise tolerance in patients with chronic airflow obstruction and mild anxiety. *Chest*, *103*, 800–804.

Smoller J., Pollack M., Wassertheil-Smoller S., Barton B., Hendrix S.L., Jackson R.D., Dicken T., Oberman A., Sheps D.S., & Women's Health Initiative Investigators. (2003). Prevalence and correlates of panic attacks in postmenopausal women. *Arch Intern Med*, *163*, 2041–50.

Smoller J.W., Pollack M.H., Otto M.W., Rosenbaum J.F., & Kradin R.L. (1996). Panic anxiety, dyspnea, and respiratory disease. Theoretical and clinical considerations. *Am J Respir Crit Care Med*, *154*(1), 6–17.

Spielberger C.E., Gorsuch R.L., & Luschene R.E. (1970). Manual for the State-Trait Anxiety Inventory. Palo Alto: Consulting Psychologist Press.

Stapleton R.D., Nielson E.L., Engelberg R.A., Patrick D.L., & Curtis J.R. (2005). Association of depression and life-sustaining treatment preferences in patients with COPD. *Chest*, *127*(1), 328–334.

Thakur N., Blanc P.D., Julian L.J., Yelin E.H., Katz P.P., Sidney S., Iribarren C., & Eisner M.D. (2010). COPD and cognitive impairment: the role of hypoxemia and oxygen therapy. *Int J Chron Obstruct Pulmon Dis*, *5*, 263–9.

Tsai T.Y., Livneh H., Lu M.C., Tsai P.Y., Chen P.C., & Sung F.C. (2013). Increased risk and related factors of depression among patients with COPD: a population-based cohort study. *BMC Public Health*, *13*, 976.

Tselebis A., Kosmas E., Bratis D., Pachi A., Ilias I., Harikiopoulou M., Theodorakopoulou E., Velentzas K., Dumitru S., Moussas G., Siafakas N., & Tzanakis N. (2014). Contribution of psychological factors in dropping out from chronic obstructive pulmonary disease rehabilitation programs. *Biomed Res Int*, 2014, 401326.

Tulek B., Atalay N.B., Yildirim G., Kanat F., & Süerdem M. (2014). Cognitive function in chronic obstructive pulmonary disease: Relationship to global initiative for chronic obstructive lung disease, 2011 categories. *Respirology*, *19*(6), 873–880.

Usmani Z.A., Carson K.V., Cheng J.N., Esterman A.J., & Smith B.J. (2011). Pharmacological interventions for the treatment of anxiety disorders in chronic obstructive pulmonary disease. *Cochrane Database Syst Rev*, 11, CD008483.

Valenza M.C., Valenza-Peña G., Torres-Sánchez .I, González-Jiménez E., Conde-Valero A., & Valenza-Demet G. (2014). Effectiveness of controlled breathing techniques on anxiety and depression in hospitalized patients with COPD: a randomized clinical Trial. *Respir Care*, *59*(2), 209–15.

Verburg K., Griez E., Meijer J., & Pols H. (1995A). Respiratory disorders as a possible predisposing factor for panic disorder. *J Affect Disord*, *33*(2), 129–34.

Verburg K., Griez E., Meijer J., & Pols H. (1995B). Discrimination between panic disorder and generalized anxiety disorder by 35% carbon dioxide challenge. *Am J Psychiatry*, *152*(7), 1081–3.

Villeneuve S., Pepin V., Rahayel S., Bertrand J.A., de Lorimier M., Rizk A., Desjardins C., Parenteau S., Beaucage F., Joncas S., Monchi O., & Gagnon J.F. (2012). Mild cognitive impairment in moderate to severe COPD: a preliminary study. *Chest*, *142*(6), 1516–23.

Vögele C., & von Leupoldt A. (2008). Mental disorders in chronic obstructive pulmonary disease (COPD). *Respir Med*, *102*(5), 764–73.

Vos P.J., Folgering H.T., & van Herwaarden C.L. (1995). Visual attention in patients with chronic obstructive pulmonary disease. *Biol Psychol*, *41*(3), 295–305.
Wagena E.J., Arrindell W.A., Wouters E.F., & van Schayk C.P. (2005). Are patients with COPD psychologically distressed? *Eur Respir J*, *26*, 242–248.
Wagena E.J., Kant I., Huibers M.J., van Amelsvoort G.L., Swaen G.M., Wouters E.F., & van Schayck C.P. (2004). Psychological distress and depressed mood in employees with asthma, chronic bronchitis or emphysema: a population-based observational study on prevalence and the relationship with smoking cigarettes. *Eur J Epidemiol*, *19*(2), 147–153.
Weaver T.E., Richmond T.S., & Narsavage G.L. (1997). An, explanatory model of functional status in chronic obstructive pulmonary disease. *Nurs Res, 46*, 26–31
Weldam S.W., Lammers J.W., Decates R.L., & Schuurmans M.J. (2013). Daily activities and health-related quality of life in patients with chronic obstructive pulmonary disease: psychological determinants: a cross-sectional study. *Health Qual Life Outcomes, 11,* 190.
Willgoss T.G., Yohannes A.M., Goldbart J., & Fatoye F. (2012). "Everything was spiraling out of control": experiences of anxiety in people with chronic obstructive pulmonary disease. *Heart Lung*, *41*(6), 562–71.
Willgoss T.G., & Yohannes A.M. (2013). Anxiety disorders in patients with COPD: a systematic review. *Respir Care*, *58*(5), 858–66.
Wilson D.K., Kaplan R.M., Timms R.M., & Dawson A. (1985). Acute effects of oxygen treatment upon information processing in hypoxemic COPD patients. *Chest*, *88*(2), 239–43.
Withers N.J., Rudkin S.T., & White R.J. (1999). Anxiety and depression in severe chronic obstructive pulmonary disease: the effects of pulmonary rehabilitation. *J Cardiopulm Rehabil*, *19*, 362–365.
Wong A.W., Gan W.Q., Burns J., Sin D.D., & van Eeden S.F. (2008). Acute exacerbation of chronic obstructive pulmonary disease: influence of social factors in determining length of hospital stay and readmission rates. *Can Respir J*, *15*(7), 361–4.
Yellowlees P., Alpers J., Bowden J., Bryant G., & Ruffin R. (1987). Psychiatric morbidity in patients with chronic airflow obstruction. *Med J Australia*, *146*, 305–7.
Yohannes A.M., & Alexopoulos G.S. (2014). Pharmacological treatment of depression in older patients with chronic obstructive pulmonary disease: impact on the course of the disease and health outcomes. *Drugs Aging*, *31*(7), 483–92
Yohannes A.M., Baldwin R.C., & Connolly M.J. (2000). Mood disorders in elderly patients with chronic obstructive pulmonary disease. *Rev Clin Gerontol*, *10*, 193–202.
Yohannes A.M., Baldwin R.C., & Connolly MJ. (2005). Predictors of 1-year mortality in patients discharged from hospital following acute exacerbation of chronic obstructive pulmonary disease. *Age Ageing*, *34*, 491–496.
Yohannes A.M., Roomi J., Waters K., & Connolly M.J. (1998). Quality of life in elderly patients with COPD: measurement and predictive factors. *Respir Med*, *92*, 1231–1236.
Yohannes A.M., Willgoss T.G., Baldwin R.C., & Connolly M.J. (2010). Depression and anxiety in chronic heart failure and chronic obstructive pulmonary disease: prevalence, relevance, clinical implications and management principles. *Int J Geriatr Psychiatry*, *25*(12), 1209–21.
Zandbergen J., Bright M., Pols H., Fernandez I., de Loof C., & Griez E.J. (1991). Higher lifetime prevalence of respiratory diseases in panic disorder? *Am J Psychiatry*, *148*(11), 1583–5.
Zarowitz B.J., & O'Shea T. (2012). Chronic obstructive pulmonary disease: prevalence, characteristics, and pharmacologic treatment in nursing home residents with cognitive impairment. *J Manag Care Pharm*, *18*(8), 598–606.
Zhang M.W.B., Ho R.C.M., Cheung M.W.L, Fu E., & Mak A. (2011). Prevalence of depressive symptoms in patients with chronic obstructive pulmonary disease: a systematic review, meta-analysis and meta-regression. *Gen Hosp Psychiatry*, *33*, 217–223.

Zheng G.Q., Wang Y., & Wang X.T. (2008). Chronic hypoxia-hypercapnia influences cognitive function: a possible new model of cognitive dysfunction in chronic obstructive pulmonary disease. *Med Hypotheses*, *71*(1), 111–3.

Zigmond A.S., & Snaith R.P. (1983). The hospital anxiety and depression scale. *Acta Psychiatr Scand*, *67*, 361–370.

Ralph J. Panos, MD

# 14 Management of Stable Chronic Obstructive Pulmonary Disease

Key Points:

1. Before initiating management, establish the diagnosis of chronic obstructive pulmonary disease (COPD):
   - respiratory symptoms: cough, phlegm production, and / or breathlessness
   - documented airflow limitation by spirometry or
   - radiographic evidence of emphysema
2. The most recent GOLD guidelines base management upon 3 factors:
   - severity of airflow limitation measured by $FEV_1$
   - respiratory healthcare visits in the prior 12 months
   - symptom score measured by the COPD Assessment Test or breathlessness measured by the modified Medical Research Council scale
3. In general, COPD pharmacologic management begins with a short acting bronchodilator and progresses with the addition of a long acting bronchodilator (either an anticholinergic or a long acting beta agonist), and lastly an inhaled corticosteroid.
4. Nonpharmacologic interventions such as oxygen, vaccinations, and pulmonary rehabilitation are essential components to comprehensive COPD management.

## 14.1 Management of Stable COPD

The prerequisite for the optimal management of COPD is the ascertainment of the correct diagnosis; COPD is diagnosed by respiratory symptoms (usually cough, sputum production, and/or dyspnea), the presence of airflow limitation ($FEV_1$/FVC < lower limit of normal), and the exclusion of other processes (see Chapter 3, COPD Recognition and Diagnosis: Approach to the Patient with Respiratory Symptoms).

The goals of COPD management are multiple and diverse: 1) reduce mortality, 2) preserve lung function, 3) decrease COPD-associated complications, 4) treat COPD-related comorbidities, 5) decrease the number and severity of COPD exacerbations, 6) relieve respiratory symptoms, especially breathlessness and cough, and 7) improve overall wellbeing. *Although exacerbation prevention, reduction in healthcare utilization, and preservation of lung function are frequently the endpoints of investigations examining the effects of pharmacologic and nonpharmacologic interventions in COPD, relief of respiratory symptoms is often the principle goal when a primary care provider sees a patient with COPD.*

The major symptoms experienced by patients with COPD are breathlessness, cough, and sputum production (Rennard, 2002; Leidy, 2003A). Assessment of these symptoms should be performed at every healthcare encounter for individuals with COPD. Numerous surveys and assessment tools have been developed to assist clinicians with the evaluation of respiratory symptoms. One such tool is the Breathlessness, Cough, and Sputum Scale, a daily diary of COPD related symptoms that correlates with lung function measured by the $FEV_1$ and sputum volume (Leidy, 2003). This scale is simple and consists of only three questions: 1) How much difficulty did you have breathing today?, 2) How was your cough today?, and 3) How much trouble was your sputum today? Each question has 5 graded responses from none to severe (Leidy, 2003A; Leidy, 2003B). This questionnaire is limited to the three major respiratory symptoms associated with COPD. Numerous other disease-specific, as well as generic surveys, have been developed to assess quality of life in individuals with COPD. In a systemic review, the best instruments were the Chronic Respiratory Questionnaire (CRQ), COPD Assessment Test (CAT), Saint George Respiratory Questionnaire (SGRQ), and Living with COPD questionnaire (LCOPD) (Weldam, 2012). The CAT has been adopted in the most recent GOLD guidelines (Jones, 2009) (Figure 14.1).

### 14.1.1 Breathlessness

Breathlessness at rest and especially with exertion is a primary symptom of COPD. Dyspnea often limits action or patients avoid activities due to the fear of developing breathlessness. The cause of breathlessness in individuals with COPD is multifactorial with contributions from bronchospasm, desaturation, secretions, and cough but the major factor is dynamic lung hyperinflation. Lung hyperinflation is an increase in the volume of air remaining in the lungs at the end of exhalation that is associated with excessive loading and functional weakness of the respiratory muscles that precipitates mechanical dysfunction and sensory dysphoria (the sensation of breathlessness). Lung hyperinflation is caused by increased lung compliance and airflow limitation. In COPD, air is easily inhaled but exhalation is impeded by airflow limitation caused by increased resistance and reduced elastic recoil; if less air is exhaled than was inhaled, the lung begins to retain air, increasing the end expiratory lung volume (EELV). As EELV increases, the volume of air inhaled during subsequent breaths is decreased due to restriction of the inspiratory capacity, reducing the tidal volume, and impairing minute ventilation. Thus, the lungs are unable to meet ventilatory and oxygenation demands. The increase in respiratory rate that occurs with exertion further augments hyperinflation by reducing expiratory time causing more air trapping and elevation of EELV. As hyperinflation increases, the respiratory muscles are stretched or loaded causing discomfort; the stretching also causes functional weakness by putting the muscles at a mechanical disadvantage. *The discomfort caused by stretching and loading of respiratory muscles by dynamic hyperinflation is a significant factor contributing to the sensation of breathlessness.* Both pharmacologic and non-pharmacologic treatments may help to ameliorate dynamic hyperinflation.

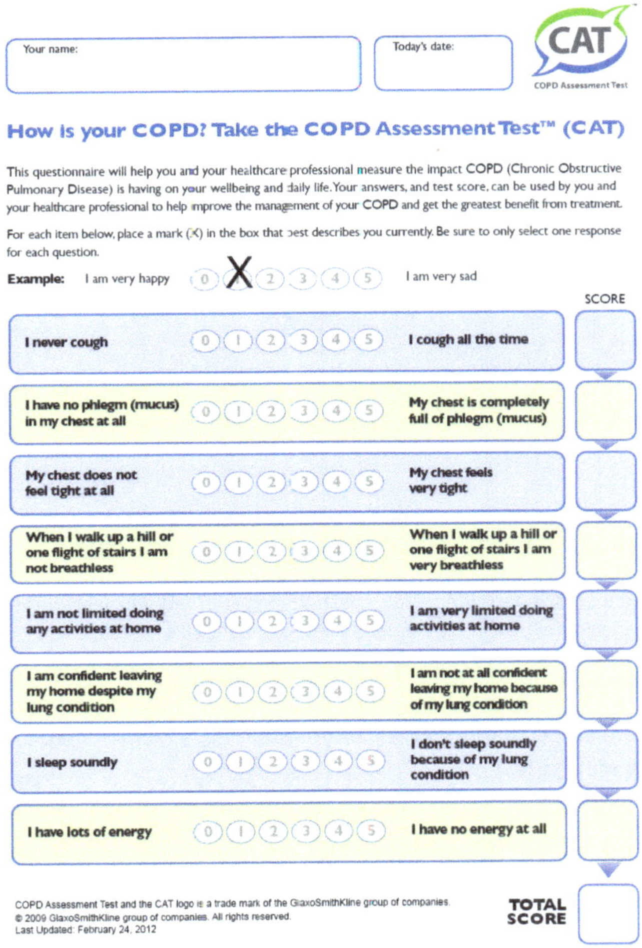

Your name: | Today's date:

CAT
COPD Assessment Test

**How is your COPD? Take the COPD Assessment Test™ (CAT)**

This questionnaire will help you and your healthcare professional measure the impact COPD (Chronic Obstructive Pulmonary Disease) is having on your wellbeing and daily life. Your answers, and test score, can be used by you and your healthcare professional to help improve the management of your COPD and get the greatest benefit from treatment.

For each item below, place a mark (X) in the box that best describes you currently. Be sure to only select one response for each question.

**Example:** I am very happy (0) X (2) (3) (4) (5) I am very sad

| | | | SCORE |
|---|---|---|---|
| I never cough | 0 1 2 3 4 5 | I cough all the time | |
| I have no phlegm (mucus) in my chest at all | 0 1 2 3 4 5 | My chest is completely full of phlegm (mucus) | |
| My chest does not feel tight at all | 0 1 2 3 4 5 | My chest feels very tight | |
| When I walk up a hill or one flight of stairs I am not breathless | 0 1 2 3 4 5 | When I walk up a hill or one flight of stairs I am very breathless | |
| I am not limited doing any activities at home | 0 1 2 3 4 5 | I am very limited doing activities at home | |
| I am confident leaving my home despite my lung condition | 0 1 2 3 4 5 | I am not at all confident leaving my home because of my lung condition | |
| I sleep soundly | 0 1 2 3 4 5 | I don't sleep soundly because of my lung condition | |
| I have lots of energy | 0 1 2 3 4 5 | I have no energy at all | |
| | | TOTAL SCORE | |

COPD Assessment Test and the CAT logo is a trade mark of the GlaxoSmithKline group of companies.
© 2009 GlaxoSmithKline group of companies. All rights reserved.
Last Updated: February 24, 2012

**Figure 14.1:** COPD Activity Test (From http://www.catestonline.org/)

Pursed lip breathing facilitates exhalation of air by creating an increased expiratory resistance that elevates the intra-airway pressure to maintain airway patency, reducing collapse due to diminished elastic recoil and increasing the amount of air expelled during exhalation. The improved expiratory airflow reduces air trapping and hyperinflation. Slow, deliberate, and controlled breathing utilizing pursed lip breathing helps to reduce the respiratory rate which increases the exhalation time that may also reduce air trapping and hyperinflation. Control of anxiety, relaxation techniques, and better awareness of the perception of breathlessness may also help reduce the rate of breathing. Oxygen and improved overall fitness from pulmonary rehabilitation or other conditioning programs may reduce ventilatory demand slowing the respira-

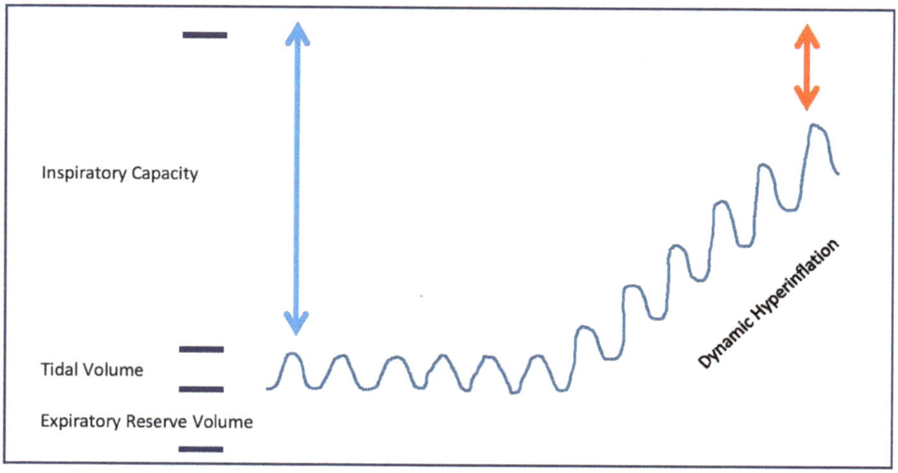


**Figure 14.2:** Dynamic Hyperinflation. During normal tidal breathing, the end expiratory lung volume is constant and the inspiratory capacity is maintained. With exercise, dynamic hyperinflation increases the end expiratory lung volume and reduces inspiratory capacity (change from baseline (blue arrow) to peak exertion (red arrow)). Respiratory muscle stretching and loading, mechanical disadvantage, and inability to inspire fully contribute to the sensation of breathlessness.

tory rate and increasing time in exhalation. Bronchodilators reduce airway resistance and permit improved lung emptying.

### 14.1.2 Cough

Chronic bronchitis is defined as cough and sputum production for at least 3 months of the year for two consecutive years. Individuals with mild to moderate airflow limitation report cough and sputum production more frequently than those with severe obstruction (von Hertzen, 2000). Causes of cough in COPD have not been well studied but inflammation, sputum clearance, and comorbidities such as bronchiectasis, gastroesophageal reflux disease, and postnasal drainage may all contribute. Early studies suggested that patients with COPD had a heightened cough response to capsaicin that was similar to individuals with asthma but further studies have been equivocal (Doherty, 2000).

Patients with COPD and chronic cough have longer durations of smoking, more impaired lung function, and are more likely to be current smokers (Kanner, 1999). The prevalence of chronic cough decreases by 80% 5 years after quitting smoking. Productive cough is a risk factor for the development of airflow limitation in nonsmokers and former smokers (Yamane, 2010).

Patients with moderately severe COPD and cough spend more time coughing during the day than at night (Smith, 2003). Cough frequency does not correlate with the severity of airflow limitation (Smith, 2003; Smith, 2004). Despite the frequent reporting of cough by patients with COPD, objective cough counts and time spent coughing, 12.3 s per hour during the day and 1.63 s per hour at night, are quite low (Smith, 2003; Smith, 2004).

Inhaled steroids do not affect cough frequency in patients with COPD (Doherty, 2000; Smith, 2004). Long acting beta agonists reduce cough more effectively than short acting beta agonists (Smith, 2004); in contrast, short acting anticholinergics reduce cough better than long acting anticholinergics (Smith, 2004). Codeine is not better than placebo in reducing cough frequency in patients with COPD (Smith, 2006).

### 14.1.3 Sputum Production

Airway mucus is usually a thin gel composed of water and mucins (glycosylated proteins) as well as components of the innate immune system: antimicrobial, immunomodulatory, and protective proteins, that line the respiratory mucosal surface. Inhaled toxins and particles are trapped within the mucus and expelled from the lungs by ciliary beating and cough (Fahey, 2010). Cigarette smoke impairs cilia structure and function, induces mucin production, and reduces mucus hydration. Thus, more airway mucus remains in the lower airway and may become colonized with bacteria which can induce inflammation and inflammatory cell migration into the airway. Neutrophil-derived DNA increases the viscosity of the airway mucus further impairing clearance.

Patients with severe COPD frequently experience increased phlegm production and have more respiratory symptoms, less emphysema, and greater airflow limitation (Kim, 2011). Approximately 14% of individuals with airflow limitation have symptoms of chronic bronchitis and, compared with those with airflow limitation but no symptoms of chronic bronchitis, have worse lung function and overall health, more respiratory symptoms and exacerbations, greater limitations in physical activity, and an increased risk of mortality (Montes de Oca, 2012; Burgel, 2009; Kim, 2011). Most recently the COPDGene Study has shown that individuals with the chronic bronchitic phenotype of COPD have an accelerated rate of decline in lung function, increased risk of respiratory infections, more frequent nasal and respiratory symptoms, and increased frequency and severity of exacerbations (Kim, 2011).

Bronchiectasis is another contributing factor to cough and sputum production. Approximately 30–60% of individuals with COPD have chest CT evidence of bronchiectasis (Bafadhel, 2011; Martinez-Garcia, 2011). The presence of bronchiectasis is associated with increased frequency of bacterial colonization of the lower airway, more severe airflow limitation, and previous hospitalizations for COPD exacerbations.

Smoking cessation is associated with a reduction in phlegm production (Kanner, 1999). Airway clearance techniques such as postural drainage, percussion, vibration, and breathing exercises do not reduce COPD exacerbations, have variable effects on lung function, improve quality of life, and may promote short term increases in phlegm production (Osadnik, 2012). Mucolytics (such as N-acetyl cysteine) reduce exacerbation rates in patients with chronic bronchitis by approximately 20% (Poole, 2012).

## 14.2 Guidelines for the Management of COPD

There are multiple guidelines for the management of COPD that have been developed by numerous national and international health organizations. The Global Initiative for Chronic Obstructive Lung Disease (GOLD) reports are the most widely disseminated international guidelines for the management of COPD and are continually updated (GOLD guidelines). Another source for practical advice for the management of COPD is the COPD Foundation Guide to COPD Diagnosis and Treatment (http://journal.copdfoundation.org/Portals/0/JCOPDF/Files/Issue1-Volume1/JCOPDF-2014-0124-Pocket-Guide.pdf).

COPD is a systemic inflammatory state with protean manifestations-*COPD is not just a lung disease!* (see Chapter 10. COPD Is a Multi-organ Disorder: Systemic Manifestations). Cardiovascular disease including coronary artery disease, stroke, and hypertension, osteoporosis, psychological disorders, especially anxiety and depression, skeletal muscle dysfunction, and lung cancer occur more frequently in individuals with COPD than in those with normal lung function even though they may have similar smoking histories. Treatment of COPD comorbidities should include optimal COPD management as well as appropriate management of the specific nonpulmonary process.

Most COPD treatment guidelines advocate an additive, incremental approach to the pharmacologic management of COPD. There has been poor adherence to most COPD guidelines and few studies have evaluated their effectiveness. At the Cincinnati VAMC, review of the prescribed respiratory medications and respiratory and nonrespiratory visits between 2000 and 2005 showed poor compliance with the GOLD pharmacologic treatment guidelines but correlation between respiratory treatments and the number of prior respiratory health care visits (Seaman, 2010). Another study from Switzerland showed that adherence to the GOLD guidelines did not affect respiratory symptoms, exacerbation rate, or lung function over 12 months (Jochmann, 2012). However, other studies have shown that better adherence with respiratory medications improves overall survival in individuals with COPD (Vestbo, 2009). *Although these earlier guidelines classified disease impairment and based treatment recommendations upon the severity of airflow limitation (usually measured by the $FEV_1$), the most recent 2012 GOLD guidelines include an assessment of respiratory symptoms and prior healthcare encounters to assist in the determination of the optimal treatment regimen.*

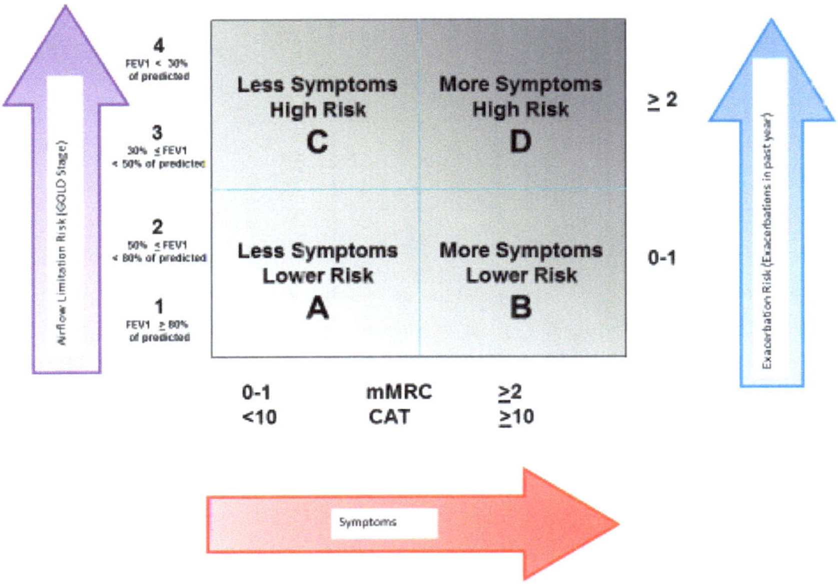


**Figure 14.3:** GOLD Guideline COPD Categories. The GOLD Guidelines categorize patient with COPD using three variables: $FEV_1$ measured by spirometry, symptoms, and exacerbation risk measured by the number of exacerbations in the previous 12 months. Although there are 4 categories of airflow limitation, patients are divided into 2 groups: those with less severe obstruction, $FEV_1$ >= 50% of predicted and more severe disease, $FEV_1$<50% of predicted. Symptoms are graded either by breathlessness measured by the modified Medical Research Council score (Table 14.2) or by the COPD Activity Test (CAT) (Figure 14.1). Exacerbations are divided into 2 groups: those with >=2 exacerbations in the past year and those with <2 exacerbations. There are 4 categories of patients: A. those with less obstruction, less symptoms and fewer exacerbations; B. those with less obstruction, fewer exacerbations, but more symptoms; C. those with worse obstruction, less symptoms, but more exacerbations, and D. those with worse obstruction, more symptoms, and more exacerbations.

### 14.2.1 GOLD Guidelines for the Management of COPD

The GOLD guidelines recommend that each individual with COPD be evaluated to determine the severity of COPD, the effect of COPD on the individual's overall health and well being, the risk of future COPD-related events (healthcare encounters or death), and COPD-related comorbidities (Figure 14.3). *COPD severity* is classified by the severity of airflow limitation measured by spirometry. The GOLD guidelines define airflow limitation as $FEV_1/FVC < 0.70$ (see Chapter 4, Pulmonary Function Testing: Presence and Severity of Airflow Limitation/Obstruction).

The effects of COPD on an individual's overall health and well being are evaluated by the COPD Assessment Test (CAT) (Figure 14.1) or the Modified British Medical Research Council (mMRC) breathlessness scale (Table 14.2).

**Table 14.1:** GOLD Classification of COPD Severity (GOLD Guidelines)

| **GOLD Classification of Airflow Limitation Severity** | | |
|---|---|---|
| GOLD 1 | Mild | $FEV_1 \geq 80\%$ of predicted |
| GOLD 2 | Moderate | $50\% < FEV_1 < 80\%$ of predicted |
| GOLD 3 | Severe | $30\% < FEV_1 < 50\%$ of predicted |
| GOLD 4 | Very Severe | $FEV_1 < 30\%$ of predicted |

**Table 14.2:** MMRC Dyspnea Scale

| **Grade** | **Description of Breathlessness** |
|---|---|
| 0 | I only get breathless with strenuous exercise. |
| 1 | I get short of breath when hurrying on level ground or walking up a slight hill. |
| 2 | On level ground, I walk slower than people of the same age because of breathlessness, or have to stop for breath when walking at my own pace. |
| 3 | I stop for breath after walking about 100 yards or after a few minutes on level ground. |
| 4 | I am too breathless to leave the house or I am breathless when dressing. |

Although there are numerous definitions of a *COPD exacerbation* (see Chapter 16, Management of Outpatient COPD Exacerbations and Chapter 17, Management of Inpatient COPD Exacerbations), the GOLD guidelines define a COPD exacerbation as an acute event characterized by worsening of the patient's respiratory symptoms that is beyond normal day-to-day variations and leads to a change in medication (GOLD Guidelines). The best predictor of future exacerbations is a history of exacerbations in the prior year (Hurst, 2010). Severity of airflow limitation and use of systemic steroids are also associated with more frequent COPD exacerbations.

The GOLD multivariable COPD assessment is complex and requires several disparate pieces of data. It classifies patients as high or low risk based upon the severity of airflow limitation and history of exacerbations and then grades them as more or less symptomatic based upon their CAT or mMRC score (Figure 14.3). Patients with less symptoms, better spirometry, and fewer exacerbations are group A; patients with more symptoms, worse spirometry, and more frequent exacerbation are group D. Groups B and C are intermediate and have either more symptoms and lower risk or less symptoms and higher risk.

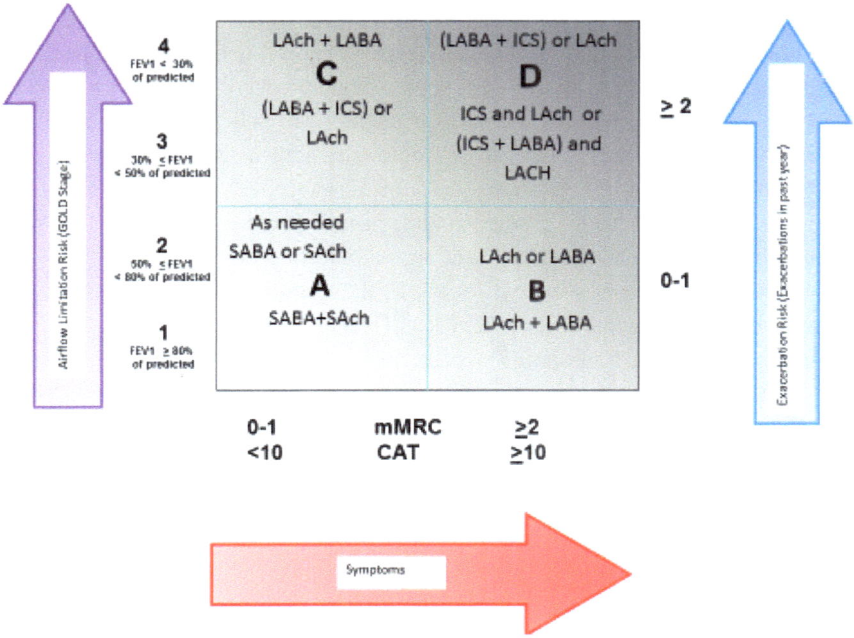


**Figure 14.4:** GOLD Guideline COPD Treatment Based upon COPD Category Pharmacologic treatment of patients in category A includes SAch or SABA or combination SAch + SABA; in category B, either LAch or LABA or combination LAch + LABA; in category C, combination LAch + LABA or combination LABA + ICS or LAch; and in category D, LAch, or combination LABA + ICS, or combination LAch + ICS, or combination LABA + LAch + ICS. Abbreviations: SABA: short acting beta agonists; LABA: long acting beta agonists; SAch: short acting anticholinergics; LAch: long acting acting anticholinergics; ICS inhaled corticosteroids.

## 14.3 Pharmacologic Treatment of COPD

Medications for the treatment of COPD consist of short acting beta agonists (SABA), long acting beta agonists (LABA), short acting anticholinergics (SAch), long acting acting anticholinergics (LAch), inhaled (ICS) and enteral corticosteroids. Other medications include phosphodiesterase inhibitors, macrolide antibiotics (used for their anti-inflammatory not antibiotic effect), and mucolytics.

SABAs are usually the initial medication and should be used on an as needed rather than scheduled basis for patients in GOLD group A. (Figure 14.4) Combinations of SABA and SAch (such as Combivent[R]) should not be prescribed regularly because SABA's should only be used on an as needed basis. If symptoms persist despite use of a SABA or if SABA use is excessive (greater than 3–4 times daily), an anticholinergic bronchodilator is usually added, GOLD Group B. LAch's are usually preferred because of the ease of use and theoretical advantage of improved adherence with less frequent dosing. A LABA may also be added. Combinations of a LABA and ICS or LABA and LACH may facilitate medication use and improve adherence, GOLD group C. ICS are recommended for patients with GOLD severe or very severe disease (FEV1<50%) and who have had two or more exacerbations in the prior year, GOLD Group D. ICS may also be beneficial in individuals who demonstrate bronchodilator responsiveness during spirometry testing (Chapter 9.4, COPD Phenotypes). *Use of triple inhalers in COPD, LAch and LABA plus ICS, improves lung function and symptoms but does not reduce exacerbations compared with either treatment alone* (Aaron, 2007).

Many patients with less severe and /or less COPD-related risk are prescribed ICS. It has been estimated that 70% of patients with COPD are treated with high-dose combination inhalers yet only 10% qualify under the current guidelines (Barnes, 2011). Similarly, significant over prescription of ICS compared with guidelines was noted among Veterans with COPD at the Cincinnati VAMC (Seaman, 2010). Use of ICS is associated with an increased risk of pneumonia in patients with COPD, OR 1.78 (95% CI, 1.50–2.12) (Kew, 2014).

Over the past 5 years, numerous new medications and novel medication combinations for the management of COPD have been approved by the US Food and Drug Administration (Table 14.3). The pharmacologic armamentarium for the treatment of COPD has doubled in the past several years and many new medications and combinations are in development.

### 14.3.1 Phosphodiesterase Inhibitors

Phosphodiesterases (PDEs) are a family of at least 11 isoenzymes that hydrolyze cAMP and cGMP. Inhibition of PDEs stimulates bronchodilation and also reduces pulmonary inflammation. Methylxanthines such as aminophylline or theophylline are nonspecific PDE inhibitors that have been used for the treatment of asthma and COPD. These medications are limited by a narrow therapeutic serum drug range, frequent interaction with other medications, and poor tolerability. Most recently, specific inhibitors of PDE isoforms, especially PDE4, have been developed and shown to be effective in the management of COPD. Roflumilast was approved by the FDA in 2011 as adjuvant treatment to reduce COPD exacerbations in patients with severe COPD associated with chronic bronchitis and a history of exacerbations (Reid, 2012).

### 14.3.2 Macrolides

Macrolides such as erythromycin and azithromycin have anti-inflammatory properties in addition to anti-microbial effects. Recent studies have shown that either daily erythromycin or azithromycin decrease the frequency of COPD exacerbations in patients with a history of exacerbations. (Martinez, 2008; Seemungal, 2008; Albert,

**Table 14.3:** Federal Drug Administration Approved Medications for COPD

| Class | Generic Name | Brand Name | FDA Approval |
|---|---|---|---|
| SABA | Albuterol | Ventolin HFA | 2001 |
| | | Proventil HFA | 1999 |
| | | Xopenex | 2002 |
| SAch | Ipratroprium | Atrovent HFA | 2004 |
| SABA + SAch | albuterol + ipratropium | Duoneb | 2001 |
| LAch | Tiotropium bromide | Spiriva HandiHaler | 2004 |
| | Umeclidinium | Incruse Ellipta | 2014 |
| | Aclidinium bromide | Tudorza Pressair | 2012 |
| LABA | Formoterol fumarate | Foradil Aerolizer | 2001 |
| | Salmeterol | Serevent Diskus | 1998 |
| | Indacaterol maleate | Arcapta | 2011 |
| | Arformoterol tartrate | Brovana | 2006 |
| | Olodaterol | Stiverdi Respimat | 2014 |
| LABA + ICS | Formoterol + Budesonide | Symbicort | 2009 |
| | Salmeterol + Fluticasone furoate | Advair Diskus | 2003 |
| | Vilanterol + Fluticasone furoate | Breo Ellipta | 2013 |
| LACH + LABA | Umeclidinium+ vilanterol | Anoro Ellipta | 2013 |
| PDE 4 Inhibitor | Roflumilast | Daliresp | 2011 |

Abbreviations: SABA: short acting bronchodilator; SACH: short acting anticholinergic; LACH: long acting anticholinergic; LABA: long acting bronchodilator; ICS: inhaled corticosteroid; PDE: phosphodiesterase

2011) Although it remains unclear which subgroup of patients with COPD will benefit best from macrolide treatment and whether dosing should be daily or thrice weekly, current recommendations are to consider daily macrolide treatment in patients who, despite maximal standard bronchodilator therapy, have at least 2 exacerbations yearly (Mammen, 2012). Potential adverse effects of prolonged macrolide use include development of bacterial resistance, cardiovascular events, and hearing loss.

### 14.3.3 Mucolytics

Mucolytics such as n-acetylcysteine and carbocysteine may reduce COPD exacerbations and improve health related quality of life in patients with COPD (Decramer, 2010). In one prospective study, n-acetylcysteine reduced hyperinflation (Stav, 2009).

### 14.3.4 Supplemental Oxygen

Supplemental oxygen improves survival in patients with hypoxemia at rest ($PaO_2$ <55 torr or $SpO_2$ <88%; or $PaO_2$ < 60 and >55 torr with evidence of cor pulmonale). The mechanism(s) by which supplemental oxygen improves mortality is not known. Oxygenation should be measured on room air at rest, with exertion, and during sleep after the administration of supplemental oxygen to insure that desaturation is prevented. Although Medicare and most insurances reimburse for supplemental oxygen during exercise or at night with evidence of exercise or nocturnal desaturation, **there is no substantive evidence that supplemental oxygen during exercise or at night is beneficial in individuals with stable COPD and normoxemia at rest.**

## 14.4 Nonpharmacologic Treatment of COPD

*Smoking cessation* is the singularly most important intervention for the prevention and treatment of COPD. Please see Chapter 7, Smoking Cessation, for further discussion of smoking cessation.

*Both influenza and pneumococcal vaccination* are recommended for individuals with COPD. Influenza vaccination reduces mortality, outpatient visits, hospitalizations, and exacerbations caused by influenza (Varkey, 2009). In contrast, although pneumococcal vaccination reduces the incidence of invasive pneumococcal disease, it has not shown any significant effect on mortality, rates of pneumonia or exacerbations, lung function, or cost effectiveness (Varkey, 2009; Walters, 2010). Vaccination against both influenza and pneumococcus may reduce COPD exacerbations more effectively than either vaccine alone (Varkey, 2009).

*Pulmonary rehabilitation* is a multidisciplinary program of education and exercise that teaches patients with COPD about their disease, its treatment, and mechanisms to cope with its consequences as well as an exercise and conditioning program. Pulmonary rehabilitation has the best effect when it is integrated into a comprehensive COPD management program that encourages behavior change and a shift from provider initiated to patient initiated care. Patients with COPD who maintain physical activity have less breathlessness with exertion, better health related quality of life, improved long term function and independence, and better psychological and physiological function.

**Table 14.4:** Medicare Oxygen Reimbursement Guidelines

| Patient Condition | $PaO_2$ | $SpO_2$ |
|---|---|---|
| Awake, at rest | < 55 mm Hg or<br>56–59 mm Hg and<br>dependent edema or<br>cor pulmonale or<br>pulmonary hypertension by right heart catheterization or ECHO or<br>P pulmonale on ECG (P wave > 3 mm in leads II, III, or AVF) or<br>erythrocythemia (HCT> 56%) | < 88% or<br>= 89% and<br>dependent edema or<br>cor pulmonale or<br>pulmonary hypertension by right heart catheterization or ECHO or<br>P pulmonale on ECG (P wave > 3 mm in leads II, III, or AVF) or<br>erythrocythemia (HCT> 56%) |
| Exercise | < 55 mm Hg and<br>Documentation that use of supplemental oxygen ameliorates the decline in oxygen levels<br>(Duration of desaturation and type/level of exertion are not specified.) | < 88% mm Hg and<br>Documentation that use of supplemental oxygen ameliorates the decline in oxygen levels<br>(Duration of desaturation and type/level of exertion are not specified.) |
| Sleep | < 55 mm Hg or<br>PaO2 declines > 10 mm Hg from awake, resting level and<br>dependent edema or<br>cor pulmonale or<br>pulmonary hypertension by right heart catheterization or ECHO or<br>P pulmonale on ECG (P wave > 3 mm in leads II, III, or AVF) or<br>erythrocythemia (HCT> 56%)<br>(Duration of desaturation and type/level of exertion are not specified.) | < 88% or<br>SpO2 declines > 5% from awake, resting level and<br>dependent edema or<br>cor pulmonale or<br>pulmonary hypertension by right heart catheterization or ECHO or<br>P pulmonale on ECG (P wave > 3 mm in leads II, III, or AVF) or<br>erythrocythemia (HCT> 56%)<br>(Duration of desaturation and type/level of exertion are not specified.) |

Physical inactivity is associated with worse survival, increased risk of respiratory-related hospitalization, lower self-reported health status, and greater systemic inflammation (Watz, 2014). Pulmonary rehabilitation improves respiratory symptoms (Lacasse, 2006). In addition to improving respiratory symptoms, pulmonary rehabilitation decreases health care utilization and may improve survival (Ries, 2008). Home based PR programs have the equivalent benefit of hospital based programs (Bourbeau, 2010).

*Lung volume reduction* either surgical or endoscopic via endobronchial valve placement may also be effective in certain patients with COPD. Surgical lung volume reduction improves exercise tolerance, quality of life, and survival in selected patients with COPD (Tidwell, 2012). LVRS is only beneficial in patients with upper lobe emphysema and poor exercise tolerance and is detrimental in individuals with $FEV_1$ < 20%

of predicted, DLCO < 20% of predicted, or diffusely distributed emphysema. Patients who are being considered for LVRS should be referred for pulmonary consultation. Endoscopic LVRS is a newer technique that may also be beneficial in select patients.

## 14.5 Management of COPD-related Nonpulmonary Co-morbidities

Because COPD is a multisystemic disorder with protean nonpulmonary manifestations, it is essential to evaluate and treat patients with COPD for conditions such as anemia, diabetes, lung cancer, and cardiovascular disease. (Reviewed in Chapter 10, COPD Is a Multi-Organ Disorder: Systemic Manifestations.)

## 14.6 Summary Points

1. Establish a definitive diagnosis of COPD before initiating treatment.
2. The principal symptoms of COPD are breathlessness, cough, and sputum production.
3. There are several well validated instruments (such as the COPD Activity Test) to assess and monitor serially COPD's effects on quality of life and respiratory symptoms.
4. Pharmacologic treatment for COPD begins with an as needed short acting bronchodilator, usually a SABA. The subsequent medication is a long acting bronchodilator, either LACH or LABA. Next, the other class of long acting bronchodilator is added and inhaled corticosteroids are usually the final inhaler category. (Individuals with COPD who have a response to bronchodilators may be more responsive to inhaled corticosteroids.)
5. Recent definitions of new COPD phenotypes will help to individualize COPD treatment regimens.
6. Dynamic hyperinflation is the major cause of exertional dyspnea and responds to pursed lip breathing and a slowing of the respiratory rate.
7. Nonpharmacologic treatments that are effective in the management of COPD include supplemental oxygen, lung volume reduction surgery, pulmonary rehabilitation and vaccinations, especially influenza.

## References

Aaron S.D., Vandemheen K.L., Fergusson D., Maltais F., Bourbeau J., Goldstein R., Balter M., O'Donnell D., McIvor A., Sharma S., Bishop G., Anthony J., Cowie R., Field S., Hirsch A., Hernandez P., Rivington R., Road J., Hoffstein V., Hodder R., Marciniuk D., McCormack D., Fox G., Cox G., Prins H.B., Ford G., Bleskie D., Doucette S, Mayers I., Chapman K., Zamel N., & FitzGerald M.; Canadian Thoracic Society/Canadian Respiratory Clinical Research Consortium.

(2007). Tiotropium in combination with placebo, salmeterol, or fluticasone-salmeterol for treatment of chronic obstructive pulmonary disease: a randomized trial. *Ann Intern Med*, *146*, 545–555.

Albert R.K., Connett J., Bailey W.C., Casaburi R., Cooper J.A. Jr, Criner G.J., Curtis J.L., Dransfield M.T., Han M.K., Lazarus S.C., Make B., Marchetti N., Martinez F.J., Madinger N.E., McEvoy C., Niewoehner D.E., Porsasz J., Price C.S., Reilly J., Scanlon P.D., Sciurba F.C., Scharf S.M., Washko G.R., Woodruff P.G., & Anthonisen N.R.; COPD Clinical Research Network. (2011). Azithromycin for prevention of exacerbations of COPD. *N Engl J Med*, *365*, 689–698.

Bafadhel M., Umar I., Gupta S., Raj J.V., Vara D.D., Entwisle J.J., Pavord I.D., Brightling C.E., & Siddiqui S. (2011). The role of CT scanning in multidimensional phenotyping of COPD. *Chest*, *140*(3), 634–42.

Barnes P.J. (2011). Triple inhalers for obstructive airways disease: will they be useful? *Expert Rev Respir Med*, *5*(3), 297–300.

Bourbeau J. (2010). Making pulmonary rehabilitation a success in COPD. *Swiss Med Wkly*, *140*, w13067.

Burgel P.R., Nesme-Meyer P., Chanez P., Caillaud D., Carré P., Perez T., Roche N.; Initiatives Broncho-pneumopathie Chronique Obstructive Scientific Committee. (2009). Cough and sputum production are associated with frequent exacerbations and hospitalizations in COPD subjects. *Chest*, *135*(4), 975–82.

de Oca M.M., Halbert R.J., Lopez M.V., Perez-Padilla R., Tálamo C., Moreno D., Muiño A., Jardim J.R., Valdivia G., Pertuzé J., & Menezes A.M. (2012). The chronic bronchitis phenotype in subjects with and without COPD: the PLATINO study. *Eur Respir J*, *40*(1), 28–36.

Doherty M.J., Mister R., Pearson M.G., & Calverley P.M. (2000). Capsaicin responsiveness and cough in asthma and chronic obstructive pulmonary disease. *Thorax*, *55*(8), 643–9.

Fahy J.V., & Dickey B.F. (2010). Airway Mucus Function and Dysfunction. *N Engl J Med*, *363*, 2233–2247

Global Initiative for Chronic Obstructive Lung Disease (GOLD). *Global Strategy for the Diagnosis, Management and Prevention of COPD, Updated 2014*. http://www.goldcopd.org/. Accessed October, 2014.

Hurst J.R., Vestbo J., Anzueto A., Locantore N., Müllerova H., Tal-Singer R., Miller B., Lomas D.A., Agusti A., Macnee W., Calverley P., Rennard S., Wouters E.F.,& Wedzicha J.A.; Evaluation of COPD Longitudinally to Identify Predictive Surrogate Endpoints (ECLIPSE) Investigators. (2010). Susceptibility to exacerbation in chronic obstructive pulmonary disease. *N Engl J Med*, *363*(12), 1128–38.

Jochmann A., Scherr A., Jochmann D.C., Miedinger D., Török S.S., Chhajed P.N., Tamm M., & Leuppi J.D. (2012). Impact of adherence to the GOLD guidelines on symptom prevalence, lung function decline and exacerbation rate in the Swiss COPD cohort. *Swiss Med Wkly*, *142*, w13567.

Jones P.W., Harding G., Berry P., Wiklund I., Chen W.H., & Kline Leidy N. (2009). Development and first validation of the COPD Assessment Test. *Eur Respir J*, *34*, 648–54.

Kanner R.E., Connett J.E., Williams D.E., & Buist A.S. (1999). Effects of randomized assignment to a smoking cessation intervention and changes in smoking habits on respiratory symptoms in smokers with early chronic obstructive pulmonary disease: the Lung Health Study. *Am J Med*, *106*(4), 410–6.

Kew K.M., & Seniukovich A. (2014). Inhaled steroids and risk of pneumonia for chronic obstructive pulmonary disease. *Cochrane Database Syst Rev*, 3, CD010115.

Kim V., Han M.K., Vance G.B., Make B.J., Newell J.D., Hokanson J.E., Hersh C.P., Stinson D., Silverman E.K., Criner G.J.; & COPDGene Investigators. (2011). The chronic bronchitic phenotype of COPD: an analysis of the COPDGene Study. *Chest*, *140*(3), 626–33.

Lacasse Y., Goldstein R., Lasserson T.J., & Martin S. Pulmonary rehabilitation for chronic obstructive pulmonary disease. *Cochrane Database Syst Rev*, 4, CD003793.

Leidy N.K., Rennard S.I., Schmier J., Jones M.K., & Goldman M. (2003). The breathlessness, cough, and sputum scale: the development of empirically based guidelines for interpretation. *Chest, 124*(6), 2182–91.

Leidy N.K., Schmier J.K., Jones M.K., Lloyd J., & Rocchiccioli K. (2003). Evaluating symptoms in chronic obstructive pulmonary disease: validation of the Breathlessness, Cough and Sputum Scale. *Respir Med*, Suppl A, S59–70.

Mammen M.J., & Sethi S. (2012). Macrolide therapy for the prevention of acute exacerbations in chronic obstructive pulmonary disease. *Pol Arch Med Wewn*, *122*(1–2), 54–9.

Martinez F.J., Curtis J.L., & Albert R. (2008). Role of macrolide therapy in chronic obstructive pulmonary disease. *Int J Chron Obstruct Pulmon Dis*, *3*(3), 331–50.

Martínez-García M.Á., Soler-Cataluña J.J., Donat Sanz Y., Catalán Serra P., Agramunt Lerma M., Ballestín Vicente J., & Perpiñá-Tordera M. (2011). Factors associated with bronchiectasis in patients with COPD. *Chest*, *140*(5), 1130–7.

Osadnik C.R., McDonald C.F., Jones A.P., & Holland A.E. (2012). Airway clearance techniques for chronic obstructive pulmonary disease. *Cochrane Database Syst Rev*, 3, CD008328.

Poole P., Black P.N., & Cates C.J. (2012). Mucolytic agents for chronic bronchitis or chronic obstructive pulmonary disease. *Cochrane Database Syst Rev*, 8, CD001287.

Reid D.J., & Pham N.T. (2012). Roflumilast: a novel treatment for chronic obstructive pulmonary disease. *Ann Pharmacother*, *46*(4), 521–529.

Rennard S., Decramer M., Calverley P.M., Pride N.B., Soriano J.B., Vermeire P.A., & Vestbo J. (2002). Impact of COPD in North America and Europe in 2000: subjects' perspective of Confronting COPD International Survey. *Eur Respir J*, *20*(4), 799–805.

Ries AL. (2008). Pulmonary rehabilitation: summary of an evidence-based guideline. *Respir Care*, 53(9), 1203–7.

Seaman J., Leonard A.C., & Panos R.J. (2010). Health care utilization history, GOLD guidelines, and respiratory medication prescriptions in patients with COPD. *Int J Chron Obstruct Pulmon Dis*, *5*, 89–97.

Seemungal T.A., Wilkinson T.M., Hurst J.R., Perera W.R., Sapsford R.J., & Wedzicha J.A. (2008). Long-term erythromycin therapy is associated with decreased chronic obstructive pulmonary disease exacerbations. *Am J Respir Crit Care Med*, *178*, 1139–1147.

Smith J., Owen E., Earis J., & Woodcock A. (2006). Effect of codeine on objective measurement of cough in chronic obstructive pulmonary disease. *J Allergy Clin Immunol*, *117*(4), 831–5.

Smith J.A., & Calverley P.M. (2004). Cough in chronic obstructive pulmonary disease. *Pulm Pharmacol Ther*, 17(6), 393–8.

Smith J.A., Hambleton E.C., Earis A., & Woodcock A.A. (2003). Measurements of cough in chronic obstructive pulmonary disease. *Thorax*, *58*(suppl III), iii48.

Stav D., & Raz M. (2009). Effect of N-acetylcysteine on air trapping in COPD: a randomized placebo-controlled study. *Chest*, *136*(2), 381–6.

Tidwell S.L., Westfall E., & Dransfield M.T. (2012). Lung volume reduction for advanced emphysema: surgical and bronchoscopic approaches. *South Med J*, *105*(1), 56–61.

Varkey J.B., Varkey A.B., & Varkey B. (2009). Prophylactic vaccinations in chronic obstructive pulmonary disease: current status. *Curr Opin Pulm Med*, *15*(2), 90–9.

Vestbo J., Anderson J.A., Calverley P.M., Celli B., Ferguson G.T., Jenkins C., Knobil K., Willits L.R., Yates J.C., & Jones P.W. (2009). Adherence to inhaled therapy, mortality and hospital admission in COPD. Thorax, *64*(11), 939–43.

von Hertzen L., Reunanen A., Impivaara O., Mälkiä E., & Aromaa A. (2000). Airway obstruction in relation to symptoms in chronic respiratory disease--a nationally representative population study. *Respir Med*, *94*(4), 356–63.

Watz H., Pitta F., Rochester C.L., Garcia-Aymerich J., ZuWallack R., Troosters T., Vaes A.W., Puhan M.A., Jehn M., Polkey M.I., Vogiatzis I., Clini E.M., Toth M., Gimeno-Santos E., Waschki B.,

Esteban C., Hayot M., Casaburi R., Porszasz J., McAuley E., Singh S.J., Langer D., Wouters E.F., Magnussen H., & Spruit M.A. (2014). An official European Respiratory Society statement on physical activity in COPD. *Eur Respir J*, *44*(6), 1521-1537

Weldam S.W, Schuurmans M.J., Liu R., & Lammers J.W. (2013). Evaluation of Quality of Life instruments for use in COPD care and research: A systematic review. Int J Nurs Stud, 50(5), 688–707.

Yamane T., Hattori N., Kitahara Y., Haruta Y., Sasaki H., Yokoyama A., & Kohno N. (2010). Productive cough is an independent risk factor for the development of COPD in former smokers. *Respirology*, *15*(2), 313–8.

Aaron M Mulhall MD

# 15 Practical Guide to Correct Inhaler Use

Key Points

1. Knowledge of proper inhaler techniques enables providers to educate patients with COPD how to use their medications correctly and achieve maximal benefits.
2. Correct inhaler use is critical to obtaining maximal therapeutic benefit.
3. Repetitive inhaler education and direct observation play crucial roles in ensuring that patients use their inhalers correctly.
4. Correct use of pressurized metered-dose inhalers (pMDIs) requires coordination between activating the canister and slowly inhaling the aerosol.
5. Using a spacer with a pMDI improves effective drug delivery to the lungs.
6. Multidose dry powder inhalers (DPIs) are inhalation-triggered by the patient and do not require activation-inhalation coordination for proper use.
7. The Respimat® Soft Mist Inhaler® (SMI) provides the same level of bronchodilatation as pMDIs without spacers and DPIs, but at roughly half the dose of medication. The Respimat® SMI has been shown to have greater lung and less oropharyngeal deposition of medication compared to pMDIs without spacers and DPIs.
8. Nebulizers are an alternative to short acting bronchodilator pMDIs when patients are unable to use a pMDI properly or when they are hospitalized. There is not a significant clinical therapeutic difference between medications delivered by pMDI with a spacer and by nebulizer.

## 15.1 Introduction

Inhaled medications have a critical role in the treatment of chronic obstructive pulmonary disease (COPD). The goals of treatment include bronchodilation, minimizing airway inflammation, preventing exacerbations, improving quality of life (QOL), and decreasing mortality (Celli, 2004). The success and potential benefits of treatment depend upon successfully delivering the drug to the appropriate location in the lungs. Inhalers, when properly used, serve to target the drug directly to the lungs (Dolovich, 2005; Ernst, 1998; Pauwels, 1997). Inhaled medications are a preferred treatment for COPD, as compared to oral or intravenous (IV) medications, because they can be distributed to the lungs as an aerosol in smaller quantities, leading to significantly fewer systemic side effects (Aerosol Consensus Statement, 1991; GOLD website).

The ability of the drug to reach the smaller, more peripheral airways of the lung is critical for inhaler efficacy. Inhaled particles that are traveling at high velocity or are too large tend to be delivered to the larger (more proximal) airways, thus not reaching their target. To reach the smaller airways, particles must be moving slowly enough

**Table 15.1:** Qualities that exemplify the "ideal" inhaler

| |
|---|
| *Readily able for patient to use* |
| – Easy to use/learn<br>– Small and portable (can keep in pocket)<br>– Ready to use<br>– Breath-actuated (breath triggers drug delivery)<br>– Can control drug delivery based on audio/visual features (ex: dose count meter)<br>– Only medication delivered (no propellants or additives)<br>– Multidose and can be reloaded/refilled<br>– Environmentally safe |
| *Drug dose and amount delivered are independent of external conditions and low inspiratory flow* |
| *Delivers drug to smaller airways* |
| – Able to deliver drug in small particles<br>– Delivers aerosol slowly<br>– Minimizes oropharyngeal delivery |

and must be small enough (1–5μm) to navigate the multiple directional bifurcations within the distal airways (Burton, 1992; Dolovich, 1991).

There are a variety of available inhalational devices that deliver medication in an aerosol form. The choice of medication, as well as the ability of the patient, ultimately determines what type of inhaler to prescribe (Broeders, 2009; Hanania, 1994; Vincken, 2010) (Table 15.1). In this chapter, we will review most commonly prescribed inhalers (pressurized metered-dose inhalers [pMDIs], multidose dry powder inhalers [DPIs], Respimat® inhaler, and nebulizers), how they work, and the correct steps to use them properly.

## 15.2 Inhaler Education and Errors in Inhaler Technique

The most commonly used inhalation devices are pMDIs, DPIs, Respimat® and nebulizers. (Table 15.2) If used properly, each of these devices can deliver a precise amount of drug in small particles that can reach the terminal airways and produce a bronchodilating effect. Incorrect inhaler use by patients decreases medication adherence and diminishes the therapeutic benefit (Crompton, 1982; McFadden, 1995). Errors in inhaler technique occur in as many as 90% of patients with COPD (Crompton, 1982; Crompton, 2006; Fink, 2005; Lavorini, 2008; McFadden, 1995; Rees, 2005; Wieshmmer, 2008). Factors associated with improper inhaler use in patients with COPD include age, impaired cognitive function, and poor training of healthcare professionals responsible for teaching correct inhaler use (Leiva-Fernández, 2012). Problems are further increased when patients use multiple inhalation delivery devices, often

**Table 15.2:** Medications commonly used for the treatment of COPD

| |
|---|
| *Pressurized Metered-Dose Inhalers (pMDIs) (Can use with a spacer)* |
| Albuterol |
| Ipratropium |
| Albuterol / Ipratropium |
| Budesonide / Formoterol |
| *Multidose Dry Powder Inhalers (DPIs)* |
| Formoterol |
| Mometasone |
| Budesonide |
| Tiotropium |
| Fluticasone / Salmeterol |
| Aclidinium |
| *Respimat® Soft Mist Inhaler (SMI)* |
| Ipratropium |
| Tiotropium |
| Albuterol / Ipratropium |
| *Nebulized Solutions* |
| Albuterol |
| Ipratropium |
| Albuterol / Ipratropium |

confusing the different techniques required for each unique device (van der Palen, 1999).

Errors in inhaler technique are often a consequence of inadequate or poor education. Inhaler education prior to initiation of inhalation therapy is critical and written instruction alone are inadequate. Verbal instruction, assessing correct inhaler technique, and reassessment decrease inhaler misuse (De Boeck, 1999; Leiva-Fernández, 2012). Patients who have recurrent inhaler education have better inhaler techniques compared with those who only receive instruction at the time of prescription (Gracia-Antequera, 1999). The Global Initiative for Chronic Obstructive Lung Disease (GOLD) and the National Institute for Health and Care Excellence (NICE) both recommend inhaler education and device training when a patient is prescribed a new inhaler (GOLD, NICE websites). They also recommend that correct inhaler technique be assessed at each patient encounter. However, up to 25% of patients do not receive any verbal instruction when prescribed an inhalational device (Lavorini, 2008).

There are several modalities used to provide inhaler education and improve correct use. Demonstration of inhaler use by healthcare professionals is effective at both teaching and assessing the correct use of inhaler devices (Bosnic-Anticevich, 2010; Nimmo, 1993). However, healthcare professionals often do not know how to

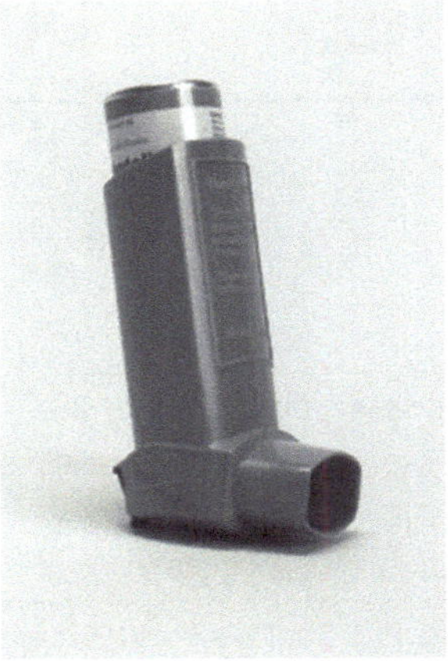

**Figure 15.1:** Pressurized metered-dose Inhalers (pMDI)

use the inhalation device and often cannot use it correctly themselves (Guidry, 1992; Hanania, 1994; Keston, 1993). Coaching has also been used to improve the ability to use inhalers; however, many patients often quickly revert back to an incorrect inhalation technique (Crompton, 1982; Duerden, 2002). For the patient to have the optimum benefit of their inhaled medication, it is of the utmost importance that the healthcare professional educating the patient has proper knowledge of the inhaler, knows what inhalers are appropriate for individual patients, and can teach correct inhaler use.

## 15.3 Inhalation Delivery Systems

### 15.3.1 Pressurized Metered-Dose Inhalers (pMDIs)

The pMDI has long been the most commonly used inhaled device because it is small, portable, inexpensive, and relatively easy to use (Vincken, 2010). Benefits of pMDIs are that they are pocket-sized, efficient, and can deliver many doses of medication quickly with precision. The pMDI is a pressurized canister filled with liquid medication placed in a chamber with a mouthpiece. Built into this system is a metering valve that delivers a specific quantity of the drug with each use. The wet aerosol is delivered to the lungs by a propellant. Historically, chlorofluorocarbon (CFC) was used as a propellant but CFC use is banned by the *Montreal Protocol on Substances that Deplete the Ozone Layer* because CFCs have been linked to depletion of the ozone layer in the upper atmosphere. CFCs have since been replaced by hydrofluoroalkanes (HFA), which are more environmentally friendly (Dolovich, 1999). The newer pMDIs formulated with HFAs have, in part, many of the same inhaler characteristics (smaller

**Table 15.3:** Correct steps for using pMDI without a spacer

| | |
|---|---|
| 1. | Shake the inhaler well immediately before each use. |
| 2. | Remove cap from mouthpiece |
| 3. | Check mouthpiece for foreign objects. |
| 4. | Make sure the canister is fully inserted into the actuator. |
| 5. | Prime inhaler if using for the first time or if the inhaler has not been used for over 2 weeks. Do this by spraying the inhaler 2–3 times away from the face. |
| 6. | Breathe out gently and fully through the mouth, trying to remove as much air from the lungs as possible. |
| 7. | Open the mouth wide, and place the open end of the mouthpiece about 1–2 inches from the mouth and inhale (slowly and deeply; as if sipping hot soup). Press canister down into the mouthpiece to actuate the aerosal at the beginning of inhalation while continuing to inhale deeply. |
| 8. | At end of inspiration, hold breath for 10 seconds, or as long as possible, then breathe out slowly. |
| 9. | If more puffs are needed (albuterol and ipratropium), wait for a few seconds before repeating steps 4–8. |

particle sized and less need for actuation-inhalation coordination) as the CFC inhalers (Leach, 1998; Melani, 2007).

pMDIs are designed to deliver an exact dose of medication to the lungs (Wilson, 1993). When the patient presses the canister, a one-way metering valve opens. The drug is aerosolized and the patient inhales it from the mouthpiece. The particle sizes within the aerosol vary, and the larger particles are deposited more proximally and the smaller particles dispersed to the smaller airways (Finlay, 2001; Hickey, 2004; Swarbrick, 2007). (Figure 15.1) For pMDIs to deliver the medication to the lungs properly, there must be coordination between canister activation and aerosol inhalation (Crompton, 1982; Larsen, 1994). pMDIs are both a reliable and effective inhaler device when used correctly. The coordinated steps that must be taken to use the pMDI correctly are shown in Table 15.3.

Determining the amount of medication remaining in the pMDI canister has been difficult to assess. The float method was used in the past to determine the amount of medication remaining in pMDIs. In the float method, the canister containing medication was placed in water. If the canister was empty if would float. How full the canister was full of medication would determine how far it would sink. Float testing is highly variable, product-specific, and a function of canister size, design, content, and method of testing (Brock, 2002). Float testing is not recommended as an appropriate method to measure medication adherence. Directly weighing the canister and dose counters are the most accurate ways to assess the medication remaining in the

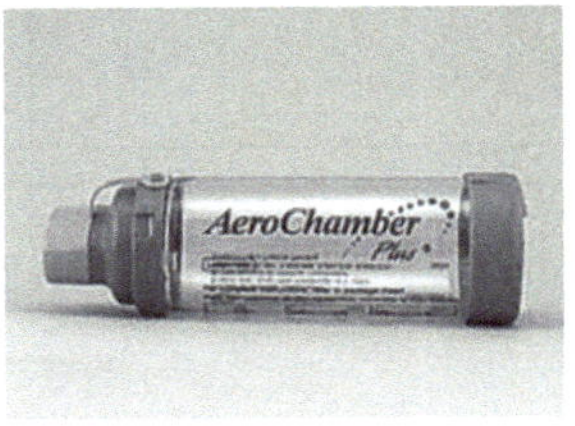


**Figure 15.2:** Spacer device for pressurized metered-dose Inhalers (pMDI)

pMDI canister. Dose counters have now been added to some pMDIs brands over the past decade. These devices display the number of doses/actuations that remain in the inhaler. The accuracy of dose counters depends upon the ability of the dose counter to decrease by one unit each time the patient actuates the inhaler. The dose counter should also be ergonomic (patient-friendly), and sustainable (lasting for the lifetime of the inhaler) (Weinstein, 2011).

### 15.3.2 Spacer Utilization

pMDIs are good inhalational devices for patients with COPD, but medication effectiveness using this type of inhaler is limited by the coordination of multiple steps, fine motor control, hand / finger strength, arthritis or other hand deformity, and, most importantly, precise hand-breath coordination. One way to minimize the issue of hand-breath coordination with a pMDI is to use a spacer. These devices improve drug delivery to the patient who is either non co-operative with pMDI use without the spacer, or unable to master correct pMDI usage. Spacers improve effective drug delivery when using the pMDI (Brennan, 2005; Melani, 2004). A spacer consists of a holding chamber with a one-way valve that connects to the mouthpiece of the pMDI. After activation of the pMDI, the medication aerosol is contained within the holding chamber and slowly inhaled by the patient. The one-way valve opens during inspiration and closes during expiration. This valve helps prevent drug loss which commonly occurs when patients cannot coordinate activating the canister and inhaling the aerosol (Dolovich, 1983). The spacer can also help to deliver the medication effectively to the smaller, more peripheral airways by slowing down the smaller particles and holding them in suspension for about one second, allowing some of the propellant surrounding the drug to evaporate. (Figure 15.2) Larger drug particles are also retained or deposited within the spacer during inhalation, thus limiting the inhaled aerosol to small particles that can reach the terminal airways (Ahrens, 1995; Barry, 1996). Another benefit is that larger particles will not reach the oropharynx, decreasing potential side effects. Spacers decrease oropharyngeal candidiasis associated with inhaled corticosteroid use; however, they do not decrease the rate of dyspho-

**Table 15.4:** Correct steps for using pMDI with spacer

| |
|---|
| 1. Shake the inhaler well before use (3–4 shakes)<br>2. Remove the cap from the inhaler, and from the spacer, if it has one<br>3. Attach the inhaler to the spacer<br>4. Breathe out, away from the spacer<br>5. Insert the spacer mouthpiece in mouth, putting the mouthpiece between teeth and closing lips around it<br>6. Activate the pMDI by pressing the top of the inhaler once; the aerosol will be sprayed into the holding chamber of the spacer<br>7. Breathe in **slowly** (as if sipping hot soup) until a full breath is taken. If the spacer whistle sounds, decrease the inspiratory speed.<br>8. Hold breath for about ten seconds or for as long as is comfortable, and then breathe out slowly.<br>9. If more puffs are needed (albuterol and ipratropium), wait for a few seconds before repeating steps 4–8. |
| To clean the spacer: |
| 1. Take the spacer apart (usually by removing the cap or flange containing the pMDI attachment port).<br>2. Clean the parts by washing in warm water with mild dish detergent. Never use boiling hot water, rubbing alcohol, or disinfectant.<br>3. Rinse the parts well in clean water.<br>4. Let spacer air dry.<br>5. Put the spacer back together. |

nia (Barnes, 1993; Dolovich, 1983; Dolovich, 2005). Despite the benefits of spacer use, they are infrequently prescribed or used. This reduced adherence may be due to the size of the spacer (they are long, bulky, and not conveniently transported), and patients are often embarrassed to use them in public. Another disadvantage of the spacer is that it requires frequent cleaning by a standard procedure (Bisgaard, 2007; Van der Palen, 1999). (Table 15.4)

### 15.3.3 Multidose Dry Powder Inhalers (DPIs)

DPIs were developed as alternative inhalers for patients who have difficulty using pMDIs and as environmentally friendly alternatives to CFC containing pMDI. DPIs specifically address issues with actuation-inhalation synchronization as well as potential allergic reactions to the propellants in the pMDIs (Beaucage, 2002). They resolve actuation-inhalation difficulties by being inhalation-triggered. They deliver medication, in the form of a dry powder, to the smaller airways. The medication is released in the form of small particles that are inhaled into the airways when the patient takes a breath. The factors that determine the amount of medication delivered by DPIs are the inspiratory volume and flow produced by the patient. There are a variety of DPIs, and

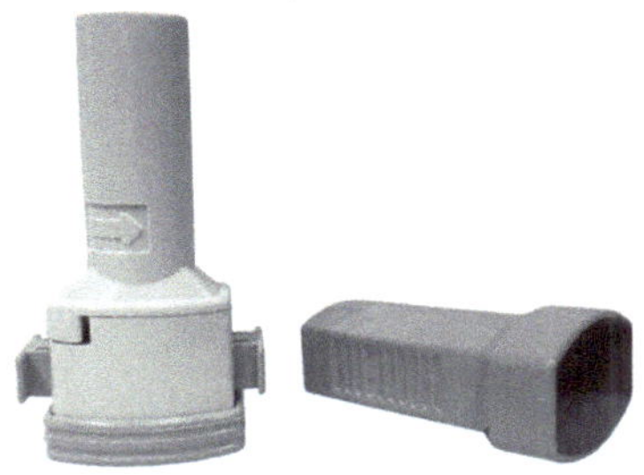

Figure 15.3: Aerolizer® multidose dry powder inhaler (DPI)

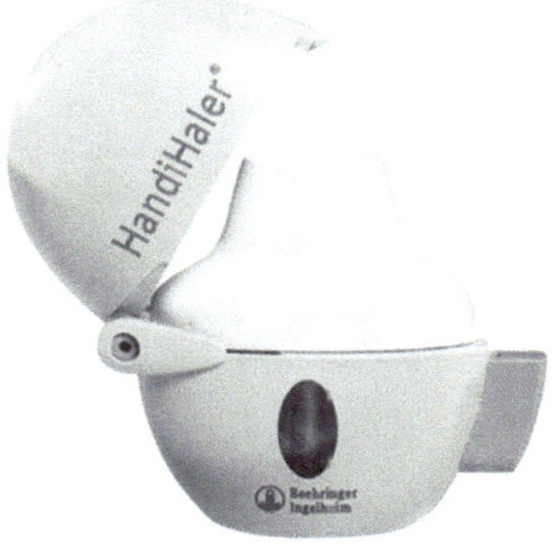


Figure 15.4: Handihaler® multidose dry powder inhaler (DPI)

Figure 15.5: Twisthaler® multidose dry powder inhaler (DPI)

**Table 15.5:** Correct steps for Using Formoterol (Foradil Aerolizer®) DPI

1. Hold the base of the inhaler firmly and twist the mouthpiece in the direction of the arrow to open.
2. Push the buttons in on each side to make sure that you can see 4 pins in the capsule-chamber of the inhaler.
3. Remove one capsule from the blister packer by peeling off the paper backing that covers one capsule, and pushing the capsule through the foil.
4. Place the capsule in the capsule-chamber in the base of the inhaler and twist the mouthpiece back to the closed position.
5. Hold the mouthpiece of the inhaler upright and press both buttons at the same time. Only press the buttons ONCE. There will be a click as the capsule is being pierced.
6. Release the buttons.
7. Keep the inhaler level, with the blue buttons to the left and right (not up and down).
8. Breathe out and exhale fully.
9. Place the mouthpiece in mouth and close lips around it.
10. Breathe in quickly and deeply. This will cause the capsule to spin around in the chamber and deliver the dose of medicine. There will be a whirring noise and a sweet taste due to the sugar filler in the capsule.
11. Remove the inhaler from mouth and continue to hold breath as long as possible, and then exhale.
12. Open the inhaler to see if any powder is still in the capsule. If any powder remains in the capsule repeat steps 8 to 11. Most people are able to empty the capsule in one or two inhalations.
13. After use, open the inhaler, remove and discard the empty capsule. Do not leave a used capsule in the chamber.
14. Close the mouthpiece and replace the cover.

**Table 15.6:** Correct steps for using Tiotropium (Spiriva Handihaler®) DPI

15. Open Handihaler by lifting the cap and the mouthpiece on the top to reveal capsule insertion site.
16. Separate one of the blisters from the blister card, open, and remove the capsule.
17. Insert the capsule and close the mouthpiece firmly against the gray base until it clicks shut.
18. Press the green piercing button once until it is flat (flush) against the base, then release.
19. Breathe out completely.
20. Place Handihaler mouthpiece in mouth and breathe in deeply until lungs are full. The capsule will vibrate (rattle).
21. To take a full daily dose, inhale **twice** from the same capsule by repeating steps 5 and 6.

with each one the amount of inspiratory flow needed to deliver the medication to the correct location varies. Examples of DPIs include the Twisthaler®, Handihaler®, and Aerolizer®. (Figures 15.3–15.5) The correct steps for commonly used DPIs are shown in Tables 15.5–15.7.

The main advantages of DPIs include: they do not requiring a propellant for aerosolization and are ecologically friendly; they are breath-triggered and do not require the precise hand-inhalation coordination of pMDIs (Melani, 2007; Virchow, 2008).

Table 15.7: Correct steps for using Mometasone (Asmanex Twisthaler®) DPI

1. Hold the inhaler upright, with the colored portion on the bottom.
2. Remove the cap of the inhaler while it is in this upright position. Holding the colored base, twist the cap in a counterclockwise direction to remove it. Removing the cap loads the inhaler with the medicine.
3. Breathe out fully.
4. Insert inhaler in mouth, holding it in a horizontal (on its side) position.
5. Firmly close lips around the mouthpiece and take in a fast, deep breath. Do not cover the ventilation holes while inhaling the dose.
6. Remove the inhaler from mouth and hold breath for about 10 seconds.
7. Wipe mouthpiece dry, if needed, place cap back on mouthpiece, and firmly close the inhaler. A "click" will signify the cap is fully closed. This is the only way to be sure that the next dose is loaded the right way.

Disadvantages of DPIs include: inability to use them with non-cooperative patients or those being ventilated via endotracheal tube or tracheotomy tube; cannot use a spacer to improve effective drug delivery; the amount of drug delivered is not as accurate, or reproducible, compared to pMDIs; patients who cannot generate appropriate inspiratory volume or flow will receive inadequate drug doses; each individual DPI has its own steps for correct use requiring dexterity and understanding of each inhaler (Clark, 1993; Fuller, 1995; Olsson, 1998; Robbins, 2005; Tarsin, 2006).

### 15.3.4 Respimat® Soft Mist Inhaler® (SMI®)

The Respimat® SMI® is the most recent inhaler delivery system to be developed as an alternative to pMDIs. The Respimat® SMI® forces a solution carrying the medication through a series of channels with two nozzles on the end. These nozzles focus two fluid jets at a convergence, producing a vapor of medication-containing droplets of a precise size that can be inhaled (Dalby, 2004; Dalby, 2011; Panos, 2013). (Figure 15.6) This inhaler was also developed to deliver the vapor at a slower velocity, thus increasing the window of time for successful inhalation, decreasing drug deposition in the oropharynx, and increasing the amount of medication successfully reaching the lungs. A number of studies have confirmed less oropharyngeal and greater lung deposition with the Respimat® SMI® compared to pMDIs without spacers and DPIs (Brand, 2008; Khachikian, 2012; Newman, 1996; Newman, 1998; Pitcairn, 2005). Another benefit of the Respimat® SMI® is that it provides the same level of bronchodilation that pMDIs offer at a much lower dose (Iacono, 2000; Kilfeather, 2004; Ram, 2011; Zuwallack, 2010).

To use the Respimat® SMI®, a medication-containing cartridge must be inserted into the delivery system. This device is activated by twisting the base 180° (half a turn) until it clicks. This twisting loads the fluid into the dosing chamber. The patient then

**Figure 15.6:** Respimat® inhaler

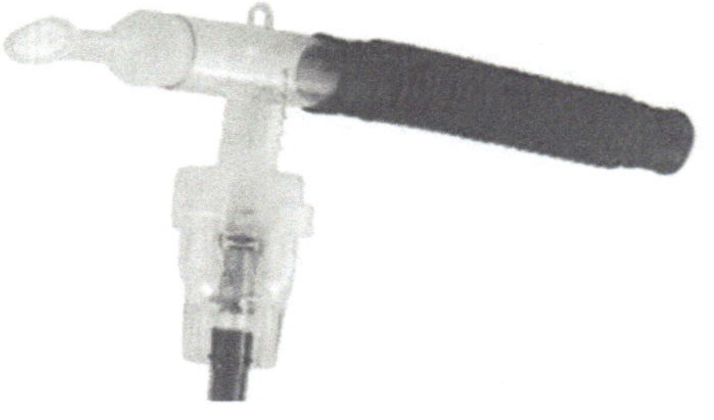

**Figure 15.7:** Nebulizer device

presses the dose-release button sending the fluid through the series of channels with nozzles at the end producing an inhalable particle vapor that exits the device. The coordinated steps that must be taken to use the Respimat® SMI® correctly are shown in Table 15.8.

### 15.3.5 Nebulized Solutions

Prior to the development of pMDIs and DPIs, inhaled medications were delivered via nebulizer. They transform the liquid form of medication into an aerosol of particles of various sizes that can be inhaled by mouthpiece or mask. The medication is inhaled while the patient is tidal breathing and does not require a deep, coordinated inspiration. To use a nebulized solution, one must have a nebulizer, air or oxygen compressor, and a mask or mouthpiece. (Figure 15.7) (Table 15.9) The types of medication delivered via nebulizer vary (steroids, short acting bronchodilators, and long acting

**Table 15.8:** Correct steps for using Respimat® SMI®

1. Remove cartridge from box and push the narrow end of the cartridge into the inhaler. The cartridge will not sit flush with the inhaler, with 1/8 of an inch of the cartridge sticking out of the inhaler.
2. Place clear base over the top of the cartridge.

**To Prime**

1. Prime inhaler if using for the first time, or if it has not been used in 3 weeks.
2. To prime, hold the inhaler upright, with the orange cap closed. Turn the clear base in the direction of the white arrows on the label until it clicks (half a turn). Flip the orange cap until it snaps fully open. Point inhaler toward the ground and press the dose release button. Repeat three more times.

**To Use**

1. Hold the inhaler upright with the orange cap closed, so it does not accidentally discharge a dose of medicine.
2. Turn the clear base in the direction of the white arrows on the label until it clicks (half a turn / 180°).
3. Flip the orange cap until it snaps fully open.
4. Breathe out slowly and fully, and then close lips around the end of the mouthpiece without covering the air vents.
5. Point inhaler to the back of throat.
6. While taking in a slow, deep breath by mouth, press the dose release button and continue to breathe in slowly for as long as possible.
7. Hold breath for 10 seconds or for as long as comfortable.

bronchodilators), and their delivery will depend on the drug's solubility and if they are in a solution or a suspension.

The ability of a nebulizer to deliver medications to the lungs successfully depends upon many factors, especially the patient's breathing pattern and the nebulizer output. As the drug is nebulized, its concentration in solution increases, leaving up to 50% of the drug in the reservoir (Johnson, 1989). The flow of gas in the nebulizer can alter the amount of drug delivered by changing particle size and nebulizer time. A flow rate between 6 and 10L/min can deliver approximately 2.5 mL of drug solution over 5–10 minutes (Muers, 1997). The patient should have a tidal (slow and regular) breathing pattern while inhaling the aerosol. It is also important to note these medications should be inhaled by breathing in and out through the mouth. Nebulizers are widely popular, often used, and are thought to be the most effective way to deliver inhaled medication. This, however, is not the case as only about 5% of the nebulized medication makes it to the smaller airways (Johnson, 1989). The rest of the medication is either delivered proximally, exhaled, or lost in the form of condensation in the reservoir, tubing, mouthpiece, or on the face.

There are a number of disadvantages to using a nebulizer. The process of delivering an inhaled medication to the lungs is long, inconvenient, and cumbersome (Melani, 2007). It is almost impossible to precisely deliver a set dose of medication with a nebulizer (Johnson, 1989). Nebulizers need to be cleaned frequently to prevent

**Table 15.9:** Correct steps for using nebulizer

| |
|---|
| 1. Remove 1 vial from the foil pouch.<br>2. Twist cap off vial and squeeze contents into nebulizer reservoir.<br>3. Connect nebulizer reservoir to the facemask/mouthpiece<br>4. Connect nebulizer to the compressor.<br>5. Sitting upright, in a comfortable position, place mouthpiece into mouth and turn on compressor.<br>6. Breathe slowly and regularly until no more mist is in the nebulizer chamber. |
| To clean weekly |
| 1. Remove the mask/mouthpiece from the reservoir. Remove the tubing and set it aside. The tubing should not be washed or rinsed. Wash the mask/mouthpiece with a mild dishwashing soap and warm water.<br>2. Rinse under a strong stream of water for 30 seconds.<br>3. Rinse the nebulizer parts under warm running water for 1 minute. Use distilled or sterile water, if possible.<br>4. Shake off excess water and air dry.<br>5. Put the mask/mouthpiece, reservoir, and tubing back together and connect the device to the compressed air machine. Run the machine for 10 to 20 seconds to dry the inside of the nebulizer thoroughly.<br>6. Disconnect the tubing from the compressed air machine. Store the nebulizer.<br>7. Clean the surface of the compressed air machine with a damp, soapy cloth, sponge, or an alcohol or disinfectant wipe. Never place the air compressor in water. Place a cover over the compressed air machine. |

contamination of the nebulized aerosols. Contamination has occurred frequently with the following microorganisms: methicillin-resistant *Staphylococcus aureus* (MRSA), *Pseudomonas aeruginosa*, *Burkholderia* species, and *Stenonotrophomonas* species (Berlinski, 2006; Melani, 2001). Most nebulizers are not portable.

There have been many studies comparing pMDIs (with a spacer) to nebulizers, showing that both are equally effective. Some studies favor pMDI use with a spacer over nebulizers in acute care and hospital settings, citing similar efficacy and potential cost savings (Comargo, 2000; Idris, 1993). The GOLD guidelines do not recommend the use of nebulizers for regular maintenance therapy in the treatment of COPD (GOLD website). The American Thoracic Society (ATS) and the European Respiratory Society (ERS) guidelines suggest that nebulizers can be used in the following situations for COPD: when using short acting bronchodilators; when patients cannot use an inhaler properly; and when patients are hospitalized (easier to deliver by respiratory therapist and requires little patient effort) (Celli, 2004).

## 15.4 Reminders to Increase Adherence

The goals of COPD treatment are to control disease symptoms, prevent chronic complications related to the disease, and prevent exacerbations. Patient adherence with inhaled medications helps to achieve these goals (GOLD website; Restrepo, 2008). Adherence is concordance between the healthcare provider's recommendations and the patient's actual behavior. This concordance requires that the patient assumes an active role in their treatment. Over half of patients with COPD adhere poorly with their treatment regimens (Bender, 2006; Haupt, 2008; Krigsman, 2007a; Krigsman, 2007b; Krigsman, 2007c; Lareau, 2010; WHO website). There are a number of reasons for poor adherence, including: the number of chronic co-morbidities; the number of prescribed medications; decreased adherence over time with chronic use of medications; impaired physical and cognitive function; lack of patient understanding about chronic nature of COPD and use of medications to prevent exacerbations; and discontinuation of medication in response to a decline in symptoms (Dolce, 1991; Krigsman, 2007b; Lareau, 2010; Meckenberg, 2008; Restrepo, 2008). Poor adherence is associated with increased risk of exacerbations and greater healthcare utilization (Isamlia, 2014; van Boven, 2014). Patients who adhere to their treatment regimens >80% of the time survive longer than less adherent patients (Vestbo, 2009).

Medication adherence among patients with COPD is affected by a number of variables related to the patient, the treatment, and society (Bourbeau, 2008; Restrepo, 2008). Patient-related factors include their physical abilities, cognitive function, and mental capabilities. For example, patients with COPD and depression adhere less well with their inhalers than those who are not depressed (DiMatteo, 2007; Lareau, 2010). An important treatment-related factor is the use of multiple inhalers, each of which often has a different inhalation technique. Societal factors include the relationship between the patient and the healthcare provider, access to medications, financial resources, ability to receive adequate inhaler education, and the patient's familial and social support system.

Assessing medication adherence can be difficult as there is no clear definition of what would be an appropriate level of compliance. A variety of methods to assess adherence have been described, including pill counting or weighing, reviewing pharmacy records, patient self-reporting, estimations made by the healthcare provider, electronic monitoring, and biological monitoring (Lareau, 2010). Each of these have their advantages and disadvantages.

Providers can perform a variety of interventions to increase inhaler adherence in patients with COPD. One of the most important factors is effective communication between the healthcare provider and the patient, as low patient satisfaction with their physician is associated with decreased adherence (George, 2005; Restrepo, 2008). Proper inhaler education for the patient is paramount in helping patients understand their drug regimen, and the reasons for taking the medication (Falvo, 1980; George, 2007; Hulka, 1976). Healthcare providers must also be well-educated about COPD treatment guidelines to educate their patients about all aspects of their disease. Adherence can also be improved by tailoring drug therapy to each patient's needs, preferences, and capabilities. Patients who are unable to use their inhalers regularly or have complex medication regimens may benefit from simplified, once-daily treatments if possible (Breekveldt-Postma, 2007). Patients who also forget to take medications might benefit from behavioral therapy, such as cueing (for example, placing inhaler on the nightstand) and self-monitoring. Patients who have issues with depression, anxiety, or cognitive impairment should be given written instructions on medication use, as they are prone to have difficulty remembering instructions. Finally, patients who intentionally do not take medication can benefit from further education, review of patient's personal goals of therapy, and medication negotiation with the patient.

## 15.5 Conclusions

In this chapter we have discussed commonly used inhalers and how to use them correctly, the importance of inhaler education for correct inhaler technique, and how to increase inhaler compliance / adherence. There are various advantages and disadvantages associated with each type of inhaler. Inhaler device selection depends on the type of medication selected, as well as the patient's preferences and abilities. The healthcare provider should have adequate knowledge of the inhalational devices being prescribed. Inhaler education including the correct steps to use the device should be provided to the patient when receiving the inhaler, and should be re-addressed at follow-up visits. If medication adherence is an issue, the healthcare provider should search for reasons why, and intervene. Finally, successful inhaler education and adherence rely on effective communication between the healthcare provider and the patient.

## 15.6 Summary Points

1. Providers should know how to use inhaled medications for COPD correctly, as well as educate patients with COPD how to use their medications appropriately.
2. Repetitive inhaler education and direct observation of inhaler technique should occur in patients with COPD.
3. A pressurized metered-dose inhaler (pMDI) should be used with a spacer. If the patient does not use a spacer, then we recommend the open-mouth technique for pMDI use (Table 15.3).
4. Nebulizers can be used as an alternative to short acting bronchodilator pMDIs when patients cannot use a pMDI properly or when they are hospitalized. A sig-

nificant clinical therapeutic difference has not been shown between medications delivered by pMDI with a spacer versus a nebulizer.
5. Inhaler adherence should be addressed by the provider at every patient encounter.

## References

Ahrens. R., Lux, C., Bahl, T., & Han, S.H. (1995). Choosing the metered dose inhaler spacer or holding chamber that matches the patient's need: evidence that the specific drug being delivered is an important consideration. *J Allergy Clin Immunol, 96*(2), 288–294.

American Association for Respiratory Care. Aerosol consensus statement. (1991). *Respir Care, 36*(9), 916–921.

Barnes, P.J., & Pedersen, S. (1992). Efficacy and safety of inhaled corticosteroids in asthma. Report of a workshop held in Eze, France, October 1992. *Am J Respir Crit Care Med, 148*(Suppl 14, part 2), S1–S26.

Barry, P.W., & O'Callaghan, C. (1996). Inhalational drug delivery from seven different spacer devices. *Thorax, 51*(8), 835–840.

Beaucage, D., & Nesbitt, S. (2002). Using inhalation devices. *Comprehensive Management of Chronic Obstructive Pulmonary Disease* (pp. 83–107). Hamilton, Ontario: BC Decker.

Bender, B.G., Pedan, A., & Varasteh, L.T. (2006). Adherence and persistence with fluticasone propionate/salmeterol combination therapy. *J Allergy Clin Immunol, 118*(4), 899–904.

Berlinski, A., & Waldrep, J.C. (2006). Nebulized drug admixtures: effect on aerosol characteristics and albuterol output. *J Aerosol Med, 19*(4), 484–490.

Bisgaard, H., Pederson, S., Anhoj, J., et al. (2007) Determinants of lung function and airway hyperresponsiveness in asthmatic children. *Respir Med, 101*(7), 1477–1482.

Bosnic-Anticevich, S.Z., Sinha, S., So, S., et al. (2010) Metered-dose inhaler technique: the effect of two educational interventions delivered in community pharmacy over time. *J Asthma, 47*(3), 251–256.

Bourbeau, J., & Bartlett, S.J. (2008). Patient adherence in COPD. *Thorax, 63*(9); 831–838.

Brand, P., Hederer, B., Austen, G., et al. (2008). Higher lung deposition with Respimat® Soft Mist inhaler than HFA-MDI in COPD patients with poor technique. *Int J Chron Obstruct Pulmon Dis, 3*(4), 763–770.

Breekveldt-Postma, N.S., Koerselman, J., Erkens, J.A., et al. (2007). Enhanced persistence with tiotropium compared with other respiratory drugs in COPD. *Respir Med, 101*(7), 1398–1405.

Brennan, V.K., Osman, L.M., Graham, H., et al. (2005). True device compliance: the need to consider both competence and contrivance. *Respir Med*, 99(1), 97–102.

Broeders, M.E., Sanchis, J., Levy, M.L., et al. (2009). The ADMIT series – Issues in Inhalation Therapy. 2) Improving technique and clinical effectiveness. *Prim Care Respir J, 18*(2), 76–82.

Burton, G., Hodgkin, J.E., & Ward, J. (1992) *Respiratory care: a guide to clinical practice. 3rd Ed.* Philadelphia, PA: JB Lippincott.

Celli B.R., MacNee, W., Agusti, A., et al. (2004). Standards for the diagnosis and treatment of patients with COPD: a summary of the ATS/ ERS position paper. *Eur Respir J, 23*(6), 932–946.

Chronic obstructive pulmonary disease. Management of chronic obstructive pulmonary disease in adults in primary and secondary care. http://www.nice.org.uk/nicemedia/live/13029/49397/49397.pdf. Accessed March 30, 2014.

Clark, A.R., & Hollingworth, A.M. (1993). The relationship between powder inhaler resistance and peak inspiratory conditions in healthy volunteers: implications for in vitro testing. *J Aerosol Med, 6*(2), 99–110.

Comargo, C.A. Jr., & Kenney, P.A. (2000). Assessing costs of aerosol therapy. *Respir Care, 45*(6), 756–763.

Crompton, G.K., Barnes, P.J., Broeders, M. et al. (2006). The need to improve inhalation technique in Europe: a report from the Aerosol Drug Management Improvement Team. *Respir Med, 100*(9), 1479–1494.

Crompton, G.K. (1982). Problems patients have using pressurised aerosol inhalers. *Eur J Respir Dis, 63*(Suppl.119), 101–104.

Dalby, R.N., Spallek, M., & Voshaar, T. (2004). A review of the development of Respimat® Soft Mist Inhaler. *Int J Pharm, 283*(1–2),1–9.

Dalby, R.N., Eicher, J., & Zierenberg, B. (2011). Development of Respimat®(®) Soft Mist™ Inhaler and its clinical utility in respiratory disorders. *Med Devices (Auckl)*, 4, 145–155.

De Boeck, K., Alifier, M., & Warnier, G. (1999). Is the correct use of a dry powder inhaler (Turbohaler) age dependent? *J Allergy Clin Immunol, 103*(5 Pt 1), 763–767.

DiMatteo, M.R., Haskard, K.B., & Williams, S.L. (2007). Health beliefs, disease severity, and patient adherence: A meta-analysis. *Med Care.* 45(6), 521–528.

Dolce, J.J., Crisp, C., Manzella, B., et al. (1991). Medication adherence patterns in chronic obstructive pulmonary disease. *Chest, 99*(4), 837–841.

Dolovich, M.B., Ruffin, R., Corr, D., & Newhouse, M. (1983). Clinical evaluation of a simple demand inhalation MDI aerosol delivery device. *Chest, 84*(1), 36–41.

Dolovich, M.B. (1991). Clinical aspects of aerosol physics. *Respir Care, 36*, 931–938.

Dolovich, M.B. (1999). New delivery systems and propellants. *Can Respir J, 6*(3), 290–295.

Dolovich, M.B, Ahrens, R.C., & Hess, D.R. (2005). Device selection and outcomes of aerosol therapy: evidence based guidelines: American College of Chest Physicians / American College of Asthma, Allergy and Immunology. *Chest, 127*(1), 335–371.

Duerden, M., & Price, D. (2002). InhalersEducation and training needs. *Current Ther*, 21–29.

Ernst, P. (1998). Inhaled drug delivery: a practical guide to prescribing inhaler devices. *Can Respir J, 5*(3), 180–183.

Falvo, D., Woehlke, P., & Deichmann, J. (1980). Relationship of physician behavior to patient compliance. *Patient Couns Health Educ, 2*(4), 185–188.

Fink, J.B., & Rubin, B.K. (2005). Problems with inhaler use: a call for improved clinician and patient education. *Respir Care, 50*(10), 1360–1374.

Finlay, W.H., (2001). *The Mechanics of Inhaled Pharmaceutical Aerosols: An Introduction*. San Diego, Ca: Academic Press.

Fuller, R. (1995). The Diskus: a new multi-dose powder device. Efficacy and comparison with Turbuhaler. *J Aerosol Med, 8*(Suppl 2), S11-S17.

George, J., Kong, D.C., Thoman, R., & Stewart, K. (2005). Factors associated with medication nonadherence in patients with COPD. *Chest, 128*(5), 3198–3204.

George, J., Kong, D.C., Stewart, K. (2007) Adherence to disease management programs in patients with COPD. *Int J Chron Obstruct Pulmon Dis,* 2(3),253–262.

Global initiative for chronic obstructive lung disease (GOLD).Global strategy for the diagnosis, management, and prevention of chronic obstructive pulmonary disease. www.goldcopd.org/uploads/users/files/GOLD_Report2014_Feb07.pdf. Accessed March 30, 2014.

Gracia-Antequera, M., & Morales Suarez-Varela, M.M. (1999). An intervention to improve the inhalatory technique of children and adolescents with asthma. *Allergol Immunopathol, 27*(5), 255–260.

Guidry, G.G., Brown, W.D., Stogner, S.W., & George, R.B. (1992). Incorrect use of metered dose inhalers by medical personnel. *Chest, 101*(1), 1256–1261.

Hanania, N.A., Wittman, R., Kesten, S., & Chapman, K.R. (1994). Medical personnel's knowldege of and ability to use inhaling devices. Metered-dose inhalers, spacing chambers, and breath-actuated dry powder inhalers. *Chest, 105*(1), 111–116.

Haupt, D., Krigsman, K., Nilsson, J.L. (2008). Medication persistence among patients with asthma/COPD drugs. *Pharm World Sci, 30*(5), 509–514.

Hickey, A.J. (2004). *Pharmaceutical Inhalation Aerosol Technology*. New York, NY: CRC Press.

Hulka, B.S., Cassel, J.C., Kupper, L.L., & Burdette, J.A. (1976) Communication, compliance, and concordance between physicians and patients with prescribed medications. *Am J Public Health, 66*(9), 847–853.

Iacono, P., Velicitat, P., Guemas, E., et al. (2000). Improved delivery of ipratropium bromide using Respimat® (a new soft mist inhaler) compared with a conventional metered dose inhaler: cumulative dose response study in patients with COPD. *Respir Med, 94*(5), 490–495.

Idris, A.H., McDermott, M.F., Raucci, J.C., et al. (1993). Emergency department treatment of severe asthma. Metered-dose inhaler plus holding chamber is equivalent in effectiveness to nebulizer. *Chest,* 103(3), 665–672.

Ismaila, A., Corriveau, D., Vaillancourt, J., et al. (2014) Impact of adherence to treatment with tiotropium and fluticasone propionate / salmeterol in COPD patients. *Curr Med Res Opin*, (Epub ahead of print).

Johnson, C.E. (1989). Principles of nebulizer-delivered drug therapy for asthma. *Am J Hosp Pharm, 46*(6), 1845–1855.

Kesten, S., Zive, K., Chapman, K.R. (1993). Pharmacist knowledge and ability to use inhaled medication delivery systems. *Chest, 104*(6), 1737–1742.

Khachikian, D. (2012) VA Pharmacy Benefits Management Services, Medical Advisory Panel, VISN Pharmacist Executives. Ipratropium/Albuterol (Combivent® Respimat®®)http://www.pbm.va.gov/ClinicalGuidance/AbbreviatedReviews/Ipratropium-albuterol(CombiventRespimat®).doc. Accessed April 15, 2014.

Kilfeather, S.A., Ponitz, H.H., Beck, E., et al. (2004). Improved delivery of ipratropium bromide/fenoterol from Respimat® Soft Mist Inhaler in patients with COPD. *Respir Med,* 98(5), 387–397.

Krigsman, K., Moen, J., Nilsson, J.L., & Ring, L. (2007). Refill adherence by the elderly for asthma/chronic obstructive pulmonary disease drugs dispensed over a 10-year period. *J Clin Pharm Ther, 32*(6), 603–611.

Krigsman, K., Nilsson, J.L., & Ring, L. (2007). Adherence to multiple drug therapies: Refill adherence to concomitant use of diabetes and asthma/COPD medication. *Pharmacoepidemiol Drug Saf, 16*(10), 1120–1128.

Krigsman, K., Nilsson, J.L., & Ring, L. (2007). Refill adherence for patients with asthma and COPD: Comparison of a pharmacy record database with manually collected repeat prescriptions. *Pharmacoepidemiol Drug Saf. 16*(4), 441–448.

Larsen, J.S., Hahn, M., Ekholm, B., & Wick, K.A. (1994). Evaluation of conventional press-and breathe metered-dose inhaler technique in 501 patients. *J Asthma,* 31(3), 193–199.

Lareau, S.C., & Yawn, B.P. (2010). Improving adherence with inhaler therapy in COPD. *Int J Chron Obstruct Pulmon Dis, 5*, 401–406.

Lavorini, F., Magnan, A., Dubus, J.C., et al. (2008). Effect of incorrect use of dry powder inhalers on management of patients with asthma and COPD. *Respir Med,* 102(4), 593–604.

Leach, C.L., Davidson, P.J., & Boudreau, R.J. (1998). Improved airway targeting with the CFC-free HFA-beclomethasone metered-dose inhaler compared with CFC-beclomethasone. *Eur Respir J,* 12(6), 1346–1353.

Leiva-Fernández, F., Leiva-Fernández, J., Zubeldia-Santoyo, F., et al. (2012). Efficacy and two educational interventions about inhalation techniques in patients with chronic obstructive pulmonary disease (COPD). TECEPOC: study protocol for a partially randomized control trial (preference trial). *Trials,* 13, 64.

McFadden, E.R. (1995). Improper patient techniques with metered dose inhalers: clinical consequences and solutions to misuse. *J Allergy Clin Immunol, 96*(2), 278–283.

Menckeberg, T.T., Bouvy, M.L., Bracke, M., et al. (2008). Patients' understanding of the reasons for starting and discontinuing inhaled corticosteroids. *Br J Clin Pharmacol, 66*(2), 255–260.

Melani, A.S., Zanchetta, D., Barbato, N., et al. (2004). Inhalation technique and variables associated with misuse of conventional metered-dose inhalers and newer dry powder inhalers in experienced adults. *Ann Allergy Asthma Immunol,* 93(5), 439–446.

Melani, A.S. (2007). Inhalatory therapy training: a priority challenge for the physician. *Acta Biomed, 78*(3), 233–245.

Melani, A.S., Sestini, P., Aiofi, S., et al. (2001). GENebu Project: home nebulizer use and maintenance in Italy. *Eur Respir J, 18*(5), 758–763.

Muers, M.F. (1997). Overview of nebuliser treatment. *Thorax, 52*(Suppl 2), S25-S30.

Newman, S.P., Steed, K.P., Reader, S.J., et al. (1996). Efficient delivery to the lungs of flunisolide aerosol from a new portable hand-held multidose nebulizer. *J Pharm Sci, 85*(9), 960–964.

Newman, S.P., Brown, J., & Steed, K.P. (1998). Lung deposition of fenoterol and flunisolide delivered using a novel device for inhaled medicines: comparison of RESPIMAT® with conventional metered-dose inhalers with and without spacer devices. *Chest, 113*(4), 957–963.

Nimmo, C.J., Chen, D.N., Matinusen, S.M., et al. (1993). Assessment of patient acceptance and inhalation technique of a pressurized aerosol inhaler and two breath-actuated devices. *Ann Pharmacother, 27*(7–8), 922–927.

Olsson, B. (1998). The revision of the Inhalandia monograph of the European Pharmacopoeia. *J Aerosol Med, 11*(Suppl 1), 13S-16S.

Panos, R.J. (2013). Efficacy and safety of eco-friendly inhalers: focus on combination ipratropium bromide and albuterol in chronic obstructive pulmonary disease. *Int J Chron Obstruct Pulmon Dis, 8*, 221–230.

Pauwels, R., Newman, S., & Borgström, L. (1997). Airway deposition and airway effects of antiasthma drugs delivered from metered-dose inhalers. *Eur Respir J, 10*(9), 2127–2138.

Pitcairn, G., Reader, S., Pavia, D., & Newman, S. (2005). Deposition of corticosteroid aerosol in the human lung by Respimat® Soft Mist inhaler compared to deposition by metered dose inhaler or by Turbuhaler dry powder inhaler. *J Aerosol Med, 18*(3), 264–272.

Ram, F.S., Carvallho, C.R., & White, J. (2011). Clinical effectiveness of the Respimat® inhaler device in managing chronic obstructive pulmonary disease: evidence when compared with other handheld inhaler devices. *Int J Chron Obstruct Pulmon Dis,* 6, 129–139.

Rees, J. (2005). Methods of delivering drugs. *BMJ, 331*(7515), 504–506.

Restrepo, R.D., Alvarez, M.T., Wittnebel, L.D., et al. (2008). Medication adherence issues in patients treated for COPD. *Int J Chron Obstruct Pulmon Dis, 3*(3), 371–384.

Robbins, R.A., Thomas, A.R., Proctor, L.M., et al. (2005). Heat decreases formoterol delivery. *Chest, 128*(6), 4036–4040.

Swarbrick, J., & Boylan, J.C. (2007). *Encyclopedia of Pharmaceutical Technology*. New York: Marcell Dekker Inc.

Tarsin, W.Y., Pearson, S.B., Assi, K.H., & Chrystyn, H. (2006). Emitted dose estimates from Seretide Diskus and Symbicort Turbuhaler following inhalation by severe asthmatics. *Int J Phar, 316*(1–2), 131–137.

van der Palen, J., Klein, J.J., van Herwaarden, C.L., et al. (1999). Multiple inhalers confuse asthma patients. *Eur Respir J, 14*(5), 1034–1037.

Vincken, W., Dekhuljzen, R., Barnes, P., et al. (2010) The ADMIT series – Issues in inhalational therapy. 4) How to choose the inhaler devices for the treatment of COPD. *Prim Care Respir J, 19*(1),10–20.

Van Boven, J.F, Chavannes, N.H., van der Molen, T., et al. (2014). Clinical and economic impact of non-adherence in COPD: a systematic review. *Respir Med, 108*(1), 103–113.

Vestbo, J., Anderson, J.A., Calverley, P.M.A., et al. (2009). Adherence to inhaled therapy, mortality and hospital admission in COPD. *Thorax, 64*(11), 939–943.

Virchow, J.C., Cromptom, G.K., & Dal Negro, R. (2008). Importance of inhaler devices in the management of airway disease. *Respir Med*, *102*(1), 10–19.

Wieshammer, S., & Dreyhaupt, J. (2008). Dry powder inhalers: which factors determine the frequency of handling errors? *Respiration*, *75*(1), 18–25.

Wilson, A.F. (1993). Aerosol delivery systems. In: Weiss, E.B., & Stein, M. (Eds.), *Bronchial asthma mechanisms and therapeutics*, (749–755). Toronto, ON: Little Brown and Company.

World Health Organization. Adherence to long-term therapies: evidence for action. Geneva Switzerland: World Health Organization. http://www.who.int/chp/knowledge/publications/adherence_full_report.pdf. Accessed April 9, 2014.

Zuwallack, R., De Salvo, M.C., Kaelin, T., et al. (2010). Combivent Respimat® Inhaler Study Group. Efficacy and safety of ipratropium bromide/albuterol delivered via Respimat® inhaler versus MDI. *Respir Med*, *104*(8), 1179–1188.

Folarin Sogbetun, MD

# 16 Management of Outpatient COPD Exacerbations

Key Points

1. COPD exacerbations are associated with an acute worsening of the underlying respiratory symptoms and chronic pulmonary and systemic inflammatory processes.
2. Patients may have a susceptibility phenotype that determines their propensity for exacerbations.
3. Patients with COPD can tell when their baseline symptoms are worsening and can recognize the increases in dyspnea, changes in nature and frequency of cough and sputum, and tachypnea.
4. Early recognition and treatment improves outcomes of COPD exacerbations.
5. Most COPD exacerbations can be safely managed at home with an action plan.
6. Management involves the use of bronchodilators (short acting beta agonists and anticholinergics), steroid therapy, and antibiotics.
7. Between 30% and 50% of COPD exacerbations are associated with a bacterial infection and benefit from antibiotic therapy; antibiotics should be rotated to minimize development of antibiotic resistance.

## 16.1 Introduction

Chronic obstructive pulmonary disease is an incurable but treatable long term condition that is usually associated with an insidiously progressive loss of lung function and increasing respiratory and systemic symptoms. The course of COPD is often marked by intermittent exacerbations: episodes of increased respiratory symptoms, especially cough, wheezing, phlegm production, and breathlessness, that vary in severity, frequency, duration, and consequence. (See Chapter 9, Natural History, Phenotypes, and Gender Differences in COPD.)

COPD exacerbations may profoundly affect an individual's health and quality of life and, collectively, exacerbations are the major contributor to the socioeconomic and health-related burden of COPD. Therefore, the treatment and prevention of COPD exacerbations are critical elements in COPD management.

Approximately half of all COPD exacerbations are not reported to healthcare providers and usually are not treated (Wilkinson, 2004). Individuals with COPD may exhibit therapeutic paralysis, attempt to "tough it out" during exacerbations, and do not seek medical attention (Mulhall, 2013). Patients with COPD delay treatment initiation by a median duration of 3.7 days even though each day without treatment prolongs the recovery time by nearly half a day (Wilkinson, 2004). Additionally, those individuals who report exacerbations and are treated have a better quality of life compared with those not treated (Wilkinson, 2004). Thus, although nearly half of all exacerbations are unreported and untreated, earlier recognition and treatment of COPD exacerbations may improve recovery and quality of life.

## 16.2 Definition and Differential Diagnosis

The Global Initiative for Chronic Obstructive Lung Disease (GOLD) report defines a COPD exacerbation as an acute event characterized by a change/increase in the patient's baseline dyspnea, cough, and/or sputum that is beyond normal day-to-day variation (Global initiative for chronic Obstructive Lung Disease (GOLD) guidelines, 2014). Because these symptoms are not specific and may be caused by numerous processes, other causes should be considered during the initial evaluation including myocardial ischemia, heart failure, pneumonia, pneumothorax, pleural effusion, cardiac dysrhythmias, and pulmonary embolism.

In addition to being subjective, the respiratory symptoms that define a COPD exacerbation are patient dependent. To provide more objective measures of COPD exacerbations, various surveys such as the Exacerbations of Chronic Obstructive Pulmonary Disease Tool, a patient-reported outcome (EXACT-PRO), have been developed (Mohan, 2014). The EXACT-PRO is a 14 question survey that is valid and reliable for the objective recognition of COPD exacerbations (Mohan, 2014).

## 16.3 Prevalence

Using a definition of COPD exacerbation as an event treated with antibiotics and/or corticosteroids, the Evaluation of COPD Longitudinally to Identify Predictive Surrogate Endpoints (ECLIPSE) study monitored exacerbations among 2,138 patients with varying COPD severity for 3 years (Hurst, 2010). During the first study year, the overall exacerbation rate was 1.21 exacerbations/participant and correlated with the severity of airflow limitation: 0.85, 1.34, and 2.00 exacerbations/participant for GOLD stages 2, 3, and 4, respectively (Hurst, 2010). 29% of the study participants had two or more exacerbations in the first year and this proportion increased with disease severity, 22%, 33%, and 47% for GOLD stages 2, 3, and 4, respectively (Hurst, 2010). Approximately half of the patients did not have an exacerbation during the first year. The propensity or resistance to COPD exacerbations was remarkably consistent throughout the study; 71% of patients who had two or more exacerbations in years 1 and 2 had frequent exacerbation in year 3 and 74% of those with no exacerbations in years 1 and 2 had no exacerbations in year 3. Frequent exacerbations were associated with a history of prior events, gastroesophageal reflux or heartburn, worse quality of life, and increased white blood cell count (Hurst, 2010). Thus, the annual frequency of COPD exacerbations ranges from approximately one quarter to one half of individuals

**Table 16.1:** Risk factors for COPD exacerbation hospitalization and readmission (Bahadori, 2007)

| |
|---|
| 1. **Increased $P_aCO_2$** is associated with increased risk of COPD hospitalization, readmission and reduced survival |
| 2. **Lower $FEV_1$** is associated with increased risk of COPD hospitalization and readmission |
| 3. **Prior COPD exacerbations** 3 or more times in the preceding year is associated with Increased risk of readmission |
| 4. **Inhaled corticosteroid** use is associated with increased risk of COPD hospitalization. |
| 5. **Oral corticosteroid** use is associated with increased risk of COPD hospitalization and readmission |
| 6. **Reported poor health related quality of life** is associated with increased risk of COPD hospitalization and readmission |
| 7. **Long term use of oxygen** is associated with increased risk of COPD hospitalization and readmission |
| 8. **History of COPD** for more than 5 years is associated with a doubling in the risk of readmission |
| 9. **Co-existing comorbidities** including coronary artery disease, congestive heart failure, or diabetes |
| 10. **Severe dyspnea** is associated with increased risk of COPD hospitalization and readmission |

with COPD depending upon the severity of their airflow limitation and the propensity toward frequent or infrequent exacerbations is stable over a several year period.

## 16.4 Etiology

COPD exacerbations are characterized by increased inflammation of the entire tracheobronchial tree with increased numbers of macrophages and CD8 T lymphocytes in the airway wall and neutrophils in the airway lumen. Systemic inflammation is also elevated (Wedzicha, 2007). Persistently elevated levels of C reactive protein (CRP) after an exacerbation are associated with failure to recover from that episode and portend another exacerbation within 50 days (Wouters, 2005; Perera, 2007). Elevation of fibrinogen levels is associated with the presence and frequency of COPD exacerbations (Duvoix, 2013). Other biomarkers include procalcitonin and peripheral blood eosinophil count (Brightling, 2013). Elevated levels of von Willebrand's factor, D dimer, and prothrombin fragment 1+2 during COPD exacerbations suggest damage to endothelial cells and activation of clotting cascades (Polosa, 2011).

70–80% of COPD exacerbations are triggered by respiratory infections, mainly viral and bacterial and the majority of the rest are due to environmental exposures and medication non-adherence (Sethi, 2008). The risk of admission for COPD exacerbation is correlated with the severity of the underlying COPD (Bahadori, 2007) and these risk factors are presented in Table 16.1.

## 16.5 Presentation

Exacerbations are associated with an acute worsening of a patient's health status and delay in treatment is associated with slower resolution and increased risk of hospitalization (Wilkinson, 2005). Consequently, a patient's early recognition of exacerbation symptoms and prompt treatment improves exacerbation recovery, reduces risk of hospitalization, and is associated with better health-related quality of life. Patients with COPD can recognize the worsening of their baseline symptoms with each exacerbation and can learn to identify these symptoms. The symptoms depend on the cause of the exacerbation and typical manifestations include cough, sputum production, dyspnea, tachypnea, wheezing, and a decrease in pulmonary function. (Table 16.2)

**Table 16.2:** Respiratory Symptoms During a COPD Exacerbation

| |
|---|
| 1. Greater dyspnea, especially with exertion |
| 2. Increase in frequency and severity of cough |
| 3. Changes in sputum production including increased volume, purulence, and blood |
| 4. Tachypnea |
| 5. Wheezing |

Physical examination findings depend on the severity of the exacerbation and typically include wheezing and tachypnea. In more severe exacerbations, patients develop difficulty speaking, use accessory respiratory muscles, and exhibit paradoxical chest and abdominal wall movements due to asynchrony between the chest and abdomen with respiration. In very severe exacerbations, patients develop hypoxemia and hypercapnia with an increase in lethargy and possible obtundation. They may have fever, chills, or night sweats if there is a precipitating bacterial infection.

## 16.6 Natural History

The median recovery time from a COPD exacerbation is 6 days for the peak expiratory flow rate (PEFR) and 7 days for daily symptoms; up to 14% of patients do not recover clinically within 35 days and some never return to baseline (Seemungal, 2000). PEFR recovery to baseline values is complete in only 75.2% of exacerbations at 35 days and, in 7.1% of exacerbations, PEFR recovery has not occurred by 91 days (Seemungal, 2000). The rate of decline in forced expiratory volume in one second ($FEV_1$) is 2–8 ml/year greater in frequent COPD exacerbators (two or more exacerbations yearly) compared with infrequent exacerbators (less than two exacerbations annually) (Donaldson, 2002; Vestbo, 2011). Quality of life is significantly affected by COPD exacerbations and, as measured by the St. George's Respiratory Questionnaire

(SGRQ), is worse in patients with more frequent exacerbations (Seemungal, 1998; Miravitlles, 2004).

## 16.7 Consequences

The consequences of ambulatory COPD exacerbations are less well studied than more severe exacerbations requiring healthcare encounters but are associated with poor outcomes (Table 16.3).

**Table 16.3:** Consequences of Frequent COPD Exacerbations (Qureshi, 2014; Chhabra, 2014)

| |
|---|
| Increased risk of future exacerbations |
| Greater mortality |
| More frequent healthcare visits |
| Faster decline in lung function |
| More inflammation |
| Worse quality of life |
| Less physical activity |
| Aggravation of co-morbidities |

## 16.8 Outpatient Management of COPD Exacerbations

### 16.8.1 Indications for Home Care

Patients with COPD can recognize the worsening of their baseline symptoms that characterize exacerbations. Common symptoms include a cold or flu, feeling run down or tired, and mood changes, such as feeling down or anxious. When these symptoms are associated with cardinal COPD symptoms including increased shortness of breath and increased amounts of cough and sputum and/or sputum changes from its normal color to a yellow, green or rust color, it is strongly suggestive of a COPD exacerbation. Patients should be given an action plan that explains how to manage exacerbations at home (Figure 16.1 and Table 16.4). The action plan is filled out by the health care provider during routine visits and is individualized for each patient. It includes a list of symptoms to aid the patient in recognizing and assessing the severity of his/her symptoms and lists appropriate next steps.

Other steps include reducing activity, resting frequently, and practicing controlled breathing and relaxation. After resolution of an exacerbation, the patient should see

**Table 16.4:** Components of a COPD action plan

| |
|---|
| 1. Assessment of symptoms and their severity |
| 2. Assessment of the need to inform primary care provider of symptoms or seek more acute medical care |
| 3. Patient initiates prescribed prednisone |
| 4. Patient starts prescribed antibiotic |
| 5. Patient takes 2–4 puffs of their rescue inhaler (albuterol) as needed, up to 4 to 8 times per day for shortness of breath |
| 6. Information about when to seek further medical care |

When you have a COPD exacerbation

1. Start your action plan as instructed by your Provider
2. If you do not feel better after 48 hours, or if you are getting worse at any time, seek medical attention immediately.
3. Schedule an appointment to see your Provider or contact your Provider to refill and maintain your COPD exacerbation medications-inhalers, antibiotics, and steroids at all times.

| Assessment of COPD Disease Activity | |
|---|---|
| **I am doing well today** | |
| Symptoms | Actions |
| Usual activity and exercise level | Take daily medicines |
| Normal amounts of cough or sputum | Use oxygen as prescribed |
| Typical level of breathlessness at rest and with exertion | Continue regular exercise/diet plan |
| Sleeping well at night | Avoid cigarette smoke and other irritants |
| Appetite is good | Plan activities and pace yourself |
| **I am having a bad day or COPD Exacerbation** | |
| Symptoms | Actions |
| More wheezy and breathless than usual | Continue daily medications and oxygen |
| Feeling run down or tired | Use quick relief inhaler (albuterol) 2-4 puffs with spacer every 2-4 hours |
| Increased cough or sputum; change in color of sputum | Start an oral corticosteroid (Prednisone 40 mg orally daily for 5 days) |
| Utilizing more reliever medication (albuterol) than usual | Start an antibiotic (Use most recently prescribed antibiotic; see chart below) |
| Swelling of ankles more than usual | Use pursed lip breathing |
| Poor sleep or loss of appetite | Use anxiety/stress management techniques |
| Cold or flu symptoms | Reduce activity and rest frequently |
| Feeling down or increased anxiety | Eat and drink well especially fluids |
| Recent weather change or exposure to air pollution or smog | Call provider if symptoms don't improve after 48hrs or if you develop any of the symptoms listed below. |
| **I need urgent medical attention** | |
| Symptoms | Actions |
| *Danger Signs* – Severe breathlessness, chest pain, fever, agitation, fear, drowsiness, confusion | Call 911 or seek medical care immediately |
| Severe shortness of breath even at rest | Show them this plan and say you have severe COPD |
| Not able to perform normal activities | |
| Not able to sleep because of breathing | |
| Fever or chills | |
| Feeling confused or very drowsy | |
| Chest discomfort/pain | |
| Coughing up blood | |

Antibiotic Rotation

After a COPD exacerbation, a different antibiotic may need to be prescribed for your next exacerbation. Help your doctor do this by keeping track of the name of the antibiotic, and when you started taking it for each COPD exacerbation. *Bring this information with you to your doctor appointments.*

| Antibiotic Name | | | |
|---|---|---|---|
| Date Antibiotic Taken | | | |

**Figure 16.1:** Generic COPD Action Plan (American Lung Association accessed December, 2014; Australian Lung Foundation accessed December, 2014; Canadian Medical Association accessed December, 2014)

Table 16.5: Indications for a Healthcare Encounter Due to a COPD Exacerbation

| |
|---|
| 1. Inadequate response to outpatient management |
| 2. Marked increase in dyspnea |
| 3. Inability to eat or sleep due to symptoms |
| 4. Worsening hypoxemia or hypercapnia |
| 5. Changes in mental status |
| 6. Inability to care for oneself |
| 7. Uncertain diagnosis |
| 8. High risk comorbidities including pneumonia, cardiac arrhythmia, heart failure, diabetes mellitus, renal failure or liver failure |
| 9. Inability to take oral medications or use inhalers correctly |

their primary care provider to obtain a different antibiotic to ensure antibiotic rotation for the next exacerbation (Postma, 1999) and minimize development of antibiotic resistance. A generic action plan derived from recommendations from the American Lung Association, the Canadian Medical Association, and the Australian Lung Foundation (American Lung Association accessed December, 2014; Australian Lung Foundation accessed December, 2014; Canadian Medical Association accessed December, 2014) is presented in Figure 16.1.

### 16.8.2 Indications for a Healthcare Encounter

Patients who are extremely breathless, anxious, panicky, confused, agitated, fearful, or drowsy should seek immediate medical attention. Other patients should start with the action plan but if there is no improvement after 48 hours, or if symptoms worsen at any time, medical attention should be sought immediately (GOLD guidelines, 2014). Other indications to escalate the level of care are presented in Table 16.5.

## 16.9 Management

### 16.9.1 Home Care

A COPD action plan (Figure 16.1) encourages early intervention by giving patients guidelines to enhance the recognition of an exacerbation and how to initiate early medical management. Action plans with limited or no self-management education (See Educational Programs below) promote patient recognition and initiation of treat-

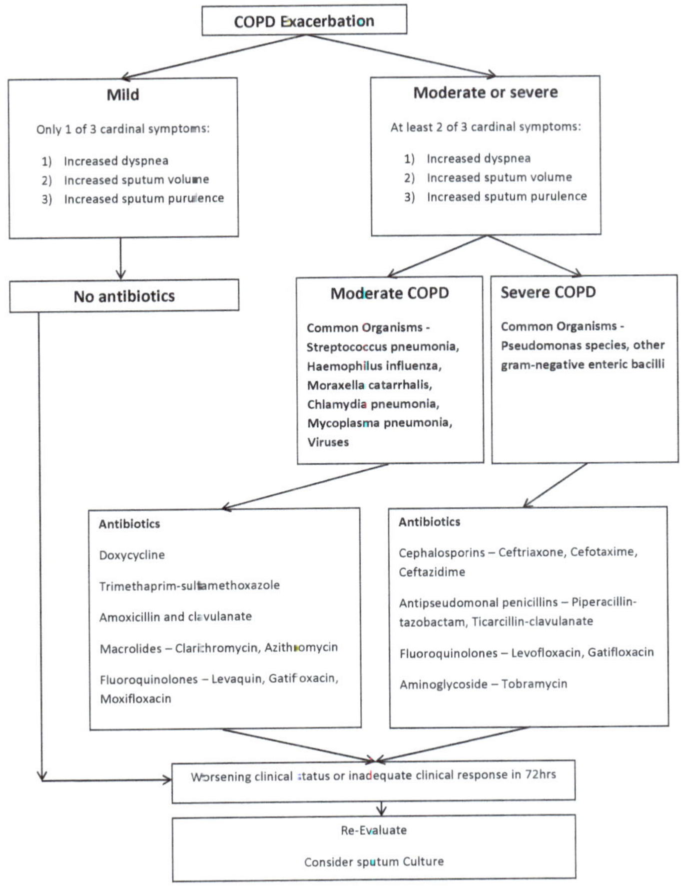


**Figure 16.2:** COPD management algorithm, modified from Anthonisen (1987), Hunter (2001) and Siddiqi (2008)

ment for COPD exacerbations but have not been demonstrated to decrease healthcare utilization or improve health-related quality of life (Walters, 2010). The action plan contains advice on how to increase the use of routine COPD medications, to use breathing exercises and relaxation techniques, to change the environment if it is causing the exacerbation, and to increase oxygen use. If the exacerbation is infectious and the dyspnea is accompanied by increased or colored sputum, antibiotics and systemic steroids are indicated (see Figure 16.2). If the condition worsens, patients are advised to visit their physician's office or the emergency department. Follow-up with their physicians either in person or via telephone or electronic communication after the episode is also recommended. Medications used to treat a COPD exacerbation are reviewed in Table 16.6. Adherence to a written action plan is associated with a reduction in exacerbation recovery time (Bischoff, 2011). Knowing the factors that are associated with proper and prompt utilization of an action plan permits healthcare professionals to direct self-management support to appropriate patients. For those individuals who are unable to adhere with a self-administered action plan, an intensive home care program, including nurse visits, home oxygen, and physical therapy, produces clinical outcomes that are equivalent to hospitalization (Postma,1999). See discussion of hospital at home below.

**Table 16.6:** Pharmacologic therapy in acute exacerbation (Updated from Stoller, 2002)

| Class | Drug | Mode of Delivery | Dose | Frequency |
|---|---|---|---|---|
| Bronchodilators | | | | |
| | Beta-adrenergic agonist | | | |
| | Albuterol | Metered-dose inhaler or<br>Nebulizer | 100–200 μg<br>0.5–2.0 mg | 4–8 times daily<br>4–8 times daily |
| | Anticholinergic agent | | | |
| | Ipratropium bromide | Metered-dose inhaler or<br>Nebulizer | 18–36 μg<br>0.5 mg | 4 times daily<br>4 times daily |
| Corticosteroids | | | | |
| | Prednisone | Pill | 30–60 mg | Daily for 5 days |

## 16.9.2 Bronchodilators

### 16.9.2.1 Short Acting Bronchodilators

**Beta adrenergic agonists:** Inhaled short-acting beta adrenergic agonists (SABA e.g. albuterol) are the mainstay of therapy for an acute exacerbation due to their rapid onset of action and efficacy in producing bronchodilation. After inhalation, the effects of SABAs begin within 5 minutes and reach maximal effect at 30 minutes. SABA's improve $FEV_1$ and FVC by 15 to 29% over a period of 60 to 120 minutes. Side-effects include tremors, headache, nausea, vomiting, palpitations, heart rate, and blood pressure variations. There is no added benefit to adding long acting beta-adrenergic agents (LABA e.g. salmeterol) in the treatment of acute exacerbations. Nebulizers and metered dose inhalers (MDI) with spacers have equal efficacy during exacerbations but patients may have difficulty with proper MDI technique during an exacerbation. There has been no demonstrated advantage to the use of a higher cumulative dose of albuterol in patients with acute exacerbation of COPD and 4 times daily dosing is usually adequate (Emerman, 1997).

**Anticholinergic agents:** Anticholinergic agents (non-selective muscarinic antagonists-SAMA e.g. ipratropium bromide) have an equivalent effect to SABA's and other factors such as the time to peak effect (slightly more rapid for SABA's) and the frequency of adverse effects (fewer and milder with ipratroprium bromide – tremors, dry mouth, and urinary retention) may influence the choice of agent for a given patient (Karpel, 1990; Rebuck, 1997; Johnson, 2002). Ipratropium's effect begins within 10–15 minutes and peaks at 30–60 minutes.

The effects of the two classes of short acting bronchodilator agents decline after 2–3 hours but can last as long as 4–6 hours. Both inhaled agents are more effective than all parenterally administered bronchodilators (methylxanthines and sympathomimetics). Unlike the management of stable COPD where the concurrent administration of albuterol and ipratroprium is more efficacious than either agent given alone (The COMBIVENT Inhalation Solution Study Group, 1997), a combination of short acting bronchodilators given sequentially in exacerbations does not provide additional benefit (Karpel, 1990; Patrick, 1990; Moayyedi, 1995).

### 16.9.3 Corticosteroid Therapy

Several randomized, placebo-controlled trials have demonstrated the benefit of systemic corticosteroid therapy in accelerating improvement in airflow, gas exchange, and symptoms, and in reducing the rate of treatment failure (Albert, 1980; Thompson, 1996; Aaron, 2003; Niewoehner, 1999; Aaron, 2003; Davies, 1999; Maltais, 2002). Benefits include a higher $FEV_1$ on day 1, lower rate of treatment failure at 30 and 90 days, and a shorter hospital stay. The optimal duration of therapy remains uncertain but some studies support a course of 5–10 days (Davies, 1999; Sayiner, 2001; Stanbrook, 2001). Patients with COPD exacerbations continue to have cumulative improvement in $FEV_1$ during a 10 day corticosteroid course. However, outcomes were no better with an 8 week course of corticosteroids compared with a 15 day course. A Cochrane review found no significant increase in treatment failure with shorter systemic corticosteroid treatment for seven days or less for acute exacerbations of COPD (Walters, 2011). More recently, the REDUCE trial demonstrated that 5 days was not inferior to 14 days of oral 40 mg prednisolone daily and there were no differences in time to the next exacerbation, mortality, restoration of lung function, and adverse events during the 6 months of follow up (Leuppi, 2013).

Oral glucocorticoids are rapidly absorbed with peak serum levels achieved at one hour after ingestion with virtually complete bioavailability. They are as efficacious as intravenous glucocorticoids for treating most exacerbations unless the patient is unable to take oral medications or has poor gastrointestinal absorption.

Most exacerbations can be treated with 30–60 mg prednisone daily for 5–7 days (Gold Guidelines, 2014) and steroid therapy can be stopped without tapering if the duration of therapy is less than 3 weeks (Gold Guidelines, 2014; Niewoehner, 1999).

Longer durations of therapy have no added benefit and a higher risk of adverse effects especially hyperglycemia. More recent findings are suggesting that shorter durations with lower doses are as effective as longer courses with higher doses of corticosteroids.

### 16.9.4 Antibiotic Therapy

Up to 50% of COPD exacerbations are associated with bacterial infections and antibiotics are indicated for these patients. Clinical criteria (increased dyspnea, sputum volume and sputum purulence) are sufficient to commence a course of antibiotics for a COPD exacerbation and sputum cultures are not usually obtained unless there is a clinical indication. Treatment is usually empirical and a low-cost antibiotic such as trimethaprim-sulfamethoxazole, azithromycin, cefuroxime, or tetracycline is adequate for mild exacerbations in relatively uncompromised patients. For more severe exacerbations, a broader-spectrum antibiotic such as moxifloxacin or levofloxacin that is effective against resistant strains of H. influenzae and S. pneumoniae is recommended. Patients with systemic symptoms such as pneumonia should be treated with a broad-spectrum antibiotic. See Figure 16.2.

### 16.9.5 Chronic Antibiotic Treatment

Long term antibiotic treatment with azithromycin, erythromycin, clarithromycin, or moxifloxacin has been demonstrated to reduce COPD exacerbations (Herath, 2013). A meta-analysis demonstrated an odds ratio of 0.55 (95% CI, 0.39–0.77) for COPD exacerbations with prophylactic antibiotic treatment and the number needed to treat was 8 (95% CI, 5–18) (Herath, 2013). Both azithromycin and erythromycin have been studied extensively and reduce the time to first exacerbation and exacerbation frequency when administered daily for one year but also adversely impair hearing and increase the prevalence of macrolide resistant bacteria in the sputa of treated patients (Ramos, 2014). Azithromycin therapy has also been associated with a prolonged QTc. (Albert, 2011). The benefit of macrolides has to be balanced against the possible development of antibiotic resistance both in the patient being treated and in other individuals. The exact mechanism of action of macrolides is not known but may be related to their antibacterial, anti-inflammatory, or immunomodulating properties (Martinez, 2008).

### 16.9.6 Phosphodiesterase 4 (PDE 4) Inhibitors

PDE-4 inhibitors, roflumilast and cilomilast, reduce inflammation and bronchoconstriction by preventing the degradation of cyclic AMP by phosphodiesterase (Beghe,

2013). PDE-4 inhibitors reduce the frequency of COPD exacerbations (OR 0.77, 95% CI 0.71, 0.83) with a number needed to treat for an additional benefit, 20 (95% CI, 16 to 27) (Chong, 2013). Adverse effects of the PDE-4 inhibitors include gastrointestinal symptoms, headache, and weight loss.

### 16.9.7 Oxygen Therapy

Alterations in oxygenation during COPD exacerbations appear to be associated with the severity of the exacerbation. A prospective study of 40 individuals with moderate to severe COPD not receiving supplemental oxygen demonstrated that the stable mean $SpO_2$ was 94.8% with a standard deviation of 1% (Hurst, 2010). The maximum reduction in the $SpO_2$ standard deviation during an exacerbation was only 1.24% suggesting that the $SpO_2$ did not decline markedly during less severe exacerbations. In contrast, in a prospective study of 2,487 patients presenting to an emergency department with a COPD exacerbation, half had an oxygen saturation < 90% (Quintana, 2014).

Patients with COPD exacerbations are given oxygen to treat hypoxemia with a goal of maintaining adequate levels of oxygenation without precipitating respiratory acidosis or worsening hypercapnia (Brill, 2014). The minimal adequate or safe level of oxygenation has not been defined definitively but most experts suggest a target $SpO_2$ range of 88–92% (Brill, 2014). The administration of oxygen has potential therapeutic benefits, which include relief of pulmonary vasoconstriction, decrease in right heart strain, and improved myocardial oxygenation. A high $F_iO_2$ is not required to correct the hypoxemia associated with most acute exacerbations and persistent hypoxemia should prompt consideration of pulmonary embolism (PE), acute respiratory distress syndrome (ARDS), pulmonary edema, or severe pneumonia. Oxygen delivery devices include face masks, Venturi masks, nasal cannulae, and non-rebreathing masks. Simple face masks can provide a $F_iO_2$ up to 55% and nasal cannulae up to 40%. Venturi masks provide a precise $F_iO_2$ from 24% to 60% and are the preferred means of oxygen delivery. Non-rebreathing masks can deliver a $F_iO2$ up to 90%.

Although a "more is better" approach to supplemental oxygen has been adopted by many providers, recent evidence suggests that hyperoxemia (defined as a $SpO_2$ greater than the target range of 88–92%) is harmful. A British study demonstrated that lower flow oxygen ($F_iO_2$ < 28%) with a goal $SpO_2$ 88–92% compared with higher flow oxygen delivered while transporting patients with COPD to the hospital reduced the proportion of complicated admissions (defined as the need for aminophylline, invasive or noninvasive ventilation, or death) to 25.2% from 40.8% (Durrington, 2005). In a prospective study comparing untitrated high flow oxygen with oxygen titrated to a target $SpO_2$ 88–92%, titrated oxygen reduced mortality among those participants with COPD by 78% and among all participants by 58% (Austin, 2010). In patients presenting to an emergency department, hyperoxemia ($PaO_2$>100 mmHg) was associated with a greater risk of adverse outcomes (hypercapnic respiratory failure, assisted ventilation, or death) OR 9.17 (95% CI, 4.08, 20.6) than hypoxemia ($PaO_2$<60 mm Hg) OR 2.16 (95% CI, 1.11, 4.20) (Cameron, 2012).

In patients who do develop hypercarbia after treatment with higher levels of oxygen, rapid cessation of supplemental oxygen may lead to "rebound hypoxemia" due to a greater reduction in the arterial oxygen level compared with the arterial carbon dioxide level upon oxygen withdrawal (Kane, 2011). Therefore, in patients who develop oxygen induced hypercarbia, treatment with invasive or noninvasive ventilation while maintaining low concentration supplemental oxygen should be considered.

### 16.9.8 Educational Programs

Multiple and varied self-management programs for patients with COPD have been developed and implemented with widely ranging results. A review of COPD educational programs revealed that 53.8% of programs incorporated 10 or more areas of instruction (Stoilkova, 2013). The most common topics were smoking cessation (80.0%), medications (76.9%), exercise (76.9%), breathing techniques (70.8%), exacerbations (69.2%), and stress management (67.7%). Most programs were led by nurses (75.8%) who supplied written information (90.5%) and utilized demonstrations or practice sessions (73.8%). A Cochrane meta-analysis demonstrated that self-management education for patients with COPD reduced hospitalizations, OR 0.57 (95% CI 0.43, 0.75) with a number needed to treat 8 (95% CI, 5, 14) for those with high risk of COPD hospitalization and 20 (95% CI, 15, 35) for those with low risk (Zwerink, 2014). Additional benefits included enhanced quality of life and reduced breathlessness. Integrated disease management incorporating a multidisciplinary team improves quality of life, reduces breathlessness, increases the distance walked in 6 minutes, and decreases the number of hospitalizations and hospitalization duration (Kruis, 2013). A randomized control trial of a Comprehensive Care Management program to prevent COPD hospitalizations (Fan, 2012) did not demonstrate decreased hospitalizations and was associated with unanticipated excess mortality. This finding may have been related to differences between patients not detectable in data or possibly to undetected delays in care in the intervention group due to a false sense of security.

### 16.9.9 Hospital at Home

An alternative to hospitalization for an acute COPD exacerbation is hospital at home, a program of intensive management of COPD exacerbations in a patient's home by visiting healthcare providers. A meta-analysis of patients presenting to the emergency department and then treated with hospital at home for COPD exacerbations demonstrated a reduction in readmission rates compared with traditional hospitalization, RR 0.76 (95% CI, 0.59, 0.99) and a trend toward reduced mortality, RR 0.65 (95% CI, 0.4, 1.04) (Jeppesen, 2012).

### 16.9.10 Respiratory stimulants

Respiratory stimulants, measures to increase mucous clearance such as acetylcysteine, nebulized magnesium, and chest physiotherapy are not beneficial in acute exacerbations.

## 16.10 Prevention of COPD Exacerbations

### 16.10.1 Pulmonary Rehabilitation

Pulmonary rehabilitation is a multidisciplinary intervention that combines education and exercise to optimize physical conditioning, adherence, and patient involvement in care (Spruit, 2006). When provided in either the stable state or after an acute exacerbation, pulmonary rehabilitation is a highly effective and safe intervention to reduce hospital admissions and mortality and to improve health-related quality of life in COPD patients (Spruit, 2014; Lacasse, 2006; Puhan, 2011). A meta-analysis of pulmonary rehabilitation after a COPD exacerbation revealed reduced mortality (OR 0.28, 95% CI 0.10, 0.84), fewer hospitalizations (OR 0.22, 95% CI 0.08, 0.58) with a number need to treat 4 (95% CI, 3 to 8), and improved quality of life and exercise capacity (Puhan, 2011).

### 16.10.2 Smoking cessation

A cohort study of 23,971 self-reported previous and current smokers demonstrated that quitting smoking is associated with fewer COPD exacerbations, HR 0.78, (95% CI 0.75,0.87) and that the effect depends upon the length of smoking cessation, 1.04 at less than one year to 0.65 at 10 or more years of smoking abstinence (Au, 2009). Smoking cessation but not smoking reduction is associated with fewer COPD hospitalizations, HR 0.57 (95% CI, 0.33, 0.99) and 0.93 (95% CI, 0.73, 1.18), respectively (Godtfredsen, 2002).

### 16.10.3 Nutritional support

Although low body mass index and weight loss are risk factors for COPD exacerbations, the effect of nutritional supplementation on exacerbation frequency is not well studied (Hallin, 2006). A meta-analysis showed that nutritional supplementation stimulates weight gain in patients with COPD and the effect is greatest in malnourished patients (Ferreira, 2012). Additional benefits of nutritional supplementation included increases in measures of fat-free body mass, respiratory muscle strength, distance walked in 6 minutes, and health-related quality of life (Collins, 2013; Ferreira, 2012).

### 16.10.4 Lung Volume Reduction Surgery (LVRS)

In patients who are appropriate candidates, LVRS reduces severe COPD exacerbations (respiratory-related emergency room visits and hospitalizations) by 29% (95% CI, 11–48%) compared with medical management (Washko, 2008). LVRS also increases the time to the first COPD exacerbation in patients with and without a history of exacerbations in the year prior to surgery (Washko, 2008).

### 16.10.5 Telehealth

Clinical information systems can monitor patients with COPD in their homes using biosensors and questionnaires. This information is transmitted to a central coordination center and reviewed by healthcare providers using data processing algorithms and alerts to monitor daily status, advise individual patients about the goals of maintenance of maximal function and independence, early detection and management of exacerbations and reducing in-person healthcare visits, and provide pulmonary rehabilitation (Goldstein, 2014; McKinstry, 2013). Use of telehealth services for patients with COPD reduces emergency room visits and hospitalizations and exacerbations, does not improve quality of life, and has no effect or may actually increase mortality rates by delaying needed in person care (Kamei, 2013; McLean, 2012; Polisena, 2010). A cost effectiveness review of telehealth for chronic conditions including COPD concluded that telehealth was not cost effective when added to usual care (Henderson, 2013).

## 16.11 Risk Factors for Relapse

Risk factors for relapse include patients requiring increased doses of nebulized bronchodilators, use of theophylline, use of supplemental oxygen at home, an ED visit in the preceding week, number of ED and urgent care visits in the past year, self-reported activity limitation, respiratory rate at ED presentation, prior relapse after a hospital visit, and preceding use of glucocorticoids or antibiotics (Kim, 2004). Proven interventions that minimize relapse include smoking cessation, pulmonary rehabilitation, and physical exercise. (See prior sections.) Other strategies to prevent relapse of exacerbations are presented in Table 16.7. Tiotropium, a long acting anticholinergic agent that causes prolonged and persistent bronchodilation, reduces COPD exacerbations and COPD-related hospitalization rates (Anzueto, 2009). Long acting beta adrenergic agonists (LABA) such as salmeterol or formoterol reduce the risk of COPD exacerbations by 23% (Puhan, 2009). Inhaled corticosteroids (ICS) have proven efficacy in reducing the number and severity of exacerbations (Alsaeedi, 2002). The combination of LABA and ICS reduces exacerbations by 25% over a one year period (Calverley, 2003).

**Table 16.7:** Strategies to Prevent Relapse After an Acute COPD Exacerbation

| |
|---|
| Pulmonary Rehabilitation |
| Smoking cessation |
| Self-management plans |
| LABAs: salmeterol, formoterol |
| Combination therapy: LABA/ICS |
| Tiotropium |
| Influenza vaccine |
| Physical exercise |
| LVRS in selected patients |

Abbreviations: LABA: long-acting β 2-agonist; ICS: inhaled corticosteroid; LVRS: lung volume reduction surgery.

## 16.12 Conclusion

The natural history of COPD is usually punctuated by exacerbations that are characterized by increased respiratory symptoms including breathlessness, cough, wheezing, and sputum production. The frequency, severity, duration, and consequences of each exacerbation vary but patients with COPD appear to exhibit frequent or infrequent exacerbator phenotypes. Nearly half of all exacerbations are not reported by patients but earlier recognition and treatment is associated with more rapid recovery and better quality of life. The main pharmacologic treatments are short acting bronchodilators, antibiotics, and corticosteroids. Factors that reduce relapse of COPD exacerbations include pulmonary rehabilitation, smoking cessation, long acting anticholinergics and beta agonists, and self-management plans.

## 16.13 Summary Points

1. COPD exacerbations are interspersed throughout the natural course of COPD but some patients are prone to frequent episodes whereas others have few or infrequent exacerbations.
2. Self-management plans aid in the recognition of exacerbations and earlier institution of treatment.
3. The principal pharmacologic treatments of COPD exacerbations are:
   - Short acting bronchodilators
   - Antibiotics which should be rotated to mitigate the selection of resistant bacteria
   - Corticosteroids which are beneficial in moderate doses (prednisone 40 mg/d orally) and short duration (5 days) that do not require tapering
4. Pulmonary rehabilitation after an acute COPD exacerbation improves survival, reduces subsequent hospitalizations, increases exercise capacity, and improves quality of life.
5. Newer modalities for the ambulatory management of COPD exacerbations include hospital at home and telemedicine.

## References

Aaron, S.D., Vandemheen, K.L. & Hebert, P. et al. (2003). Outpatient oral prednisone after emergency treatment of chronic obstructive pulmonary disease. *N Engl J Med*, 348, 2618–2625.

Afessa, B., Morales, I.J., Scanlon, P.D., Peters & S.G. (2002). Prognostic factors, clinical course, and hospital outcome of patients with chronic obstructive pulmonary disease admitted to an intensive care unit for acute respiratory failure. *Crit Care Med*, 30(7), 1610–5.

Albert, R.K., Martin, T.R. & Lewis, S.W. (1980). Controlled clinical trial of methylprednisolone in patients with chronic bronchitis and acute respiratory insufficiency. *Ann Intern Med*, 92(6),753–8.

Albert, R.K., Connett, J., Bailey, W.C., Casaburi, R., Cooper, J.A. & Criner, G.J., et al. (2011). Azithromycin for prevention of exacerbations of COPD. New England Journal of Medicine, 365:689–98

Papi, A., Luppi, F., Franco, F. & Fabbr,i L.M. (2009). Pathophysiology of Exacerbations of Chronic Obstructive Pulmonary Disease. *The Proceedings of the American Thoracic Society*, 3(3), 245–251.

Alsaeedi, A., Sin, D.D. & McAlister, F.A. (2002). The effect of inhaled corticosteroids in chronic obstructive pulmonary disease: a systematic review of randomized placebo-controlled trials. *Am J Med*, 113, 59–65.

American College of Chest Physicians (1997). COMBIVENT Inhalation Solution Study Group Routine nebulized ipratropium and albuterol together are better than either alone in COPD. *Chest*, 112(6),1514–21.

American Lung Association COPD Exacerbation Action Plan (Accessed December, 2014) http://www.lung.org/lung-disease/copd/living-with-copd/copd-management-tools.html.

Anthonisen, N.R., Manfreda, J., Warren, C.P.W., Hershfield, E.S., Harding, G.K.M. & Nelson, N.A. (1987). Antibiotic Therapy in Exacerbations of Chronic Obstructive Pulmonary Disease. *Annals of internal medicine*, 106(1), 196–204.

Anzueto, A. & Miravitlles, M. (2009). Efficacy of tiotropium in the prevention of exacerbations of COPD. *Ther Adv Respir Dis*, 3(3),103–11.

Au, D.H., Bryson, C.L., Chien, J.W., Sun, H., Udris, E.M., Evans, L.E. & Bradley, K.A. (2009). The effects of smoking cessation on the risk of chronic obstructive pulmonary disease exacerbations. *J Gen Intern Med*, 24(4), 457–63.

Austin, M.A., Wills, K.E., Blizzard, L., Walters, E.H. & Wood-Baker, R. (2010). Effect of high flow oxygen on mortality in chronic obstructive pulmonary disease patients in prehospital setting: randomised controlled trial. *BMJ*, 341, c5462.

Australian Lung Foundation COPD Exacerbation Action Plan (Accessed December, 2014) http://lungfoundation.com.au/health-professionals/clinical-resources/copd/copd-action-plan/.

Bahadori, K. & FitzGerald, J.M. (2007). Risk factors of hospitalization and readmission of patients with COPD exacerbation – systematic review. Int J Chron Obstruct Pulmon Dis, 2(3): 241–251

Beghè, B., Rabe, K.F. & Fabbri, L.M. (2013). Phosphodiesterase-4 inhibitor therapy for lung diseases. *Am J Respir Crit Care Med*, 188(3), 271–278.

Bischoff, E.W., Hamd, D.H., Sedeno, M., Benedetti, A., Schermer, T.R., Bernard, S., Maltais, F. & Bourbeau, J. (2011). Effects of written action plan adherence on COPD exacerbation recovery. *Thorax,* 66(1), 26–31.

Brightling, C.E. (2013). Biomarkers that predict and guide therapy for exacerbations of chronic obstructive pulmonary disease. *Ann Am Thorac Soc*, 10Suppl, S214–9.

Brill, S.E. & Wedzicha, J.A. (2014). Oxygen therapy in acute exacerbations of chronic obstructive pulmonary disease. *Int J Chron Obstruct Pulmon Dis*, 9, 1241–1252.

Calverley, P., Pawels, R. & Vestbo, J., et al. (2013). Combined salmeterol and fluticasone in the treatment of chronic obstructive pulmonary disease: a randomised controlled trial, *Lancet*, 361, 449–456.

Cameron, L., Pilcher, J., Weatherall, M., Beasley, R. & Perrin, K. (2012). The risk of serious adverse outcomes associated with hypoxaemia and hyperoxaemia in acute exacerbations of COPD. *Postgrad Med J*, 88(1046), 684–9.

Canadian Medical Association COPD Exacerbation Action Plan (Accessed December, 2014) http://www.bcguidelines.ca/guideline_copd.html.

Chhabra, S.K. & Dash, D.J. (2014). Acute exacerbations of chronic obstructive pulmonary disease: causes and impacts. *Indian J Chest Dis Allied Sci,* 56(2), 93–104.

Chong, J., Leung, B. & Poole, P. (2013). Phosphodiesterase 4 inhibitors for chronic obstructive pulmonary disease. *Cochrane Database Syst Rev*, 11:CD002309.

Collins, P.F., Elia, M. & Stratton, R.J. (2013). Nutritional support and functional capacity in chronic obstructive pulmonary disease: a systematic review and meta-analysis. *Respirology*, 18(4), 616–29.

Connors, A.F. Jr, Dawson, N.V., Thomas, C., et al. (1996). Outcomes following acute exacerbation of severe chronic obstructive lung disease. The SUPPORT investigators (Study to Understand Prognoses and Preferences for Outcomes and Risks of Treatments). *Am J Respir Crit Care Med*, 154, 959.

Davies, L., Angus, R.M. & Calverley, P.M. (1999). Oral corticosteroids in patients admitted to hospital with exacerbations of chronic obstructive pulmonary disease: a prospective randomised controlled trial. *Lancet*, 354,456–460.

Donaldson, G., Seemungal, T., Bhowmik, A. & Wedzicha, J. (2002) Relationship between exacerbation frequency and lung function decline in chronic obstructive pulmonary disease. *Thorax*, 57, 847–852.

Durrington, H.J., Flubacher, M., Ramsay, C.F., Howard, L.S. & Harrison, B.D. (2005). Initial oxygen management in patients with an exacerbation of chronic obstructive pulmonary disease. *QJM*, 98(7), 499–504.

Duvoix, A., Dickens, J., Haq, I., Mannino, D., Miller, B., Tal-Singer, R. & Lomas, D.A. (2013). Blood fibrinogen as a biomarker of chronic obstructive pulmonary disease. *Thorax*, 68(7), 670–6.

Emerman, C.L. & Cydulka, R.K. (1997). Effect of different albuterol dosing regimens in the treatment of acute exacerbation of chronic obstructive pulmonary disease. *Ann Emerg Med*, 29(4),474–8.

Esteban, A., Frutos-Vivar, F., Ferguson, N.D., Arabi, Y., Apezteguía, C., González, M., Epstein, S.K., Hill, N.S., Nava, S., Soares, M.A., D'Empaire, G., Alía, I. & Anzueto, A. (2004). Noninvasive positive-pressure ventilation for respiratory failure after extubation. *N Engl J Med*, 350(24), 2452–60.

Fan, V.S., Gaziano, M., Lew, R. et al. (2012). A Comprehensive Care Management Program to Prevent Chronic Obstructive Pulmonary Disease Hospitalizations: A Randomized, Controlled Trial. Ann Intern Med. 156(10):673–683

Farah, R. & Makhoul, N. (2011). Optimal time needed for withdrawal of mechanical ventilation in patients with chronic obstructive pulmonary disease. *Isr Med Assoc J*, 13(10),609–12.

Global strategy for the diagnosis, management, and prevention of chronic obstructive pulmonary disease (Accessed December, 2014): *http://www.goldcopd.org*.

Godtfredsen, N.S., Vestbo, J., Osler, M. & Prescott, E. (2002). Risk of hospital admission for COPD following smoking cessation and reduction: a Danish population study. *Thorax*, 57(11), 967–72.

Goldstein, R.S. & O'Hoski, S. (2014). Telemedicine in COPD: time to pause. *Chest*, 145(5), 945–9.

Hallin, R., Koivisto-Hursti, U.K., Lindberg, E. & Janson, C. (2006). Nutritional status, dietary energy intake and the risk of exacerbations in patients with chronic obstructive pulmonary disease (COPD). *Respir Med*, 100(3), 561–7.

Henderson, C., Knapp, M., Fernández, J.L., Beecham, J., Hirani, S.P., Cartwright, M., Rixon, L., Beynon, M., Rogers, A., Bower, P., Doll, H., Fitzpatrick, R., Steventon, A., Bardsley, M., Hendy, J. & Newman, S.P.; (2013). Whole System Demonstrator evaluation team. Cost effectiveness of telehealth for patients with long term conditions (Whole Systems Demonstrator telehealth questionnaire study): nested economic evaluation in a pragmatic, cluster randomised controlled trial. *BMJ*, 346, f1035.

Herath, S.C. & Poole, P. (2013). Prophylactic antibiotic therapy for chronic obstructive pulmonary disease (COPD). *Cochrane Database Syst Rev*, 11, CD009764.

Hunter, M.H. & King, D.E. (2001) Exacerbations of Chronic Stable Disease. *American Family Physician*, 64 (4), 603–612.

Hurst, J.R., Donaldson, G.C., Quint, J.K., Goldring, J.J., Patel, A.R. & Wedzicha, J.A. (2010). Domiciliary pulse-oximetry at exacerbation of chronic obstructive pulmonary disease: prospective pilot study. *BMC Pulm Med*, 10, 52.

Hurst, J.R., Vestbo, J., Anzueto, A., Locantore, N., Müllerova, H., Tal-Singer, R., Miller, B., Lomas, D.A., Agusti, A., Macnee, W., Calverley, P., Rennard, S., Wouters, E.F. & Wedzicha, J.A. (2010). Susceptibility to exacerbation in chronic obstructive pulmonary disease; Evaluation of COPD Longitudinally to Identify Predictive Surrogate Endpoints (ECLIPSE) Investigators. *N Engl J Med*, 363(12), 1128–1138.

Jeppesen, E., Brurberg, K.G., Vist, G.E., Wedzicha, J.A., Wright, J.J., Greenstone, M. & Walters, J.A., (2012). Hospital at home for acute exacerbations of chronic obstructive pulmonary disease. *Cochrane Database Syst Rev*, 5. CD003573.

Johnson, M.K. & Stevenson, R.D. (2002). Management of an acute exacerbation of COPD: are we ignoring the evidence?, *Thorax*, 57(2), ii15–ii23.ii23.

Kane, B., Turkington, P.M., Howard, L.S., Davison, A.G., Gibson, G.J. & O'Driscoll, B.R. (2011). Rebound hypoxaemia after administration of oxygen in an acute exacerbation of chronic obstructive pulmonary disease. *BMJ*, 342, d1557.

Karadag, F., Kirdar, S., Karul, A.B. & Ceylan, E. (2008). The value of C-reactive protein as a marker of systemic infl ammation in stable chronic obstructive pulmonary disease. *Eur J Int Med.*, 19(2), 104–8.

Karpel, J.P., Pesin, J. & Greenberg, D. et al. (1990). A comparison of the effects of ipratropium bromide and metaproterenol sulfate in acute exacerbations of COPD. *Chest*, 98(4), 835–9.

Kim, S., Emerman, C.L., Cydulka, R.K., Rowe, B.H., Clark, S. & Camargo, C.A.; MARC Investigators. (2004). Prospective multicenter study of relapse following emergency department treatment of COPD exacerbation. *Chest*, 125(2), 473–481.

Kruis, A.L., Smidt, N., Assendelft, W.J., Gussekloo, J., Boland, M.R., Rutten-van Mölken & V., Chavannes, N.H. (2013). Integrated disease management interventions for patients with chronic obstructive pulmonary disease. *Cochrane Database Syst Rev*, 10, CD009437.

Lacasse, Y., Goldstein, R., Lasserson ,T.J. & Martin, S. (2006). Pulmonary rehabilitation for chronic obstructive pulmonary disease. *Cochrane Database Syst Rev*, 18(4):CD003793.

Leuppi, J.D., Schuetz, P., Bingisser, R., et al. (2013). Short-term vs conventional glucocorticoid therapy in acute exacerbations of chronic obstructive pulmonary disease: the REDUCE randomized clinical trial. *JAMA*, 309(21), 2223–2231.

MacIntyre, N.R., Cook, D.J., Ely, E.W. Jr, Epstein, S.K., Fink, J.B., Heffner, J.E., Hess, D., Hubmayer, R.D. & Scheinhorn, D.J.; American College of Chest Physicians; American Association for Respiratory Care; American College of Critical Care Medicine. (2001) Evidence-based guidelines for weaning and discontinuing ventilatory support: a collective task force facilitated by the American College of Chest Physicians; the American Association for Respiratory Care; and the American College of Critical Care Medicine. *Chest*, 120(6 Suppl), 375S-95S.

Maltais, F., Ostinelli, J., Bourbeau, J. et al. (2002). Comparison of nebulized budesonide and oral prednisolone with placebo in the treatment of acute exacerbations of chronic obstructive pulmonary disease: a randomized controlled trial. *Am J Respir Crit Care Med*, 165, 698–703.

Martinez, F.J., Curtis, J.L. & Albert, R. (2008). Role of macrolide therapy in chronic obstructive pulmonary disease. *Int J Chron Obstruct Pulmon Dis*, 3(3), 331–50.

McCrory, D.C., Brown, C., Gelfand, S.E., et al. (2001). Management of acute exacerbations of COPD: a summary and appraisal of published evidence. *Chest*, 19, 1190–1209.

McKinstry, B. (2013). The use of remote monitoring technologies in managing chronic obstructive pulmonary disease. *QJM*, 106(10), 883–5.

McLean, S., Nurmatov, U., Liu, J.L., Pagliari, C., Car, J. & Sheikh, A. (2012). Telehealthcare for chronic obstructive pulmonary disease: Cochrane Review and meta-analysis. *Br J Gen Pract*, 62(604), e739–49.

Miravitlles, M., Ferrer, M., Pont, A., Zalacain, R., Alvarez-Sala, J.L., Masa, F., Verea, H., Murio, C. & Ros, F., Vidal, R. (2004). Effect of exacerbations on quality of life in patients with chronic obstructive pulmonary disease: a 2 year follow up study. *Thorax*, 59(5), 387–395.

Moayyedi, P., Congleton, J. & Page, R.L. et al. (1995). Comparison of nebulised salbutamol and ipratropium bromide with salbutamol alone in the treatment of chronic obstructive pulmonary disease. *Thorax*, 50(8), 834–837.

Mohan, A. & Sethi, S. (2014). The reliability and validity of patient-reported chronic obstructive pulmonary disease exacerbations. *Curr Opin Pulm Med*, 20(2), 146–52.

Mulhall, A.M., Lac,h L.A., Krzywkowski-Mohn, S.M, Welge, J.A. & Panos, R.J., (2013). Therapeutic paralysis in veterans with COPD. *Respir Med*, 107(10), 1547–57.

National Institute for Clinical Excellence (NICE). (2004). Chronic obstructive pulmonary disease: national clinical guideline for management of chronic obstructive pulmonary disease in adults in primary sand secondary care. *Thorax*, 59, i131–i156(Suppl I).

Nevins, M.L. & Epstein, S.K. (2001). Predictors of outcome for patients with COPD requiring invasive mechanical ventilation. *Chest*, 119(6),1840–1849.

Niewoehner, D.E., Erbland, M.L., Deupree, R.H. et al. (1999). Effect of systemic glucocorticoids on exacerbations of chronic obstructive pulmonary disease. *N Engl J Med*, 340(25), 1941–1947.

Ntoumenopoulos, G. & Physiother, J. (2011). Using titrated oxygen instead of high flow oxygen during an acute exacerbation of chronic obstructive pulmonary disease (COPD) saves lives. *BMJ*, 57(1), 55.

Patil, S.P., Krishnan, J.A., Lechtzin, N. & Diette, G.B. (2003). In-hospital mortality following acute exacerbations of chronic obstructive pulmonary disease. *Arch Intern Med*, 163(10), 1180–6.

Patrick, D.M., Dales, R.E. & Stark, R.M. et al. (1990). Severe exacerbations of COPD and asthma. Incremental benefit of adding ipratropium to usual therapy. *Chest*, 98(2), 295–7.

Perera, W.R., Hurst, J.R., Wilkinson, T.M., Sapsford, R.J., Müllerova, H., Donaldson, G.C. & Wedzicha, J.A. (2007). Inflammatory changes, recovery and recurrence at COPD exacerbation. *Eur Respir J.*, 29(3), 527–534.

Polisena, J., Tran, K., Cimon, K., Hutton, B., McGill, S., Palmer, K. & Scott, R.E. (2010). Home telehealth for chronic obstructive pulmonary disease: a systematic review and meta-analysis. *J Telemed Telecare*, 16, 120–127.

Polosa, R., Malerba, M., Cacciola, R., Morjaria, J., Maugeri, C. & Prosperini, G. *et al.* (2011) Effect of acute exacerbations on circulating endothelial, clotting, and fibrinolytic markers in COPD patients. *Intern Emerg Med*, 1–8, 567–674.

Postma, D.S., Ten Hacken, N.H., Kerstjens, H.A. & Koëter, G.H. (1999). Home treatment of COPD exacerbations. *Thorax*, 54(2), 8–13.

Puhan, M.A., Bachmann, L.M., Kleijnen, J., et al. (2009). Inhaled drugs to reduce exacerbations in patients with chronic obstructive pulmonary disease: a network meta-analysis. *BMC Med*, *7*, 2.

Puhan, M.A., Gimeno-Santos, E., Scharplatz, M., Troosters, T., Walters, E.H. & Steurer, J. (2011). Pulmonary rehabilitation following exacerbations of chronic obstructive pulmonary disease. *Cochrane Database Syst Rev*, (10), CD005305.

Quintana, J.M., Esteban, C., Unzurrunzaga, A., Garcia-Gutierrez, S., Gonzalez, N., Barrio, I., Arostegui, .I, Lafuente, I., Bare, M., Fernandez-de-Larrea, N. & Vidal, S., IRYSS-COPD group. (2014). Predictive score for mortality in patients with COPD exacerbations attending hospital emergency departments. *BMC Med*, 12, 66.

Ram, F.S., Picot, J., Lightowler, J. & Wedzicha, J.A. (2004). Non-invasive positive pressure ventilation for treatment of respiratory failure due to exacerbations of chronic obstructive pulmonary disease. *Cochrane Database Syst Rev*, (3):CD004104.

Ramos, F.L. & Criner, G.J. (2014). Use of long-term macrolide therapy in chronic obstructive pulmonary disease. *Curr Opin Pulm Med*, 20(2), 153–158.

Rebuck, A.S., Chapman, K.R. & Abboud, R. et al. (1987). Nebulized anticholinergic and sympathomimetic treatment of asthma and chronic obstructive airways disease in the emergency room, *Am J Med*, 82(1), 59–64.

Rodríguez-Roisin, R. (2006). COPD exacerbations.5: management. *Thorax*, 61(6), 535–44.

Rothberg, M.B., Pekow, P.S., Lahti, M., Brody, O., Skiest, D.J. & Lindenauer, P.K. (2010). Antibiotic therapy and treatment failure in patients hospitalized for acute exacerbations of chronic obstructive pulmonary disease. *JAMA*, 303(20), 2035–2042.

Sayiner, A., Aytemur, Z.A., Cirit, M. & Unsal, I. (2001). Systemic glucocorticoids in severe exacerbations of COPD, *Chest*, 19, 726–730.

Seemungal, T.A., Donaldson, G.C., Bhowmik, A., Jeffries, D.J. & Wedzicha, J.A. (2000). Time course and recovery of exacerbations in patients with chronic obstructive pulmonary disease, *Am J Respir Crit Care Med,* 161(5), 1608–13.

Seemungal, T.A., Donaldson, G.C., Paul, E.A., Bestal,l J.C., Jeffries, D.J. & Wedzicha. (1998). Effect of exacerbation on quality of life in patients with chronic obstructive pulmonary disease, *JA. Am J Respir Crit Care Med*, 157(5 Pt 1), 1418–22.

Sethi, S. & Murphy, T.F. (2008). Infection in the pathogenesis and course of chronic obstructive pulmonary disease, *N Engl J Med,* 359, 2355–2365.

Siddiqi, A. & Sethi, S. (2008). Optimizing antibiotic selection in treating COPD exacerbations. *Int J Chron Obstruct Pulmon Dis,* 3(1), 31–44.

Soto, F.J. & Varkey, B. (2003). Evidence-based approach to acute exacerbations of COPD, *Curr Opin Pulm Med,* 9(2), 117–24.

Spruit, M.A., Singh, S.J , Garvey, C., ZuWallack, R., Nici, L., Rochester, C., Hil,l K., Holland, A.E., Lareau, S.C., Man, W.D., Pitta, F., Sewell, L., Raskin, J., Bourbeau, J., Crouch, R., Franssen, F.M., Casaburi, R., Vercoulen, J.H., Vogiatzis, I., Gosselink, R., Clini, E.M., Effing, T.W., Maltais, F., van der Palen, J., Troosters, T., Janssen, D.J., Collins, E., Garcia-Aymerich, J., Brooks, D., Fahy, B.F., Puhan, M.A., Hoogendoorn, M., Garrod, R., Schols, A.M., Carlin, B., Benzo, R., Meek, P., Morgan, M., Rutten-van Mölken, M.P., Ries, A.L., Make, B., Goldstein, R.S., Dowson, C.A., Brozek, J.L., Donner, C.F. & Wouters, E.F. (2013) ATS/ERS Task Force on Pulmonary Rehabilitation. (2013). An official American Thoracic Society/European Respiratory Society statement: key concepts and advances in pulmonary rehabilitation. *Am J Respir Crit Care Med*, 188(8), 13–64.

Stanbrook, M.B. & Goldstein, R.S (2001). Steroids for acute exacerbations of COPD: how long is enough?. *Chest*, 119, 675–6.

Stoilkova, A, Janssen, DJ & Wouters, EF. (2013). Educational programmes in COPD management interventions: a systematic review. *Respir Med*, 107(11), 1637–1650.

Stoller, J.K. (2002). Clinical practice. Acute exacerbations of chronic obstructive pulmonary disease. *N Engl J Med*, 346(13), 988–94.

The COMBIVENT Inhalation Solution Study Group. (1997). Routine nebulized ipratropium and albuterol together are better than either alone in COPD. *Chest*, 112(6), 1514–21.

Thompson, W.H., Nielson, C.P., Carvalho, P. et al. (1996).Controlled trial of oral prednisone in outpatients with acute COPD exacerbation. *Am J Respir Crit Care Med,* 154(2 Pt 1), 407–12.

Wilkinson, M.A., Donaldson, C., Hurst, R., Seemungal, A.R. & Wedzicha, A. (2004). Early Therapy Improves Outcomes of Exacerbations of Chronic Obstructive Pulmonary Disease. *Am J Respir Crit Care Med*, 169(12), 1298–1303. 171(3), 292.

Vestbo, J., Lisa, D., Scanlon, P., Yates, J., Agusti, A., Bakke, P., et al. (2011) Changes in forced expiratory volume in 1 second overtime in COPD. *N Engl J Med*, 365, 1184–1192

Walters, J.A., Turnock, A.C., Walters, E.H. & Wood-Baker, R. (2010). Action plans with limited patient education only for exacerbations of chronic obstructive pulmonary disease. *Cochrane Database Syst Rev*, (5), CD005074.

Walters, J.A., Wang, W., Morle,y C., Soltani, A. & Wood-Baker, R. (2011). Different durations of corticosteroid therapy for exacerbations of chronic obstructive pulmonary disease. *Cochrane Database Syst Rev.*, (10), CD006897

Washko, G.R. , Fan, V.S. & Ramsey, S.D., et al, (2008). National Emphysema Treatment Trial Research Group . The effect of lung volume reduction surgery on chronic obstructive pulmonary disease exacerbations. *Am J Respir Crit Care Med,* 177( 2 ), 164–169.

Wedzicha, J.A. & Seemungal, T.A. (2007). COPD exacerbations: defining their cause and prevention. *Lancet*, 370(9589), 786–96.

Wilkinson, T.M., Donaldson, G.C., Hurst, J.R., Seemungal, T.A. & Wedzicha, J.A. (2004). Early therapy improves outcomes of exacerbations of chronic obstructive pulmonary disease. *Am J Respir Crit Care Med*, 169(12), 1298–303.

Wouters, E.F. (2005). Local and systemic inflammation in chronic obstructive pulmonary disease. *Proc Am Thorac Soc.*, 2(1), 26–33.

Zwerink, M., Brusse-Keizer, M., van der Valk, P.D., Zielhuis, G.A., Monninkhof, E.M., van der Palen, J., Frith, P.A. & Effing, T. (2014). Self management for patients with chronic obstructive pulmonary disease. *Cochrane Database Syst Rev*, 3, CD002990.

Nishant Gupta, MD

# 17 Inpatient Management of Acute COPD Exacerbations

Key Points

1. Acute exacerbations of COPD are a leading cause of morbidity and mortality worldwide. The majority of acute exacerbations of COPD are triggered by bacterial and viral infections.
2. The presence of severe symptoms (breathlessness, cough, wheezing), hemodynamic instability, hypoxemia or hypercarbia, severe underlying disease/comorbidities, and lack of adequate support at home, are some of the factors which should trigger inpatient management as compared to home management of an acute exacerbation.
3. Supplemental oxygen should be provided to target oxygen saturations between 88 – 92%.
4. Moderate dose glucocorticoids for a short duration (40mg prednisone for 5 days) are sufficient for most patients with an acute exacerbation.
5. Use of Noninvasive Positive Pressure Ventilation (NIPPV) reduces mortality and improves outcomes in hypoxemic/hypercapnic patients with acute exacerbations of COPD, and, unless absolutely contraindicated, should be the modality of choice for ventilatory support.

## 17.1 Introduction

Chronic obstructive pulmonary disease (COPD) is characterized by persistent airflow limitation that is usually progressive and associated with an enhanced chronic inflammatory response in the airways and lungs to noxious stimuli or gases (Global initiative for chronic Obstructive Lung Disease (GOLD) guidelines, 2014). It represents a major public health challenge. The prevalence and burden of COPD are projected to increase in the coming years due to continued exposure to COPD risk factors and the aging population (Mathers, 2006). In addition to being a leading cause of mortality and morbidity, COPD poses a significant economic and social burden. In the United States, the estimated direct costs from COPD are 29.5 billion dollars and indirect costs are 20.4 billion dollars (NHLBI Mortality & Morbidity chartbook, 2012). The majority of this cost burden is attributable to COPD exacerbations. In the subsequent sections we will review the salient features of COPD exacerbations and the management of hospitalized patients with COPD exacerbations.

## 17.2 Definition and Risk Factors

A COPD exacerbation is defined as an acute event characterized by worsening of the patient's respiratory symptoms that is beyond normal day-to-day variations and leads to a change in medication (GOLD guidelines, 2014). It is accompanied by a change in one or all of the following symptoms:

1. Increase in cough severity and frequency
2. Change in sputum color or consistency
3. Increase in baseline dyspnea

## 17.3 Risk Factors for COPD Exacerbations

Multiple studies have attempted to identify factors which might predispose patients to frequent exacerbations. In an observational study, Miravitlles et al (Miravitlles, 2000) found that increasing age, severity of $FEV_1$ impairment, and presence of chronic mucus hypersecretion were independently associated with the risk of having 2 or more exacerbations per year. Additionally, the severity of $FEV_1$ impairment and the presence of co-morbid conditions were associated with a higher risk of hospitalization (Miravitlles, 2000). In another study, chronic cough and sputum production were associated with frequent COPD exacerbations including frequent hospitalizations for severe exacerbations (Burgel, 2009). Niewoehner et al (Niewoehner, 2007) created a multi-variate model and found that older age, severity of $FEV_1$ impairment, productive cough, duration of COPD, hospitalization for COPD in the previous year, and theophylline use at baseline predicted a higher risk of future exacerbations. In the same study, older age, percentage of predicted $FEV_1$, unscheduled clinic/emergency department visits for COPD in the prior year, any cardiovascular comorbidity, and prednisone use at baseline were associated with a greater risk of hospitalization (Niewoehner, 2007).

Perhaps the best appraisal of COPD exacerbations comes from the Evaluation of COPD Longitudinally to Identify Predictive Surrogate Endpoints (ECLIPSE) study (Hurst, 2010). This study followed more than 2000 patients with COPD for a period of 3 years and observed the frequency of COPD exacerbations. They found that exacerbations became more frequent and more severe as the severity of COPD increased. **The single best predictor of exacerbations, across all GOLD stages, was a history of prior exacerbations.** Other factors associated with an increased frequency of exacerbations were the presence of gastroesophageal reflux disease (GERD), poorer quality of life, and elevated white blood cell (WBC) count (Hurst, 2010).

COPD is frequently characterized by evidence of increased low grade systemic inflammation (Gan, 2004). Recently, Thomsen et al hypothesized that elevated levels of inflammatory biomarkers in patients with stable COPD are associated with an increased risk of exacerbations. They identified 6574 patients with COPD from the

**Table 17.1:** Factors predicting an increased risk of exacerbations in patients with COPD.

| |
|---|
| 1. History of prior exacerbations |
| 2. Disease Characteristics:<br>– Worsening underlying disease based on $FEV_1$ impairment & GOLD classification<br>– Chronic cough and sputum production<br>– Prednisone and/or theophylline use at baseline |
| 3. Presence of comorbidities:<br>– Gastroesophageal reflux disease<br>– Pre-existing cardiovascular comorbidities<br>– Poor quality of life at baseline |
| 4. Laboratory characteristics:<br>– Elevated white blood cell count<br>– Elevated fibrinogen levels<br>– Elevated levels of C-reactive protein |

participants of Copenhagen City Heart Study and the Copenhagen General Population Study and followed them prospectively to assess for exacerbations. They found that elevated levels of inflammatory biomarkers at baseline (CRP, Fibrinogen and WBC count) were associated with an increased risk of future exacerbations, even in patients with mild disease and no prior history of exacerbations (Thomsen, 2013).

## 17.4 Etiology of COPD Exacerbations

COPD exacerbations can be triggered by several factors. The most common cause of an acute exacerbation is a respiratory tract infection (viral or bacterial). Bacterial pathogens are believed to be responsible for up to 50% of the COPD exacerbations (Sethi, 2008). Rosell et al performed bronchoscopic sampling of lower airways and found clinically significant bacterial concentrations in 54% of patients with COPD exacerbations as opposed to 4% of healthy adults (Rosell, 2005). Acquisition of new bacterial strains may play a central role in the pathogenesis of COPD exacerbations (Sethi, 2008). Respiratory viral infections can account for exacerbations in up to one-third of patients (Mohan, 2010). A range of respiratory viruses are linked to COPD exacerbations. The most common viruses associated with exacerbations of COPD are rhinoviruses, but in more severe exacerbations requiring hospitalization, influenza is more common (Seemungal, 2001; Rohde, 2003; Greenberg, 2000).

Air pollution can trigger exacerbations in patients with COPD (Ling, 2009). In up to 30% of patients with an acute exacerbation, no particular etiology is identified (Sapey, 2006). Recent evidence suggests that pulmonary embolism (PE) might account for a significant proportion of these exacerbations. A single center prospective cohort

**Table 17.2:** Common etiologies responsible for acute exacerbations of COPD

| | |
|---|---|
| Bacterial infections | *Haemophilus influenza, Streptococcus pneumonia, Moraxella catarrhalis, Pseudomonas aeruginosa, Chlamydophila pneumonia, Mycoplasma pneumonia* |
| Viral infections | Rhinovirus, Influenza and Parainfluenza virus, Respiratory syncytial virus, Coronavirus, Adenovirus, Human metapneumovirus |
| Air pollution | |
| Pulmonary embolism | |
| Comorbid conditions such as congestive heart failure, pneumonia | |
| Other/Idiopathic | |

study found that in patients requiring hospitalization secondary to a severe COPD exacerbation, PE was identified in 25% cases (Tillie-Leblond, 2006). These results were further supported by a meta-analysis (Rizkallah, 2009).

## 17.5 Triage to Home Versus Hospital for Management of Exacerbations

The assessment of a patient with COPD exacerbation begins with a complete medical history and physical examination. It is important to have a broad initial set of differential diagnoses when evaluating a patient with COPD presenting with worsening dyspnea. Alternate diagnoses to consider include congestive heart failure, pulmonary thromboembolism, pneumonia, pneumothorax and worsening anemia. Zvezdin et al (Zvezdin, 2009) reviewed the medical records of 43 patients who died within 24 hours of admission for an acute exacerbation of COPD. The primary cause of death was heart failure (37%), pneumonia (28%), and pulmonary thromboembolism (21%); respiratory failure due to COPD progression occurred in only 14% of the patients (Zvezdin, 2009).

The medical history should include an assessment of COPD severity (usually based upon prior spirometry measuring the $FEV_1$ % predicted), presence/worsening of new/existing symptoms, and their comorbidities. Physical examination should focus on identifying signs which might suggest acute decompensation, such as the use of accessory muscles of respiration, paradoxical movement of the chest and abdomen, development of cyanosis, peripheral edema, change in mental status, and hemodynamic instability. In addition, the following tests may be of additional value to assess severity of the exacerbation and exclude alternate diagnoses:

1. Pulse oximetry and arterial blood gas measurement to analyze oxygenation and acid-base status

**Table 17.3:** Criteria to trigger hospitalization for patients with COPD exacerbations.

| |
|---|
| – Marked increase in intensity of symptoms, such as sudden development of resting dyspnea |
| – Severe underlying COPD |
| – Onset of new physical signs (e.g. peripheral edema, cyanosis) |
| – Failure of outpatient/emergency room management |
| – Presence of other co-morbidities (e.g. heart failure, arrhythmias) |
| – History of frequent exacerbations |
| – Older age |
| – Inadequate home support |
| – Change in mental status |

2. Chest radiographs are especially useful as they can help exclude alternate diagnoses such as heart failure, pneumonia and pneumothorax. A clear chest radiograph might provide a clue to the presence of pulmonary thromboembolism, especially if the dyspnea and hypoxemia seem out of proportion to the degree of cough/sputum production.
3. Electrocardiogram to diagnose arrhythmias or cardiac ischemia.
4. Complete blood count to look for polycythemia, leukocytosis, thrombocytopenia or anemia.
5. Metabolic panel to evaluate electrolytes and blood sugar.

The first question to answer in the management of COPD exacerbations is to determine whether the patient needs hospitalization or can they be safely managed at home. Over 80% of exacerbations can be safely managed at home with antibiotics, corticosteroids, and bronchodilators (Hurst, 2010; Tashkin, 2008). Intensive home care or "Hospital at home" programs for management of COPD exacerbations deliver similar clinical outcomes compared with hospitalization but provide substantial financial savings (Ram, 2004). However, such an approach requires a dedicated support team and resources which are not widely available at the current time.

Overall, there is a paucity of literature when it comes to guidance in making the decision to hospitalize a patient with an acute exacerbation of COPD. To some extent this decision has to be individualized based on the available hospital and community resources. In general, criteria that might trigger hospitalization are provided by the GOLD guidelines (GOLD guidelines, 2014). These criteria can be divided into clinical, laboratory/radiologic, and psychosocial factors. Clinical examination findings such as hemodynamic instability, altered mental status, use of accessory muscles of respiration, new oxygen requirement, presence of cyanosis, severe underlying COPD, history of frequent exacerbations, failure of outpatient management, and significant comorbid conditions should prompt consideration of hospitalization. Laboratory findings such as respiratory acidosis, elevated white blood cell count, and chest radiograph showing a lobar pneumonia or significant pulmonary edema should also prompt consideration of inpatient admission. Finally, psychosocial factors, such as older age, presence or absence of support at home, and availability of outpatient appointments for quick follow up should be evaluated prior to discharging patients from the emergency room or office.

Once a decision has been made to admit a patient with an acute exacerbation, the next step is to decide whether the patient can be safely managed on the ward or requires an ICU admission. Patients with a life threatening exacerbation should be promptly triaged to the ICU. Presence of hemodynamic instability, respiratory muscle fatigue, respiratory acidosis, persistent severe hypoxemia, need for mechanical ventilation, and altered mental status should prompt admission to the ICU. Table 17.4 summarizes the indications that warrant ICU admission for patients with an acute exacerbation of COPD. Patients not meeting these indications can generally be safely triaged to the wards. Patients with a mild exacerbation and good social support at home can be admitted under observation (less than 48 hour hospital stay) with a plan to complete the remainder of their therapy at home. This decision can be further guided by the emergency department course of these patients. Patients who start to show improvement in their symptoms in the emergency department after a few hours of treatment can generally be safely admitted for observation. However, patients with more severe exacerbations, especially patients with severe underlying disease, history of frequent exacerbations, and presence of significant cardiovascular comorbidities should be admitted to the inpatient setting with a plan to monitor them for a few days until they start to show signs of clinical improvement/stabilization.

**Table 17.4:** Indications for ICU admission for patients with acute exacerbations of COPD

| |
|---|
| – Changes in mental status |
| – Persistent and/or worsening hypoxemia ($pO_2$ < 40 mmHg) despite supplemental oxygen |
| – Presence of respiratory acidosis |
| – Hemodynamic instability |
| – Need for mechanical ventilation |

## 17.6 Hospital Management of COPD Exacerbations

The major components of management in COPD exacerbations include reversal of airflow obstruction with short acting bronchodilators and systemic glucocorticoids, identifying and treating the trigger(s) of the exacerbation, especially treating infectious processes with antibiotics, and ensuring adequate oxygenation. In the following sections we will cover the pharmacologic management of COPD exacerbations, followed by the role of mechanical ventilation in the management of COPD exacerbations.

### 17.6.1 Pharmacologic Therapies for the Management of COPD Exacerbations

#### 17.6.1.1 Supplemental Oxygen

Supplemental oxygen is a key therapy for management of COPD exacerbations. However, the use of supplemental oxygen should be judicious. Administration of high flow oxygen can lead to worsening hypercapnia and worse outcomes. The exact mechanisms for worsening hypercapnia after administration of supplemental oxygen are not clear, but likely include a combination of the following factors:

1. Worsened ventilation-perfusion matching due to attenuation of hypoxic pulmonary vasoconstriction (Aubier, 1980).
2. Haldane effect – release of carbon dioxide bound to hemoglobin due to rightward displacement of CO2-hemoglobin dissociation curve in the presence of increased oxygen saturation (Christiansen, 1914).
3. Decreased minute ventilation (Robinson, 2000).

In a prospective, randomized trial, paramedics treating patients with COPD exacerbations provided either high flow oxygen irrespective of the patient's pulse oximeter saturations ($SpO_2$) or supplemental oxygen titrated to achieve $SpO_2$ between 88 – 92%. The mortality rate in the high flow oxygen group was 9% whereas mortality rate in the oxygen titration group was 4%. Thus, in patients with an acute exacerbation of COPD, using supplemental oxygen titrated to maintain $SpO_2$ between 88 – 92% reduced mortality by 58% compared with unconstrained high flow oxygen (Austin, 2010). This trial forms the basis of our recommendation to titrate supplemental oxygen to a $SpO_2$ of 88 – 92% in patients with COPD exacerbations.

#### 17.6.1.2 β Adrenergic Agonists

Inhaled short acting β-adrenergic agonists (albuterol, levalbuterol) are the mainstays of pharmacological management to reverse air flow obstruction. They can be administered via a metered dose inhaler (MDI) with/without a spacer or via nebulization. Current evidence suggests that both approaches (nebulization versus MDI) are equivalent in terms of drug delivery and treatment of bronchospasm (Turner, 1997). Despite this evidence of clinical equivalency and increased cost, clinicians tend to prefer nebulized therapy on the pretext of a more uniform/reliable drug delivery.

Typical doses of albuterol are 2.5 mg by nebulizer every one to four hours as needed, or four to eight puffs (90 mcg per puff) by MDI with a spacer every one to four hours as needed. Increasing the dose of nebulized albuterol to 5 mg or using continuous nebulized β-agonists does not have a significant impact on spirometry or clinical outcomes (Nair, 2005), but might lead to increased adverse effects such as tachycardia, tremors, and hypokalemia.

Patients with severe COPD are at higher risk of hypercapnia with supplemental oxygen (discussed in the section above). This phenomenon has been observed with the use of oxygen-driven nebulizers (Edwards, 2012). Thus, bronchodilators to be administered via nebulization should be given via compressed air nebulization rather than oxygen driven nebulization (O'Driscoll, 2008).

#### 17.6.1.3 Anticholinergic Agents

Short acting inhaled anticholinergic agents (ipratropium) are commonly employed in conjunction with β-adrenergic agonists for treatment of COPD exacerbations. The typical dose for ipratropium in this setting is 500 mcg by nebulizer every four – six hours as needed. Alternatively, two to four puffs (18 mcg per puff) can be administered by MDI with a spacer every four – six hours as needed.

The evidence for this practice is conflicting. There are studies showing an additive bronchodilator effect by adding short acting anticholinergics to inhaled β-agonists (O'Driscoll, 1989). However, there is contrasting evidence that showed no additive bronchodilation was observed with the addition of inhaled anticholinergics to β-agonists (McCrory, 2002).

We recommend giving a trial of inhaled anticholinergics in conjunction with β-agonists to see if patients derive symptomatic benefit. However, in the absence of robust clinical evidence behind this practice, caution should be exercised in administering anticholinergics to elderly patients with a history of benign prostatic hyperplasia. They should not be given any more frequently than every 4 hours in order to prevent anticholinergic side effects.

#### 17.6.1.4 Glucocorticoids

Systemic corticosteroids, when given in conjunction with bronchodilators, can improve symptoms and shorten the hospital length of stay for patients with an acute exacerbation of COPD (Niewoehner, 1999; Quon, 2008). Corticosteroids have a nearly 100% oral bioavailability and, thus, should be administered orally unless patients are unable to take oral medications (e.g. intubated and mechanically ventilated patients). De Jong et al (de Jong, 2007) compared intravenous prednisone to oral prednisone in patients admitted with COPD exacerbation and found no difference in the rates of treatment failure, spirometric and quality of life improvement, and length of hospital stay.

The optimal dose and duration of corticosteroids for treatment of COPD exacerbations has been a subject of debate for the past few years. De Jong et al (de Jong, 2007) and Lindenauer et al (Lindenauer, 2010) compared low dose oral prednisone to high dose intravenous prednisone and found similar outcomes. Niewoehner et al (Niewoehner, 1999) conducted a double blind, randomized trial comparing a 2 week with an 8 week course of steroids for COPD exacerbations. They found that a 2 week course of steroids was similar in efficacy and outcomes to an 8 week course. This trial formed the basis for the standard 14 day steroid course for COPD exacerbations over the past decade. More recently, the 14 day steroid course was compared with a 5 day course and the authors found similar outcomes and less corticosteroid exposure from a 5 day steroid course (REDUCE trial) (Leuppi, 2013). The dose of prednisone used in the REDUCE trial was 40 mg prednisone daily. Nebulised budesonide alone may be an alternative to systemic corticosteroids in the management of hospitalized patients with acute exacerbations of COPD (Maltais, 2002; Gunen, 2007).

Tapering of systemic corticosteroids, although a common practice, is unnecessary in most circumstances. The risk of hypothalamic-pituitary-adrenal-axis suppression is negligible when low dose, short duration corticosteroid regimens are used. No evidence exists to suggest that abruptly stopping a low-dose steroid regimen will increase the risk of disease relapse. In addition, patients find tapered regimens confusing which commonly leads to incorrect dosing (Vondracek, 2006). We recommend not initiating a tapering course of steroids unless the duration of treatment will exceed 14 days.

In summary, the trend in corticosteroid dosing is shifting to a paradigm of low to moderate doses given for a relatively short duration. Based upon the findings from the REDUCE trial (Leuppi, 2013) and the GOLD guidelines (GOLD guidelines, 2014), oral 40 mg prednisone daily for 5 days should suffice for most patients with acute exacerbations of COPD.

#### 17.6.1.5 Antibiotics

While the utility of antibiotics is less established for mild exacerbations managed in the outpatient setting, the role of antibiotics is more established in moderate-severe exacerbations requiring hospitalization. Anthonisen (Anthonisen, 1987) compared antibiotic administration with placebo in patients with acute exacerbations of COPD and found a higher treatment success rate in patients who received antibiotics with no increase in adverse effects. Nouira et al (Nouira, 2001) compared oral ofloxacin to placebo in mechanically ventilated patients with COPD exacerbation and showed that the combined frequency of death and need for additional antibiotics, as well as duration of hospital stay and mechanical ventilation were lower in the group treated with ofloxacin. Similar improvements in outcomes after administration of antibiotics have been reported by multiple other studies (Roede, 2009; Rothberg, 2010; Daniels, 2010; and Stefan, 2013). Vollenweider et al (Vollenweider, 2012) conducted a meta-analysis of all randomized control studies on this subject and found high quality evidence supporting the role of antibiotics in the management of severe COPD exacerbations requiring hospitalization, especially patients admitted to the ICU or requiring mechanical ventilation. Similar benefit was not found in cases of mild exacerbations managed in the outpatient setting.

Based upon the above data, the GOLD guidelines recommend antibiotic administration to patients with COPD exacerbations requiring mechanical ventilation (invasive or non-invasive) or patients with increased sputum volume or purulence (GOLD guidelines, 2014). The recommended length of therapy is 5 days for most patients.

Falagas et al (Falagas, 2008) perfomed a meta-analysis comparing short duration antibiotic courses (5 days) with longer duration courses (7 – 10 days) and found similar treatment success rates in both groups. Additionally, patients treated with a shorter course of antibiotics had fewer adverse events.

The optimal choice of antibiotic for use in COPD exacerbations is not well established, and to some extent is dependent upon the local bacterial resistance pattern. Usual first line therapy should target the common bacterial pathogens *(Haemophilus influenzae, Moraxella catarrhalis*, and *Streptococcus pneumonia*) and consists of a macrolide antibiotic, penicillin, or doxycycline (Dimopoulos, 2007). In patients with severe disease, history of frequent exacerbations and/or history of exacerbation requiring mechanical ventilation, consideration must be given to the possibility of resistant organisms such as *Pseudomonas* species which will not be adequately covered by the above antibiotics. Cultures from sputum and/or lung should be performed in these high risk patients and broad spectrum antibiotics administered with a plan to de-escalate based upon the culture and susceptibility results (Soler, 1998; Miravitlles, 1999).

Measurement of serum procalcitonin should be considered in patients with acute exacerbations of COPD. Serum procalcitonin is elevated in response to bacterial infections and thus can be a useful biomarker to help decide initiation/duration of antibiotics. A recent Cochrane analysis found that use of serum procalcitonin measurement in cases of respiratory tract infections (including COPD exacerbations) did not affect mortality or treatment failure but led to a significant reduction in antibiotic exposure (Schuetz, 2012). This practice could reduce the overall cost of treatment, prevent unnecessary adverse events associated with exposure to antibiotics and also prevent emergence of resistant organisms.

#### 17.6.1.6 Other Therapies

Adjuvant therapies in addition to the above measures that might benefit a hospitalized patient with an acute exacerbation of COPD include the following:

1. *Smoking cessation*: Hospitalization provides a great opportunity to get patients to quit smoking. The admission itself can act as a strong deterrent against continued active smoking (Rigotti, 2008; Keenan, 2009). Intensive counseling for smoking cessation during hospitalization (at least one contact during the hospital stay with continued support for at least one month after discharge) increased the likelihood of smoking cessation (relative risk (RR) 1.37, 95% confidence interval (CI) 1.27–1.48) (Rigotti, 2012). Addition of nicotine replacement therapy to the counselling can further increase the rates of smoking cessation (RR 1.54, 95% CI 1.34–1.79) (Rigotti, 2012).
2. *Thromboprophylaxis*: PE accounts for a significant proportion of acute exacerbations of COPD. As discussed earlier in this chapter, PE is the trigger for up to a quarter of COPD exacerbations in patients without an identified exacerbation

cause or in patients with non-resolving symptoms (Tillie-Leblond, 2006; Rizkallah, 2009). Additionally patients with COPD are at increased risk for development of venous thromboembolism and PE (Bertoletti, 2012). Adequate pharmacologic measures should be taken to prevent this complication in hospitalized patients (Kahn, 2012). Physicians should maintain a high index of suspicion to look for a deep vein thrombosis (DVT) or PE in cases of COPD exacerbations.

3. *Nutritional support*: Patients with an acute exacerbation of COPD tend to have negative nitrogen balance and use of nutritional supplements to target a daily caloric intake of 1.5 times their resting energy expenditure leads to modest improvements in lung function and general well-being scores (Saudny-Unterberger, 1997).
4. *Management of comorbidities*: COPD coexists with multiple other comorbidities which can negatively affect patients' prognosis (Barnes, 2009). Cardiovascular disease is the most frequent comorbidity in patients with COPD and frequently complicates the hospital course and management of patients admitted with a COPD exacerbation (Almagro, 2012). The major cardiovascular comorbidities coexisting with COPD include hypertension, ischemic heart disease (IHD), heart failure (CHF), and atrial fibrillation (Almagro, 2012). Distinction between heart failure and COPD exacerbation can sometimes be difficult based on history, and further investigations such as chest radiographs, serum brain natriuretic peptide (BNP), and echocardiography may be helpful in distinguishing the two conditions. In general, these comorbidities should be managed according to their respective guidelines, as there is no evidence to suggest that these manifestations should be treated differently in the presence of COPD (GOLD guidelines, 2014).

   There is an increased risk of myocardial ischemia in patients admitted with acute exacerbations of COPD (Donaldson, 2010). The biggest management conundrum in the presence of combined COPD and cardiovascular disease is the ability to use β-blockers. β-blockers have a significant mortality benefit in cases of ischemic heart disease and congestive heart failure (Hunt SA, 2009; Kushner FG, 2009), and are under-utilized because of concern for worsening bronchospasm (Stefan, 2012). Multiple studies have shown that selective $b_1$-blockers can be safely administered to patients with COPD (Stefan, 2012; Salpeter, 2005). In a cohort study of patients with COPD, Quint et al (Quint, 2013) found that use of β-blockers either started at presentation for MI or continuation of previously prescribed β-blockers was associated with a reduction in mortality. Thus, the benefits of β-adrenergic blockade in cases of IHD or CHF far outweigh any concerns for worsening bronchospasm and should not be withheld from patients with COPD exacerbations.
5. Other therapies such as mucolytic agents e.g. N-acetylcysteine, methylxanthines e.g. theophylline and aminophylline, and chest physiotherapy have not been shown to be beneficial in management of COPD exacerbations, and, thus, should not be routinely used for these patients (Black, 2004; Snow, 2001).

### 17.6.2 Mechanical Ventilation for Acute Exacerbations of COPD

#### 17.6.2.1 Noninvasive Positive Pressure Ventilation *(NIPPV)*:

NIPPV refers to positive pressure ventilation delivered via a noninvasive interface (nasal mask, oral mask or nasal prongs) as opposed to an invasive interface (endotracheal tube, tracheostomy). The use of NIPPV is becoming more common as we realize the benefits offered by this modality compared to invasive mechanical ventilation.

Perhaps, the best studied use of NIPPV has been in cases of hypoxemic and hypercapnic respiratory failure from COPD exacerbations. NIPPV reduces arterial carbon dioxide levels, corrects acidosis, decreases work of breathing, decreases hospital length of stay, and avoids complications of mechanical ventilation such as ventilator associated pneumonia. More importantly, use of NIPPV improves overall survival compared with invasive mechanical ventilation (Brochard, 1995; Plant, 2000; Chandra, 2012; Ram, 2004; Conti, 2002). In a meta-analysis by Ram et al (Ram, 2004), the use of NIPPV for COPD exacerbations was associated with almost 50% reduction in mortality (11% versus 21%). Thus, NIPPV is probably the treatment modality offering the largest mortality benefit in cases of acute exacerbations of COPD.

An oronasal mask might confer the most physiologic advantage in these patients (Navalesi, 2000) but, in reality, the choice of mask is more dependent upon patient comfort. A starting inspiratory pressure (IPAP) of 8–12cms $H_2O$, and an end expiratory pressure (EPAP) of 4–6 cms $H_2O$ is a reasonable start for most patients. Further titration of inspiratory and expiratory pressures is based on the clinical condition and gas exchange parameters. Patients initiated on NIPPV should be closely monitored and a repeat blood gas obtained after 1–2 hours of NIPPV. Improvement of pH and carbon dioxide within this time frame portends a good prognosis (Anton, 2000). As a corollary to this, if patients fail to show improvement/stabilization in their gas exchange parameters or clinical condition within the first two hours after initiation of NIPPV, they should be intubated and placed on invasive mechanical ventilation.

**Table 17.5:** Indications for initiation of Noninvasive Positive Pressure ventilation (NIPPV)

| |
|---|
| At least one of the following: |
| – Respiratory acidosis (Arterial pH ≤ 7.35, or PaCO2 > 45 mmHg) |
| – Severe persistent hypoxemia (Arterial PaO2 < 40 mmHg) |
| – Severe dyspnea with clinical signs suggestive of respiratory muscle fatigue |
| – Increased work of breathing, as evidenced by use of accessory muscles of respiration, paradoxical motion of abdomen, or intercostal muscle retraction |

**Table 17.6:** Contraindications for use of Noninvasive Positive Pressure ventilation (NIPPV)

| |
|---|
| At least one of the following: |
| – Aspiration risk |
| – Altered mental status |
| – Hemodynamic instability |
| – Cardiac/respiratory arrest |
| – Severe agitation |

**Table 17.7:** Indications to initiate invasive mechanical ventilation

| |
|---|
| – Failure to tolerate NIPPV |
| – Contraindications to the use of NIPPV |
| – Failure to improve gas exchange parameters after trial of NIPPV (2 hours) |
| – Massive aspiration |
| – Inability to handle respiratory secretions |

#### 17.6.2.2 Invasive Mechanical Ventilation

Endotracheal intubation and invasive mechanical ventilation is typically reserved as the last resort in the management of COPD exacerbations, and are used when patients have either failed or not tolerated a trial of NIPPV or there are contraindications to the use of NIPPV (Table 17.6). The goals of invasive mechanical ventilation are the same as NIPPV and include reduction in work of breathing, correction of acidosis, and prevention of dynamic hyperinflation. Volume controlled modes of ventilation are most commonly used for this purpose with assist control mode (AC) being the most common mode of mechanical ventilation.

With mechanical ventilation, careful attention has to be given to avoid overventilation that can lead to air trapping and dynamic hyperinflation. Dynamic hyperinflation can lead to barotrauma and decreased venous return causing cardiovascular collapse and death (Tobin, 2001). Dynamic hyperinflation is characterized by increased levels of intrinsic positive end expiratory pressure (Auto-PEEP). Auto-PEEP is very common in patients with COPD (MacIntyre, 1997) and can lead to significantly increased work of breathing (Coussa, 1985). An indication of the presence of auto-PEEP can be the presence of one or more of the following: 1) ineffective triggering on the ventilator, 2) increasing peak pressures, 3) the beginning of inspiratory flow before expiratory flow reaches zero (Ranieri, 1995). Auto-PEEP can be quantitatively assessed by measuring the airway opening pressure during an end-expiratory pause (Pepe, 1982). The quantitative measurement might be helpful as it provides a guide to the amount of extrinsic PEEP that should be used. As a rough estimate, the applied or extrinsic PEEP should be approximately 80% of the auto-PEEP (Ranieri, 1993). Other strategies to reduce auto-PEEP include reducing the minute ventilation and prolong-

**Table 17.8:** Summary of management of hospitalized patients with an acute exacerbation of COPD.

| |
|---|
| – Diagnostic testing<br>– Assess oxygen saturation with pulse oximetry<br>– Routine labs such as CBC, Renal panel<br>– Chest x-ray to assess for pneumonia, heart failure, pneumothorax etc<br>– Arterial blood gas in severe exacerbations or patient exhibiting signs of respiratory distress |
| – Supplemental oxygen: Titrate to keep oxygen saturation between 88 – 92% |
| – Inhalers:<br>– β-adrenergic agonists (Albuterol) and anticholinergic agents (Ipratropium).<br>– Avoid aggressive use of anticholinergic agents to prevent side effects especially in elderly patients.<br>– Use compressed air nebulizers rather than oxygen driven nebulizers |
| – Glucocorticoids:<br>– Moderate dose glucocorticoids are as effective as high dose.<br>– Oral steroids have similar efficacy to intravenous steroids |
| – Antibiotics:<br>– Macrolide, or respiratory fluoroquinolone as first line agents<br>– May have to alter antibiotic choice based on likely pathogens and local antibiograms |
| – Mechanical Ventilation:<br>– Noninvasive positive pressure ventilation (NIPPV), is the preferred mode of mechanical ventilation, unless absolute contraindications exist<br>– Consider for patients with respiratory acidosis, hypoxemia, or signs of respiratory distress/ fatigue<br>– Close monitoring to assess for need of invasive mechanical ventilation<br>– Use NIPPV to assist with weaning from invasive mechanical ventilation |

ing the expiratory time (de Durante, 2002; Marini, 2003). Close attention must be paid to the size of the endotracheal tube in mechanically ventilated patients with COPD. Whenever possible, avoid smaller diameter endotracheal tubes as increased resistance through the smaller tube can contribute to Auto-PEEP. Occasionally, patients can present with severe auto-PEEP causing decreased venous return and cardiovascular collapse. Immediate, short duration disconnection from the ventilator (to allow "deflation" and reduction in hyperinflation) can be a lifesaving maneuver in this circumstance. Mechanical ventilation can then be resumed with reductions in minute ventilation and the addition of extrinsic PEEP.

COPD exacerbations that require mechanical ventilation are associated with worse outcomes and increased mortality (Seneff, 1995). Thus, every effort should be made to identify the patient's wishes (advance directives or living will) prior to initiating mechanical ventilation.

Weaning from mechanical ventilation can be difficult in patients with COPD. The major determinant in a patient's ability to be liberated from the ventilator is the ability of the respiratory muscles to cope with the ventilatory load (Purro, 2000). Use of NIPPV to facilitate weaning can significantly improve the chances of successful extubation (Nava, 1998). In addition, early use of NIPPV in patients with hypercapnia following a spontaneous breathing trial reduced the risk of respiratory failure and improved 90 day mortality (Ferrer, 2009).

## 17.7 Hospital Discharge and Follow up

The optimal duration of inpatient stay for management of COPD exacerbations is unclear. Length of stay of 6–7 days has been quoted based on the results by Mushlin et al (Mushlin, 1991). However, in today's age, with better organized transitions of care between inpatient and outpatient teams, the optimal length of stay is likely shorter for most patients. A patient's home medications should be initiated prior to discharge to ensure efficacy of the regimen. It might be prudent to continue inhaled corticosteroids even in the presence of systemic steroids, in order to emphasize adherence and ensure continuity of the home regimen after systemic steroids are discontinued. The requirement for supplemental oxygen should be addressed at rest and with exertion prior to discharge.

**Table 17.9:** Items to assess prior to discharge from hospital

- Smoking cessation
- Ensure efficacy of home inhaler regimen
- Reassess inhaler technique
- Need for supplemental oxygen, at rest and with exercise
- Adequate outpatient follow up
- Management and follow up plan for other comorbidities
- Ensure patient and/or home caregivers understand the management plan and provide written instructions for the same

The goal after hospital discharge is to prevent future exacerbations and hospitalizations. Prior hospital admissions, use of oral corticosteroids, long term oxygen use, poor health related quality of life, and lack of physical activity are associated with an increased rate of readmissions (Bahadori K, 2007). Effective communication between hospital providers, patient/family, and outpatient physicians is critical to prevent future readmissions. These patients should be reassessed 4 – 6 weeks after hospital discharge. Smoking cessation, effectiveness of the outpatient medical regimen, inhaler technique and vaccination status should be addressed during this follow up. In patients with frequent exacerbations, long term use of macrolides such as azithromycin (Albert, 2011), or phosphodiesterase inhibitors such as roflulimast (Chong, 2013) should be considered in order to reduce the frequency of exacerbations. When compared to conventional care, pulmonary rehabilitation after an acute exacerbation of COPD reduces mortality by 72% and readmission by 78% with a number needed to treat of only 6 and 4, respectively (Puhan, 2011). Health related quality of life and exercise capacity were increased above the minimally important difference (Puhan, 2011).

## 17.8 Conclusion

Acute exacerbations of COPD are a leading cause of morbidity and mortality worldwide. The majority of these exacerbations can be successfully treated in the outpatient setting; however, severe cases require hospitalization. Detailed investigations to determine etiology of exacerbations as well as management of underlying comorbidities is essential for successful management of these patients. Careful attention must be paid to the presenting symptoms and underlying comorbidities in order to properly triage these patients from the emergency room. The use of NIPPV has led to significant reduction in mortality from acute exacerbations of COPD. Effective communication between inpatient providers, patients, families and primary care providers is essential in order to prevent recurrent hospitalizations from COPD exacerbations.

## 17.9 Summary Points

1. Acute exacerbations of COPD are significant contributing factors to the morbidity and mortality burden of COPD.
2. The distinction between COPD exacerbations and underlying cardiovascular comorbidities can be difficult but must be done promptly as it can have a significant impact on management and subsequent mortality.
3. History of frequent exacerbations, severity of underlying disease, and the presence of significant cardiovascular comorbidities are the main factors predicting future exacerbations as well as increased risk of hospitalization.
4. Avoid excessive use of anticholinergic inhalers in order to prevent adverse effects, especially in elderly patients.
5. Administration of β-blockers is safe in patients with COPD and should not be withheld, especially in patients with significant cardiac history.
6. Early use of NIPPV should be considered in severe exacerbations for initial mechanical ventilator support as well as to facilitate weaning and liberation from invasive mechanical ventilation.

## References


Albert, R.K., Connett, J., Bailey, W.C., et al. COPD Clinical Research Network. (2011). Azithromycin for prevention of exacerbations of COPD. *The New England Journal of Medicine, 365*(8), 689–698.

Almagro, P., Cabrera, F.J., Diez, J., et al. Working Group on COPD , Spanish Society of Internal Medicine. (2012). Comorbidities and short-term prognosis in patients hospitalized for acute exacerbation of COPD: The EPOC en servicios de medicina interna (ESMI) study. *Chest, 142*(5), 1126–1133.

Anthonisen, N.R., Manfreda, J., Warren, C.P., et al. (1987). Antibiotic therapy in exacerbations of chronic obstructive pulmonary disease. *Annals of Internal Medicine, 106*(2), 196–204.

Anton, A., Guell, R., Gomez, J., et al. (2000). Predicting the result of noninvasive ventilation in severe acute exacerbations of patients with chronic airflow limitation. *Chest, 117*(3), 828–833.

Aubier, M., Murciano, D., Milic-Emili, J., et al. (1980). Effects of the administration of O2 on ventilation and blood gases in patients with chronic obstructive pulmonary disease during acute respiratory failure. *The American Review of Respiratory Disease, 122*(5), 747–754.

Austin, M.A., Wills, K.E., Blizzard, L., et al. (2010). Effect of high flow oxygen on mortality in chronic obstructive pulmonary disease patients in prehospital setting: Randomised controlled trial. *BMJ (Clinical Research Ed.), 341*, c5462.

Bahadori, K., & FitzGerald, J.M. (2007). Risk factors of hospitalization and readmission of patients with COPD exacerbation--systematic review. *International Journal of Chronic Obstructive Pulmonary Disease, 2*(3), 241–251.

Barnes, P.J., & Celli, B.R. (2009). Systemic manifestations and comorbidities of COPD. *The European Respiratory Journal, 33*(5), 1165–1185.

Bertoletti, L., Quenet, S., Mismetti, P., et al. RIETE Investigators. (2012). Clinical presentation and outcome of venous thromboembolism in COPD. *The European Respiratory Journal, 39*(4), 862–868.

Black, P.N., Morgan-Day, A., McMillan, T.E., et al. (2004). Randomised, controlled trial of N-acetyl-cysteine for treatment of acute exacerbations of chronic obstructive pulmonary disease (ISRCTN21676344. *BMC Pulmonary Medicine, 4*, 13.

Brochard, L., Mancebo, J., Wysocki, M., et al. (1995). Noninvasive ventilation for acute exacerbations of chronic obstructive pulmonary disease. *The New England Journal of Medicine, 333*(13), 817–822.

Burgel, P.R., Nesme-Meyer, P., Chanez, P., et al. Initiatives Bronchopneumopathie Chronique Obstructive Scientific Committee. (2009). Cough and sputum production are associated with frequent exacerbations and hospitalizations in COPD subjects. *Chest, 135*(4), 975–982.

Chandra, D., Stamm, J.A., Taylor, B., et al. (2012). Outcomes of noninvasive ventilation for acute exacerbations of chronic obstructive pulmonary disease in the united states, 1998–2008. *American Journal of Respiratory and Critical Care Medicine, 185*(2), 152–159.

Chong, J., Leung, B., & Poole, P. (2013). Phosphodiesterase 4 inhibitors for chronic obstructive pulmonary disease. *The Cochrane Database of Systematic Reviews, 11*, CD002309.

Christiansen, J., Douglas, C.G., & Haldane, J.S. (1914). The absorption and dissociation of carbon dioxide by human blood. *The Journal of Physiology, 48*(4), 244–271.

Conti, G., Antonelli, M., Navalesi, P., et al. (2002). Noninvasive vs. conventional mechanical ventilation in patients with chronic obstructive pulmonary disease after failure of medical treatment in the ward: A randomized trial. *Intensive Care Medicine, 28*(12), 1701–1707.

Coussa, M.L., Guerin, C., Eissa, N.T., et al. (1993). Partitioning of work of breathing in mechanically ventilated COPD patients. *Journal of Applied Physiology (Bethesda, Md.: 1985), 75*(4), 1711–1719.

Daniels, J.M., Snijders, D., de Graaff, C.S., et al. (2010). Antibiotics in addition to systemic corticosteroids for acute exacerbations of chronic obstructive pulmonary disease. *American Journal of Respiratory and Critical Care Medicine, 181*(2), 150–157.

de Durante, G., del Turco, M., Rustichini, L., et al. (2002). ARDSNet lower tidal volume ventilatory strategy may generate intrinsic positive end-expiratory pressure in patients with acute respiratory distress syndrome. *American Journal of Respiratory and Critical Care Medicine, 165*(9), 1271–1274.

de Jong, Y.P., Uil, S.M., Grotjohan, H.P., et al. (2007). Oral or IV prednisolone in the treatment of COPD exacerbations: A randomized, controlled, double-blind study. *Chest, 132*(6), 1741–1747.

Dimopoulos, G., Siempos, I.I., Korbila, I.P., et al. (2007). Comparison of first-line with second-line antibiotics for acute exacerbations of chronic bronchitis: A metaanalysis of randomized controlled trials. *Chest, 132*(2), 447–455.

Donaldson, G.C., Hurst, J.R., Smith, C.J., et al. (2010). Increased risk of myocardial infarction and stroke following exacerbation of COPD. *Chest, 137*(5), 1091–1097.

Edwards, L., Perrin, K., Williams, M., et al. (2012). Randomised controlled crossover trial of the effect on PtCO2 of oxygen-driven versus air-driven nebulisers in severe chronic obstructive pulmonary disease. *Emergency Medicine Journal : EMJ, 29*(11), 894–898.

Falagas, M.E., Avgeri, S.G., Matthaiou, D.K., et al. (2008). Short- versus long-duration antimicrobial treatment for exacerbations of chronic bronchitis: A meta-analysis. *The Journal of Antimicrobial Chemotherapy, 62*(3), 442–450.

Ferrer, M., Sellares, J., Valencia, M., et al. (2009). Non-invasive ventilation after extubation in hypercapnic patients with chronic respiratory disorders: Randomised controlled trial. *Lancet, 374*(9695), 1082–1088.

Gan, W.Q., Man, S.F., Senthilselvan, A., & Sin, D.D. (2004). Association between chronic obstructive pulmonary disease and systemic inflammation: A systematic review and a meta-analysis. *Thorax, 59*(7), 574–580.

Global strategy for the diagnosis, management, and prevention of COPD: Revised 2014. global initiative for chronic obstructive lung disease (GOLD). http://www.goldcopd.org. (accessed on february 7 2014).

Greenberg, S.B., Allen, M., Wilson, J., & Atmar, R.L. (2000). Respiratory viral infections in adults with and without chronic obstructive pulmonary disease. *American Journal of Respiratory and Critical Care Medicine, 162*(1), 167–173.

Gunen, H., Hacievliyagil, S.S., Yetkin, O., et al. (2007). The role of nebulised budesonide in the treatment of exacerbations of COPD. *The European Respiratory Journal, 29*(4), 660–667.

Hunt, S.A., Abraham, W.T., Chin, M.H., et al. American Heart Association. (2009). 2009 focused update incorporated into the ACC/AHA 2005 guidelines for the diagnosis and management of heart failure in adults A report of the american college of cardiology Foundation/American heart association task force on practice guidelines developed in collaboration with the international society for heart and lung transplantation. *Journal of the American College of Cardiology, 53*(15), e1-e90.

Hurst, J.R., Vestbo, J., Anzueto, A., et al. Evaluation of COPD Longitudinally to Identify Predictive Surrogate Endpoints (ECLIPSE) Investigators. (2010). Susceptibility to exacerbation in chronic obstructive pulmonary disease. *The New England Journal of Medicine, 363*(12), 1128–1138.

Kahn, S.R., Lim, W., Dunn, A.S., et al. American College of Chest Physicians. (2012). Prevention of VTE in nonsurgical patients: Antithrombotic therapy and prevention of thrombosis, 9th ed: American college of chest physicians evidence-based clinical practice guidelines. *Chest, 141*(2 Suppl), e195S-226S.

Keenan, P.S. (2009). Smoking and weight change after new health diagnoses in older adults. *Archives of Internal Medicine, 169*(3), 237–242.

Kushner, F.G., Hand, M., Smith, S.C.,Jr, et al. (2009). 2009 focused updates: ACC/AHA guidelines for the management of patients with ST-elevation myocardial infarction (updating the 2004 guideline and 2007 focused update) and ACC/AHA/SCAI guidelines on percutaneous coronary intervention (updating the 2005 guideline and 2007 focused update) a report of the american college of cardiology Foundation/American heart association task force on practice guidelines. *Journal of the American College of Cardiology, 54*(23), 2205–2241.

Leuppi, J.D., Schuetz, P., Bingisser, R., et al. (2013). Short-term vs conventional glucocorticoid therapy in acute exacerbations of chronic obstructive pulmonary disease: The REDUCE randomized clinical trial. *JAMA : The Journal of the American Medical Association, 309*(21), 2223–2231.

Lindenauer, P.K., Pekow, P.S., Lahti, M.C., et al. (2010). Association of corticosteroid dose and route of administration with risk of treatment failure in acute exacerbation of chronic obstructive pulmonary disease. *JAMA : The Journal of the American Medical Association, 303*(23), 2359–2367.

Ling, S.H., & van Eeden, S.F. (2009). Particulate matter air pollution exposure: Role in the development and exacerbation of chronic obstructive pulmonary disease. *International Journal of Chronic Obstructive Pulmonary Disease, 4*, 233–243.

MacIntyre, N.R., Cheng, K.C., & McConnell, R. (1997). Applied PEEP during pressure support reduces the inspiratory threshold load of intrinsic PEEP. *Chest, 111*(1), 188–193.

Maltais, F., Ostinelli, J., Bourbeau, J., et al. (2002). Comparison of nebulized budesonide and oral prednisolone with placebo in the treatment of acute exacerbations of chronic obstructive pulmonary disease: A randomized controlled trial. *American Journal of Respiratory and Critical Care Medicine, 165*(5), 698–703.

Marini, J.J., & Brower, R.G. (2003) Auto-peep with low tidal volume. *American Journal of Respiratory and Critical Care Medicine, 167*(8), 1150–1; author reply 1151.

Mathers, C.D., & Loncar, D. (2006). Projections of global mortality and burden of disease from 2002 to 2030. *PLoS Medicine, 3*(11), e442.

McCrory, D.C., & Brown, C.D. (2002). Anti-cholinergic bronchodilators versus beta2-sympathomimetic agents for acute exacerbations of chronic obstructive pulmonary disease. *The Cochrane Database of Systematic Reviews, (4)*(4), CD003900.

Miravitlles, M., Espinosa, C., Fernandez-Laso, E., et al. (1999). Relationship between bacterial flora in sputum and functional impairment in patients with acute exacerbations of COPD. study group of bacterial infection in COPD. *Chest, 116*(1), 40–46.

Miravitlles, M., Guerrero, T., Mayordomo, C., et al. (2000). Factors associated with increased risk of exacerbation and hospital admission in a cohort of ambulatory COPD patients: A multiple logistic regression analysis. the EOLO study group. *Respiration; International Review of Thoracic Diseases, 67*(5), 495–501.

Mohan, A., Chandra, S., Agarwal, D., et al. (2010). Prevalence of viral infection detected by PCR and RT-PCR in patients with acute exacerbation of COPD: A systematic review. *Respirology (Carlton, Vic.), 15*(3), 536–542.

Mushlin, A.I., Black, E.R., Connolly, C.A., et al. (1991). The necessary length of hospital stay for chronic pulmonary disease. *JAMA : The Journal of the American Medical Association, 266*(1), 80–83.

Nair, S., Thomas, E., Pearson, S.B., & Henry, M.T. (2005). A randomized controlled trial to assess the optimal dose and effect of nebulized albuterol in acute exacerbations of COPD. *Chest, 128*(1), 48–54.

National heart, lung and blood institute. morbidity and mortality chartbook on cardiovascular, lung and blood diseases. bethesda, maryland: US department of health and human services, public health service, national institutes of health. (2012). Retrieved from http://www.nhlbi.nih.gov.proxy.libraries.uc.edu/research/reports/2012-mortality-chart-book.htm

Nava, S., Ambrosino, N., Clini, E., et al. (1998). Noninvasive mechanical ventilation in the weaning of patients with respiratory failure due to chronic obstructive pulmonary disease. A randomized, controlled trial. *Annals of Internal Medicine, 128*(9), 721–728.

Navalesi, P., Fanfulla, F., Frigerio, P., et al. (2000). Physiologic evaluation of noninvasive mechanical ventilation delivered with three types of masks in patients with chronic hypercapnic respiratory failure. *Critical Care Medicine, 28*(6), 1785–1790.

Niewoehner, D.E., Erbland, M.L., Deupree, R.H., et al. (1999). Effect of systemic glucocorticoids on exacerbations of chronic obstructive pulmonary disease. department of veterans affairs cooperative study group. *The New England Journal of Medicine, 340*(25), 1941–1947.

Niewoehner, D.E., Lokhnygina, Y., Rice, K., et al. (2007). Risk indexes for exacerbations and hospitalizations due to COPD. *Chest, 131*(1), 20–28.

Nouira, S., Marghli, S., Belghith, M., et al. (2001). Once daily oral ofloxacin in chronic obstructive pulmonary disease exacerbation requiring mechanical ventilation: A randomised placebo-controlled trial. *Lancet, 358*(9298), 2020–2025.

O'Driscoll, B.R., Howard, L.S., Davison, A.G., & British Thoracic Society. (2008). BTS guideline for emergency oxygen use in adult patients. *Thorax, 63 Suppl 6*, vi1–68.

O'Driscoll, B.R., Taylor, R.J., Horsley, M.G., et al. (1989). Nebulised salbutamol with and without ipratropium bromide in acute airflow obstruction. *Lancet, 1*(8652), 1418–1420.

Pepe, P.E., & Marini, J.J. (1982). Occult positive end-expiratory pressure in mechanically ventilated patients with airflow obstruction: The auto-PEEP effect. *The American Review of Respiratory Disease, 126*(1), 166–170.

Plant, P.K., Owen, J.L., & Elliott, M.W. (2000). Early use of non-invasive ventilation for acute exacerbations of chronic obstructive pulmonary disease on general respiratory wards: A multicentre randomised controlled trial. *Lancet, 355*(9219), 1931–1935.

Puhan, M.A., Gimeno-Santos, E., Scharplatz, M., et al. (2011). Pulmonary rehabilitation following exacerbations of chronic obstructive pulmonary disease. *The Cochrane Database of Systematic Reviews, (10):CD005305. doi*(10), CD005305.

Purro, A., Appendini, L., De Gaetano, A., et al. (2000). Physiologic determinants of ventilator dependence in long-term mechanically ventilated patients. *American Journal of Respiratory and Critical Care Medicine, 161*(4 Pt 1), 1115–1123.

Quint, J.K., Herrett, E., Bhaskaran, K., et al. (2013). Effect of beta blockers on mortality after myocardial infarction in adults with COPD: Population based cohort study of UK electronic healthcare records. *BMJ (Clinical Research Ed.), 347*, f6650.

Quon, B.S., Gan, W.Q., & Sin, D.D. (2008). Contemporary management of acute exacerbations of COPD: A systematic review and metaanalysis. *Chest, 133*(3), 756–766.

Ram, F.S., Picot, J., Lightowler, J., & Wedzicha, J.A. (2004). Non-invasive positive pressure ventilation for treatment of respiratory failure due to exacerbations of chronic obstructive pulmonary disease. *The Cochrane Database of Systematic Reviews, (3)*(3), CD004104.

Ram, F.S., Wedzicha, J.A., Wright, J., & Greenstone, M. (2004). Hospital at home for patients with acute exacerbations of chronic obstructive pulmonary disease: Systematic review of evidence. *BMJ (Clinical Research Ed.), 329*(7461), 315.

Ranieri, V.M., Giuliani, R., Cinnella, G., et al. (1993). Physiologic effects of positive end-expiratory pressure in patients with chronic obstructive pulmonary disease during acute ventilatory failure and controlled mechanical ventilation. *The American Review of Respiratory Disease, 147*(1), 5–13.

Ranieri, V.M., Mascia, L., Petruzzelli, V., et al. (1995). Inspiratory effort and measurement of dynamic intrinsic PEEP in COPD patients: Effects of ventilator triggering systems. *Intensive Care Medicine, 21*(11), 896–903.

Rigotti, N.A., Clair, C., Munafo, M.R., & Stead, L.F. (2012). Interventions for smoking cessation in hospitalised patients. *The Cochrane Database of Systematic Reviews, 5*, CD001837.

Rigotti, N.A., Munafo, M.R., & Stead, L.F. (2008). Smoking cessation interventions for hospitalized smokers: A systematic review. *Archives of Internal Medicine, 168*(18), 1950–1960.

Rizkallah, J., Man, S.F., & Sin, D.D. (2009). Prevalence of pulmonary embolism in acute exacerbations of COPD: A systematic review and metaanalysis. *Chest, 135*(3), 786–793.

Robinson, T.D., Freiberg, D.B., Regnis, J.A., & Young, I.H. (2000). The role of hypoventilation and ventilation-perfusion redistribution in oxygen-induced hypercapnia during acute exacerbations of chronic obstructive pulmonary disease. *American Journal of Respiratory and Critical Care Medicine, 161*(5), 1524–1529.

Roede, B.M., Bresser, P., Prins, J.M., et al. (2009). Reduced risk of next exacerbation and mortality associated with antibiotic use in COPD. *The European Respiratory Journal, 33*(2), 282–288.

Rohde, G., Wiethege, A., Borg, I., et al. (2003). Respiratory viruses in exacerbations of chronic obstructive pulmonary disease requiring hospitalisation: A case-control study. *Thorax, 58*(1), 37–42.

Rosell, A., Monso, E., Soler, N., et al. (2005). Microbiologic determinants of exacerbation in chronic obstructive pulmonary disease. *Archives of Internal Medicine, 165*(8), 891–897.

Rothberg, M.B., Pekow, P.S., Lahti, M., et al. (2010). Antibiotic therapy and treatment failure in patients hospitalized for acute exacerbations of chronic obstructive pulmonary disease. *JAMA : The Journal of the American Medical Association, 303*(20), 2035–2042.

Salpeter, S., Ormiston, T., & Salpeter, E. (2005). Cardioselective beta-blockers for chronic obstructive pulmonary disease. *The Cochrane Database of Systematic Reviews, (4)*(4), CD003566.

Sapey, E., & Stockley, R.A. (2006). COPD exacerbations . 2: Aetiology. *Thorax, 61*(3), 250–258.

Saudny-Unterberger, H., Martin, J.G., & Gray-Donald, K. (1997). Impact of nutritional support on functional status during an acute exacerbation of chronic obstructive pulmonary disease. *American Journal of Respiratory and Critical Care Medicine, 156*(3 Pt 1), 794–799.

Schuetz, P., Muller, B., Christ-Crain, M., et al. (2012). Procalcitonin to initiate or discontinue antibiotics in acute respiratory tract infections. *The Cochrane Database of Systematic Reviews, 9*, CD007498.

Seemungal, T., Harper-Owen, R., Bhowmik, A., et al. (2001). Respiratory viruses, symptoms, and inflammatory markers in acute exacerbations and stable chronic obstructive pulmonary disease. *American Journal of Respiratory and Critical Care Medicine, 164*(9), 1618–1623.

Seneff, M.G., Wagner, D.P., Wagner, R.P., et al. (1995). Hospital and 1-year survival of patients admitted to intensive care units with acute exacerbation of chronic obstructive pulmonary disease. *JAMA : The Journal of the American Medical Association, 274*(23), 1852–1857.

Sethi, S., & Murphy, T.F. (2008). Infection in the pathogenesis and course of chronic obstructive pulmonary disease. *The New England Journal of Medicine, 359*(22), 2355–2365.

Snow, V., Lascher, S., Mottur-Pilson, C., & Joint Expert Panel on Chronic Obstructive Pulmonary Disease of the American College of Chest Physicians and the American College of Physicians-American Society of Internal Medicine. (2001). Evidence base for management of acute exacerbations of chronic obstructive pulmonary disease. *Annals of Internal Medicine, 134*(7), 595–599.

Soler, N., Torres, A., Ewig, S., et al. (1998). Bronchial microbial patterns in severe exacerbations of chronic obstructive pulmonary disease (COPD) requiring mechanical ventilation. *American Journal of Respiratory and Critical Care Medicine, 157*(5 Pt 1), 1498–1505.

Stefan, M.S., Rothberg, M.B., Priya, A., et al. (2012). Association between beta-blocker therapy and outcomes in patients hospitalised with acute exacerbations of chronic obstructive lung disease with underlying ischaemic heart disease, heart failure or hypertension. *Thorax, 67*(11), 977–984.

Stefan, M.S., Rothberg, M.B., Shieh, M.S., et al. (2013). Association between antibiotic treatment and outcomes in patients hospitalized with acute exacerbation of COPD treated with systemic steroids. *Chest, 143*(1), 82–90.
Tashkin, D.P., Celli, B., Senn, S., et al. UPLIFT Study Investigators. (2008). A 4-year trial of tiotropium in chronic obstructive pulmonary disease. *The New England Journal of Medicine, 359*(15), 1543–1554.
Thomsen, M., Ingebrigtsen, T.S., Marott, J.L., et al. (2013). Inflammatory biomarkers and exacerbations in chronic obstructive pulmonary disease. *JAMA : The Journal of the American Medical Association, 309*(22), 2353–2361.
Tillie-Leblond, I., Marquette, C.H., Perez, T., et al. (2006). Pulmonary embolism in patients with unexplained exacerbation of chronic obstructive pulmonary disease: Prevalence and risk factors. *Annals of Internal Medicine, 144*(6), 390–396.
Tobin, M.J., Jubran, A., & Laghi, F. (2001). Patient-ventilator interaction. *American Journal of Respiratory and Critical Care Medicine, 163*(5), 1059–1063.
Turner, M.O., Patel, A., Ginsburg, S., & FitzGerald, J.M. (1997). Bronchodilator delivery in acute airflow obstruction. A meta-analysis. *Archives of Internal Medicine, 157*(15), 1736–1744.
Vollenweider, D.J., Jarrett, H., Steurer-Stey, C.A., et al. (2012). Antibiotics for exacerbations of chronic obstructive pulmonary disease. *The Cochrane Database of Systematic Reviews, 12*, CD010257.
Vondracek, S.F., & Hemstreet, B.A. (2006). Is there an optimal corticosteroid regimen for the management of an acute exacerbation of chronic obstructive pulmonary disease? *Pharmacotherapy, 26*(4), 522–532.
Zvezdin, B., Milutinov, S., Kojicic, M., et alO. (2009). A postmortem analysis of major causes of early death in patients hospitalized with COPD exacerbation. *Chest, 136*(2), 376–380.

Sara M. Krzywkowski-Mohn Ed.D, FNP

# 18 Primary Care and Interaction with Specialty Care for the COPD Patient

Key Points

1. The Primary Care team will ultimately manage the care of the patient with COPD in close collaboration with Pulmonary Services.
2. Relationships between Primary Care and Pulmonary Specialists must be collaborative, fluid, and respectfully recognize each provider's unique role in the care of the patient.
3. Traditional management of the COPD patient in the primary arena setting has changed and includes expanding roles and responsibilities of all team members.

## 18.1 Introduction: A Healthcare System in Crisis and New Models of Care

The U.S. Healthcare System continues to face a challenging environment including rising healthcare costs while achieving mediocre health outcomes for its population of 311 million people. The current healthcare system is saturated with inconsistent coordination and discontinuous care, poor access to both Primary Care and Specialty Services (Pulmonary; Cardiology) and increasing numbers of emergency room visits, hospitalizations and hospital readmissions (Ewing, 2013). In addition, the US spends approximately $3.6 trillion dollars per year on healthcare which is an average of over $8000.00 per citizen. In addition, the US population is living longer with an average life expectancy of 82.2 years for women and 77.4 years for men. With this aging population, the process of chronic disease management becomes critical in the Primary Care setting (Wat, 2014). The percentage of Americans struggling with a chronic disease such as cardiac disease, diabetes, hypertension, chronic obstructive pulmonary disease, obesity and cancer is staggering and affects at least 133 million adults which is nearly one in two adults. Seven percent of U.S. children also suffer from at least one chronic disease including diabetes, hypertension, and obesity. The consequences of these chronic disorders are sobering; 70% of all adult deaths are attributed to chronic diseases and more than 75% of the U.S. health care budget is spent on the management of chronic disease (Richmann, 2014). These results have stimulated the examination and testing of other models of providing and managing Primary Care to the U.S. population. One proposed solution is a redesign of the primary care outpatient setting called the Patient Centered Medical Home (Higgins, 2013).

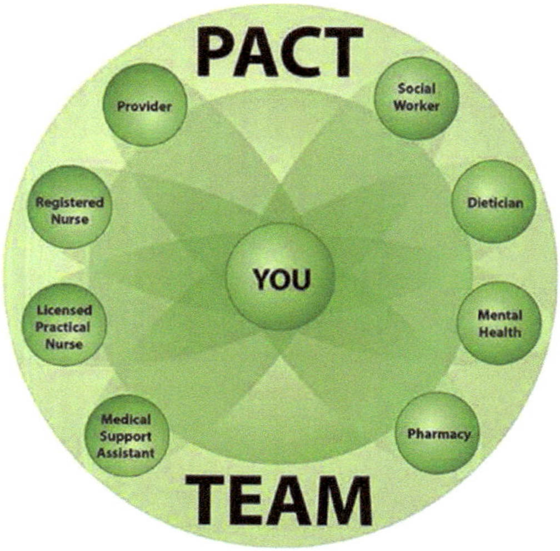


**Figure 18.1:** Organization of the Patient Aligned Care Team (VA Team Training, 2014)

## 18.2 The Patient Centered Family Medical Home Model

The Patient Centered Care Medical Home Model is a patient driven, team based approach that delivers efficient, comprehensive, and continuous care through active communication and coordination of healthcare services (Daschle, 2013). It is based on a set of seven principles: 1) respect for the patient; 2) coordination and integration of care; 3) emphasis on communication and education between the patient and staff; 4) emphasis on physical comfort; 5) emotional support/alleviation of fear and anxiety; 6) involvement of family and friends and 7) attention to transition and continuity of care and improved access (Jackson, 2013). The Patient Centered Care Medical Home Model is also known by a variety of other names such as the Patient Aligned Care Team or PACT (Veterans Administration System). This team structure has the patient at the center of the process and dictates that the patient is no longer the passive recipient of healthcare but rather is viewed as an integral and active participant. In fact, the patient is recognized as the most important member of the health care team. Thus, the patient and provider are reconfigured into a shared decision making model where the patient ultimately will decide on the unique plan of his/her care. The matriarchal/patriarchal all-knowing physician is no longer viewed as the epitome of medical care. Surrounding that unique patient are the members of the Primary Care Team consisting of a Primary Care Provider (medical doctor, nurse practitioner or physician assistant), registered nurse, licensed practical nurse and medical support assistant. In addition, integrated into the Primary Care Team are allied health providers including nutrition, pharmacy, social work, and mental health (Yoon, 2013). (Figure 18.1).

To complicate improvement in primary care further, the U.S. continues to face a growing need for primary care physicians and will need an additional 52,000 doctors by 2025. The reasons for the primary care physician shortage are complex and include population growth, an aging population, the rising cost of medical school, more lucrative specialty care opportunities, and scope of practice laws. There is projected to be a substantial shortage of non-primary care specialists of 33,100 in specialties such as cardiology, oncology, and emergency medicine. Thus, other providers such as nurse practitioners and physician assistants are helping to fill the gap in care. In addition, other allied health providers such as nutritionists, pharmacists, mental health providers, and physical therapists are being relied upon more frequently to help in the management of chronic disease and lifestyle issues (Herman, 2014).

Specialty care is viewed as a secondary tier and to be consulted only when primary care has a question or problem with a complex patient. In this model, only the most complex and sickest patients are seen by specialty care. This practice redesign creates improved access for specialty care; however, it conversely increases the workload for the primary care team. It is expected that the primary care team will manage most of the care of the patient including specialty services. This assumes that the primary care team has additional skills, experience and professional development to feel comfortable in managing the complex specialty patient (Pagan, 2013).

## 18.3 How Does the PACT Team Differ from Traditional Roles/ Responsibilities?

The Family Medical Home or Patient Aligned Care Team must have an organizational foundation of patient centeredness, continuous improvement, and adequate resources. The very structure of the team is built on patient access, care management, and coordination and practice redesign. Patient access to the team is a cornerstone of practice; however, the traditional face-to-face provider patient visit is rapidly being reconstructed to include non-traditional visits such as scheduled telephone visits when a physical exam is not needed, secure messaging (email), and group medical appointments for chronic disease management. The patient is typically seen on an annual basis for a wellness exam and certainly for ill visits when a physical exam is imperative. Thus, the non-traditional visits allow improved access via alternative pathways for patients to interact with their family medical home. In addition, other allied professionals including nutrition, social work, mental health, pharmacy and, in some settings, substance abuse, chronic disease case management (COPD/Diabetes), and physical therapy are relied upon for their expertise. These professionals are integrated directly into the teams. In this way, patients are able to access a variety of professionals at point of care in the primary care setting as a formalized appointment or as a "warm handoff" (Roseland, 2013).

**Figure 18.2:** PACT Team Pillars. (VA Team Training 2014).

Patient care management and coordination are key to the family medical home. In particular, the team identifies those patients who are at higher risk for emergency room visits and inpatient hospitalizations due to their complex medical and psychological histories. Chronically ill patients (COPD, diabetes, coronary artery disease) are followed more closely utilizing non-traditional visits with the team nurses and allied health professionals. Team care is focused on prevention, management of chronic disease, and coordinating transitions of care. In particular, continuity of care can be challenging when patients are seen by specialty care, in the emergency room and/or admitted and discharged from inpatient hospital stays. The problems most commonly encountered include discrepancies in medication management, failure to understand medications, and overall lack of understanding in the plan of care. This is true not only for the patient but often for the primary care team and creates tension often between services. Primary care often feels as if they are responsible for coordinating the care for a patient with limited communication from specialty care (Plaisance, 2010; Kilo, 2010; Gardner, 2014).

Finally practice redesign has been instrumental in the reconfiguration of how primary care is provided to the patient. The family medical home has expanded the roles, responsibilities, and tasks of each member of the team. Each team member is encouraged to practice at the top of their educational level (Swartwout, 2014). This team approach enables its members to value each member's skills and expertise, thereby promoting communication and teamwork. Frequently teams have designated weekly meetings to discuss high risk patients and management strategies. During these team meetings, workload dealing with both patient visits and non-visit work such as paperwork for family medical leave is discussed and distributed as dictated by time, skill level, educational competencies, and training. In this way, all visit and non-visit work is distributed amongst the team members, freeing up the provider to focus on patient management (Coulmont, 2013). (Figure 18.2)

## 18.4 General Roles of the PACT Team

The patient centered primary care team includes the patient, clerical associate, clinical associate, nurse care manager and the provider. Each team member is responsible for a specific function within the PACT. The patient is central to the entire team and has the responsibility to schedule appointments as needed, participate in face to face visits, prepare for primary care visits, and participate in all care. The clerical associate specializes in customer service, team work, and clerical office support. Direct patient care, secure messaging, care management, teamwork, patient education and clinical support are the duties of a PACT clinical associate. The nurse care manager anchors the team with a multitude of duties including: direct patient care, group visits, patient/family education, disease management, daily huddles, team meetings, health education, and patient coaching. Finally, the provider focuses on the management of complex patients through direct patient care, group visits, telephone visits, and secure messaging (Maeng, 2013; Hoff, 2013; Baxter, 2013).

## 18.5 Care Management of the COPD Patient PACT Roles and Responsibilities

Comprehensive care management of the total patient is the cornerstone of PACT team practice. Importantly, the patient is at the center of the structure of his/her management. For a patient with COPD, this structure becomes even more critical to optimize pulmonary health and prevent further disease progression. Surrounding that structure are the tools necessary to help the patient maintain optimal health including: personalized health care planning, labs/imaging studies, medication reconciliation, preventive services, protocols, consults, referrals, and local community resources (Comlossy, 2012).

### 18.5.1 The Patient

First and foremost, the patient is involved at the very beginning of his/her primary care visit and plan of specialty care. This model dictates that the patient is responsible for scheduling appointments, preparing for appointments, and participating in his/her unique plan of care. The personalized health plan (PHP) is a tool used to individualize the care provided by the team for that patient. It is patient driven, holistic in approach, and offers the patient a choice of what area of their health care they would like to improve. There are a variety of models but they all center around the broader questions of why health is important to the patient and the patient's selection of the primary health focus. The tools present areas of health assessment and prevention such as: be tobacco free, eat wisely, be physically active, limit alcohol, feel spiritually connected, manage stress, and be involved in one's healthcare. Thus, the patient chooses their area of focus and the team becomes more of a coach to help that patient achieve their self-determined goal. This approach is a fundamental change in how health care is now being delivered in the United States. Historically, it was the provider (almost always a physician) who dictated to the patient the plan of care. There was almost always no negotiation, limited discussion, and minimal education given to the patient. Now the patient has become the central player in the delivery of his/her own healthcare and as such the process has become more equalized and a more shared decision making process (Jarousse, 2013; Berryman, 2013). For the patient with COPD, the PHP can focus on tobacco cessation, medication review, proper use of inhalers and participation in pulmonary rehabilitation. The plan may also focus on a mental health issues common to COPD patients such as depression or anxiety.

Laboratory and imaging studies are important diagnostic tools used to diagnose and treat illness. In this model, the patient is able to obtain his/her results by accessing a secure website which includes all the components of the patients' electronic medical chart or EMC. In this way, the patient again has access to critical data in the individualized plan of care (Jampel, 2013; Mancuso, 2013).

### 18.5.2 Clerical Associate (CA)

This member of the team is the first line of contact with the patient and the very face of the PACT Team. As such, all initial communication relating to patient visits and concerns are triaged through this team member including such things as scheduling, reminder calls, managing sick and informational calls to the team, obtaining outside records, faxing information back to outside facilities, and issues with customer service. Clerical associates are experts in day to day mechanics of running an outpatient office. For the COPD patient, the clerical associate will need a basic understanding of the disease so that when a patient calls, the clerical associate can assist in triaging the severity of the patient's symptoms and can schedule an emergent ill visit with a provider or other appropriate healthcare visit. Integral to the management of a specialty patient, any recent change in care such as an inpatient stay or change in medication will need to be verified though acquirement of records (McNellis, 2013).

### 18.5.3 The Clinical Associate

The clinical associate is the first clinical person to assess the patient after they are checked into the PACT Team. As such, the associate performs the initial assessment of the patient including collection of data related to the visit, vital signs, prevention screening, and administration of immunizations, medications, and treatments. This team member is the initial responder to triaged messages (secure messaging) as well as telephone messages related to clinical concerns. It is often this team member who reminds the provider that the patient with COPD requires immunizations such as influenza and pneumonia vaccinations. The clinical associate is also trained to do point of care screening with spirometry for the patient suspected of having a pulmonary disorder. This clinical member is often the educator and instructs the patient on the use of his/her inhalers and the use of a spacer. The personalized health care plan for the COPD patient is often started by the clinical associate. Often this clinical member is the first to initiate treatment or other medications promptly (True, 2013).

### 18.5.4 Nurse Case Manager

This professional registered nurse anchors the team and provides direct patient care, triaging and clinically responding to secure messaging, phone calls and walk-in ill visits. The nurse is responsible for assisting with chronic disease management, coordinating transitions of care, and daily team work.

This team member is an expert in medication reconciliation which is especially important for the patient with COPD. Medication reconciliation continues to be one of the most important tasks for both the team and patient and it may be extremely time consuming to perform medication reconciliation correctly. Often medications are changed during a specialty visit or inpatient hospital stay and poorly communicated to both the patient and the PACT. The nurse case manager is an expert educator and reviews each medication with the patient including its purpose and how and when it is to be administered. The nurse is able to assess clinically a specialty patient and determine the needs of that patient in consultation with the primary care provider. This team member has a huge role in both family and patient education, coordination of transitions of care referrals such as pulmonary rehabilitation, home care, palliative care and hospice. The care manager also has a vast knowledge of outside community resources which may be of use for a COPD patient including meals on wheels, the Council On Aging and the American Cancer Society (Worth, 2012; Lewis, 2012).

### 18.5.5 The Provider

The provider in a PACT is an expert in direct patient care. Direct patient care as redesigned in PACT includes not only traditional face-to-face visits (well and ill visits) but also non-traditional visits such as telephone visits, secure messaging, and group medical appointments. The use of alternative visits theoretically improves patients' access to their provider and teams. Telephone visits are used when a physical exam is not necessary and the patient issue can be resolved on the telephone. Telephone visits are frequently used for a follow up from a previous visit, medication titration, discussion related to labs and imaging and plan of care. Secure messaging (by email) is an easy way for a provider to answer a question, renew a medication, or assess a patient issue in writing. Group visits are used to educate and manage chronically ill patients with the same diagnosis. The provider's main role is to provide care for patients through disease management of both complex and stable/chronic patients, preventative care, record review, view alerts, review of diagnostic results, referrals to specialty care, final medication reconciliation, initiation of the personalized health care plan, narcotic contracts, and referrals to additional community resources and services (Hoff, 2012; VA Teamlet training 2013).

## 18.6 COPD and PACT

The recognition and diagnosis of COPD are the initial steps in the provision of COPD care management. All patients with a history of tobacco use and/or environmental exposure and respiratory symptoms should be evaluated with spirometry to determine the presence of airflow limitation. Spirometry and pulmonary function tests are interpreted by specialty care; however, the interpretation and results still need to be reviewed and understood by the provider. In many cases, patients are assigned a diagnosis of COPD without adequate diagnostic testing. This leads to incorrect diagnosis and treatment. After diagnosis, the provider will need to determine what medications should be ordered for the patient based on the physical assessment and patient evaluation. The provider should be familiar with the different classes of respiratory medications such as short and long acting β adrenergic agonists and anti-cholinergics commonly used for the treatment of COPD. A basic understanding of aerosol inhalers, the use of spacers, and the ability to instruct patients how to use their inhalers correctly is critical. Other basics needed to properly assess the COPD patient are baseline studies such as chest x-rays, electrocardiogram, and annual labs. Preventative immunizations (influenza and pneumococcal vaccines) are essential. Tobacco cessation should always be discussed and assessed as stopping smoking is the single most important life change a COPD patient can make. An emergency plan is critical when exacerbations are expected and should include a treatment plan (antibiotics and steroids) and the patient must be instructed on how and when to use the emergency plan. Pulmonary rehabilitation should always be discussed with patients and they should be referred when appropriate. Medication reconciliation is imperative for both the provider and the COPD patient. Finally, it is the provider who should finish the personalized health care plan and negotiate goal setting and subsequent primary care appointments with the patient (Panos, 2013).

In conclusion, care management for the COPD patient is complex and requires a team approach to meet the patient's needs. Several areas of management can be initiated by all clinical team members including direct patient care, medication reconciliation, required referrals, and initiation of the PHP. (Figure 18.3).

**Figure 18.3:** Patient Centered Model for the Management of Chronic Obstructive Pulmonary Disease (VA Team Training, 2014)

The Primary Care Provider and PACT team are the patients' first line of entry into the health care system. The team needs to be familiar with the recognition and early diagnosis of COPD to properly manage these complex patients.

It is important to note that primary care PACTs may need extra training and education to feel comfortable when managing complex chronically ill pulmonary patients. Providers who attended a six week mini-COPD residency at the Cincinnati VA Medical center found that they were more comfortable with the COPD patient. This education provided the PACTs and the specialists time to get to know one another and to learn each other's role in keeping the COPD patient healthy. The residency was a series of six lectures on the basics of COPD, early recognition and diagnosis, spirometry and interpretation of pulmonary function tests, medications specific to COPD and proper use of inhalers and spacers, smoking cessation, Motivational Interviewing and multiple case studies for review (Panos, 2013).

A team approach with not only the PACT but integrating the pharmacist and the social worker into the team is instrumental. In a 2013 qualitative study, COPD patients were unclear of their medications, had multiple social and mental health issues and needed extra nursing education to better manage their chronic disease (Mulhall, 2013).

Specialty care is an important piece of the COPD patient's overall plan of care. Pulmonologists should be utilized for those complex respiratory patients who are difficult to manage. They should be used a resource service and provide expert guidance on the management of the COPD patient. A COPD nurse educator or manager of pulmonary rehabilitation may also be used by the PACT as a resource for patient education, clinical questions, and may act as a bridge to connect the inpatient and outpatient services ensuring continuity of care.

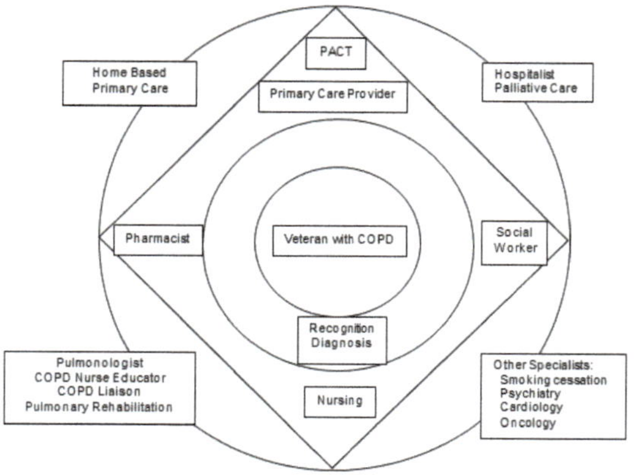


**Figure 18.4:** Patient-Centered Model for the Management of Chronic Obstructive Pulmonary Disease (Panos, 2014).

Finally, the COPD patient will typically have exacerbations and remissions of their chronic disease state and may require hospitalizations to stabilize their pulmonary status. Thus, hospitalists will be managing the patient while they are inpatients and may request input from specialty care. Again, communication is at the forefront of transitions of care and the individualized plan of care needs to be communicated back to that primary care provider and PACT (Panos, 2013). A transition of care discharge summary note to help to direct care at patient discharge should be written by the hospitalist/pulmonologist and flagged to the team. This communication ensures continuity of care and helps the team manage the COPD patient in the outpatient setting.

COPD patients are not only complex medically but often need additional support from other specialists including mental health and tobacco cessation counselors. These additional professionals can help in the management of tobacco use/abuse and mental health issues such as anxiety and depression (Bao, 2013).

In conclusion, a partnership needs to exist between the patient, the primary care PACT, the pulmonary specialist and allied health providers. Through this partnership (Figure 18.4), the patient should obtain the best care for a long, active, and meaningful life (Pourat, 2013).

## 18.7 Summary Points

1. The US health care delivery system is evolving toward a Patient Centered Family Medical Home Model.

2. Comprehensive care management focuses all team members including administrative/clerical, nursing, and provider staff on the patient and everyone functions at their maximal level.
3. Management of patients with COPD involves a cadre of primary care team members and specialists whose collaboration, integration, and communication is essential for optimal care.

## References

Bao, Y., Casalino, L.P., & Pincus, H.A. (2013). Behavioral health and health care reform models: patient-centered medical home, health home, and accountable care organization. *Journal of Behavioral Health Services and Research, 40(1)*, 121–132.

Baxter, L. & Nash, D.B. (2013). Implementing the patient-centered medical home model for chronic disease care in small medical practices: practice group characteristics and physician understanding. *American Journal of Medical Quality, 28(2)*, 113–119.

Berryman, S.N., Palmer, S.P., Kohl, J.E., & Parham, J.S. (2013). Medical home model of patient-centered health care. *MEDSURG Nursing, 22(3)*, 166–171.

Capko, J. (2014). The patient-centered movement. *Journal of Medical Practice Management, 29(4)*, 238–242.

Comlossy, M. (2012). The medical home model of care: reducing costs and improving quality. *Ncsl Legisbrief, 20(33)*, 1–2.

Coulmont, M., Roy, C., & Dumas, L. (2013). Does the Planetree Patient-Centered Approach to Care Pay Off? A Cost-Benefit Analysis. *Health Care Manager, 32(1)*, 87–95.

Daschle, T., Domenici, P., Frist, W., & Rivlin, A. (2013). Prescription for patient-centered care and cost containment. *New England Journal of Medicine, 369(5)*, 471–474.

Department of Veterans Affairs. (2014). VA Teamlet Training.

Ewing, M. (2013). The patient-centered medical home solution to the cost-quality conundrum. *Journal of Healthcare Management, 58(4)*, 258–266.

Gardner, R., Li, Q., Baier, R.R., Butterfield, K., Coleman, E.A., & Gravenstein, S. (2014). Is implementation of the care transitions intervention associated with cost avoidance after hospital discharge? *Journal of General Internal Medicine, 29(6)*, 878–874.

Herman, P.M., Dodds, S.E., Logue, M.D., Abraham, I., Rehfeld, R.A., Grizzle, A.J., Urbine, T.F., Horwitz, R., Crocker, R.L., & Maizes, V.H. (2014). IMPACT- Integrative Medicine PrimAry Care Trial: protocol for a comparative effectiveness study of the clinical and cost outcomes of an integrative primary care clinic model. *BMC Complementary and Alternative Medicine, 14(1)*, 132.

Higgins, S., Chawla, R., Colombo, C., Snyder, R., & Nigam, S. (2014). Medical homes and cost and utilization among high-risk patients. *American Journal of Managed Care, 20(3)*, 61–71.

Hoff, T. (2013). Medical home implementation: a sensemaking taxonomy of hard and soft best practices. *Milbank Quarterly, 91(4)*, 771–810.

Jackson, G.L., Powers, B.J., Chatterjee, R., Bettger, J.P., Kemper, A.R., Hasselblad, V., Dolor, R.J., Irvine, R.J., Heidenfelder, B.L., Kendrick, A.S., Gray, R., & Williams, J.W. (2013). Improving patient care. The patient centered medical home. A systematic review. *Annals of Internal Medicine, 158(3)*, 169–178.

Jampel, H.D. (2013). Patient-centered outcomes research: evolution, definition, and implications. *Ophthalmology, 120(4)*, 655–656.

Jarousse, L.A. (2013). Patient-centered care. *Hospitals and Health Networks, 87(7)*, 53–63.

Kilo, C.M., & Wasson, J.H. (2010). Practice redesign and the patient-centered medical home: history, promises, and challenges. *Health Affairs, 29(5)*, 773–778.

Lewis, P.C. & Holcomb, B. (2012). A model for patient-centered Army primary care. *Military Medicine, 177(12)*, 1502–1507.

Maeng, D.D., Davis, D.E., Tomcavage, J., Graf, T.R., & Procopio, K.M. (2013). Improving patient experience by transforming primary care: evidence from Geisinger's patient-centered medical homes. *Population Health Management, 16(3)*, 157–163.

Mancuso, J.M. (2013). Capsule commentary on True et al., open access in the patient centered medical home: lessons from the Veterans Health Administration. *Journal of General Internal Medicine, 28(4)*, 568.

Mcnellis, R.J., Genevro, J.L, & Meyers, D.S. (2013). Lessons learned from the study of primary care transformation. *Annals of Family Medicine, 11(1)*, S1-S5.

Mulhall, A.M., Lach, L.A., Krzywkowski-Mohn, S.M., Welge, J.A., & Panos, R.J. (2013). Therapeutic paralysis in veterans with COPD. *Respiratory Medicine, 107(10)*, 1547–1557.

Pagan, J.A., & Carlson, E.K. (2013). Assessing long-term health and cost outcomes of patient-centered medical homes serving adults with poor diabetes control. *Journal of Primary Care and Community Health, 4(4)*, 281–285.

Panos, R.J. COPD mini-residency primary care. Cincinnati, Ohio. 2014.

Panos, R.J., Krzywkowski-Mohn, S.M., Sherman, S.M., & Lach, L.A. (2013). Patient determinants of health: a qualitative analysis of veterans with Chronic Obstructive Pulmonary Disease at the Cincinnati VAMC. *COPD, 10(3)*, 333–347.

Plaisance, N.H. (2012). Care coordination a fundamental pillar to PCMH, but some find it easier than others to implement. *MGMA Connexion, 12(1)*, 42–43.

Pourat, N., Lavarreda, S.A., & Snyder, S. (2013). Patient-centered medical homes improve care for adults with chronic conditions. *Policy Brief (UCLA Center for Health Policy Research, 2013(3)*, 1–8.

Richman, M., Sklaroff, L.M., Hoang, K., Wasson, E., & Gross-Schulman, S. (2014). Innovative use of technologies and methods to redesign care: the problem of care transitions. *Journal of Ambulatory Care Management, 37(2)*, 100–105.

Rosland, A.M., Nelson, K., Sun, H., Dolan, E.D., Maynard, C., Bryson, C., Stark, R., Shear, J.M., Kerr, E., Fihn, S.D., & Schectman, G. (2013). The patient-centered medical home in the Veterans Health Administration. *American Journal of Managed Care, 19(7)*, 263–272.

Swartwout, K., Murphy, M.P., Dreher, M.C., Behal, R., Haines, A., Ryan, M., Ryan, N., & Saba, M. (2014). Advanced practice nursing students in the patient-centered medical home: preparing for a new reality. *Journal of Professional Nursing, 30(2)*, 139–148.

True G., Butler, A.E., Lamparska, B.G., Lempa, M.L., Shea, J.A., Asch, D.A. & Werner, R.M. (2013). Open access in the patient-centered medical home: lessons from the Veterans Health Administration. *Journal of General Internal Medicine, 28(4)*, 539–545.

Wat, D., Glossage, E., Hampson, O., & Sibley, S. (2014). Reducing admissions with patient group directions. *Nursing Times, 110(16)*, 18–20.

Worth, T. (2012). Saving primary care. Why PCMH and team-based models could rescue and transform healthcare delivery. *Medical Economics, 89(22)*, 24–26, 30–31.

Yoon, J., Rose, D.E., Canelo, I., Upadhyay, A.S., Schectman, G., Stark, R. Rubenstein, L.V., & Yano, E.M. (2013). Medical home features of VHA primary care clinics and avoidable hospitalizations. *Journal of General Internal Medicine, 28(9)*, 1188–1194.

Ralph J. Panos, MD

# 19 Integrating Supportive, Palliative, and End of Life Care for COPD

Key Points:

1. COPD is a chronic disease with a trajectory and natural history that is poorly predicted for any individual patient.
2. The prognosis of COPD is frequently as poor as lung cancer but patients with COPD often do not have discussions about advanced care planning with their providers.
3. Because disease trajectory is not well predicted for individual patients with COPD, advanced care planning should be incorporated into chronic disease management beginning at the time of diagnosis.
4. Advanced care planning includes information about COPD, its natural history, pharmacologic and nonpharmacologic management, comorbidities, potential for exacerbations, treatments for breathlessness, anxiety, and depression, and life sustaining interventions including invasive mechanical ventilation and resuscitation.
5. Multidisciplinary teams may enhance advanced care planning.
6. Patients' families and other caregivers should participate in advanced care planning.

## 19.1 Introduction

Chronic obstructive pulmonary disease (COPD) is a progressive, incurable yet treatable disorder that is a significant cause of disability, morbidity, and mortality. COPD is one of the few chronic processes that is increasing in prevalence and is predicted to become the third leading cause of death and fourth leading cause of worldwide disability in 2020. Although new and effective treatments are now available that reduce COPD's morbidity and mortality, there is no cure and many individuals die of or with COPD. During the course of their illness, patients with COPD frequently experience insidiously progressive breathlessness, physical and emotional deterioration, and social isolation. Advanced care planning is the process through which providers communicate with patients and their families and support networks to prepare a comprehensive COPD management strategy. Advanced care planning incorporates therapeutic, supportive, palliative, and end of life care. Therapeutic and supportive care is treatment that helps patients and their families cope with COPD and its treatment from pre-diagnosis, diagnosis, and care into chronic management, continued illness, death, and, finally, bereavement (www.endoflifecumbriaandlancashire.org.uk/info_patients_carers/definitions.php accessed 2014). (Figure 19.1)

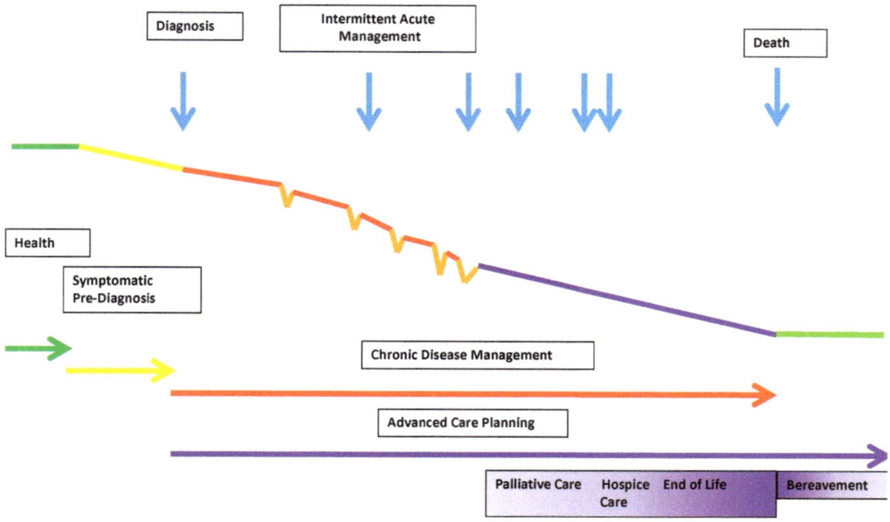


**Figure 19.1:** Stages of COPD. During the course of their illness, patients with COPD pass through various stages starting with good health, pre-diagnostic decline, development of respiratory symptoms, or even exacerbations, diagnosis, and then relentless disease progression. Frequently they experience insidiously progressive breathlessness, physical and emotional deterioration, and social isolation. Advanced care planning is the process through which providers communicate with patients and their families and support networks to prepare a comprehensive COPD management strategy. Advanced care planning incorporates therapeutic, supportive, palliative, and end of life care. Therapeutic and supportive care is treatment that helps patients and their families cope with COPD and its treatment from pre-diagnosis, diagnosis, and care into chronic management, continued illness, death, and, finally, bereavement.

## 19.2 COPD Disease Course and Management

Palliative care is an approach that improves the quality of life of patients and their families facing the problem(s) associated with life-threatening illness through the prevention and relief of suffering by means of early identification and impeccable assessment and treatment of pain and physical, psychosocial and spiritual care. (www.who.int/cancer/palliative/definition/en/, accessed 2014) Palliative care is multidimensional and its critical elements are presented in Table 19.1.

In addition to acute management, palliative care includes enhancing quality of life, helping with medical decision making, and identifying the goals of care, addressing the needs of family and other formal and informal caregivers, and providing opportunities for personal growth (National Consensus, 2004). End-of-life care encompasses the final stage of life during the terminal phase of the disease process and provides care for the dying person and their family and support network (Curtis, 2008).

**Table 19.1:** Critical Elements of Palliative Care (www.who.int/cancer/palliative/definition/en/, accessed 2014)

| Essential Components of Palliative Care |
|---|
| – Provides relief from pain and other distressing symptoms; |
| – Affirms life and regards dying as a normal process; |
| – Intends neither to hasten nor postpone death; |
| – Integrates the psychological and spiritual aspects of patient care; |
| – Offers a support system to help patients live as actively as possible until death; |
| – Offers a support system to help the family cope during the patient's illness and in their own bereavement; |
| – Uses a team approach to address the needs of patients and their families, including bereavement counseling, if indicated; |
| – Will enhance quality of life and may also positively influence the course of illness; |
| – Is applicable early in the course of illness, in conjunction with other therapies that are intended to prolong life, such as chemotherapy or radiation therapy, and includes those investigations needed to better understand and manage distressing clinical complications. |

## 19.3 Patient and Caregiver Burden

COPD is a persistent, treatable yet incurable, chronic disorder that is marked by exacerbations with intensification of respiratory symptoms; in early disease, the major causes of death are cardiac and oncologic comorbidities; whereas in later disease, respiratory failure predominates (discussed in Chapter 9, Natural History, Phenotypes, and Gender Differences in COPD; and Chapter 10, COPD Is a Multi-organ Disorder: Systemic Manifestations). Patients' health and quality of life are eroded by not only the respiratory manifestations of COPD but also the associated nonpulmonary processes (discussed in Chapter 10, COPD Is a Multi-organ Disorder: Systemic Manifestations). Current pharmacologic and nonpharmacologic treatments have significantly improved respiratory symptoms, reduced the frequency and severity of exacerbations, and consequences of COPD, but, nevertheless, the decline in respiratory function progresses as patients with COPD age. Patients with COPD often note what McMillan Boyles and colleagues (McMillan Boyles, 2011) have described as the invisible disability of COPD: the disparity between their outward normal appearance and their impaired functional status. Pinnock and coworkers (Pinnock, 2011) describe COPD not as an illness but an altered way of life. As functional impairment progresses, individuals with COPD enter a downward spiral. Their increasing physical limitations prompt a more sedentary life style restricting social interactions and activities that further reduces physical conditioning and function precipitating feelings of low self worth and depression. The less they do, the less they are able to do and a downward spiral ensues. COPD is associated with ubiquitous and insidiously pervasive effects on all aspects of life (Table 19.2)

**Table 19.2:** COPD's Effects on Patients' Lives (Panos, 2013)

| **Effects of COPD** |
|---|
| Physical and Functional Limitations: |
| – Work and employment constraints |
| – Recreation restrictions |
| – Limits on activities of daily living |
| – Reduced sexuality |
| – Concerns about housing and finances |
| – Physical symptoms |
| Restricted Social Interactions/Altered Social Networks: |
| – Altered relationships with friends and family |
| – Reliance upon family and care givers; |
| Emotional Effects: |
| – Reduced self-worth |
| – Vulnerability |
| – Depression |
| – Hopelessness |
| – Fear |
| – Lack of control |

(Panos, 2013). The trajectory of decline is not predictable for an individual patient with COPD.

Retrospective studies of the needs of patients with COPD during the last year of life reveal that nearly all of them experienced breathlessness (98%), fatigue or weakness (96%), low mood (77%), and pain (70%) (Elkington, 2005). Symptom relief was poor with only half experiencing relief of breathlessness and 82% not receiving treatment for their mood. Many, 41%, were housebound, leaving their home once or less monthly.

Patients with COPD often have a poor understanding of this disease. They may be unaware of its chronic, progressive course despite concerns that their condition might deteriorate, and are often unaware that COPD can cause death even though they worry about the manner of their death, especially a fear of dying with breathlessness or suffocation. These issues and fears are not always discussed with a caregiver (Gardiner, 2009). Patients with COPD adapt to an "abnormal normal" life style and accept their limitations rather than express a desire or need for assistance (Habraken, 2008; Panos, 2013). During exacerbations or episodes of breathlessness, they "tough it out" rather than seek medical attention or increased medication use (Panos, 2013). A cross sectional study of interviews with 163 patients with severe COPD showed that 57% had severe breathlessness and 92% said breathlessness was their most important problem (White, 2011). Despite its chronicity, patients and their families often lack information about COPD, its consequences, treatment, effects on psychosocial well-being, and inevitable decline in health. (Table 19.3)

**Table 19.3:** COPD Burden for Patients and Family/Caregivers (Yohannes, 2007; White, 2011)

| **Burden of COPD on Patients and their Social Support Networks** |
|---|
| Patients |
| – Intractable and inexorable dyspnea |
| – Reduced self-efficacy |
| – Poor quality of life |
| – Fatigue |
| – Disability |
| – Social isolation |
| – Anxiety depression |
| – Family/Caregivers should be aligned under Patients and should not have a – in front of it because it is an equivalent subject heading in the table |
| – Insidious encroachment upon their lives |
| – Medical, psychosocial care |
| – Lack of supportive services |

## 19.4 Prognostication of Duration and Quality of Life in COPD

Disease trajectory is difficult to predict in COPD. Although multivariate predictive models have greatly improved prognostication in COPD, there is significant individual variation and uncertainty. This prognostic imprecision may contribute to providers' timidity and tentativeness in initiating palliative or end of life discussions with patients with COPD. Although patients frequently request predictive information by asking "How long do I have to live?", primary care providers feel ill prepared to respond, believe that patients want more accurate predictions than they can provide and will then judge them based upon their response, and prefer to reinforce positive prospects (Rogg, 2009; Christakis, 1998).

In general, patients with COPD have a very poor prognosis after an exacerbation. In the 1990's, patients older than 65 years admitted to an ICU with a COPD exacerbation had a 30% mortality which increased to 60% over the ensuing year (Seneff, 1995). Although this mortality rate has declined to 28%, 48%, and 74% at 1, 2, and 5 years after an initial acute exacerbation treated with noninvasive ventilation in the early 21st century, the prognosis for patients with COPD who experience exacerbations remains poor. (Chung, 2010). Overall mortality in the year after hospitalization for a COPD exacerbation may be as high as 23–50% (Groenewegen, 2003; Chung, 2010; Batzlaff, 2014) but the 6 month mortality rate for elderly patients with mild COPD admitted with nonacidotic COPD exacerbations is 20% (Ranieri, 2008). A retrospective review of patients admitted to the medical intensive care unit from 1995 to 2009 revealed a one year mortality of 50% and that age and hospital length of stay were independent determinants of death (Batzlaff, 2014). Nearly 4 of every 5 patients hospitalized for a COPD exacerbation die within 9 years and the median survival is approximately 1000 days for those with severe airflow obstruction and 2500 days for those with mild disease (Gudmundsson, 2012). However, up to 30% of patients with severe COPD have not been hospitalized in the preceding 2 years (White, 2011).

Comorbidities, especially cardiovascular disease and cancer, are the major causes of death in individuals with less severe airflow limitation whereas respiratory failure is the top cause of mortality in those individuals with worse physiological obstruction. (See Chapter 10, COPD Is a Multi-organ Disorder: Systemic Manifestations) Thus, it is very difficult to predict the disease course in COPD and unexpected deaths occur frequently whereas other patients with severe derangements of lung function may survive for long periods of time (Fox, 1999; Coventry, 2005).

## 19.5 Advanced Care Planning Discussions Between Providers and Patients with COPD and Their Families

Very few patients with COPD have end of life or palliative care discussions with their providers and fewer still are actually offered these services. Only 13% of National Health Service units in the UK provided end of life care information to patients with stable COPD (Royal College of Physicians, 2008). Only 19% of patients with COPD entering pulmonary rehabilitation had discussed advanced directive plans with their physician (Heffner, 1996). A survey of 115 Veterans with COPD requiring supplemental oxygen demonstrated that only 32% reported a discussion about end of life issues with their self-identified primary COPD provider (Knauft, 2005). Although the majority of general practitioners in the UK believe that discussions of prognosis are important for patients with COPD, most did not have these discussions with their patients and approximately half were undecided as to whether patients wanted to know their prognosis (Elkington, 2001). Only 13% of pulmonologists discussed advanced care planning with most patients, 31% with half, 50% with few, 6% with none or almost none. Although most pulmonologists, 57%, preferred outpatient conversations, most discussions occurred as inpatients. The key elements discussed were diagnosis, treatment purpose, and incurability of COPD; items that were not discussed included appointment of a health care proxy, patients' values and goals, and palliative care options (Smith, 2013). Comparative studies suggest that the prevalence of end of life discussions between providers and patients with COPD is low and there are significant differences in the quality of COPD prognosis discussions internationally (Mulcahy, 2005; Janssen, 2011). Impediments and promoters of advanced care planning discussions are presented in Table 19.4.

Not only are patients under- or mis-informed about COPD and its management and natural history, but their families frequently have inadequate information about the diagnosis, prognosis, and management (Patel, 2012). Family and friends assist 95% of patients with COPD with household tasks, personal care, or medications

**Table 19.4:** Factors Aiding and Impeding Palliative Care Discussions (Knauft, 2005; Gott, 2009; Patel, 2012)

| **Patient and Physician Impediments and Promoters for Discussions about Palliative and End of Life Care** |
|---|
| Patients |
| – Impediments |
| – Preference for life maintaining rather than end of life discussion |
| – Multitude of providers with uncertainty as to which provider will discuss prognosis and care decisions |
| – Negative stigmata of a perceived self-induced disease |
| – Lack of or incorrect medical information |
| – Promoters |
| – Family or friends who have died |
| – Trust in medical provider |
| – Sense of confidence in medical provider's competence |
| – Caring relationship with provider |
| – Confidence in provider's reliability |
| – Prior illness |
| – Worry about becoming a burden for friends and family if illness progresses |
| – Concern about future quality of life |
| Physicians |
| – Impediments |
| – Inadequate time/reimbursement for discussion |
| – Imperfect predictive information about the course of COPD |
| – Lack of consensus about when, where, and with whom these discussions should occur |
| – Connotations of comparing COPD with cancer |
| – Potential/perceived conflict between chronic disease management goals and advanced care planning |
| – Poor understanding and training in palliative care and end of life care |
| – Uncertainty about how patients perceive the discussion of COPD prognosis |
| – Promoters |
| – Good relationship between provider and patient |
| – Experience with lung disease |
| – Patient's prior exacerbations and severity of illness |
| – Duration of relationship with patient |

during the last year of life (Elkington, 2005). Nearly 40% were not aware that their relative with COPD might die even though most would have preferred to have known (Elkington, 2005). Caring for individuals with COPD profoundly affects care providers and the nature of their caring tasks, relationship to the patient, and expectations evolve as the disease progresses (Philip, 2014). There are multiple barriers to identifying patient care givers including a gradual transition into the caring role during which the care giver does not recognize the adoption of this function, the care giver role's insidious encroachment upon the care giver's self needs, and ambiguous responsibility and relationship of health care providers to care givers (Carduff, 2014). Despite the apparent importance of family and friend care providers for individuals with COPD and their involvement in surrogate end of life decision making, very little is known about their needs, requirements, and involvement in the advanced care planning process (Caress, 2009).

## 19.6 Timing and Content of Discussions

### 19.6.1 Early Stage COPD

The entire spectrum of advanced care planning can be overwhelming to patients, their families, and health care providers. Therefore, the goals of these discussions may evolve with the course of disease; however, very little is known about the structure, content, or frequency of advanced care planning during the early stages of COPD as most research has studied the latter stages of COPD. The time of diagnosis is an opportunity to begin to educate both the patient and their family about COPD, its management, and its natural history. As a part of chronic disease management, advanced care planning should begin at the time of diagnosis. (Figure 19.1) There are few if any guidelines for approaching advanced care planning at this stage of COPD but providers should present a realistic picture of the disease and its course. Back and colleagues (Back, 2003) have advocated a "hope for the best, and prepare for the worst" agenda for patients with advanced disease but it is not known if this approach is ideal or how it is received by patients and their families during the early stages of COPD. Recent advances in management and improvements in outcomes (discussed in Chapters 14, Management of Stable COPD; 16, Management of Outpatient COPD Exacerbations; 17, Management of Inpatient COPD Exacerbations) should be discussed. Dialogue about advanced directives, appointment of surrogate healthcare decision makers, and promotion of familial discussions about health and contingencies for care might be initiated during this period. In subsequent discussions, the provider can begin discussions of palliative care and end of life issues including review of advanced directives and surrogate healthcare decision makers, use of mechanical ventilation, critical care, and resuscitation status. Involvement of care providers is essential as COPD progresses and patients became more reliant upon others (see Chapter 13, Psychosocial and Familial Consequences of COPD). The extent and breadth of these discussions can be daunting to providers, patients, and their families and they are best approached incrementally once open avenues of dialogue are established between the provider and patient and family. Although referral to multidisciplinary services may also facilitate these discussions, most palliative and hospice care teams become involved with patients during later stage disease (Cambell, 2014; Curtis, 2014; Dando, 2014).

### 19.6.2 Later Stage COPD

The timing of advanced care planning discussions for the latter stages of COPD is difficult because the disease trajectory and natural history varies widely. Many studies have attempted to identify the characteristics of individuals with COPD who have a limited, less than one year, prognosis. (Table 19.5)

**Table 19.5:** Indications for End of Life Discussions with Patients who have COPD (Curtis, 2008; Benzo, 2013; Reinke, 2008; Matkovic, 2012)

| **Characteristics of Candidates for End of Life Discussion** |
|---|
| – FEV1 <30% predicted |
| – Supplemental oxygen therapy |
| – One or more COPD exacerbations in the prior year requiring hospital admission, especially if associated with either hypoxemia or hypercarbia |
| – Left heart failure/other comorbidity |
| – Weight loss/cachexia |
| – Reduced functional status causing activity limitations/change to a very sedentary life style |
| – Increasing dependence upon others |
| – Age > 70 years |
| – Decrease in gait speed or distance walked in 6MT |
| – Decrease in maximal inspiratory pressure |
| – Feeling downhearted or upset |
| – Decline in PaO2 by 5 mm Hg |
| – Increase in PaCO2 by 3 mm Hg |

These characteristics can help health care providers recognize individuals with COPD who are candidates for palliative and end of life advanced care planning. For those individuals who have not yet started the advanced care planning process, this recognition is critical for the initiation and possible acceleration of advanced care planning if discussions about palliative care, hospice, advanced directives, and end of life management have not yet been initiated. For those in whom the planning process has started, the development of these signs and symptoms is a signal to progress to the next stage of planning (Seamark, 2007).

In 2000, a comparison study of 100 patients, half with COPD and half with nonsmall cell lung cancer, showed that, whereas 30% of patients with lung cancer received palliative care services, none of the patients with COPD received palliative care (Gore, 2000). More recently, in 2013, only 20% of patients with COPD were referred to palliative care compared with 34% of patients with heart failure, 37% with severe dementia, and 60% with cancer (Beernaert, 2013) despite worse quality of life among those with COPD compared with advanced nonsmall cell lung cancer (Habraken, 2009). Further, among patients who do not receive palliative care consultations, those with COPD more often received curative or life-prolonging treatments and less often palliative or comfort management compared with patients with other chronic disorders (Beernaert, 2013). The Study to Understand Prognosis and Preferences for Outcomes and Treatments (SUPPORT, 1999) enrolled patients with nine chronic disorders including COPD in five American hospitals (SUPPORT, 1999; Claessens, 2000). Although most patients with COPD preferred comfort rather than life prolonging treatment, they were more likely to experience severe breathlessness, be placed on mechanical ventilator support in an intensive care unit, and receive tube feedings and cardiopulmonary resuscitation than patients with lung cancer (Claessens, 2000). During the last 6 months of life, Veterans with COPD received fewer opiates and benzodiazepine prescriptions, were twice as likely to be admitted to an ICU, had longer ICU length of stays, and greater healthcare costs than Veterans with lung cancer (Au, 2006). The median time between palliative care referral and death was only 10 days for patients with COPD compared with 20 days for those with cancer in the Flanders Study to Improve End-of-Life Care and Evaluation Tools (FLIECE-project) (Beernaert, 2013).

Although patients with COPD desire information about diagnosis, management, prognosis, death, and advanced care, they prefer these discussions occur when they are in relatively good health (Hardin, 2008; Gardiner, 2009; Reinke, 2008). Even though most patients with COPD desire better education and information about their condition and feel they have not received enough information about their prognosis and future care, they often prefer deferring end of life discussions until their disease is more advanced (Gore, 2000; Gysels, 2010; Gaber, 2004). Very often, patients expect their providers to initiate advanced care discussions and, when these topics are not discussed, assume that advanced care is not relevant to them (McCormick, 2009). However, even when advanced care discussion is offered, some patients will not engage due to denial or fear of COPD (Gardiner, 2009). Most patients do not want to receive detailed information that they perceive as distressing and prefer broad indications of prognosis (Gore, 2000). Some patients with COPD may prefer to focus discussions on alleviation of symptoms rather than end of life care (White, 2011). Others prefer not to discuss end of life and these individuals usually describe an excellent prognosis, good quality of life, and do not want to be involved actively in decision making (Barclay, 2009; Hoffman, 1997). COPD comorbidities, especially anxiety and depression, may also impede patients and their families from engaging in advanced care discussions and may influence their decisions about mechanical ventilation and resuscitation (Simpson, 2008; Omachi, 2010; Stapleton, 2005). There is limited awareness and understanding of palliative care among individuals with COPD (Fahim, 2013). Providers report that end of life discussions occur late in the course of COPD, often when patients are unable to make decisions (Gott, 2009; Sullivan, 1996). They are uncertain when to discuss end of life with patients with COPD and rarely have these discussions early in the disease course (Gott, 2009; Momen, 2012).

The quality of patient-provider discussions of end of life care for COPD can be improved. One trial showed that when providers received a one page report summarizing a patient's responses to a questionnaire eliciting their preferences for communication, life-sustaining therapy, and experiences at the end of life, the number of discussions increased to 30% from 11% compared with providers who did not receive a report (Au, 2012). In addition, patients in the intervention group felt that the quality of the discussions was better. Experiential skills building communication training also enhances providers' proficiency with end of life communication (Fallowfield, 2002; Back 2007).

## 19.7 Symptom Management

### 19.7.1 Dyspnea

Breathlessness is the principal respiratory symptom affecting patients with COPD. Breathlessness in COPD may be multifactorial with contributions from bronchospasm, dynamic hyperinflation, comorbidities especially heart failure and anemia, muscle weakness, anxiety and fear. Bronchospasm is often amenable to treatment with beta agonist and anticholinergic bronchodilators (discussed in management of stable COPD and COPD exacerbations). Dynamic hyperinflation is caused by airtrapping and may be reduced by bronchodilators, reduction in respiratory rate, and breathing techniques such as pursed lip breathing (discussed in management of stable COPD). Heart failure is treated with diuretics, nitrates, and afterload reduction. Red blood cell transfusions may alleviate breathlessness associated with anemia. Muscle weakness may cause decreased minute ventilation and hypercarbia that may be improved with noninvasive ventilation. Anxiolytics such as benzodiazepines may alleviate anxiety and fear. A 2010 Cochrane analysis found that benzodiazepines provided no significant benefit for the relief of breathlessness in patients with COPD (Simon, 2010). Benzodiazepines caused less drowsiness than morphine but more than placebo.

Qualitative studies show that opioids provide a sense of calm, improved quality of life, and relieved dyspnea in patients with COPD. Caregivers noted that opioids helped patients to breath more normally, improved their anxiety and depression while also reducing caregivers' anxiety. However, physicians were reluctant to prescribe opioids for severe breathlessness due to lack of knowledge and experience and concerns about untoward effects and legal consequences (Rocker, 2012). Although opiates are effective treatment for breathlessness in individuals with COPD, concern has been raised that opiates may cause respiratory depression and thus accelerate death (Varkey, 2010). The principle of double effect proposes that, when appropriately used with the intent of relieving suffering, opiates may be administered to relieve breathlessness or pain even if they might hasten death (Sulmasy, 1999; Quill, 1997). Observational studies suggest that, when appropriately used, opiates do not hasten death (Chan, 2004; Bercovitch, 1999; Sykes, 2003). Enteral or intravenous routes are preferred as review of nebulized morphine trials suggest that this route of administration is not effective for the relief of refractory dyspnea (Brown, 2005; Foral, 2004).

The perception of breathlessness is mediated through peripheral and central nervous system pathways and influenced by physical, psychosocial, and spiritual factors (Davidson, 2011). Supplemental oxygen prolongs life for individuals with COPD who are hypoxemic at rest despite maximal pharmaceutical treatment. Oxygen does not appear to be beneficial in individuals with refractory breathlessness and mild hypoxemia or normoxemia (Davidson, 2011; Abernethy, 2005) even though nearly one third of supplemental oxygen costs in Canada are for palliative care (Abernethy, 2005; Guyatt, 2000). A Cochrane analysis of the treatment of dyspnea with supplemental oxygen in individuals with COPD and mild hypoxemia or normoxemia demonstrated that oxygen can effectively reduce breathlessness but that oxygen treatment should be evaluated on an individual basis and discontinued if it is ineffective (Uronis, 2011). However, a subsequent double blind randomized trial comparing room air with oxygen in patients with refractory dyspnea demonstrated no benefit (Abernethey, 2010). Compared with compressed air, oxygen does not improve dyspnea, quality of life, or functional status in home based, nonhypoxemic patients with COPD (Moore, 2011). Mixtures of oxygen and helium may help relieve breathlessness in individuals with COPD but have not been evaluated in large, long term trials (Laude, 2007).

Nonpharmacological treatments, including breathing training, walking aids, neuro-electrical muscle stimulation, and chest wall vibration, were found to be effective treatments for breathlessness in a Cochrane review in 2008 (Bausewein, 2008); that review is currently undergoing revision (Bausewein, 2013).

### 19.7.2 Anxiety and Depression

Pharmacologic management of anxiety and depression in individuals with COPD has only recently been evaluated and their treatment in palliative care of patients with COPD is even less well studied (see Chapter 13, Psychosocial and Familial Consequences of COPD).

Comprehensive, multidisciplinary pulmonary rehabilitation ameliorates anxiety and depression in patients with moderate to severe COPD as well as improves quality of life and exercise capacity (Coventry, 2009; Coventry, 2011; McCormick, 2009).

### 19.7.3 Other Symptoms

Patients with COPD may have significant comorbidities, anorexia, cachexia, poor nutritional intake, and fatigue. Management of these symptoms is discussed in chapters on comorbidities and management of stable COPD. Lung volume reduction surgery reduces the rate of decline in quality of life of individuals with COPD, especially those with upper lobe predominant emphysema (Benzo, 2009).

## 19.8 Bereavement

Advanced care planning does not end with death; care for both the patient's family/friends as well as health care providers should be part of the advanced care plan. (Figure 19.1) Caretakers of individuals with COPD experienced carer burden, limited access to support services, and need for both palliative and bereavement support (Hasson, 2009).

## 19.9 Effectiveness of Palliative Care

Advanced care planning improves patient satisfaction, increases the proportion of at home deaths, and use of hospice services (Tierney, 2001; Hammes, 1998). Provider goals of advanced care planning are outlined in Table 19.6.

**Table 19.6:** Goals for Advanced Care Planning (Halliwell, 2004)

| **Provider Goals for Advanced Care Planning** |
| --- |
| – Awareness of the implications of a COPD diagnosis |
| – Use of uncertainty to ease discussion |
| – Building relationships with patients |
| – Being caring and respectful |
| – Beginning discussion early in the disease course |
| – Identifying and using opportunities to discuss prognosis |
| – Working as a team |

The COPD IMPACT study evaluated a customized home-based palliative care service for patients and caregivers and found, that although palliative care services were valued, health related quality of life, caregiver burden and symptom severity did not change (Horton, 2013). Despite a desire to die at home with supportive care, many patients died in hospital because patients' needs exceeded caregivers' ability to cope precipitating hospital admission (Horton, 2013). A Cochrane review of home palliative services for individuals with multiple disorders including COPD concluded that home palliative care improved the chances of dying at home and reduced symptom burden but did not affect caregiver grief (Gomes, 2013). Thus, there are conflicting reports on the benefits of palliative and hospice care for individuals with COPD. Differences in program components, level of involvement, and COPD stage at the initiation of services may be variables that influence a program's effectiveness.

## 19.10 Conclusion

COPD is a chronic, progressive disorder that is treatable but not curable. The natural course of COPD is marked by exacerbations, episodes of increased respiratory symptoms, and development of nonpulmonary co-morbidities. Many current treatments reduce the frequency and severity of COPD exacerbations and may improve survival. Advanced care planning is the process through which providers communicate with patients and their families/support networks to prepare a comprehensive COPD management strategy and integrate therapeutic, supportive, palliative, and end of life care. Because the disease trajectory is unpredictable for an individual patient with COPD, advanced care planning should begin at the time of diagnosis by providing both the patient, their family, and support network education about COPD, its management, and its natural history. As a part of chronic disease management, dialogue about advanced directives, appointment of surrogate healthcare decision makers, and promotion of familial discussions about health and contingencies for care should be initiated. In subsequent discussions, the provider can begin discussions of palliative care and end of life issues including review of advanced directives and surrogate healthcare decision makers, use of mechanical ventilation, critical care, and resuscitation status. Involvement of care providers is essential as COPD progresses and patients became more reliant upon others. Breathlessness is the most severe and devastating symptom of COPD; effective treatments depend upon the cause but include bronchodilators, oxygen, pulmonary rehabilitation, and opiates.

## 19.11 Summary Points

1. Although there are many effective treatments for COPD, there is no cure and many patients die of or with COPD.
2. Advanced care planning is the process through which providers communicate with patients and their families and support networks to prepare a comprehensive COPD management program that incorporates therapeutic, supportive, palliative, end of life, and bereavement care.
3. Because the disease trajectory for an individual patient is highly variable and unpredictable, advanced care planning for COPD should begin at the time of diagnosis and incrementally proceed as the disease progresses.
4. Effective treatments for the management of breathlessness, anxiety, and depression associated with COPD include pharmacologic and nonpharmacologic interventions.

## References

Abernethy, A.P., Currow, D.,C., Frith, P., & Fazekas, B.S. (2005). Prescribing palliative oxygen: a clinician survey of expected benefit and patterns of use. *Palliative Med*, *19*, 168–170.

Abernethy, A.P., McDonald,C.F., Frith, P.A., Clark, K., Herndon, J.E., Marcello, J., Young, I.H. Bul , J., Wilcock, A., Booth, S., Wheeler, J.L., Tulsky, J.A., Crockett, A.,J, & Currow, D.C. (2010). Effect of palliative oxygen versus room air in relief of breathlessness in patients with refractory dyspnoea: a double-blind, randomised controlled trial. *The Lancet*, *376*, 784–793.

Au, D.H., Udris, E.M., Engelberg, R.A., Diehr, P.H., Bryson, C.L., Reinke, L.F., & Curtis, J.R. (2012). A randomized trial to improve communication about end-of-life care among patients with COPD. *Chest*, *141*(3), 726–35.

Au, D.H., Udris, E.M., Fihn, S.D., McDonell, M.B., & Curtis, J.R. (2006). Differences in health care utilization at the end of life among patients with chronic obstructive pulmonary disease and patients with lung cancer. *Arch Intern Med*, *166*, 326–331.

Back, A.,L, Arnold, R.M. , Baile, W.F., Fryer-Edwards, K.A., Alexander, S.C., Barley, G.E., Gooley, T.A., & Tulsky, JA. (2007). Efficacy of communication skills training for giving bad news and discussing transitions to palliative care. *Arch Intern Med*, *167*(5), 453–460.

Back, A.L., Arnold, R.M., & Quill, T.E. (2003). Hope for the best, and prepare for the worst *Ann Intern Med*,*138*(5), 439–443.

Barclay, S., & Case-Upton, S. (2009). Knowing patients' preferences for place of death: how possible or desirable? *Br J Gen Pract*, *59*, 642–3.

Batzlaff, C.M., Karpman, C., Afessa, B., & Benzo, R.P. (2014). Predicting 1-Year Mortality Rate for Patients Admitted With an Acute Exacerbation of Chronic Obstructive Pulmonary Disease to an Intensive Care Unit: An Opportunity for Palliative Care. *Mayo Clin Proc*, *89*(5), 638–643.

Bausewein, C., Booth, S., Gysels, M., & Higginson, I.J. (2013). Non-pharmacological interventions for breathlessness in advanced stages of malignant and non-malignant diseases. *Cochrane Database of Systematic Reviews*, 11, CD005623.

Bausewein, C., Booth, S., Gysels, M., & Higginson, I.J. (2008). Non-pharmacological interventions for breathlessness in advanced stages of malignant and non-malignant diseases. *Cochrane Database of Systematic Reviews*, 2, CD005623.

Beernaert, K., Cohen, J., Deliens, L., Devroey, D., Vanthomme, K., Pardon, K., & Van den Block, L. (2013). Referral to palliative care in COPD and other chronic diseases: a population-based study. *Respir Med*, *107*(11), 1731–9.

Benzo, R., Farrell, M.H., Chang, C.C., Martinez, F.J., Kaplan, R., Reilly, J., Criner, G, Wise, R., Make, B., Luketich, J., Fishman, A.P., Sciurba, F.C.; & NETT Research Group. (2009). Integrating health status and survival data: the palliative effect of lung volume reduction surgery. *Am J Respir Crit Care Med*, *180*(3), 239–46.

Benzo, R., Siemion, W., Novotny, P., Sternberg, A., Kaplan, R.M., Ries, A., Wise, R., Martinez, F., Utz, J., Sciurba, F.; & National Emphysema Treatment Trial Research Group. (2013). Factors to inform clinicians about the end of life in severe chronic obstructive pulmonary disease. *J Pain Symptom Manage*, *46*(4), 491–499.

Bercovitch, M., Wall, A., & Adunsky, A. (1999). High dose morphine use in the hospice setting: a database survey of patient characteristics and effect on life expectancy. *Cancer*, *86*, 871–877.

Brown, S.J., Eichner, S.,F, & Jones, J.R. (2005). Nebulized morphine for relief of dyspnea due to chronic lung disease. *Ann Pharmacother*, *39*(6), 1088–92.

Cambell, F., Leek, J., Hudson, S., Colclough, R., Pereira, B., Sullivan, A., & Davies, C. (2014). A space to breathe; a hospice based, multidisciplinary, palliative care programme for people with severe copd. *BMJ Support Palliat Care*, Suppl 1, A95.

Carduff, E., Finucance, A., Kendall, M., Jarvis, A., Harrison, N., Greenacre, J., & Murray, S., (2014). Understanding the barriers to identifying carers of people with supportive and palliative care needs in primary care. *BMJ Support Palliat Care*, *4* Suppl 1, A17.

Caress, A.L., Luker, K.A., Chalmers, K.I., & Salmon, M.P. (2009). A review of the information and support needs of family carers of patients with chronic obstructive pulmonary disease. *J Clin Nurs*, *18*(4), 479–91.

Chan, J.D., Treece, P.D., Engelberg, R.A., Crowley, L., Rubenfeld, G.D., Steinberg, K.P., & Curtis J.R. (2004). Narcotic and benzodiazepine use after withdrawal of life support: association with time to death? *Chest*, *126*, 286–293.

Christakis, N.A., & Iwashyna, T.J. (1998). Attitude and self-reported practice regarding prognostication in a national sample of internists. *Arch Intern Med*; *158*, 2389–2395.

Chung, L.P., Winship, P., Phung, S., Lake, F., & Waterer, G. (2010). Five-year outcome in COPD patients after their first episode of acute exacerbation treated with non-invasive ventilation. *Respirology*, *15*, 1084–1091.

Claessens, M.T., Lynn, J., Zhong, Z., Desbiens, N.A., Phillips, R.S., Wu, A.W., Harrell, F.E., & Connors, A.F. (2000). Dying with lung cancer or chronic obstructive pulmonary disease: insights from SUPPORT. *J Am Geriatr Soc*, *48*, Suppl. 5, S146–S153.

Coventry, P.A., Grande, D.A., Richards, D.A., & Todd, C.J. (2005). Prediction of appropriate timing of palliative care for older adults with non-malignant life-threatening disease: a systematic review. *Age Ageing*, *34*, 218–27.

Coventry, P.A., & Hind, D. (2007). Comprehensive pulmonary rehabilitation for anxiety and depression in adults with chronic obstructive pulmonary disease: systematic review and meta-analysis. *J Psychosom Res*, *63*(5), 551–65.

Coventry, P.A. (2009). Does pulmonary rehabilitation reduce anxiety and depression in chronic obstructive pulmonary disease? *Curr. Opin. Pulm.Med*, *15*, 143–9.

Curtis, C., Challand, S., Harrison, S., Turner, M., & Bevan-Smith, E. (2014). Integrated palliative care/ advanced respiratory disease (ard) clinics - a multi-centre pilot project. *BMJ Support Palliat Care*, *4* Suppl 1, A94–5.

Curtis, J.R. (2008). Palliative and end-of-life care for patients with severe COPD. *Eur Respir J*, *32*, 796–803.

Dando, N., & Chiverton, J. (2014). An evaluation of a community multidisciplinary team meeting for patients with end stage respiratory disease. *BMJ Support Palliat Care*, *4* Suppl 1, A94.

Davidson, P.M., & Johnson, M.J. (2011). Update on the role of palliative oxygen. *Curr Opin Support Palliat Care*, *5*(2), 87–91.

Downey, L., Au, D.H., Curtis, J.R., & Engelberg, R.A. (2013). Life-sustaining treatment preferences: matches and mismatches between patients' preferences and clinicians' perceptions. *J Pain Symptom Manage*, *46*(1), 9–19.

Elkington, H., White, P., Addington-Hall, J., Higgs, R., & Edmonds, P. (2005). The healthcare needs of chronic obstructive pulmonary disease patients in the last year of life. *Palliat Med*, *19*(6), 485–91.

Elkington, H., White, P., Higgs, R., & Pettinari, C.J. (2001). GPs' views of discussions of prognosis in severe COPD. *Fam Pract*, *18*, 440–444.

Foral, P.A., Malesker, M.A., Huerta, G., & Hilleman, D.E. (2004). Nebulized opioids use in COPD. *Chest*, *125*(2),691–4.

Fox, E., Landrum-McNiff, K., Zhong, Z., Dawson, N.V., Wu, A.W., & Lynn, J. (1999). Evaluation of prognostic criteria for determining hospice eligibility in patients with advanced lung, heart or liver disease. SUPPORT investigators. Study to Understand Prognoses and Preferences for Outcomes and Risks of Treatments. *JAMA*, *282*(17), 1638–1645.

Gaber, K.A., Barnett, M., Planchant, Y., & McGavin, C.R. (2004). Attitudes of 100 patients with chronic obstructive pulmonary disease to artificial ventilation and cardiopulmonary resuscitation. *Palliat Med*, **18**, 626–629.

Gardiner, C., Gott, M., Small, N., Payne, S., Seamark, D., Barnes, S., Halpin, D., & Ruse, C. (2013). Living with advanced chronic obstructive pulmonary disease: patients concerns regarding death and dying. *Palliat Med*, *23*(8), 691–7.

Gomes, B., Calanzani, N., Curiale, V., McCrone, P., & Higginson, I.J. (2013). Effectiveness and cost-effectiveness of home palliative care services for adults with advanced illness and their caregivers. *Cochrane Database Syst Rev*, 6, CD007760.

Gore, J.M., Brophy, C.J., & Greenstone, M.A. (2000). How well do we care for patients with end stage chronic obstructive pulmonary disease (COPD)? A comparison of palliative care and quality of life in COPD and lung cancer. *Thorax*, *55*, 1000–6

Gott, M., Gardiner, C., Small, N., Payne, S., Seamark, D., Barnes, S., Halpin, D., & Ruse, C. (2009). Barriers to advance care planning in chronic obstructive pulmonary disease. *Palliat Med*, *23*(7), 642–8.

Groenewegen, K.H., Schols, A.M., & Wouters, E.F. (2003). Mortality and mortality-related factors after hospitalization for acute exacerbation of COPD. *Chest*, *124*, 459–67.

Gudmundsson, G., Ulrik, C.S., Gislason, T., Lindberg, E., Brøndum, E., Bakke, P., & Janson, C. (2012). Long-term survival in patients hospitalized for chronic obstructive pulmonary disease: a prospective observational study in the Nordic countries. *Int J Chron Obstruct Pulmon Dis*, *7*, 571–6.

Guyatt, G.H., McKim, D.A., Austin, P., Bryan, R., Norgren, J., Weaver, B., & Goldstein, R.S. (2000). Appropriateness of domiciliary oxygen delivery. *Chest*, *118*, 1303–1308.

Gysels, M., & Higginson, I.J. (2010). The experience of breathlessness: the social course of chronic obstructive pulmonary disease. *J Pain Symptom Manage*, *39*, 555–563.

Habraken, J.M., ter Riet, G., Gore, J.M., Greenstone, M.A., Weersink, E.J., Bindels, P.J., & Willems, D.L. (2009). Health-related quality of life in end-stage COPD and lung cancer patients. *J Pain Symptom Manage*, 37(6), 973–81.

Habraken, J.M., Pols, J., Bindels, P.J., & Willems, D.L. (2008). The silence of patients with end-stage COPD: a qualitative study. *Br J Gen Pract*, *58*(557), 844–9.

Halliwell,J., Mulcahy, P., Buetow, S., Bray, Y., Coster, G., & Osman, L.M. (2004). Discussion of prognosis with patients with severe chronic obstructive pulmonary disease: a qualitative study. *Br J Gen Pract*, *54*, 904–8

Hammes, B.J., & Rooney, B.L. (1998). Death and end-of-life planning in one midwestern community. *Arch Intern Med*, *158*, 383–90

Hardin, K.A., Meyers, F., & Louie, S. (2008). Integrating palliative care in severe chronic obstructive lung disease. *COPD*, *5*, 207–220.

Hasson, F., Spence, A., Waldron, M., Kernohan, G., McLaughlin, D., Watson, B., & Cochrane, B. (2009). Experiences and needs of bereaved carers during palliative and end-of-life care for people with chronic obstructive pulmonary disease. *J Palliat Care*, *25*(3), 157–63.

Heffner, J.E., Fahy, B., Hilling, L., & Barbieri, C. (1996). Attitudes regarding advance directive education among patients in pulmonary rehabilitation. *Am. J. Respir. Crit. Care Med*, *154*, 1735–40.

Heffner, J.E. (2011). Advance care planning in chronic obstructive pulmonary disease: barriers and opportunities. *Curr Opin Pulm Med*, *17*(2), 103–9.

Hoffman, J.C., Wenger, N.S., Davis, R.B., Teno, J., Connors, A.F. Jr, Desbiens, N., Lynn, J., & Phillips, R.S. (1997). Patient preferences for communication with physicians about end-of-life decisions. *Ann Intern Med*, *127*, 1–12.

Horton, R., Rocker, G., Dale, A., Young, J., Hernandez, P., & Sinuff, T. (2013). Implementing a palliative care trial in advanced COPD: a feasibility assessment (the COPD IMPACT study). *J Palliat Med*, *16*(1), 67–73.

http://www.endoflifecumbriaandlancashire.org.uk/info_patients_carers/definitions.php; Accessed October, 2014.

Janssen, D.J.A., Curtis, J.R., Au, D.H., Spruit, M.A., Downey, L., Schols, J.M.G.A., Wouters, E.F.M., & Engelberg, R.A. (2011). Patient–clinician communication about end-of-life care for Dutch and US patients with COPD. *Eur Respir J*, *38*, 268–276

Knauft, E., Nielsen, E.L., Engelberg, R.A., Patrick, D.L., & Curtis, J.R. (2005). Barriers and facilitators to end-of-life care communication for patients with COPD. *Chest*,*127*(6), 2188–96.

Laude, E.A., & Ahmedzai, S.H. Oxygen and helium gas mixtures for dyspnoea. (2007). *Curr Opin Support Palliat Care*, *1*(2), 91–5.

Matkovic, Z., Huerta, A., Soler, N., Domingo, R., Gabarrús, A., Torres, A., & Miravitlles, M. (2012). Predictors of adverse outcome in patients hospitalised for exacerbation of chronic obstructive pulmonary disease. *Respiration*, *84*(1), 17–26.

McCormick, J.R. Pulmonary rehabilitation and palliative care. (2009). *Semin Respir Crit Care Med*, *30*(6), 684–99.

McMillan Boyle, C., Bailey, P.H., Mossey, S. (2011). Chronic obstructive pulmonary disease as disability: dilemma stories. *Qualitative Health Research*, *21*, 187–198.

Momen, N., Hadfield, P., Kuhn, I., Smith, E., & Barclay, S. (2012). Discussing an uncertain future: end-of-life care conversations in chronic obstructive pulmonary disease. A systematic literature review and narrative synthesis. *Thorax*, *67*(9), 777–80.

Moore, R., Berlowitz, D., Denehy, L., Jackson, B., & McDonald, C.F. (2011). A randomised trial of domiciliary, ambulatory oxygen in patients with COPD and dyspnoea but without resting hypoxaemia. *Thorax*, *66*, 32–37.

Mulcahy, P., Buetow, S., Osman, L., Coster, G., Bray, Y., White, P., & Elkington H. (2005). GPs' attitudes to discussing prognosis in severe COPD: an Auckland (NZ) to London (UK) comparison. *Fam Pract*, *22*, 538–540.

National Consensus Project for Quality Palliative Care: Clinical Practice Guidelines for quality palliative care, executive summary. (2004). *J Palliat Med*, *7*, 611–627.

Omachi, T.A., Katz, P.P., Yelin, E.H., Iribarren, C., Knight, S.J., Blanc, P.D., & Eisner, M.D. (2010). The COPD Helplessness Index: a new tool to measure factors affecting patient self-management. *Chest*, *137*, 823–830.

Panos, R.J., Krywkowski-Mohn, S.M., Sherman, S.N., & Lach, L.A. (2013). Patient reported determinants of health: a qualitative analysis of veterans with chronic obstructive pulmonary disease. *COPD*, *10*(3), 333–47.

Patel, K., Janssen, D.J.A., & Curtis, J.R. (2012). Advance care planning in COPD. *Respirology*, *17*, 72–78.

Philip, J., Gold, M., Brand, C., Miller, B., Douglass, J., & Sundararajan, V. (2014). Facilitating change and adaptation: the experiences of current and bereaved carers of patients with severe chronic obstructive pulmonary disease. *J Palliat Med*, *17*(4), 421–7.

Pinnock, H., Kendall, M., Murray, S.A., Worth, A., Levack, P., Porter, M., Macnee, W., & Sheikh, A. (2011). Living and dying with severe chronic obstructive pulmonary disease: multi-perspective longitudinal qualitative study. *BMJ Support Palliat Care*, *1*(2), 174–83.

Quill, T.E., Dresser, R., & Brock, D.W. (1997). The rule of double effect: a critique of its role in end-of-life decision making. *N Engl J Med*, *337*, 1768–1771.

Ranieri, P., Bianchetti, A., Margiotta, A., Virgillo, A., Clini, E.M., & Trabucchi, M. (2008). Predictors of 6-month mortality in elderly patients with mild chronic obstructive pulmonary disease discharged from a medical ward after acute nonacidotic exacerbation. *J Am Geriatr Soc*, *56*(5), 909–13.

Reinke, L.F., Engelberg, R.A., Shannon, S.E., Wenrich, M.D., Vig, E.K., Back, A.L., & Curtis, J.R. (2008). Transitions regarding palliative and end-of-life care in severe chronic obstructive pulmonary disease or advanced cancer: themes identified by patients, families, and clinicians. *J Palliat Med*, *11*(4), 601–9.

Rocker, G., Young, J., Donahue, M., Farquhar, M., & Simpson, C. (2012). Perspectives of patients, family caregivers and physicians about the use of opioids for refractory dyspnea in advanced chronic obstructive pulmonary disease. *CMAJ*, *184*(9), E497–504.

Rogg, L., Loge, J.H., Aasland, O.G., & Graugaard, P.K. (2009). Physicians' attitudes towards disclosure of prognostic information: a survey among a representative cross-section of 1605 Norwegian physicians. *Patient Educ Couns*, *77*(2), 242–7.

Royal College of Physicians, British Thoracic Society, British Lung Foundation. Report of the national COPD audit 2008: resources and organisation of care in acute NHS units across the UK, London: UK. Royal College of Physicians, British Thoracic Society, British Lung Foundation; 2008.

Seamark, D.A., Seamark, C.J., & Halpin, D.M. (2007). Palliative care in chronic obstructive pulmonary disease: a review for clinicians. *J R Soc Med*, *100*(5), 225–33.

Seneff, M.G., Wagner, D.P., Wagner, R.P., Zimmerman, J.E., & Knaus, W.A. (1995). Hospital and 1-yearsurvival of patients admitted to intensive care units with acute exacerbation of chronic obstructive pulmonary disease. *JAMA*, *274*, 1852–1857.

Simon, S.T., Higginson, I.J., Booth, S., Harding, R., & Bausewein, C. (2010). Benzodiazepines for the relief of breathlessness in advanced malignant and non-malignant diseases in adults. *Cochrane Database Syst Rev*, (1), CD007354.

Simpson, A.C., & Rocker, G.M. (2008). Advanced chronic obstructive pulmonary disease: impact on informal caregivers. *J Palliat Care*, *24*, 49–54.

Smith, T.A., Kim, M., Piza, M., Davidson, P.M., Clayton, J.M., Jenkins, C.R., & Ingham, J.M. (2013). Specialist respiratory physicians' attitudes to and practice of advance care planning in COPD. A pilot study. *Respir Med*, *108*(6), 935–939.

Stapleton, R.D., Nielsen, E.L., Engelberg, R.A., Patrick, D.L., & Curtis, J.R. (2005). Association of depression and life-sustaining treatment preferences in patients with COPD. *Chest*, *127*, 328–334.

Sullivan, K.E., Hebert, P.C., Logan, J., O'Connor, A.M., & McNeely, P.D. (1996). What do physicians tell patients with end-stage COPD about intubation and mechanical ventilation? *Chest*, *109*(1), 258–64.

Sulmasy, D.P., & Pellegrino, E.D. (1999). The rule of double effect: clearing up the double talk. *Arch Intern Med*, *159*, 545–550.

Sykes, N., & Thorns, A. (2003). The use of opioids and sedatives at the end of life. *Lancet Oncol*, *4*, 312–318.

The Hospice and Palliative Medicine National Consensus Guidelines, 2004. www.nationalconsensusproject.org Accessed October, 2014.

The SUPPORT Principal Investigators. (1995). A controlled trial to improve care for seriously ill hospitalized patients: The Study to Understand Prognoses and Preferences for Outcomes and Risks of treatments (SUPPORT). *JAMA*, 274, 1591–1598.

Tierney, W.M., Dexter, P.R., Gramelspacher, G.P., Perkins, A.J., Zhou, X.H., & Wolinsky, F.D. The effect of discussions about advance directives on patients' satisfaction with primary care. J Gen Intern Med, *16*, 32–40

Uronis, H., McCrory, D.C., Samsa, G., Currow, D., & Abernethy, A. (2011). Symptomatic oxygen for non hypoxaemic chronic obstructive pulmonary disease. *Cochrane Database of Syst Rev*, 15(6), CD006429.

Varkey, B. (2010). Opioids for palliation of refractory dyspnea in chronic obstructive pulmonary disease patients. *Curr Opin Pulm Med*, *16*(2),150–4.

White, P., White, S., Edmonds, P., Gysels, M., Moxham, J., Seed, P., & Shipman, C. (2011). Palliative care or end-of-life care in advanced chronic obstructive pulmonary disease: a prospective community survey. *Br J Gen Pract*, *61*(587), 362–70.

White, P., White, S., Edmonds, P., Gysels, M., Moxham, J., Seed, P., & Shipman, C. (2011). Palliative care or end of-life care in advanced chronic obstructive pulmonary disease: a prospective community survey. *Br J Gen Pract*, *61*(587), 362–70.

WHO Definition of Palliative Care http://www.who.int/cancer/palliative/definition/en/ Accessed April, 2014.

Yohannes, A.M. (2007). Palliative care provision for patients with chronic obstructive pulmonary disease. *Health Qual Life Outcomes*, *5*, 17.

# Index

5 A's Model 116
α-1 antitrypsin 39
α1-antitrypsin 78, 81
β adrenergic agonists 341, 342, 348
β blocker 191
γδ T cells 85
acetylation 79
action 131, 132, 133, 134, 135, 139, 140, 145, 146, 150, 151, 152, 153, 154, 157
Action 114, 115
action plan 131, 132, 133, 135, 139, 140, 146, 150, 151, 152, 153, 154, 157, 312, 316, 318, 329
activity 250, 251, 253, 262, 264, 265
acute exacerbations 159, 160, 161, 165, 166, 170, 174, 186, 187
adherence 132, 135, 136, 137, 139, 140, 143, 154, 155, 156, 157
Adherence 305
advanced care discussions 378
advanced care planning 10, 369, 374, 375, 376, 377, 381, 382
Advanced care planning 369, 370, 381, 382
advanced directive plans 374
advanced directives 376, 377, 382
Advanced Imaging Techniques in COPD 72
Aerolizer® 299, 300
age 15, 16, 19, 25, 26
effect on lung function 163
airflow limitation 1, 2, 3, 4, 5, 6, 7, 9, 14, 15, 18, 105, 215, 216, 221, 226, 250, 252, 255, 258, 264, 275, 276, 273, 279, 280, 281, 282
Airflow limitation 4, 6
airflow obstruction 1, 2, 3, 4, 6, 8, 11, 12, 21, 24, 26, 27, 31, 34, 37, 38, 39, 40, 41
Airflow Obstruction Pattern 52
air pollutants 14, 16, 23, 24, 27, 29
air pollution 17, 26, 27, 29
Air pollution 17, 26, 27
air trapping 219, 224
Air-trapping 68
Airway Changes in COPD 69
airway epithelial cells 76, 80, 83
Airway mucus 279
alpha 1-antitrypsin 159, 163, 168, 169, 170
alpha-1-antitrypsin 8
Alpha 1-antitrypsin deficiency 168
alveolar epithelial cells 76, 80
anemia 198, 199, 200, 207, 208
angiogenesis 238, 242
antibiotic 312, 317, 318, 322, 330, 333
Antibiotic 332
antibiotics 312, 313, 319, 322, 327, 339, 340, 343, 344, 352, 355
anticholinergic agents 342, 348
Anticholinergic agents 321
anticholinergics 222, 312, 328
Antidepressants 253
antioxidants 80
antiproteases 76, 80
anxiety 140, 143, 148, 157, 249, 250, 251, 252, 253, 254, 255, 256, 258, 261, 262, 263, 264, 265, 266, 267, 268, 269, 270, 271, 272, 273, 274, 369, 378, 379, 380, 382, 384
Anxiety 250, 251, 252, 253, 254, 255, 256, 264, 265, 266, 267, 268, 270, 272, 273, 373
apneas 214, 216, 218, 221
apoptosis 77, 79, 82, 83, 86, 87, 94
arterial blood gas 338
arterial stiffness 221
Ask–Elicit–Tell–Elicit 111
asthma 2, 4, 5, 8, 9, 12, 36, 37, 38, 41
Asthma 41
atonia 218
atrial fibrillation 216, 221, 225, 227
Auto-PEEP 347
azithromycin 284
Azithromycin 174
bacterial 312, 314, 315, 322
B cells 88, 89, 90
Ben-Yehuda, Nachman. *see* moral panic
benzodiazepines 379
Benzodiazepines 258
Bereavement 381
Berlin questionnaire 217
Biomarkers 165
biomass fuels 17
biomass smoke 2
BODE index 160
breathlessness 6, 9, 10, 31, 33, 131, 135, 140, 144, 154, 212, 251, 252, 253, 254, 255, 256, 258, 263, 264, 265, 268, 275, 276, 277, 278, 281, 282, 286, 288, 290, 312, 327, 369, 370, 372, 378, 379, 380, 382, 383, 385, 387
Breathlessness 276, 282, 290, 379, 382

bronchiectasis 278, 279, 290
Bronchiectasis 279
bronchodilator 4, 5, 8, 12
Bronchodilator Response 63
bronchodilator responseness 4
Bronchodilator responseness 5
Bronchodilator responsiveness 4, 164
phenotype 172
bronchodilators 4, 5, 320, 321, 326, 327, 328, 339, 340, 342, 353
Calcium channel blockers 239
cardiac disease 190
Cardiopulmonary exercise testing 41
Cardiovascular Disease 91
caregivers 262, 263, 266
care management 359, 360, 361, 364
care providers 373, 375, 376, 377, 381, 382
CAT 276, 281, 282
cathepsin G 84
CD3+ T cells 87
CD4+ 81, 87, 88, 89
CD8+ 77, 87, 88, 89
CD8+ T cells 77, 87, 88, 89
CFC 295, 298, 309
change 131, 132, 133, 134, 135, 140, 142, 143, 144, 147, 148, 150, 153, 154, 157
chemokines 87, 89
Chest CT 10
chest radiograph 31, 36, 41
Chest Radiograph 66
Chest radiographs 339
chest radiography 234, 245
chest x-ray 10
chlorofluorocarbon 295
chronic bronchitis 2, 8, 11, 15, 17, 18, 20, 24, 26, 27, 28, 76, 92
Chronic bronchitis 77, 278
chronic disease management 357, 359, 363
Chronic Disease Self-Management Program 133, 142, 144, 145, 146, 150, 151, 152, 154, 156
chronic illness model 106
chronic obstructive pulmonary disease 357
clerical associate 361, 362
Clinical Associate 362
Codeine 279
cognitive behavioral therapy 258, 265, 269
cognitive dysfunction 259, 260, 264, 274
Cognitive dysfunction 249, 266, 271
cognitive impairment 249, 259, 260, 264, 265, 266, 267, 270, 271, 272, 273
Cognitive impairment 260, 265, 266
collagen 78
Collins, Patricia Hill. *see* intersubjectivity
compliance 136, 137, 139, 144, 154, 155, 157
computed tomography 7
congestive heart failure 216
connective tissue growth factor 78
contemplation 134
Contemplation 113
continuous positive airway pressure 224, 226, 229
Controversy for Determination of Airflow Limitation/Obstruction 62
COPD 1, 2, 3, 4, 5, 6, 7, 8, 9, 10, 11, 12, 13, 14, 15, 16, 17, 18, 19, 20, 21, 22, 23, 24, 25, 26, 27, 28, 29, 30, 31, 32, 33, 34, 36, 37, 38, 39, 40, 41, 76, 77, 78, 79, 80, 81, 82, 83, 84, 85, 86, 87, 88, 89, 90, 91, 92, 93, 94, 104, 105, 106, 107, 108, 110, 123, 124, 125, 128, 129, 130, 131, 132, 133, 134, 135, 136, 139, 140, 141, 142, 143, 144, 148, 149, 150, 151, 152, 153, 154, 155, 156, 157, 189, 190, 191, 192, 193, 194, 197, 198, 199, 200, 201, 202, 203, 204, 205, 206, 207, 208, 209, 210, 211, 212, 213, 214, 215, 216, 217, 219, 220, 221, 222, 223, 224, 225, 226, 227, 228, 229, 230, 231, 232, 233, 234, 235, 236, 237, 238, 239, 240, 241, 242, 243, 244, 246, 247, 248, 249, 250, 251, 252, 253, 254, 255, 256, 257, 258, 259, 260, 261, 262, 263, 264, 265, 266, 267, 268, 269, 270, 271, 272, 273, 275, 276, 277, 278, 279, 280, 281, 282, 283, 284, 285, 286, 287, 288, 289, 290, 291, 292, 293, 294, 297, 304, 305, 306, 307, 308, 309, 310, 312, 313, 314, 315, 316, 317, 318, 320, 321, 322, 323, 325, 327, 328, 329, 330, 331, 332, 333, 357, 359, 360, 361, 362, 363, 364, 365, 366, 368, 369, 370, 371, 372, 373, 374, 375, 376, 377, 378, 379, 380, 381, 382, 383, 384, 385, 386, 387
COPD Assessment Test (CAT) 276, 281
COPD-Asthma overlap syndrome 172
COPD exacerbation 139, 143, 153, 154, 336
- Beta-blockers 345
- Corticosteroids 342
- Hospitalization 339
- pulmonary rehabilitation 349
- Supplemental oxygen 341

COPD exacerbations 15, 17, 21, 29, 84, 86, 93, 275, 279, 280, 282, 284, 286, 335, 336, 337, 338, 339, 340, 341, 342, 343, 344, 345, 346, 347, 348, 349, 350, 352, 355
COPD phenotypes 70
cor pulmonale 191, 286, 287
corticosteroid 321, 327, 333
corticosteroids 223, 231, 313, 321, 322, 327, 328, 330, 339, 342, 343, 349, 352
cost 14, 21, 22, 23, 24, 25, 28
cough 8, 9, 10, 31, 36, 39, 104, 105, 108, 213, 217, 220, 225, 227, 230, 231, 275, 276, 278, 279, 288, 289, 290, 291, 312, 313, 314, 315, 316, 327, 335, 336, 337, 339
Cough 276, 278, 279, 289, 290
CPAP 213, 222, 223, 224, 225, 226, 228, 229, 230, 231
C reactive protein 314
CT 234, 246, 247
CTGF 78
CT scan 41, 67, 193
Cytokines 84, 89
d-dimer 248
D-dimer 240
death 14, 20
Death Penalty. *see* Baldus Study
decision-making 131, 134, 146
Decision-making 131, 151, 152, 153
Declaration of Independence. *see* Lemert, Charles
deep vein thrombosis 240
Dendritic Cells 89
depression 139, 140, 143, 148, 157, 249, 250, 251, 252, 253, 255, 256, 261, 262, 263, 264, 265, 266, 267, 268, 269, 270, 271, 272, 273, 274, 369, 371, 373, 378, 379, 380, 382, 384, 387
Depression 249, 251, 252, 253, 254, 263, 264, 265, 266, 268, 273, 372, 380
desaturation 215, 217, 220, 225, 226, 227
diabetes 203, 208, 209
diaphragm 217, 218, 219, 228
diet 131, 135, 150, 154
diffusing capacity 39, 41
direct medical costs 15, 21
disability 14, 22, 24
DPIs 292, 293, 294, 298, 300, 301, 302
dust 14, 16, 17, 23, 24
dynamic hyperinflation 379
Dynamic hyperinflation 347, 379
dynamic lung hyperinflation 276
dysanapsis 18
dyspnea 33, 34, 35, 36, 39, 232, 234, 236, 240, 241, 255, 258, 265, 267, 271, 272, 275, 288, 312, 313, 315, 318, 319, 322, 373, 379, 380, 383, 387
Dyspnea 33, 276, 282, 379
early disease 164
echocardiogram 233
elastase 79, 84
elastin 79, 81, 87, 89
Electrocardiogram 339
emphysema 1, 2, 7, 8, 10, 11, 15, 18, 19, 20, 25, 26, 76, 77, 79, 80, 81, 84, 85, 86, 88, 89, 92, 94, 192, 194, 195, 196, 198, 200, 205, 207, 211
effect on lung function 163
genetic predisposition 163
Emphysema 67
endo-bronchial valves 172
endo-bronchinal coils 172
End of Life 369, 375, 377
End-of-Life 149
end of life care 369, 370, 374, 375, 378, 382
End-of-life care 370
end of life discussions 373, 374, 378
endothelial dysfunction 238
environmental risk factors 14, 29
environmental tobacco smoke 16
Environmental Tobacco Smoke 16
Eosinophils 84
epidemiology 14, 19, 27, 28, 29
gender differences 178
epigenetics 9
Epigenetics 79
Epithelium 83
Epworth sleepiness scale 217, 228
Epworth Sleepiness Scale 215
erythromycin 284, 290
exacerbation 2, 21, 23, 28, 30, 191, 200, 205, 206, 208, 211, 232, 240, 245, 247, 373, 384, 385, 386, 387
– effect of emphysema 164
– factors associated with 166
– Role of 165
exacerbations 4, 6, 7, 10, 13, 104, 105, 212, 220, 224, 225, 226, 231, 232, 234, 240, 242, 248, 249, 252, 253, 255, 257, 259, 260, 261, 262, 263, 264, 271, 335, 336, 337, 338, 339, 340, 341, 342, 343, 344, 345,

346, 348, 349, 350, 351, 352, 353, 354, 355, 356
Exacerbations 312, 313, 315, 316, 325, 328, 333
EXACT-PRO 313
examination 338, 339
exercise 131, 135, 140, 141, 142, 143, 148, 150, 154, 156, 232, 233, 239, 244, 245, 246, 247, 248
exercise training 253
falls 201, 209
FEV1 336, 337, 338
fibrinogen 314, 330
fibrosis 76, 78, 84, 94
Formoterol 294, 300
fracture 200, 201, 206, 208
Frequent exacerbator 173
fumes 14, 16, 23, 24
functional status 256, 273
gender differences 176, 179, 180
genetics 76, 90
Genetic susceptibility 163
Global Initiative for Chronic Obstructive Lung Disease 280, 289
glucocorticoids 335, 340, 348, 354
GOLD 275, 276, 280, 281, 282, 283, 289, 290
Goode, Erich. *see* moral panic
granzyme B 86
Handihaler® 299, 300
healthcare 357, 358, 362, 368
healthcare costs 14, 21, 22, 23, 29
healthcare utilization 4, 6, 249, 256, 263
health related quality of life 252, 255
heart failure 190, 191, 204, 208, 210
Heart failure 379
HFA 295, 307, 309
histone deacetylase 79
history 31, 36, 38, 39, 40, 336, 337, 338, 339, 340, 342, 344, 345, 350
HIV 18, 25, 26, 29, 30
hospice 376, 377, 381, 383, 384
Hospital at home 23, 339, 354
hospitalization 242, 245, 315, 320, 327, 336, 337, 338, 339, 343, 344, 350, 351
hospitalizations 14, 15, 20, 21, 22, 23, 139, 140, 144, 145, 150, 155
human immunodeficiency virus 14, 23, 25
Hydralazine 239
hydrofluoroalkanes 295
hypercapnia 315, 318, 323, 341, 349, 355
hypercarbia 219, 220, 224, 225, 226, 377, 379
hyperinflation 10, 216, 219, 224, 276, 277, 278, 286, 288
hypertension 215, 216, 221, 226, 228, 230
hypopneas 218, 221
hypoponeas 214
hypoventilation 212, 223, 224, 225
hypoxemia 196, 198, 201, 202, 212, 216, 219, 220, 221, 222, 223, 225, 238, 239, 240, 244, 252, 259, 260, 272, 318, 323, 324
ICU 340, 343
IFNγ 82, 88, 89
IL-4 88
IL-4 84
IL-5 84
IL-8 83, 84
immune function 76
Importance and Confidence Rulers 106
Indirect Costs 22
infection 337, 353
Infection 333
inflammation 2, 5, 8, 11, 76, 77, 80, 82, 85, 87, 90, 91, 92, 93, 94, 189, 193, 198, 200, 202, 203, 208, 219, 220, 223, 238, 240, 242, 314, 316, 322, 334, 336, 352
inflammatory mediators 78, 83, 84, 89, 91
influenza 286, 288
inhaled corticosteroids 170, 173, 174, 179
inhaler 136, 137, 151, 152, 155, 157
Inhaler Education 293
Inhalers 292, 294
insomnia 213, 216, 223, 252
inspiratory muscle training 141, 155
Integrated Care Teams 150
Interpretation of Spirometry Results 54
interstitial lung disease 36
Interventions 117, 123, 124
invasive mechanical ventilation 346, 347, 348, 350
Invasive mechanical ventilation 347
Auto-PEEP 347
Jasanoff, Sheila. *see* co-production of knowledge
KEAP1 82, 83
knowledge-based economy. see knowledge economy
Living Well with COPD 142, 144, 150, 156
long acting acting anticholinergics 283
long acting anticholinergics 279
long acting beta agonists 283
Long acting beta agonists 279

lung 1, 2, 3, 4, 5, 6, 7, 3, 9, 10, 12
lung age 110, 111, 128, 130
Lung age 2
lung cancer 104, 105, 108, 128, 190, 192, 193, 194, 197, 204, 205, 206, 207, 208, 209, 210, 211
lung elasticity 76, 77
lung function 104, 110, 111
– factors influencing 160
lung volume reduction 172
Lung volume reduction 287, 290
lung volumes 40
lymphocytes 77, 83, 83, 91, 94
macrolide 283, 285, 290
macrolides 349
macrophages 79, 81, 84, 86, 87, 89, 94
Macrophages 84
maintenance 134, 158
Maintenance 115, 116
Management 331
Mast Cells 85
matrix metalloproteinases 80
McCall, Leslie. *see* intersubjectivity
Measurements from Spirometry Testing 52
medical decision making 370
medication adherence 131, 135, 150, 153
medullary ventilator center 217
memory impairment 259, 268
men 18, 19, 20
Methylxanthines 284
MI 110, 121, 123, 128
MICA 86
minute ventilation 218, 219
Mixed Impairment 54
MMP 80, 81, 84, 88
MMPs 80
mMRC score 282
Modified British Medical Research Council 281
Mometasone 294, 301
morbidity 232, 240
mortality 4, 8, 104, 105, 128, 129, 220, 222, 224, 225, 230, 232, 233, 241, 242, 247, 249, 250, 252, 253, 256, 260, 263, 265, 266, 271, 273
– effect of exacerbations 166
Motivational interviewing 110
Motivational Interviewing 121, 123, 128, 129
MRI scan 73
mucolytic agents 345
mucolytics 283
Mucolytics 280, 286
mucus 76, 77, 80, 87, 89
multidose dry powder inhalers 293
Multidose Dry Powder Inhalers (DPIs) 294, 298
Muscle weakness 379
muscular hyperplasia 237
myocardial infarction 104, 105, 128, 190, 191, 206, 208, 209
myocardial ischemia 345
n-acetylcysteine 286
natural history 369, 374, 376, 377, 382
Natural history 159
Nebulizers 292, 303
neurocognitive dysfunction 222
Neurological Disorders 93
neutrophils 79, 81, 83, 87, 89, 94
Neutrophils 83
never smokers 16, 19
nicotine 213, 214, 227, 228, 231
nicotine dependence 105, 129
nicotine replacement 110, 112, 113, 114, 115, 117, 124, 125, 127, 128
Nicotine replacement therapies 104, 125
Nighttime Symptoms of COPD Instrument 213, 217
NIPPV 335, 346, 347, 348, 349, 350
nitric oxide 238, 239, 243, 244, 246, 247, 248
Nitric oxide 238
NK cells 77, 86
NKG2D 86
NKT 86
noninvasive positive pressure ventilation 212, 225, 226, 231
Noninvasive positive pressure ventilation 346
noninvasive ventilation 224, 225
NRF2 protein 82
nurse care manager 361
Nurse Case Manager 363
nutrition 142, 143
Nutritional Abnormalities 92
Nutritional support 329
obesity 224, 226, 227
obstruction 76, 77, 78, 88
obstructive sleep apnea 212, 216, 226, 227, 228, 229, 230, 231
of bronchodilators 312
opiates 378, 379, 382
opioids 379, 384, 387
OSA 212, 213, 214, 215, 216, 217, 218, 219, 220, 221, 222, 223, 224, 225, 226, 230

osteopenia 200, 201, 209
osteoporosis 200, 201, 204, 206, 207, 208, 209
Osteoporosis 93
Outpatient 328
overlap syndrome 212, 214, 215, 216, 217, 219, 220, 221, 222, 224, 225, 226, 227, 228, 229, 230
Overlap Syndrome 212, 214, 215, 219, 231
oxidative stress 76, 77, 79, 80, 83, 92, 94
Oxidative stress 76
oximetry 338, 348
oxygen 213, 215, 217, 218, 219, 220, 223, 225, 226, 227, 228, 229, 230, 232, 233, 237, 239, 242, 243, 244, 246, 248, 252, 256, 260, 265, 268, 269, 272, 273, 319, 323, 324, 326, 329, 330, 331, 332, 335, 339, 340, 341, 348, 349, 351, 352, 354, 355, 374, 377, 380, 382, 383, 384, 385, 386, 387
Oxygen 277, 286, 287
PA 234, 243
PaCO2 212, 217, 218, 221, 224
PACO2 224, 225
PACT 358, 359, 360, 361, 362, 363, 364, 365, 366
palliative 369, 370, 371, 373, 374, 375, 376, 377, 378, 380, 381, 382, 383, 384, 385, 386, 387, 388
Palliative 369, 370, 371, 375, 383, 384, 386, 387, 388
Panic attack 257
panic attacks 249, 256, 257, 258, 270, 272
panic disorder 254, 257, 258, 264, 265, 267, 268, 270, 272, 273
Panic disorder 257, 266
panic disorders 249, 258, 259, 264
PaO2 212, 217, 218
patient 357, 358, 359, 360, 361, 362, 363, 364, 365, 366, 367, 368
Patient Aligned Care Teams 358
Patient Centered Medical Home 357
patient-provider relationship 131, 134, 148, 150
Patterns of Spirometry Impairment or Limitation 52
periodic limb movement syndrome 213
personalized health care plan 363, 364
PET scans 72
PH 232, 233, 234, 235, 237, 238, 239, 241, 242
phenotype 160, 167, 168, 170, 171, 172, 173, 176, 186, 188
frequent exacerbator 159, 160, 167, 173, 188
phenotypes 1, 8, 9, 11
phlegm 275, 279, 280
Phosphodiesterase 4 329
phosphodiesterase inhibitors 283
Phosphodiesterase inhibitors 239
physical examination 31, 36, 40
Platelet derived growth factor 238
pMDIs 292, 293, 294, 295, 296, 297, 298, 300, 301, 302, 304, 306
pneumococcal vaccination 286
pneumonia 190
pollution 2
polycythemia 198
polysomnography 214, 215, 216
practice redesign 359, 360
Precede-Proceed Model 144
precontemplation 134, 147
Precontemplation 112
prednisone 317, 321, 328, 333
preparation 134
Preparation 114
pressurized metered-dose inhalers 292, 293
Pressurized Metered-Dose Inhalers (pMDIs) 294, 295
prevalence 18, 19, 20, 23, 24, 25, 27, 28, 29, 212, 213, 214, 215, 220, 221, 225, 228
preventable 1, 2, 3
Primary Care 357, 358, 365, 368
primary care provider 10
Primary Care Provider 358, 365
primary care team 359, 360, 361
problem solving 134, 144, 145
problem-solving 131, 134, 145, 153
procalcitonin 344
progressive 1, 2, 3, 8
proteases 76, 79, 84
proteinase-3 84
proteolytic imbalance 76
provider 357, 358, 359, 360, 361, 362, 363, 364, 366
Provider 363
providers 131, 134, 140, 144, 146, 149, 150, 151, 152
psychosocial manifestations 6
Psychotherapy 256
pulmonary arteries 234, 237, 238, 243, 244, 245, 246, 247, 248
pulmonary artery 233, 234, 235, 236, 237, 245, 246, 247, 248
pulmonary artery pressures 233, 236, 237

pulmonary embolism 337, 355
pulmonary fibrosis 193, 195, 196, 198, 205, 207
pulmonary function testing 20
pulmonary hypertension 191, 197, 216, 221, 225, 226, 227, 232, 234, 236, 237, 241, 243, 244, 245, 246, 247, 248
pulmonary pressures 232, 233, 234, 235, 236, 239, 240, 242
pulmonary rehabilitation 23, 26, 253, 254, 256, 261, 263, 265, 267, 268, 269, 273, 277, 287, 288, 289, 374, 380, 382, 384, 385
Pulmonary rehabilitation 143, 155, 194, 209, 249, 253, 261, 286, 289, 290
Pulmonary Rehabilitation 327, 333
pulmonary thromboembolism 338
pulmonary vascular disease 232, 234, 238, 239
pulmonary vasculature 6
pulse oximetry 217, 220, 230
pursed lip breathing 277, 288
Pursed lip breathing 277
quality of life 4, 10, 11, 131, 139, 140, 141, 143, 144, 150, 251, 252, 255, 256, 260, 262, 264, 265, 270, 271, 273
Quality of life 315
effect of exacerbations 166
rapid eye movement 222
relapse 106, 107, 112, 115, 121, 124, 125
REM 212, 213, 215, 218, 219, 220, 225
resource utilization 131, 134, 153
Respimat® 292, 293, 294, 301, 302, 303, 307, 308, 309, 310, 311
Respimat® Soft Mist Inhaler (SMI) 294, 301
respiratory failure 189, 190, 207
respiratory symptoms 212, 213, 216, 217, 225, 226, 228
Respiratory Symptoms 31
Restrictive Lung Defect Pattern 54
reversible 1, 2, 3, 4
RHC 233, 234, 236
right heart catheterization 233, 236
right heart failure 234, 236, 240, 248
right ventricle 234, 237, 245
right ventricular hypertrophy 232, 234
Risk Factors 15
Risk factors for relapse 326
RNS 80
Roflumilast 174, 176, 284, 285, 290
ROS 80
RV hypertrophy 233
Screening Recommendations 106
second hand smoke 16
self-management 131, 132, 133, 134, 135, 139, 140, 142, 143, 144, 145, 146, 148, 150, 151, 152, 153, 154, 157
Self-management programs 131, 142, 154
Self-Management Programs 142, 151, 152
Self-management tasks 131
serotonin receptor agonist 256
serotonin reuptake inhibitor 256
serotonin reuptake inhibitors 253, 259
short acting anticholinergics 279, 283
short-acting beta adrenergic agonists 320
short acting beta agonists 279, 283, 312
shortness of breath 31, 33
sildenafil 239, 243
skeletal muscle dysfunction 202
Skeletal muscle dysfunction 202, 207
Skeletal Muscle Dysfunction 92
small airway disease 76
smoke 2, 14, 15, 16, 17, 18, 19, 23, 24, 26, 29, 30, 77, 78, 79, 80, 83, 84, 86, 87, 88, 89, 90, 93, 213
smokers 2, 8, 14, 15, 16, 19, 20, 25, 26, 28, 29, 104, 105, 106, 108, 112, 113, 114, 115, 116, 117, 125, 127, 128, 129, 130
smoking 15, 16, 18, 19, 25, 26, 27, 28, 29, 30, 232, 237, 239, 242, 244, 278, 280, 286, 289
gender differences 177
susceptibility 177
Smoking 213, 214, 231
adolescent smoking 162
effect on lung function 162
maternal smoking 161
smoking cessation 3, 10, 104, 106, 107, 110, 114, 116, 123, 124, 125, 128, 129, 130, 232, 239, 242, 344, 354
Smoking cessation 15, 280, 286, 327
Smoking Cessation 2, 10
smoking-related interstitial lung diseases 71
smooth muscle 76, 77, 78
snoring 214, 216, 227
social interactions 6
social isolation 249, 255, 262
social movements. *see* Olesen
social network 261
social networks 249
Social Norms and Roles. *see* Rommetveit Ragnar
social support 253, 255, 261, 262, 264, 266, 269, 270

socio-legal positivist theory of law. *see* Tamanaha, Brian
spacer 292, 294, 296, 297, 298, 301, 304, 306, 307, 310
Spacers 297
Specialty care 359, 365
spirometry 1, 2, 4, 7, 11, 31, 36, 37, 38, 41, 110, 111
Spirometry 45
Spirometry Screening for COPD 47
sputum 9, 10, 31, 36, 39, 104, 105, 275, 278, 279, 288, 289, 290, 312, 313, 315, 316, 319, 322, 327
stage of change 104, 128
stages of change 132, 133
steroids 279, 282, 289
stroke 104, 105, 128, 190, 206
structural shifts. *see* Pescosolido
Sun-style t'ai chi 141
supplemental oxygen 286, 287, 288
supportive 369, 370, 373, 381, 382, 384
Supportive 369
supportive counseling 110
surveillance for lung cancer 72
survival 223, 226
systemic inflammation 5, 8, 253
tachypnea 312, 315
taking action 131, 134, 153
taterne. *see* Roma
T cell 85, 87, 89, 90
T cells 85, 87, 89, 90
TGFβ 78, 79
Th1 88, 89
The Five R's – Strategies to Enhance Motivation to Quit 107
Tiotropium 294, 300
tobacco 2, 8, 104, 105, 106, 107, 108, 109, 110, 114, 115, 116, 121, 122, 123, 124, 125, 127, 128, 129, 130
tobacco cessation 131, 150, 153
transforming growth factor β 78
Transtheoretical Model of Change 111, 134
treatable 1, 2, 3
tricyclic antidepressant 256
tricyclic antidepressants 253, 259
tuberculosis 14, 16, 18, 23, 24, 26, 27, 30
Twisthaler® 299, 300, 301
vagrants. *see* Roma
Vascular endothelial growth factor 238
vasodilators 232, 239, 242, 243
venous thromboembolism 232, 240, 243
ventilation-perfusion 212, 220, 225
ventilation/perfusion matching 239
Venturi masks 323
viral 314
Viral infections 338
Visual Pillbox 137, 154
VTE 232, 234, 240, 241, 242
ward 340, 351
weaning 348, 349, 350, 354
wheezing 31, 39
women 17, 18, 19, 20, 29, 30. *see* gender
World Health Organization 236, 247

FSC
www.fsc.org
MIX
Papier | Fördert gute Waldnutzung
FSC® C083411

Kolibri 360 GmbH
Ferdinand-Jühlke-Straße 7
99095 Erfurt, Deutschland
produktsicherheit@kolibri360.de